HANDBOOK ON CRITICAL GE
OF MIGRATION

RESEARCH HANDBOOKS IN GEOGRAPHY

Series Editor: Susan J. Smith, *Honorary Professor of Social and Economic Geography* and *The Mistress of Girton College, University of Cambridge, UK*

This important new *Handbook* series will offer high quality, original reference works that cover a range of subjects within the evolving and dynamic field of geography, emphasising in particular the critical edge and transformative role of human geography.

Under the general editorship of Susan J. Smith, these *Handbooks* will be edited by leading scholars in their respective fields. Comprising specially commissioned contributions from distinguished academics, the *Handbooks* offer a wide-ranging examination of current issues. Each contains a unique blend of innovative thinking, substantive analysis and balanced synthesis of contemporary research.

Titles in the series include:

Handbook on Geographies of Technology
Edited by Barney Warf

Handbook on the Geographies of Money and Finance
Edited by Ron Martin and Jane Pollard

Handbook on the Geographies of Regions and Territories
Edited by Anssi Paasi, John Harrison and Martin Jones

Handbook on the Geographies of Power
Edited by Mat Coleman and John Agnew

Handbook on the Geographies of Corruption
Edited by Barney Warf

Handbook on Critical Geographies of Migration
Edited by Katharyne Mitchell, Reece Jones and Jennifer L. Fluri

Handbook on Critical Geographies of Migration

Edited by

Katharyne Mitchell

Dean of the Division of Social Sciences, University of California, Santa Cruz, USA

Reece Jones

Department of Geography and Environment, University of Hawai'i, USA

Jennifer L. Fluri

Department of Geography, University of Colorado Boulder, USA

RESEARCH HANDBOOKS IN GEOGRAPHY

Edward Elgar
PUBLISHING

Cheltenham, UK • Northampton, MA, USA

Published by
Edward Elgar Publishing Limited
The Lypiatts
15 Lansdown Road
Cheltenham
Glos GL50 2JA
UK

Edward Elgar Publishing, Inc.
William Pratt House
9 Dewey Court
Northampton
Massachusetts 01060
USA

Paperback edition 2020

A catalogue record for this book
is available from the British Library

Library of Congress Control Number: 2018960590

This book is available electronically in the **Elgar**online
Social and Political Science subject collection
DOI 10.4337/9781786436030

Printed on elemental chlorine free (ECF)
recycled paper containing 30% Post-Consumer Waste

ISBN 978 1 78643 602 3 (cased)
ISBN 978 1 78643 603 0 (eBook)
ISBN 978 1 83910 985 0 (paperback)

Typeset by Servis Filmsetting Ltd, Stockport, Cheshire
Printed and bound in the USA

Contents

PART III   BORDERS, VIOLENCE AND THE EXTERNALIZATION OF CONTROL

PART IV   CAMPS, DETENTION AND PRISONS

PART V   TRANSNATIONALISM AND DIASPORA

Figures

Contributors

Jennifer Allsopp, University of Exeter, UK

Ilker Ataç, University of Vienna, Austria

Nazgol Bagheri, University of Texas, USA

Alison Blunt, Queen Mary, University of London, UK

Jayani Bonnerjee, Centre for Social Sciences and Humanities, Delhi, India

Andrew Burridge, University of Exeter, UK

Maribel Casas-Cortes, University of North Carolina at Charlotte, USA

Abel Chikanda, University of Kansas, USA

Sebastian Cobarrubias, University of North Carolina at Charlotte, USA

Kate Coddington, University at Albany, State University of New York, USA

Michael Collyer, University of Sussex, UK

Deirdre Conlon, University of Leeds, UK

Jonathan Crush, Balsillie School, Canada, and University of Cape Town, South Africa

Thom Davies, University of Nottingham, UK

Surindar Dhesi, University of Birmingham, UK

Patricia Ehrkamp, University of Kentucky, USA

Jennifer L. Fluri, University of Colorado, USA

Glenda Garelli, DePaul University, USA

Nick Gill, University of Exeter, UK

Mary Gilmartin, Maynooth University, Ireland

Charmian Goh, National University of Singapore, Singapore

Melanie Griffiths, University of Exeter, UK

Elaine Lynn-Ee Ho, National University of Singapore, Singapore

Jennifer Hyndman, York University, Canada

Arshad Isakjee, University of Liverpool, UK

Reece Jones, University of Hawai'i, USA

Bernd Kasparek, EU border monitoring, Germany

Philip Kelly, York University, Canada

Saskia Kok, University of Amsterdam, Netherlands

Anna-Kaisa Kuusisto-Arponen, University of Tampere, Finland

Rodrigo Bueno Lacy, Radboud University, Netherlands

Jenna M. Loyd, University of Wisconsin at Madison, USA

Key MacFarlane, University of California, Santa Cruz, USA

Cindy Maharaj, York University, Canada

Lauren Martin, Durham University, UK

Daniel E. Martínez, George Washington University, USA

Elizabeth Mavroudi, Loughborough University, UK

Cecilia Menjívar, University of Kansas, USA

Katharyne Mitchell, University of California, Santa Cruz, USA

Benjamin J. Muller, King's University College, Canada

Polly Pallister-Wilkins, University of Amsterdam, Netherlands

Natalia Paszkiewicz, University of Exeter, UK

Timothy Raeymaekers, University of Zurich, Switzerland

Richard Rogers, University of Amsterdam, Netherlands

Rebecca Rotter, University of Exeter, UK

Anu Sabhlok, Indian Institute of Science Education and Research, India

Robyn Sampson, Swinburne University of Technology, Australia

Matthias Schmidt-Sembdner, University of Göttingen, Germany

Anna Secor, University of Kentucky, USA

Jeremy Slack, University of Texas at El Paso, USA

Elias Steinhilper, Scuola Normale Superiore, Pisa, Italy

Martina Tazzioli, Swansea University, UK

Henk van Houtum, Radboud University, Netherlands, and University Eastern Finland, Finland

Shannon Drysdale Walsh, University of Minnesota, USA

Margaret Walton-Roberts, Balsillie School and Wilfrid Laurier University, Canada

Kellynn Wee, National University of Singapore, Singapore

Yolanda Weima, York University, Canada

Brenda S.A. Yeoh, National University of Singapore, Singapore

Introduction to the *Handbook on Critical Geographies of Migration*

Katharyne Mitchell, Reece Jones and Jennifer L. Fluri

Why critical geographies of migration? We felt that while there are currently a number of excellent monographs on migration, there are few edited volumes that are focused on the geographies of migration with a specifically critical lens. Our aims for the *Handbook* are to develop an exciting new introduction to critical migration research that draws on the work of leading scholars in the field, to offer a comprehensive overview of key themes in spatial and geographical scholarship in migration, and to highlight a range of ideas, methods, and regions in migration research, while remaining attuned to the underlying politics that brings critical scholars together. Along with perennial issues of relevance such as the shifting nature of borders, camps, and refugee management, some emergent thematic areas include the impact of new technologies on forms of communication and systems of surveillance and mapping, as well as a heightened focus on embodiment and affective practices. Other threads include the changing nature of humanitarian aid and its implications for refugee governance and political activism, and the new ways that time is calculated and experienced vis-à-vis detainment, waiting, and local and transnational forms of im/mobility. In each of these areas, contributors bring a renewed focus on spatial analysis and geographical context.

Migration and borders are central issues in academic debates around the state and the nation but, in recent years, they have also come to dominate public debates about identity and justice in the era of globalization. The so-called European migration crisis of 2015 raised global attention to the issue of violent borders, but countries around the world had been hardening their edges for decades. New walls, more sophisticated surveillance technology, additional border agents, and stricter immigration laws have been implemented in countries as diverse as Australia, Botswana, Thailand, and the United States.

On the one hand, there are more people on the move today than in previous decades. The United Nations High Commissioner for Refugees (UNHCR) reported that in 2017 there were over 68 million people displaced by conflict, the highest number ever recorded (UNHCR, 2018). In response, across Europe and North America, anti-immigrant political parties rallied their supporters with stories of migrant crime, cultural change, and lost jobs, echoing the anti-immigrant language of nativists for generations. In the United States, the same timeworn, and false, claims of the civilizational threat posed by immigration was used by the Know Nothings of the 1850s, the Chinese exclusion campaigners of the 1880s, and the supporters of national origins quotas in the 1920s. The effectiveness of anti-immigrant organizing was evident in the 2016 Brexit vote in the United Kingdom, in the consolidation of power by right-wing governments in Hungary, Poland, and Austria, in the election of an anti-immigrant coalition in Italy, and in the rise of Donald Trump in the United States whose campaign was launched by attacking immigrants as rapists, murders, and criminals (Kopan, 2016).

On the other hand, despite the media and political circus, the total number of irregular migrant arrivals in the European Union (EU) and North America remains relatively modest. Even in the unusual year of 2015, there were only 1.3 million new asylum applications in the EU, which was double the previous year's total of 626,000, but represents only a tiny fraction of the EU's total population of over 500 million people. It was also fewer than the 2 million legal immigrants who arrived in the EU during the same period (Eurostat, n.d.). In the United States, despite the global increase in the number of people displaced by conflict, irregular arrivals have declined substantially since their peak around the dawn of the new millennium. In 2000, the US Border Patrol made 1.68 million apprehensions but by 2017 it was only 310,000 (US Border Patrol, 2017). None of the top ten countries hosting refugees are located in Europe or North America (UNHCR, 2017).

The contribution scholars have made to these debates is to contextualize and historicize the contemporary moment. Rather than accepting the overheated rhetoric about migration and borders, critical geographers of migration have mapped out the geography of contemporary migration and have situated it within the fabric of the larger political, economic, and social history. Scholars have provided the data to demonstrate that today's migrations are not unique but instead have echoes in past mass migrations that were driven by economic restructuring and demographic changes. In the nineteenth century, Europe was at the center of another mass migration, but then the continent sent people around the world as agricultural lands were enclosed and the urban slum populations of London and Manchester grew. From 1815 to 1915, 30 million migrants from Europe arrived in the United States.

In order to understand the causes of contemporary migration, scholars have emphasized the role of past colonial economic exploitation and political meddling by European and North American states in many of the migrant-sending countries. Many of the borders that cross over historical, cultural, or political groups in Asia, Africa, and the Middle East were drawn by Europeans as they left behind their colonial claims. These deep histories shape today's migrations. Finally, critical scholars have also highlighted the geopolitics and geoeconomics behind the emergence of a border security industry that profits from the deep pockets of states interested in managing and directing migrant flows through the construction of walls, the deployment of larger security forces, and the creation of a vast network of camps to detain people on the move. The contributions here tell these stories by drawing on detailed field research that is situated within the academic literature and on the ground experience of contemporary migration.

Some of these situated stories involve humanitarian efforts on behalf of migrants, including the practices of aid workers and organizations at the border itself. Critical geographers interrogating the impact of humanitarianism question both the motivations and the impacts of these actions. Who is involved and what exactly does the presence of humanitarian actors do in specific contexts? While previous research in this area focused largely on the actions of inter-governmental organizations such as the UNHCR (cf. Hyndman, 2000), current critical work has considered a greater variety of organizations and actors. The operations of philanthropists, non-governmental organizations, non-profits, local providers, and faith-based organizations are scrutinized for their roles in the migration 'industry,' as well as for the ways in which they may help to normalize violent border practices, inadequate forms of government care, or passivity among recipients. Contemporary work on humanitarianism thus enlarges the frame, enabling new ways of seeing the relationship between philanthropic actors, aid institutions, and migrants in the context of advanced capitalism, as well as the various ramifications of different forms of help. Additionally, the rapid increase in new kinds of humanitarian public-private partnerships and the rise of new forms of measurement and accountability is itself an important object of study, as neoliberal globalization shifts the terrain in which everyone must operate.

In addition to shifts in humanitarian partnerships and practices, geoeconomic considerations are also implicated in new experiences of the asylum system and detention, where many migrants have been forced to endure longer and longer periods of waiting, and of time that stretches out indefinitely with no hope of forward mobility. This kind of slow violence is manifested in refugee management systems globally, where hundreds of thousands of people remain trapped in various camps and prisons, perennially waiting for a resolution that never arrives. This form of purgatory is the new normal, evidence of a broken system, in which many nations are unwilling to formally withdraw from the 1951 Refugee Convention, yet at the same time, equally unwilling to provide the services needed to grant due process rights to asylum seekers. The passage of time, which used to be investigated more in relation to questions of integration and second generation advancement, is now frequently examined in terms of migrants' experiences of entrapment and immobility such as these. Some migrants – from the Lampedusa in Hamburg activist group to the City Plaza squatters in Athens (see Mitchell and Sparke, 2018) – have taken up their own causes, fighting physically and publicly for their right to be part of their surroundings and to work and move and be educated. Others, such as several refugee children in Sweden, have reacted to their situation by completely giving up on life, going to bed and not getting up again for months or even years (Aviv, 2017). In both these cases, it is the lack of forward mobility, the profound stasis and sense of limbo, the passage of time and of life itself that the migrants are experiencing and challenging.

Feminist geographers have examined migration through the lens of gender, embodiment, and affect in an effort to draw attention to the physical and emotional experiences of migrants such as these. For example, Pratt's (2012) extensive research on Philippine domestic workers in Canada illustrates in ethnographic detail the emotional and physical stress on female domestic laborers who are separated from their children. The division of families, often across several countries, remains an outgrowth of economic migration and therefore an increasing site of geographic analysis. Family divisions also occur across several countries and have developed into extensive multi-country diasporas, particularly for individuals from countries embroiled in protracted conflict such as Afghanistan, Iraq, Syria, Somalia, and South Sudan. Disparate attempts to remain connected to family members or maintain cultural and national identities occur through extensive networks to ensure connectedness, which are often mitigated by a variety of gendered practices (Yeoh, 2016). Examinations of 'embodied mobilities' by geographers brings into focus the ways in which social categories and identities are interconnected and experienced by migrants in different locations (Sabhlok, 2017). In some geographic contexts one's gender, race, language, or nationality may be an asset leading to job opportunities, while in others these identity markers may marginalize one from accessing resources. Additionally, age has become a focus of analysis, particularly the politicized vulnerability of children, such as unaccompanied minors and the geopolitics of care work (Swanson and Torres, 2016). Micro and intimate scales of migration and vulnerability are further examined through analyses of transnational refugee processing centers that pathologize mental health experiences by way of bureaucratic processes that determine whether or not one is worthy of resettlement (Loyd et al., 2018). Thus, as feminist and other critical geography scholars have shown, examining micro-scale, embodied, and affective experiences of migration exposes compelling, complex, and often complicated narratives of mobility.

In Part I of the volume, we explore these new issues in critical migration research in key areas such as gender and violence as well as on borders, displacement, and questions of permanence and impermanence. These five chapters address disparate themes with an eye towards future developments in the field. In Chapter 1, for example, we learn about the siting of critical geographies of migration as Gilmartin and Kuusisto-Arponen theorize the importance of bringing geopolitical and biopolitical approaches together. Beginning with a discussion of the two most studied aspects of migration – the causes of migration and the effects of it – they go on to discuss how these early research foci led critical theorists to analyse not just causes but also *restrictions* to free movement (the geopolitical); additionally, they note how, alongside examining the effects of migration, critical geographers explore in greater depth the embodied *experiences* of migrants (the biopolitical), especially those who are particularly vulnerable to exploitation. The authors then introduce critical border studies and studies on migrant bodies, highlighting the need to think about both the border *and* the body to gain a sufficiently holistic understanding of any given context. Looking to the future, Gilmartin and Kuusisto-Arponen argue for the necessity of critical migration scholarship that is reflexive of its 'own omissions and contradictions,' such as in the area of the classification of migrant bodies and experiences. While critical geographers have paid great attention to migrants living in conditions of economic precarity, for example, this has led to relatively less attention given to other forms of social differentiation, and to some of the ways that migrants are pitted against each other. The authors call for expanding our conceptualizations of both borders and bodies and 'considering their connections with broader socio-spatial formations.'

In Chapter 2, Weima and Hyndman address some similar issues in their examination of displacement and the management regime of humanitarian governance. They argue that theories of migrant management are often too territorially static and state-centric – following too closely the geopolitical logic of the two key spatialities of exclusion, those of containment and securitization. Exploring the idea of transnational displacement enables new ways of conceptualizing alternative frameworks of both humanitarian management and migrant agency. An alternative view of migrant mobility and geographic circularity alleviates the territorial trap, allowing for greater understandings of the various types of 'ruptures and sutures of displacement, return, and return again' experienced by so many migrants. In examining the transnational movements and networks of migrants, the authors see and articulate the multiple ways that refugees negotiate their own paths of safety and security within a broader system of humanitarian governance and the zones of violence and insecurity in which all operate.

In Chapter 3, Menjívar and Walsh attend to women's experiences of physical violence in Central America along with the structural forms of violence that both compel and impede migration. They link the continuation of violence in the wake of the extensive history of US intervention in Latin America with contemporary decisions to escape violence through migration abroad. Endemic poverty has become an outgrowth of entrenched violence, which has had disproportionately negative effects on Central American spaces, economies, and societies as compared to the United States. The authors intricately illustrate the interconnected links between structural, criminal, and political violence with gender-based violence. In many cases gender-based violence remains a compelling reason to migrate. However, the process of migrating, particularly to the United States, is further marked by sexual violence, which is predominantly experienced by female migrants. Many women endure multiple forms of violence throughout their journey as well as additional layers of structural and bureaucratic violence at the border and in US detention facilities. Women who seek asylum in the United States are faced with an uneven and often unjust system, which is difficult to navigate and often re-traumatizes victims of sexual and gender-based violence. Menjívar and Walsh explicate the difficulties experienced by female migrants by analysing inequities through the lens of 'legal violence.' Their chapter provides an innovative approach to understanding the multiple layers of gender-based violence and migration from the bodies of women to the scale of institutions that should protect vulnerable persons but often perpetuate structural and physical violence.

In Chapter 4, Timothy Raeymaekers theorizes how the dislocation of borders through externalization and internalization of border work challenges our notion of migrant mobility. He contends that these new configurations of border policing at locations far from the line itself create new spaces of enforcement and politics of mobility. Raeymaekers argues for an embodied analytics that considers the structured agency produced through new tensions between displacement and enforcement, sovereignty and governmentality, and negation and negotiation of rights; and illustrates these new spaces, politics, and tensions through an analysis of changes to the migration regime in Italy since 2011.

Benjamin Muller delves into the technologies employed by states to track the movement of people in Chapter 5. In this chapter Muller defines the biometric border and explains the history of the technologies that have transformed how bodies pass through border spaces and how agents of the state decide which of those bodies will receive further scrutiny. He argues that the use of biometric data at the border is only one aspect of a larger trend towards the biometric state that uses data to monitor the population. Mountains of data about individuals from commerce, through the use of mobile devices, and through internet searches allows for the creation of profiles and categories that border agencies use to prescreen many travelers before they even reach the border line. Therefore, Muller argues that biometric borders are 'instrumental facilitators in the proliferation and permanence of this discretionary sovereign power.'

Part II of the volume, entitled 'Corporeal and Gendered Geographies of Migration,' emphasizes the body and gender as central to analyses of disparate patterns of migration. Gender provides a lens through which to examine the multiple and intersecting identities, such as race, ethnicity, religion, caste, class, and social status, which influence individual reasons for and experiences of migration (Hyndman, 2010). Analyses of migration at the scale of the body explicates critical geographies of migration through intimate experiences and practices that elucidate the multiple influences on decision making as well as the processes, flows, difficulties, and politics associated with this form of mobility (Kuusisto-Arponen and Gilmartin, 2015). While economic opportunity remains a clear motivating factor for many forms of migration, feminist geographers have shown that other social dynamics, such as status, religion, citizenship, caste, class, and of course gender roles/relations have been significant motivators for migrants (Pratt, 2012; Silvey 2003, 2004; Yeoh et al., 2005). Additionally, gendered migration takes several different forms. Some situations and locations encourage male migration, while female migration is more encouraged in other contexts (Silvey, 2006). States seeking tax remittances have implemented campaigns to encourage labor migration, while other states seek foreign laborers to address shortfalls in their domestic labor force. Forced migration such as individuals fleeing conflict is discussed through the lens of geopolitics, citizenship, and liminal spaces (also see Ashutosh and Mountz, 2011; Ehrkamp, 2017).

Chapters 7 and 8 examine circular forms of labor migration throughout Asia (Chapter 7) and within India (Chapter 8). Chapters 6, 9, and 10 examine vulnerability, agency, embodiment, and gender through the lens of forced migration and flight from conflict zones. These chapters analyse the spatial, social, and situational complexities of migration from unaccompanied minors in Europe (Chapter 6), to the ways in which trauma has become a geopolitical method for determining legible and legitimate asylum cases (Chapter 9) and the multifarious, continual, and often circular migrations of individuals from Afghanistan over the course of nearly 40 years of sustained political conflict (Chapter 10).

In Chapter 6, Kuusisto-Arponen and Gilmartin examine embodied experiences of migration and geographies of care through an analysis of unaccompanied minors in Europe, with a specific focus on Finland. They analyse embodied migration and geographies of care through three interrelated classifications. First, they examine the processes of creating a sense of belonging. Second, they explicate the material, spatial, and psycho-social systems of care relations. The authors identify the need for psycho-social support for unaccompanied minors, and the importance of accepting their agency and abilities. They call for new modes of interaction between unaccompanied minors and caregivers that assist children with cultivating their agency rather than treating them as 'victims or passive beneficiaries.' They further challenge institutional assumptions that stress belonging as territorially bound, and suggest more interaction among students from various countries including young people from the host country. Third, the authors argue for more analytical attention to translocal and transcultural experiences of unaccompanied minors and how they develop a sense of belonging. This sense of belonging for many minors develops through cross-cultural relationships with children from different home countries but similar experiences of displacement and resettlement in Finland. The authors argue that transcultural ties need to be 'recognized and deemed worthy of acknowledgement' from adult caregivers in institutionalized settings.

In Chapter 7, Yeoh, Wee, and Goh highlight the gendered and embodied experiences of temporary labor migrants in Asia. International migration within Asia continues to grow as several countries seek temporary and foreign-born laborers to work within various economic sectors, from construction to housekeeping. This chapter highlights the temporary-ness of migration patterns in Asia. Several countries (i.e., Singapore, Hong Kong, Japan, South Korea, and Taiwan) in response to low fertility rates and rising quality of life and life expectancy seek foreign workers to fill jobs that are identified as 'dirty, difficult, and dangerous.' Additionally, countries seek laborers who are flexible and temporary by initiating policies that make it difficult, if not impossible, for migrant laborers to settle permanently. By focusing on the body as a primary site of analysis, the authors elucidate the intimate and emotional experiences of transient work and transnational family life. They further identify how bodies are gendered at the border and in relation to work. For example, women's care work is often valorized while their reproductive abilities become scrutinized as sites of surveillance, such as in Singapore where female migrants in low-wage jobs are subject to medical screenings and deported if they become pregnant.

In Chapter 8, Anu Sabhlok examines the internal migration of construction workers in India. She emphasizes the circular and cyclical patterns of this form of temporary work, its links to nationalist discourse, and the disparate constructions of laborer masculinity. Masculinity in this context is spatial and differentially performed during one's journey to the work site, labor at the work site, and upon his return home. Her chapter carefully charts the arduous journey male temporary laborers take to reconstruct India's northern border roads. The roads have become both material and symbolic representations of Indian nationalism, while the physical and mentally difficult work, and dangerous work conditions experienced by the laborers remain invisible. Thus, she explains the ways in which citizenship is differentially and hierarchically applied, privileging the citizens who will traverse these roads and the soldiers that monitor them, over the laborers who build and rebuild them each summer.

In Chapter 9, Ehrkamp, Loyd, and Secor theoretically and empirically extend existing analyses of corporeal geographies of migration by focusing on the geopolitics of trauma experienced by Iraqi refugees. Their research identifies the ways in which post-traumatic stress disorder (PTSD) has become a ubiquitous diagnostic tool for what they identify as 'trauma practices.' They show how diagnosing PTSD among refugees can pathologize them and create a 'refugee condition.' By following the multiple layers of bureaucracy and institutionalized frameworks for managing refugee trauma, the authors illustrate how trauma becomes quantified, calculated, and categorized. They further remind readers that only a small fraction of all forcibly displaced persons are recognized by the UNHCR. In order to be recognized individuals must undergo extensive screenings, protocols, and interviews to determine if they have a 'credible fear of future persecution.' Once this process has been completed refugees continue on a more uncertain path towards asylum and resettlement, which requires additional medical screenings, interviews, and legal procedures, which often drag on for years. The authors explicate how identifying and classifying relational trauma resonates geopolitically. For example, requiring refugees to retell traumatic events in order to seek asylum in the United States both reflects geopolitical events and has the potential to 'remake political geographies.' The authors provide a detailed narrative to explain how storytelling identifies traumatic events and places them temporally in the past, while the lingering memories and corporeal experiences continue to affect individuals in their daily life.

In Chapter 10, Bagheri and Fluri address flight from conflict by examining the multiple and cyclical migrations of Afghans regionally and to western countries, centering on the United States. This chapter provides a historical overview of the various phases of conflict in Afghanistan and subsequent waves of migration to neighboring countries, Iran and Pakistan. The gendering of migration in this chapter focuses on changing gender roles and relations mitigated by migration, and the laws and expectations of host countries. For example, in Iran, inter-national marriages between Iranian men and Afghan women are automatically legitimate and children from this union receive citizenship. Conversely, marriages between Afghan men and Iranian women must receive approval from the state and if they are not legitimated, children from this union are not granted citizenship. Masculinity is often measured by Afghan migration experiences, where travel for work in Iran is viewed as a right of passage and process of becoming a man within one's home community. Afghan migration experiences in Pakistan have been diverse based on expected affiliations with disparate resistance factions and the political configuration and management of different refugee camps, from feminist to Islamic extremist. The authors also include migration and mobility practices of Afghans – motivated by economic opportunity rather than flight from conflict – by discussing extensive economic networks among individuals in the diaspora. The chapter concludes by examining cyclical migration patterns of Afghans regionally and in the United States, which pushes against mainstream assumptions that moving to the United States provides greater physical and economic security.

The corporeal and gendered geographies of migration discussed in each chapter in this part provide a micro-scale lens through which to interpret massive macro-scale process, procedures, and pressures to migrate. Time is a key component of several chapters in this part as experiences of migration are often cyclical, circular, and constrained by time-horizons directed by states and employers rather than individual migrants.

Part III of the volume, entitled 'Borders, Violence and the Externalization of Control,' focuses on the experience of people on the move as they encounter the increasingly hardened and militarized edges of the state. Over the past 30 years, countries around the world built dozens of border walls, expanded border security budgets, deployed new surveillance technologies, and hired thousands of new agents (Andersson, 2014; Jones, 2016; Jones and Johnson, 2016; Vallet, 2014). These expansive new security practices at borders have transformed border landscapes from liminal and remote edges of state authority into legible and governed state spaces where agents gain firmer control over movement (Ferdoush, 2018). The result of the hardening of borders has been changes in migration routes as easier crossings in urban areas are closed down and new corridors have emerged, often in more dangerous locations in remote deserts or across dangerous bodies of water (Jones et al., 2017). The global media attention to migration pushed many governments to reformulate border control in an effort to further disrupt migration routes to prevent people from even reaching the edges of the state (Casas-Cortes et al., 2015). The chapters in this part delve into the present moment of hardened borders and immigration controls by documenting the impact of border security on migration journeys, theorizing the efforts to control migration in distant locations well beyond the edges of the state, and reconfiguring how we understand the relationship between development, humanitarianism, and border security.

In Chapter 11, Slack and Martínez examine the grisly relationship between expanded border security and the increase in deaths at borders. They focus on the seeming paradox at the United States-Mexico border where the rate of migrant deaths is increasing even as the US Border Patrol reports steep declines in apprehensions at the border. The authors break migrant deaths down into two categories: those who die at the border due to increased security forcing them over more rugged and dangerous terrain and those that do not even make it to the border, but pass away en route through Mexico. The authors also contextualize the complexities of naming and counting migrant deaths, which is fraught with ambiguity and can be perceived as exploiting the individual's suffering for political or academic benefit. They conclude that despite the discomfort inherent in talking about an individual's death, the policy implications are significant and require more research and discussion of the 'linkages between (im)mobility, violence, and death' at increasingly militarized borders. Therefore, it is important to count migrant deaths but also to humanize them by thinking of each as a person who had dreams and aspirations and with a family left behind who is mourning their loss.

In Chapter 12, Van Houtum and Bueno Lacy analyse how maps of undocumented migration developed by the European border agency Frontex create a particular narrative of threat and enforcement. The authors deconstruct the map by considering the work done by its constituent parts of grids, arrows, and frames to argue that the map not only reproduces a nativist discourse of migration but exacerbates it by visually creating an image of invasion that does not exist in practice. The map erases the vulnerability and insecurity of people on the move and replaces it with the perception of vulnerability and insecurity for the people of Europe, in the process manufacturing a threat that requires further militarization and securitization of the borders of the European Union.

Michael Collyer investigates the connections between development aid and migration in Chapter 13. For decades, wealthy countries have thought of development aid as a mechanism to keep the poor in place by improving economic conditions in order to deter migration. These efforts generally fail because they misunderstand the relationship between development and migration. It is often not the poorest of the world who migrate. Instead, research suggests that, up to a point, increasing wealth in a country also increases migration as people have the means to make a longer journey and the knowledge of what opportunities might exist on the other end of the endeavor (Clemens and Postel, 2018). Collyer finds that as development as a means of dissuading migration has failed, many countries are turning to more coercive and violent means to prevent the movement of others.

In Chapter 14, Garelli and Tazzioli delve further into the uncomfortable connections between humanitarian aid work and border militarism by focusing on migration in the Mediterranean Sea. The authors emphasize the spatiality of migration policing by arguing that new policies criminalizing aid work by migrant rescue ships, new zones of operation by military and coast guard patrols, and renewed crackdowns on smuggling networks create new geographies of migration and enforcement in the Mediterranean. The authors conclude by proposing new research agendas in light of the military-humanitarian nexus in the governance of refugees and migration into the European Union.

Casas-Cortes and Cobarrubias provide a genealogy of the geographic imaginaries that underpin the externalization of border controls in the European Union in Chapter 15. Border externalization is a key facet of how the European Union, the United States, and Australia attempt to prevent people on the move from getting anywhere near the borders of the state. These efforts include direct funding to source and transit countries as well as military interventions to disrupt migration networks and routes. In this chapter, the focus is on how the spatial imaginary of border externalization is created, perpetuated, and enacted. Drawing on archival research, the chapter excavates a history of concentric circles of influence and control that shape how the European Union practices border externalization in the Mediterranean, North Africa, and beyond.

In Chapter 16, Kasparek and Schmidt-Sembdner use a case study of the village of Brennero on the Italian-Austrian border to analyse how internal policing for people on the move has evolved in the post-2015 era in the European Union. The authors introduce the concepts of the 'ethnographic border and migration regime analysis' and then use these tools to demonstrate how they form the context of the border enforcement regime at the Italian-Austrian border. The result is an illustration of how enforcement and migration create new configurations and peculiar political spaces within the European Union.

Part IV of the volume, entitled 'Camps, Detention and Prisons,' looks at different strategies of containment states engage in after they locate people on the move. As immigration enforcement budgets have increased in many wealthy states, there has been a simultaneous rise in the perceived need for detention facilities to house people without the proper documents to remain in a country. The news spaces produced by containment strategies have proved to be productive arenas for scholars to reconsider the relationships between the state, sovereignty, and the control of the mobility of subjects and non-subjects alike. These new spaces range from informal camps along new migration corridors to private prisons that funnel state dollars into corporate coffers as each migrant body generates more revenue. Other novel practices have also emerged including community detention, in which people are officially detained but allowed to live in society as long as they regularly report back to the authorities. In each of these instances, the idea of the border materializes in locations far from the actual borderline as the informal camps, prisons, and the bodies of migrants become the embodiment of the border of the state.

In Chapter 17, Davies, Isakjee, and Dhesi analyse informal camps as quintessential spaces of modern migration. Scholars have long engaged with formal refugee camps, studying the organization of the space, the distribution of services, and the relations with neighboring host country officials and residents (Martin, 2015; Minca, 2005, 2015; Ramadan, 2013). The recent period of migration, however, has created new corridors of movement as many people avoid formal camps because they realize if they settle there, they could be stuck there for many years or even decades because the rate of third country resettlement is very low (Mountz et al., 2013). Instead, many people have set out directly for their destination countries, which has resulted in many informal camps along the route, particularly at chokepoints where movement is slowed or even completely stopped. The authors focus on the jungle camp at Calais, France, and argue that the informality of these camps is a critical space for scholars to consider within the larger context of migration.

In Chapter 18, Kate Coddington describes Australia's 'border continuum' strategy that attempts to deter, divert, and detain people on the move before they reach Australia's shores. Australia's aggressive interventions in migration routes and its offshore detention facilities in Nauru and Manus Island, Papua New Guinea, have resulted in criticism from human rights groups, but also are often held up as a model by other governments attempting to crack down on movement. Coddington outlines the components of the program that attempt to shrink the scope of refugees' ability to claim asylum, but also argues there are fissures in the border continuum that make visible the potential spaces for change.

Lauren Martin describes the links between the criminal justice system and migrant detention in the United States in Chapter 19. In the past, most people picked up on immigration violations in the United States were either released or immediately taken to the border with Mexico and returned. As immigration police forces have expanded through new Border Patrol and Immigration and Customs Enforcement hires, there has been a similar growth in detention facilities. Martin describes the expanding pipeline between immigration policing, detention centers, and deportation to countries of origin. She concludes that these new detention practices are part of the broader strategy to 'widen the net' of containment and deportation for people on the move in the United States.

In Chapter 20, Robyn Sampson discusses alternatives to immigration detention. The author focuses on the emerging practice of community detention and analyses it through the lens of biopolitics and Agamben's notion of the homo sacer. Sampson argues that the embedding of individuals in a community, who are simultaneously under detention orders but also not physically confined, creates an embodied border that travels with them and can reconfigure their spatial experiences of belonging and home as their body hosts the border, and all of the exclusions it entails.

In Part V, entitled 'Transnationalism and Diaspora,' the focus is on the movement of people over the course of generations and in patterns that differ from and often defy conventional assumptions about migration 'from' one region 'to' another. Transnationalism generally refers to the possibilities of living bi-nationally, with actors moving and communicating across international divides on a fairly regular basis. It is conceptualized in terms of stretched social relations and multiple attachments, where migrant lives are understood to be formed in new kinds of intertwined spaces and worlds and where receiving and sending societies must be conceptualized in terms of a single field of analysis (Levitt and Sørenson, 2004). Diaspora likewise is concerned with questions of mobility over time, but more often explores the questions of individuals and populations living outside of or away from a perceived 'homeland' from which they are separated. This separation may be voluntary, but more often is understood as a form of exile, either real or imagined. The term thus evokes and questions notions of home and belonging, a politics of return, and place-based notions of identity.

Both concepts raise questions about political allegiance, cultural and performative expression, and emotional affinity, in addition to material concerns relating to development, citizenship, and the possibilities of economic integration. Furthermore, new technologies create new geographies, where the distances of prior eras shrink and shrink again with each passing decade. At the same time, new forms of media alter when and how information is processed and disseminated, shifting the timing of reactions to events far removed, but also the terms of national and regional debates and the emotional reactions to them.

For critical geographers these material and emotional questions of economic integration and development, cultural belonging and identity, and the politics of return are infused with a spatial set of inferences and logics. Contributors in this part examine all of these areas with different emphases, but always with a keen geographical eye and imagination. In Chapter 21, Blunt and Bonnerjee interrogate the dynamics of diaspora through a focus on the scale of the home. They examine how the experiences and understandings of home for people living in diaspora can be conceptualized in relation to a sense of diasporic home-making, urban belonging, and in the contested feelings of 'homeland' and diaspora. The investigation of the city as a site of diasporic attachment is particularly interesting for geographers because it provides a powerful analytical frame between the scale of the nation (homeland) and the domestic (see also Brickell and Datta, 2011; Oswin and Yeoh, 2010). It facilitates a view onto the specific processes of migrant incorporation and cultural interactions between differing actors on the ground, as well as the specific ways in which migrants participate in the production of urban space. Blunt and Bonnerjee conclude by bringing these analytical vantage points into dialogue with their own research on the experiences of diasporic Anglo-Indian and Chinese communities from Calcutta living in Toronto and London, arguing for views that highlight the 'multi-scalarity of home and diaspora and the connections between them.'

In Chapter 22, Elizabeth Mavroudi looks at diaspora as a process, beginning with an analysis of the meanings of diaspora, and then focusing more closely on the performative aspects of diaspora, including questions of timespace and representation. In this theoretical chapter, she helps the reader identify and critique concepts of diaspora that have been adopted by numerous scholars, arguing ultimately that conceptualizing diaspora as process enables a more ecumenical understanding of the term. 'Rather than seek to close or box in, categorise, attribute characteristics to those in diaspora, the notion of process is more open and inclusive.' Mavroudi's geographical contribution rests in her further exploration of diaspora as process in performative timespace, where she brings in questions of time alongside those of space. She contends that the notion of timespace provides the possibility of capturing the experiences and feelings of those in diaspora in a more holistic manner.

In Chapter 23, Walton-Roberts, Crush, and Chikanda approach diasporas with more attention to their specific material effects, especially with respect to their capacity to contribute to national development. In this chapter, the authors investigate some of the repercussions of contemporary interest by many nation-states in harnessing the economic power of diasporic communities to boost national development agendas. They caution against an uncritical celebration of this type of diaspora engagement, however, showing some of the ways in which this new policy orthodoxy can lead to increased polarization of wealth in remittance-receiving areas, as well as increased forms of securitization of various diaspora groups. In conclusion, they put forward four intersecting issues they believe to be critical in any current research framing of diaspora; these include questions of the new economy, gender and identity, information technologies, and processes of marginalization.

In Chapter 24, Elaine Lynn-Ee Ho examines the affective practices of Chinese diasporic descendants in Myanmar. She focuses, in particular, on the ways in which emotions towards transnational migration play a significant role in not just the experience of belonging, but also in expressions of citizenship. Moreover, these experiences and expressions are even more profoundly connected to the constitution of political subjectivity through generations in the Chinese diasporic population. The chapter contributes to current debates on the political integration of transnational migrants and diasporic populations into nation-states over time. Whereas many scholars have analysed the impact of labor market opportunities or racism on immigrant integration, Ho's research highlights a more elusive yet equally enduring factor: the long-term effects of emotional practices wherein diasporic residents 'approximate' the cultural values of citizenship in order to secure their community's safety and belonging over time. These emotional practices produce a habitus, or way of life, that continues through the generations, and which is implicated in their expressions of political subjectivity.

In 'Geographies of the next generation' (Chapter 25), Kelly and Maharaj employ a spatial lens in analysing the outcomes for the children of immigrants in the United States and Canada. While acknowledging the vast sociological literature on second generation immigrants, they contend that there is still room for a more holistic spatial understanding of next generation outcomes. In this pursuit they propose three key spatialities: the role of place – specifically schools, neighborhoods, and cities; the importance of territory, in which they include legal questions and border regimes and how these impact labor market entry; and transnationalism – especially the impact of contemporary colonialisms that continue to negatively affect those identified as racial minorities in white-dominant societies. In each of these three spatialities, they delineate the ways that place shapes youth outcomes in multiple ways, including education and employment. In conclusion, Kelly and Maharaj argue that a critical geographical perspective is essential for understanding the processes of second generation integration and the outcomes of youth development and wellbeing in every area of life.

In Chapter 26, Kok and Rogers demonstrate the importance of social media for migrants, for migration research, and for political outcomes connected to migration and diaspora. Drawing on the Rwandan diaspora's connections and use of Facebook, they contend that the uses of social media such as this have important political implications for national narratives – such as those of repatriation and return – and it is imperative for migration scholars to identify and pinpoint why, how, for what purposes, and with what effects these types of social media are being employed. In the chapter, Kok and Rogers note how concepts such as the 'connected migrant' (e.g., Diminescu, 2008) emphasize positive networked forms of mobility and social connectivity, including through digital technologies, but often omit the equally important questions related to how digital data collections might also be used by governments in political ways. In their work they call for a cross-fertilization of social media analysis and migration scholarship, indicating how 'social media data may be used to study connected migration, and how migration research may benefit from relying on digital data for studying social and political inference.'

In the concluding part of the volume, entitled 'Refugees, Asylum, Humanitarianism,' we highlight work that explores the current configurations of actors, institutions, and events connected with humanitarian governance and refugees in the twenty-first century. This is a rapidly growing area of migration scholarship, one that investigates those individuals and institutions who aim to help, as well as those who are exploited, vulnerable and/or targeted as in need of help. In both of these categories questions of governance and agency are raised, as are broader implications about changes in the constitution of humanitarianism in the neoliberal era.

In Chapter 27, Steinhilper and Ataç contend that much of migration scholarship emphasizes refugees as passive victims or grateful receivers of liberal humanitarian handouts. By contrast, they focus on the voices, practices, and social movements of refugees in Austria and Germany, arguing that these types of self-organized activities are far more prevalent worldwide than generally acknowledged (cf. Mudu and Chattopadhyay, 2017). In their work, they draw on two case studies to explore the spatialities of refugee activism. In both cases, the refugee protest movements were shaped by mobility, place, and social space in ways that profoundly altered their trajectories. The specific spatial effects were most broadly connected to the ways in which refugees were able to escape from isolation and exclusion through their contentious strategies of visibility, voice, representation, and resistance. They used mobile tactics such as marches and bus tours, they occupied buildings, and they raised public attention through their claims to central urban spaces and resources. In their active responses to the depredations and indignities of detention and waiting, they became recognized as 'political subjects with rights and voices rather than passive victims or stigmatized outsiders.'

In Chapter 28, in their work on the law and court system in the United Kingdom, Gill, Allsopp, Burridge, Griffiths, Paszkiewicz, and Rotter interrogate the absence rather than the presence of refugee voices and political subjectivities. Drawing on a number of refugee claims cases that went through the UK courts in recent years, they demonstrate how the law's privileging of bodily presence worked to the detriment of numerous asylum claimants, who were unable to advocate for themselves or even fully understand the situation they were in. Whether owing to fear, pain, lack of comprehension, or some combination of these factors, many refugees were effectively excluded from access to justice despite their physical presence at their asylum hearings. In this chapter, the authors review and expand on analytical approaches to concepts of absence and presence and offer a typology of how different forms of presence might be 'translated into the legal context.' Through this process they hope to both reveal and resist the many exclusions that arise from the legal system in UK-based refugee claim determinations.

Polly Pallister-Wilkins, in Chapter 29, approaches questions of migration and humanitarianism through looking at their intersection in border spaces. In recent years, as the world's borders have become increasingly violent, there has been a corresponding rise of humanitarian actors in these liminal spaces. Pallister-Wilkins examines some of the intended and unintended consequences of this humanitarian presence, including the relationship between humanitarian practices and the political regimes responsible for these violent borders – and the increasingly risky strategies of mobility used by migrants to navigate them. Using the concept of triage she examines the way that the humanitarian care of bodies at the border becomes sorted and rationalized as a form of pre-emptive risk management – one that does not disturb or call attention to the larger forces that create such violent regimes of mobility in the first place (cf. Mitchell and MacFarlane, 2016). She argues for the importance of a deepened awareness and critical concern for the ways in which im/mobility interacts with humanitarian practices of this type.

In Chapter 30, Deirdre Conlon examines the asylum process in the United States through the lens of neoliberal governmentality. She examines multiple aspects of the application and adjudication of asylum claims to unpack how actors are positioned and governed within the asylum system. She finds that the process is complicated, messy, and often contradictory. While rational and effective practices and subjects may be desired and demanded, the asylum process itself is mired in bureaucracy and scarcity, thus creating the conditions in which inefficiencies and irrationalities multiply. At the same time, while neoliberal governmentality presupposes the constitution of calculating, entrepreneurial actors, the asylum process encourages and necessitates both enterprising behavior but also compliance and passivity on the part of asylum seekers. Conlon concludes by noting the importance of attending to the heterogeneous, unstable, and paradoxical spaces and processes of the asylum process to better understand the complexity of neoliberal forms of governance as they play out on the ground.

In Chapter 31, Tazzioli and Garelli scrutinize refugee governance and the policies and politics of asylum by taking up the question of mapping. In their analysis, they show how normative refugee mapping imposes a Westphalian imaginary that is both territorially fixed and static. They argue for a 'counter-mapping' approach with respect to the geographies of the asylum system. By this, they mean an approach that embraces a reflexive cartography, one in which the practice of mapping is constantly interrogated, thus helping to unsettle and unpack 'the spatial assumptions upon which migration maps are crafted.' Tazzioli and Garelli thus frame counter-mapping not merely in terms of resistance to a linear, territorial, and statist view from above, but more broadly as an epistemological move in which the cartographic visibility, representation, and mobility of migrants itself is constantly questioned and examined.

Katharyne Mitchell and Key MacFarlane take up the question of refugee protection by faith-based actors in Chapter 32. Their study focuses on the transnational practices and relationships between European churches and allies that form what they call a sanctuary network. They are interested in the ways that the sanctuary network's cross-border relationships and implicit assumptions about the necessity and value of alternative forms of justice have existed for centuries, and can be called on and reactivated by multiple actors at different historical junctures. Drawing on interviews as well as archival data, Mitchell and MacFarlane show how contemporary church-based sanctuary networks are now operating in Europe, how they are linked to previous transnational sanctuary movements, and how they are both similar to and different from other types of transnational social movements. They contend that the sanctuary network demonstrates a bundle of spatially embedded solidarities across both space and time that is important to consider in the history of refugee justice movements and transnational social movements more generally.

REFERENCES

Andersson, R. (2014), *Illegality, Inc.: Clandestine Migration and the Business of Bordering Europe*. Oakland, CA: University of California Press.

Ashutosh, I. and Mountz, A. (2011), Migration management for the benefit of whom? Interrogating the work of the International Organization for Migration. *Citizenship Studies*, **15**(1), 21–38.

Aviv, R. (2017), The trauma of facing deportation. *The New Yorker*, April 3.

Brickell, K. and Datta, A. (2011), *Translocal Geographies: Space, Places and Connections*. London: Routledge.

Casas-Cortes, M., Cobarrubias, S., and Pickles, J. (2015), Riding routes and itinerant borders: autonomy of migration and border externalization. *Antipode*, **47**(4), 894–914.

Clemens, M. and Postel, H. D. (2018), Emmigration with foreign aid: an overview of the evidence from low-income countries. Center for Global Development Policy Paper 119, February.

Diminescu, D. (2008), The connected migrant: an epistemological manifesto. *Social Science Information*, **47**, 565–79.

Ehrkamp, P. (2017), Geographies of migration I: refugees. *Progress in Human Geography*, **41**(6), 813–22.

Eurostat (n.d.), Migration and migrant population statistics. Accessed 11 October 2018. http://ec.europa.eu/eurostat/statistics-explained/index.php/Migration_and_migrant_population_statistics#Migration_flows:_2_million_non-EU_immigrants.

Ferdoush, M.A. (2018), Seeing borders through the lens of structuration: a theoretical framework. *Geopolitics*, **23**(1), 180–200. https://doi.org/10.1080/14650045.2017.1341406.

Hyndman, J. (2000), *Managing Displacement: Refugees and the Politics of Humanitarianism*. Minneapolis, MN: University of Minnesota Press.

Hyndman, J. (2010), Introduction: the feminist politics of refugee migration. *Gender, Place & Culture*, **17**(4), 453–9.

Jones, R. (2016), *Violent Borders: Refugees and the Right to Move*. New York: Verso.

Jones, R. and Johnson, C. (2016), Border militarization and the rearticulation of sovereignty. *Transactions of the Institute of British Geographers*, **41**, 187–200.

Jones, R., Johnson, C., Brown, W., Popescu, G., Pallister-Wilkins, P., Mountz, A., and Gilbert, E. (2017), Interventions on the state of sovereignty at the border. *Political Geography*, **59**, 1–10.

Kopan, T. (2016), What has Donald Trump said about Mexico and vice versa. *CNN*. Accessed 11 October 2018. https://www.cnn.com/2016/08/31/politics/donald-trump-mexico-statements/index.html.

Kuusisto-Arponen, A.-K. and Gilmartin, M. (2015), The politics of migration. *Political Geography*, **48**, 143–5.

Levitt, P. and Sørensen, N.N. (2004), Global migration perspectives: the transnational turn in migration studies. *Global Migration Perspectives*, No. 6, Global Commission on International Migration, October. Accessed 8 October 2018. https://www.iom.int/jahia/webdav/site/myjahiasite/shared/shared/mainsite/policy_and_research/gcim/gmp/gmp6.pdf.

Loyd, J.M., Ehrkamp, P., and Secor, A. (2018), A geopolitics of trauma: refugee administration and protracted uncertainty in Turkey. *Transactions of the Institute of British Geographers*, **43**(3), 377–89.

Martin, D. (2015), From spaces of exception to 'campscapes': Palestinian refugee camps and informal settlements in Beirut. *Political Geography*, **44**, 9–18.

Minca, C. (2005), The return of the camp. *Progress in Human Geography*, **29**(4), 405–12.

Minca, C. (2015), Geographies of the camp. *Political Geography*, **49**, 74–83.

Mitchell, K. and MacFarlane, K. (2016), Crime and the global city: migration, borders, and the pre-criminal. In *Oxford Handbooks Online.* New York: Oxford University Press. doi: 10.1093/oxfordhb/9780199935383.013.45.

Mitchell, K. and Sparke, M. (2018), Hotspot geopolitics versus geosocial solidarity: contending constructions of safe space for migrants in Europe. *Environment and Planning D: Society and Space.* https://doi.org/10.1177/0263775818793647.

Mountz, A., Coddington, K., Catania, R.T., and Loyd, J.M. (2013), Conceptualizing detention: mobility, containment, bordering, and exclusion. *Progress in Human Geography*, **37**(4), 522–41.

Mudu, P. and Chattopadhyay, S. (2017), *Migration, Squatting and Radical Autonomy.* London: Routledge.

Oswin, N. and Yeoh, B. (2010), Introduction: mobile city Singapore. *Mobilities*, **5**(2), 167–75.

Pratt, G. (2012), *Families Apart: Migrant Mothers and the Conflicts of Labor and Love.* Minneapolis, MN: University of Minnesota Press.

Ramadan, A. (2013), Spatialising the refugee camp. *Transactions of the Institute of British Geographers*, **38**(1), 65–77.

Sabhlok, A. (2017). 'Main Bhi to Hindostaan Hoon': gender and nation-state in India's Border Roads Organisation. *Gender, Place & Culture*, **24**(12), 1711–28.

Silvey, R. (2003), Spaces of protest: gendered migration, social networks, and labor activism in West Java, Indonesia. *Political Geography*, **22**(2), 129–55.

Silvey, R. (2004), Transnational domestication: state power and Indonesian migrant women in Saudi Arabia. *Political Geography*, **23**(3), 245–64.

Silvey, R. (2006), Geographies of gender and migration: spatializing social difference. *International Migration Review*, **40**(1), 64–81.

Swanson, K. and Torres R.M. (2016), Child migration and transnationalized violence in Central and North America. *Journal of Latin American Geography*, **15**(3), 23–48.

UNHCR (2017), Poorer countries host most of the forcibly displaced, report shows. New York: United Nations Publishing. Accessed 11 October 2018. http://www.unhcr.org/en-us/news/latest/2017/2/58b001ab4/poorer-countries-host-forcibly-displaced-report-shows.html.

UNHCR (2018), *Global Trends: Forced Displacement in 2017.* New York: United Nations Publishing. Accessed 11 October 2018. http://www.unhcr.org/5b27be547.

US Border Patrol (2017), Total illegal alien apprehensions by fiscal year. Accessed 11 October 2018. https://www.cbp.gov/sites/default/files/assets/documents/2017-Dec/BP%20Total%20Apps%2C%20Mexico%2C%20OTM%20FY2000-FY2017.pdf.

Vallet, E. (2014), *Borders, Fences, and Walls: States of Insecurity?* London: Routledge.

Yeoh, B.S. (2016), Migration and gender politics in Southeast Asia. *Migration, Mobility, & Displacement*, **2**(1), 75–88.

Yeoh, B.S., Huang, S., and Lam, T. (2005), Transnationalizing the 'Asian' family: imaginaries, intimacies and strategic intents. *Global Networks*, **5**(4), 307–15.

PART I

NEW ISSUES IN CRITICAL MIGRATION RESEARCH

1. Borders and bodies: siting critical geographies of migration

Mary Gilmartin and Anna-Kaisa Kuusisto-Arponen

INTRODUCTION

The place of migration in the discipline of Geography is changing. Once clearly located within population geography, and studied in terms of its role in population change, migration studies has spilled out beyond these sub-disciplinary confines. What Ehrkamp calls the "geographies of migration" now takes in much more than the role of migration in population change (Ehrkamp 2017). Geographers studying migration now draw on a much wider range of influences, which include the cultural turn, the mobilities turn and transnational approaches (King 2012), as well as geopolitics (Ehrkamp 2017), legal geographies (Strauss 2017) and labour geographies (Buckley et al. 2017). Smith has described this as "the ascendancy of migration studies" (Smith 2018, p. 297).

The opening up of migration studies in geography has led to a proliferation of research on the topic, using a wide diversity of theoretical and empirical approaches. Despite this, there are two clear areas of focus. The first considers the causes of migration. This is a concern that stretches all the way back to Ravenstein's formulation of laws of migration in the 1880s (Ravenstein 1885, 1889). However, the emphasis now is increasingly on the broader issues of the migration-development relationship and the role of migration policy (see, e.g., Czaika and De Haas 2013; De Haas 2010; Skeldon 2008). The second considers the effects of migration and, increasingly, migrant experiences. Geographers have traditionally paid considerable attention to effects of migration on place, for example, through mapping residential segregation (see, e.g., Ellis et al. 2004). However, the growing emphasis on embodiment has led to a broader conceptualization of migrant experiences (see, e.g., Gorman-Murray 2009; Pratt 2012).

In this chapter, our focus is specifically on what we call critical geographies of migration. We define critical geographies of migration as spatially informed theories and practice explicitly directed towards understanding and challenging migration as a site of exploitation. Critical geographies of migration are certainly concerned with the causes of migration though, in many instances, they focus on efforts to restrict people's movements across national borders, whether legally or physically. However, the more significant emphasis is on the effects of migration, particularly through a focus on the experiences of migrants who are vulnerable, marginalized or exploited. These experiences are intersectional, and critical geographies of migration are increasingly addressing the relationship between migrant status, race and sexuality, adding to a longer-standing interest in migration and gender. In considering the causes and effects of migration, critical geographers are informed by two broad theoretical approaches – geopolitics and biopolitics – with an increasing emphasis on biopolitical approaches in recent years.

We begin the chapter by locating the critical geographies of migration. We identify and interrogate two key sites that are studied: the border and the body. We then reflect on the theoretical and scalar shifts that have occurred within critical approaches to migration in geography. We conclude with our brief reflections on the future for critical geographies of migration.

LOCATING CRITICAL GEOGRAPHIES OF MIGRATION

Critical geographies of migration are concerned with identifying and challenging the processes that serve to marginalize and oppress migrants. From our perspective, we are concerned with how these processes are spatialized and spatially grounded. Given this, we consider that there are two key sites where critical geographers interested in the issue of migration have directed their attention: the border and the body. Each of these sites is complex and multifaceted and, consequently, provides important insights into how critical geographies of migration are imagined and operationalized. We first discuss borders, paying attention to significant borders and the practices of bordering in relation to migrants, including the increasing reliance on detention as a bordering practice. We then discuss the body. First, we show how migrant bodies are hierarchized with particular reference to status, and how these hierarchies shape the engagement of critical geographers. Through a focus on work, specifically precarity and care work, we then discuss embodied geographies in more detail.

The Border

Specific borders, namely, the European Union's external border and the border between the USA and Mexico, have received considerable attention. Van Houtum and Pijpers (2007) described the European Union (EU) as a gated community and its border and immigration regime as two-faced, highlighting the stratification of people into different immigrant statuses based on their perceived desirability. The effects of this regime were clearly shown by Collyer (2007), who charted the difficult, fragmented journeys of trans-Saharan migrants as they tried to get to the EU, and described the common experiences of "isolation, uncertainty and hardship" (Collyer 2007, p. 685), which on occasion resulted in death (Van Houtum and Pijpers 2007, pp. 298–9). These "deaths at the border" of the EU, an ongoing and persistent issue, have come under more sustained scrutiny in recent years with the advent of the so-called migrant or refugee crisis (Kynsilehto 2017). This particular crisis is defined in terms of a rapid increase in the numbers of people seeking to enter Europe, often along hazardous routes. Stories of Mediterranean shipwrecks and drownings, treacherous land journeys across Balkan countries, and violent border enforcement inside the Schengen border regime provide one means of framing this "crisis" of human mobility. Yet, as De Genova points out, the crisis is also framed as "a crisis of control over the ostensible borders of Europe" (De Genova 2016, p. 37), and their perceived porosity in relation to undesirable migrants and, increasingly, terrorism. This, too, has been a focus of the work of critical geographers, who have drawn attention to the ways in which the EU has been attempting to securitize its borders by externalizing migration management. The EU's Global Approach to Migration and Mobility (GAMM) is a key policy framework for border externalization. GAMM began in 2005.[1] It provides the framework for how the EU engages with countries outside the EU in relation to migration and asylum, primarily in order to prevent irregular migration to Europe (Hampshire 2016). Casas-Cortes et al. (2015) show both the spatial ambition and reach of GAMM, and the difficulties in its implementation, not least because of the actions of migrants who resist being contained by official migrant routes.

Critical research on the EU border emphasizes the importance of naming and understanding borders as practice. As De Genova writes, "the agonistic coherence and ostensible fixity of borders – their thing-like qualities – only emerge as the *effect* of active processes by which borders must be made to appear *thing-like*" (De Genova 2016, p. 47, emphases in the original). This focus on borders as practice has also marked work on the USA-Mexico border. Nevins describes some of the ways in which the "thing-like" border was delineated and enforced, beginning in the 1980s. This included installing high-intensity floodlights, erecting steel walls, and increasing the number of Border Patrol agents in order to deter migration from Mexico to the USA (Nevins 2002, p. 65). The physical border between the USA and Mexico was, of course, central to the presidential campaign of Donald Trump. The specifications for the expanded USA-Mexico wall announced in March 2017 included that it be "physically imposing in height" and able to deter "for a minimum of 1 hour . . . a physical breach of the wall" by tools that include a sledgehammer, car jack or battery operated cutting tools (quoted in Jusionyte 2017, p. 16).

The discussion of borders has moved way beyond physical boundaries. While the EU border has been externalized, the USA-Mexico border has been internalized. Coleman describes the process as "the growth of interior immigration policing practices" (Coleman 2007, p. 55), which includes the devolution of federal immigrant powers to non-federal officers such as local police. In this sense, the USA-Mexico border is now policed all across the USA (Coleman and Kocher 2011), with a consequential rise in the numbers of forced removals, or deportations, from the country. There were 4.3 million forced removals between 2000 and 2013, over 93 per cent of which were to Latin America. The majority related to immigration rather than criminal offences, and often included people from non-border states who had been living in the USA for at least three years (Price and Breese 2016, pp. 367–9). The effects of the interiorization of USA border enforcement are evident in the lives of migrant workers. Research with migrant dairy workers in Wisconsin highlighted "a pervasive sense of surveillance and fear of apprehension" (Harrison and Lloyd 2012, p. 376). People they interviewed told stories about workplace raids, apprehension and detention, leading to what Harrison and Lloyd identified as their "deportability" (Harrison and Lloyd 2012, p. 366). At the same time, critical geographers have highlighted the contrast with the treatment of the other significant US land border, that with Canada (Sparke 2006).

In addition to work on the shifting forms of the EU and US borders, critical geographers have also investigated other sites that are central to practices of migration control. Mountz describes these sites as an "enforcement archipelago" (Mountz 2011a), implicated in processes of migrant detention (Mountz et al. 2013). Mountz focuses on islands, and lists the wide range of sites – from Guam in the USA to Lampedusa in Italy to

---

[1]   When first introduced, it was known as GAM (Global Approach to Migration). The name changed in 2011.

Nauru – where asylum seekers are detained and, in some instances, prevented from applying for asylum (Mountz 2011a, p. 121). But islands are just one example of the range of sites of detention, many of which operate as extrajudicial for migrants who are detained. Other examples include camps, prisons and specifically designated immigration detention centres (Davies and Isakjee 2015; Moran et al. 2013; Mountz et al. 2013). For Mountz et al., the proliferation of spaces of migrant detention "elucidates a conceptual and material crossroads between the domestic and foreign, the intimate and geopolitical, the detention centre and the prison" (Mountz et al. 2013, p. 536). In their account of the Calais refugee camp and its inhabitants, Davies and Isakjee (2015) illustrate this crossroads, and its contradictions, in a vivid and powerful way.

Practices of migrant detention have shifted the location of the border for migrants, as has technology. Amoore (2006) drew attention to this when she introduced the concept of the biometric border. Her specific focus was the War on Terror, and how electronic personal data was increasingly being used to "classify and govern the movement of people across borders" (Amoore 2006, p. 341). As a consequence, then, borders have become mobile. As Amoore writes, the body "becomes the carrier of the border as it is inscribed with multiple encoded boundaries of access" (Amoore 2006, pp. 347–8). The implications of the biometric border for migrants were clear for Amoore, who described how the category "immigrant" was becoming a signifier of illegitimate mobility. This was further developed in later studies of biometric border control regimes, such as the Temporary Resident Biometrics Project in Canada (Pero and Smith 2014). Coleman and Stuesse characterize this as a shifting emphasis on policing immigrant bodies rather than just borders (2014), though they, with others, also acknowledge the increasing levels of state border militarization around the world. This includes more border walls and fences; border guards and uniformed troops, both privatized and public; and surveillance hardware such as drones, helicopters and armoured vehicles (Jones and Johnson 2016). These militarization efforts often target particular migrants, as is the case for the EU and the USA-Mexico border. In the process, borders are increasingly inscribed on the bodies of migrants. We turn to the body in the next subsection.

The Body

Our second site of interest is the body. We argue that the body has been put to use by critical geographers of migration in two key ways. The first is by highlighting the ways in which migrant bodies are categorized and hierarchized, and the effects of these processes. The second involves highlighting the embodied experiences of migrants. In this chapter, we show the broader critical potential of this focus on embodied experience by highlighting just one of the many areas of investigation, namely, migrant experiences of/at work.

Critical geographers have paid particular attention to the categorization of migrant bodies. There has been a sustained focus on migrant status, and on particular groups of migrants defined in terms of status. Such groups include forced migrants (a term inclusive of asylum seekers and refugees) and undocumented migrants, many of whom are understood as vulnerable to exploitation. Much of this work is ethnographic in scope, and is highly aware of the ethics of research with vulnerable migrants (Griffiths 2018; Korjonen-Kuusipuro et al. 2018; Kynsilehto 2016). Collyer interviewed over 130 undocumented migrants in Morocco – 85 per cent male – about the dangers they faced on their "fragmented journeys". These dangers included natural obstacles, the actions of traffickers and smugglers, and state violence. For those undocumented migrants who were stranded in Morocco, unable to reach Europe, their situation was often quite desperate. A 29-year-old from Cameroon, who had been sleeping rough in Morocco for five years, said, "I no longer have the courage to fight any more" (Collyer 2010, p. 283). This focus on forced and undocumented migrants draws particular attention to their experiences of hardships and exploitation.

The impact of enforced waiting has been discussed in detail by feminist geographers as well. Mountz, for example, described the poignancy of "life in limbo, efforts to seek asylum elsewhere and frustration with the length of their wait" for Afghan asylum seekers detained on the island of Lombok in Indonesia (Mountz 2011b; see also Hyndman and Giles 2017). Within this category, there has also been attention to the specific experiences of children and young people, most often those in the asylum regimes of European countries. Crawley worked with separated minors in the UK to chart their experiences of the asylum interview, which is carried out with an asylum seeker by the UK Border Agency, and then given a prominent place when the application for asylum is being determined. She points out the ways in which children were listened to but not heard, and argues for the need to recognize both the principle of child agency and children's voices in the asylum process (Crawley 2010).

The significant increase in research on forced migration and, by association, forced migrants has led to suggestions that the topic may now be over-researched, particularly in the Middle East and North African regions (Pascucci 2017). When it comes to research with other (non-forced) types of undocumented migrants, however, the approach taken by critical geographers differs slightly. This is particularly the case in the USA, where the category of "undocumented migration" receives more attention than "forced migration". In the USA, there is a stronger concern with the consequences of lack of status, such as deportability (Harrison and Lloyd 2012). In contrast, ethnographic research in the USA often includes undocumented migrants without necessarily prioritizing this aspect of their identity. Winders provides a clear example of this approach in her detailed study of the lives of Latino immigrants in Nashville, Tennessee – a new immigrant destination. While she acknowledges that most of the immigrants who participated in her research were undocumented, Winders's focus is on their everyday lives and on their encounters with long-term residents, rather than on their vulnerabilities (Winders 2013). The politics of understatement employed here, which focuses less on status and more on everyday experiences, serves as a useful contrast to the politics of hyper-visibility in research on forced migrants. Yet, the politics of understatement creates its own difficulties, given the size of the population of undocumented migrants in the USA – estimated at 11.4 million in 2012 (Baker and Rytina 2013). The interest in and emphasis on migrants whose status makes them vulnerable to exploitation is understandable for critical geographers. However, the contrast in treatment raises broader concerns about how status and space influence these critical approaches. Ehrkamp insists that critical geographers should "carefully examine the terms and categories we use to describe people who move across spaces because these categories have the potential to inflict epistemological violence" (Ehrkamp 2017, p. 814). The terms and categories that are used – for example, forced and undocumented migrants – are defined and shaped by states, and serve to create hierarchies of migrants. When this translates into contrasting methodologies, such as defining some groups in terms of vulnerabilities and hardships only, critical geographers have to be aware of how their practices may, in turn, serve to further reinforce the hierarchies created by states. The example of unaccompanied refugee minors illustrates this point. Researchers who focus on the protection and institutional care of unaccompanied refugee minors minimize the reality that, as minors, they do not have family reunification rights (see Kuusisto-Arponen and Gilmartin, Chapter 6 in this volume; also Herz and Lalander 2017).

While critical geographic research on forced and undocumented migrants certainly engages with embodied experiences, we want to discuss the issue of embodiment in more detail through a focus on work. Migration research in general is characterized by a preoccupation with work, which stems from the common sense belief that most migration is for the purposes of economic gain through work. As a consequence, the experiences of migrants at work are subject to intense investigation. Among these broad areas of focus are experiences of exploitation and discrimination and sectoral concentration (e.g., Martin and Prokkola 2017; Vaittinen 2014). We first explore exploitation and discrimination as it is framed by recent critical geographies of precarity. We then highlight care work as a feminized sectoral concentration for migrants. The intersections between precarity and care provide important insights into the embodied experiences of migrants that, while concentrated on work, have broader critical implications.

Waite uses the example of migrant labourers to argue for the analytical significance of precarity, which she defines as "life worlds that are inflected with uncertainty and instability" (Waite 2009, p. 416). She makes the case that migrant labourers in the UK "may experience insecure contracts, poor conditions at work, eroded rights at work and generalised exploitation" (Waite 2009, p. 423), yet also points to the problems with labelling groups or categories and homogenizing their experiences. As a result, she suggests that a more useful approach is to consider the spatiotemporal moments when migrant labourers might work as a precariat, if only temporarily. More recent research suggests, however, that those spatiotemporal moments are becoming more common. As Lewis et al. insist, certain migrants are now a crucial part of the low-wage economies of wealthier countries: without their presence and their exploitation, those low-wage economies could not continue to function (Lewis et al. 2015; see also Scott 2013). However, they argue that precarity is now a function of many working experiences regardless of migration status, and so the term is insufficient to capture the realities for many migrants. As a result, they introduce the term *hyper*-precarity in order to show the additional vulnerabilities that result from the insecurities of immigration regimes. Hyper-precarity is "produced by the nexus of employment and immigration precarity", and it is experienced through deportability, risk of injury without access to adequate healthcare, and a reliance on overtly transactional relationships (Lewis et al. 2015, pp. 593–4). Experiences of precarity and hyper-precarity are grounded in a range of case studies that explore what Lorey elsewhere calls precarization – a form of governance that destabilizes both employment and the conduct of life (Lorey 2015, p. 13). The interplay between immigration status and work is highlighted in research on the Temporary Foreign Worker Program in Canada, which shows how a "continuum of exploitation" is created (Strauss and McGrath 2017). Similarly, Axelsson et al. show that while Swedish migration policies create the conditions for the exploitation of migrant workers who are required to be hyper-flexible, those workers in turn accept precarious conditions in a trade-off for the promise of permanent residency (Axelsson et al. 2017). In their study of migrant workers in three different sectors in Finland, Martin and Prokkola (2017) argue that context-specific forms of precarity are a result of the strategic territorialization of borders by the state and by employers. This precarization affects both skilled and unskilled workers (Martin and Prokkola 2017).

Issues of vulnerability and precarity are clearly evident in the experiences of migrants employed in care work, which includes domestic work, child and elder care, as well as more formalized forms of care work through medical centres such as hospitals. The work itself is intimate, often dealing with vulnerable bodies: it is usefully characterized as "body work" that, by nature of its feminization, is also devalued (Kofman 2013; Walton-Roberts 2012). The spatial concentration of care work in domestic homes creates exposure to exploitation for many migrant care workers, and critical geographers – particularly feminists – have been at the forefront in documenting and analysing these experiences. For example, Geraldine Pratt's long and sustained engagement with Filipino domestic workers in Vancouver, recruited as part of the Live-In Caregiver Program in Canada, has highlighted their difficult experiences as workers as well as the toll of long-term separation from their families (Pratt 2012). The abuse of migrant domestic workers is addressed more directly by Huang and Yeoh, who use court and press reports to document the deeply troubling experiences of some "foreign maids" in Singapore. The reports document the physical, sexual and psychological abuse endured by women from a range of Asian countries, including Indonesia, the Philippines and India, for misdemeanours that included poor laundry, ironing and kitchen skills (Huang and Yeoh 2007).

Critical geographers have also paid attention to other forms of migrant care workers, such as nurses and doctors (see, e.g., Dyer et al. 2008; Walton-Roberts 2012). Importantly, though, this research insists on the importance of an understanding of migrant experiences that extends beyond work. As Kofman suggests, leaving the circuits of family and work disconnected results in "hanging onto traditional gendered knowledge in terms of categories of migration" (Kofman 2012, p. 145). For Kofman and Raghuram (2015), this means a focus on the broader question of social reproduction. In migration research, social reproduction is sometimes conceptualized as "migrant trajectories", which have transformative power through "the capacity of the migrant body to tie together different networks of relatedness, when navigating through global space" (Vaittinen 2014, p. 197). Thus, the embodied presence and movement of migrants simultaneously reproduces and challenges the "perceived" order of global economic space, bordering practices and multiscalar migration governance. We argue, with Vaittinen, that labour migration articulates both global political and power structures and also multiple embodiments of human and institutional settings, which are part of the wider processes of social reproduction.

CONNECTING GEOPOLITICS AND BIOPOLITICS

Our discussion of the critical geographies of migration has focused on two key sites, the border and the body. This emphasis reflects two broad theoretical approaches: geopolitics and biopolitics. Elsewhere, we argued that geopolitical and biopolitical theory underpin much research on migration within political geography which, in turn, shapes the study of migration within the discipline of geography as a whole (Kuusisto-Arponen and Gilmartin 2015). However, this is not sufficient to capture the diversity of ways in which critical geographers have approached the study of migration. In this section, we develop our understanding of the relationship between geopolitics and biopolitics, and highlight how this understanding is enhanced by a focus on how migrant bodies and mobilities actively work against bordering practices.

As Coleman and Stuesse point out, there is a general impasse in the social sciences and humanities "which insists on biopolitics and geopolitics as opposed models of power" (Coleman and Stuesse 2014, p. 37). Their particular concern is border studies, and they argue that geopolitics and biopolitics or, in their formulation, topography and topology, are interlinked rather than separate when it comes to the policing of migrants and migration. Our wider discussion of the border and the body show these interconnections clearly. The border, we argue, is more than the physical barrier that separates one nation-state from another, but is also a practice that is increasingly inscribed on the bodies of migrants. Similarly, the migrant body is the object of geopolitical and geoeconomic processes, whether through state-defined migrant statuses or the increasing precarity of work. These processes intersect in the embodied experiences of migrants.

The interconnections of geopolitical and biopolitical approaches to critical geographies of migration are clear through processes of hierarchization. States create and reinforce migrant status hierarchies, deciding who has permission to enter and live in a country and under what conditions. However, hierarchies are also created and reinforced through everyday practices, such as through the figure of the "good migrant". Findlay et al. (2013) provide a fascinating insight into how the good migrant is understood and reproduced in their account of research with recruitment agents and employers in the UK and Latvia. They chart the physical and behavioural characteristics that are favoured: young and healthy, flexible, compliant and self-regulated. In doing so, they insist that the production of the idealized migrant worker is a dual process "in which migrants self-regulate themselves as well as being directly regulated by recruiters" (Findlay et al. 2013, p. 163).

The nod to migrant agency in this discussion of the "good worker" is important, because it highlights another, important way in which geopolitics and biopolitics intersect. This is through a focus on the geopolitical practices of migrants, whether local, national or transnational. For Casas-Cortes et al., this is apparent in the mobility practices of migrants which act as a "collective force re-making space", thus departing from approaches that construct migrants as victims (2015, pp. 898–9). Other critical geographers emphasize acts of solidarity. No More Deaths/No Más Muertes, a volunteer organization working in the Arizona-Sonora borderlands, places water, food and other crucial supplies along busy desert routes for migrants. In his participatory research with the organization, Johnson shows how the border site itself is important for organizing and sustaining social movement activity. This is because the everyday lives of volunteers "are surrounded by material evidence of migration enforcement and filled with narratives and anecdotes about encounters with migrants or Border Patrol" (Johnson 2015, p. 1255).

Johnson focuses on camps in the desert, in contrast to most work on solidarity which emphasizes urban settings because of their potential for alliances between disadvantaged groups (Bauder 2016, p. 258). One such focus is on Sanctuary cities, which have policies that aim to provide services to residents regardless of migration status (Ridgley 2013). Others focus on the emergent politics of migration in cities, where the tensions between governmental attempts to control migrants and migrants' desire to control their own lives and mobilities play out in a striking way (Collins 2016; Darling 2017). More recently, research on gay, lesbian and queer migration has highlighted the draw of urban areas for coming-out and for work, while recognizing that cities, particularly for ethnic and racial minorities, are often spaces of exclusion (Lewis 2012; Lewis and Mills 2016). It is also important to emphasize the ways in which many critical geographers actively work in collaboration with migrants to actively challenge their exploitation and marginalization. Geraldine Pratt's long collaboration with the Philippine Women Centre of BC (Vancouver, British Columbia) provides an excellent example of critical and engaged research that is both locally and translocally situated and is directed towards meaningful social and political change (Pratt 2012). While processes of hierarchization differentiate migrants on the basis of legal status, creating insecurity and vulnerability, migrant lives are more complex than status alone. Critical geographic work that emphasizes networks, connections, and acts of political protest and solidarity offers an important corrective to research and broader discourses that posit migrants as either helpless or dangerous but, in either case, not fully belonging to the places where they live.

LOOKING TO THE FUTURE

In the field of critical geographies of migration, there is an increasing focus on the intersection of geopolitical and biopolitical theory, with particular attention to how borders and hierarchies are created and enforced. This work is nuanced and politically engaged yet, at times, insufficiently reflexive on its own omissions and contradictions. In this regard, Pascucci's identification of over-research is particularly important. Her particular concern is based on her experiences of fieldwork in Egypt, which she saw as enabled and shaped by a broader humanitarian infrastructure that, in turn, led to certain places and groups of people being over-studied (Pascucci 2017). Though grounded in a particular place and time, we believe that Pascucci raises issues of broader relevance for critical geographers of migration. Specifically, to what extent does our research reinforce rather than challenge hierarchies, and what does this mean for the future of migration research?

In our discussion of the body, we highlighted the classification of migrant bodies, and how this has led to a concentration on particular types of migrant bodies, defined in terms of status. Critical geographers have paid most attention to forced and undocumented migrants, and to migrants in precarious employment, in part because their experiences illuminate the effects of status hierarchies for those with the least power. However, paying critical attention to other migration streams – for example, those defined as highly skilled – would also provide important insights into the pernicious effects of hierarchization, particularly as it pits migrants against each other (Mitchell 1998; see also Martin and Prokkola 2017). Given this, broader attention to questions of intersectionality is also required, since migrants enter and live in places that are marked by other forms of social differentiation. Racial and ethnic hierarchies are of particular relevance here, since their spatial articulation may place migrants in different, and perhaps challenging, positions (Pulido 2018). The emphasis on precarity as experienced by many workers, and not just migrant workers, provides one example of how other aspects of identity might be reconsidered.

Our discussion of the border highlights research that operates within a border ontology. By this, we mean that it takes the existence of borders for granted, even when assessing their form and meaning from a critical perspective (Gilmartin 2018). Given this, it seems crucial for critical geographers of migration to provide an expanded account of how borders work. We outlined work on the spatial and technological siting of borders, which brings together geopolitics and biopolitics. It is clear, though, that work from a critical legal geography perspective is also required, given the significance of law in defining and enforcing borders. Courtroom battles in the USA over President Trump's travel ban, first introduced in 2017, provide a timely example of the pressing need to bring critical legal perspectives to bear on the border.

Critical geographers of migration already provide crucial insights into how migrants experience injustice. Those insights are spatially grounded in studies of borders and bodies. Expanding the conceptualizations of both, and considering their connections with broader socio-spatial formations, will enhance our ability to understand migration not as exceptional, but as central to and illuminating of the contemporary human condition.

ACKNOWLEDGEMENTS

Kuusisto-Arponen wishes to thank the Academy of Finland for funding: projects SA 266161 and SA 304146.

REFERENCES

Amoore, L. (2006), "Biometric borders: governing mobilities in the war on terror", *Political Geography*, **25**, 336–51.

Axelsson, L., B. Malmberg and Q. Zhang (2017), "On waiting, work-time and imagined futures: theorising temporal precariousness among Chinese chefs in Sweden's restaurant industry", *Geoforum*, **78**, 169–78.

Baker, B. and N. Rytina (2013), "Estimates of the unauthorized immigrant population residing in the United States, January 2012", Department of Homeland Security, accessed 15 July 2017 at http://www.dhs.gov/immigration-statistics/population-estimates/unauthorized-resident.

Bauder, H. (2016), "Possibilities of urban belonging", *Antipode*, **48** (2), 252–71.

Buckley, M., S. McPhee and B. Rogaly (2017), "Labour geographies on the move: migration, migrant status and work in the 21st century", *Geoforum*, **78**, 153–8.

Casas-Cortes, M., S. Cobarrubias and J. Pickles (2015), "Riding routes and itinerant borders: autonomy of migration and border externalization", *Antipode*, **47** (4), 894–914.

Coleman, M. (2007), "Immigration geopolitics beyond the Mexico-US border", *Antipode*, **39** (1), 54–76.

Coleman, M. and A. Kocher (2011), "Detention, deportation, devolution and immigrant incapacitation in the US, post 9/11", *The Geographical Journal*, **177** (3), 228–37.

Coleman, M. and A. Stuesse (2014), "Policing borders, policing bodies: the territorial and biopolitical roots of US immigration control", in R. Jones and C. Johnson (eds), *Placing the Border in Everyday Life*, Farnham: Ashgate, pp. 33–63.

Collins, F.L. (2016), "Migration, the urban periphery, and the politics of migrant lives", *Antipode*, **48** (5), 1167–86.

Collyer, M. (2007), "In-between places: trans-Saharan transit migrants in Morocco and the fragmented journey to Europe", *Antipode*, **39** (4), 668–90.

Collyer, M. (2010), "Stranded migrants and the fragmented journey", *Journal of Refugee Studies*, **23** (3), 273–93.

Crawley, H. (2010), "'No one gives you a chance to say what you are thinking': finding space for children's agency in the UK asylum system", *Area*, **42** (2), 162–9.

Czaika, M. and H. De Haas (2013), "The effectiveness of immigration policies", *Population and Development Review*, **39** (3), 487–508.

Darling, J. (2017), "Forced migration and the city: irregularity, informality, and the politics of presence", *Progress in Human Geography*, **41** (2), 178–98.

Davies, T. and A. Isakjee (2015), "Geography, migration and abandonment in the Calais refugee camp", *Political Geography*, **49**, 93–5.

De Genova, N.P. (2016), "The 'crisis' of the European border regime: towards a Marxist theory of borders", *International Socialism*, **150**, 31–54.

De Haas, H. (2010), "Migration and development: a theoretical perspective", *International Migration Review*, **44** (1), 227–64.

Dyer, S., L. McDowell and A. Batnitzky (2008), "Emotional labour/body work: the caring labours of migrants in the UK's National Health Service", *Geoforum*, **39** (6), 2030–38.

Ehrkamp, P. (2017), "Geographies of migration I: refugees", *Progress in Human Geography*, **41** (6), 813–22.

Ellis, M., R. Wright and V. Parks (2004), "Work together, live apart? Geographies of racial and ethnic segregation at home and at work", *Annals of the Association of American Geographers*, **94** (3), 620–37.

Findlay, A., D. McCollum, S. Shubin, E. Apsite and Z. Krisjane (2013), "The role of recruitment agencies in imagining and producing the 'good' migrant", *Social & Cultural Geography*, **14** (2), 145–67.

Gilmartin, M. (2018), "Beyond walls: border epistemologies and the politics of migration", *Political Geography*, **66**, 206–8.

Gorman-Murray, A. (2009), "Intimate mobilities: emotional embodiment and queer migration", *Social & Cultural Geography*, **10** (4), 441–60.

Griffiths, M. (2018), "For speaking against silence: Spivak's subaltern ethics in the field", *Transactions of the Institute of British Geographers*, **43** (2), 299–311.

Hampshire, J. (2016), "European migration governance since the Lisbon Treaty: introduction to the special issue", *Journal of Ethnic and Migration Studies*, **42** (4), 537–53.

Harrison, J.L. and S.E. Lloyd (2012), "Illegality at work: deportability and the productive new era of immigration enforcement", *Antipode*, **44** (2), 365–85.

Herz, M. and P. Lalander (2017), "Being alone or becoming lonely? The complexity of portraying 'unaccompanied children' as being alone in Sweden", *Journal of Youth Studies*, **20** (8), 1062–76.

Huang, S. and B.S.A. Yeoh (2007), "Emotional labour and transnational domestic work: the moving geographies of 'maid abuse' in Singapore", *Mobilities*, **2** (2), 195–217.

Hyndman, J. and W. Giles (2017), *Refugees in Extended Exile: Living on the Edge*, London and New York: Routledge.

Johnson, L. (2015), "Material interventions on the US-Mexico Border: investigating a sited politics of migrant solidarity", *Antipode*, **47** (5), 1243–60.

Jones, R. and C. Johnson (2016), "Border militarisation and the re-articulation of sovereignty", *Transactions of the Institute of British Geographers*, **41** (2), 187–200.

Jusionyte, I. (2017), "The wall and the wash: security, infrastructure and rescue on the US-Mexico border", *Anthropology Today*, **33** (3), 13–16.

King, R. (2012), "Geography and migration studies: retrospect and prospect", *Population, Space and Place*, **18**, 134–53.

Kofman, E. (2012), "Rethinking care through social reproduction: articulating circuits of migration", *Social Politics*, **19** (1), 142–62.

Kofman, E. (2013), "Gendered labour migrations in Europe and emblematic migratory figures", *Journal of Ethnic and Migration Studies*, **39** (4), 579–600.

Kofman, E. and P. Raghuram (2015), *Gendered Migrations and Global Social Reproduction*, Houndmills and New York: Palgrave Macmillan.

Korjonen-Kuusipuro, K., A.-K. Kuusisto and J. Tuominen (2018), "Everyday negotiations of belonging – making Mexican masks together with unaccompanied minors in Finland", *Journal of Youth Studies*. https://doi.org/10.1080/13676261.2018.1523539

Kuusisto-Arponen, A.K. and M. Gilmartin (2015), "The politics of migration", *Political Geography*, **48**, 143–5.

Kynsilehto, A. (2016), "Resisting borders: mobilities, gender, and bodies crossing the Mediterranean, Refugee Watch", *A South Asian Journal of Forced Migration*, **47**, 10–19.

Kynsilehto, A. (2017), "Mobilities, politics and solidarities", *Peace Review*, **29** (1), 48–54.

Lewis, H., P. Dwyer, S. Hodkinson and L. Waite (2015), "Hyper-precarious lives: migrants, work and forced labour in the Global North", *Progress in Human Geography*, **39** (5), 580–600.

Lewis, N.M. (2012), "Remapping disclosure: gay men's segmented journeys of moving out and coming out", *Social & Cultural Geography*, **13** (3), 211–31.

Lewis, N.M. and S. Mills (2016), "Seeking security: gay labour migration and uneven landscapes of work", *Environment and Planning A*, **48** (12), 2484–503.

Lorey, I. (2015), *States of Insecurity: Government of the Precarious*, London and New York: Verso.

Martin, L. and E.-K. Prokkola (2017), "Making labour mobile: borders, precarity and the competitive state in Finnish migration politics", *Political Geography*, **60**, 143–53.

Mitchell, K. (1998), "Reworking democracy: contemporary immigration and community politics in Vancouver, Chinatown", *Political Geography*, **17** (6), 729–50.

Moran, D., N. Gill and D. Conlon (eds) (2013), *Carceral Spaces: Mobility and Agency in Imprisonment and Migrant Detention*, Farnham: Ashgate.

Mountz, A. (2011a), "The enforcement archipelago: detention, haunting, and asylum on islands", *Political Geography*, **30** (3), 118–28.

Mountz, A. (2011b), "Where asylum-seekers wait: feminist counter-topographies of sites between states", *Gender, Place & Culture*, **18** (3), 381–99.

Mountz, A., K. Coddington, R.T. Catania and J.M. Loyd (2013), "Conceptualizing detention: mobility, containment, bordering, and exclusion", *Progress in Human Geography*, **37** (4), 522–41.

Nevins, J. (2002), *Operation Gatekeeper: The Rise of the "Illegal Alien" and the Making of the U.S.-Mexico Boundary*, New York: Routledge.

Pascucci, E. (2017), "The humanitarian infrastructure and the question of over-research: reflections on field-work in the refugee crises in the Middle East and North Africa", *Area*, **49** (2), 249–55.

Pero, R. and H. Smith (2014), "In the 'service' of migrants: the temporary resident biometrics project and the economization of migrant labor in Canada", *Annals of the Association of American Geographers*, **104** (2), 401–11.

Pratt, G. (2012), *Families Apart: Migrant Mothers and the Conflicts of Labor and Love*, Minneapolis, MN: University of Minnesota Press.

Price, M. and D. Breese (2016), "Unintended return: U.S. deportations and the fractious politics of mobility for Latinos", *Annals of the Association of American Geographers*, **106** (2), 366–76.

Pulido, L. (2018), "Geographies of race and ethnicity III: settler colonialism and non-native people of color", *Progress in Human Geography*, **42** (2), 309–18.

Ravenstein, E.J. (1885), "The laws of migration", *Journal of the Statistical Society of London*, **48** (2), 167–235.

Ravenstein, E.J. (1889), "The laws of migration", *Journal of the Royal Statistical Society*, **52** (2), 241–305.

Ridgley, J. (2013), "Cities of refuge: immigration enforcement, police, and the insurgent genealogies of citizen-ship in U.S. Sanctuary cities", *Urban Geography*, **29** (1), 53–77.

Scott, S. (2013), "Labour, migration and the spatial fix: evidence from the UK food industry", *Antipode*, **45** (5), 1090–109.

Skeldon, R. (2008), "International migration as a tool in development policy: a passing phase?" *Population and Development Review*, **34** (1), 1–18.

Smith, D.P. (2018), "Population geography I: human trafficking", *Progress in Human Geography*, **42** (2), 297–308.

Sparke, M. (2006), "A neoliberal nexus: economy, security and the biopolitics of citizenship on the border", *Political Geography*, **25** (2), 151–80.

Strauss, K. (2017), "Sorting victims from workers: forced labour, trafficking, and the process of jurisdication", *Progress in Human Geography*, **41** (2), 140–58.

Strauss, K. and S. McGrath (2017), "Temporary migration, precarious employment and unfree labour relations: exploring the 'continuum of exploitation' in Canada's Temporary Foreign Worker Program", *Geoforum*, **78**, 199–208.

Vaittinen, T. (2014), "Reading global care chains as migrant trajectories: a theoretical framework for under-standing of structural change", *Women's Studies International Forum*, **47**, 191–202.

Van Houtum, H. and R. Pijpers (2007), "The European Union as a gated community: the two-faced border and immigration regime of the EU", *Antipode*, **39** (2), 291–309.

Waite, L. (2009), "A place and space for a critical geography of precarity", *Geography Compass*, **3** (1), 412–33.

Walton-Roberts, M. (2012), "Contextualizing the global nursing care chain: international migration and the status of nursing in Kerala, India", *Global Networks*, **12** (2), 175–94.

Winders, J. (2013), *Nashville in the New Millennium: Immigrant Settlement, Urban Transformation, and Social Belonging*, New York: Russell Sage Foundation.

2. Managing displacement: negotiating transnationalism, encampment and return
Yolanda Weima and Jennifer Hyndman

INTRODUCTION

Migration management influences humanitarian governance and human displacement in multiple ways, with geopolitics a salient force in shaping responses. Humanitarian donors have a dual imperative: to help people survive their displacement, but also to manage it far from the borders of global North countries. The externalization of asylum (Huysmans, 2006) and the containment of refugees in global South locations (Castles, 2008) are not new, but these salient geopolitical discourses embody practices that are important to understanding international efforts to manage displacement. Asylum seekers, refugees, and migrants are managed through a nexus of systematic, expensive enforcement regimes, but also bilateral and multilateral agreements (or "pacts") in which global North states pay transit states (and refugee-hosting countries) to prevent asylum seekers from leaving to global North locations. While much has been written about the immobilizing effects of these state-led and exclusionary arrangements of power, not nearly as much is known about how such arrangements are negotiated by refugees and those who return home. How migrants, asylum seekers, refugees, returnees and others navigate migration policies and humanitarian governance structures, or find themselves in conditions of "involuntary immobility" (Lubkemann, 2008) is analysed far less than regimes of exclusion.

As a particular kind of political migrant, refugees are an expression of the salience of states, international borders, and their crossing in contemporary political discourse. In other words, they are an expression of state-centric "ways of seeing" migration, which in turn shape how one might analyse the governance of refugees as migrants forced to leave their country and seek asylum. Legally, refugees are persons fleeing persecution or targeted violence in another country.[1] And yet the category "refugee" is also exclusionary, and leaves out many people fleeing immediate violence and state-led human rights atrocities (Crawley and Skleparis, 2017). What does one call a person who flees her country to seek asylum, is granted refugee status, returns home when violence declines, only to flee again and seek asylum but this time be refused by the same government? This chapter focuses on such circuits of displacement and return to highlight the highly embodied but

---

[1]   This legal definition applies in signatory countries of the United Nations 1951 Geneva Convention and 1967 Protocol on Refugees. The 1969 Organisation of African Unity Convention Governing the Specific Aspects of Refugee Problems in Africa, and the 1984 Cartegena Declaration by Central American states were based on more regionally specific contextual analyses, by states whose experiences of large-scale forced migration differed from the European context which the Geneva Convention was designed to address. Both regional agreements provide critical interpretations of the causes of forced migration, and broader recognition of refugees, including those forced to move due to events "seriously disturbing the public order." While implementation varies, the regional agreements are actually existing legal frameworks that provide different ways of understanding and governing migration.

largely invisible strategies that asylum seekers, refugees, and migrants – sometimes the same person at different junctures – employ to forge their own safety in fluid and insecure conditions.

At the end of 2016, the United Nations High Commissioner for Refugees (UNHCR) counted some 22.5 million refugees worldwide, and more than 40 million more displaced within the borders of their countries of origin (UNHCR, 2017). This global scale of displacement is unprecedented since the Second World War, hence the management of refugees is an issue of importance to forced migration studies. Refugees are often assisted through humanitarian aid provided by host governments, foreign governments, and/or international non-governmental organizations (NGO). Such aid is technically governed by principles of International Humanitarian Law, but practically is never separate from the geopolitics that produce refugees and the anxieties such displacements generate (Hyndman, 2018). Hence refugees are managed, even governed, by "humanitarians" and by the host states that provide them with a safe, if temporary, place to stay.

Refugee management in such cases refers to a blended strategy – providing the basic necessities of life (sufficient to survive but not to live a normal life with many basic human rights) while maintaining refugees in their *regions of origin*. This specific geography of managing refugees "over there" has characterized asylum since the end of the Cold War (Castles, 2008). Such management is achieved through the securitization of refugees, including asylum seekers, in the global North, and the provision of humanitarian aid in mostly global South locations. More than 90 percent of the world's refugees live in the "global South," a vague and imperfect geographical reference that includes the Middle East and suggests a very uneven distribution of the displaced persons across world regions. Refugee encampment is often justified as both providing security *for* refugees, and security *from* refugees. While more and more refugees are also residing outside of camps, theories of "the camp" often retain relevance for the political and social conditions they may encounter in other settings.

In this chapter we outline the salient spatial configurations of humanitarian efforts and refugee management to contain people on the move, including the creation of camps, and the phenomenon to "return," sometimes called repatriation. This provides a backdrop and context for refugees' own experiences and subjectivities that demonstrate much more fraught transnational spatialities, power negotiations, and politics.

Both encampment and broader containment in *regions of origin* are tied to a strong emphasis on ultimate return of refugees to their countries of origin as the ideal solution for refugees. Although little refugee scholarship focuses on repatriation, the return-orientation is an important aspect of the spatiality of managing migration, and is accordingly discussed in this chapter. Even as refugee numbers are increasing, voluntary returns have declined. In 2016, two-thirds of all refugees were in what UNHCR terms "protracted refugee situations," meaning that they had been refugees for over five years (UNHCR, 2017). Some 4.1 million people had been registered as refugees for more than 20 consecutive years (UNHCR, 2017). While few contest the need for life saving aid when people are facing death, managing migration seems far less justifiable and less human when refugees remain in camps with curtailed rights for decades (Agier, 2003; Hyndman and Giles, 2017).

Focusing solely on camps as technologies of control and experiences of encampment misses any analysis of how migrants and refugees negotiate safety through extensive and often transnational networks involving placement and displacement, refuge and return, stasis and movement. "On the ground" border-crossers are managing their own security, livelihoods, and families, sometimes in exile, often transnationally, and always in ways that defy easy theorizing. The idea of *transnational* displacement as an alternate theoretical framing and empirically observable pathway to safety is explored later in this chapter through a case study of Burundian refugees and returnees. This example demonstrates how "grand theories of humanitarian government" cannot fully capture the ruptures and sutures of displacement, return, and return again that may occur in the lives of families caught between violence, starvation, and family separation. The messiness of this case study demonstrates both a "pushback" to the unidirectional flow of refugees (either to seek asylum or to repatriate when safe to do so), but also challenges the very categories we use to understand protection among those displaced, especially where displacement occurs multiple times.

MANAGING DISPLACEMENT: SPATIALITIES OF CONTAINMENT AND HUMANITARIAN GOVERNANCE

In her analysis of the scholarship pertaining to refugees, geographer Patricia Ehrkamp (2016) notes three main trends in the refugee studies literature: the securitization of migration, including territorial and spatial strategies of migration management; protracted displacement in camps and cities; and refugee subjectivities. Our chapter examines these politics and processes at work, but particularly traces the geographies of seeking safety that defy easy categorization.

"Migration management," broadly conceived, is largely a state practice exercised on migrant (including refugee) bodies, normally with the aim of exclusion from a territory (Geiger and Pécoud, 2010). Humanitarian governance, on the other hand, has a more specific focus on assisting those who are facing the possibility of death, fleeing violence, and/or in need of protection, both social and political. Refugees are one of the largest groups of humanitarian beneficiaries, but others include civilians located in conflict zones or at home where governments cannot or will not provide the necessities of life to their own citizens. Migration management overlaps with humanitarian governance, but the articulations between the two are rarely made. In this section, we offer a brief overview of the "minimalist" biopolitics (Redfield, 2005) of providing a means of survival for those whose lives are at risk in humanitarian emergencies. We focus on the spatialities of this humanitarian biopolitics that aims to contain refugees both in "regions of origin" and through the sited technology of encampment. Normally, the imperatives of states, and especially "national security," trump humanitarian principles of neutrality, impartiality, and independence, and can even threaten the prerogative to ensure the "right to life."

Containment works at the macro-scale as "global North" states seek to keep "global South" border-crossers in their regions of origin. Asylum seekers are currently being managed through a series of ad hoc, expensive bilateral and multilateral agreements (or "pacts") in which global North states pay transit states (and refugee-hosting countries) to prevent asylum seekers from leaving to global North locations. While International Humanitarian Law dictates neutrality and impartiality, aid to refugees often has geopolitical antecedents and generates immobilizing effects (Hyndman and Giles, 2011). Nowhere but in Turkey, Jordan, and Lebanon is this more vivid: the European Union

(EU) promised in excess of $8 billion to the Turkish Government until 2018 to keep asylum seekers en route to the EU in Turkey instead. Jordan and Lebanon have also received "cash for containment" in the form of EU investment in economic activities and other concessional perks. While controversial, this approach has nevertheless been promoted by some refugee scholars as a solution to protracted refugee situations (Betts and Collier, 2017; for a critique see Crawley, 2017).

At a more localized scale, the creation of camps has long been a key spatial tactic of containment. Refugee protection can be elided by state security concerns. Even though refugees are fleeing violent conditions, they may be framed as an even greater threat themselves, and states justify the encampment of refugees for the protection of their own populations. The grouping of refugee populations in camps and away from other residents emphasizes the fact that they do not belong (Hovil, 2014). National security concerns may link-up with global geopolitics, such as the American "War on Terror," contributing to even greater securitization and militarization of camps, and greater limitations on refugee rights and mobilities.

Just as encampment facilitates the efficient surveillance and securitization of refugee populations, it also creates convenience for humanitarian management. The stark visibility of needs and aid in camps may help in humanitarian fundraising (Hyndman and Giles, 2017). Camps, although they may host residents for decades, are said to only be temporary measures – in place until populations can return home.

One well-known humanitarian organization, Médecins Sans Frontières (MSF, or Doctors Without Borders), is the subject of an ethnography by Peter Redfield (2005). MSF often provides medical services in refugee camps. Redfield examines the approach, practice, and politics of MSF in such contexts: "members of MSF rarely suggest that their work will directly build a better social order or achieve a state of justice. The goal is to agitate, disrupt, and encourage others to alter the world by practicing humanitarian medicine 'one person at a time'" (MSF cited in Redfield, 2005, p. 334). Redfield draws on Foucault and Agamben to create his own analysis of MSF's biopolitical approach to humanitarianism. From Agamben, he notes that the camp, not the city, is the fundamental biopolitical paradigm of the West: "One might say that the ancient right to take life or let live was replaced by a power to foster life or disallow it to the point of death" (Foucault cited in Redfield, 2005, p. 339). A refugee camp is a site of biopolitics where survival is central and lives have either been abandoned or put at risk, an "attenuated form of government" (Foucault cited in Redfield, 2005, p. 341).

Some of the most insightful analyses of the camp are those made by geographer Adam Ramadan who, in a series of articles, takes on different humanitarian rationalities. While scholars like Hyndman (2000) and Redfield (2005) conceive of the refugee camp as a space of biopolitical care and control, Ramadan (2013) acknowledges this biopolitical impulse but shows how the camp is distinctive as a *productive* political space where vital subjectivities emerge, national powers circulate, and evolving diaspora politics are everywhere.

Although the institutional nature of refugee camps has established them as a dominant mode of humanitarian management of refugees, more and more of the world's refugees are residing outside of camps, and many humanitarian organizations are advocating alternatives to encampment. While the new global compact on refugees has claimed to push for greater refugee rights and reduced encampment, the lack of genuine funding to do so has led Tanzania to withdraw from its key pilot program, the Comprehensive Refugee Response Framework (CRRF). This highlights the global North's inability to genuinely share fiscal responsibility for displacement in which its own imperial history often plays a role.

Based on recent fieldwork in Lebanon, where the government has specifically established a "no-camp" policy for Syrian refugees, geographer Romola Sanyal highlights the importance of adapting camp-focused theories of refugee management to address seemingly divergent spatialities of refugee management (Sanyal, 2017). Without formal camps for Syrians, two informal solutions have emerged: highly varied private accommodation, with varying degrees of formality, particularly in urban areas; and deregulated, informal, unrecognized settlements, often in rural areas. These settlements are negotiated with individual land owners, and consequently are quite uneven in terms of the quality of accommodation, basic services, and access to the settlements by NGOs – they are socially and spatially uneven as they depend on ongoing negotiations of power relations by many stakeholders due to their lack of formal humanitarian status.

Drawing on scholarship related to urban informality and camp theorization, Sanyal argues that we can no longer treat "camp" and "city" as binary spatio-political categories. As these settlements vary widely, they exist in a theoretical continuum between theorizations of the camp and informality in the city. While some theorists celebrate informality, and see these liminal spaces as offering potentiality and opportunities for agency that are not present in much more disciplined camps, Sanyal is cautious. The lack of formal definition or status can itself be disempowering and can produce marginality. Furthermore, it does not offer a clear position from which to make claims. Informality can be confining and restrict mobility because of precarity outside of camps. Such status can produce conditions as bleak as encampment, but without even the minimum guarantees of humanitarian service provision accorded to "camp refugees" (Sanyal, 2017).

CAMP GOVERNMENTALITIES: NEGOTIATING PARTICIPATION, POWER, AND POLITICS

Humanitarian agencies attempt to formally manage refugee political contestation of humanitarian "apolitical" sovereignties in camps by creating official spaces for "apolitical" but "democratic" refugee participation in camp management and programs. Such participation is also meant to respond to the contradictions of supposed humanitarian protection of human rights and democracy in exceptional spaces where subjects lack basic rights. Concepts such as "participation" and "self-management" have been key principles in camp management for over two decades. Participatory schemes are often envisaged as a way of empowering refugees, who are framed by relief organizations as passive and reliant on aid (Hyndman, 1997; Turner, 2010). While differently understood, and at times opposed even from within the relief organizations that seek to implement self-management principles, they generally refer to seeking the inclusion of refugees in decision making, service delivery, and project implementation, ostensibly with some degree of democratic reworking of "top-down" management.

The promotion of refugee participation is fraught with ambivalence – it may come from a genuine self-critique by relief organizations that "the status quo is undesirable and perhaps unacceptable," but it is hindered by limitations on what types of decisions refugees are able to make (for example, withholding financial decisions), and a real fear of the implications of shifting power relations (Hyndman, 1997, p. 21). The power-geometries of refugee participation vary empirically in different camps or through time within a camp, as well as in theoretical interpretations by scholars.

Drawing on research in Lukole camp for Rwandan and Burundian refugees in Tanzania, Simon Turner (2010) highlights an aspect of ambivalence in tracing the desire of camp managers to promote "good participation" as an alternative to "bad politics." "Bad politics" is understood narrowly as relating to formal politics, particularly groups aspiring to challenge home-country political regimes, and is banned and disciplined in refugee camps as threatening the neutrality of aid. Bans on "politics" are often ineffective, and Turner discusses how Lukole remained, covertly, a hyper-politicized space. "Bad politics" is often associated with the conflict causing displacement, and insecurity within camps, threatening to "the community" (Turner, 2010).

Scholars have challenged an idea promoted by relief organizations that the population of a refugee camp is a harmonious "community"; rather, the camp should be conceptualized as an *assemblage* as Ramadan argues, or an institutional invention of the UN (Hyndman, 2000; Ramadan, 2013). "The community," for the purposes of participatory governance, is based on ideals of perceived harmony, even when camp populations include diverse groups and interests. At the same time, participation is meant to contribute to rebuilding social cohesion, imagined as damaged due to displacement. Because the community is envisaged as homogeneous, participatory schemes are imagined as modeling good governance, and even democratic practices such as voting for representatives, but at the same time "being void of politics, [and] also void of power relations." Without "politics," the problems of camp management through participation become "merely a question of finding the optimal solution to the interests of the community" from the perspective of relief organizations (Turner, 2010, p. 56).

Geographers theorize the political broadly, as concerning negotiations and "distributions of power" – so that participation schemes can also be understood as political in how they attempt to govern populations, beginning with their framing of camp residents as a community (Agnew and Muscara, 2012; Hyndman, 1997). In Foucauldian terms, through participatory schemes and empowerment, camp management seeks to move from a disciplinary mode of government to shaping or governing the mentalities of refugees. It aims to transform a population framed as powerless victims to empowered and participating subjects, who facilitate program implementation and service delivery. The goal is for refugees to *feel* involved and choose to conduct themselves in the manner desired, *not to* change the actual structures of management (Turner, 2010).

Also countering the idea of refugees as passive, Elizabeth Holzer (2015) argues that participation was not just a pragmatic way to govern conduct or to seek to "empower" refugees but was imperative to the management of Buduburam camp for Lebanese refugees in Ghana. By comparing the camp to other poor municipalities, Holzer argues that refugee participation is a form of resilient and indispensable civic engagement in the face of crises. With few public services, little public administration, and scarce resources, the camp relied on its residents to cope with frequent breakdowns in the delivery of aid. Without refugee participation they simply could not manage: "Civic engagement in Buduburam was not a luxury; it was necessity" (Holzer, 2015, p. 40).

Holzer (2015) employs a broad conception of "civic life," including fleeting, informal acts, and the "everyday small acts of helping," which she interprets as "all the more powerful" in the refugee camp context. Yet, definitions of the "civic" are usually tied to citizenship, originating in belonging to the *polis* – urban political space – which Michel Agier (2003) argues cannot be found in camps because they never move from emergency management to enduring political recognition even when other characteristics of the urban may be emergent. Nevertheless, rather than a binary contrast of the urban and the camp, Agier terms these enduring spaces as city-camps (*villes-camp*) (Agier, 2003). This creates liminal space for debate as to whether refugee participation in essential service delivery can be considered "civic engagement," even without the foundational urban political space of the "polis."

Beyond participating in camp governance structures or programs, or tolerated everyday activities, refugees can and do choose to subvert and rework aspects of the rules and conditions which govern life in camps. Indeed, just as participating in "civic" activities may be necessary to life in the camp, so may be subversion of camp limitations on necessary activities such as running small businesses, reselling aid, seeking informal employment or land to cultivate outside of a camp, or collecting resources such as firewood from the surrounding locale (Agier, 2003). In some cases, such activities may transcend more than camp boundaries, as camps are linked in to cross-border trade networks. Such activities are passively tolerated by camp officials in some contexts, recognizing that aid only is often insufficient to live. Officially, such practices are often disallowed, contributing to the precarity that refugees face in undertaking them without legal protection.

Further countering claims of passivity, refugees actively resist and dispute conditions within camps. Protests, particularly when related to demands for adequate aid, are seen as obstructing humanitarian aid, and sometimes framed as proof of dependency, rather than seen as voicing legitimate concerns about their lives and their futures. Shutting down such protests is framed as "for their own good" or protecting "vulnerable refugees" – yet, Holzer notes, other impediments to humanitarian aid are deemed legitimate, such as donor lack of generosity and responsibility sharing (Holzer, 2015). In spite of human rights rhetoric, the response to resistance in camps is often "state violence, greater securitization of aid delivery and the violent clamping down on claims-making refugee organizations" (Daley, 2013, p. 909). Refugees who are seen to encourage others to resist or protest may be imprisoned, or even extradited to their countries – a kind of disciplinary governance meant to discourage dissent (Holzer, 2015; Hovil and Mbazumutima, 2012). Such punishment nonetheless underscores the volition and political lives of refugees in camps and conditions of extended exile.

Ramadan (2013) illustrates how Palestinian camps in Lebanon are *assemblages* of people, institutions, and the built environment that produce particular practices and values. He goes beyond the biopolitical analysis of camps to argue that their constrained temporality and liminality in relation to states create a particular "time-space" from which the camp draws its meaning and provides a grounding for everyday geopolitics, "understanding the small moments and acts that negotiate and constitute broader geopolitical architectures in the spaces of the camp and beyond" (Ramadan, 2013, p. 67). He illustrates that both biopolitical control and active political subjectivities are at play in camps, but goes beyond this not so subtle binary tension and argues that they are places of politics, diasporic and otherwise: "Being an active Palestinian instead of a passive and placeless refugee therefore becomes a source of strength, and makes people part of a political constituency that is concentrated and reproduced in camps." While Hyndman's work on refugee camps highlights them as sites of intensified biopolitical management, Ramadan brings nuance to such evidence: "The refugee camp is more than just a humanitarian space of physical relief and welfare, more than a space of exception and intensified biopolitical control. For Palestinians in Lebanon, it is also a space of refuge from the bewildering disorientation, insecurity and marginality of exile" (p. 74).

AFTER THE CAMP: MANAGING DURABLE SOLUTIONS

UNHCR's mandate, in addition to protection and humanitarian assistance, is ultimately to seek durable solutions for refugees that resolve their refugee status and need for UNHCR's protection (UNHCR, 2013). The agency endorses three solutions that aim to provide long-lasting protection: local integration in the initial country of refuge; resettlement to a third country; or voluntary return to one's country of origin. Repatriation, also referred to simply as return, remains the preferred solution of UNHCR, and remains within its mandate during refugees' initial period of (re)integration (UNHCR, 2013, n.d.). Nevertheless, return has seen a downward trend since the 1990s "decade of repatriation" (Crisp, 2014; UNHCR, 2015, n.d.). At its best, return is seen by many as the ideal way to redress the loss of domicile and the fact of displacement, to repair exclusions from citizenship rights and state institutions, and to promote reconciliation. For some, return can be a way of asserting belonging to a place and within a nation, affirming political victory, or minimally, a return to greater security after conflict (Fresia, 2014; Hammond, 2004; Long, 2012).

In increasingly protracted refugee situations, "return" may be a misnomer – multiple generations born in exile may in fact be "returning" to a place they had never previously lived. Repatriation may also be a misnomer – it implies renewed inclusion in citizenship, when those forced to flee may never have enjoyed full rights within their country of origin. Accordingly, Katy Long differentiates a physical process of return – simply crossing a border to one's state of official citizenship, or returning to a specific location of prior residence – and a political and social process of repatriation – becoming a fully included member of the nation (Long, 2013).

The figure of the refugee is a paradigmatic sign of the aberration of the nation-state-territory triad, and related essentialized conceptions of identity, autochthony, and belonging. Repatriation, then, is the resolution that most normatively upholds this same system (Malkki, 1992, 1995). Critical scholars question the efficacy of the emphasis on these "solutions" in resolving the question of citizenship protections and home for refugees in increasingly protracted refugee situations (Chimni, 2004; Daley, 2013; Hyndman and Giles, 2017). An emphasis on these solutions can draw attention away from the broader geopolitical and political economic causes of conflict and displacement (Chimni, 2004; Daley, 2013). It may also defer solutions indefinitely to only when return or resettlement can occur, so that new possibilities for restoring political being and basic rights within the reality of protracted situations have not been adequately explored (Hyndman and Giles, 2017). Most worryingly, the emphasis on repatriation as the ideal solution may contribute to the premature cessation of protection, and even *refoulement* (forced return) (Bradley, 2008; Chimni, 2004).

The actual level of involvement of refugees in the decision if, when, and how to return to their countries of origin, or to participate in other durable solutions, varies greatly. The case of Guatemalan Maya (who actively participated in negotiations around their return while still in exile) provides an interesting example of the possibilities when space is created for refugee voices in decisions around durable solutions (Bradley, 2014; Long, 2013). This case also suggests that political re-engagement and recognition, as well as claims-making and the recognition of political community, can begin prior to (and potentially without) actual physical return. It initially disrupted the nation-state-territory nexus by recognizing citizenship and belonging beyond borders (Long, 2013). Yet, participation is not straightforward, as one cannot assume specific refugee populations are necessarily one united community (Holzer, 2015; Hyndman, 1997). Indeed, refugees may have diverse political factions and varied perspectives on ideal solutions or necessary conditions for return (Ramadan, 2013; Turner, 2010).

When UNHCR and the states hosting refugees deem that the situation from which refugees fled no longer presents a real danger of persecution to those in exile, they may choose to invoke the cessation clause, ending refugee status for those in exile, and often requiring return (where local integration or other solutions are not offered). Return may also be strongly encouraged prior to the invocation of the cessation clause. For example, measures may be taken to make life in camps less liveable, such as reducing food rations, closing schools, prohibiting livelihood activities, and increasing security (IRRI and Rema Ministries, 2012). Additionally, repatriation may be incentivized through aid packages for returnees (Haver et al., 2009). "Illegal migrants" who do not have recognized refugee status, even though they may have left their countries of origin under similar conditions to recognized refugees, get little recognition because they have not engaged with humanitarian management systems which would require them to live in camps. In such scenarios, "voluntary repatriation" may be a perversely ironic term, through which coerced or even forced return migration becomes a sanctioned solution to initial forced migration.

Refugee negotiations of decisions about their management and protection continue throughout return processes, and may be shaped by process beyond those addressed by humanitarian programming. For example, research suggests that in Bosnia, many displaced people returned only as long as needed to access reparations of property and indemnifications that were not otherwise available, only to later sell or rent out their properties and continue to reside elsewhere (Black, 2002; Black and Koser, 1999; Jansen, 2007; Ó Tuathail and O'Loughlin, 2009). Many displaced people were uncomfortable returning to past homes that were now sites of traumatic memories. Further, the drastic changes in the larger political economic context were not addressed in return programs, and many displaced people were no longer able to access livelihoods in their former places of residence even if they desired to return. A comprehensive and workable approach to return requires taking into consideration factors beyond refugee and repatriation management. Economic restructuring is increasingly central to peace agreements and neoliberal reconstruction plans often rely on market-based strategies (Haynes, 2010). Such political-economic transformations shape labour markets, social services, and ultimately the livability and durability of solutions, like return, for former refugees. Displacements due to neoliberal accumulation by dispossession and exacerbated patterns of uneven geographical development may compound initial forced displacement. Decisions to move are forged within local and regional contexts of containment, under conditions not of refugees' own making.

CASE STUDY: LANDLESS BURUNDIAN RETURNEES

The balance of this section is based on original graduate research conducted by co-author Yolanda Weima (2015). The case study of Burundian returnees unable to access land on return highlights how "grand theories of humanitarian government" cannot fully capture the ruptures and sutures of displacement, return, and migration again (and again) that may occur over the lifetimes of families caught between violence, starvation, and family separation. Following genocide targeting educated Hutu by the military in 1972, and protracted warfare in the 1990s, hundreds of thousands of Burundians sought refuge both in neighbouring countries and in sites for internally displaced people, or were forced into internal "regroupment" camps (Daley, 2008; Lemarchand, 2011). Refugee return was promoted at many points over the following decades, including prior to the violence in the 1990s, and especially following the signing of peace accords in 2000, even though they did not end the violence in Burundi. Over 700,000 Burundians were repatriated in the 12 years following the peace accords.

Challenges to the durability of supposed "durable solutions" for refugees, as well as refugee negotiation of processes and decisions about their "management," can be seen in the Burundian context, particularly in the case of returnees who were not able to access land upon return. Crudely framed as "where to put" landless returnees, villagization programs explicitly sought to regroup people of different ethnicities, a sort-of socio-spatial engineering of social cohesion meant to promote long-term peace as well as modernization and development (Newbury, 2005; Purdeková, 2017). While the villages were meant to contribute to returnee reintegration and self-sufficiency, less than half of the villagers where research was conducted had received land to cultivate. The little land that was given often had very poor soil (Weima, 2015). Few other livelihood opportunities existed in such remote locations (Falisse and Niyonkuru, 2015).

Many of those residing in these villages returned to Burundi against their will due to camp closures in Tanzania, or through deportation after being identified as illegal migrants rather than refugees, as they had self-settled after fleeing and made lives in Tanzanian communities outside of camps (Hovil and Mbazumutima, 2012; IOM, 2014; IRRI and Rema Ministries, 2012). Others were ambivalent about their return – they had been told that they would be able to have their properties restored or to receive land from the government, to return to their regions of origin, and to no longer face exclusions and persecutions they had as refugees or under past regimes in Burundi. Some had desired return and eagerly or pragmatically engaged with the new political order, seeking opportunities from which they had previously been excluded. Some returned because they felt discomfort and threat due to the political rhetoric in Tanzania that conveyed they were no longer welcome; they no longer felt at home in a place that had, over decades, become home. Emphasis on return to the territory of a "state of origin" as a return "home" by regional states and refugee agencies neglects the many ways in which former refugees had, over decades, built and experienced home in other countries (IRRI, 2013; IRRI and Rema Ministries, 2009; Weima, 2015).

For villagized returnees settled in their specific region of origin, renewed ties with family members did offer important support in reintegration. For many families, however, return created new ruptures and challenges, especially for those who had self-settled in Tanzania. This included separation from Tanzanian spouses or adoptive families, and separation from children who more successfully "passed" as Tanzanian and who had not been caught and/or forced to return. Even when families returned together, the difficult conditions in the villages created new kinds of dislocation and isolation (Weima, 2015).

Despite these ruptures, returnees worked hard to make life in the villages more liveable, and to shape the space in which they found themselves – as many had previously done multiple times, in multiple places, due to multiple displacements. For example, returnee villagers re-established traditions of community support for neighbours in both celebration and hardship. They shaped their physical space – for example, by decorating houses with simple drawings of flowers, people, and messages about their return, or creating kitchen buildings and outhouses that had not initially been provided. When the simple mudbrick houses originally provided in one "peace village" literally crumbled – the soil from which they had been constructed was not suitable for durable bricks, particularly in the rainy season – other residents sheltered neighbours in their own small homes, and rebuilt houses as they were able (Weima, 2015).

Although repatriation technically restores *de jure* citizenship to former refugees, returnees were still managed as an aid-dependent and helpless population. They were framed as needing to be empowered, to learn work-ethic and self-sufficiency as though they were still refugees, not citizens. Contradictorily, the framing of returnees as mendicants was most poignant when village residents attempted to protest a meagre distribution of food aid. The aid was given through the government in recognition that it was impossible for most villagized returnees to meet their own needs. Residents were shocked by the insufficiency of the distribution – enough food for a couple of meals, but which was meant to last them several months. Village residents decided to refuse to accept the aid or participate in its distribution, demanding adequate food to live given their lack of land or livelihood opportunities (Weima, 2015).

In response to this protest, the refugees' former status as displaced people was used to cast them as dependent mendicants, rather than rights-claiming citizens, even though mendicancy does not describe their experiences as refugees. Many of the returnees were self-sufficient outside of camps for decades before being brought to camps prior to their repatriation. Several had learned trades and specialized skills; most of those in the camps had worked outside the camps as agricultural labourers; others had risked getting caught crossing the borders in small-trading; others participated in local leadership in the camp, or had remunerated work as teachers or water-tank guards. Yet, because of their status as "returnees," understanding of their prior experience as refugees and their resultant character was homogenized. They were told to passively take the food distribution, or they would not receive any aid in the future. Their renewed citizenship, then, was not associated with renewed voice, entitlements or rights, but with continued discipline to accept aid. Self-sufficiency of returnees was the stated goal, but without adequate provision to catalyse such a transition (Weima, 2015).

One of the results of insufficient aid and livelihood opportunities is that several returnee families who had been resettled in the village had again left Burundi by 2014. They moved on, seeking land and labour opportunities in Democratic Republic of Congo

(DRC), Tanzania, or further afield. Many other households relied on the labour migration remittances of young Burundian men who returned to Tanzania. Often households drew on transnational networks of friends and family, knowledge of and past experience in other places, and de facto belonging to communities elsewhere (Weima, 2015). In this way, returnees sought their own de facto solutions, which crossed borders, transcended nationalisms, and avoided official state management both of refuge and return. Labour migration and other forms of survival migration are shaped by and not entirely separate from previous displacements (both in seeking refuge and in return), nor are they necessarily "voluntary" despite the framing of workers having "freedom" to sell their labour within a capitalist economic system (Harvey, 2006; Mezzadra and Neilson, 2013). This continued movement defies the sedentarist emphasis on return to "home" countries (Long, 2009; Weima, 2017). However, not all households had the resources or capacity to undertake such strategies, and those unable to continue to move – the "involuntarily immobile" returnees – were often the most vulnerable (Lubkemann, 2008).

Notably, in 2014, Tanzania granted citizenship to over 170,000 Burundians who had been refugees since 1972 (or who had been born in Tanzania to that cohort of refugees). The Tanzanian government is now adamant that those who returned to Burundi, even if they belonged to that cohort, forfeited this opportunity. In 2015, political violence resurged around the national election in Burundi. Soon after, several regions suffered from drought and extreme weather. Camps in Tanzania, Rwanda, and the DRC were reopened or expanded to manage renewed large-scale forced migration. Official numbers are not likely to include those who have relied on prior experience and networks in Tanzania to settle outside of camps, including those who left prior to 2015, though border region monitoring is making it difficult for even those with decades of experience to continue this informal practice. Only two years later, with political stability and security still elusive, repatriation is again being strongly encouraged by politicians in both Tanzania and in Burundi. Some refugees are choosing to return, but the majority remain wary. The humanitarian response has been severely hampered by a lack of funding, leading to cuts in food rations which then became consistently below recommended caloric minimums. Although no longer classified as an emergency, the conditions in the camps are those of an ongoing humanitarian crisis – a silent violence, far from the shores of Europe, or geopolitical concerns of the West (Watts, 2013).

WITHOUT CONCLUSION

The spatialized tactics of "managing migration" operate at regional scales that deepen North/South divides and, at finer scales, through encampment which creates social and political isolation through spatial exclusion. States create enforcement regimes and practice exclusion in relation to all but the most elite migrants, whereas asylum seekers creatively subvert or work around the biometric visas, safe third country agreements, and other "policy walls" that prevent them from getting to countries of the global North. Humanitarian organizations voice neutrality while still enmeshed in this geopolitical system of securitization and containment.

While the enforcement and humanitarian impulses of global North states remain in tension, the highly spatialized tactics of managing personal security among refugees, asylum seekers, and migration through ongoing migration across borders is underrepresented in the forced migration literature. Encampment remains a dominant spatiality of state management of refugees, often legitimized through arguments of service provision and safety. Yet camps are porous, and at times are transformed into more permanent settlements that become destinations for those who return.

Encampment is tied to the state-centric orientation to return as a "durable solution." Yet encampment may extend displacement, and return itself can be experienced as renewed transnational displacement. Ultimately, refugees negotiate their own safety both within and beyond the humanitarian governance system, through extensive and often transnational networks.

REFERENCES

Agier, M. (2003). Between War and City: Towards an Urban Anthropology of Refugee Camps. *Ethnography*, 3(3), 317–41.

Agnew, J. and Muscara, L. (2012). *Making Political Geography*, second edn. Lanham, MD: Rowman and Littlefield.

Betts, A. and Collier, P. (2017). *Refuge: Transforming a Broken Refugee System*. London: Allen Lane.

Black, R. (2002). Conceptions of "Home" and the Political Geography of Refugee Repatriation: Between Assumption and Contested Reality in Bosnia-Herzegovina. *Applied Geography*, 22, 125–38.

Black, R. and Koser, K. (1999). *The End of the Refugee Cycle? Refugee Repatriation and Reconstruction*. New York: Berghahn Books.

Bradley, M. (2008). Back to Basics: The Conditions of Just Refugee Returns. *Journal of Refugee Studies*, 21(3), 285–304. doi:10.1093/jrs/fen023.

Bradley, M. (2014). Rethinking Refugeehood: Statelessness, Repatriation, and Refugee Agency. *Review of International Studies*, 40(1), 101–23. doi:10.1017/s0260210512000514.

Castles, S. (2008). The Politics of Exclusion: Asylum and the Global Order. *Metropolis World Bulletin*, 8, 3–6.

Chimni, B.S. (2004). From Resettlement to Involuntary Repatriation: Towards a Critical History of Durable Solutions to Refugee Problems. *Refugee Survey Quarterly*, 23(3), 55–73.

Crawley, H. (2017). Refugee Economics. [Review of the book *Refuge: Transforming a Broken Refugee System* by Alexander Betts and Paul Collier]. *Nature*, 544, 26–7.

Crawley, H. and Skleparis, D. (2017). Refugees, Migrants, Neither, Both: Categorical Fetishism and the Politics of Bounding in Europe's "Migration Crisis." *Journal of Ethnic and Migration Studies*, 1–17. doi:10.1080/1369183x.2017.1348224.

Crisp, J. (2014). In Search of Solutions: Refugees are Doing It for Themselves. Paper presented at the Refugee Voices (Opening Plenary), Oxford.

Daley, P. (2008). *Gender & Genocide in Burundi: The Search for Spaces of Peace in the Great Lakes Region*. Oxford: James Currey.

Daley, P. (2013). Refugees, IDPs and Citizenship Rights: The Perils of Humanitarianism in the African Great Lakes Region. *Third World Quarterly*, 34(5), 893–912. doi:10.1080/01436597.2013.800740.

Ehrkamp, P. (2016). Progress Report: Geographies of Migration I: Refugees. *Progress in Human Geography*, 41(6), 813–22. doi: 10.1177/0309132516663061.

Falisse, J.-B. and Niyonkuru, R.C. (2015). Social Engineering for Reintegration: Peace Villages for the "Uprooted" Returnees in Burundi. *Journal of Refugee Studies*, 28(3), 388–411. doi:10.1093/jrs/fev002.

Fresia, M. (2014). Performing Repatriation? The Role of Refugee Aid in Shaping New Beginnings in Mauritania. *Development and Change*, 45(3), 434–57.

Geiger, M. and Pécoud, A. (2010). *The Politics of International Migration Management*. Basingstoke, UK: Palgrave Macmillan.

Hammond, L. (2004). *This Place Will Become Home: Refugee Repatriation to Ethiopia*. Ithaca, NY: Cornell University Press.

Harvey, D. (2006). *The Limits to Capital*. London and New York: Verso.

Haver, K., Hatungimana, F., and Tennant, V. (2009). *Money Matters: An Evaluation of the Use of Cash Grants in UNHCR's Voluntary Repatriation and Reintegration Program in Burundi*. Geneva: UNHCR.

Haynes, D.F. (2010). Lessons From Bosnia's Arizona Market: Harm to Women in a Neoliberalized Postconflict Reconstruction Process. *University of Pennsylvania Law Review*, 158(6), 1779–829.

Holzer, E. (2015). *The Concerned Women of Buduburam: Refugee Activists and Humanitarian Dilemmas.* Ithaca, NY and London: Cornell University Press.

Hovil, L. (2014). Local Integration. In E. Fiddian-Qasmiyeh, G. Loescher, K. Long, and N. Sigona (eds), *The Oxford Handbook of Refugee Studies and Forced Migration* (pp. 488–98). Oxford: Oxford University Press.

Hovil, L. and Mbazumutima, T. (2012). Tanzania's Mtabila Camp Finally Closed. *Pambazuka News*, December 13. Retrieved October 1, 2018 from http://www.pambazuka.org/governance/tanzania's-mtabila-camp-finally-closed.

Huysmans, J. (2006). *The Politics of Insecurity: Fear, Migration, and Asylum in the EU.* Oxford: Routledge.

Hyndman, J. (1997). Refugee Self-management and the Question of Governance. *Refuge*, **16**(2), 16–22.

Hyndman, J. (2000). *Managing Displacement: Refugees and the Politics of Humanitarianism.* Minneapolis, MN: University of Minnesota Press.

Hyndman, J. (2018). To Help or Not to Help? Humanitarian Spaces, Power and Government. In M. Coleman and J. Agnew (eds), *Handbook on the Geographies of Power.* Cheltenham, UK and Northampton, MA, USA: Edward Elgar Publishing.

Hyndman, J. and Giles, W. (2011). Waiting for What? The Feminization of Asylum in Protracted Situations. *Gender, Place & Culture*, **18**(3), 361–79.

Hyndman, J. and Giles, W. (2017). *Refugees in Extended Exile.* New York: Routledge.

IOM (2014). IOM Assists Returnees Expelled from Tanzania in Burundi and Uganda. November 2. Retrieved October 1, 2018 from http://www.iom.int/news/iom-assists-returnees-expelled-tanzania-burundi-and-uganda.

IRRI (2013). "I can't be a citizen if I am still a refugee." Former Burundian Refugees Struggle to Assert their New Tanzanian Citizenship. Retrieved October 1, 2018 from http://www.refworld.org/docid/53b3da324.html.

IRRI and Rema Ministries (2009). "Two People Can't Share the Same Pair of Shoes": Citizenship, Land and the Return of Refugees to Burundi. Citizenship and Forced Migration in the Great Lakes Region, Working Paper. Retrieved October 1, 2018 from https://www.ssrc.org/publications/view/52FF4E58-22D5-DE11-9D32-001CC477EC70/.

IRRI and Rema Ministries (2012). An Urgent Briefing on the Situation of Burundian Refugees in Mtabila Camp in Tanzania. Retrieved October 1, 2018 from https://reliefweb.int/sites/reliefweb.int/files/resources/Mtabila%2520FINAL.pdf.

Jansen, S. (2007). The Privatisation of Home and Hope: Return, Reforms and the Foreign Intervention in Bosnia-Herzegovina. *Dialectical Anthropology*, **30**(3–4), 177–99. doi:10.1007/s10624-007-9005-x.

Lemarchand, R. (2011). Burundi 1972: Genocide Denied, Revised, and Remembered. In R. Lemarchand (ed.), *Forgotten Genocides: Oblivion, Denial and Memory* (pp. 37–50). Philadelphia, PA: University of Pennsylvania Press.

Long, K. (2009). Extending Protection? Labour Migration and Durable Solutions for Refugees. New Issues in Refugee Research, Working Paper 176. Geneva.

Long, K. (2012). Statebuilding Through Refugee Repatriation. *Journal of Intervention and Statebuilding*, **6**(4), 369–86. doi:10.1080/17502977.2012.714236.

Long, K. (2013). *The Point of No Return: Refugees, Rights, and Repatriation.* Oxford: Oxford University Press.

Lubkemann, S.C. (2008). Involuntary Immobility: On a Theoretical Invisibility in Forced Migration Studies. *Journal of Refugee Studies*, **21**(4), 454–75. doi:10.1093/jrs/fen043.

Malkki, L.H. (1992). National Geographic: The Rooting of Peoples and the Territorialization of National Identity among Scholars and Refugees. *Cultural Anthropology*, **7**(1), 24–44.

Malkki, L.H. (1995). Refugees and Exile: From "Refugee Studies" to the National Order of Things. *Annual Review of Anthropology*, **2**, 495–523.

Mezzadra, S. and Neilson, B. (2013). *Border as Method, Or, the Multiplication of Labor.* Durham, NC and London: Duke University Press.

Newbury, D. (2005). Returning Refugees: Four Historical Patterns of "Coming Home" to Rwanda. *Society for Comparative Study of Society and History*, **47**(2), 252–85.

Ó Tuathail, G. and O'Loughlin, J. (2009). After Ethnic Cleansing: Return Outcomes in Bosnia-Herzegovina a Decade Beyond War. *Annals of the Association of American Geographers*, **99**(5), 1045–53. doi:10.1080/00045600903260671.

Purdeková, A. (2017). Respacing for Peace? Resistance to Integration and the Ontopolitics of Rural Planning in Post-war Burundi. *Development and Change*, **48**(3), 534–66. doi:10.1111/dech.12305.

Ramadan, A. (2013). Spatialising the Refugee Camp. *Transactions of the Institute of British Geographers*, **38**(1), 65–77. doi:10.1111/j.1475-5661.2012.00509.x.

Redfield, P. (2005). Doctors, Borders, and Life in Crisis. *Cultural Anthropology*, **20**(3), 328–61.

Sanyal, R. (2017). A No-camp Policy: Interrogating Informal Settlements in Lebanon. *Geoforum*, **84**, 117–25.

Turner, S. (2010). *Politics of Innocence: Hutu Identity, Conflict and Camp Life.* Oxford: Berghahn Books.

UNHCR (2013). Note on the Mandate of the High Commissioner for Refugees. Geneva. Retrieved October 1, 2018 from http://www.unhcr.org/526a22cb6.pdf.

UNHCR (2015). *UNHCR Global Report 2014*. Geneva. Retrieved October 1, 2018 from http://www.unhcr.org/gr14/index.xml.

UNHCR (2017). *Global Report 2016*. Geneva. Retrieved October 1, 2018 from http://www.unhcr.org/the-global-report.htm.

UNHCR (n.d.). Voluntary Repatriation: Going Back Home. Retrieved October 1, 2018 from http://www.unhcr.org/pages/49c3646cfe.html.

Watts, M.J. (2013). *Silent Violence: Food, Famine, and Peasantry in Northern Nigeria*. Athens, GA: University of Georgia Press.

Weima, Y. (2015). Villagisation for Our Times: Neoliberal Governmentality and the Experiences of Villagised Burundian Returnees. MA unpublished manuscript thesis, Queen's University, Kingston, ON.

Weima, Y. (2017). Refugee Repatriation and Ongoing Transnationalisms. *Transnational Social Review*, **7**(1), 113–17. doi:10.1080/21931674.2016.1277857.

3. Gender, violence and migration
Cecilia Menjívar and Shannon Drysdale Walsh

Sara, who fled Honduras and sought asylum in the United States, explained: *"Coming here was like having hope that you will come out alive."* (Cardoletti-Carroll et al., 2015, p. 41, emphasis added)

24-year-old Saudi Arabian Dina Ali Lasloom was fleeing domestic abuse to seek asylum in Australia. At her layover in the Manila airport, authorities "confiscated [her] passport and boarding pass to Sydney and held her at an airport hotel until her uncles arrived. When they did, they beat her and forcibly repatriated her." She was "dragged onto a plane from Manila to Riyadh with her mouth taped shut and her arms and legs bound . . ." (Eltahawy, 2017)

Across the globe, the decision of women to migrate is often driven by the need to flee from violence. Reports such as those quoted above reveal that this is a common thread in women's experiences, even from countries as different as Honduras and Saudi Arabia. Women's pathways to migration are commonly part of a continuum of violence in their lives, marked with state failures in responsiveness to violence against women, weak and ineffective justice system institutions, and dangerous journeys to seek asylum elsewhere. If women seek safety in the United States, the asylum system often exposes them to further violence in detention centers and re-victimization and even humiliation in immigration courts. In addition, courts reproduce cultural stereotypes about "machismo" as a cause of violence while denying the role of broader processes, such as the receiving countries' government complicity in the persistent violence in sending countries. In the end, some women are granted asylum, while others are sent back to the same dangerous conditions from which they fled.

The structure of legal and justice systems in countries of origin, along the migration route, and in receiving countries, have harmful impacts on female migrants. We describe these harms as "legal violence," which is the *normalized but cumulatively injurious effects of laws* (Menjívar and Abrego, 2012, p. 1380), a concept that applied to this case permits us to see how women are propelled through a continuum of violence before and during the migration progress. Legal violence encompasses structural violence, the institutionalized inequalities that systematically discriminate against women – for example, keeping them marginalized, poor, and vulnerable – as well as symbolic violence, that is, the naturalized inequalities, categories of domination, and internalization of social asymmetries that sustain hierarchies of power.

In addition, there are gender-specific reasons for women's migration that have received less attention in the scholarly literature that are related to, but distinct from, legal violence. These include violence within families and in society that disadvantages women; symbolic violence (e.g., stigma and discrimination after divorce or union dissolution); and discriminatory labor practices, among others. Much of the scholarship on migration has focused on factors such as work and family as motives for migration, but less attention has been given to violence as a driver of migration. We demonstrate how the migration process can create, reproduce, and exacerbate many of the forms of gender-based violence that initiate women's migration in the first place (see also Parish, 2017). Although the conditions we examine are present in other parts of the world, we draw primarily on examples from Central American countries. This region is the focus of our research and of our pro bono work on cases of women seeking asylum in the United States. And although we recognize that gender-based violence similarly shapes the migration process of LGBT individuals, in this chapter we focus on women as they are the focus of our research.

In the following, we provide an overview of gender-based violence worldwide and the context of violence in Central America. We then follow the continuum of violence that women typically experience before and during their migratory experiences, from violent conditions in their home country, harrowing journeys, to their struggles in seeking asylum at entry. We argue that the legal and justice systems and policy decisions in countries throughout women's migratory routes amount to legal violence as they enable these harrowing experiences by creating a continuum of violence in sending, transit, and receiving countries.

GENDER, VIOLENCE, AND MIGRATION: A BRIEF OVERVIEW

Gender violence is widespread and worldwide. According to the United Nations and World Health Organization, one in three women worldwide have experienced physical and/or sexual violence at some point in their lives, and for these women such violence comes from an intimate partner at some point in their lives (United Nations Statistics Division, 2015; World Health Organization, 2013, 2016). Women make up two in three victims of intimate partner/family-related homicides worldwide (United Nations Statistics Division, 2015). While there is some variation in levels and types of violence worldwide, there is also significant variation in how states attempt to prevent it and respond to it (Menjívar and Walsh, 2016). The countries from which women seek to flee most often have legal and justice systems that have repeatedly failed to protect them (Walsh and Menjívar, 2016).

Women's experiences of gender-based violence occur throughout the life course, and while it affects all populations, some groups of women, such as girls, are more vulnerable than others (see Santibáñez et al., 2017). Girls under 18 often face (forced) marriage at very young ages (United Nations Statistics Division, 2015, p. 147). While boys are sometimes also married as children, girls are disproportionately affected (United Nations Statistics Division, 2015, p. 147). Early marriage is accompanied by pregnancy, which is particularly detrimental for girls in the short and in the long term as it interrupts their schooling and development and places their health at risk (Menjívar and Walsh, 2016). Older women are also at increased risk of violence, including physical, sexual, and psychological violence as well as financial exploitation or neglect (United Nations Statistics Division, 2015).

Women often experience these various forms of violence – all at once – in an intertwined fashion, with varying degrees of intensity according to their social position, such as social class and/or race/ethnicity (see Menjívar, 2011). Also, visible and recognizable forms of violence – physical, sexual, emotional – occur within contexts of structural, symbolic, and political violence. Unequal power relations create and reproduce conditions for gender-based violence that women seek to escape; such conditions are often condoned in intimate relations in families (Parish, 2017). However, not all women who experience violence are able to flee such conditions; social class, race, age, and other social positions intersect

(Crenshaw, 1991) so that only certain women can seek protection in other countries. Thus, as in other migratory flows, factors such as having access to social networks and information (Massey et al., 1990) and access to financial resources are needed to realize the motivation to migrate. Similar to other migratory flows, therefore, the women who manage to flee violent conditions, organize their journeys, pay for their trip, and arrive at their destination are only a small proportion of those who endure multiple forms of violence around the world today.

Structural Violence, Violent Crime, and Gender Violence as Precursors to Migration

A long history of US intervention in Latin America has left a legacy of violence, contributing to the dangerous conditions that compel migration. While some US policies have aimed at economic development, most interventions, particularly those that seek political stability, have ignored or undermined other goals and resulted in political violence. Among many examples, the United States adopted an anti-communist "national security doctrine" that supported repressive military dictatorships responsible for massive human rights violations throughout Latin America – including the utilization of death squads, torture, murder, and disappearance (Cullather, 1999; Menjívar and Rodríguez, 2005). In Central America during the 1980s, the United States used Honduras as a staging ground for military operations in the region, supported repressive regimes in El Salvador and Guatemala, and armed counter-revolutionaries (contras) in Nicaragua (Reichman, 2011). Complicity in Central American violence and state terror against citizens has left a legacy of human rights violations, weak democratic institutions, and impunity in the region (Booth et al., 2015; Cullather, 1999; LaFeber, 1993; Menjívar and Rodríguez, 2005). Such a legacy is manifested though current engagement with neoliberal economic practices that keep people, and especially women, poor and vulnerable to violence as well as Central American economies subordinate to US interests (Hartviksen, 2014; Weissman, 2010).

The end of the conflicts in Central America in the 1990s did not mean an end to violence, poverty, or migratory flows, particularly from the three northernmost countries, which have been disproportionately impacted by a deteriorated economic infrastructure and violence (Carey and Torres, 2010). In addition to contributing to direct violence during the civil wars, the United States has supported economic policies that exert impoverishment and increase inequality. Central American governments began US-backed neoliberal economic reforms in the 1980s as armed conflicts were ongoing, which contributed to the loss of land, natural resources, and public safety nets, leading to increased inequality. Such reforms cut jobs in four main sectors: tourism, textile maquiladoras, agro-industry, and electronic manufacturing (Varela Huerta, 2017). Today, US support of economically repressive policies such as the North American Free Trade Agreement (NAFTA) and the Central America Free Trade Agreement (CAFTA) have put regular Central American citizens at the receiving end of unfavorable trade relations, further impoverishing the poor – especially women and Afro-Caribbean and indigenous groups (Hartviksen, 2014).

Central America is one of the poorer and more unequal regions of Latin America, a region that in turn has the most unequal distribution of resources in the world (Hoffman and Centeno, 2003). It is estimated that 59 percent of Guatemalans, 63 percent of Hondurans, and 33 percent of Salvadorans lived below their national poverty levels in 2014 (World Bank, 2015). Structural violence (e.g., structural processes and policies that manifest in profound inequality and poverty) and "common" or everyday crime are a deadly combination, making contemporary northern Central American countries some of the most violent on the planet (UNDP, 2009–10). Structural violence in the region is widespread, in the form of limited employment opportunities, poverty-level wages, and limited access to resources (Menjívar, 2011). Additionally, gender-segregated labor markets and wages limit women's access to employment. Women fleeing violence from the three northernmost Central American countries are overwhelmingly poor and socioeco-nomically vulnerable, a significant factor in their lack of protection by their governments.

Social and legal marginalization based on ethnicity exacerbates vulnerabilities for Afro-descendants and indigenous people. Indigenous Maya, who make up more than half of Guatemala's population, have been found at a disadvantage on every social indicator. Mayan women are disproportionately rural, poor, discriminated against, and lack support from the police as well as access to justice system institutions (Carey, 2006). When indig-enous Maya women seek justice for the violence they endure, they are the least likely to be heard (Carey and Torres, 2010). The combined effect of inequality and vulnerabilities in various social positions has made violence in the lives of women (especially poor women) reach crisis levels in Guatemala, Honduras, and El Salvador.

The migration of Central Americans that increased with the armed conflicts in the 1980s continued into the 1990s as more Central Americans migrated in search of better life opportunities and security (Asakura and Torres Falcon, 2013). By 2015, approxi-mately 19 percent of Salvadoran citizens, 7.5 percent of Hondurans, and 6 percent of all Guatemalans lived outside their country of origin (International Organization for Migration, 2015). Research on Central American immigrant women identifies violence as two of the three main reasons compelling women's migration, which include (1) extortion and death threats from delinquent groups; (2) threats and violence suffered from their male partners; and (3) family subsistence (see Willers, 2016 on immigrants in Mexico; Cardoletti-Carroll et al., 2015 on immigrants in the United States).

Given the presence and comingling of various forms of violence – structural, political, and common crime – as well as the legal violence in the form of states' failure to protect women, it is not surprising that Guatemalan, Honduran, and Salvadoran women have been emigrating at high rates. However, continuing the practice during the Central American civil wars, the US government has been classifying Central American women seeking asylum as "regular" (and undocumented) immigrants, rather than bona fide refugees, as many organizations (such as the Center for Gender and Refugee Studies)[1] have categorized them. With these general considerations in mind, we now turn to the case of Central American women fleeing violence to illustrate the main points of this piece and their relevance to other regions of the world.

GENDER VIOLENCE IN CENTRAL AMERICA

Although women have always migrated, it has not been until the last few decades that scholars have noted women as economic migrants in their own right, not just as family

---

[1]   Center for Gender and Refugee Studies. University of California Hastings College of the Law. Accessed July 13, 2017 at http://cgrs.uchastings.edu/publications.

members accompanying others (American Immigration Council, 2017; Hondagneu-Sotelo, 1994; Parreñas, 2001). Oftentimes women, many of whom are mothers at very young ages, migrate in search of better employment opportunities to sustain their families back home, even as family reunification is commonly perceived to be the main reason for women's migration (Salcido and Menjívar, 2012). Women make up approximately half of the total migrant population worldwide, and slightly over half of all Latin American migrants (United Nations, Department of Economic and Social Affairs, 2016).

Legal violence – in the form of failing laws and justice system institutions to address women's safety – compels women to migrate from violent conditions. Increasingly, women flee generalized conditions of violence, which is an amalgamated form of structural, symbolic, and political violence, as well as violence from "common" crime (Menjívar, 2011). In addition, they migrate to avoid violence directed at women in particular. An estimated 52.6 percent of Central American women have migrated due to gender-based violence since the 1990s (Varela Huerta, 2017). Structural and normalized gender violence puts women's lives at risk and limits their life chances; the violence they seek to escape comes from intimate interactions or criminal organizations (Asakura and Torres Falcon, 2013) but it also comes from institutional structures and societal practices (Menjívar and Walsh, 2016) that reproduce profound gender inequalities. Thus, whereas women migrate to escape immediate violence in their lives, the impunity for crimes against them, institutional non-response when women seek protection from violence, and states' unwillingness to enforce laws create powerful contexts of legal violence that women flee.

A context of legal violence often drives women to attempt migration from the three northernmost countries of Central America (El Salvador, Guatemala, and Honduras), typically through Mexico to the United States. These countries are embroiled in generalized violence, with some of the highest murder rates in the world (UNODC, 2012).[2] According to the UNODC report on homicides in 2012, the murder rate in Honduras was 90 per 100,000 population, followed by El Salvador (41), Guatemala (40), Nicaragua, (11), and Costa Rica (8.5). By contrast, the United States' was 4.7 and Canada's was 1.6. This violence is mediated by social cleavages and thus it is classed, raced, and gendered (Menjívar and Walsh, 2016). The resulting sharp increase in migrants from this region has recently been described as a refugee crisis at the US border (Semple, 2016), and similar situations exist in other places around the world, most highly publicized in the European Union.

While a general context of violence has been driving this general pattern of migration, gender-based violence in a context of impunity is the catalyst for many of the women who migrate. According to a regional study in 12 countries of Latin America, close to 25 percent of women reported experiencing physical violence by an intimate partner in Guatemala and El Salvador in 2008 (these estimates were higher in Bolivia, with 52 percent, and lower in Haiti, with 13.4 percent) (Bott et al., 2012). Feminicide, the alarming phenomenon of gender-motivated killings of women in the face of impunity and lack of state response (Lagarde, 2010; Sanford, 2008), is widespread in Latin America. Of the countries with the highest rates of feminicide in the world, more than half are located in Latin America; El Salvador and Guatemala are in the top three (Waiselfisz, 2015).

---

[2] Data from the United Nations Office on Drugs and Crime (UNODC). These rates are reported at the country level, usually through the national police, and are more conservative than other estimates.

Violence against women remains underreported. Still, Central American countries including El Salvador, Honduras, and Guatemala have some of the highest rates of reported violence, especially feminicide, in the world. In Honduras between January and June of 2016, 227 women were murdered; in this same period, 1,498 attacks and 1,375 incidents of sexual violence against women were recorded (Amnesty International, 2017). At the same time, emergency contraception is banned and abortion is criminalized as homicide. These laws leave women who are raped or otherwise coerced into sex with limited options for taking care of themselves or their children. Such acts amount to legal violence as they further impoverish women and render them vulnerable to violence. These expressions of violence are produced and sustained by a social system that legitimates and reproduces patriarchal structures (Beramendi et al., 2015). We add that this social system is reinforced through the legal violence in the justice system.

GENDER VIOLENCE IN TRANSIT

The structure of US law makes it necessary for the vast majority of Central American women seeking asylum to do so from within the United States. While visa opportunities include employment-based, family reunification, tourist, among others, there are no similar visas for these women, as they do not qualify for refugee protection outright. US policy requires that asylum seekers *are already on US soil* in order to apply. Thus, a typical route to access the US asylum system is for a woman to make the dangerous journey through Mexico. But when women leave a context of legal violence in their home countries, they often encounter legal violence in transit (see Colegio de México/ONU Mujeres, 2017; Parish, 2017). Being outside one's home country produces a new kind of vulnerability for those who are undocumented and avoiding being sent back to dangerous conditions in their home country. Thus, the violence that Central American women escape from does not abruptly end as they exit their countries. Structural, gender-based, and sexual violence continue through the journey, emerging in different forms as women make their way north. In addition, these women's experiences of violence during the journey accumulate, build up, and exacerbate the various forms of violence they flee from such that when they arrive in the United States they have acquired multiple layers of violent experiences. This process mirrors what women who traverse territories and cross borders by land or sea face in other parts of the world.

In 2015, 121,260 Central American migrants were apprehended and deported by Mexican authorities, a substantial increase since 2010 when 65,802 migrants were apprehended and deported from Mexico (Consejo Nacional de Población, 2016). Most of these migrants were from Guatemala (46 percent), Honduras (34 percent), and El Salvador (20 percent) and about 23 percent of those apprehended in 2015 were women (Consejo Nacional de Población, 2016). Most of the migrants in transit through Mexico are apprehended in the Mexican state of Chiapas (42 percent), which borders Guatemala (Consejo Nacional de Población, 2016).

Along with increased efforts to control migration flows both at the US-Mexico border as well as Mexico's interior, migrants crossing through Mexico today face exponential levels of violence. Organized crime has become increasingly involved in the smuggling of migrants (who do not have visas to enter the United States), which has resulted in diverse forms of trafficking and skyrocketing rates of kidnappings (Izcarra Palacios, 2015). In just the 2009–10 period, there were over 10,000 kidnappings documented by civic organizations in Mexico (Izcarra Palacios, 2015; Kuhner, 2011). Migrants are vulnerable to kidnappings by smugglers and gangs, but according to human rights organizations, migrants who cross Mexico also face extortion by the police, physical and verbal abuse, robbery, life-threatening accidents, forced labor, and various forms of gender-based violence (Kuhner, 2011; Schmidt and Buechler, 2017).

A common mode of transportation to cross Mexico, especially for migrants with few resources (e.g., who do not have enough to afford a smuggler) (see Sládková, 2010), is to ride on the roof of the notoriously dangerous train known as *La Bestia* "The Beast" (Dominguez Villegas, 2014) going to the north of Mexico. Many migrants suffer life-threatening accidents as they fall off the train or have their arms and/or legs crushed by the wheels (Vogt, 2013). In an attempt to avoid travel by way of *La Bestia*, most women travel through even more clandestine routes utilizing smugglers and organized trafficking networks that provide false documentation to travel by bus or airplane. When smugglers demand more money during the trip and the women are unable to produce it, they are held until their family members put together the money the smugglers are demanding. While awaiting extortion payments, women are compelled to provide sex and/or do chores such as food preparation and cleaning. Although these routes seem safer than riding the train, they often become even more dangerous as women become vulnerable to sexual violence and dependent on the traffickers (Kuhner, 2011). Migrants crossing Mexico must bribe their way through, dealing with extortion, robberies, unscrupulous enforcement agents, and physical attacks (Cardoletti-Carroll et al., 2015).

The various forms of violence that migrant women face as they cross Mexico are underreported (Cardoletti-Carroll et al., 2015) as the police and immigration authorities are often involved in their trafficking. Sexual violence has been so normalized in these women's journeys that criminal gangs often view it as part of the "price" that women must pay to pass thorough their territories (Amnesty International, 2010), to the degree that many women take contraceptives as they begin their journeys (Amnesty International, 2010). Women have reported that police and immigration officers often coerce them into forced sex in exchange for letting them go through without being detained or deported (Schmidt and Buechler, 2017), and are often threatened with deportation if they report the abuse (Kuhner, 2011). Being coerced into survival sex in a context where they are not protected by the state puts women at high risk of other forms of abuse such as sex trafficking and dire health consequences such as HIV (Dewey, 2012; Goldenberg et al., 2013; Shannon et al., 2008; Wojcicki, 2002). Thus, human traffickers and other forms of criminal organizations, in collusion with authorities, use rape and sexual violence to terrorize women during the journey (Schmidt and Buechler, 2017). But even if Central American women report these assaults, Mexican authorities have never prosecuted any cases of sexual violence, including rape, against these women (Schmidt and Buechler, 2017). Contexts of legal violence are characterized by institutional indifference (or by direct actions or through policies that harm certain groups), lack of responsiveness, and impunity. These contexts sustain and amplify the same messages that women received in the home countries from which they fled – that their lives are not valued and that their plights are unimportant.

RE-VICTIMIZATION, STEREOTYPING, AND THE US ASYLUM SYSTEM

Legal violence does not end, even if Central American women reach the United States and apply for asylum. Just as gender-based violence and state failure to respond to it are drivers of migration, there is also gender-based violence that women face when they seek asylum (see also McKinnon, 2016). Not only does the state often fail to protect women who are seeking safety, it can put these women in further danger and add to the harm. In the United States, the legal system is not prepared to recognize these women's need for protection, as extant definitions of who deserves protection (e.g., UN definitions) do not recognize their plight. A general lack of formal or legal categories of admission for women fleeing extreme conditions of gender-based violence creates a fractured asylum system where some women receive asylum while others do not.[3] In June 2018, Attorney General Jeff Sessions announced that domestic and gang violence will no longer constitute grounds for asylum, a decision that is having far-reaching implications for Central American women seeking asylum in the United States. Thus, when Central American women seek asylum in the United States, they are often re-victimized within the US immigration and asylum system.

Since the structure of US law requires that anyone seeking asylum apply for it from within the United States, women seeking protection must cross the border to apply for asylum on US soil. Thus, legal violence continues in these women's lives, as crossing the border without inspection constitutes a misdemeanor (re-entry after deportation becomes a felony) and thus the law criminalizes these women from the start. These women are usually apprehended or they turn themselves in at the border. Upon interrogation by immigration authorities, they declare their intention to file for asylum. If they are found to have a credible fear of return to their home country, they are usually held in detention while awaiting a hearing. But the process of applying for asylum until a final ruling takes years, so women (but not men) are often released on bond or through the Alternatives to Detention Programs and under surveillance (e.g., with check-ins with the immigration authorities and/or ankle bracelets for monitoring their movement).[4] Detention centers add a layer of trauma for these women as these spaces are increasingly akin to prisons (Gómez Cervantes et al., 2018), and there have been reports of women abused by guards while detained (USGAO, 2013).

We have both served as pro bono expert witnesses on several cases of women seeking asylum in the United States from situations of violence in the northern countries of Central America. We have interacted with the minority of female asylum applicants who have been able to gain access to a competent pro bono lawyer. Speaking from these experiences, a common thread among these cases is that immigration officials treat women with very little respect, and subject them to a line of questioning that assumes they are

---

[3]   Although gender is not included in the categories recognized in international protocols as qualifying for refuge or asylum, there are some cases that have set narrow and very limited precedent for women in the United States to qualify for asylum, such as Guatemalan women in marital unions. However, even in these scenarios, lawyers cannot assume that cases will be successful.

[4]   It is difficult to follow the logic of these surveillance programs because they are supposed to be for people who are a flight risk. However, the women who are fleeing violence in their home countries, who have equal or even more traumatic experiences during the journey, and are asking for protection so they are not sent back, may not logically represent flight risk.

lying or aims to trip them up about the consistency of their story. Women are not usually offered legal counsel, and are often unaware that it is necessary or could be beneficial.[5] Many Central American women testify before immigration judges without an advocate of any sort and face hostile questioning by US immigration lawyers, whose career incentives include deporting as many asylum seekers as possible.[6] While it is the duty of US immigration officials to only grant asylum to those with meritorious cases, the process need not be so contentious. Nor does it need to make invisible the discrimination against women in the United States, and US complicity in creating and sustaining conditions for violence in Central America. This situation has been made much more difficult with the recent decision by Attorney General Sessions, as there is increased need for experienced legal counsel in these cases.

In addition, those in the immigration bureaucracy (e.g., judges and adjudicators) expect these women to position themselves as victims of violent cultural practices that allow men to abuse them. We argue that such expectations reproduce stereotypes that leave unquestioned fundamental aspects of the violence that women experience throughout their migratory experience, at exit and during the journey. Those expectations ignore the legal violence of domestic laws and institutions in sending countries that the receiving countries could help change if the interests of women's safety were not outweighed by political goals (such as maintaining "friendly" relations with countries that have "women-unfriendly" laws and institutions such as Saudi Arabia). We do not argue that the United States has a higher moral authority to police these issues, that its domestic violence laws are not imperfect, or that this problem does not exist in the United States. Our point here is to note the political and foreign policy entanglements that undermine potentially beneficial projects that the United States can undertake to improve the conditions for women in other countries of the world.

If asylum applicants have legal representation, there is an incentive for lawyers to frame the story of the applicant to conform to, and therefore perpetuate, judges' stereotypes of women suffering at the hands of individual macho men produced by a chauvinistic culture that views women as property. Further, in appealing to government lawyers and immigration judges, asylum applicants' lawyers erase any mention of the role of the US involvement in governments that have committed and perpetuated violence that, in turn, has contributed to women's vulnerability. These court narratives often represent Central American countries as "uncivilized" nations, in contrast to the "civilized" United States, appealing to existing views of immigration and court officials (Berger, 2009). This is despite the fact that chauvinism and institutional discrimination against women are long-standing problems in the United States, which have been exacerbated in the current political environment. While chauvinistic cultural patterns are certainly present in origin countries, these court narratives tend to ignore how women's lives are linked to broader institutional patterns that enable the expression of machismo through the police, courts, and laws.

The prevailing narratives in US immigration courts ignore and implicitly deny US complicity with the root causes of gender violence in Central America and other countries

---

[5]   For further discussion on the obstacles women asylum seekers in the United States face, see Parish (2017).
[6]   Menjívar and Walsh have both observed these practices in the course of their experiences serving as pro bono expert witnesses for asylum cases.

(see also McKinnon, 2016). This system and the narratives it creates obfuscate the US role in Central American violence and ignore institutional factors that could be mitigated by transnational advocates. Thus, pointing to machismo and focusing on understanding intentionality in individual acts of violence, pinning individual violent acts to entire cultures or regions (McKinnon, 2016), misrepresents the context of violence from which women flee. Such a focus exculpates the United States from any responsibility for the people who seek asylum from such conditions. At the same time, it creates a narrative that positions the United States as the innocent and benevolent "hero" that occasionally "rescues" refugees that fit the US immigration courts' stereotypes of deserving victims. In shifting the focus away from the historical roots of the context from which women flee, the courts function in such a way that focusing on violent citizens erases and ignores structural inequalities at the international level that continue to enable the perpetuation of impunity.[7]

CONCLUSION

A context of legal violence exerts itself upon migrant women throughout their journey from their home country, in transit, and in receiving countries. The specific manifestation of legal violence varies in each country, but it imposes a continuum of violence in the lives of women migrants. There are several reasons why women migrate, including drivers of migration that parallel those of men, such as economic, family reunification, disasters, and political conflicts. These reasons also include various forms of gender-based violence, such as domestic abuse and intimate partner violence that can be manifested in extreme forms, such as killings of women (e.g., feminicide). Although gender-specific reasons for migrating are present in women's migration in all regions of the world, we focus on the experiences of Central American women (Guatemala, El Salvador, and Honduras) to provide an in-depth view of conditions that are relevant to other cases. Across the globe, seemingly individual acts of violence (e.g., intimate partner violence or abuse in the home and in families) intertwine with and result from a context where multiple forms of violence, such as structural and everyday violence, coalesce. These forms of violence are distinctive for women, and are often more extreme for women who are positioned in particularly marginalized subgroups (e.g., according to class, race, and ethnicity). Thus, a lens of intersectionality can be mapped on to this analysis to account for these distinctions (Crenshaw, 1991).

Framing the context from which women flee through the lens of legal violence allows us to redirect attention away from individuals and to focus on institutions and structures in the origin countries that make possible the violence the women experience but also send messages that women's lives are disposable. This framing on broader structures also sheds light on the key role that the receiving country's foreign policy plays in creating the conditions of violence that makes women's migration imperative. As poor women desperately seeking to escape those conditions cannot avail themselves of the legal means to do so because there are no visas available for them, and refuge is not an option for them

---

[7]   For a set of articles that connects the linkages between intimate violence and systemic, institutional, structural, and state violence, see Fluri and Piedalue (2017).

from overseas, they risk their lives by traveling by land through Mexico. These journeys are harrowing as women experience extortion, robbery, kidnappings, torture, rape and sexual violence, and death. Those who make it alive arrive at their destination often more traumatized than when they left the violence in their homes.

Upon arrival, admission guidelines in the US asylum system do not extend *de jure* protection to these women who are de facto refugees. They often end up re-victimized and detained. Furthermore, this system ignores the fact that the United States has played a central role in creating the violent conditions from which women flee and therefore has an obligation to extend them protection. Instead, successful asylum cases often rely on narratives that portray Central American men as violent abusers and the *culture* in the home countries as the force behind the women's victimization because this will resonate in immigration courts. Violent abusers exist in every country, but it is the general context of violence and impunity – that the United States has contributed to producing – that enables the continued violence in the lives of women in sending countries. Immigration judges' tendency to focus on individual motivations and cultural background reproduces a system that differentially racializes asylum seekers and ignores the historically imbalanced power relations between the sending and receiving states (McKinnon, 2016). In this chapter, we have called attention to the continuum of violence behind Central American women's migration. We have shed light on the links among institutions, structures, and violence, which guide the entire migratory process, from the context women leave, through their journeys, to the system they enter. Although we have focused on Central American countries, the conditions of legal violence we have examined are also applicable in other parts of the world.

REFERENCES

American Immigration Council (2017), *The Impact of Immigrant Women on America's Labor Force*, Washington, DC. https://www.americanimmigrationcouncil.org/research/impact-immigrant-women-americas-labor-force. Accessed July 1, 2017.

Amnesty International (2010), *Invisible Victims: Migrants on the Move in Mexico*, London. https://fusiondotnet.files.wordpress.com/2014/09/amr410142010eng.pdf. Accessed June 30, 2017.

Amnesty International (2017), *Amnesty International Report 2016/17*, London.

Asakura, H. and M. Torres Falcon (2013), "Migración Femenina Centroamericana Y Violencia de Género: Pesadilla Sin Límites", *Zona Franca. Revista Del Centro de Estudios Interdisciplinario Sobre Mujeres*, **XXI**(22), 75–88.

Beramendi, C., L. Fainstain, and A. Tuana (2015), "Mirando Las Violencias Contra Las Mujeres Desde La Perspectiva International. Desafíos Teóricos Y Metodológicos Para Su Conceptualización Y Medición", in Gabriel Guajardo Soto and Christian Rivera Viedma (eds), *Violencias contra las mujeres: Desafíos y aprendizajes en la cooperacion Sur-Sur en America Latina y el Caribe*, Santiago, Chile: FASCO-Chile, pp. 55–80.

Berger, S. (2009), "Production and Reproduction of Gender and Sexuality in Legal Discourses of Asylum in the United States", *Signs: Journal of Women in Culture and Society*, **34**(3), 659–85.

Booth, J.A., C.J. Wade, and T.W. Walker (2015), *Understanding Central America: Global Forces, Rebellion, and Change*, 6th edn, Boulder, CO: Westview Press.

Bott, S., A. Guedes, M. Goodwin, and J. Adams Mendoza (2012), *Violence against Women in Latin America and the Caribbean: A Comparative Analysis of Population-based Data from 12 Countries*, Washington, DC: Pan American Health Organization and Centers for Disease Control and Prevention.

Cardoletti-Carroll, C., A. Farmer, and L. Velez (2015), *Women on the Run*, United Nations High Commission for Refugees. http://www.unhcr.org/5630f24c6.html. Accessed March 11, 2016.

Carey Jr., D. (2006), *Engendering Mayan History: Mayan Women as Agents and Conduits of the Past, 1875–1970*, New York: Routledge.

Carey Jr., D. and M.G. Torres (2010), "Precursors to Femicide: Guatemalan Women in a Vortex of Violence", *Latin American Research Review*, **45**(3), 142–64.

Colegio de México/ONU Mujeres (2017), *Situación de las Mujeres Trabajadoras Migrantes*, México, DF.

Consejo Nacional de Población (2016), *Anuario de Migración Y Remesas México 2016*, Mexico City, Mexico. https://www.gob.mx/cms/uploads/attachment/file/109457/Anuario_Migracion_y_Remesas2016.pdf. Accessed May 28, 2017.

Crenshaw, K. (1991), "Mapping the Margins: Intersectionality, Identity Politics, and Violence against Women of Color", *Stanford Law Review*, **43**(6), 1241–99.

Cullather, N. (1999), *Secret History: The CIA's Classified Account of Its Operations in Guatemala, 1952–1954*, 2nd edn, Stanford, CA: Stanford University Press.

Dewey, S. (2012), "Rethinking Survival Sex and Trafficking in Conflict and Post-conflict Zones: The Case of Bosnia-Herzegovinia", *Wagadu: A Journal of Transnational Women's & Gender Studies*, **10**, 15–31.

Dominguez Villegas, R. (2014), *Central American Migrants and "La Bestia": The Route, Dangers, and Government Responses*, Washington, DC: Migration Policy Institute. http://www.migrationpolicy.org/article/central-ameri can-migrants-and-"la-bestia"-route-dangers-and-government-responses. Accessed March 29, 2017.

Eltahawy, M. (2017), "Why Saudi Women are Literally Living 'The Handmaid's Tale'", *New York Times*, May 24. https://www.nytimes.com/2017/05/24/opinion/why-saudi-women-are-literally-living-the-handmaids-tale. html?_r=0. Accessed July 1, 2017.

Fluri, J.L. and A. Piedalue (2017), "Embodying Violence: Critical Geographies of Gender, Race, and Culture", *Gender, Place & Culture*, **24**(4), 534–44.

Goldenberg, S.M., J.G. Silverman, D. Engstrom, I. Bojorquez-Chapela, and S.A. Strathdee (2013), "'Right Here is the Gateway': Mobility, Sex Work Entry and HIV Risk Along the Mexico-US Border", *International Migration*, **52**(4), 27–40.

Gómez Cervantes, A., D. Alvord, and C. Menjívar (2018), "'Bad Hombres:' The Effects of Criminalizing Latino Immigrants through Law and Media in the Rural Midwest", *Migration Letters*, **15**(2), 182–96.

Hartviksen, J. (2014), "Towards a Historical Materialist Analysis of Femicide in Post-conflict Guatemala," MA Thesis, Graduate Program in Global Development, Queen's University, Kingston, Ontario.

Hoffman, K. and M.A. Centeno (2003), "The Lopsided Continent: Inequality in Latin America", *Annual Review of Sociology*, **29**, 363–90.

Hondagneu-Sotelo, P. (1994), *Gendered Transitions: Mexican Experiences of Immigration*, Berkeley, CA: University of California Press.

International Organization for Migration (2015), *Global Migration Flows*. https://www.iom.int/world-migration. Accessed May 26, 2017.

Izcarra Palacios, S.P. (2015), "Los Transmigrantes Centroamericanos en México", *Latin American Research Review*, **50**(4), 49–68.

Kuhner, G. (2011), "La Violencia Contra Las Mujeres Migrantes En Tránsito Por México", *Defensor: Revista de Derechos Humanos*, **6**, 19–26.

LaFeber, W. (1993), *Inevitable Revolutions: The United States in Central America*, 2nd edn, New York: W.W. Norton.

Lagarde, M. (2010), "Preface: Feminist Keys for Understanding Feminicide: Theoretical, Political, and Legal Construction", in Rosa-Linda Fregoso and Cynthia Bejarano (eds), *Terrorizing Women, Feminicide in the Américas*, Durham, NC: Duke University Press, pp. xi–xx.

Massey, D.S., R. Alarcón, J. Durand, and H. González (1990), *Return to Aztlán: The Social Process of International Migration from Western Mexico*, Berkeley, CA: University of California Press.

McKinnon, S. (2016), *Gendered Asylum: Race and Violence in U.S. Law and Politics*, Chicago, IL: University of Illinois Press.

Menjívar, C. (2011), *Enduring Violence: Ladina Women's Lives in Guatemala*, Berkeley, CA: University of California Press.

Menjívar, C. and L.J. Abrego (2012), "Legal Violence: Immigration Law and the Lives of Central American Immigrants", *American Journal of Sociology*, **117**(5), 1380–421.

Menjívar, C. and N.P. Rodríguez (eds) (2005), *When States Kill: Latin America, the U.S., and Technologies of Terror*, Austin, TX: University of Texas Press.

Menjívar, C. and S.D. Walsh (2016), "Subverting Justice: Socio-legal Determinants of Impunity for Violence against Women in Guatemala", *Laws*, **5**(3), 1–20.

Parish, A. (2017), *Gender-based Violence against Women: Both Cause for Migration and Risk Along the Journey*, Washington, DC: Migration Policy Institute. http://www.migrationpolicy.org/article/gender-based-violence-against-women-both-cause-migration-and-risk-along-journey. Accessed September 23, 2017.

Parreñas, R.S. (2001), *Servants of Globalization: Women, Migration and Domestic Work*, Stanford, CA: Stanford University Press.

Reichman, D. (2011), *The Broken Village: Coffee, Migration, and Globalization in Honduras*, Ithaca, NY: Cornell University Press.

Salcido, O. and C. Menjívar (2012), "Gendered Paths to Legal Citizenship: The Case of Latin-American Immigrants in Phoenix, Arizona", *Law & Society Review*, **46**(2), 335–68.

Sanford, V. (2008), "From Genocide to Feminicide: Impunity and Human Rights in Twenty-first-Century Guatemala", *Journal of Human Rights*, **7**, 104–22.

Santibáñez, J., S.I. Palma, H. Ramírez Reyes, N. Hidalgo, and A-M. Urban (2017), *Estudio Cualitativo Sobre Mujeres Jóvenes Y La Violencia En Centroamérica: Efecto En Condiciones de Salida Y Retorno de Menores Migrantes*, Banco Interamericano de Desarrollo. https://publications.iadb.org/handle/11319/8160. Accessed September 30, 2018.

Schmidt, L.A. and S. Buechler (2017), "'I Risk Everything Because I Have Already Lost Everything': Central American Female Migrants Speak Out on the Migrant Trail in Oaxaca, Mexico", *Journal of Latin American Geography*, **16**(1), 139–64.

Semple, K. (2016), "Fleeing Gangs, Central American Families Surge Toward U.S.", *New York Times*, November 12. https://www.nytimes.com/2016/11/13/world/americas/fleeing-gangs-central-american-families-surge-toward-us.html. Accessed July 12, 2017.

Shannon, K., T. Kerr, S. Allinott, J. Chettiar, J. Shoveller, and M.W. Tyndall (2008), "Social and Structural Violence and Power Relations in Mitigating HIV Risk of Drug-using Women in Survival Sex Work", *Social Science & Medicine*, **66**, 911–21.

Sládková, J. (2010), *Journeys of Undocumented Honduran Migrants to the United States*, El Paso, TX: LFB Scholarly Publishers.

UNDP (United Nations Development Programme) (2009–10), *Opening Spaces to Citizen Security and Human Development, Human Development Report for Central America*.

United Nations, Department of Economic and Social Affairs (2016), *International Migration Report 2015*. http://www.un.org/en/development/desa/population/migration/publications/migrationreport/docs/MigrationReport2015.pdf. Accessed May 26, 2017.

United Nations Statistics Division (2015), *The World's Women 2015: Trends and Statistics*. https://unstats.un.org/unsd/gender/chapter6/chapter6.html. Accessed May 17, 2017.

UNODC (United Nations Office on Drugs and Crime) (2012), *Global Study on Homicide: Homicide Counts and Rates, Time Series 2000–2012*. http://www.unodc.org/gsh/en/data.html. Accessed July 1, 2017.

USGAO (United States Government Accountability Office) (2013), *Immigration Detention: Additional Actions Could Strengthen DHS Efforts to Address Sexual Abuse*. November.

Varela Huerta, A. (2017), "La Trinidad Perversa de La Que Huyen Las Fugitivas centroamericanas: Violencia Feminicida, Violencia de Estado y Violencia de Mercado", *Debate Feminista*, **53**, 1–17.

Vogt, W.A. (2013), "Crossing Mexico: Structural Violence and the Commodification of Undocumented Central American Migrants", *American Ethnologist*, **40**(4), 764–80.

Waiselfisz, J.J. (2015), "Mapa Da Violência 2015: homocídio de Mulheres no Brasil", FLACSO Brazil. http://www.mapadaviolencia.org.br/pdf2015/MapaViolencia_2015_mulheres.pdf. Accessed July 2, 2017.

Walsh, S.D. and C. Menjívar (2016), "Impunity and Multisided Violence in the Lives of Women in Latin America: El Salvador in Comparative Perspective", *Current Sociology*, **64**(4), 586–602.

Weissman, D.M. (2010), "Global Economics and Their Progenies: Theorizing Femicide in Context," in R.L. Fregoso and C.L. Bejarano (eds), *Terrorizing Women: Feminicide in the Américas*, Durham, NC: Duke University Press, pp. 225–424.

Willers, S. (2016), "Migración Y Violencia: Las Experiencias de Mujeres Migrantes Centroamericanas En Tránsito Por México", *Sociológica*, **31**(89), 163–95.

Wojcicki, J.M. (2002), "'She Drank His Money': Survival Sex and the Problem of Violence in Taverns in Gauteng Province, South Africa", *Medical Anthropology Quarterly*, **16**(3), 267–93.

World Bank (2015), *Data for Mexico, Guatemala, Honduras, El Salvador*. http://data.worldbank.org/?locations=MX-GT-HN-SV. Accessed May 26, 2017.

World Health Organization (2013), *Global and Regional Estimates of Violence against Women: Prevalence and Health Effects of Intimate Partner Violence and Non-partner Sexual Violence*. http://apps.who.int/iris/bitstream/10665/85239/1/9789241564625_eng.pdf?ua=1. Accessed May 23, 2017.

World Health Organization (2016), "Violence against Women: Intimate Partner and Sexual Violence against Women Fact Sheet". http://www.who.int/mediacentre/factsheets/fs239/en/. Accessed May 16, 2017.

4. The laws of impermanence: displacement, sovereignty, subjectivity
Timothy Raeymaekers

MIGRANT SUBJECTIVITY I

To talk about borders and migration today may sound a bit like the chicken-and-the-egg debate. On the one hand, the challenge of migration has arguably forced governments to become more mobile, including in the very techniques that track, channel, filter and differentiate people's mobility across the globe. Alison Mountz's term "archipelago of sovereign control" (2011b) captures quite well how governments are continuously externalizing the cost and responsibility of asylum to third – frequently unaccountable – bodies. She explains how sovereign bodies (which include but are not limited to state government authorities) often exploit distance, precariousness and ambiguous political status as ways to deflect migration and responsibility over refugee rights. Typically, this process involves certain tactics of spatial distancing, exclusion and segregation, exemplified for instance in practices of offshore detention, the establishment of legal no-man's lands and security valves, and increasingly privatized surveillance (see also Jones 2016).

On the other hand, though, and often anticipating this very move, existing infrastructures (i.e., what Lindquist et al. 2012 call the "black box") of migration (the "institutions, networks and people that move migrants from one point to another") are also undergoing fundamental changes. To connect the different dots, some authors have started to contemplate the emergence of a "middle space" of migration (McKeown 2012): an ambiguous intersecting space occupied by mediators of various kinds. This space not only allows for a multitude of passages through contemporary boundaries (in other words, the concept contests the notion of single, unidirectional flows), but it also opens our minds to the involvement of organizations that are located within, outside, as well as on the brink of state government (in other words, it shifts our lens from state to global governmentalities). Slightly moving away from the classic, social network focus on embeddedness and nested scales (see, e.g., Portes and Sensenbrenner 1993; Portes 1995; Swyngedouw 1997), the emerging vocabularies of mobile "channels", "infrastructures", "punctuations", and "circulations" (e.g., Smart and Smart 2008; Tsing 2009; Elyachar 2010; Lindquist 2017), have become the initial nodal points of such a "multi-scalar" method that is capable of identifying "strategic sites" where critical engagement can be grounded (Mezzadra and Neilson 2013; Xiang 2013, p. 282).

While today's paradigm of mobile borders is certainly a very useful one, two further signposts have to be erected here. First, the idea of the mobility of borders and their relation to regimes of classification, sorting and hierarchization is certainly not a new one. In fact, the entire endeavour of postcolonial studies has been to unveil how the colonial project was also a cultural process that sought legitimation through discourses of difference and superiority. Typically, these strategies of differentiation were actively implemented through essentialist boundaries of difference (for an overview see Nash 2004). So rather than asserting uniqueness, a more useful way to analyse current transformations is to ask how current strategies, of punctuation, channelling and filtering take on distinct forms and modalities in the current conjuncture.[1] Second, mobile borders also produce important territorial *effects* (Van Houtum and Van Naerssen 2002; Painter 2010). When it comes to today's technologies of migrant asylum, for instance, they typically continue to crystallize into quite heterogeneous places such as (ex-colonial) prisons, (contemporary) reception and asylum centres, "informal" settlements, "jungles", "shantytowns and ghettos" (Deleuze 1992, p. 7) that are in various ways interconnected both with each other and with the wider systems of government that project and sustain them.

One important question that remains somewhat undervalued in the current debate is how migrant subjectivities are actively translated through the embodied experience of contemporary border politics. This is nonetheless an important question. It is important because, as Agier and Lecadet (2014) write, the daily experience of migration, which involves both the materiality and socialization that unfolds in the heterogeneous places of border governance, gives us a more concrete notion not so much of the "camp form" as a presumably unifying structure of migrant containment (for a critical overview see Minca 2015) but rather about its ambivalence. Such embodied narrative of migration can tell us something about the way exile and displacement become integrated into possible futures, of urbanization, of citizenship, and of territorial interconnectedness; in other words, of the ways citizens and non-citizens are being separated socially, culturally, politically. To quote Agier once more (2016, p. 7), borders represent a time-space that somehow ritualizes our relationship with the Other, either through negation or negotiation, but always through cultural *mediations*. This seems to me a crucial insight for geographers, sociologists and anthropologists interested in the concrete experience of alterity and what it does to people's everyday lives. Based on the recognition that human mobility is in itself a highly differentiated and differentiating activity, it becomes our task, then, to assess how the boundaries of migration are actively promoted through strategies of differentiation, hierarchization and stratification, and how these become conducive in the making of migra(n)t(ing) political subjects. We need not romanticize or demonize "migrants" and "nomads" as political categories. But we need to provide situated and provisional accounts of their movement in space (Cresswell 1997). The literature on political subjectivity offers one lens to situate migrant experiences in such a *relational* field of power (Das et al. 2000; Biehl et al. 2007; Das 2008).[2] In this chapter, I will focus on two of its contributions. First, I will focus on the acts of *translation* through which this differentiation is actively performed, practised and embodied (see also Isin 2008; Andrijasevic 2009). On the other hand, I will concentrate more prominently on the historical legacies of subordination, racism and colonial imperialism through which migrant differentiation continues to be informed and enacted today. In order to argue these two points, the rest of this chapter will develop as follows: after a short introduction into the concept of mobile bordering processes, I ask what kind of migrant subjectivity such processes potentially

---

[1] I thank Camilla Hawthorne for this extremely useful insight.
[2] I base part of these insights on previous ethnographic reflections in Greenhouse et al. (2002), Vigh (2008, 2009) and Arnaut et al. (2008).

produce. Through the example of my fieldwork in the domain of the Italian asylum system, I develop a few thoughts about the relationships between migration, sovereignty and violence. In the final section, the conceptual framework of political subjectivity and of diffuse governance will help me to deconstruct the spatial processes through which social abandonment is performed, embodied and enacted in the domain of contemporary border management. The focus of the chapter involves practices of refugee asylum in Italy. Within the context of the current migration "crisis" across the Mediterranean, I present this research as a way to understand how relationality and translation play an increasingly prominent role in the subjectivation of migrant would-be (or non-)citizens in the current paradigm of diffuse territorial borders.

TERRITORIALITY I

From the perspective of migration, the tendency nowadays is to talk about territorial borders in topological rather than topographic terms (Raeymaekers 2014). Amilhat-Szary and Giraut (2015, p. 6) write we are witnessing a kind of epistemological breakdown currently, from the definition of the border as a palimpsest that fixes the memory of past movements, to an analysis of *mobile* bordering *processes*. Borders are complex assemblages that are not situated at the presumed margins, but in the heart of the contemporary political sphere, Balibar (2002) writes. And from there, they are capable of recalibrating the technologies of government in substantial new ways.

For our current purpose, this means, essentially, two things. For one, it is important that we continue to deconstruct the tautological relationship between territories, nations and states with regard to contemporary bordering processes. The border as a neat "line in the sand" (Williams 2006) is not only dead, but it may never have existed (Amilhat-Szary and Giraut 2015, p. 9). Borders have become more fluid, more networked, more web-like. And their function has more prominently become that of a sorting device, a mobile "dispositif" (Deleuze and Guattari 1993) that serves to channel, categorize and distinguish "legitimate" from "illegitimate", "legal" from "illegal" flows. Rather than fixating movement in place, therefore, the function of territorial borders is to make authority valid in space, to regulate flows at a distance (Rose 1999; Allen 2003; Walters 2006).

Second, the complex interplay between the functions and forms of territorial borders in today's international system also highlights a renewed temporality of the border. Through the emerging technoscapes of mobile databases and technologies, borders also assume an important temporal dimension. While there exists indeed a dynamic relationship between cross-border movements, on the one hand, and the agents, devices and technologies that attempt to channel these movements, on the other, the aim of the latter is to accelerate certain flows while slowing down others. Consequently, and much in line with the observation that the territorialization of state power constitutes an effect of boundary-making practices rather than its cause (Mitchell 1991; Elden 2009; Novak 2011), the current, web-like epistemology of territorial bordering processes forces us to consider the assemblages of power that actively channel and direct flows across multiple spaces (Klatt and Anderson 2012).

TERRITORIALITY II

If we accept, then, that borders are dynamic processes that may be associated with technologies working both through and beyond territorial states, the question becomes how sovereign power substantiates and materializes itself with regard to migrating subjects that are moving within as well as across such bordered spaces.

For the last five years, I have tried to understand this tension within the context of the so-called Mediterranean "migration crisis" – which was, arguably also, a crisis of the European border regime (Bojadžijev and Mezzadra 2015). In the aftermath of the 2010–11 Arab Revolutions – which later exploded into full-scale war in Libya and Syria – migrants from North and West Africa have been travelling in great numbers across the Mediterranean, frequently with deadly consequences. Rather than treating the Mediterranean as a conceptual "dead zone" (Saucier and Woods 2014, p. 57) marred by spectacularized demise and borderization (De Genova 2013; Cuttitta 2014), I became more interested in the ways contemporary bordering techniques remain informed by histories of racial formation and colonial memorization. Following the lead of radical feminists like bell hooks, Adrian Piper and Kimberle Crenshaw who have described marginality as a site of both separation and resistance (hooks 1990), I started to imagine contemporary border regimes as part of longer histories of displacement, segregation and persecution.[3] The purpose of this research has also been to unravel the acts of translation through which migrants are both encapsulated and excluded from contemporary "acts of citizenship" (Isin 2008) – particularly with regard to the actualization of refugee rights. As Cristiana Giordano (2008, p. 592, emphasis added) writes, "the possibility of being a migrant subject [needs to be situated] *at the threshold* of institutional languages and their inability to provide a narrative that can account for the migrant's experience, while at the same time providing the possibility of becoming visible and recognizable as a subject" (see also Blommaert 2009; Pinelli 2013). It is this threshold, or "middle space" (McKeown 2012), that stands at the centre of my current research purpose.

Within this domain, an interesting discussion has been going on about the wider implications of the politics of historical memory, on what Judith Butler (2003, p. 52) has called the "diffuse" governmentality of undesired subjects. Reflecting on the tragedy that unfolded in the night of 2–3 October 2013, and where 386 Eritrean, Somali and Ghanaian migrants drowned in waters off the Sicilian island of Lampedusa, some authors have been prone to invoking a kind of Sophoclean drama. On the one hand, the very act of mourning these deaths potentially raised the need to imagine a community "of a more complex order" (Butler 2003, p. 22) underpinned by the recognition of universal precarity and ethical responsibility (see also Gilroy 2015). On the other hand, European governments have continued to insist on the message that "Europe has to choose to be or not to be . . ." (as Italy's Minister Alfano termed it on 3 October 2013) – a message that has generally resulted in more securitization, surveillance and closed border policies. More often than not though, the implementation of these bordering strategies have been diverted and diluted to organizations that have little accountability to sovereign territorial states. Just as Butler warns us, this tension risks resulting in a kind of "diffuse" governmentality,

---

[3]   For Italy, see for instance Carter (2010), Merrill (2014), Hawthorne (2017).

whereby the right to sovereign violence is being redistributed among a range of "rogue" administrators and actors that take over the prerogatives of rule in a context of state absence. So, rather than assuming the camp form as a unifying, segregating structure, we ought to ask ourselves what this tension between migrant precarity and sovereign displacement has produced within this new constellation of the Mediterranean migration "crisis".

As the dead bodies of travelling migrants continued to wash ashore on the Sicilian coast, the Lampedusa crisis quickly intensified this Sophoclean dynamic. On the one hand, it brought about a movement of solidarity between European and African citizens across the continent that was in many ways inspired by the slogan that "we are all on the same boat". Some people joined hands with the aim of replacing national categories with new forms of transnational collaboration and belonging. Throughout 2013–14, different "migrant" occupations emerged, which waved the banner of Lampedusa as a sign of connectivity and resistance across the continent. When I started to visit some of these locations more closely in the city of Bologna, on the other hand, it quickly became clear how they also blended into existing spatial arrangements. This was particularly the case for a specific category of so-called return migrants: those refugees who, after making unsuccessful asylum claims in a second European state, were being actively sent back to Italy within the context of the Dublin Regulations (in Italian: *dublinati*; Bertin et al. 2013). For them, the participation in such squatting operations often became a matter of utter necessity, as they were both spatially and legally placed "out of sight" (MSF 2016). In 2016, Doctors without Borders (or Médecins Sans Frontières, MSF) used this metaphor to denounce the more or less 10,000 refugees and asylum seekers who were living in such "informal" settlements.[4] Unable to legally leave the country, and often without access to an official residence, many of these *dublinati* remained literally stuck in these places without a proper right to the city. Consequently, their faith became illustrative of a new kind of private-public assemblage (Raeymaekers 2019 forthcoming) that is fundamentally reconfiguring migrant rights in this context.

MIGRANT SUBJECTIVITY II

The example of Bologna's *dublinati* illustrates well how migrant asylum can quickly transform itself into a permanent threshold, or a grey zone of excluded existence that reiterates rather than challenges the premises of the territorial nation-state. Caught by the isomorphism between national belonging, territorial integrity and sovereign autonomy, return refugees are actually being denied their basic human rights in the current context of diffuse border and migration governance. In Bologna, the situation unfolded like this: while various autonomous groups continued to actively propagate a political resistance to Europe's border regime over the course of 2011–15, a swathe of non-governmental

---

[4] Quite significantly, these "informal settlements" did not include what MSF depicted as the more or less permanent labour camps in Italy's industrial agriculture areas, such as Piedmont and Puglia, where thousands of migrants flock together each year to harvest grapes, oranges and tomatoes. Part of my endeavour, and that of other scholars (see, e.g., Andrijasevic and Sacchetto 2015; Dines and Rigo 2015) has been to analyse how they are related.

organizations gradually sought to fill the gap by providing aid in the form of legal advice and medical assistance to displaced people that had been literally abandoned by the system. Most of these latter organizations operated under the form of certain government "concessions", in which they acquired the active temporary right to implement state regulations under condition of conscious government withdrawal (for comparison see, e.g., Kritzman-Amir 2011). To some extent, therefore, this changing temporality of refugees' evictability in Europe's asylum regime reflected a kind of corrugation (or folding back) of its deterritorialized border politics in the Southern Mediterranean. One thinks automatically of countries like Libya, Senegal and Mauritania, where European states have been collaborating for years with Frontex and national border guards to hold back trans-Mediterranean migration. Politically speaking, such concessionary asylum politics actually highlights the more pressing question of who decides over people's rights, and who implements territorial sovereignty there where state governments consciously decide to outsource or even withdraw from their prerogatives to implement refugee rights. From a postcolonial perspective, this situation raises an interesting paradox, because it shows the perennially tentative character of territorial sovereignty there where the ability to decide over people's rights is actively dispersed among often competing actors and institutions (Mbembe 2001; Hansen and Stepputat 2006). Strikingly similar to the context Judith Butler is describing (of Guantanamo prison), this legal suspension has created the conditions for a privatized form of sovereign violence to take root, embodied by various "petty" sovereigns (rogue administrators, unaccountable bodies) who literally take over the power to render unilateral decisions and rule over those "ungrievable" effaced bodies whose lives are accountable to no law and do not necessitate the intervention of a legitimate authority. This ambivalence between sovereign violence and its dislocation constitutes at once the centre of the problem of contemporary migration management across the Mediterranean, because it is through the actual *displacement* of control that the im/mobility of migrants' rights and freedoms are being *enforced* in the everyday (Mountz 2011a).

The next question in this context then becomes whether the current threshold of contemporary migration regimes represents a negation, or rather a renegotiation of migrants' political subjectivity.[5] The answer is, again, not a straightforward one. For one, one cannot draw a sharp line between regulating institutions and collective actions in this context, because the violence underpinning displacement thoroughly creates, sustains and transforms the interconnections between lived values and contested meanings (Biehl et al. 2007; Das 2008). Personally, I like to imagine today's asylum system in Europe as a legal and cultural *grey zone*: it is a liminal space, where non-citizens are made explicitly complicit in their own impermanence (Levi 1991; Raeymaekers 2019 forthcoming). Second, and rather than limiting our view to the sites of encampment, imprisonment and exclusion that migrants continue to be subjected to in this contemporary constellation, we should also continue to highlight the underlying processes of illegalization and racialization, of social and political differentiation, of protection and surveillance, of mobility and immobility, that continue to shape and modulate migrant experiences in this context. As I hopefully made clear, this process is not merely driven by the techniques

---

[5] Again, I want to thank Camilla Hawthorne for this very useful question.

of filtering, hierarchization and selection embodied in contemporary bordering policies. It also involves an important cultural process, which – through acts of translation and mediation – continues to reproduce, contest and transform migrants' deterritorialized and racialized status.

At the very least, therefore, these observations highlight the necessity to further deconstruct the spatial processes through which the social abandonment of migrant subjects (and particularly of refugees) is performed, embodied and enacted. Besides governing technologies, these include the everyday tactics of navigation that connect displaced people to livelihood opportunities, the brokers and mediators that both facilitate and oppress them in their determination to sustain their lives. At the same time, this contemporary condition of the displaced also tells us something about the way sovereign power, or the ability to "kill, punish and discipline with impunity" (Hansen and Stepputat 2006, p. 295) has increasingly been downgraded, outsourced and disaggregated among unaccountable actors who are not always aware of their role in sustaining this process of enforcement. Such actors include but are not limited to local volunteers and associations, as well as brokers of various kinds who are actively involved in the domain of labour intermediation, housing and social "service delivery". Following anthropological work on the postcolony, one could argue that the "margin" of the state in Europe effectively represents this expanding grey zone of relative indistinction, between the law as abstract norm (*de iure*), and the practice of sovereign violence by those agents who, de facto, execute and interpret its application (Das and Poole 2004). The terminology of diffuse governance explicitly extends this right to presumably autonomous groups, non-governmental organizations and other agencies that are not exercising state power in a formal sense, but, through the gaps and fissures generated by this absence, acquire a de facto right to do so.

CONCLUSION: AFTER THE SPECTACLE

After these observations it is time to go back to our main question: if, indeed, we accept that human mobility is challenging the paradigms of government nowadays, in particular in the form of partially delocalized and deterritorialized bordering processes, then how is the subjectivity of migrating subjects affected by such bordering technologies and vice versa? In the current, critical paradigm, this relationship is frequently depicted as a spectacle. In his much quoted piece, Nicholas De Genova (2013) shows how, in the context of US deportation policies, the border sets a scene of exclusion that verifies, validates and legitimates migrants' subaltern status within the receiving society through a narrative of il/legality. At the same time, however, this scene is accompanied by a shadowy and often disacknowledged *obscene*, which reinforces the migrants' precarious inclusion into territorial state and market dynamics. Comparing migrants' subjectivities beyond the experience of deportable subjects clearly asks for an expansion of this "shadowy" space of inclusion. In this chapter, I have tried to explain what the diffuse governmentality of contemporary bordering processes means for migrants', and particularly for refugee rights in Europe, as well as the manner in which decisions about them become entangled with the dynamics of their cultural and political renegotiation. As Judith Butler writes, diffuse governance involves the systematic outsourcement of sovereign power in the context of a (total or partial) legal abstention. Though this withdrawal has been pretty much noticeable in the domain of migration and border "management" across the globe, the outcomes of this process are never straightforward: in some cases, government withdrawal may produce a "rogue" administration characterized by arbitrariness and random violence.[6] In other cases, it might produce an ambiguous grey zone in which undesired subjects are made complicit in their own impermanence. In the example of Italian asylum politics I briefly touched upon in this chapter, the conscious withdrawal of formal government from the domain of migration "management" to some extent has contributed to an expanding grey zone that confirms the migrants', and particularly refugees' legal limbo. But this political constellation is also altering the political subjectivity of Europe's internal borders to some extent. Particularly the rights of so-called return migrants (or *dublinati*) has been paradoxical in this respect. On the one hand, their hypermobile trajectories make it extremely difficult for them to get rooted into their new environments. While intentions to leave remain thwarted, and desires to stay made liable on all sorts of uncertain premises, they experience a kind of permanent threshold, or a "double absence" that continues to mark the boundary between being and non-being politically recognized and protected (Sayad 1999). On the other hand, however, the lack of official residence of these refugees in many cases is leading to a static territorial existence that reiterates rather than challenges the premises of the nation-state boundaries their rights are meant to overcome. Like the victims of the Lampedusa shipwrecks, therefore, they remain caught in a kind of Sophoclean drama whereby the sanctuary of overarching human principles is being replaced by an actual denial of their rights.

The literature on subjectivity helps us untangle two important dimensions of that process. First, it highlights the historical legacies, of racial subordination, discrimination and (neo-)colonialist practices, through which the current differentiation of migrant rights continues to be informed and enacted in many places around the world. Insisting on the "embodied effects" of practices of government (Fanon 2002, cited in Browne 2015, p. 20), we are made aware of the laws of impermanence that make forced displacement today not just an epistemological but also an ontological crisis (Mountz 2011a). It is a crisis that remains fundamental to the reproduction of precarity, which leading scholars identify as the underpinning drivers of capitalist expansion across the globe (Bauman 2000; Sassen 2006; Mezzadra 2011; De Genova 2013). But it is also a crisis of routines, of predictability, and of people's normative horizons that continue to separate "the actual from the possible" in people's everyday lives (Vigh 2008, p. 10). Whether this crisis is a temporary situation or a permanent "pervasive state" (Vigh 2008, p. 16) we get to understand only when connecting our analysis of the technologies of exclusion and separation with the embodied practices that make or do not make them be worked out in space. To quote John Berger and Jean Mohr (2010, p. 11, my quotation marks): "unfreedom can only be fully recognized if an 'objective' economic system is related to the 'subjective' experience of those trapped within it".

---

6   In this context, the case of the German town of Burbach springs to mind. In 2014, police investigated the alleged abuse of asylum seekers in a shelter home by the staff of a private security company. The two suspects, both men in their forties, filmed and photographed each other while placing their boots on the head of an unidentified asylum seeker. To some extent, these sorts of excesses also highlight the relative arbitrariness that marks the pathways of candidate citizens towards their suspended insertion or expulsion.

REFERENCES

Agier, Michel (2016), *Borderlands: Towards an Anthropology of the Cosmopolitan Condition*, Cambridge and Malden, MA: Polity Press.

Agier, Michel and C. Lecadet (2014), *Un monde de camps*, Paris: La Decouverte.

Allen, John (2003), *Lost Geographies of Power*, RGS-IGB Book Series, Oxford: Blackwell.

Amilhat-Szary, Anne-Laure and F. Giraut (2015), "Borderities: the politics of contemporary mobile borders", in *Borderities and the Politics of Contemporary Mobile Borders*, London: Palgrave Macmillan, pp. 1–19.

Andrijasevic, Rutvica (2009), "Sex on the move: gender, subjectivity and differential inclusion", *Subjectivity*, **29** (1), 389–406.

Andrijasevic, Rutvica and D. Sacchetto, D. (2015), "Against the day: migrant workers and new forms of exploitation: Europe and beyond", *South Atlantic Quarterly*, **114** (1), 192–4.

Arnaut, K., C. Hojbjerg, and T. Raeymaekers (eds) (2008), "Gouvernance et ethnographie en temps de crise: de l'étude des ordres émergents dans l'Afrique entre guerre et paix", *Politique africaine*, no. 111 (dossier).

Balibar, Etienne (2002), "What is a border?" in *Politics and the Other Scene*, London: Verso, pp. 75–86.

Bauman, Zygmunt (2000), *Liquid Modernity*, Cambridge and Malden, MA: Polity.

Berger, John and J. Mohr (2010), *A Seventh Man*, London: Verso.

Bertin, Francesca, E. Fontanari and L. Gennari (2013), *At the Limen. The Implementation of the Return Directive in Italy, Cyprus and Spain*, Ilmenau, bis500 Digitaldruck (http://www.bis500druck.de), December.

Biehl, Joao, B. Good and A. Kleinmann (2007), *Subjectivity: Ethnographic Investigations*, Berkeley, Los Angeles, CA and London: University of California Press.

Blommaert, Jan (2009), "Language, asylum, and the national order", *Current Anthropology*, **50** (4), 415–41.

Bojadžijev, Manuela and S. Mezzadra (2015), "Refugee crisis or crisis of European migration policies?" *FocaalBlog*, 12 November.

Browne, Silvia (2015), *Dark Matters: On the Surveillance of Blackness*, Durham, NC: Duke University Press.

Butler, Judith (2003), *Precarious Life: The Power of Mourning and Violence*, London: Verso.

Carter, Donald M. (2010), *Navigating the African Diaspora: The Anthropology of Invisibility*, Minneapolis, MN: University of Minnesota Press.

Cresswell, Tim (1997), "Imagining the nomad: mobility and the postmodern primitive", in Georges Benko and U. Strohmayer (eds), *Space and Social Theory: Interpreting Modernity and Postmodernity*, Malden, MA: Blackwell, pp. 360–79.

Cuttitta, Paolo (2014), "Borderizing the island: setting and narratives of the Lampedusa border play", *ACME*, **13** (2), 196–219.

Das, Veena (2008), "Violence, gender, and subjectivity", *Annual Review of Anthropology*, **37**, 283–99.

Das, Veena, A. Kleinmann, M. Ramphele and S. Reynolds (2000), *Violence and Subjectivity*, Berkeley, Los Angeles, CA and London: University of California Press.

Das, Veena and D. Poole (2004), *Anthropology in the Margins of the State*, Santa Fe, School of American Research Press.

De Genova, Nicholas (2013), "Spectacles of migrant 'illegality': the scene of exclusion, the obscene of inclusion", *Ethnic and Racial Studies*, **36** (7), 1180–98.

Deleuze, Gilles (1992), "Postscript on the Societies of Control", *October*, **59** (Winter), 3–7.

Deleuze, Gilles and F. Guattari (1993), *A Thousand Plateaus: Capitalism and Schizophrenia*, Minneapolis, MN: University of Minnesota Press.

Dines, Nick and E. Rigo (2015), "Postcolonial citizenships and the 'refugeeization' of the workforce: migrant agricultural labor in the Italian Mezzogiorno", in Sara Ponzanesi and G. Colpani (eds), *Postcolonial Transitions in Europe: Contexts, Practices and Politics*, Lanham, MD: Rowman International.

Elden, Stuart (2009), *Terror and Territory: The Spatial Extent of Sovereignty*, Minneapolis, MN: Minnesota University Press.

Elyachar, Julia (2010), "Phatic labor, infrastructure, and the question of empowerment in Cairo", *American Ethnologist*, **37** (3), 452–64.

Fanon, Franz (2002), *Les Damnes de la terre*, Paris: Editions la decouverte et Syros.

Gilroy, Paul (2015), "Offshore humanism", Antipode RGS-IBG Lecture, Exeter.

Giordano, Cristiana (2008), "Practices of translation and the making of migrant subjectivities in contemporary Italy", *American Ethnologist*, **35** (4), 588–606.

Greenhouse, Carol J., E. Mertz and K.B.B. Warren (eds) (2002), *Ethnography in Unstable Places: Everyday Lives in Contexts of Dramatic Political Change*, Durham, NC: Duke University Press.

Hansen, Thomas B. and F. Stepputat (2006), "Sovereignty revisited", *Annual Review of Anthropology*, **35**, 295–315.

Hawthorne, Camilla (2017), "In search of black Italia", *Transition*, **123**, 152–74.

hooks, b. (1990), "Marginality as site of resistance", in Russell Ferguson, M. Gever, M.T. Minh-ha and C. West (eds), *Out There: Marginalization and Contemporary Cultures*, Cambridge, MA: MIT Press, pp. 341–3.

Isin, Elin (ed.) (2008), *Acts of Citizenship*, London and New York: Zed Books.

Jones, Reece (2016), *Violent Borders: Refugees and the Right to Move*, London: Verso.

Klatt, Martin and D.J. Anderson (2012), *The Border Multiple: The Practicing of Borders between Public Policy and Everyday Life in a Re-scaling Europe*, London and New York: Routledge.

Kritzman-Amir, Talin (2011), "Privatization and delegation of state authority in asylum systems", *Law & Ethics of Human Rights*, **5** (1), 193–215.

Levi, Primo (1991), *I sommersi e i salvati*, Torino: Einaudi.

Lindquist, J. (2017), "Brokers, channels, infrastructure: moving migrant labor in the Indonesian-Malaysian oil palm complex", *Mobilities*, **12** (2), 213–26.

Lindquist, J., B. Xiang, and B.S.A. Yeoh (2012), "Opening the black box of migration: brokers, the organization of transnational mobility and the changing political economy in Asia", *Pacific Affairs*, **85** (1), 7–19.

Mbembe, Achille (2001), *On the Postcolony*, Berkeley, CA: University of California Press.

McKeown, A. (2012), "How the box became black: brokers and the creation of the free migrant", *Pacific Affairs*, **85** (1), 21–45.

Merrill, Heather (2014), "Postcolonial borderlands: black life worlds and relational place in Turin, Italy", *ACME*, **13** (2), 263–94.

Mezzadra, Sandro (2011), "How many histories of labour? Towards a theory of postcolonial capitalism", *Postcolonial Studies*, **14** (2), 151–70.

Mezzadra, Sandro and B. Neilson (2013), *Border as Method, or, the Multiplication of Labor*, Durham, NC and London: Duke University Press.

Minca, Claudio (2015), "Geographies of the camp", *Political Geography*, **49** (November), 74–83.

Mitchell, Tim (1991), "The limits of the state. Beyond statist approaches and their critics", *American Political Science Review*, **85** (1), 77–96.

Mountz, Alison (2011a), "Specters at the port of entry: understanding state mobilities through an ontology of exclusion", *Mobilities*, **6** (3), 317–34.

Mountz, Alison (2011b), "The enforcement archipelago: detention, haunting, and asylum on islands", *Political Geography*, **30** (3), 118–28.

MSF (2016), *Out of Sight: Asylum Seekers and Refugees in Italy, Informal Settlements and Social Marginalization*, Brussels: Médecins Sans Frontières.

Nash, Carolyn (2004), "Postcolonial geographies: spatial narratives of inequality and interconnection", in Paul Cloke and P. Crang (eds), *Envisioning Human Geographies*, London and New York: Routledge, pp. 114–27.

Novak, Paolo (2011), "The flexible territoriality of borders", *Geopolitics*, **16** (4), 741–67

Painter, John (2010), "Rethinking teritory", *Antipode*, **42** (5), 1090–118.

Pinelli, Barbara (2013), "Silenzio dello stato, voce delle donne: abbandono e sofferenza nell'asilo politico e nella sua assenza", *Antropologia*, **15**, 85–108.

Portes, Alajandro (ed.) (1995), *The Economic Sociology of Immigration: Essays on Networks, Ethnicity, and Entrepreneurship*, New York: Russell Sage Foundation.

Portes, Alajandro and J. Sensenbrenner (1993), "Embeddedness and immigration: notes on the social determinants of economic action", *American Journal of Sociology*, **98** (6), 1320–50.

Raeymaekers, T. (2014) *What is a Border?* Posted on http://www.timothyraeymaekers.net/2014/10/518/.

Raeymaekers, T. (forthcoming 2019), "The deep border: migrant ghettos and the Mediterranean crisis", *Social and Cultural Geography*.

Rose, Nicholas (1999), *Powers of Freedom: Reframing Political Thought*, Cambridge: Cambridge University Press.

Sassen, Saskia (2006), *Territory, Authority, Rights: From Medieval to Global Assemblages*, Princeton, NJ: Princeton University Press.

Saucier, Khalil and T.P. Woods (2014), "Ex aqua: the Mediterranean basin, Africans on the move and the politics of policing", *Theoria*, **61** (141), 55–75.

Sayad, Abdelmalek (1999), *La double absence: des illusions de l'émigré aux souffrances de l'immigré*, Paris: Editions Seuil.

Smart, Alan and J. Smart (2008), "Time-space punctuation: Hong Kong's border regime and limits on mobility", *Pacific Affairs*, **81** (2), 175–93.

Swyngedouw, Eric (1997), "Neither global nor local: 'glocalization' and the politics of scale", in K. Cox (ed.), *Spaces of Globalization. Reasserting the Power of the Local*, New York: The Guilford Press, pp. 137–66.

Tsing, Anna (2009), "Supply-chains and the human condition", *Rethinking Marxism: A Journal of Economics, Culture & Society*, **21** (2), 148–76.

Van Houtum, Henk and T. Van Naerssen (2002), "Bordering, ordering and othering", *Journal or Economic and Social Geography*, **93** (2), 125–36.

Vigh, Henrik (2008), "Crisis and chronicity: anthropological perspectives on continuous conflict and decline", *Ethnos*, **73** (1), 5–24.

Vigh, Henrik (2009), "Motion squared: a second look at the concept of social navigation", *Anthropological Theory*, **9** (4), 419–38.

Walters, William (2006), "Rethinking borders beyond the state", *Comparative European Politics*, **4**, 141–59.

Williams, John (2006), *The Ethics of Territorial Borders: Drawing Lines in the Sifting Sand*, Basingstoke: Palgrave Macmillan.

Xiang, Biao (2013), "Multi-scalar ethnography: an approach for critical engagement with migration and social change", *Ethnography*, **14** (3), 282–99.

5. Biometric borders
Benjamin J. Muller

ENCOUNTERS

You suddenly realize that your planned trip is only three weeks away; you should book your airline ticket right away. As you complete the booking online, you are asked to add details such as your passport number and your trusted traveler status. Several verifications and ticked boxes for privacy (or an assumed lack thereof) pop up, which you click and dispatch rapidly. Paying little attention, you may not recognize that you have acknowledged that your personal data, including biometric information, will already cross the border, weeks before your physical departure.

The travel day arrives. As you approach the customs and border checkpoint in the airport, which so happens to be an extra-territorial border crossing inside your domestic airport, you reach into your pocket to retrieve your passport and your trusted traveler card. As differing national and even sub-national jurisdictions have myriad regulations about which precise forms of identification are acceptable, you carry both. As far as you know, the trusted traveler card, which is in year 3 of its five-year term, has been risk assessed half a dozen times in the past two months; or never. It certainly may or may not have any correlation with your physical visits to the border. As you approach the checkpoint you are confronted with a series of electronic kiosks, and you choose those associated with the trusted traveler program. You pass your card over the reader and then use the iris and fingerprint scanners for verification. Something appears to be malfunctioning, and you're directed to the border agent. Your nervous unease shifts to frustration with inefficient and malfunctioning technology that seems intended to save you time, but has simply enhanced frustration and added complication.

Out of habit, the customs and border security agent asks for your passport, so you reach into your pocket and produce your biometric passport. Unfortunately, in this case, the state you wish to enter requires a visa, which also happens to be biometric. You place all fingers on the readers and stare into the iris scanner. You are then also asked to produce your boarding pass. You fumble in your bag to retrieve your iPhone and use the biometric scanner to unlock and show the eBoarding pass. After what feels like a prolonged silent stare at a concealed computer screen, the boarding agent says, "welcome" and hands you back your documents and mobile phone. You are granted entry.

To members of the traveling public and to scholars in border and borderlands studies, this vignette is likely familiar. We live in a time of transition and flux, in terms of the management and security of borders and the bodies that cross them. The relatively routine border crossing in an international airport or at a territorial land border, regardless of frequency, often involves uncertainty, virtuality, and opacity. Both spatially and temporally, the border expands, thickens, proliferates, and goes virtual. Contemporaneous with the equally prolific penchant for walls and the accompanying violent and exclusionary ramifications (Bebout, 2016; Brown, 2014; Casey and Watkins, 2014; Dear, 2013; Jones,

2012; Rael, 2017; Vallet, 2014), biometrics and biometric borders conceal the violence and exclusion, in more "sterile" forms of social sorting. In this sense, biometric borders are like all forms of surveillance and identification technologies in contemporary everyday life. As Monahan notes, surveillance and identification technologies serve to secure "social relations, institutional structures, and cultural dispositions that – more often than not – aggravate existing social inequalities and establish rationales for increased, invasive surveillance of marginalised groups" (Monahan, 2006, p. ix). As such, to unpack the biometric border is, to some extent, to reflect on trends towards the "biometric state" (Breckenridge, 2014; Muller, 2010a) and the politics of surveillance and identification in everyday life.

What is the biometric border? How did it emerge and to what extent have biometric technologies changed borders and the experience and articulation of the bodies that cross them? Although the use of biometrics in border security and visa and migration management are presented as enabling verification and authentication of identity, deeper trends towards what for lack of a better term we might refer to as a "biometric state" are part of this story. It is as much about the increasing interoperability and interchangeability of border security and identity management tactics that biometrics promises (which is hindered by a general lack of global harmonized standards) as it is about proliferating and enhancing sovereign power as global commerce and mobility challenge the state's resilience. Referred to as emergency or exception, biometric borders are instrumental facilitators in the proliferation and permanence of this discretionary sovereign power. Furthermore, it's not accidental or trivial that the US extra-territorial border crossings in airports around the world often include some ersatz Statue of Liberty and various other plastic patterns of power. What amounts to kitsch chauvinism is an essential part of biometric borders and the biometric state, as plastic performances of state power are intended to supplant the lived experiences of borderlands that extol the virtues of universality and inclusion, rather than the exclusionary particularity of the sovereign state narrative.

The analysis begins by reviewing the key literature on this issue, focusing on the impact of biometrics on contemporary border politics. As any epoch will attest, borders are easily beholden to primal discourses of exclusion, often celebrating material and metaphorical walls as effective and legitimate strategies to insure supposed civilized politics of the inside from the alleged barbarism of the outside. Indeed, US President Donald Trump regularly seems to conflate civilization and the political vision of the walled-off world. The re-emergence of walls is not unrelated to the near obsessive fetish with technologies of surveillance and identification in the service of a seemingly unquenchable thirst for technology at the border (Muller, 2010b; Salter and Mutlu, 2012). The biometric border, and the emerging biometric state for which the biometric border is an integral part, is an essential part of this reassertion of sovereign power. This is not only about the so-called "exception as the norm" or the way unelected portions of the state security apparatus have come to take on more significant portions of state governance (Ackerman, 2010; Agamben, 2005; Alford, 2017; Glennon, 2014). It is also about reasserting the sovereign story of state identity, (rein)forcing the rituals and performances of state identity that conflict with the histories and identities of the borderlands. During "engagements" with scholarly literature on biometric borders, we also entertain, however briefly, the institutional and geopolitical changes that have helped to contribute to the emergence of biometric borders: namely, state, bilateral and multilateral policies and agreements, international organizations and international regimes that have contributed directly to the emergence of biometric borders. Finally, the chapter ends with some potential eventualities of biometric borders; in other words, where are we headed?

ENGAGEMENTS

Nick Vaughan-Williams points out, "the border is no longer where it is supposed to be" (Vaughan-Williams, 2012). But what does this mean? It teases out the fact that borders and border politics – which encompasses the state to state interactions, and mobile bodies that cross them, and the national and international political agents scuffling for the management of borders – is undergoing significant change, much like the political more generally. As a scholar of politics and international relations, Vaughan-Williams brings specific competence to the understanding of borders. Throughout global politics the border is perceived to be the limit of the political, the line or liminal space between civilization and barbarians, us and them, inside and outside (Walker, 1993). As such, it is a kind of "ground zero" of the political; the precise locale of differentiation. Similarly, the biometric border serves as this hyper political site of the biometric state. The mistake is to understand this in solely territorial terms, which oddly, scholars of international relations (IR) and politics fall prey to far more than geographers.

John Agnew famously and astutely noted that the discipline of IR/Global Politics was beholden to a "territorial trap" (Agnew, 1994). Although geography and geopolitics is more explicitly the study of the "earth," denoted by the Greek *ge*, geographical engagements with the study of borders are more hesitant to theorize the border as a limit in the manner that IR scholars do. For geographers, mobility is a rich, complex, and fecund concept, which informs their understanding of borders and borderlands as sites of opportunity, heterogeneity, and complexity, not fear (Adey, 2017). Whereas IR scholars tend to perceive mobility through a lens of civilization: either marauding barbarians confront the walls and gates of civilization; or the civilized, often through barbaric acts "outside" the sovereign state are engaged in civilizing missions (Salter, 2002).[1] Rich, ethnographic understandings of borders and borderlands from anthropology place borders in even sharper relief.

Although the study of borders and borderlands is undoubtedly an interdisciplinary and multidisciplinary exercise, anthropology has had a significant role in the emergence and development of this field of study. As "frontiers of identity," borders and borderlands are articulated through ethnographic research as complex cultural spaces/places; both institutions and processes (Donnan and Wilson, 1999, p. 5). Although the role borders play in making national identity is captured by political analysis and IR, border cultures and ethnicities that undermine the chauvinism of national identity is the purview of anthropology (Donnan and Wilson, 1999, p. 5).

---

[1] This particular issue is addressed later in the chapter, as the history of colonialism is deeply integrated with the history of IR. As such, the tactics to sort, categorize, and "know" the colonial other by the imperial overloads has a closely related genealogy to the identity management tactics that are integral to the biometric borders of today (see Appadurai, 1996).

In sharp contrast, biometric borders assert a specific political articulation as opposed to an ethnographic one. Representing a series of complex and intense power relations and political challenges and resolutions that have been instrumental in rearticulations of notions of sovereign power (discretionary, exception, norm) as well as notions of political identity and the *body* politic, biometric borders embrace the border as *limit*. As a direct and intentional challenge to ethnographic borders and borderlands, biometric borders are about (re)introducing performances of nationalism and statehood that reassert exclusionary, nationalist, sovereigntist thinking (see Shapiro, 2004).[2] Moreover, there is an intimate relationship between some emerging scholarship in IR and comparative politics that validates articulations of sovereign power over the fluid, ethnographic accounts of borderland identities.

Among the actions taken by the US in response to the events of September 11, 2001, the immediate but temporary closure of the US border was among the most significant. Ongoing wars on foreign soil which have led to catastrophic loss of life and regional and global geopolitical instability is in no way eclipsed by the actions taken by US officials to close the US border. However, together with significant institutional and policy changes in terms of border security and mobility management, the changes to the border, not only in the US, but globally, remain spectacularly important, and ubiquitous. The emerging biometric borders embrace the civilization/barbarian dichotomy, the chauvinisms of national identity and the long-held Hobbesian-inspired vision of the border as the limit of the political. As a direct challenge to the ethnically diverse "border mentality," this "security state of mind" (see also Salter and Mutlu, 2012; Schneier, 2008) strangles borderland claims of heterogeneity and productive if not harmonious diversity. The pincers of local and global that threaten the jingoistic possibilities of sovereignty's grip on the political imagination are kept at bay by biometric borders and the ersatz symbols of liberty and justice stationed there. In this sense, it is clear that biometric borders, although novel in the specifics of the technology used, and the enhanced capacity to categorize and sort at the border, are nonetheless consistent with the long-standing function of nation state borders as zones of exclusion and indistinction (see Edkins, 2000).

While in very real terms the border is mobile, the bordering practices of risk assessment, security, and clearance occur physically and symbolically *away* from the border. Facilitated by the ubiquitous reliance on biometric technologies in border management, this has allowed the border and its accompanying politics of exceptionalism to proliferate locally and globally. As such, this "exception as norm," which has often been the case in the borderlands, but not beyond, together with the wider civil and commercial reliance on biometric technologies and related forms of surveillance help create an emerging "biometric state."

The biometric border is also not unique. In other words, the border and the biometric border are increasingly synonymous. As Frowd and others have shown, the biometric border is throughout the developing world often motivated by geopolitical pressures from

---

2   Shapiro's 2004 text, *Methods and Nations*, provides a rich and persuasive account of the role of IR and comparative politics *thinking* in the construction of not only the academy, but also the politics of development, difference, and otherness. As Shapiro notes, "Pierre Bourdieu has pithily summarized one of the consequences: 'if the state is so difficult to think, it is because we are the states' thinkers, and because the state is in the head of the thinkers'" (Shapiro, 2004, p. 5; see also Scott, 1998).

more powerful states or blocs, namely, the US and European Union (EU) (Frowd, 2014; Leite and Mutlu, 2017; Mutlu, 2011). As Nevins explains in his astute and comprehensive analysis of US "Operation Gatekeeper" along the Mexico-US border, policy directions often form a mutually constitutive relationship with the use of biometric technologies and, hence, biometric borders (Nevins, 2013). Effective and necessary in the erasure of the local lived experiences that form the identities of those in the borderlands, biometrics and the policies that serve to mutually constitute the biometric border wrestle the history and identity of borderlands from their inhabitants and recast this through the lens of the state – trying desperately for borderland identities to instead "see like a state" (Scott, 1998). The extent to which those in a borderland share much in the past and present, and the particularity of that experience in comparison to other borderlands is ground under the biometric border's wheel of standardization and interoperability. Whether it happens to be relatively bizarre towns like Derby Line, Vermont, and Standstead, Quebec, where the civic buildings that were intentionally constructed on the Canada-US border to thwart such state-centric imaginaries, or the San Xavier Mission south of Tucson, Arizona, which sits at the crossroads of Native American, Spanish, Mexican, and American histories and identities, biometric borders serve to challenge these borderland identities. As such, biometric borders bring with them their own set of rituals and performances (concealed in apolitical and ahistorical packaging) to challenge the long-standing shared histories, identities and mobilites that are integral to the borderlands. Therefore, this shift towards all borders as biometric borders not only connotes changing policies and institutions that manage the border, but also a series of different but relatively uniform rituals that serve to reassert sovereignty in the borderlands, where its hold on the political imagination has often been tenuous.

A variety of academic analysts provided keen insight into the new direction border management appeared to be taking, from asking how smart the border might become (Salter, 2004) to ideas of a biometric border (Amoore, 2006) and even a biometric state (Muller, 2010a) that dramatically altered the way in which the border and the bodies that crossed (or attempted to cross) were managed. Nominally, there appears to be an ongoing obsession with making the border "smarter," however anthropomorphic such an idea might be, but the ideal border seems to be more preoccupied with exclusivity and exclusion rather than intelligence per se. As Amoore argues, the biometric border "not only signals the introduction of digital technologies, molecular techniques, and data analytics in the politics of the border and its management. It simultaneously dissects bodies into granular degrees of risk, such that mobile subjects are inscribed with, and carry with them, plural encoded borderlines" (Amoore, 2013, p. 82; see also Hall, 2015). Among the various questions one might ask is to what extent biometric technologies and what has come to be referred to as the biometric border serve this objective? The simple answers here are: they do. As Popescu notes, the topology of borders is decentered and mobile, reaching into the everyday lives of sovereign subjects, unsettling the liminal understanding of the border (Popescu, 2015). However, in order to get to this analysis, we must address in more material terms what the biometric border is. For what is this moniker shorthand? Bound up within this is a series of moves which have helped to dislocate and deterritorialize borders and even lead to the proliferation of borders and bordering practices. The discretionary sovereign power often found only in the borderlands of liberal democratic states has grown and expanded, and the reliance on various identification and surveillance technologies, not least biometrics, has contributed to this directly. Unfortunately, with very few exceptions, what might be perceived as destabilizing trends to deterritorialize and dislocate borders has in fact led to the opposite: a general normalization of exceptional sovereign politics vis-à-vis something we call the "biometric border."

To some extent, the biometric border is not new. The collection and surveillance of personal data have been integral to the governance of mobility for a very long time, and, indeed, the use of personal data for the purpose of population management, often times to categorize and sort along gendered, racial and socio-economic classes, has also been an essential part of population management, or what Michel Foucault refers to as *biopolitics* and *governmentality*. Furthermore, the extent to which technologies of rule have been a part of identifying, categorizing, and sorting populations also has a long and rather disturbing history. Biometrics itself has a similar history that has reified racial, gendered and class-based forms of social sorting (Pugliese, 2012), and as research on facial recognition and body scanners illustrates, many of the same biases remain bred into contemporary biometric applications (Hall, 2015; Wilcox, 2015).

EXPOSITION

As noted earlier, biometric borders are not altogether unique; they continue to function like political borders always have. Functions of sorting, categorizing, and excluding, as well as playing an instrumental role in the imagined community and the ways in which identity and technologies of rule have intermingled. Biometrics emerged and continues to be an integral part of contemporary "identity management." As the border moved away from customs, excise, and examination and towards surveillance and risk assessment, identity management has become a mutually constitutive aspect of border security (Muller, 2004, 2005; Salter, 2004). The cornerstone of contemporary identity management is biometric technology and surveillance, and, thus, biometric borders.

The history of fingerprinting (Cole, 2002) and of biometrics (Pugliese, 2012) clearly indicate the extent to which these technologies that have contributed to what we now refer to as "identity management" are bound up with the accelerated categorization and control of racialized, gendered, and class-based social categories. Although there is far more to say about this, it is important to keep in mind the extent to which this is a part of the genealogy of biometric borders, and, as a result, how it places a dark shadow over discourses of fairness, equity, and the alleged lack of racial profiling and enhanced efficiency that are the kinds of claims that ground biometric borders (see also Amoore, 2006). Much like the genealogy of biometrics itself, the genealogy of biometric borders is closely tied to the obsession with enumeration and "body counts" in the management of colonial subjects (Appadurai, 1996). Drawing on Appadurai, Amoore notes in her text on the biometric border: "classification . . . disciplines the unruly body, bringing it back into a zone of calculation and manageability, recuperating it and accounting for it within 'normal' ranges of acceptability" (Appadurai in Amoore, 2006, p. 341). Amoore goes on to highlight that biometric borders, in a quest to render all bodies knowable and manageable, create a series of "boundaries around homogeneous bodies" (Amoore, 2006, p. 342) that, as other observers of surveillance and identification technologies have noted, flatten and erase difference through a kind of self-discipline, rendering all differences as calculable along a spectrum of risk.

One of the most sustained and developed material examples in the growing biometric border is the US Office of Biometric Identity Management (OBIM). Formerly known as the United States Visitor Immigration Status Indicator Technology or US-VISIT, OBIM supports all aspects of the Department of Homeland Security's (DHS) biometric programs. For a government agency, OBIM has a particularly clean and elegant vision: "A more secure nation through advanced biometric identification, information sharing, and analysis" (Office of Biometric Identity Management, Department of Homeland Security, n.d.). Although last, among the guiding principles, the protection of privacy is listed. As with most biometric identity management programs, a key tension lay between the stated aims of information collection and sharing and the commitment to the protection of privacy. Although some skepticism and critique from members of the public and scholars often derives from the use of biometrics itself, the primary site of tension is between information sharing and privacy protection. Motivated by the kind of longing to calculate and pre-assess the risk of difference, as discussed vis-à-vis Amoore and Appadurai, biometric borders as manifest through OBIM and a wide range of so-called "trusted traveler" programs operate on a number of assumptions and pre-existing categories of risk. As such, biometric borders are by design "multi-lane and multi-speed" borders; crossings with pre-assumed categories of risk and levels of pre-assessment or the lack thereof will inhibit or accelerate crossing (Muller, 2010b; Sparke, 2006). Biometric borders therefore blur the lines between the commercial and the civil, as one's level of neoliberal engagement comes to have a mutually constitutive relation with their level of risk. As I reflect in the conclusion, the contemporary status of biometric borders, and where they appear to be headed in the future, indicate an acceleration of these trends, where the various applications of biometrics from commercial to civil and political are murkier and mutually re-enforcing, leading ever closer to the kind of divided and disaggregated "dividual" described by Amoore (2013, p. 92), rather than the robust mobile citizen imagined in the early twentieth century (Marshall, 1950).

Since September 11, 2001, the changes to the border have been significant. The emerging reliance on biometrics is a significant part of this change, which was accelerated by domestic and international institutional changes. Many of these changes were directly related to the alleged need to wrestle control of the border from local borderlands and into federal control (Konrad and Nicol, 2008; Muller, 2010b). Although significant institutional changes in the US became best practice in border security management, international institutions and regimes, such as the International Civil Aviation Organization (ICAO), have also played a significant role in promoting the norm of Machine Readable Travel Documents (MRTD), which are reliant on biometrics. As part of the international passport regime, these forces further enhance biometric borders as the sole model of advanced identity management.

EVENTUALITIES

As a former Canadian Minister of Citizenship and Immigration noted in 2003, "the biometrics train has left the station" (Muller, 2005). But what does this mean? In 2017 INTERPOL requested a report on a series of questions related to the status of harmonized global standards in biometrics. What was evident, not only from the research but more importantly from the questions asked, was how committed INTERPOL and other agencies remain to biometric borders. Moreover, the relatively uncritical embrace of biometrics, criticized regularly in the years after 2001, appears stable. The general lack of a robust international regime upon which harmonized global standards might emerge, the paucity of international norms about the use of biometrics, and the regular failure to acknowledge public suspicion and skepticism about these technologies are peripheral to the discussion. Visions committed to the alleged promise of biometric technologies and consequently biometric borders to predictive policing and widespread risk assessment verge on the kind of fetishized status biometric technologies (and other surveillance and identification technologies) have had for governments and law enforcement. As noted elsewhere, "surveillance practices and moves towards increased reliance on risk management as a governance framework help shape and are shaped by contemporary norms, ideas, identities and behaviors, dystopian visions often bordering on alarmist and simultaneously fetishized Hollywood images that embrace those norms and practices" (Muller, 2008, p. 217).

The point here is not to make an overtly normative claim about biometric borders. Identification technologies and surveillance, and the manner in which the increasing reliance on the panoply of these technologies is not by definition evil or unjust. However, the relatively uncritical embrace of these technologies, and the manner in which this embrace is motivated by a commitment to the violent, exclusionary performances and rituals of sovereign statehood is cause for deep reflection if not criticism. The complex, interwoven histories and identities of borderlands are not without violence or lines of inclusion and exclusion. However, mobility itself was deemed to be an essential part of the borderland identities and histories. In contrast, biometric borders flatten the diversity, quench neoliberalism's thirst for uniformity, and with the exception of particular forms of labor and capital, render mobility itself as a category of suspicion. Although the story of biometric borders going forward need not be so troubling, without deeper, critical engagement with "identity management" and the ramifications of this for borders and the bodies that cross them, the violent universality of the neoliberal state will likely intensify its grasp on the dominant understandings of borders, borderlands, and mobility.

REFERENCES

Ackerman, Bruce A. (2010). *The Decline and Fall of the American Republic*, Cambridge, MA: Harvard University Press.

Adey, Peter (2017). *Mobility*, London: Routledge.

Agamben, Giorgio (2005). *State of Exception*, Chicago, IL: University of Chicago Press.

Agnew, J. (1994). "The territorial trap: the geographical assumptions of International Relations theory," *Review of International Political Economy*, **1**(1), 53–80.

Alford, Ryan Patrick (2017). *Permanent State of Emergency: Unchecked Executive Power and the Demise of the Rule of Law*, Montreal: McGill-Queen's University Press.

Amoore, L. (2006). "Biometric borders: governing mobilities in the war on terror," *Political Geography*, **25**(3), 336–51. https://doi.org/10.1016/j.polgeo.2006.02.001.

Amoore, L. (2013). *The Politics of Possibility: Risk and Security Beyond Probability*, Durham, DC: Duke University Press.

Appadurai, Arjun (1996). *Modernity at Large: Cultural Dimensions of Globalization*, Minneapolis, MN: University of Minnesota Press.

Bebout, Lee (2016). *Whiteness on the Border: Mapping the U.S. Racial Imagination in Brown and White*, New York: New York University Press.

Breckenridge, Keith (2014). *Biometric State: The Global Politics of Identification and Surveillance in South Africa, 1850 to the Present*, New York: Cambridge University Press.

Brown, Wendy (2014). *Walled States, Waning Sovereignty*, New York: Zone Books.

Casey, Edward S. and Mary M. Watkins (eds) (2014). *Up Against the Wall: Re-imagining the U.S.-Mexico Border*, Austin, TX: University of Texas Press.

Cole, Simon A. (2002). *Suspect Identities: A History of Fingerprinting and Criminal Identification*, Cambridge, MA: Harvard University Press.

Dear, M.J. (2013). *Why Walls Won't Work: Repairing the US-Mexico Divide*, New York: Oxford University Press.

Donnan, Hastings and Thomas M. Wilson (1999). *Borders: Frontiers of Identity, Nation and State*, New York: Berg.

Edkins, J. (2000). "Sovereign power, zones of indistinction and the camp," *Alternatives*, **25**, 3–25.

Frowd, P.M. (2014). "The field of border control in Mauritania," *Security Dialogue*, **45**(3), 226–41. https://doi.org/10.1177/0967010614525001.

Glennon, M.J. (2014). *National Security and Double Government*, New York: Oxford University Press.

Hall, D.R. (2015). *The Transparent Traveler: The Performance and Culture of Airport Security*, Durham, NC: Duke University Press.

Jones, Reece (2012). *Border Walls: Security and the War on Terror in the United States, India, and Israel*, New York: Zed Books.

Konrad, Victor A. and Heather N. Nicol (2008). *Beyond Walls: Re-inventing the Canada-United States Borderlands*, Aldershot, UK: Ashgate.

Leite, C.C. and C.E. Mutlu (2017). "The social life of data: the production of political facts in EU policy governance," *Global Governance*, **23**(1), 71.

Marshall, T.H. (1950). *Citizenship and Social Class and Other Essays*, Cambridge: Cambridge University Press.

Monahan, Torin (2006). *Surveillance and Security: Technological Politics and Power in Everyday Life*, New York: Routledge.

Muller, B.J. (2004). "(Dis)qualified bodies: securitization, citizenship and 'identity management'", *Citizenship Studies*, **8**(3), 279–94. https://doi.org/10.1080/1362102042000257005.

Muller, B. (2005). "Borders, bodies and biometrics: towards identity management," in M.B. Salter and E. Zureik (eds), *Global Surveillance and Policing*, Abingdon: Willan Publishing, pp. 83–96.

Muller, B.J. (2008). "Securing the political imagination: popular culture, the security dispositif and the biometric state," *Security Dialogue*, **39**(2–3), 199–220. https://doi.org/10.1177/0967010608088775.

Muller, B.J. (2010a). *Security, Risk and the Biometric State: Governing Borders and Bodies*, London: Routledge.

Muller, B.J. (2010b). "Unsafe at any speed? Borders, mobility and 'safe citizenship'", *Citizenship Studies*, **14**(1), 75–88. https://doi.org/10.1080/13621020903466381.

Mutlu, C.E. (2011). "A de facto cooperation? The increasing role of the European Union in improved relations between Georgia and Turkey," *Comparative European Politics*, **9**(4–5), 543–61. https://doi.org/10.1057/cep.2011.16.

Nevins, J. (2013). *Operation Gatekeeper and Beyond: The War On "Illegals" and the Remaking of the U.S.-Mexico Boundary* (2nd edn), New York: Routledge.

Office of Biometric Identity Management, Department of Homeland Security (n.d.). Retrieved May 27, 2018 from https://www.dhs.gov/obim.

Popescu, Gabriel (2015). "Topological imagination, digital determinism and the mobile border paradigm," *Nordia*, **44**(4), 49–55.

Pugliese, J. (2012). *Biometrics: Bodies, Technologies, Biopolitics*, New York: Routledge.

Rael, R. (2017). *Borderwall as Architecture: A Manifesto for the U.S.-Mexico Boundary*, Oakland, CA: University of California Press.

Salter, Mark B. (2002). *Barbarians and Civilization in International Relation*, London: Pluto Press.

Salter, M.B. (2004). "Passports, mobility, and security: how smart can the border be?" *International Studies Perspectives*, **5**(1), 71–91. https://doi.org/10.1111/j.1528-3577.2004.00158.x.

Salter, M.B. and C.E. Mutlu (2012). "Psychoanalytic theory and border security," *European Journal of Social Theory*, **15**(2), 179–95. https://doi.org/10.1177/1368431011423594.

Schneier, Bruce (2008). *Schneier on Security*, Indianapolis, IN: Wiley.

Scott, P.J.C. (1998). *Seeing Like a State: How Certain Schemes to Improve the Human Condition Have Failed*, New Haven, CT: Yale University Press.

Shapiro, Michael J. (2004). *Methods and Nations: Cultural Governance and the Indigenous Subject*, New York: Routledge.

Sparke, M.B. (2006). "A neoliberal nexus: economy, security and the biopolitics of citizenship on the border," *Political Geography*, **25**(2), 151–80. https://doi.org/10.1016/j.polgeo.2005.10.002.

Vallet, E. (ed.) (2014). *Borders, Fences and Walls: State of Insecurity?* London: Routledge.

Vaughan-Williams, Nick (2012). *Border Politics: The Limits of Sovereign Power*, Edinburgh: Edinburgh University Press.

Walker, R.B.J. (1993). *Inside/Outside: International Relations as Political Theory*, Cambridge: Cambridge University Press.

Wilcox, L.B. (2015). *Bodies of Violence: Theorizing Embodied Subjects in International Relations*, Oxford: Oxford University Press.

PART II

CORPOREAL AND GENDERED GEOGRAPHIES OF MIGRATION

6. Embodied migration and the geographies of care: the worlds of unaccompanied refugee minors
Anna-Kaisa Kuusisto-Arponen and Mary Gilmartin

INTRODUCTION

Migration is an embodied practice. It is not just an act of people moving from place A to place B, but it is also a relational socio-spatial and bodily experience. There are several studies that focus on migrant narratives (see Datta et al., 2009; Lawson, 2000; Ní Laoire, 2008; Rogaly, 2015 as examples of this extensive literature). However, less attention has been given to the embodied nature of migration, particularly among children and young people on the move, whether historically or in contemporary societies (cf. Kaukko, 2015, 2016; Kohli, 2006, 2011, 2014; Kuusisto-Arponen 2015, 2016a, 2016b; Kuusisto-Arponen and Savolainen, 2016; Ní Raghallaigh, 2013; Wernesjö, 2012). In our chapter we focus on embodied migration and related geographies of care. Embodied migration refers to narrated and bodily memorised experiences of being on the move, passing through several places, arriving to a new society and the daily negotiations of identity and belonging. This embodied migration is experiential but simultaneously influenced by and structured around the dynamics of global migration governance.

Quite often international migrants are viewed as care-givers when working as domestic workers, nannies, nurses and in other low skilled occupations (Anderson and Shutes, 2014). Moreover, translocal lives are often discussed in relation to the families and relatives who remain in the country of origin, for example, through the concept of the global care chain (Yeates, 2008). Here we focus on the less discussed perspective of migrants and refugees as care-receivers and how they construct their transcultural subjectivity through everyday socio-spatial encounters near and far. In this chapter, therefore, we define "geographies of care" as the practices and actions taken by institutional actors and individuals to provide protection, support and wellbeing in the new host country. Geographies of care should not be understood as unquestionably positive. As a socio-political practice, care is constituted through uneven and complex power relations (Raghuram, 2016). Even though the production of particular social spaces of caring may be based on an ethos of empathetic and compassionate engagements, it may simultaneously construct care recipients as passive victims (see Conradson, 2003; Korjonen-Kuusipuro et al., 2018).

In this chapter we discuss embodied migration and its relationship to geographies of care. We particularly focus on how governing practices and even institutional care challenge the idea of lived transcultural belonging. We explore this through an empirical investigation of a specific group of care recipients, namely, unaccompanied refugee minors (UMs) in Europe and particularly in Finland. Our discussion is based on ethnographic fieldwork conducted by Anna-Kaisa in Finland, between 2014 and 2017, which foregrounded the experiences of UMs.

EMBODIMENT AND CARE

Approaches to understanding the migratory movement of people often focus on global issues, such as economic differences, geopolitics and security. While global issues are prevalent in explanatory approaches, there is an increasing awareness of their impacts on migrants. Embodied migration is evident in and through several biopolitical governing attempts of the state apparatus and supranational enforcement practices to control the movement of people, such as the European Union-Turkey deal (Rygiel et al., 2016). This does not mean, however, that migrants do not actively resist these practices of governing in their daily life. Quite often this resistance is silent and embodied and thus requires research to highlight the variety of practices of expression. Following on from this, global trends also affect the possibilities for migrant belonging (Antonsich, 2010). Here, we see belonging as a daily negotiation of transcultural identity that occurs through multiple narrative and embodied expressions of translocal ties.

The concept of subaltern geopolitics provides an important insight into the situation of migrants. It suggests that the position of some people is not completely other, resistant or alternative, but *ambiguously marginal* (hooks, 1990; Sharp, 2011). We propose that displaced people, and especially migrant and refugee children and young people, practise subaltern geopolitics in their everyday lives while trying to reconstruct the ties and sites of belonging. They are not outside the state or other such institutional settings, but their practices are affected by the asymmetry of power relations and subordinated modes of representation (see hooks, 1990; Sharp, 2011). Often displaced children's home-making practices, daily social and ethno-cultural encounters, experiences of chronic waiting and other *everyday negotiations of belonging* have not gained much attention in research (see, e.g., Kohli, 2006; Wernesjö, 2014, p. 24). Thus, embodied migration has remained hidden, both in relation to young people's subjectivity as migrants or refugees and also as ordinary young people growing up in the new host country, in our case Finland.

We analyse embodied migration through three key arenas. First, forced migration creates a need for legal protection, social support and (institutional) care for young people who are on the move. In our chapter we discuss particularly the connections between practices of care and embodied migration in creating a sense of belonging. Second, geographies of care can be understood as an umbrella term for the bundle of spatial, material and psycho-social practices and relations of care. We illustrate how these are experienced in UMs' daily lives in Finland. Third, we argue that an analytical focus on the transcultural and translocal sense of belonging of UMs forms the key element in understanding the embodiment of forced displacement. Thus, in this respect the concept of spatial trauma is a powerful way to understand the long-lasting effects of displacement (Kuusisto-Arponen, 2015). Spatial trauma refers to how forced displacement creates drastic, often bodily experienced and memorised, psycho-social experiences. It is characterised by a prolonged sense of placelessness, difficulties in narrative expressions of displacement experiences, and blurred memories of travelling, in addition to extremely accurate and vivid memories of specific emotional events and places. Often, these memories are triggered by smells, sounds, events or social interactions. They may appear very suddenly and sometimes are characterised with mis-timings or even psychological dissociation (Kuusisto-Arponen, 2015). These memories of displacement are not remembered solely for the purpose of retelling; rather, their nature is more existential and relates to affective subjectivities of the displaced people in general. Traumatic experiences of displacement continue to affect autobiographical memory as displaced children and adults narrate their childhood experiences (e.g., Howe et al., 2004; Peltonen and Punamäki, 2010, pp. 97–8). For these reasons, the concept of spatial trauma offers a way to elaborate altered dynamics in the existential interconnectedness of self, place and memory due to forced displacement (Kuusisto-Arponen, 2015).

Thus, we argue that a sense of belonging is not only achieved through identification with groups or individuals, but through performative repertoires and memories that are expressive and embodied (cf. Hetherington, 1998; see also Kuusisto-Arponen, 2014). These embodied repertoires and memories are extremely important in conflict and war situations where forced displacement changes the daily social and geographical environment (Curti, 2008; Venken, 2009). In these situations, repertoires and memories create comfort and moreover reconstruct the ties and sites of belonging. The *situated knowledge* (Rose, 1997) of forced displacement is approached through the daily practices of (be)longing and through narratives of migration memories (see also Korjonen-Kuusipuro and Kuusisto-Arponen, 2012). We argue that focusing on the particular care environments and place-based subjectivities of migrant and refugee youths creates a new standpoint for recognising and understanding the practices and politics of care. This approach also appreciates the displaced children's and young people's own presence as political selves in their life and provides a critical perspective on the spatiality of care (e.g., Conradson, 2003, p. 453; Philo and Smith, 2003).

MIGRANT EXPERIENCE AS TRANSCULTURAL PHENOMENA

Many European states are experiencing institutional uncertainty in relation to migration governance. This is for a variety of reasons, including the significant increase in the numbers of all migrant groups, including UMs; the recent proliferation of ad hoc restrictions in national immigration and family reunification legislation in European Union states; and limits to the supranational governance of migration. The implications of this for UMs are far-reaching. In particular, the bureaucratic asylum process takes a lot of time and no one takes overall responsibility for the situation and lives of UMs. Their lives become an endless chain of incidents: arriving in one particular country or region in Europe; meeting new adults who represent local governing and caring practices; and simultaneously trying to uphold transcultural ties. Moreover, several national policies have for many years tried to address the systemic-level integration of UMs in European societies, but it has been acknowledged that the provision of nationally standardised solutions of institutional care, schooling and social services for UMs is seriously limited and does not recognise the needs of minors (Korjonen-Kuusipuro et al., 2018). One of the main reasons behind this is that the daily realities of UMs are not captured by simplistic, objectifying and territorially restrictive social integration measures and schemes.

Transcultural belonging is an existential condition for many international migrants including UMs and thus should be seen at least as a basic need, but preferably as a right, in these people's life. We argue that there are four key features to be recognised in order to understand what transcultural belonging means in the daily social encounters of UMs. First, the existential loneliness experienced by UMs has long-term effects on their wellbeing, agency and selfhood. New psycho-social interventions have been developed to help children with trauma memories (Peltonen and Punamäki, 2010). However, along with this psychological support, new ways to deal with the loss and alteration of important social and spatial relations are needed. Second, UMs are active agents with multiple capabilities and resources. New modes of interaction between UMs and their carers are needed to support and enable this agency, rather than treating them as victims or passive beneficiaries. Third, many contemporary institutional agents that provide care and protection still emphasise belonging as something territorially bound. They thus operate with nationalistic imageries, such as framing integration primarily through language, and developing partly separated education and work training schemes. For example, in Finland all non-Finnish and migrant children and young people attend a separate preparatory class when they enter the Finnish education system. As a consequence, they have limited interaction with their Finnish peers, resulting in social enclaves in the school setting. Fourth, UMs hope to gain new friends and an expanded social life among their peers in their new host societies, but find this hard to accomplish. These peer relations have to be actively supported in schools and through multicultural child and youth work. Social relations require facilitation and extra efforts of trust building (Ní Raghallaigh, 2013). Moreover, social integration requires a compassionate understanding of the migratory movement and the experiences of the UMs in wider society, particularly in daily encounters with peer groups and adults (Korjonen-Kuusipuro et al., 2018).

The reality, however, is that migrant identities are governed in an embodied manner that emphasises migrants as objects of mistrust, which in turn affects migrant belonging. This is exacerbated for UMs, for whom the question of identity is extremely complicated and simultaneously constituted at several scales of governance. These young people have their own narratives of who they were and what they are now, but often this is challenged by the practices of immigration officials. The asylum process is not, however, the only way in which UMs experience socio-spatial liminality. Another example relates to the lack of official identification, which serves to keep them in the margins and under suspicion. Here, the Finnish case is illustrative. In Finland, an "alien passport" or a residence permit card is not an official identification document. The Finnish Migration Office's English translated webpage states:

An alien's passport and a refugee travel document are travel documents given instead of a national passport. They are not official identification documents even when they do not state "unverified identity." (Migri, 2017a)

A remark "Identity not verified" will be added to your alien's passport or refugee travel document if it has not been possible to verify your identity. (Migri, 2017b)

This means that many unaccompanied youths are unable to obtain an official identification document, which is only issued on the basis of a passport or other validated document. The lack of access to official identification also creates difficulties for handling money. Many UMs are unable to access internet banking, which is based on electronic verification, but only after the provision of official identification.

This kind of identification governance helps to keep UMs ambiguously marginal in their daily encounters in the new society. One youngster, who had just turned 18 (the legal age in Finland), described the following event during the discussion of fieldwork conducted in 2014–15.

He tells about his new friend who he met through skype. He was skyping the Swedish reception centre where one person of his home village was living at that moment. Somehow in the Swedish reception centre there was a young boy with same name as him. They also started to chat and during the years they have became friends. [The youth has told us earlier that he only has three friends in his life that he can trust and this boy living in Sweden is one of them.] Now they have planned that they will meet in Finland during Christmas holidays. We discuss their plans and he first happily says that they at least will go dancing . . . if they are able. Continuing from this ambivalent notion he starts to tell another story of visiting Helsinki a few months ago. He had made plans to have a nice evening with his friends and go dancing. "We tried to go to a disco, but I only had my alien passport, they said that I can not come in, then I tried to explain that I do not have any other documentation of my identity. They did not care, we had to go home . . . It was so embarrassing, girls had put their make-ups for hours and we had to go home." (Field notes, 8.1.2015)

This extract from field notes illustrates vividly the multiple forms of embodied migration, particularly in relation to migrant belonging. Living far away from family and friends is one key factor in the transcultural belonging of UMs. Ties and sites of belonging are not just spatial locations. Rather, relational geographies of belonging also consist of mindscapes and virtual relations through social media. In addition, migration management creates new borders of mistrust within nation-states. These borders are actualised in the daily encounters of young people. In these encounters, their identity is constantly questioned, they are not able to use services that other people can, and, moreover, they are not viewed as any ordinary young person but mostly through past experiences which are further boosted by a "climate of suspicion" in society at large (e.g., Ní Raghallaigh, 2013, pp. 91–2). Thus, it is not surprising that many UMs find it hard to develop trusting relationships with the people around them. Trust is a crucial element in establishing relationships in social environments (Withers, 2017). Gaining trust is complex, and should be seen as an active process that requires time and concerted effort (Ní Raghallaigh, 2013, pp. 92–6) and that may, in time, lead to intimacy (Oswin and Olund, 2010). In principle, caring environments are built on trust and empathy, but in practice these spaces and relationships are loaded with power relations, illustrating the (geo)politics of both trust and intimacy (Pain and Staeheli, 2014). For example, Family Group Homes are sites where the lives of UMs are regulated by Finnish authorities. UMs have to act according to rules posed on them and thus feel constantly evaluated through their behaviour. Care practitioners are paid workers, which further complicates relationships with UMs, at times making young people feel like "products" (also Herz and Lalander, 2017, pp. 1071–2). Being subjected to institutional care practices and systems may thus actually intensify the experience of being lonely or left outside the society in large. We discuss the relationship between care and belonging in more detail in the next section, where we focus on practices and experiences in a housing unit for UMs in Finland.

CARE AND BELONGING IN A FINNISH FAMILY GROUP HOME

UMs are taken care of by many institutional agents, and in settings that include schools, housing and in social and youth work. Family Group Homes, residential units with 24-hour staffing that house a maximum of 24 UMs, are a good example. Prior to 2015, most of the UMs arriving in Finland were housed in these residential units. Though there have been many recent changes in national immigration policies in Finland, these have not affected how the needs of UMs are viewed in the governing and daily practices of care. Additionally, recent changes to laws and policies on family reunification have created new and significant difficulties for UMs who wish to apply for family reunification. Even prior to the recent changes, reunification applications had to be made in the country of origin and by the family members living there. However, the changes have introduced a new income requirement. This has made the process of family reunification even more demanding and difficult for the family and for the separated child who often lacks the necessary resources and competences. The application process now takes more time and effort, including travelling to another country for interviews conducted in the Finnish embassy, and additional costs for travel documents and visas. In many instances, refugee families are undocumented and thus travelling to another country is impossible. Moreover, applications for family reunification of UMs are most often turned down in Finland (Kuusisto-Arponen, 2016a). As a result, UMs living in Finland may have to remain apart from their families for the rest of their lives. This legally created nation-state-based territorial trap results in new existential boundaries for transcultural subjects that are formed in and through international mobility. In this peculiar setting it is even more important to ask how their sense of belonging is formed and lived daily and what kind of social and spatial liminalities define their lives (Kuusisto-Arponen, 2016a, 2016b).

Institutional care is the main protective structure in the lives of these young people. However, it also results in moments of emotive-spatial confusion and traps of liminality. These experiences of liminality are not openly discussed due to high political sensitivity. This happens because many protection and integration practices do not recognise the needs of UMs and actually inhibit their ability to develop and renegotiate a sense of belonging. This constant neglect of experiential knowledge also means that much of children's daily life, negotiations and emotional investment might be incorrectly understood, if heard or seen at all. Institutional care is based on the concept of the child's best interest, but in this case it provides narrow grounds for understanding the lives and the "best interest" of unaccompanied children. In order to emphasise this point, we show how "being in the world" is formed in the transcultural lives of these children and how their subjectivity and agency are constructed.

As subjects, unaccompanied youths should not be defined only through the frames provided by institutional care. Their subjectivity is transcultural and formed in and through silent and outspoken negotiations: who am I and where do I belong? The past experiences are present in daily life, but not only in a negative sense: sometimes as sorrow, loneliness and longing, but on other occasions as joy, for example, when using one's native language or celebrating familiar cultural festivals. One's family cannot be replaced, but gradually new peer families and ties of transcultural belonging start to appear. UMs in the Family Group Home understand each other's situation intuitively, although on many occasions – particularly right after arrival in the country – they do not share a common language. Living and growing together requires a significant effort from these young people. Sometimes they search for closeness, while on other occasions personal limits are tested and sometimes crossed, and arguments and misunderstandings occur. The core of everyday life in the housing unit is living together, taking part in discussions and being involved in daily practices of the emerging transcultural extended family. The Family Group Home is also a site of transnational friendships. UMs have family and relative networks in different parts of the world: in former home countries or in diaspora in a third country. These spheres create the overlapping realities in which subjectivity and everyday agency is negotiated.

We will illustrate this through an in-depth analysis of an afternoon in the housing unit in Finland where one of the authors of this chapter, Anna-Kaisa Kuusisto-Arponen, conducted ethnographic fieldwork for seven months in 2014–15. Field notes recount a period of about 20 minutes when Anna-Kaisa and two girls were watching and discussing music videos from YouTube. Here the extract is divided into three parts to emphasise the key concepts of embodiment, care and transcultural belonging. The original discussion was in Finnish, except the parts that the girls discussed in Somali. We use pseudonyms to distinguish the two girls.

I am in the front hall of the family group home and I hear music. Someone is listening to music on upstairs' computer. I look up and Iana is sitting in front of the computer. She has wrapped herself in a blanket.
A-K: are you cold?
Iana: hrrr, yes I am!
We start to discuss what music she is listening to. She tells me that it is Somali music and she likes it very much.
Iana says: I remember my home country when I am listening to this.
A-K: What the lyrics are about?
Iana explains: Well it is about life, everything, like love and such. The singer is from here . . . Iana stands up and goes to world map which is hanging on upstairs wall. She points to Somalia and says: "But this is Djibouti. They are Somalis too but speak French."

We go back to computer and she searches more videos from YouTube.
A-K: Is the singer still living in Djibouti?
Iana: No, he lives in Canada now.
A-K: But you understand what he is singing?
Iana says with more emphasis: Yes, he sings in Somali!

We watch many videos from this same singer. Iana's friend, another unaccompanied youth, comes to see us. The girls greet each other in Somali but then Nafiso says in Finnish: Iana do you like that?
Iana replies: yes me likes!
Nafiso continues: I do not like.
A-K asks Nafiso why she does not like and she says: I like different kind of music (and then she continues wandering around the house with phone connected to Spotify, she is listening to music too).

Everyday life is full of identity negotiations in the lives of UMs. In the housing unit with almost 20 young people, staff are busy with daily routines and there is limited time for hanging out with the young people. As a researcher, Anna-Kaisa spent several hours per week just chatting and listening to the youngsters. These occasions were all very much as described above; moments where one or two young people are spending time in their home, but no one really pays attention to what they are doing or asks what they are watching, for example, on YouTube. Most of the evenings the shared computer was used by some of the youths to listen to music, watch football or follow an Imam's speech.

As the first part of the extract illustrates, music invokes the feeling of diaspora belonging (Leurs, 2015, pp. 215–16). Iana is not just listening to the music but also uses it to explain how Somalis living in different parts of the world are connected to each other. At the same time, there is a short exchange about music preferences between the two girls.

Multilingual communication is also a crucial element. Both girls use Finnish with Anna-Kaisa, while they first greet each other in Somali. However, they start using Finnish again, because they wish Anna-Kaisa to understand what they are saying about their musical tastes. Operating with multiple languages in daily encounters is a defining feature in these young people's life. It can also be used as a way to resist adults, especially when young people know that the adult cannot understand their native language. Thus, language can create a private space for a few people from the same linguistic group that, at the same time, excludes others. In this way, young people are able to create intimate, if temporary, sites of belonging among the daily routines of their lives.

> Iana shows a video of people dancing disco in a big party. The music is in Somali and Iana starts to move her hands to the rhythm of the music and imitate the other dancers. Her moves are a bit careful and not as brave as in the video. Suddenly she says that this is traditional dance in her home country and she remembers when she was a little girl that she also knew how to dance this. Then she says enthusiastically: "look at her, that small girl there, she can also do that, and those old people. Everybody knows how." We watch the video and Iana starts moving more and more with the rhythm. Now she is moving her upper body and not only hands as in the beginning. Few minutes later she goes to google and carries out a search: she wants me to see what the traditional clothes look like in her country. Now in the video young boys and girls are dancing in rows and wearing traditional clothes. All have white clothes but boys have colourful belts and girls have scarf like thing on their other shoulder. Girls are wearing hijabs. Iana says: "look how difficult, look feet and hands go at different times and then the head." We watch how the dance develops.

Iana's embodied description of the moves of the traditional dance and the memory of actual practice of dancing it when she was a small girl in Somalia can be seen as a trace of spatial trauma. This moment vividly recalls and expresses fractures in her sense of place. Embodied memories of childhood festivities and kinaesthetic knowledge of the dance movements surface to her mind by watching the music video. Iana's narrative explains what she wants me to see in the video. How she memorises past events through her body is equally significant. This kind of recalling is quite typical for any traumatic memory, and can be seen as a way to deal with the loss of place and cultural community through the development of a new transcultural subjectivity. Therefore, utilising social media is not just about hanging out and spending time online. Rather, it can evoke bodily memories from the childhood, create affective connections to distant locations and support the transcultural reality that these youths belong to (see, e.g., Leurs, 2015). Part of this reality is the use of online cultural substitutes for translocal familial ties that are "denied" by the state authorities and often also unrecognised by the care environment. This kind of banal transculturality is not supported in integration policies either, particularly when these markers do not carry Western cultural values. For example, while Somali or Afghan music and hijabs were daily matters and part of the visual and soundscape of the home, these were not often discussed by the care practitioners and young people. This should be carefully rethought in the provision of social support for UMs, to ensure that their transcultural ties and needs are recognised and deemed worthy of acknowledgement from caring adults. This support does not have to be more than adults' genuine interest in issues that are important in the UMs' ethno-cultural backgrounds. Moreover, this would help tackle the loneliness that many UMs carry in them. Being separated from many familial relations, UMs often describe themselves as being trapped in loneliness because of their separation from family and friends, and this is exacerbated by care practices that position them as victims and sometimes even "potential terrorists" (Herz and Lalander, 2017). Instead of focusing solely on loneliness, we claim here that building transcultural belonging in care practices is not in opposition to societal integration. Studies have shown that stable and loving home ties at both individual and community levels are important factors in supporting resilience in UMs' lives (e.g., Nardone and Correa-Velez, 2016). While these home ties are not often possible with many UMs, the socio-cultural ties can provide at least a partial substitute. Thus, it is crucial that care providers give space to young people to relate to familiar childhood experiences and interests such as language, clothes and cultural traditions, even if through virtual and temporary channels.

> Suddenly she goes to Google again: a new video. There is a Somali man who sings to a woman sitting on the stairs.
> Iana says: Where can I find that hat (laughs happily) (woman is wearing striped felt hat).
> A-K: Ou, that hat, well that is nice indeed. I think you could find one somewhere.
> Iana: maybe!
> A-K continues: Could you wear that without your hijab?
> Iana: Of course I can if I want! (with very strong voice)
> A-K: Ok.
> We do not discuss the hat anymore. Nafiso comes back and they start to discuss something in Somali. Girls go downstairs for 5 minutes and I am left alone with the computer. Later Iana comes back with food plate. We discuss how girls are planning to go to swim soon, because it is women's shift in swimming pool on that day. Simultaneously, phone rings and she talks in Somali again. After the call Iana explains: "She was my friend from the school, I told her that I cannot meet because it is Wednesday and I need to go to swimming". (On Wednesdays there is a shift for only women in the local swimming hall, in the area where majority of immigrants live in the city). (Field notes, 17.11.2014)

One aspect of embodied migration is the relationship to and the stance taken on cultural traditions in the home country and the country of residence. One's own decisions are weighed against social and cultural memories of the past and the practices of the present. UMs, like other young people, also experience peer pressure, the influence of relatives and the demands made by Finnish society. As the extract above shows, it is not always easy to navigate these competing demands. On the one hand, fashionable things and global youth culture are important but, on the other hand, Somali culture and Muslim traditions are an important component of belonging. As Iana's narrative illustrates, hijab, hat and swimming create a moment of emotive-spatial confusion. For her, it is not so clear what she actually can do and what she might prefer to do.

As the three extracts have shown, daily care environments are full of micro moments where both longing and belonging are present. These are not loud and expressive moments but fundamental embodiments of migration experience. These moments where transcultural belonging is created need to be better understood and recognised by the care practitioners. For example, the Finnish Family Group Home is much more than a place to house and integrate UMs. It should also be viewed as a care environment and site of belonging which opens up in multiple and changing directions, to include Finnish society, global ties of diaspora communities, places of journeying, and other familial but distant places. As such, it is also a site for the negotiation of the complexities of belonging, including both the joy of developing new social relations and building trust, as well as difficult emotions such as sorrow and loss. This entire range of emotional geographies and subjective experiences needs to be considered equally important in the lives of UMs (see also Sharp, 2009).

CONCLUSION

UMs are politicised by varying agents, whether as targets of (trans)national bordering practices, as recipients of institutional care or as transmitters of this lived liminality. These all contribute to migration as an embodied experience, which expands our understanding beyond the act of the journey to and resettlement in the new society. We argue that migration must be understood as a lived and embodied experience that continues to affect everyday social and cultural encounters long after the actual journey to the new society has ended. Through ethnographic research in a Finnish Family Group Home, we showed how daily encounters in an institutional setting provide an illustrative example of geographies of care. UMs are recipients of protective care. This may, in turn, help to support their transcultural agency and belonging, but only if their daily encounters – which are not easily narrated – are recognised and acknowledged, and they are able to build trust. Geographies of care, such as those in the Family Group Home, have the potential to facilitate and enable migrant belonging. However, other power relations, such as European Union migration enforcement and national migration and integration legislation and policies, are inherent in this site too. Thus, rather than providing a care-full environment for UMs, at times care environments impose multiple positionings on UMs and sometimes even actively work against their embodied transcultural and translocal belonging. This is the case, for example, when care practices position UMs in ambiguously marginal positions such as in preparatory classes in school or without suitable identification documents.

Many established societies perceive irregular migration as a problem (Kynsilehto, 2017). In particular, the position of UMs is very challenging in relation to global mobility, migration governance and the provision of care. For the new host, societies providing state care and protecting the best interest of the child should be of utmost importance, but there is considerable variation in how European countries fulfil these basic rights for UMs. The neglect of the recognition of belonging in institutions that are nominally focused on care has led to increasing challenges in wellbeing among UMs and decreased the effectiveness of integration policies in respective national contexts. In this way, the practices of institutions of care, informed by national integration schemes, might exacerbate migrant loneliness, rather than support the complexity and breadth of migrant embodied belonging. More importantly, as an experiential phenomenon, care providers need to recognise the worlds that UMs carry in them: UMs encounter chronic loneliness, long for familial ties, and simultaneously belong to several cultural communities. These are embodied experiences that give rise to transcultural and translocal belonging.

ACKNOWLEDGEMENTS

Kuusisto-Arponen wishes to thank the Academy of Finland for funding: projects SA 266161 and SA 304146.

REFERENCES

Anderson, B. and I. Shutes (eds) (2014), *Migration and Care Labour, Theory, Policy and Politics*, Basingstoke, Hampshire: Palgrave Macmillan.

Antonsich, M. (2010), "Searching for belonging – an analytical framework", *Geography Compass*, **4** (6), 644–59.

Conradson, D. (2003), "Geographies of care: spaces, practices, experiences", *Social and Cultural Geography*, **4** (4), 451–4.

Curti, G.H. (2008), "From a wall of bodies to a body of walls: politics of affect, politics of memory and politics of war", *Emotion, Space and Society*, **1** (2), 106–18.

Datta, K., C. McIlwaine, J. Herbert, Y. Evans, J. May and J. Wills (2009), "Men on the move: narratives of migration and work among low-paid migrant men in London", *Social and Cultural Geography*, **10** (8), 853–73.

Herz, M. and P. Lalander (2017), "Being alone or becoming lonely? The complexity of portraying 'unaccompanied children' as being alone in Sweden", *Journal of Youth Studies*, **20** (8), 1062–76.

Hetherington, K. (1998), *Expressions of Identity. Space, Performance, Politics*, London: Sage.

hooks, b. (1990), "Marginality as a site of resistance", in R. Ferguson, M. Gever, T.T. Minh-ha and C. West (eds), *Out There: Marginalisation and Contemporary Cultures*, Cambridge, MA: MIT Press, pp. 341–3.

Howe, M.L., D. Cicchetti, S.L. Toth and B.M. Cerrito (2004), "True and false memories of maltreated children", *Child Development*, **75**, 1402–17.

Kaukko, M. (2015), *Participation in and Beyond Liminalities. Action Research with Unaccompanied Asylum-seeking Girls*, Oulu: Acta Universitatis Ouluensis, p. 156.

Kaukko, M. (2016), "The P, A and R of participatory action research with unaccompanied girls", *Educational Action Research*, **24** (2), 177–93.

Kohli, R. (2006), "The sound of silence: listening to what unaccompanied asylum-seeking children say and do not say", *British Journal of Social Work*, **36**, 707–21.

Kohli, R. (2011), "Working to ensure safety, belonging and success for unaccompanied asylum-seeking children", *Child Abused Review*, **20**, 311–23.

Kohli, R. (2014), "Protecting asylum seeking children on the move", *Revue Européenne des Migrations Internationales*, **30** (1), 83–104.

Korjonen-Kuusipuro, K. and A.-K. Kuusisto-Arponen (2012), "Emotional silences: the rituals of remembering the Finnish Karelia", in B. Törnquist-Plewa and N. Bernsand (eds), *Painful Pasts and Useful Memories. Remembering and Forgetting in Europe*, Lund University, CFE Conference Papers Series, Vol. 5, Lund: Centre for European Studies, pp. 109–26.

Korjonen-Kuusipuro, K., A.-K. Kuusisto and J. Tuominen (2018), "Everyday negotiations of belonging – making Mexican masks together with unaccompanied minors in Finland", *Journal of Youth Studies*, https://doi.org/10.1080/13676261.2018.1523539.

Kuusisto-Arponen, A.-K. (2014), "Silence, childhood displacement and spatial belonging", *ACME: An International Journal for Critical Geographies*, **13** (3), 434–41.

Kuusisto-Arponen, A.-K. (2015), "Relating self, place and memory: spatial trauma among the British and Finnish War children", in C. Harker, T. Skelton and K. Hörschelmann (eds), *Geographies of Children and Young People: Conflict, Violence and Peace*, Singapore: Springer, pp. 307–25.

Kuusisto-Arponen, A.-K. (2016a), "Perheettömiksi suojellut: yksin tulleiden alaikäisten oikeus perheeseen" (Protected to live without familial ties: unaccompanied minor's right to family), in O. Fingerroos, A.-M. Tapaninen and M. Tiilikainen (eds), *Perheenyhdistäminen: kuka saa perheen Suomeen ja kuka ei? (Family Reunification: Who Can and Cannot have their Family to Finland)*, Tampere: Vastapaino, pp. 89–109.

Kuusisto-Arponen, A.-K. (2016b), "Myötätunnon politiikka ja tutkimusetiikka Suomeen yksin tulleiden maahanmuuttajanuorten arjen tutkimisessa" (Politics of compassion and research ethics in studying the encounters of unaccompanied refugee youth), *Sosiologia*, **53** (4), 396–415.

Kuusisto-Arponen, A.-K. and U. Savolainen (2016), "The interplay of memory and matter: narratives of former Finnish Karelian child evacuees", *Oral History Journal*, **44** (2), 59–68.

Kynsilehto, A. (2017), "Mobilities, politics and solidarities", *Peace Review: A Journal of Social Justice*, **29**, 48–54.

Lawson, V. (2000), "Arguments within geographies of movement: the theoretical potential of migrants' stories", *Progress in Human Geography*, **24** (2), 173–89.

Leurs, K. (2015), *Digital Passages: Migrant Youth 2.0. Diaspora, Gender and Youth Cultural Intersections*, Amsterdam: Amsterdam University Press.

Migri (2017a), "Travel documents. Alien's passport", accessed 5 June 2017 at http://www.migri.fi/travel_documents.

Migri (2017b), "Identity not verified", accessed 5 June 2017 at http://www.migri.fi/asylum_in_finland/applying_for_asylum/obtaining_a_travel_document/identity_not_verified.

Nardone, M. and I. Correa-Velez (2016), "Unpredictability, invisibility and vulnerability: unaccompanied asylum-seeking minors' journeys to Australia", *Journal of Refugee Studies*, **29** (3), 295–314.

Ní Laoire, C. (2008), "'Settling back'? A biographical and life-course perspective on Ireland's recent return migration", *Irish Geography*, **41** (2), 195–210.

Ní Raghallaigh, M. (2013), "The causes of mistrust amongst asylum seekers and refugees: insights from research with unaccompanied asylum-seeking minors living in the Republic of Ireland", *Journal of Refugee Studies*, **27** (1), 82–100.

Oswin, N. and E. Olund (2010), "Guest editorial: Governing intimacy", *Environment and Planning D: Society and Space*, **10**, 60–67.

Pain, R. and L. Staeheli (eds) (2014), "Special section: Intimacy, geopolitics, violence", *Area*, **46** (4), 344–60.

Peltonen, K. and R.-L. Punamäki (2010), "Preventive interventions among children exposed to trauma of armed conflict: a literature review", *Aggressive Behaviour*, **36**, 95–116.

Philo, C. and F. Smith (2003), "Guest editorial: Political geographies of children and young people", *Space and Polity*, **7**, 99–115.

Raghuram, P. (2016), "Locating care ethics beyond the Global North", *ACME: An International Journal for Critical Geographies*, **15** (3), 511–33.

Rogaly, B. (2015), "Disrupting migration stories: reading life histories through the lens of mobility and fixity", *Environment and Planning D: Society and Space*, **33** (3), 528–44.

Rose, G. (1997), "Situated knowledges: positionalities, reflexivities and other tactics", *Progress in Human Geography*, **21**, 305–20.

Rygiel, K., F. Baban and S. Ilcan (2016), "The Syrian refugee crisis: the EU-Turkey 'deal' and temporary protection", *Global Social Policy*, **16** (3), 315–20.

Sharp, J. (2009). "Geography and gender: what belongs to feminist geography? Emotion, power and change", *Progress in Human Geography*, **33**, 74–80.

Sharp, J. (2011), "A subaltern critical geopolitics of the 'war on terror': postcolonial security in Tanzania", *Geoforum*, **42**, 297–305.

Venken, M. (2009), "Bodily memory: introducing immigrant organizations and the family", *The History of the Family*, **14**, 150–64.

Wernesjö, U. (2012), "Unaccompanied asylum-seeking children: whose perspective?", *Childhoods*, **19** (4), 495–507.

Wernesjö, U. (2014), *Conditional Belonging. Listening to Unaccompanied Young Refugees' Voices*, Digital Comprehensive Summaries of Uppsala Dissertations from the Faculty of Social Sciences, 93, Uppsala: Acta Universitatis Upsaliensis.

Withers, C. (2017), "Trust – in geography", *Progress in Human Geography*, **42**, 489–508.

Yeates, N. (2008), *Globalizing Care Economies and Migrant Workers*, Basingstoke, Hampshire: Palgrave Macmillan.

7. Corporeal geographies of labor migration in Asia
Brenda S.A. Yeoh, Kellynn Wee and Charmian Goh

TEMPORARY LABOR MIGRATION IN ASIA

In Asia, the increased volume and velocity of transnational migration based on work contracts within and beyond the region is a phenomenon symptomatic of the flexibilization of life and labor under neoliberal capitalism and uneven development. As Mackie (2010, p. 81) put it, 'to trace the circuits of labor mobility in the Asia-Pacific region is also to map the patterns of economic inequality in the region.' In this context, the corporeal geographies of migration are increasingly marked by temporariness. Transience and transitoriness are becoming fundamental characteristics of labor migration flows worldwide, but these features resonate particularly strongly in Asia, where migration regimes are underscored by enforced temporariness (Castles et al., 2014). Migrant bodies in Asia are allowed to labor, but are usually not allowed to stay. While migrants in Europe have been offered pathways – however fraught – towards permanent residency and eventual incorporation into society as ethnic minorities, migrants in Asia circulate between 'home' and 'host' societies. They swing pendulum-like from impoverished circumstances at home to precarious conditions at destination (Piper et al., 2017), often moving to replace successive cohorts of labor in response to the ebb and flow of market demand (Piper, 2010).

Not all geographies are created equal. Migrants are often stratified in many ways – embodied characteristics such as race and gender, for example, frequently structure labor market incorporation – but one of the most powerful ways in which migrants are differentiated is through the perceived worth of their labor. As a result, a migrant's potential claim to become a 'citizen is contingent upon one's value as a laborer' (Dauvergne and Marsden, 2014, p. 239). Occupying one end of the spectrum is the hypermobile global elite comprising mainly highly skilled professional migrants and capital-rich entrepreneurs; at the other are low-waged labor migrants, who face a gauntlet of restrictions surrounding their access to mobility, social benefits, housing, and job security (May et al., 2007). As Theodore (2003, p. 1812) wrote, 'conditions of precariousness do not fall randomly across urban labor markets,' but are concentrated in particular segments, rendering these groups that much more vulnerable.

In contrast to Europe, where enforced transience as a fundamental governing principle of major labor migration regimes rose and fell alongside the 'guest worker' schemes, labor-importing nation-states in Asia have always foregrounded temporary labor migration in their social and economic policies (Piper, 2010). Temporary labor migration regimes gained popularity following the oil price hike in 1973, where oil-rich but labor-short states in the Gulf and the Middle East began to import contract labor to build large-scale infrastructural projects (Castles et al., 2014). Eventually, employers and governments began to prefer recruiting Asian workers over Arab ones, as the former lacked sufficient linguistic and cultural capital, and were hence less able to make their dissent against poor working conditions known (Fargues, 2011). As intra-Asia labor migration expanded in the wake of decolonization and nation-state building, countries began to occupy positions in the labor migration market as countries of origin, countries of destination, and countries which experience both flows simultaneously (Kaur, 2010). Migration flows in Southeast Asia have also become increasingly feminized, as women are drawn and incorporated into the gender-segmented global economy as nurses, factory workers, intimate laborers, domestic workers, and care workers, often also on the basis of transient work contracts. In this context, temporariness is here to stay: short-term, contract-bound labor migration in Asia continues to dominate as a consequence of continued labor market segmentation, the rapidly expanding migration industry of private brokers, and the growth of social and kinship networks amongst migrants themselves (Hugo, 2012).

There are particular features specific to temporary labor migration in the Asian context. Low-waged transnational migrants often take on unwanted, dangerous, and socially devalued jobs, such as construction, domestic, and care work (Hugo, 2012). Usually shunned by the citizen workforce, these occupations are considered undesirable in large part because they involve demanding physical labor performed over long hours and in dirty or hazardous environments; in the case of care work, the intimate maintenance of ailing or infirm bodies is expected. Other features of temporariness in labor migration regimes include the use of short-term, time-bound contracts that automatically lapse without continual renewal, with little to no possibility of family reunification or permanent settlement; in other words, bodies may labor, but not go into labor (Kaur, 2010). Furthermore, on the basis of their transience, low-waged labor migrants are frequently excluded or only partially incorporated into labor laws, with minimal access to the full range of rights available to citizens (Hewison and Young, 2006). Their bodies are seen as deportable (De Genova, 2002), and their continued socio-legal status in countries of destination depend on the decisions of employers (Rosewarne, 2010). While laboring in countries of destination, transnational migrants' bodies are often rendered docile and deferential through 'technologies of servitude' (Rudnyckyj, 2004) at work while perceived to be dangerous and disposable beyond the sphere of work. These features of temporariness conflate to place migrants in situations that are hyper-precarious (Lewis et al., 2014).

Facilitated by time-space compression brought about by rapid advancements in transport and communication technologies, the rise of temporary labor migration is in large part a response to the flexibilization of contemporary life and work cultures under neoliberal capitalist conditions. Neoliberal globalization has polarized labor markets, devalued old skills, eroded job security, and given rise to global commodity chains. Labor has become increasingly informalized; alongside temporariness, subcontracting and casualization have become everyday features of labor migration (Castles et al., 2014). The vertically integrated employing organization has dissolved, and work is becoming outsourced and offshored (Rubery, 2015). These processes of deregulation and flexibilization have undercut the bargaining power of workers' unions and heightened the precarity of low-waged labor migrants: Overbeek (2002, p. 85) wrote that this 'neoliberal defensive' has created an 'emerging global regime for labor [that] involves both the disciplining of labor and the selective freeing of the mobility of labor.'

Neoliberal capitalism does not only shape the conduct of life and labor in countries of destination to suit flexible accumulation. Arguably, countries of origin have also absolved themselves of accountability for their citizens, 'outsourcing' development to the remittances sent home by temporary labor migrants (Ferguson and McNally, 2015). Piper et al. (2017)

noted that temporary labor migration is an attractive 'safety valve' (p. 1095) for countries of origin that grapple with high unemployment rates, the decline of rural livelihoods, and job shortages. Policymakers at both origin and destination countries hence have a stake in championing temporary labor migration schemes as a 'win–win–win' policy solution: admitting 'temporary' labor into the national geobody purportedly addresses labor market shortages while allowing governments of countries of destination to maintain control of their borders and calibrate migration numbers according to the needs of the market. The policy argument is that this arrangement offers people who might otherwise be unemployed or underemployed the opportunity to chase higher wages abroad; additionally, the temporariness of the arrangement ensures citizens' continued remittances and investment in countries of origin. Temporariness, therefore, is a 'crucial, though little articulated, ingredient in the migration-development nexus' (Rosewarne, 2010, p. 103). Dauvergne and Marsden (2014) unraveled how this ideology of temporariness in labor migration has been normalized as natural and inevitable, suggesting that we are 'remarkably unselfconscious' (p. 232) about falling back on economic analyses, assuming that labor markets exist independently of the state, and reducing people to units of labor.

In this chapter, we draw on the growing scholarship on temporary labor migrants in Asia in order to spotlight the embodied experiences of low-waged migrant workers in the region. Training the analytical lens of corporeal geographies on migrant workers who labor under a patterned set of structural constraints in Asia yields a sense of context and coherence, but also gives rise to productive comparisons. In the next section, we provide a mapping of theoretical approaches relevant to understanding corporeal geographies of migration, before turning, in the third section, to illustrate significant themes that have emerged in this literature with particular reference to temporary labor migration in the context of Asia.

CORPOREAL GEOGRAPHIES AS ANALYTICAL LENS

Recently, geographers have traced the growing prominence of bodies within the discipline (Longhurst and Johnston, 2014; Mountz, 2018; Silvey, 2017). A distinct focus on bodies, whether as a starting point, a fuller engagement, or attendance to its mess, is 'the geography closest in' (Longhurst, 1994). Bodies, as an analytic and scale, accomplishes several ends. It carefully negotiates the binaries of mind/body, male/female, subject/object, sex/gender, constructivism/essentialism, structure/agency, culture/nature, public/private, and discourse/materiality that pervade scholarship (Dunn, 2010; Fluri and Piedalue, 2017; Longhurst, 1995; Longhurst and Johnston, 2014; Moss and Dyck, 2003; Nast and Pile, 1998). Foregrounding bodies and embodiment demonstrates the mutual constitution of these binaries, destabilizes them, and challenges binary thinking in discipline-specific ways. Humanistic geographers spotlight the phenomenological body – the sensorial, experiential, emotive, and affective elements of embodiment – as a valuable end in itself, and as constitutive of place-making processes. Political geographers deploy bodies to apprehend power operating at larger scales and to reveal its dialectical construction (Herod, 2011; Mountz, 2018). The global, geopolitical, national, and economic are intimately experienced by bodies, which in turn become arenas for contestation and reconfiguring scales (Andrucki and Dickinson, 2015). Within economic geography and migration studies, centering the body as a scale of analysis has entailed shifting the emphasis from migration to migrants, asking what the 'push and pull' or 'costs and benefits' of migration mean to them, and foregrounding their desires and experiences (Dunn, 2010; Silvey, 2012).

Corporeal geographies encompass a spectrum of analytical approaches to understanding bodies and embodiment. Before turning to a thematic discussion of bodies, we first consider a number of seminal approaches to bodies: poststructural theory; feminist and critical race scholarship; encounter geographies; emotional, affective, and visceral geographies; and the mobilities paradigm. While these bodies of work are far from exhaustive, they are most relevant to low-waged labor migration.

Poststructuralist scholarship has been formative to corporeal geographies, particularly in its study of the production of bodies. Foucault examined the imbrication of bodies in the microphysics of power across historical contexts: both the disciplinary techniques of surveilling, counting, and classifying individual bodies according to institutionalized knowledge systems and the biopolitics that regulate populations and harness the productive forces of the body. This vein of scholarship emphasizes the contested practices and discourses that inscribe and mark particular bodies as normal or deviant (Silvey, 2017). Scholars, for instance, considered how migrant women's bodies are known, idealized, disciplined, and desexualized within low-waged domestic work (Moukarbel, 2009; Pratt, 1998; Silvey, 2012). Besides Foucault, Butler's notion of performativity has also gained traction within poststructuralist work on bodies. Performativity, or the mimetic gestures that produce the effects of gender and other identifications on the surface of the body, allows for an anti-foundationalist approach to identities, subjectivity, and space (Andrucki and Dickinson, 2015; Butler, 1988; Gregson and Rose, 2000; Moss and Dyck, 2003). Since then, geographers have been careful to rework notions of performance and performativity, such as in non-representational formulations, to retain the subject's agency and the body's materiality without dissolving into discourse (Macpherson 2010; McCormack, 2003; Nelson, 1999; Slocum, 2008; Thrift, 2008).

Feminist geographers and critical race scholars have wielded a wide diversity of approaches to the body over time, transcending earlier notions of socialized and socially constructed bodies with a spotlight on the material and fleshly struggles of embodiment (Longhurst, 1997; Slocum, 2008). While poststructuralist theory treats the body as 'text' or surface of inscription that accrues meaning within historically situated discourses and relations of power, feminist standpoint theory treats the body as a site of experience (Dyck, 1997; Grosz, 1994; Harding, 2004). The latter debunks disembodied research proposing a 'view from nowhere' by producing 'situated knowledge' from the experiences of socially located subjects at intersections of gender, race, class, nationality, religion, among other axes (Haraway, 1988; Harding, 2004; Silvey, 2012). Attending to difference serves as a basis for rethinking fundamental concepts, revealing absences in normative and hegemonic frameworks, and destabilizing macro narratives (Dunn, 2010; Fluri, 2015; Longhurst, 1994; Mountz, 2018). Critical race and postcolonial work draws attention to the (un)conscious histories of epistemic violence targeted at and inherited by black bodies who must navigate the 'whiteness of space' (Ahmed, 2007; Silvey, 2017). In contemporary debates, scholars continue to grapple with analysing the corporeality and matter of gendered and raced bodies without reifying difference (Herod, 2011; Price, 2013; Slocum, 2008).

As per the insight of critical race scholars, differences among bodies materialize in the co-presence of multiple bodies and the dynamics of situated encounters. The congregation of differentially privileged bodies is a powerful political force to be reckoned with (Mountz, 2018; Saldanha, 2008; Silvey, 2017). But 'more than the coming together of different bodies,' Wilson (2016, p. 455, emphasis in the original) argued, 'encounters *make* difference.' The configuration of encounters allows for contingent identities and fluid differences to exceed the mediation of institutionalized categories. Besides setting in motion processes of differentiation, encounters also have powerful spatial implications. The emplacement of encounters, the circulation of bodies within 'contact zones,' and embodied social relations of difference are crucial to the making of places (Massey, 1994; Price, 2013; Silvey, 2017; Wilson, 2016).

Exploring the limits, discreteness, and relationality of bodies opens up lines of inquiry about emotional, affective, and visceral geographies (Abrahamsson and Simpson, 2011). As scholars return to emotional geographies to remedy its marginalization in masculinist corners of the discipline, they map the articulation of emotions with thinking, remembering, socializing, and place-making, hence re-invoking the body as the most intimately felt geography (Anderson and Smith, 2001; Davidson and Milligan, 2004; Nash, 1998). Increasingly, scholars turn from emotional to affectual geographies to consider sensations that precede economies of meaning and reflective thinking, to focus on the immediate and the virtual, to attend to the place of the affective in the market, and to rethink ethics in geographical research (Akalin, 2015; McCormack, 2003). An attention to affect troubles notions of objectified bodily boundaries by reconceptualizing bodies as contingent processes that emerge from material entanglements with its surroundings (Abrahamsson and Simpson, 2011; Macpherson, 2010; Silvey, 2017). Seizing a similarly dynamic conception of bodies, visceral geographies advance discussions on the centrality of material bodies and agentic matter (Hayes-Conroy and Hayes-Conroy, 2010).

The 'mobilities turn' – a theoretical paradigm that crosscuts encounter geographies, a relational approach to bodies, and a host of other disciplines – has also contributed richly to our understanding of corporeal geographies (Sheller and Urry, 2006). Mobilities, more than the fact of movement, encompass the representations and embodied practice of bodies moving. Eschewing the sedentarist and deterritorial assumptions of social science, the 'new mobilities paradigm' explores the interdependent mobilities and immobilities of bodies, things, and ideas across multiple scales. The politics of mobility is especially relevant to our study of corporeal geographies of migration; it foregrounds the uneven access people have to mobilities based on their embodied differences (Cresswell, 2010; Massey, 1994).

MIGRANT BODIES AND 'OTHER' MATTERS

While there are different conceptual pathways towards understanding the corporeal geographies of labor migration, these approaches coalesce in giving heightened attention to bodily experience and body politics: that is, the way the corporeal experience of migration is structured by, and in reaction to, power geometries based on the intersecting axes of class, gender, race, religion, nationality, citizenship, and so on. Such an approach treats the migrant (and non-migrant) body as 'both a site for political geographical analysis and a methodology for destabilizing disembodied macro-scale study of politics and space' (Fluri, 2015, p. 239). To illustrate the way corporeal geographies have been used as an approach in the study of labor migration in Asia, we draw out three significant themes for discussion. First, we examine migrant bodies and the politics of border control. Second, we pay attention to the politics of control and care in migrant encounters, enclavement, and enclosure. Finally, we explore the complex relationship between corporeal absence and mediated intimacy, and the implications for the conduct of transnational family life.

Migrant Bodies and the Politics of Border Control

As Silvey (2007, p. 266) observed, 'low-income migrant workers both challenge and define socio-spatial marginality, and in doing so they embody and enact the (re)production of the boundaries of the nation-state.' Focusing on the immigration gates of international airports in Indonesia as sites where 'multiple overt forms of discipline and regulation' are exerted on repatriating contract workers to 'reclaim' their labor power, Silvey (2007, pp. 266, 277) showed how terminal design and the practices of immigration officials work to segregate migrants from 'general' passengers, serving as a 'funnel' through which 'bodies and incomes of returning overseas workers are renationalized and reterritorialized.' The homeward border that has to be crossed for return migrants – where they are drilled, questioned, evaluated, categorized, channeled, monitored, and compelled to perform the role of the citizen-subject benefitting from the protective power of the state – is a powerful expression of state control. Operating at the edges on migrant bodies, dispersed state power thus produces marginal, 'other' subjects. As Mackie (2010, p. 72) puts it, the 'management of borders' is rooted in the 'management of bodies': while migrant workers attempt to maximize their incomes by crossing national borders, nation-states are also interested in regulating these flows of people and money through enacting border control.

In equally consequential ways, managing the selectively porous borders of host nation-states involves the intricate work of categorizing and channeling migrant bodies. As Yamanaka (2000, p. 63) pointed out, 'immigration policy has created a labor force rigidly stratified by such collective characteristics as legal status, ethnicity, nationality, gender and skill level.' The state imposes spatial and temporal disciplinary strategies in at least three ways. First, by policing territorial borders as a form of spatial control that works through the bureaucratization and commercialization of the border. Second, temporalizing presence by setting limits on the temporal length of stay permitted, leading to 'legal' migrants being transformed into 'illegal' overstayers once contracts or visas expire. Finally, by limiting human rights to discourage belonging and instead increasing the sense of insecurity by immobilizing legal migrants in the job market, making them dependent on their employers, and defining them as purely and exclusively temporary labor to render them 'deportable subjects' (Garcés-Mascareñas, 2010).

In advanced Asian economies such as Hong Kong, Japan, Korea, Singapore, and Taiwan struggling with ultra-low fertility rates, rising life expectancies, and rapidly ageing citizen-populations, the logics involved in recruiting labor power from foreign sources to fill 'dirty, difficult and dangerous' jobs are predicated on a body politics that accords different treatment to different bodies. In Mackie's (2010, p. 81) words, 'the body comes into play in distinguishing between prestigious and skilled occupations and less prestigious ones which are seen as unskilled and are often seen as involving physical or manual labor.' By relegating marginalized occupations to transient migrant laborers who have no foothold in society in general, members of 'mainstream' society are able to 'imagine themselves as fully middle class,' distinguished by the association with white-collar 'mental' work and the distancing of 'manual' labor (Mackie 2010, p. 75).

Border control to secure the geobody of the host nation-state can also be highly gendered. On the one hand, women's bodies are valorized as caregivers as they are expected to be 'infused with affective histories of maternal care' (Akalin, 2015, p. 65), on the other, the gendered and reproductive corporeality of female migrants may attract additional measures of control and governance to guard against unsanctioned fecundity (Kaur, 2010). For example, in Singapore, the bodies of migrant domestic workers are subject to periodic medical screening for pregnancy as part of surveillance to ensure that migrant bodies remain transient with those failing the medical examination subject to almost immediate repatriation (Yeoh et al., 2017b). Such exclusionary measures targeted at banishing the procreating body are doubly ironic in the context of rapidly plummeting fertility in Singapore, escalating state anxieties about the failure of the nation to reproduce itself, and the multiple waves of pro-natalist measures to encourage more babies among the Singaporean citizenry. In discussing the recruitment of Southeast Asian women to address care deficits in Taiwanese households, Lan (2003, p. 525) made a similar point in observing that foreign domestic workers are 'the perfect example of the intimate Other – they are recruited by host countries as desired servants and yet rejected citizens.'

Migrant Encounters, Enclavement, and Enclosure

With the growing everyday presence of migrant workers in globalizing cities, migration scholars are beginning to put emphasis on the need to examine informal social interactions in the 'doing' of cross-cultural encounters, where 'differences are negotiated on the smallest of scales' (Wilson, 2011, p. 635) and 'often in unpanicked and routine ways' across a range of urban localities and sites (Neal and Vincent, 2013, p. 911). Migrant-local encounters reveal 'the embodied nature of social distinction and the contingency of identity and belonging' (Wilson, 2016, p. 452). While 'embodied difference influences the ways that individual migrants are received' (Collins, 2016, p. 1175) in the host society, racialization tends to take root as a critical force in scaled-up encounters in the asymmetrically inflected contact zones between peoples with different histories and geographies (Pratt, 1992). Categories of social difference like race and ethnicity emerge in sensorial engagement with other bodies and non-living entities, while racial privilege and disadvantage hinge on the politics of (in)visibility (Price, 2013).

In Asian cities dependent on large numbers of temporary labor migrants, the contradictions between the need for a large, low-waged migrant population which is supposed to be transient, on the one hand, and the fear of 'diversity' associated with the large influx of migrant others, on the other hand, are most palpable when urban dwellers confront migrant 'concentrations' and 'hotspots' which are highly visible and patently permanent. As Collins (2016, p. 1170) observed, the everyday regulation of migrant bodies is 'an important element of maintaining their position in the lateral spaces of society, where they can contribute to the productive work of businesses without disrupting the normative orientations of urban life.' Paying attention to corporeal geographies alerts us to the way transnational migrants' bodies are often rendered docile, immobile, segregated or invisibilized through spatial measures that target bodies. For example, in her work on foreign domestic workers in Singapore, Jackson (2016) showed how stigmatization of the migrant body as 'low status' creates both physical and metaphorical territorial distinctions between the migrant body and Singaporean society. In turn, these migrant women construct emotionally and geographically separate 'micro-territories' in which they demonstrate resistance through the performative aspects of dress, comportment, food, and language. Bodily borders are hence leveraged as sites of 'continual struggles and negotiation' (Jackson, 2016, p. 297). In a similar fashion, Seo and Skelton (2017, p. 159) showed that, as temporary sojourners, Nepalese migrant workers are effectively excluded from Korean society; however they are also able to leverage 'Nepal Town' in Seoul as 'a site of spatial agency and praxis' and create spaces of possibility through 'the potentialities of reactive ethnicity.' Such 'resistive tactics' are rooted in the politics of embodiment: making their bodies visible through walking, gathering, and loitering in public spaces allows them to insist on social recognition as 'full actors who can display their own identity and specificity in public space' (Seo and Skelton, 2017, p. 160, quoting Saint-Blancat and Cancellieri, 2014, p. 646), while also countering isolation and fear through connecting themselves with co-ethnics and migrant organizations. Also focused on Seoul, Collins (2016, p. 1180) argued that 'tactics for generating visibility by migrants themselves can also serve as a potential avenue for responding to the forms of domination that characterize labor migration regimes, particularly when such visibility challenges the normative placement of migrants in the periphery.' The continual presence of migrant workers in public space does not only physically transform the city but potentially 'disrupts the established notions of temporariness' created by temporary labor migration regimes (Seo and Skelton, 2017, p. 167; see also Law, 2002; Yeoh and Huang, 1998).

As congregations of high density and marked difference, migrant enclaves are often associated with public disorder and tend to provoke social anxieties, moral panics, and calls to tighten control and surveillance. In the aftermath of what became known as Singapore's Little India riot of December 2013 which involved 300 migrant workers, scholars discussed how the area – which is both a historic district showcasing Singapore's Indian ancestral culture and a 'weekend enclave' for low-waged migrant workers from South Asia – became zoned as a space of exception featuring a ban on alcohol sales and increased police surveillance (Hamid, 2015; Yeoh et al., 2017a). Apart from the imposition of extraordinary measures of bodily control at the site of the enclave, mega-dormitories to house migrant workers were also built at peripheral areas as 'spaces of enclosure' in order to constrain the movement of migrant bodies and divert them from more centrally located co-ethnic enclaves (Yea, 2017; Yeoh et al., 2017a). In other words, when it comes to bodily control, the excesses of enclavement are more effectively regulated by strategies of enclosure. At these mega-dormitories, numerous CCTV cameras and demarcated spaces that can only be accessed via a biometric system of fingerprint scanning are integrated with food outlets, entertainment amenities, remittance services, and a help center. In this way, these mega-dormitories serve as containment measures that conjoin control with care. Minimizing unruly migrant encounters in the ethnicized enclaves and fashioning the compliant migrant subjects are 'not only dependent on discipline and surveillance, but are also inextricably conjoined to notions of pastoral care' (Yeoh et al., 2017a).

Corporeal Absence, Mediated Intimacy, and Transnational Family Life

With little chance of sustainable employment in their home countries where they hold citizenship papers and even less likelihood of becoming immigrants-turned-citizens in the host countries where they have secured (low-waged) employment, contract migrant workers become figures locked into unending circuits of transnational care, affection, money, and material goods between 'home' and 'host' countries in sustaining family life. In short, they are transnationally mobile bodies by necessity rather than choice, whose everyday familial practices generate an 'emotional economy' across the transnational stage. In this context, the corporeal geographies approach to migration opens a conceptual window to understanding the spatial and bodily elements of mobility, as well as the multiple temporalities – both organic and imposed on bodies in motion (Cresswell, 2010) – at work in the 'doing' of transnational family life.

Particularly with the increasing feminization of labor migration in Southeast Asia as more women migrants shoulder primary breadwinning responsibilities for their families, the significance of gendered corporeality to the experience of care and intimacy in familial relations has attracted both popular and scholarly attention. This is precipitated by the rapid advancement and widening penetration of new communication technologies which have transformed the norms and forms of 'staying connected' in order to 'do family' and perform care work across national borders (Asis et al., 2004; Peng and Wong, 2013; Platt et al., 2016). Portable mobile phones, followed by 'smart phones' with internet capabilities, have become more affordable for many (but not all) migrant contract workers in Asian host countries and are often preferred as a means of communication with left-behind families as these devices afford real-time communication through mediated 'on-line presence' or virtual 'co-presence.'

The relationship between corporeality and care, and the mediating role of communication technologies, has attracted much debate. In writing against 'culturalist and classist assumptions' about intimacy rooted in Western, middle class norms, scholars working in a Southeast Asian context such as McKay (2007, p. 179) made the point that intimacy need not be associated only with face-to-face connections and 'does not necessarily preclude long-distance and technologically mediated forms of closeness.' Critical of what she saw as the care chains approach to treating intimacy as only 'truly' possible when there is physical presence, McKay (2007, p. 191) claimed that 'culturally inflected forms of economic exchange have always been fundamental to familial intimacies [across distance], with transfers of value enacting the practical love and care necessary to show and share feeling.' In tandem, Parreñas (2014, p. 426) engaged with a similar debate by differentiating between what she calls 'intimacy across distance [that] is constructed primarily via routine' and 'intimacy in proximity [that] is mainly premised on instantaneity.' The former is based on careful time management while the latter depends on the privilege of immediate access. Arguing that instantaneity, or 'absent presence' (Pertierra, 2006), as a feature of intimacy is a gendered expectation tied more to transnational mothering (where the maternal body acts as 'the privileged site of intimacy' (Tan, 2012, p. 117) than transnational fathering, Parreñas (2014) urged the valorization of different temporal modalities in performing intimate labor that is integral to constructing and maintaining '*routine rhythms* of family life,' so as to avoid diminishing, or even demonizing, the intimate work that migrant women do across distance.

At the same time, mediated intimacy and corporeal absence need not be substitutable, and the disjuncture between 'imagined proximity and physical separation' may catalyse new sources of conflict, such as the unfulfilled expectation to be 'always present' or the moralized subtext embedded in acts of disengagement or the creation of social distance

(Wilding, 2006, p. 133). The 'ubiquity and affordances of polymedia environments' (Madianou, 2016, p. 198) can heighten interpersonal conflict within the family in cases where relationships are already weak and unstable because of the implications of shared social fields for increased surveillance, just as they can open up new ways of coming together as a family across distance in cases where members enjoy strong relationships with one another. It should also be noted that while increasingly ubiquitous, the use of new information and communication technologies among migrants in building connected relationships with family members continues to be characterized by unevenness of access (for example, different degrees of freedom during work hours), purchasing power, and media literacy (Madianou and Miller, 2013; Thompson, 2009; Wilding, 2006). For example, in their research with Indonesian domestic workers in Singapore, Platt et al. (2016, p. 2211) demonstrated how mobile phone technologies sustain family ties in Indonesia both in times of crisis and more often in mundane ways by maintaining the status quo, albeit in a way that requires women to 'negotiate the inequalities inscribed upon their status as a foreign domestic worker.'

CONCLUSION

In Asia, contract-based migrant workers and their families must contend with modes of temporariness that are institutionalized as a fundamental principle in neoliberal labor migration regimes. In applying a corporeal geographies lens to the study of temporary labor migration, scholars have engaged with a wide spectrum of concepts to help focus attention on the 'body' as a key site and scale of analysis, and to shift the frame from the economic to the socio-political in understanding 'corporeal mobilities' (Gogia, 2006, p. 360). This is an important development in the labor migration literature, which has until recently 'tended to reflect a series of reductive assumptions about the motivations, experiences and practices of workers who cross borders from the global South as asexual accumulators of capital, driven by little other than a narrowly defined, "rational" commitment to the material betterment of themselves and their kin' (Ahmad, 2009, p. 309).

Managing migrants' bodies as part of managing the borders of the nation-state is part and parcel of governmental strategies to resolve the fundamental dilemma between the demands of 'markets [that] require a policy of open borders to provide as many migrant workers as demanded,' and those of 'citizenship [that] require some degree of closure to the outside so as to protect the economic, social, political and cultural boundaries of the nation-state' (Garcés-Mascareñas, 2010, p. 87). States try to resolve the dilemma by managing migrants as units of labor that can be governed by erecting multiple barriers to control inclusion and exclusion, an often Sisyphean task at best as migrants are irreducible to pure labor but continue to act as social, political, psychological, emotional, and relational subjects.

Borders, and comparable spatial concepts like the skins of places, margins, boundaries, and frontiers, are salient not just as zones of contact and contradiction where encounters occur; encounters are also central in the unraveling and reshaping of spatial, conceptual, and bodily borders (Wilson, 2016). The enclavement and enclosure of migrant bodies are symptomatic of the fear of diversity in cities and other places, but are never irrevocable in their effect on migrant lives, and instead may engender spaces of possibility and hope. The proximities and encounters of transnational bodies generate a spectrum of visceral responses, from anxieties and hostilities of the migrant 'other,' to a diasporic sense of connection to 'home' through sharing food (Dunn, 2010; Longhurst et al., 2009; Yeoh and Huang, 2010).

Indeed, as transnational bodies in constant motion, temporary migrants negotiate long-distance relationships of care with family members through the complex politics of mediated intimacy and corporeal absence/presence. As Madianou (2016, p. 185) cautioned, there is a danger in romanticizing the role of communication technologies for maintaining familyhood because 'as with non-mediated practices, acts of mediated communication can have complex consequences, both positive and negative, depending on a number of factors, including the relationships themselves.' A more rounded understanding of migrant lives and their transnational relationships with left-behind families will need a close analysis of the entangled threads of the gendered division of care labor, the politics of corporeality and identity, and the relationality of communication technologies.

REFERENCES

Abrahamsson, S. and Simpson, P. (2011). The limits of the body: boundaries, capacities, thresholds. *Social & Cultural Geography*, **12**(4), 331–8.

Ahmad, A.N. (2009). Bodies that (don't) matter: desire, eroticism and melancholia in Pakistani labor migration. *Mobilities*, **4**(3), 309–27.

Ahmed, S. (2007). A phenomenology of whiteness. *Feminist Theory*, **8**(2), 149–68.

Akalin, A. (2015). Motherhood as the value of labor: the migrant domestic workers' market in Turkey. *Australian Feminist Studies*, **30**(83), 65–81.

Anderson, K. and Smith, S.J. (2001). Emotional geographies. *Transactions of the Institute of British Geographers*, **26**(1), 7–10.

Andrucki, M.J. and Dickinson, J. (2015). Rethinking centers and margins in geography: bodies, life course, and the performance of transnational space. *Annals of the Association of American Geographers*, **105**(1), 203–18.

Asis, M.M.B., Huang, S., and Yeoh, B.S.A. (2004). When the light of the home is abroad: unskilled female migration and the Filipino family. *Singapore Journal of Tropical Geography*, **25**(2), 198–215.

Butler, J. (1988). Performative acts and gender constitution: an essay in phenomenology and feminist theory. *Theatre Journal*, **40**(4), 519–31.

Castles, S., de Haas, H., and Miller, M.J. (2014). *The Age of Migration: International Population Movements in the Modern World*. Basingstoke, Hampshire: Palgrave Macmillan.

Collins, F.L. (2016). Migration, the urban periphery, and the politics of migrant lives. *Antipode*, **48**(5), 1167–86.

Cresswell, T. (2010). Towards a politics of mobility. *Environment and Planning D: Society and Space*, **28**(1), 17–31.

Dauvergne, C. and Marsden, S. (2014). The ideology of temporary labor migration in the post-global era. *Citizenship Studies*, **18**(2), 224–42.

Davidson, J. and Milligan, C. (2004). Embodying emotion sensing space: introducing emotional geographies. *Social & Cultural Geography*, **5**(4), 523–32.

De Genova, N.P. (2002). Migrant 'illegality' and deportability in everyday life. *Annual Review of Anthropology*, **31**(1), 419–47.

Dunn, K. (2010). Embodied transnationalism: bodies in transnational spaces. *Population, Space and Place*, **16**(1), 1–9.

Dyck, I. (1997). Dialogue with difference: a tale of two studies. In J.P. Jones, J J. Nast, and S.M. Roberts (eds), *Thresholds in Feminist Geography* (pp. 183–202). Lanham, MD: Rowman & Littlefield.

Fargues, P. (2011). Immigration without inclusion: non-nationals in nation-building in the Gulf States. *Asian and Pacific Migration Journal*, **20**(3–4), 273–92.

Ferguson, S. and McNally, D. (2015). Precarious migrants: gender, race and the social reproduction of a global working class. *Socialist Register*, **51**, 1–23.

Fluri, J.L. (2015). Feminist political geography. In J.A. Agnew, V. Mamadouh, A. Secor, and J. Sharp (eds), *The Wiley-Blackwell Companion to Political Geography* (pp. 235–47). Chichester: Wiley-Blackwell.

Fluri, J.L. and Piedalue, A. (2017). Embodying violence: critical geographies of gender, race, and culture. *Gender, Place, and Culture*, **24**(4), 534–44.

Garcés-Mascareñas, B. (2010). Legal production of illegality in a comparative perspective. The cases of Malaysia and Spain. *Asia Europe Journal*, **8**, 77–89.

Gogia, N. (2006). Unpacking corporeal mobilities: the global voyages of labor and leisure. *Environment and Planning A*, **38**(2), 359–75.

Gregson, N. and Rose, G. (2000). Taking Butler elsewhere: performativities, spatialities and subjectivities. *Environment and Planning D: Society and Space*, **18**(4), 433–52.

Grosz, E.A. (1994). *Volatile Bodies: Toward a Corporeal Feminism*. Indiana, IN: Indiana University Press.

Hamid, W. (2015). Feelings of home amongst Tamil migrant workers in Singapore's Little India. *Pacific Affairs*, **88**(1), 5–25.

Haraway, D. (1988). Situated knowledges: the science question in feminism and the privilege of partial perspective. *Feminist Studies*, **14**(3), 575–99.

Harding, S.G. (ed.) (2004). *The Feminist Standpoint Theory Reader: Intellectual and Political Controversies*. New York and London: Routledge.

Hayes-Conroy, J. and Hayes-Conroy, A. (2010). Visceral geographies: mattering, relating, and defying. *Geography Compass*, **4**(9), 1273–83.

Herod, A. (2011). *Scale: Key Ideas in Geography*. New York: Routledge.

Hewison, K. and Young, K. (2006). *Transnational Migration and Work in Asia*. New York: Routledge.

Hugo, G. (2012). International labor migration and migration policies in Southeast Asia. *Asian Journal of Social Science*, **40**, 392–418.

Jackson, L. (2016). Experiencing exclusion and reacting to stereotypes? Navigating borders of the migrant body. *Area*, **48**(3), 292–9.

Kaur, A. (2010). Labour migration in Southeast Asia: migration policies, labor exploitation and regulation. *Journal of the Asia Pacific Economy*, **15**(1), 6–19.

Lan, P. (2003). Negotiating social boundaries and private zones: the micropolitics of employing migrant domestic workers. *Social Problems*, **50**(4), 525–49.

Law, L. (2002). Defying disappearance: cosmopolitan public spaces in Hong Kong. *Urban Studies*, **39**(9), 1625–45.

Lewis, H., Dwyer, P., Hodkinson, S., and Waite, L. (2014). Hyper-precarious lives: migrants, work and forced labor in the Global North. *Progress in Human Geography*, **39**(5), 580–600.

Longhurst, R. (1994). The geography closest in – the body . . . the politics of pregnability. *Geographical Research*, **32**(2), 214–23.

Longhurst, R. (1995). Viewpoint: The body and geography. *Gender, Place & Culture*, **2**(1), 97–106.

Longhurst, R. (1997). (Dis)embodied geographies. *Progress in Human Geography*, **21**(4), 486–501.

Longhurst, R. and Johnston, L. (2014). Bodies, gender, place and culture: 21 years on. *Gender, Place & Culture*, **21**(3), 267–78.

Longhurst, R., Johnston, L., and Ho, E. (2009). A visceral approach: cooking 'at home' with migrant women in Hamilton, New Zealand. *Transactions of the Institute of British Geographers*, **34**(3), 333–45.

Mackie, V. (2010). Managing borders and managing bodies in contemporary Japan. *Journal of the Asia Pacific Economy*, **15**(1), 71–85.

Macpherson, H. (2010). Non-representational approaches to body-landscape relations. *Geography Compass*, **4**(1), 1–13.

Madianou, M. (2016). Ambient co-presence: transnational family practices in polymedia environments. *Global Networks*, **16**(2), 183–201.

Madianou, M. and Miller, D. (2013). Polymedia: towards a new theory of digital media in interpersonal communication. *International Journal of Cultural Studies*, **16**(2), 169–87.

Massey, D. (1994). *Place, Space and Gender*. Minneapolis, MN: University of Minnesota Press.

May, J., Wills, J., Datta, K., Evans, Y., Herbert, J., and McIlwaine, C. (2007). Keeping London working: global elites, the British state and London's new migrant division of labor. *Transactions of the British Institute of Geographers*, **32**, 151–67.

McCormack, D.P. (2003). An event of geographical ethics in spaces of affect. *Transactions of the Institute of British Geographers*, **28**(4), 488–507.

McKay, D. (2007). 'Sending dollars shows feeling' – emotions and economies in Filipino migration. *Mobilities*, **2**(2), 175–94.

Moss, P. and Dyck, I. (2003). Embodying social geography. In K. Anderson, M. Domosh, S. Pile, and N. Thrift (eds), *Handbook of Cultural Geography* (pp. 58–73). London: Sage.

Moukarbel, N. (2009). Not allowed to love? Sri Lankan maids in Lebanon. *Mobilities*, **4**(3), 329–47.

Mountz, A. (2018). Political geography III: Bodies. *Progress in Human Geography*, **42**(5), 759–69.

Nash, C. (1998). Mapping emotion. *Environment and Planning D: Society and Space*, **16**, 1–9.

Nast, H.J. and Pile, S. (1998). Introduction: making places bodies. In H.J. Nast and S. Pile (eds), *Places through the Body* (pp. 1–20). London and New York: Routledge.

Neal, S. and Vincent, C. (2013). Multiculture, middle class competencies and friendship practices in super-diverse geographies. *Social & Cultural Geography*, **14**(8), 909–29.

Nelson, L. (1999). Bodies (and spaces) do matter: the limits of performativity. *Gender, Place & Culture: A Journal of Feminist Geography*, **6**(4), 331–53.

Overbeek, H. (2002). Neoliberalism and the regulation of global labor mobility. *Annals of the American Academy of Political and Social Science*, **581**, 74–90.

Parreñas, R.S. (2014). The intimate labor of transnational communication. *Families, Relationships and Societies*, **3**(3), 425–42.

Peng, Y. and Wong, O.M.H. (2013). Diversified transnational mothering via telecommunication: intensive, collaborative, and passive. *Gender & Society*, **27**(4), 491–513.

Pertierra, R. (2006). *Transforming Technologies: Altered Selves.* Manila: De La Salle University Press.

Piper, N. (2010). All quiet on the Eastern front? – Temporary contract migration in Asia revisited from a development perspective. *Policy and Society*, **29**, 399–411.

Piper, N., Rosewarne, S., and Withers, M. (2017). Migrant precarity in Asia: 'networks of labor activism' for a rights-based governance of migration. *Development and Change*, **48**(5), 1089–110.

Platt, M., Yeoh, B.S.A., Acedera, K.A., Yen, K.C., Baey, G., and Lam, T. (2016). Renegotiating migration experiences: Indonesian domestic workers in Singapore and use of information communication technologies. *New Media & Society*, **18**(10), 2207–23.

Pratt, G. (1998). Inscribing domestic work on Filipina bodies. In H. Nast and S. Pile (eds), *Places through the Body* (pp. 283–304). London and New York: Routledge.

Pratt, M.L. (1992). *Imperial Eyes: Travel Writing and Transculturation.* London: Routledge.

Price, P.L. (2013). Race and ethnicity II: skin and other intimacies. *Progress in Human Geography*, **37**(4), 578–86.

Rosewarne, S. (2010). Globalization and the commodification of labor: temporary labor migration. *Economic and Labour Relations Review*, **20**(2), 99–110.

Rubery, J. (2015). Change at work: feminization, flexibilization, fragmentation and financialization. *Employee Relations*, **37**(6), 633–44.

Rudnyckyj, D. (2004). Technologies of servitude: governmentality and Indonesian transnational labor migration. *Anthropological Quarterly*, **77**(3), 407–34.

Saldanha, A. (2008). The political geography of many bodies. In K. Cox, M. Low and J. Robinson (eds), *The Sage Handbook of Political Geography* (pp. 323–34). London: Sage.

Seo, S. and Skelton, T. (2017). Regulatory migration regimes and the production of space: the case of Nepalese workers in South Korea. *Geoforum*, **78**, 159–68.

Sheller, M. and Urry, J. (2006). The new mobilities paradigm. *Environment and Planning A*, **38**(2), 207–26.

Silvey, R. (2007). Unequal borders: Indonesian transnational migrants at immigration control. *Geopolitics*, **12**(2), 265–79.

Silvey, R. (2012). Gender, difference, and contestation: economic geography through the lens of transnational migration. In T.J. Barnes, J. Peck, and E. Sheppard (eds), *The Wiley-Blackwell Companion to Economic Geography* (pp. 420–30). Chichester: Wiley-Blackwell.

Silvey, R. (2017). Bodies and embodiment. In D. Richardson, N. Castree, M.F. Goodchild, A. Kobayashi, W. Liu, and R.A. Marston (eds), *The International Encyclopedia of Geography: People, the Earth, Environment, and Technology* (pp. 1–7). Oxford: Wiley.

Slocum, R. (2008). Thinking race through corporeal feminist theory: divisions and intimacies at the Minneapolis Farmers' Market. *Social & Cultural Geography*, **9**(8), 849–69.

Tan, J.P. (2012). Missing mother: migrant mothers, maternal surrogates, and the global economy of care. *Thesis Eleven*, **112**(1), 113–32.

Theodore, N. (2003). Political economies of day labor: regulation and restructuring of Chicago's contingent labor markets. *Urban Studies*, **40**(9), 1811–28.

Thompson, E.C. (2009). Mobile phones, communities and social networks among foreign workers in Singapore. *Global Networks*, **9**(3), 359–80.

Thrift, N. (2008). *Non-representational Theory: Space, Politics, Affect.* London and New York: Routledge.

Wilding, R. (2006). 'Virtual' intimacies? Families communicating across transnational contexts. *Global Networks*, **6**(2), 125–42.

Wilson, H.F. (2011). Passing propinquities in the multicultural city: the everyday encounters of bus passengering. *Environment and Planning A*, **43**, 634–49.

Wilson, H.F. (2016). On geography and encounter: bodies, borders, and difference. *Progress in Human Geography*, **41**(4), 451–71.

Yamanaka, K. (2000). Nepalese labor migration to Japan: from global warriors to global workers. *Ethnic and Racial Studies*, **23**(1), 62–93.

Yea, S. (2017). The art of not being caught: temporal strategies for disciplining unfree labor in Singapore's contract migration. *Geoforum*, **78**, 179–88.

Yeoh, B.S.A. and Huang, S. (1998). Negotiating public space: strategies and styles of migrant female domestic workers in Singapore. *Urban Studies*, **35**(3), 583–602.

Yeoh, B.S.A. and Huang, S. (2010). Sexualized politics of proximities among female transnational migrants in Singapore. *Population, Space and Place*, **16**(1), 37–49.

Yeoh, B.S.A., Baey, G., Platt, M., and Wee, K. (2017a). Construction workers and the politics of (im)mobility in Singapore. *City*, **21**(5), 641–9.

Yeoh, B.S.A., Platt, M., Khoo, C.Y., Lam, T., and Baey, G. (2017b). Indonesian domestic workers and the (un)making of transnational livelihoods and provisional futures. *Social & Cultural Geography*, **18**(3), 415–34.

8. Seasonal migration and the working-class laboring body in India
Anu Sabhlok

INTRODUCTION

Circuits of labor and capital are intimately connected to migration – mobile bodies whose labor creates value. In the fast developing urban contexts of India, it is common to see migrant men (and sometimes women) gathered early in the morning to make themselves available as laboring bodies for the small and large infrastructure projects of the city. Many of them have traveled from the poorer regions of the country and now inhabit the dense urban fringes in order to sell their only asset – their body. Labor chowks are sites of intense activity in the mornings. In these busy mornings, one sees cars stopping by, negotiations between prospective day employers and the laborers, some laborers cleaning and polishing their tools, sharing an early morning snack out of their tiffin, others waiting with anticipation clearly visible in their alert eyes. One sees the laborers running in herds towards any new car that has stopped, then groups walking back to their original location with one elated laborer awkwardly making his way into the car. All this clears by around 11 am when you see only a few somewhat dejected men sitting around and playing cards to pass time in the hope that they still might get picked up. Later in the day, there are no signs that this crossing was a hub of activity for labor hiring.

In this chapter, I focus on these links between seasonal migration and the working-class laboring body in India. Here I use the term body to refer to two related aspects: the embodied aspects of identity such as gender, race and caste, and the material body composed of flesh, blood, bones and hormones. Migration very clearly involves the movement in time and space of bodies and as the laborers move from one place to the other they literally produce space (Mitchell, 2008). It is estimated that one-sixth of India's population moves every year (Rogaly, 1998). Most of these migrants move internally to work as wage laborers in agriculture, construction and industry. It is widely known that most migration takes place within national borders and yet it seems that most of the academic and political focus has been on transnational movement. It is important to nuance this categorization as migrants form networks with their kin and village brethren that often transcend national boundaries and it is not always possible to segregate local and transnational migration streams (Parry, 2003).

Labor mobility within the Indian context has been steadily on the rise and many of these migrations are short term, seasonal and circular (Breman and Das, 2000). Official statistics such as the Survey of India are unable to map this mobility as they limit their survey instruments primarily to more permanent forms of migration (Keshri and Bhagat, 2012). More recently, however, the National Sample Survey has incorporated temporary migrations and is identifying destinations that are within the same state. This affords some opportunity to make sense of the numbers at multiple scales. The routes of seasonal migration reflect historical patterns of uneven development in the country, current trends in urban infrastructure development and governmental policies related to employment, infrastructure, education and transport, agricultural cycles and rural aspirations. I start with reviewing the literature on labor migration, particularly circular migration in India, highlighting critical perspectives and approaches that pay attention to the embodiment of laboring identities. I then illustrate some of these perspectives adding the material dimensions of the body, through my study of migrant laborers who travel every May to the upper Himalayas to build roads for the Border Roads Organisation, returning home to Jharkhand in November. The narratives from this study reveal patterns of circular migration, some of the ways in which it is organized and the embodied experiences of the migrant labor during the journey, in the work sites and in their home villages. The narratives of migrant laborers draw connections between the scale of the laboring body and the construction of the nation-state.

LABOR MIGRATION IN THE INDIAN CONTEXT

In the past two decades, there has been an unprecedented increase in both the number of labor migrations within India and in the spatial range of these migrations. While rural-rural or rural-urban migration in the surrounding contexts persist, it is not uncommon to see migrant laborers today making long journeys to remote regions of the country and to far away metropolises in search for work. Seasonal migration has long been a significant livelihood strategy for the poor and occurs both as a routine phenomenon and in times of crises such as conflict or disasters. Very often "distress migration" and "labor migration" have a visible continuum blurring the lines between voluntary and involuntary migration (Richmond and Valtonen, 1994). Scholars have made the case that contrary to the widely circulated myth of sedentary lives as the norm, it is in fact "migration that is often the rule, rather than the exception" (McDowell and De Haan, 1997, p. 1). According to the National Commission on Rural Labor (NCRL), about 10 million people migrate seasonally from rural areas. Of these, 4.5 million are inter-state migrants such as the BRO laborers traveling from Jharkhand to Himachal; 6 million migrate within the same state, for example, women from Dumka district in Jharkhand migrate for a month every year to help with rice harvesting in the neighboring districts. Circular or seasonal migration in the Indian context is typically short term, repetitive and cyclical in nature in a way that accommodates the annual agricultural cycle (Deshingkar and Start, 2003). A majority of the migrants are employed in highly embodied forms of labor such as in plantations, brick kilns, construction sites, farming and fish processing. They are a visible part of the Indian landscape – often seen pulling rickshaws, carrying stacks of bricks as head loaders, bending down all day on rice fields or stamping clay with their feet in brick kilns. However, very little attention is paid to the corporeal experiences of what migrants do when they move in time and space and how their bodies are read in the multiple spaces they inhabit.

EMBODIED MOBILITIES: CASTE, CLASS AND GENDER IN LABOR MIGRATION

Migration is contingent upon how productive and reproductive labor is organized at the various scales of the household, community, village and the nation (Chant, 1992).

Migration patterns reveal uneven geographical development in the country and make visible the histories of agrarian and caste-based systems in rural areas, which then are intimately connected to patterns of movement and urban development (Carswell, 2013). The casualization of rural labor and the gradual removal of patronage relations in the twentieth century freed rural migrants from a system of bonded labor while at the same time exposing them to the vagaries of the capitalist markets (De Neve, 2019). Breman's lifelong work (1994, 1996) with landless laborers in Gujarat shows how these changes in agrarian social relations created a category of the "footloose proletariat hunting and gathering for waged work" (De Neve, 2017). Coining the term "neo-bondage," Breman shows how labor mobility continues to act in the interest of the employer. In a study conducted in the states of Andhra Pradesh and Madhya Pradesh, Deshingkar and Start (2003) found that caste dynamics of migrant communities are influenced by particularities of the village social relations. For example, in Andhra Pradesh the Scheduled Tribes (STs) were six times more likely to migrate than the upper castes, the Scheduled Castes five and a half times and the Other Backward Castes were three and a half times more likely to migrate. The evidence from Madhya Praesh (MP), on the other hand, showed that in that context even the upper castes migrated even though the STs still made up the largest group of migrants with 84.5 percent of them migrating. The wealthy Thakurs (58.9 percent) and the Brahmins (23.5) from MP also had a significant percentage of their populations migrating on a seasonal basis (Deshingkar and Start, 2003). Moreover, regional differences intersect in the kinds of work assigned to the migrant laborers. As Shah's study (2006) in a brick factory in Bengal outlines, it is usually the lower caste Bihari laborers who are assigned to molding bricks, Bengali laborers are used for extracting clay and the Scheduled Castes' and Scheduled Tribes' laborers from Jharkhand are the ones to carry headloads of bricks from the kiln to the trucks. The women carry about 8–10 unbaked bricks on their heads while men receive the bricks and line them up along the furnace. A gendered, geographical and caste-based spatiality then produces the space of the brick kiln in which migrant workers are employed.

Intersectionality between caste and gender relations is evident when it comes to geographies of migration (Carswell, 2016). It is very often that men migrate, particularly when it comes to upper castes where it is seen as shameful for the women to work outside their homes. Amongst the tribal populations, women's participation in the migratory labor markets is widespread although there are limitations to the spatial and temporal aspects of their work. Particularly in Bengal, Jharkhand and Bihar, men migrate much larger distances and many women are involved in seasonal migration to neighboring villages at times of harvesting or sowing while also taking care of their small land holdings. Harriss-White and Janakarajan (2004) assert that women now provide over half of all agricultural labor in the country, predominantly as casual wage laborers. This feminization of agricultural labor has resulted from and enabled the mobility of men accessing non-farm-based work in regions of the country far away (Rogaly, 2003). In other words, the far and wide spatial extent of men's migration pattern often relies on women's back-breaking labor at home.

More often than not seasonal migration has been correctly regarded as exploitative and not allowing accumulation, but it also holds a liberatory potential albeit limited. For example, lower caste groups experience a sense of freedom from humiliation once they migrate to other parts of the country (Agnihotri and Mazumdar, 2009). Many migrants see migration as an enabling respite from rural social structures and norms. Based on interviews with migrant men and women in the brick kilns of Orissa, Shah (2006) avers that migrants "view their migration as a temporary escape from a problem at home and an opportunity to explore a new country, gain independence from parents, and live out prohibited amorous relationships" (p. 93). Where Shah's field narratives discuss the somewhat more playful and consensual sexual relations in brick kilns, Parry's (2014) account of unorganized workers in the Bhilai steel factory is different. Parry argues that class and gender relations are mutually constituted, making women from the "labor class" particularly vulnerable to unwanted sexual advances. Men and women from the "labor classes" are both demeaned through narratives that construct women who have left their homes to labor as "loose" and men who allowed their women to do so as "little better than pimps" (Parry, 2014, p. 1251). Caste hierarchies rely on these gendered narratives of women's chastity and spatial confines for work. Regional differences too have been observed in some studies. For example, it is argued that North Indians usually migrate as single men, bringing in their families much later. South Indians, on other hand, generally migrate as a family (Crook, 1993). Migrants from North-eastern India face immense discrimination and racism in the urban centers of North India where the racial slur "chinky" works to construct them as "unwanted outsiders." Regional, caste and religious differences become sedimented in the urban contexts when migrants from varying groups get assigned to segregated ghettos. Thus, we see how embodied characteristics of gender, caste, class, religion, region and so on are central to how migration is organized and experienced.

When bodies move from one place to the other, they carry with them objects, ideas and identities. Moreover, laboring bodies mostly move in labor gangs, that is, groups of workers usually hailing from the same village or region. Gangs usually consist of 2–40 laborers, organized by a middle man/team leader, who is referred to as a mate. The mate manages recruitment, travel and stay logistics and is the contact person between the laborers and the employers. The mate's role is central to the exploitative structure of seasonal migration. Gang labor is not unique to the Indian context and has historically been a way to "produce" labor for intensive agricultural and industrial zones. While the system of organization is similar, that is, a group of laborers contracted with the help of a mate, gangmaster, contractor and so on, there are historical and geographical differences in the role gang labor has played across the world. For example, gang labor was associated with slave plantation labor in the United States while it carries the connotation of coercive but "free" labor contracting in the neoliberal UK and India (Strauss, 2013).

Considering that it is gangs and not individuals that are migrating makes it easier to visualize the various ways in which migrant laborers produce space at multiple scales. Labor geographers brought worker agency into focus by arguing that it is not merely capital that produces space but also the workers (Herod, 2001). However, their focus remained limited to organized labor and did not take into consideration the vast chunk of migrant labor that is mostly seasonal and unorganized (Lier, 2007). Starting from the act of migration itself, to somewhat mundane acts of setting up camps and organizing food on the move, Ben Rogaly (2009) sheds light on the agency of informal sector migrant laborers in India in an effort to bridge this gap in labor geography. Through a study of the temporary migrant worker, Rogaly shows that it is not merely capital that seeks a "spatial fix" but so does labor. In finding their "spatial fix", migrant workers adapt to, transform and represent the places they come from, move to and work in. Much of this work happens in and through the body. "Spaces are experienced through the psyche as well as the body; the experience and meaning of space are subjective and do matter" (Rogaly, 2009, p. 1979). Drawing from feminist literature, Gidwani and Sivaramakrishnan (2003b) follow the lives of migrant laborers who through their travels acquire political sensibilities which are then expressed in their villages as "body politics" evident from their cosmopolitan attire and display of consumer goods. Moreover, circular migration allows laborers to creatively engage with discourses and behavior since their sites of work and those of living are segregated. In my work with migrant laborers from Jharkhand working in the upper reaches of the Himalayas, I experienced two very different personalities in these two sites. The same laborers who were docile, coated in dust and crammed into tents on road building sites in Himachal were transformed into jazzy, cell phone-carrying shiny heroes in their home villages in Jharkhand. In the next section, I will delve into the bodily experiences of these road construction migrant laborers in the different spaces of home, on the journey and at work sites.

THE NATION AND THE CORPOREAL EXPERIENCES OF ITS MIGRANT LABORERS

This narrative discusses a seasonal cycle of migration that has been persistent at least since the 1960s. Although rooted in a very particular regional and social context this study brings our attention to links between development and migration, national imaginations and migrant bodies, and the gendered caste system that structure these migrations. The laborers in question move every year from Dumka district in Jharkhand to the upper reaches of the Himalayas to build roads for India's defense and development. Their employer is the semi-military government organization called the Border Roads Organisation (BRO). The BRO constructs critical infrastructure in the border areas (Kashmir, Ladakh, North Eastern Frontier (NE), Lahaul-Spiti and so on) for defense, in "troubled" interiors such as the Naxal belts of Andhra Pradesh, Chattisgarh, Maharashtra for increased legibility and mobility of the state, as well as in international locations (Bhutan, Afghanistan) for facilitating strategic alliances. It was formed in 1960 by then Prime Minister Jawaharlal Nehru to sew together the disparate pieces of a newly emerging and fragile nation-state and to protect it from external exigencies. The BRO employs more than 100,000 casual paid laborers that are primarily seasonal migrants (www.bro.nic.in). Because much of their work is set in extremely remote locations, often on partially constructed roads, the life of the migrant laborer is hidden to the public eye. I have been following the BRO laborers for over six years as they move between their homes and the Himalayan regions seasonally. Their journey begins in May when they board the train to get to Jammu and they return to their homes in October/November. Their employment with the BRO lasts only for 179 days. This is a governmental strategy to avoid paying benefits as according to labor laws, anyone employed for more than 180 days in a year is considered a regular employee, eligible for benefits. I meet gangs of laborers as I travel across the Indo-Tibetan border road and the Manali-Leh highway every summer and I meet individuals when I visit them in their homes in Jharkand in December. The laborers are accompanied by a mate who contracts them in Jharkhand and travel and work in a gang of approximately 30–40 men.

Migration from Jharkhand for laboring on roads, plantations, railways and urban development has a long history dating back at least to colonial times. Being part of

India's poorest state (then Bihar), the districts in the Santhal Paragana region (now predominantly in Jharkhand) have been attractive to labor contractors and governments who have been coming into this area for recruitment. Ironically, the government itself uses uneven development within the country in its search of "surplus labor" for projects of "national development." In Jharkhand, I was told several stories about the 1960s when military men would come and literally beat the drums in the village/town squares calling for laborers to accompany them as construction laborers into India's border areas. This has recently stopped, after Jharkhand became a state independent of Bihar and has instituted policies limiting recruitment of laborers from their state. These policies piggy back on identity politics in Jharkhand, self-described as a tribal state but in the absence of other opportunities, migration chains already set in motion still continue. Now (with military recruiters no longer allowed free access), the BRO laborers make the journey to India's border at their own expense as part of labor gangs led by their mate.

In what follows, I weave in the travel and work accounts of these migrant laborers paying particular attention to the descriptions of the corporeal body – its experiences, its pains and its pleasures.

Journey and Recruitment

Anwar boarded the train from Jasidhi in Jharkhand to Jammu in the northern most state of India along with 40 of his gang members, and the mate. The mate had brought the group together from three different villages in Dumka district, and many of the members of his gang were related to each other (either as cousins or through marriage). Mostly, the group was composed of tribals and Muslims and I did not come across any upper caste laborer on this journey. In order to avoid paying a reservation charge and unable to plan the travel too much in advance, the mate had the laborers climb onto an unreserved coach. Anwar expressed, based on his perceptions, that there must have been thousands of people already inside the coach when they tried to enter. There was no sitting space and he stood for a large part of the two-day journey. He remembers feeling like a "commodity packed for sale," being pushed and shoved around "inside the package." The most difficult part of the journey, he explains, was using the toilet – one had to be carried above by other passengers, near the ceiling of the train and then negotiate with those sitting inside the toilet to make space for a bit. Comparing the open fields that he had been used to until then to this claustrophobic experience, Anwar questioned his decision to migrate so far from home, but the contractual agreement with the mate (albeit verbal) did not allow him to turn back.

I met Anwar, once he had reached Nagrota, in Jammu and was camping on a vast recruitment site, awaiting his turn to be registered with the BRO for employment this season along with his gang members. His mate bought a large blue tarpal (plastic sheet) from the local market and they were busy trying to erect a tent with poles they had found and a flimsy rope. A few of his gang members were attempting to light a fire and cook dal and rice – their first hot meal after a long journey. Although most of them had carried few clothes, their entourage included a large pressure cooker, two large pans and a huge kadai (wok) along with other cooking equipment from their village. The recruitment site had at least 10,000 men waiting in their gangs for their turn, squatting on a vast open field in the summer heat. There were two air-cooled tents that housed the BRO officials conducting the recruitment including one for taking photographs, one tent where medical examinations were being conducted and another where a bank account was being opened for the laborers, referred to by the BRO as Imported Casual Paid Laborers (ICPL). Men were huddled around each of these tents, with their shirtless bodies lined up in front of the medical examination tent and marked (selected) bodies lined up outside the photo and bank tents. All others were patiently awaiting their turn in the sweltering heat of Jammu in May, passing time by playing cards, sharing jokes or napping when possible.

The potential ICPL are examined for two things before being hired – a strong body capable of doing the hard labor in high altitudes and a docile nature that will endure the hierarchies of military style workings. Those that passed this test were boarded onto military trucks and transported to their respective Road Construction Companies (RCC) usually another few hundred miles away. Anwar recalls feeling nauseated and trapped as the truck rolled along the windy mountain roads with about 80–90 men inside. Many ICPL reported severe headaches, fatigue and shortness of breath upon arrival as the RCC were located at high altitudes – ranging from 10,000 to 19,000 feet above sea level. Coupled with the discomfort, Anwar recalls a feeling of excitement and anticipation for being able to see snow-clad peaks and a whole different geography – he almost felt like a tourist asserting to me, "you pay money to travel here, we are paid to travel to these mountains." Anwar's travels sound comfortable compared to the first round of ICPL that cross these same mountainous slopes on foot. Their job is to cross over the high passes and clear them of the snow so that the vehicles can access them – a journey that is extremely precarious and tough on the unacclimatized body. Several narratives from the ICPL that I interviewed describe this journey by making allusions to highly masculinized images of taming the mountains, male solidarity amidst danger and conquering death.

Academic investigations of migration and labor primarily focus on source and destination points. However, I argue that the journey itself constitutes a large part of the experience and is central to the changing subjectivities and identities. How networks are formed with their kin, with other travelers, the manner in which they experience their body when traveling and how interactions on travels across the country shape their political sensibilities are important for a more nuanced understanding of migration. Challenging the prominent view that migrants are misfits within the nation, Gidwani and Sivaramakrishnan (2003b) argue that circular migrants within the country might actually be the vehicles through which ideologies of belonging to the nation are transmitted. Migrant bodies intermingle with other bodies, disrupt local markers of identity through acquired dress sensibilities and language, and contribute literally and materially to nation building when they build roads, buildings and dams.

Working Bodies on the Move

Observation of the ICPL, living and working alongside the road, that winds up and down steep rocky slopes, is an overwhelming experience. It is difficult to differentiate between the hand that holds the hammer, the hammer, and the stone that is struck by the hammer – all of these are an undifferentiated grey, the same dust covering everything. The same dust percolates into the lungs of the laborers as they break the rocks into smaller and smaller pieces and spread them over the road before pouring hot tar. Most of this work is accomplished with the bare minimum of machinery using simple hand tools. An interview with the BRO facility officer at Upshi on the Manali-Leh highway revealed that they see about 15–20 cases of respiratory illnesses every day (the BRO are responsible for a unit of 3,000 workers). Dust from the road combined with high altitudes and cold weather that most laborers are unaccustomed to leads to several corporeal ailments ranging from skin irritation to pulmonary oedema. Taken for granted routines, like taking care of the body, become difficult during migrant journeys and at work sites. For example, many ICPL working in the higher altitudes complain about the lack of warm water and the inability to have a bath for several months. Traveling and migration are not merely about economics or culture but have very significant impacts on workers' material bodies that sometimes last a lifetime (Sabhlok et al., 2015).

Marxist accounts about the processes of assimilation of the body into technologies of capitalism and Weber's discussion related to rationalization and instrumentalization of the body both reveal a concern for the corporeal body, but are less explicit about the materiality of the laboring body. Critical and feminist geographers have paid significant attention to the body particularly in terms of scale (Silvey, 2005), performativity (Nelson, 1999) and as intimately felt geographies (Longhurst, 1995; Longhurst et al., 2008). Yet there is very little attention paid to the corporeal experience of the migrant and laboring body (Breman, 1996; Dyck, 2006). Some exceptions are Lovelock's (2011) study that describes instances of injury and fatality amongst agricultural workers. Søgaard et al. (2006) focus on the microdynamics of muscle movement, cardiovascular pressures and bodily positions involved in different cleaning tasks. Much research on embodiment has focused on issues central to more developed economies such as obesity, bodily representation, manipulation and identity politics but questions of bodily health have largely been ignored (Dorn and Laws, 1994). Embodiment research has often neglected the "physical presence of the body" (Parr, 1998, p. 28), the health or impairment of "blood, brains and bones" (Hall, 2000, p. 22). Migrant laborers from India's poorer states are often seen as "disposable," and are kept in employment "long enough to extract their usefulness until the process of injury, illness, and death overcome them" (Wright, 2006). Governments too focus their health initiatives on the more sedentary populations and therefore it becomes imperative to bring attention back to the laboring body of the migrant toiling far away from their homes.

The migrant laborers working for the BRO live alongside the road that they are constructing, in tents made from plastic sheets held down by large boulders gathered from the vicinity. Most of the living arrangements I saw consisted of two tents – a living tent where 40 men slept side by side in two rows – their meager belongings hanging on a rope behind them next to the tent wall. The second tent stored food supplies and they cooked their meals in that tent. However, at the much higher altitudes, I saw that the same tent or temporary structure made of tin barrels was used for sleeping and cooking resulting in a constant smell of kerosene fumes inside the tent. Anwar and his gang members were vocal about comparisons between their comfortable village homes and the precarious living arrangements in Himachal. Comparisons of another kind were also common when they expressed their frustration at the infrastructural, educational and health-related development activity that was so prominent in Himachal but did not exist in their home location in Jharkhand. Constituted through travel and inhabiting multiple spatialities, migrants have important perspectives to share regarding uneven development, differently gendered, caste-based and class experiences in the multiple contexts and embodied experiences of multiple geographies. Thus, it is important for critical geographers to focus on this "between-ness" of migrant lives.

The bodily proximity of the 40 or so men in the same tent created a sense of solidarity and in these work sites boundaries of religion and caste were set aside. The ICPL joked about their adventures and struggles together sharing stories of drunken nights, emotional arguments and hooting at the intimate scenes when watching the rare rental film. Many discussed the hardships of living away from home when simple tasks like gathering firewood for cooking or finding a stream for washing clothes is a challenge.

Migration entails both an adventure and a challenge. Living away from home enables new networks and associations but it uproots the migrant from the very structures that gave comfort and provided strength. Sometimes when one of the ICPL was humiliated by a BRO supervisor at the work site, they would quietly listen to the chiding at the RCC. However, in Jharkhand these same laborers, with much more assertive body language, told me that if such an incident had happened on their turf, they would have shown their anger to the supervisor and made him regret his "superior attitude." Scholars have shown how technologies of governmentality and servitude produce docile laboring bodies (Rudnyckyj, 2004). What we also need to pay attention to is how these laboring bodies navigate such technologies especially when they inhabit multiple spaces as migrants. Docile bodies in one space are sometimes very assertive bodies in another place.

The Hero Returns

Gidwani and Sivaramakrishna (2003a) show how seasonal migration of the "footloose proletariat" transforms their lives in visible ways: through dress styles, bodily demeanour, modes of consumption and amendments in language. Alongside this, it is also important to direct attention to the other things the migrants bring back with them – degraded bodies, chronic diseases and injured limbs. The journey back home has different meanings for the many laborers. Some who have managed to save some money return joyous. Those that might have lost most of their money either to gambling or the unfair calculations of the mate return somewhat dejected. There are those who return with a lost limb and there are others who never return.

Anwar was one of the lucky ones and he very excitedly recounted his journey back home with his gang. He was particularly eager as he had left his newly married bride, Shahana, only about 15 days after his marriage. I met Shahana too, and she told me that she would never have married Anwar had she known that he had plans of leaving her with his parents and going off for six months. It did not take Shahana a long time to get over her resentment and I met the couple, a few days later, visibly happy together. Anwar came back not just with money, but gifts and lots of stories and pictures. He did not tell Shahana about all the discomfort and humiliation they endured. The standard joke that the ICPL shared with me is that they wash away all these memories in the first river/pond they find on the way home. This is literally the case, for many of them had not had a chance to have a real bath in six months and all of them are covered in dust with their clothes in tatters. Once they reach the Jasidhi or Asansol railway station a few hours drive from their homes, they collectively rent the finest looking taxi around. On the way, they have a bath in the river, buy new clothes and gifts and arrive home to a hero's welcome.

Inhabiting multiple spaces allows the migrant laborers to engage creatively with discourses of gender, caste, religious and national identity (Sabhlok, 2017). In recruitment camps, migrant laborers are examined for their bodily strengths while at the same time being rewarded for docility. The mates construct the laborers as effeminate and immature – in need of supervision and control. In their living spaces alongside the road, the ICPL share food and sleeping arrangements with men from other castes and religions. These relationships and hierarchies of caste and gender transform when the ICPL return home to Jharkhand. A heightened masculinity is apparent as men assume the figure of the returning hero and caste segregations resume earlier configurations wherein each caste/tribe inhabits a separate settlement space. The stories of the ICPL reveal contradictions within their own and stereotypical ideas about their subjectivities. Their seasonal migration transforms, erases and reproduces gendered subjectivities as they travel across space and time. Being in two different spaces allows them to creatively engage with discourses that surround migrant labor lives.

CONCLUSIONS

India is a fast growing economy and so much of the nation's assets and infrastructures are being constructed through the labor of migrant bodies. There is hardly any recognition of this labor and migration of the rural poor is considered more of an aberration than the norm. Developmental policies, ironically, are focused towards sedentary populations, whereas seasonal mobility is a way of life for at least one-sixth of India's population. In this chapter, I have made four related arguments. Illustrating circular migration stories through narratives of ICPL employed seasonally by the BRO, I argue for the need to incorporate an understanding of the journey into migration research, moving away from a sole focus on source and destination points. Secondly, I have emphasized the need to look at both the embodied constructs of gender, caste, regional and tribal identity in understanding seasonal migratory patterns in India and different experiences of men, women, North Indians, South Indians, Scheduled Castes and Tribes and so on. Thirdly, the material body that experiences pain, pleasure, discomfort and injury is yet to be fully articulated in research on seasonal migration and labor geographies. Lastly, as critical scholars of development, let us create a space for critiques of uneven development, articulated by the migrant laborers themselves – we will be surprised at the clarity and experiential analysis that they bring to the table.

REFERENCES

Agnihotri, I. and Mazumdar, I. (2009), Dusty trails and unsettled lives: women's labour migration in rural India. *Indian Journal of Gender Studies*, 16(3), 375–99.

Breman, J. (1994), *Wage Hunters and Gatherers: Search for Work in the Urban and Rural Economy of South Gujarat*. New Delhi: Oxford University Press.

Breman, J. (1996), *Footloose Labour: Working in India's Informal Economy* (Vol. 2). Cambridge: Cambridge University Press.

Breman, J. and Das, A.N. (2000), *Down and Out: Labouring under Global Capitalism*. Amsterdam: Amsterdam University Press.

Carswell, G. (2013), Dalits and local labour markets in rural India: experiences from the Tiruppur textile region in Tamil Nadu. *Transactions of the Institute of British Geographers*, 38(2), 325–38.

Carswell, G. (2016), Struggles over work take place at home: women's decisions, choices and constraints in the Tiruppur textile industry, India. *Geoforum*, 77, 134–45.

Chant, S. (1992), *Gender and Migration in Developing Countries*. London: Belhaven Press.

Crook, N. (1993), *India's Industrial Cities: Essays in Economy and Demography*. New Delhi: Oxford University Press.

De Neve, G. (2019), *The sociology of labour in India*. In: S. Srivastava, J. Abraham and Y. Arif (eds), *Critical Themes in Indian Sociology*. SAGE Publications (forthcoming).

Deshingkar, P. and Start, D. (2003), *Seasonal Migration for Livelihoods in India: Coping, Accumulation and Exclusion* (Vol. 111). London: Overseas Development Institute.

Dorn, M. and Laws, G. (1994), Social theory, body politics, and medical geography: extending Kearns's invitation. *The Professional Geographer*, **46**(1), 106–10.

Dyck, I. (2006), Travelling tales and migratory meanings: South Asian migrant women talk of place, health and healing. *Social & Cultural Geography*, **7**(1), 1–18.

Gidwani, V. and Sivaramakrishnan, K. (2003a), Circular migration and rural cosmopolitanism in India. *Contributions to Indian Sociology*, **37**(1–2), 339–67.

Gidwani, V. and Sivaramakrishnan, K. (2003b), Circular migration and the spaces of cultural assertion. *Annals of the Association of American Geographers*, **93**(1), 186–213.

Hall, E. (2000), "Blood, brain and bones": taking the body seriously in the geography of health and impairment. *Area*, **32**(1), 21–9.

Harriss-White, B. and Janakarajan, S. (2004), *Rural India Facing the 21st Century*. London: Anthem Press.

Herod, A. (2001), *Labor Geographies: Workers and the Landscapes of Capitalism*. New York: Guilford Press.

Keshri, K. and Bhagat, R.B. (2012), Temporary and seasonal migration: regional pattern, characteristics and associated factors. *Economic & Political Weekly*, January 28, 81–8.

Lier, D.C. (2007), Places of work, scales of organising: a review of labour geography. *Geography Compass*, **1**(4), 814–33.

Longhurst, R. (1995), Viewpoint: The body and geography. *Gender, Place & Culture*, **2**(1), 97–106.

Longhurst, R., Ho, E., and Johnston, L. (2008), Using "the body" as an "instrument of research": kimch'i and pavlova. *Area*, **40**(2), 208–17.

Lovelock, Kirsten. (2012), "The injured and diseased farmer: occupational health, embodiment and technologies of harm and care." *Sociology of Health & Illness*, **34**(4): 576–90.

McDowell, C. and De Haan, A. (1997), Migration and sustainable livelihoods: a critical review of the literature. IDS Working Paper 65, IDS, Brighton.

Mitchell, D. (2008), New axioms for reading the landscape: paying attention to political economy and social justice. In *Political Economies of Landscape Change* (pp. 29–50). Dordrecht: Springer.

Nelson, L. (1999), Bodies (and spaces) do matter: the limits of performativity. *Gender, Place & Culture: A Journal of Feminist Geography*, **6**(4), 331–53.

Parr, H. (1998), Mental health, ethnography and the body. *Area*, **30**(1), 28–37.

Parry, J.P. (2003), Nehru's dream and the village "waiting room": long-distance labour migrants to a central Indian steel town. *Contributions to Indian Sociology*, **37**(1–2), 217–49.

Parry, J. (2014), Sex, bricks and mortar: constructing class in a central Indian steel town. *Modern Asian Studies*, **48**(5), 1242–75.

Richmond, A.H. and Valtonen, K. (1994), Global apartheid: refugees, racism, and the new world order. *Refuge: Canada's Journal on Refugees*, **14**(6).

Rogaly, B. (1998), Workers on the move: seasonal migration and changing social relations in rural India. *Gender & Development*, **6**(1), 21–9.

Rogaly, B. (2003), Who goes? Who stays back? Seasonal migration and staying put among rural manual workers in Eastern India. *Journal of International Development*, **15**(5), 623–32.

Rogaly, B. (2009), Spaces of work and everyday life: labour geographies and the agency of unorganised temporary migrant workers. *Geography Compass*, **3**(6), 1975–87.

Rudnyckyj, D. (2004), Technologies of servitude: governmentality and Indonesian transnational labor migration. *Anthropological Quarterly*, **77**(3), 407–34.

Sabhlok, A. (2017), "Main Bhi to Hindostaan Hoon": gender and nation-state in India's Border Roads Organisation. *Gender, Place & Culture*, 1–18.

Sabhlok, A., Cheung, H., and Mishra, Y. (2015), Narratives of health and well-being. *Economic & Political Weekly*, **50**(51), 71–6.

Shah, A. (2006), The labour of love: seasonal migration from Jharkhand to the brick kilns of other states in India. *Contributions to Indian Sociology*, **40**(1), 91–118.

Silvey, R. (2005), Borders, embodiment, and mobility: feminist migration studies in geography. In L. Nelson and J. Saeger (eds), *A Companion to Feminist Geography*. Hoboker, NJ: Blackwell, pp. 138–49.

Søgaard, K., Blangsted, A.K., Herod, A. and Finsen, L. (2006), "Work design and the labouring body: examining the impacts of work organization on Danish cleaners' health." *Antipode*, **38**(3), 579–602.

Strauss, K. (2013), Unfree again: social reproduction, flexible labour markets and the resurgence of gang labour in the UK. *Antipode*, **45**(1), 180–97.

Wright, M.W. (2006), *Disposable women and other myths of global capitalism*. New York: Routledge.

9. Embodiment and memory in the geopolitics of trauma
Patricia Ehrkamp, Jenna M. Loyd and Anna Secor

INTRODUCTION

Trauma has become a ubiquitous framework for attempts to conceptualize the after-effects of violent and life-disruptive experiences. While the post-traumatic stress disorder (PTSD) construct has precursors, it was formalized as a psychiatric diagnosis in the early 1980s (Young, 1997). This universalization of human experience across agents and subjects of violence (categories that are not mutually exclusive) renders both as undifferentiated survivors. Trauma as an individualized, psychologized construct can work to center the geopolitics of war, empire, and dislocation exclusively on the body-minds of individuals and thereby obscure the power relations of war and its afterlives. As such, trauma is an important discursive practice through which to consider how militarized violence persistently escapes from ideologically circumscribed war zones and their discrete temporalities.

PTSD, while pervasive as a diagnostic framework, is only one form of what we call *trauma practices*. In this chapter, we establish that multiple conceptualizations of trauma – including those used by health and psy- sciences, social theorists, artists, and displaced people alike – are at work to make sense of the mind-embodied experiences of violence, displacement, and remaking lives. We focus on trauma practices within refugee resettlement processes specifically for Iraqi refugees since the 2003 US-led invasion and occupation of Iraq. As of 2017, 2.9 million Iraqis remain internally displaced (UNHCR, 2017).

In her influential contribution to critical refugee studies, anthropologist Liisa Malkki (1995) observed that the category of refugee has become synonymous with trauma: 'It is striking how often the abundant literature claiming refugees as its object of study locates "the problem" not first in the political oppression or violence that produces massive territorial displacements of people, but within the bodies and minds of people classified as refugees' (Malkki, 2012, p. 8). Malkki does not dispute the distressing experiences that refugees face but is troubled by the effects of fixing the problem of international conflict onto the bodies and minds of displaced peoples. When put into practice through humanitarian, biomedical, psychosocial, and refugee resettlement practices, this problematization runs the risk of pathologizing refugees, creating what Mimi Thi Nguyen (2012) terms 'the refugee condition.' The simultaneous lumping and individuation of the 'refugee condition' creates a categorical means through which individuals are inserted into the resettlement process.

Critical scholars and individuals working with refugees have challenged the pathologization of refugees within the PTSD framework. They counter that refugees are not categorically traumatized. Rather, individuals may experience emotional and physical (mind-body) distress as a consequence of enduring or witnessing violence or encountering social environments and protocols that create distressing feelings, sensations, and cognitive responses. This framing of trauma conceptualizes trauma not as an interior property or diagnosis of individuals, but understands individuals in dynamic relation to their environments. As such, 'trauma' is imminent to conditions and events (or 'triggers') that individuals encounter in the course of their lives, yet has no necessary relationship to any one event, place, or person.

This chapter demonstrates the tension between trauma practices that conceptualize trauma as *within* individual body-minds and trauma practices that understand experiences of trauma as relational, or emergent from particular social environments and legal procedures that individuals encounter. This latter, relational conceptualization arguably diverges from PTSD as an 'interior' psychological framework, provoking the question of how different conceptualizations of refugee trauma jostle against each other in the institutions responsible for assessing, managing, caring for, and serving refugees. As part of a strategy to dislodge dominant conceptualizations of 'the refugee condition,' we then turn to the narratives and creative practices of Iraqis who have been exiled, and in particular in this chapter to one woman's memoir. Through Alia Al-Ali's narrative we demonstrate how a relational understanding of trauma unfolds an intimate, affective geopolitics that cannot be extracted from historical geographies of US imperialism, war, and displacement.

CONTEXT

Only a tiny portion of people who are displaced outside of their countries of origin are ever formally recognized by the United Nations High Commissioner for Refugees (UNHCR) as refugees. Of this group, less than 1 percent is resettled. The refugee resettlement process involves coordination and negotiations among United Nations, individual states, and non-governmental organizations. Except in circumstances when refugee status is afforded en masse, individuals must complete a series of interviews and screening protocols to establish their past persecution or credible fear of future persecution (and thereby their eligibility for formal UN recognition of refugee status), that they do not pose a security threat, and that they do not exhibit health symptoms that would bar them from admission to another country. While there is no universally applied protocol for physical and mental health screenings (Lawrance and Ruffer, 2015), people providing psycho-social services for refugees in Turkey and Jordan whom we interviewed noted that US criteria for (in)admissibility often shaped other countries' criteria.

In order to be admitted to the US, all refugees go through a rigorous and lengthy security and health screening process (see USCIS, 2013 for process at that time). Currently, there are four medical grounds for exclusion: (1) a communicable disease of 'public health significance'; (2) failure to provide proof of immunizations; (3) a physical or mental 'disorder with associated harmful behavior'; and (4) drug abuse or addiction (USCIS, 2017). These latter two grounds of exclusion are particularly pertinent to people who have experienced distressing events and, as a result, may have wanted to harm themselves or have relied on alcohol or drugs to cope with their circumstances. Next, an individual's medical records are transmitted to the resettlement agency so that they are apprised of health needs. Once admitted to the US, refugees go through another medical screening in their new place of residence, a process that sometimes involves a mental health screening. It is unknown how many people are categorized as inadmissible on medical grounds or if there are any socio-spatial patterns to these exclusions.

Medical diagnostics in US migration policy have never been neutral scientific exercises. Rather, physical and mental health screenings have been integral tools in efforts to exclude undesirable groups on geopolitical, racial-ethnic, ableist, class, and heteronormative grounds (Coleman, 2008; Luibhéid, 2002). Between 1882 and the mid-1920s, the grounds for medical and racial/ethnic exclusion were both expanded. In the 1882 Chinese Exclusion Act, Congress authorized government agents to deny entry to 'any convict, lunatic, idiot, or any person unable to take care of himself or herself without becoming a public charge.' The Immigration Act of 1917 expanded grounds of inadmissibility, barring people from a geographic area called the Asiatic Barred Zone, and the following:

> All idiots, imbeciles, feeble-minded persons, epileptics, insane persons; persons who have had one or more attacks of insanity at any time previously; persons of constitutional psychopathic inferiority; persons with chronic alcoholism; paupers; professional beggars; vagrants; persons afflicted with tuberculosis in any form or with a loathsome or dangerous contagious disease; persons not comprehended within any of the foregoing excluded classes who are found to be, and are certified by the examining surgeon as being mentally or physically defective, such physical defect being of a nature which may affect the ability of such alien to earn a living.

People from Iraq, Palestine, Syria, Lebanon, and elsewhere in the Middle East were not expressly excluded from emigrating under the aforementioned acts, yet the quota system enacted in the Johnson-Reed Immigration Act of 1924 significantly diminished migration from these countries. It would not be until 1965 in the Hart-Celler Act that country quotas were rescinded and a new system of hemispheric visa caps, family reunification, and skilled worker visas was implemented, resulting in a major shift in immigration patterns. Between 1965 and 2000, over 630,000 Arab people immigrated to the US (Cainkar, 2009, p. 82). Of this group, almost 88,000 were Iraqi, constituting 17 percent of Arab immigrants in 2000 (Cainkar, 2009, p. 16).

Following September 11, racialized ideas of categorical Arab and Muslim difference and dangerousness were marshaled to rationalize federal anti-terrorism policies that singled out people thought to be Arab or Muslim. The federal government conducted mass arrests and detentions, implemented a registry for Arab and Muslim men, massively expanded surveillance practices, placed a temporary hold on visa applications submitted by men from 26 countries, and additionally scrutinized the visas of Arab and Muslim residents. As of 2008, the government had issued at least 13,500 removal (deportation) orders (Cainkar, 2009, p. 142). Refugee resettlement into the US was halted entirely for a time and the Bush administration sharply reduced the numbers of refugees who would be admitted. Additional security screening measures led to a decline in the number of refugees who would actually be resettled. Admission rates in 2009 remained at 79 percent of 2000 levels (Barkdull et al., 2012).

While Iraqi people, particularly professionals, had emigrated to the US before 1980, several moments of conflict are responsible for significant migration out of Iraq in the latter part of the twentieth century and into the twenty-first century: the Iran-Iraq War (1980–89), Iraq's invasion of Kuwait, the Gulf War (1991–92), international sanctions, and the 2003 invasion of Iraq by the US and its allies, and ensuing civil conflict. Not all Iraqis settled in the US, of course, but almost 80,000 Iraqi refugees were resettled in the US after the first Gulf War (Inhorn, 2016, p. 178). US State Department Worldwide Refugee Admissions Processing System data indicate that 142,534 Iraqi refugees have been resettled in the US through the US Refugee Admission Program (USRAP) between October 1, 2006 and October 2, 2017 (Refugee Processing Center, 2017). In addition, 17,754 people who worked with the US government or contractors (as interpreters, for example) have been admitted through the Special Immigrant Visas (SIV) program (Refugee Processing Center, 2017).

The medical grounds of inadmissibility to the US have been substantially revised since the 1920s, most notably with the removal of the homosexuality bar in 1990 and HIV bar in 2010. Echoes of early twentieth-century exclusion criteria remain, including chronic use of drugs and alcohol. Moreover, self-sufficiency, the stated objective of refugee resettlement, resonates both with historical efforts to deny entry to those 'likely to become a public charge' and class-based narratives of personal responsibility in mid-1990s welfare reforms. Refugees are provided with medical insurance and cash assistance for the first eight months of their time in the US, after which they are expected to have found employment, to pay rent, and so on. According to our interviews with service providers involved in refugee resettlement in the US, it is very common that symptoms of distress among refugees recur at this moment, when many feel a material disjuncture in the quality of their former and present lives.

CONTEXTUALIZING TRAUMA, EMBODIMENT, AND MEMORY

While Malkki and Mimi Nguyen rightfully caution against the pathologization of refugee experience, it remains that diagnoses of PTSD and depression, for example, do become part of the admissions and resettlement process. The question becomes *how* formal diagnoses, services, and treatments are mobilized to care for refugees and facilitate individuals to carry on in a new place. Different conceptualizations of trauma mobilize different conceptualizations of mind-embodiment, and of how responses are to be diagnosed, treated, managed, rehabilitated, and prevented (Clare, 2017, p. 70). The dichotomizing medico-legal structure of 'normal' and 'abnormal' responses is arguably hegemonic, yet it is also deeply contested by health practitioners, refugee resettlement workers, and individuals themselves. Attention to how trauma practices become elements of geopolitics is a feminist geopolitical concern in that we seek to understand the power relations at work in particular deployments of trauma and individual interpretations of their own mind-embodiment (Loyd et al., 2018; Mountz, 2017a).

In 1999, the UNHCR issued guidance for health and other professionals involved in documenting torture and other forms of cruel, inhuman or degrading punishment. Known as the Istanbul Protocol, this non-binding document nonetheless has become an international standard that informs (albeit unevenly) medical, psychological, and legal assessment procedures and ethical obligations of health and legal professionals (Lawrance and Ruffer, 2015, p. 3). The protocol prefaces its discussion of then-current understandings of psychological effects of violence by acknowledging that 'The idea that mental suffering represents a disorder that resides in an individual and features a set of typical symptoms may be unacceptable to many members of non-Western societies' (UNHCR, 2004, p. 46).

Notwithstanding this caveat, the protocol goes on to observe that 'while the utility of this diagnosis [PTSD] in non-Western cultures has not been established,' efforts have been made to document prevalence of PTSD and major depressive symptoms among refugees from many different backgrounds (UNHCR, 2004, p. 45). Since the Istanbul Protocol was issued, instruments for diagnosing PTSD cross-culturally (e.g., the Harvard Trauma Questionnaire) have been used to establish that refugees from every part of the world have experienced symptoms of anxiety and distress following traumatic events (Fazel et al., 2005). Within this medicalized account of bio-psychological distress, researchers have documented a notably high incidence of PTSD among Iraqi refugees (Slewa-Younan et al., 2015), as a result of having experienced war, multiple relocations and protracted waiting, deprivation, deaths of family and friends, and torture (El-Shaarawi, 2015; Jamil et al., 2007; Loyd et al., 2018; Taylor et al., 2013).

As the Istanbul Protocol acknowledged, the development of cross-cultural and other biomedical, psychometric diagnostics has not been without its critics. Anthropologist Allan Young, for example, reminds that the PTSD diagnosis is historically and geographically contingent. The 'disorder is not timeless, nor does it possess an intrinsic unity. Rather, it is glued together by the practices, technologies, and narratives with which it is diagnosed, studied, treated, and represented and by the various interests, institutions, and moral arguments that mobilized these efforts and resources' (Young, 1997, in Summerfield, 2001, p. 97). For medical doctor Derek Summerfield, the 'diagnosis of post-traumatic stress disorder lacks specificity: it is imprecise in distinguishing between the physiology of normal distress and the physiology of pathological distress' (2001, p. 97).

Lurking in Summerfield's quotation is a curious adherence to affixing binary categorizations of normality and pathology to distressing experiences, which arguably undercuts his broader critique of 'the medicalization of life,' a double-edged process whereby 'distress is relocated from the social arena to the clinical arena' (Summerfield, 2001, p. 98). Yet, this tension within the histories of diagnostics and symptomologies also speaks to dilemmas within trauma practices of cross-cultural understanding, difficulties and politics of working through language interpreters, differing distinctions between 'treatments' and 'diagnoses,' and how responding to human needs itself blurs categories of biomedicine, psy- sciences, social work, and legal and political advocacy. The Istanbul Protocol, for example, recommends that health practitioners involved in making a professional assessment of individual suffering should assume 'an attitude of informed learning . . . rather than one of rushing to diagnose and classify. Ideally, this attitude will communicate to the victim that his or her complaints and suffering are being recognized as real and expectable under the circumstances' (UNHCR, 2004, p. 46).

A growing body of critical health, social science, and humanities literatures suggests that symptoms associated with 'traumatic' stressors – such as flashbacks, or recurrent, intrusive memories; emotional numbing; avoidance; heightened vigilance; general anxiety; trouble sleeping; depression; dissociation; and somatic pain – cannot be understood merely as individual psychological (or even biochemical) experiences. Rather, these experiences, and the language used to discuss stressors (or 'triggers') and make meaning of violence are embedded in specific social, cultural, and geopolitical contexts (Young, 1997). For example, the common conception that refugee experience necessarily results in trauma that originates in a war-space in the past has been challenged by studies that have documented the post-resettlement stressors that contribute to distress. These include structural racism and experiences with xenophobic hostility, language barriers, poverty, inability to continue working in one's profession, shifting gender and family norms, and government surveillance (Cainkar, 2009; El-Shaarawi, 2015; Jamil et al., 2007).

Rather than conceptualizing trauma as within individuals and within the past, such research instead understands individuals as living within shifting political geographies that themselves create the conditions for distress and for reconfiguring self and institutions of care. Marshall and Sousa's work on trauma in Palestine, for example, examines how individualized, politically neutral notions of trauma can sidestep 'the specific *political* nature of violence under occupation, thus stripping children from their social and cultural contexts and their historical and political narratives' (2014, p. 4, original emphasis). Such relational conceptualizations of trauma, place, and memory are well developed in geography (Entrikin, 2007; Perera, 2010; Till, 2005) and American studies (Espiritu, 2006; M.T. Nguyen, 2012; V.T. Nguyen, 2016). Karen Till, for example, contends that the 'memory-work and creative practices of . . . displaced residents' can contribute to political challenges to authorities that continue to marginalize city residents who themselves experienced violence (2012, p. 4).

The relationality and stakes of 'trauma' are geopolitical. Espiritu writes with regard to the Vietnamese refugee subject that

> instead of producing narratives of traumatized refugees, in which trauma is conceptualized only as pain, suffering, and distress, we can read trauma productively as a disruption of the US myth of 'rescue and liberation' that enunciates violence and recovery simultaneously. That is, we can read trauma as the condition that makes visible the relationship between war, race, and violence. (Espiritu, 2006, pp. 421–2)

For literary scholar Viet Thanh Nguyen, a just memory of the war the US engaged in Vietnam, Laos, and Cambodia is geopolitical, as are powerful entreaties to forgive and forget. Rather, Nguyen contends, 'The sign of unjust forgetting is repetition' (2016, p. 284). While forgiveness for the past may be possible in the abstract, this past is complicated by the 'time warp of perpetual violence' in which the US is engaged (Nguyen, 2016, p. 284). Writing on the US-Iraq context, Iraqi feminist scholars Nadje Al-Ali and Deborah Al-Najjar observe that 'It is difficult to speak of posttraumatic stress syndrome, as Iraqis are continuing to experience various forms of individual and collective traumas both within Iraq as well as within the diaspora' (2013, p. xxv). Trauma, conceived relationally, becomes generative of transnational historical geographies, properties of US imperialism that are both repeated and reworked in different historical conjunctions.

Geographers have also explored such repetitious, non-linear, folded, and transitive qualities of trauma (Blum and Secor, 2014; Coddington, 2017; Coddington and Micieli-Voutsinas, 2017; Micieli-Voutsinas, 2017; Mountz, 2017b). Jacque Micieli-Voutsinas's research on the September 11 memorial at the former World Trade Center II site explores how visitors to this site are 'encouraged to *feel* absence and *sense* presence' (2017, p. 94, original emphasis) in ways that 'teach museum visitors (how to feel) about the traumatic past' (p. 100). Blum and Secor draw on Freud and Lacan's efforts to explain the repetition of some people's mind-body experiences of distress. For Blum and Secor, trauma 'is *topological*, which is to say that the "origin" of trauma is not a single event localizable in time and space, but rather a topological constellation in which ordinary ideas of space (such as distance or location) are distorted and subject to ongoing transformations' (2014, p. 105, emphasis in the original).

Repetition is thereby not sameness, but a new configuration that may still be distressing, but also may do something else. Kate Coddington's (2017) work on experiences of advocates for asylum seekers in Australia theorizes how trauma moves among people. Transmitted akin to a contagion, trauma is expansive, yet the affective conditions it creates shrink advocates' capacity to respond. Alison Mountz (2017b) also traces the transitive quality of trauma in her work on island detention. While one imperative of prison facilities is confinement, they cannot confine people's trauma. Mountz conceptualizes the transmission of trauma as moments of 'affective eruptions' during which 'the past erupts into the present, rendering more visible the haunting of geopoliticized fields of power' (p. 75). What these critical accounts of trauma insist upon is not mere recounting of the horrors of the prevailing geopolitical order, but also how trauma can remake political geographies.

NARRATING TRAUMA

Literary scholar Ann Cvetkovich contends that

> thinking about trauma from the same depathologizing perspective that has animated queer understandings of sexuality opens up possibilities for understanding traumatic feelings not as a medical problem in search of a cure but as felt experiences that can be mobilized in a range of directions, including the construction of cultures and publics. (2003, p. 47)

Similarly, for Al-Ali and Al-Najjar, 'Trauma not only destroys but creates' (2013, p. xxvi). They write this not to condone war and occupation, but to insist that survivors continue to make art and to mobilize politically, even in the most difficult of circumstances.

We use these theoretical and political insights to read the narrative of a young Iraqi woman, Alia Al-Ali, who left Iraq to seek asylum first in Syria and later in the US. Her account is part of the Veterans Book Project (2009–12), a collaborative effort between artist Monica Haller and US soldiers and Iraqi refugees. Through a series of workshops, participants each wrote a book, which incorporated digital images from their personal files. Haller explains that the aim of the project was to 'design a framework, a system-wide *objects for deployment*' 'within which these experiences would become socially meaningful' (Pederson, 2013, p. 22, emphasis in the original). The result is an archive of 50 books that are available online or may be printed on demand.

Alia Al-Ali's narrative begins with a photographic image of Alia walking the dog of her host family in Minnesota, explaining that she left Iraq soon after she finished high school. Images of her hometown in Iraq are interspersed with text explaining the effects of growing sectarianism in the midst of the US occupation. This was not the only war whose effects were being felt.

> My dad was paralyzed after the 1991 war. He had a tumor in his spinal cord . . . We don't know if the tumor was caused by war, because there were so many cluster bombs that bombed the area close to the refinery, or if it was because he worked in an oil refinery, a place with lots of chemicals. (Al-Ali, 2012, p. 17)

The uncertainty of what caused so many more people's neurological and other disorders was compounded by sanctions.

Alia's father's confinement to a wheelchair changed the family. He could no longer work, his wife also had to stop working as a nurse in order to care for him, and his daughters assumed many of the chores that he customarily did. As Cynthia Enloe (2010) reminds, the stresses and traumas of war are gendered. And so it was in the midst of heightened sectarian violence that Alia seems to affix more blame to her father than to the sanctions and Gulf War that she previously named. Ibrahim, a man thought to be a family friend, had begun to pressure her parents to marry her sister, Jamila. Her parents persistently refused, yet the man intimated that he was keeping them safe from Al Qaeda. The message was clear: if they did not agree to the marriage, then the entire family would be in danger.

After several months in this relationship, Jamila fled back home saying that she 'couldn't be the family's sacrifice anymore' (Al-Ali, 2012, p. 52). Ibrahim came to their home with police to retrieve her. Feeling 'really humiliated for my family being pushed around like this,' Alia 'rushed into the living room' and then

> rushed into him [Ibrahim] and pushed him away violently. I lost my mind. I said every cursing word that I could think of. He did nothing because he was so shocked I did this. I threatened him and the policemen that if they did not leave I would call the U.S. Army. This was the lie that saved my sister's life. (pp. 55–6)

The lie that saved her sister's life also spurs Alia to begin to consider leaving. Jamila goes on to study engineering and another sister nursing, yet Alia's experiences with discrimination at school, 'for no other reason than being Shiite' (p. 77), relegates her to study at an agricultural school rather than medicine. Alia told her father she wanted to leave, a decision not supported by her parents. 'People in Iraq learn to normalize war, loss, and chaos. Loss happens frequently and loses its shock. The war becomes part of them' (p. 81). Alia did not want this to happen to her too.

Alia takes a bus to the Syrian border where 'they looked at my eyes with some weird science fiction machine that takes your eye prints' (p. 96). Following this biometric documentation, she is granted asylum in December 2010. She then applies and is admitted to a program in the US for Iraqi refugees wishing to continue their undergraduate education and, at some point, to return to help rebuild their country. After living in the US for some time, Alia begins to feel alienated from her past:

> I have left everything behind – my memories, clothes, my room, home, friends and most importantly, my family. I sometimes get very busy with my life here and cannot Skype with my family. I start to forget even how my mom looks. I start to act weird around my friends or at school, but I don't realize it's because I'm homesick. (p. 131)

The formal structure of Alia's book helps tell the experience of disjunction and how she struggles with war (not) becoming part of her. The color of pages on which she narrates her and her family's lives is a light shade of brown, evoking perhaps the earth. Interspersed with these pages are photographs. And then, in the midst of one of her stories, two light blue pages appear. These pages unexpectedly jar her account, and always speak of sleepless nights, nights filled with nightmares, or visions of events she saw or fears seeing. She writes, 'Sometimes, I want to go to sleep, but instead I stay up very, very late – perhaps until four or five a.m. Sometimes I can't even sleep. I'm not like normal people. I cannot just rest' (p. 31). And later, 'My dreams are not clear. Sometimes I have dreams about my mom driving. Then she gets hit by a car, and we find her all bloody, and I wake up and find myself crying' (p. 59). Alia's mother is alive, but her nightmare suggests a topological relocation: the memory of a particularly terrifying drive through Baghdad occupies the same place as present-day fears for her mother's safety. Alia suggests this topological relation when she explains, 'You don't react to the intense atmosphere of war in daily life; it just arrives in dreams' (p. 150).

These blue pages also punctuate her movement across boundaries – from Iraq to Syria to the US – and how she experiences home. Alia describes homesickness as being out of time and space. 'I start to feel like I have no beginning or end, no family or home' (p. 132). Elsewhere, she explains the feeling that she is in two places at once. When a professor at the university she attends in the US calls to her by her name, a name that marked her as Shia in Iraq, Alia observes, 'I still have this fear inside me. It makes school like war' (p. 137). Her name being called out in a US classroom transports her to an Iraqi classroom and the discrimination she faces as a Shia in Iraq and an Iraqi in the US resonate affectively across time and space. A few pages later, Alia writes, 'In my dreams, I am always in both places at the same time. Sometimes I see myself walking the dog, Max, in Iraq. And I wonder, why am I here in Iraq? And it gets mixed up with shooting and soldiers' (p. 143).

If we follow Blum and Secor's conclusion that 'A new topological cut or connection must be made in order to escape the repetitions of the traumatic constellation' (2014, p. 107), we might read Alia's book as both an attempt to make sense of her life within a particular geopolitical context and a commentary on the US imperial conceit that war and its effects are confined over there. However much she does not want to normalize war by staying in Iraq – and her sleepless nights remind her that she does not feel 'like normal people' – she also rejects how US citizens seem to normalize war when they imagine they can 'remain neutral about war' (Al-Ali, 2012, p. 146). 'Would you accept it for yourself, your country, and your children? I do not believe so. Then how do you accept it for other people to live through murder and loss?' (p. 146).

This imperial geopolitical imaginary that partitions wartime 'for other people' creates the conditions for repetition, or 'unjust memory' in the sense that Viet Thanh Nguyen suggests. This dichotomous imagination of peace and war fails to grapple with the complexities of war that Alia necessarily navigates.

> If I were to say that war is wrong, people might say it's probably because I was not affected by Saddam. We had a surface level of safety under Saddam. But we lived, and we didn't have this massive number of people dying. My family had many people arrested by Saddam's forces. (p. 147)

Her critique of the neutral imperial affect informing US politics is not a criticism of individual Americans. 'I made many friends among the soldiers, and I am still in touch with many of them. I see them suffering now, too' (p. 172).

Alia concludes her book observing, 'It is very hard to be peaceful inside. Only when I'm with people, I can feel that peace' (p. 202). The geography of this peace is not of Alia's choosing. She fears return to Iraq because of security issues and regards people's sugges-tions that she return to help rebuild as 'mostly unrealistic' (p. 194). While in Iraq she feels safe only with her family; she alone cannot create the conditions for a 'post-war' Iraq. Nor does she control the process to get her family admitted to the US as asylees. More within Alia's control are her efforts to partition her past into events (p. 191) filled with happiness, pleasure trips, delicious food, her mother's smile. Yet, this move comes at a cost. This 'past life became like a dream. I have a dead life there. But when I have to listen to the news, I feel how distant I am. It's painful to follow up with the news and the updates in Iraq now' (p. 148). Alia suggests that this temporalization and spatialization of trauma as in the past and over there fails, despite her efforts, because she is still affected by and in some sense inscribed within the many lives being lived and events transpiring in Iraq.

CONCLUSION

In this chapter, we focused on the geopolitics of trauma for Iraqi refugees. Trauma is not a singular concept. Rather, different conceptualizations of trauma inform trauma practices in medicine, refugee resettlement, social criticism, art, and personal narrative. These conceptualizations are historically and geographically contingent, yet not separate from US histories of medical and racial-ethnic migration exclusion. We then turned to how traumatic events are known to enter into refugee resettlement processes. These practical understandings generated on the part of practitioners resonate with recent theorizations of trauma from geography, American studies, and the humanities. Finally, we turn to Alia Al-Ali's narrative of her experiences with war in Iraq and asylum in the US to explore both repetition and topologies (geopolitics) that might be otherwise.

If trauma can be creative (Al-Ali and Al-Najjar, 2013) and can be used to create publics (Cvetkovich, 2003), what does recounting Alia's narrative do? How does her narrative speak back to trauma practices that would either name her as a traumatized individual or normalize her experiences? Beyond the retinal scan, Al-Ali does not describe the screening process she went through en route to the US, but we can be certain that her admission has required exams. Her experience as a university student in the US also differed from many adult refugee experiences because the government stipulates paid work as the marker of 'self-sufficiency.' Alia also does not discuss the refugee resettlement agencies involved in her making a new life, so we do not know which of the myriad conceptualizations of trauma she has encountered. Her account, nonetheless, supports the idea of a relational conceptualization in which peace feels temporary and tied to other people.

Alia bristles at the normalization of war within Iraq and the US even as she grapples with wanting to sleep like a normal person. She uses the word trauma to talk about seeing her father in the hospital as a six-year-old girl, yet not elsewhere. Alia's narrative performs a critical resistance to any reductive reading that would make it a document of PTSD or an artifact of 'the refugee condition.' Our use of the word 'trauma' here is not to mark a pathology inhering in the body or mind of an individual, but instead to signal what Alia reveals to us: a relational topology that enfolds violent and threatening events within the ordinary of the here and now. In the form and content of her book, Alia shows how, in the singularity of her life, moments, places, events, bodies, and affective conditions overlay, transform, and call forth one another. These spatio-temporal foldings both enact and contest an embodied and affective geopolitics of US imperialism, war, and displacement – not because Alia as refugee somehow carries this geopolitics within her, but because geopolitics itself is intimate and affective (Brickell, 2014; Dixon, 2015; Laketa, 2016; Pain, 2009; Smith, 2012).

Trauma practices work to translate the geopolitics of war and displacement into individualized geographies of care and security. The more relational conceptualizations of trauma that we explored remain in tension with formal, often inquisitorial, legal processes that assess credibility, and hence rights and benefits, based upon consistent, coherent recountings of past experiences (Lawrance and Ruffer, 2015). These medico-legal processes themselves are known to act as stressors, yet within the context of increasing restrictions on immigration and asylum, legal scholars Lawrance and Ruffer contend that 'the lower threshold for establishing the "credibility" of a claimant is increasingly conflated with the much higher barrier of "proof"' (2015, p. 5). Pathologization, or distinguishing normalcy from abnormality, re-enters despite efforts to the contrary. This repetition is not sameness, though, because critics, health workers, and refugees push back. Yet, this persistence of pathologization *and* violence on the part of the US is nonetheless possible in part because of an unjust memory (Nguyen, 2016) and imperial imagined geography of war confined to people over there. We suggest that conceiving of a geopolitics of trauma destabilizes the spatial and temporal distance imagined between geographies of war and peace, creating intimate connections among violence, wellbeing, and possibilities for *non*-repetition.

REFERENCES

Al-Ali, Alia (2012), *Objects for Deployment*, Veterans Book Project, accessed April 6, 2017 at https://issuu.com/veteransbookproject/docs/alia_web_a88e6118edcf7d.

Al-Ali, Nadje and Al-Najjar, Deborah (2013), 'Writing trauma, memory, and materiality', in Nadje Al-Ali and Deborah Al-Najjar (eds), *We are Iraqis: Aesthetics and Politics in a Time of War*. Syracuse, NY: Syracuse University Press, pp. xxv–xl.

Barkdull, C., Weber, B., Swart, A. and Phillips, A. (2012), 'The changing context of refugee resettlement policy and programs in the United States', *Journal of International Social Issues*, 1(1), 107–19.

Blum, Virginia L. and Secor, Anna (2014), 'Mapping trauma: topography to topology', in Paul Kingsbury and Steve Pile (eds), *Psychoanalytic Geographies*. Farnham, UK: Ashgate, pp. 103–16.

Brickell, K. (2014), '"The whole world is watching": intimate geopolitics of forced eviction and women's activism in Cambodia', *Annals of the Association of American Geographers*, 104(6), 1256–72.

Cainkar, Louise (2009), *Homeland Insecurity: The Arab American and Muslim American Experience after 9/11*. New York: Russell Sage Foundation.

Chinese Exclusion Act of 1882, Sess. I, Chap 126; Stat. 58, 47th Congress.

Clare, Eli (2017), *Brilliant Imperfection: Grappling with Cure*. Durham, NC: Duke University Press.

Coddington, Kate (2017), 'Contagious trauma: reframing the spatial mobility of trauma within advocacy work', *Emotion, Space and Society*, http://dx.doi.org/10.1016/j.emospa.2016.02.002.

Coddington, Kate and Micieli-Voutsinas, Jacque (2017), 'On trauma, geography, and mobility: towards geographies of trauma', *Emotion, Space and Society*, http://dx.doi.org/10.1016/j.emospa.2017.03.005.

Coleman, M. (2008), 'US immigration law and its geographies of social control: lessons from homosexual exclusion during the Cold War', *Environment and Planning D: Society and Space*, 26(6), 1096–114.

Cvetkovich, Ann (2003), *An Archive of Feelings: Trauma, Sexuality, and Lesbian Public Cultures*. Durham, NC: Duke University Press.

Dixon, Deborah P. (2015), *Feminist Geopolitics: Material States*. Farnham, UK: Ashgate.

El-Shaarawi, N. (2015), 'Living an uncertain future: temporality, uncertainty, and well-being among Iraqi refugees in Egypt', *Social Analysis*, 59(1), 38–56.

Enloe, Cynthia (2010), *Nimo's War, Emma's War: Making Feminist Sense of the Iraq War*. Berkeley, CA: University of California Press.

Entrikin, J. Nicholas (2007), 'Place, destruction, and cultural trauma', in Isaac Reed and Jeffrey C. Alexander (eds), *Culture, Society, and Democracy: The Interpretive Approach*. Boulder, CO: Paradigm Publishers, pp. 163–79.

Espiritu, Yen Le (2006), 'Toward a critical refugee study: the Vietnamese refugee subject in US scholarship', *Journal of Vietnamese Studies*, **1**(1–2), 410–33.

Fazel, M., Wheeler, J. and Danesh, J. (2005), 'Prevalence of serious mental disorder in 7000 refugees resettled in western countries: a systematic review', *Lancet*, **365**(9467), 1309–14.

Immigration Act of 1917, 39 Stat 874.

Inhorn, Marcia (2016), 'Multiculturalism in Muslim America? The case of health disparities and discrimination in "Arab Detroit," Michigan', in Moha Ennaji (ed.), *New Horizons of Muslim Diaspora in North America and Europe*. Houndmills, Basingstoke: Palgrave Macmillan, pp. 177–87.

Jamil, H., Nassar-McMillan, S.C. and Lambert, R.G. (2007), 'Immigration and attendant psychological sequelae: a comparison of three waves of Iraqi immigrants', *American Journal of Orthopsychiatry*, **77**(2), 199–205.

Laketa, Sunčana (2016), 'Geopolitics of affect and emotions in a post-conflict city', *Geopolitics*, **21**(3), 661–85.

Lawrance, Benjamin N. and Ruffer, Gayla (2015), 'Witness to persecution? Expertise, testimony, and consistency in asylum adjudication', in Benjamin N. Lawrance and Gayla Ruffer (eds), *Adjudicating Refugee and Asylum Status: The Role of Witness, Expertise, and Testimony*. Cambridge: Cambridge University Press, pp. 1–24.

Loyd, Jenna, Ehrkamp, Patricia and Secor, Anna (2018), 'A geopolitics of trauma: refugee administration and protracted uncertainty in Turkey', *Transactions of the Institute of British Geographers*, doi: 10.1111/tran.12234.

Luibhéid, Eithne (2002), *Entry Denied: Controlling Sexuality at the Border*. Minneapolis, MN: University of Minnesota Press.

Malkki, Liisa A. (1995), 'Refugees and exiles: from "refugee studies" to the national order of things', *Annual Review of Anthropology*, **24**, 495–523.

Malkki, Liisa A. (2012), *Purity and Exile: Violence, Memory, and National Cosmology among Hutu Refugees in Tanzania*. Chicago, IL: University of Chicago Press.

Marshall, David J. and Sousa, Cindy (2014), 'Decolonizing trauma: liberation psychology and childhood trauma in Palestine', in Christopher Harker, Kathrin Hörschelmann and Tracey Skelton (eds), *Conflict, Violence and Peace, Geographies of Children and Young People*, Vol. 11. Singapore: Springer, pp. 1–20. doi: 10.1007/978-981-4585-98-9_7-1.

Micieli-Voutsinas, Jacque (2017), 'An absent present: affective heritage at the National September 11th Memorial & Museum', *Emotion, Space and Society*, **24**, 93–104.

Mountz, Alison (2017a), 'Political geography III: bodies', *Progress in Human Geography*, doi: 10.1177/0309132517718642.

Mountz, Alison (2017b), 'Island detention: affective eruption as trauma's disruption', *Emotion, Space and Society*, **24**, 74–82.

Nguyen, Mimi Thi (2012), *The Gift of Freedom: War, Debt, and Other Refugee Passages*. Durham, NC: Duke University Press.

Nguyen, Viet Thanh (2016), *Nothing Ever Dies: Vietnam and the Memory of War*. Cambridge, MA: Harvard University Press.

Pain, Rachel (2009), 'Globalized fear? Towards an emotional geopolitics', *Progress in Human Geography*, **33**(4), 466–86.

Pederson, Claudia C. (2013), 'The Veterans Book Project: a conversation with Monica Haller', *Afterimage*, **41**(2), 21–5.

Perera, Suvendrini (2010), 'Torturous dialogues: geographies of trauma and spaces of exception', *Continuum: Journal of Media & Cultural Studies*, **24**(1), 31–45.

Refugee Processing Center (2017), 'Cumulative arrivals by state for refugee and SIV – Iraq', October 2, http://www.wrapsnet.org/admissions-and-arrivals/ (last accessed October 3, 2018).

Slewa-Younan, S., Uribe Guajardo, M.G., Heriseanu, A. and Hasan, T. (2015), 'A systematic review of post-traumatic stress disorder and depression amongst Iraqi refugees located in western countries', *Journal of Immigrant and Minority Health*, doi: 10.1007/s10903-014-0046-3.

Smith, Sara (2012), 'Intimate geopolitics: religion, marriage, and reproductive bodies in Leh, Ladakh', *Annals of the Association of American Geographers*, **102**(6), 1511–28.

Summerfield, D. (2001), 'The invention of post-traumatic stress disorder and the social usefulness of a psychiatric category', *British Medical Journal*, **322**, 95–8.

Taylor, E.M., Yanni, E.A., Pezzi, C. et al. (2013), 'Physical and mental health status of Iraqi refugees resettled in the United States', *Journal of Immigrant and Minority Health*, **16**(6), 1130–37.

Till, Karen E. (2005), *The New Berlin: Memory, Politics, Place*. Minneapolis, MN: University of Minnesota Press.

Till, Karen E. (2012), 'Wounded cities: Memory-work and a place-based ethics of care', *Political Geography*, **31**(1), 3–14.

UNHCR (2004), *Istanbul Protocol: Manual on the Effective Investigation and Documentation of Torture and Other Cruel, Inhuman or Degrading Treatment or Punishment*. New York and Geneva: United Nations.

UNHCR (2017), 'Iraq emergency', accessed April 6, 2018 at http://www.unhcr.org/en-us/iraq-emergency.html.

USCIS (US Citizenship and Immigration Services) (2013), 'Iraqi refugee processing fact sheet', accessed April 6, 2018 at https://www.uscis.gov/humanitarian/refugees-asylum/refugees/iraqi-refugee-processing-fact-sheet.

USCIS (US Citizenship and Immigration Services) (2017), *Policy Manual, Volume 8 – Admissibility*, accessed April 6, 2018 at https://www.uscis.gov/policymanual/HTML/PolicyManual-Volume8-PartB-Chapter1.html#footnotelink-2.

Young, Allan (1997), *The Harmony of Illusions: Inventing Post-Traumatic Stress Disorder*. Princeton, NJ: Princeton University Press.

10. Gendered circular migrations of Afghans: fleeing conflict and seeking opportunity
Nazgol Bagheri and Jennifer L. Fluri

INTRODUCTION

Afghanistan has been embroiled in war and related political conflicts since the 1978 communist coup, which toppled the government, killing the president and establishing a communist state. The People's Democratic Party of Afghanistan (PDPA), under the leadership of President Taraki, retained authority and sought communist-based social and political reforms. The PDPA was significantly influenced by the Soviet Union, which sought political and territorial expansion into Afghanistan through its support of the PDPA. Various Afghan communities, throughout the country, opposed and resisted the reform efforts initiated by this new regime. Local leaders in various provincial areas extensively criticized land tenure restructuring and reforms that targeted women (such as compulsory education) because these proposed changes challenged the foundations of their authority. Opposition to the central government took shape through disparate forms of resistance including violent conflict. In addition to public dissent, infighting grew among the PDPA leadership, which culminated in President Taraki being overthrown by his former advisor Hafizullah Amin, who later had Taraki executed. Afghan leader, Babrak Karmal and his allies conspired with the Soviet Union to remove Amin from office. Amin was assassinated in the wake of the Soviet military invasion/assistance to the Afghan communist-government in December 1979, with Babrak Karmal taking over as leader of the Afghan government.

In response to the Soviet military occupation, the United States (US) with the assistance of Pakistan and Saudi Arabia, funded and supported seven disparate resistance groups in opposition to the Soviet occupation and support of the Afghan communist government. The opposition groups, known as the mujahideen, were divided along ethnic and Islamic religious lines. While all groups incorporated Islam as part of their resistance efforts against the Soviet-backed government, each group ascribed to different versions/ interpretation of Islam, drew alliances from within specific ethnic groups, and provided funds and weapons from a variety of international actors.

The US support of the mujahideen began as a covert effort with the assistance of Pakistan. Saudi Arabia was another major donor and several Saudi men, including Osama bin Laden, came to Afghanistan to assist the mujahideen to fight against Soviet occupation along with support from several other countries. "With the support of capitals ranging from Washington, London, Cairo, and Tel Aviv, to Riyadh, Islamabad, Tehran, and Beijing (not to mention the backing of grassroots Arab volunteers and charities), the mujahideen rebellion against the Afghan Communist government was an unprecedented global-jihadi phenomenon that seemed destined to achieve a quick victory" (Williams, 2014, p. 927). However, a quick victory never transpired, and the Soviet Union's military occupied Afghanistan until 1989, when a withdrawal was orchestrated with the assistance of the United Nations (UN) and included representatives from the US and the Soviet Union, while mujahideen leaders were not included in these negotiations (Rubin, 2002). Additionally, the Soviet withdrawal led to a decline in financial support for the mujahideen along with a significant decrease in aid/development assistance (Edwards, 2002; Rubin, 2002).

The Soviet occupation included military operations throughout the provincial areas in Afghanistan and led to extensive numbers of internally displaced persons (IDPs) and refugees fleeing to neighboring countries, mostly Iran and Pakistan. The mujahideen had significant influence over international assistance programs in Pakistani refugee camps, leading to coercive practices that included exchanging humanitarian assistance for political affiliation and recruiting young Afghan men from the camps into different groups (Nojumi, 2002).

After the Soviet military withdrawal in 1989, the Soviet Union continued to support the Afghan government, under the leadership of Mohammad Najibullah. When the Soviet Union collapsed in 1991, the Afghanistan communist government remained in power with a tenuous hold on the capital city, Kabul. Najibullah along with other key government officials took refuge in the UN compound, while various mujahideen groups began to jockey for power and control of the capital city. Fighting among these disparate mujahideen groups grew to full-scale civil war between 1992 and 1996, which destroyed much of Kabul. This led to another wave of refugees migrating to neighboring countries.

Refugee camps in Pakistan once again became a space for recruiting young boys and men, this time for the Taliban. Pakistan's Inter-Services Intelligence (ISI) was instrumental in helping to create the Taliban by recruiting young men and boys from refugee camps and in Pashtun-majority areas in the Northwest Frontier Province and Federally Administered Tribal Areas. The Taliban began to make their presence known in southern Afghanistan in 1994 and by 1996 they captured Kabul. Several mujahideen regrouped and some aligned to form the Northern Alliance (previously known as the United Front) to fight against Taliban encroachment into provinces in northern Afghanistan (Edwards, 2002; Rubin, 2002). When the Taliban took control of Kabul they stormed the UN compound and captured former president, Najibullah. In one of many subsequent uses of public, performative, and punitive violence the Taliban publicly beat, castrated, and killed Najibullah by hanging.

The Taliban used public executions, floggings, and corporeal amputations as a method of social control, turning the internationally sponsored soccer stadium in Kabul into a space for public punishment. The Taliban also prevented women from traversing public space without a burqa/chadri and the accompaniment of a *mahram*.[1] Women were barred from working outside the home, going to school, or seeking medical attention from a male doctor. The removal of women from public space and the harsh treatment of both male and female Afghan citizens drew international scrutiny. Additionally, some Afghan feminist organizations sought assistance from international organizations and individuals to help them resist Taliban rule. The fledgling Afghan economy during the civil war

---

[1] A *mahram* is a family member who a woman cannot marry (i.e., brother, father, uncle) or is married to, who accompanies her for her protection. A woman can be a *mahram* for another woman, although in Afghanistan *mahram* are mostly men.

continued to worsen under the Taliban, sending more Afghans to neighboring countries to seek respite from the Taliban along with the hope of securing economic opportunities. Arab resistance fighters, espousing conservative and extremist interpretations of Islam, significantly influenced both the mujahideen and the Taliban. Additionally, the international organization, Al Qaeda (the base) used spaces in Afghanistan as training grounds for its soldiers to commit acts of violence against the US and other states.[2]

After the attacks against the US on September 11, 2001, the US government led an invasion of Afghanistan on October 7, 2001 to capture Osama bin Laden, the leader of Al Qaeda and identified "mastermind" behind the September 11 attacks. US efforts in Afghanistan further sought to bolster the leadership and authority of several mujahideen groups (particularly the Northern Alliance), which led to localized control by "warlords" over various provincial areas throughout the country. Additionally, the US early military interventions were marked by several missteps, failures, and the ability to locate bin Laden. In response, US public and geopolitical discourse shifted to "saving" and assisting Afghan women as part of its military, aid, and development efforts. The geopolitical discourse focused on "saving" Afghan women culminated with Laura Bush's (former first lady of the US) use of the presidential radio address to call for action in support of Afghan women and children and to reinforce the need for US military action in Afghanistan:

> Because of our recent military gains in much of Afghanistan, women are no longer imprisoned in their homes. They can listen to music and teach their daughters without fear of punishment. Yet the terrorists who helped rule that country now plot and plan in many countries. And they must be stopped. The fight against terrorism is also a fight for the rights and dignity of women. (Bush, November 17, 2001)

The geopolitical discourse to assist/save Afghan women continued through various aid/development projects (Fluri and Lehr, 2017). The US-led military operations in Afghanistan were soon followed by extensive US-led international humanitarian aid and economic development. Over 50 countries have operated various aid/development projects and programs in Afghanistan along with several multi-national non-governmental organizations (NGOs). The UN expanded its operations in Afghanistan known as the UN Assistance Mission in Afghanistan (UNAMA). The aid/development funds allocated to Afghanistan were extensive, while organizations often competed with each other rather than attempting cooperative and coordinated international efforts to rebuild Afghanistan.

The various waves of refugees fleeing conflict and persecution in Afghanistan is further complicated by the disparate experiences of different ethnic and language groups as well as across socioeconomic levels.[3] Afghan elites, and many within the upper and middle economic strata, were able to migrate outside the region to countries in Europe, the US, Canada, and Australia. Those without financial or familial connections abroad that sought to migrate outside the region for better job opportunities and security had more economic difficulty in neighboring host countries. While those who traveled outside the region may have had more economic ability when starting their journey, many also experienced significant hardship and difficulty traversing borders and seeking asylum

---

[2]   Al Qaeda is a Sunni-Islamic organization that represents an extremist and minority interpretation of Islam.

[3]   Afghanistan is home to over 30 different ethnic groups and it is a multilingual society, with two national languages, Dari (Persian) and Pashto. There are over 40 minority languages and 200 different dialects.

(Mountz, 2010). The following sections provide an overview of gendered experiences and circular migrations of Afghans to neighboring countries – Iran and Pakistan – as well as distant locations such as the US.

GENDERED AFGHAN MIGRATION TO IRAN

For many years after the initial stages of Afghan political instability began to unfold, the Iranian government welcomed Afghan refugees in religious solidarity, as many who fled were Shi'a Muslims. Since the Soviet military occupation of Afghanistan, an estimated 2.6 million Afghan refugees (approximately) have immigrated to Iran (Rajaee, 2000; Jazayery, 2002), which includes 1.5 million documented and 1 million undocumented (Abbasi-Shavazi and Sadeghi, 2016). In the 2016 Iranian census, about 1.5 million Afghan migrants were recorded; among them, about half were born in Iran and are considered second generations. Unlike nearby Pakistan (in the earlier years of Afghan immigration) Iran set up refugee camps for Afghans, but approximately 10 percent of immigrants lived in camps, because at that time Afghans were able to integrate and take part in Iranian society (Rajaee, 2000). Currently, more than 70 percent of Afghans live in urban areas and only 3 percent live in refugee camps.

Despite early attempts at integrating Afghans into Iranian societies, Afghans have not been given the same social or political opportunities as naturalized Iranian citizens. Afghans have further been relegated or coerced into different labor-intensive job sectors, such as construction. This work has mostly been informal with much lower pay than their Iranian counterparts (Rajaee, 2000). Job insecurity along with various forms of inequality led to outrage amongst Afghan immigrants and subsequent political turmoil by Iranians acting on their behalf. Considering that Afghans do not have the same rights as naturalized Iranians (i.e., the children of Afghan immigrants who are born in Iran are not citizens unless the father is Iranian) this left Afghans with little to no political/social representation and provoked the Iranian government to pursue various programs to encourage Afghans to leave the country in an effort to restore political order.

In recent years, the Iranian government has insisted upon the involuntary deportation of Afghan immigrants by using methods such as refusing to renew their legal documents (thus, giving them an "illegal" status). Similarly, in conjunction with the United Nations High Commissioner for Refugees (UNHCR), Iran offered to give immigrant families compensation in the form of food, clothing, and money in return for "voluntary repatriation," in other words, simply leaving Iran without resisting.

According to UNHCR, the top five counties in Iran that host the most Afghan refugees are Saveh (in Markazi province), Rafsanjan and Bardsi (in Kerman province), Ardakan and Meybod (in Yazd province) (Wickramasekara et al., 2006, pp. 14–17). Similarly, these five counties can be found in three provinces, Markazi, Kerman, and Yazd, which range from east to west, geographically and respectively. However, the county hosting the most refugees, Saveh, is ironically found in eastern Iran (opposite the Afghan border). In 2016 alone, 953,447 refugees from Afghanistan immigrated to Iran (Wickramasekara et al., 2006, pp. 95–112).

While immigration laws have made migration and permanent residency in Iran difficult for Afghans, language similarities between Farsi and Dari have made it easier for Afghan immigrants to assimilate in Iran. Farsi, Iran's national language, is similar to Dari, one of Afghanistan's two official languages. Pashto-speaking Afghans usually choose to migrate to Pakistan (Adelkah and Olszewska, 2007). During the 1998–99 school year, approximately 14,000 children were being taught in informal Afghan schools in Iran, and this number has increased since 2004. Afghan children have not been able to attend Iranian public school without paying tuition; thus, keeping the pressing need for localized Afghan education more relevant in Iran (Adelkah and Olszewska, 2007).

Migration as a Male "Rite of Passage"

Afghan male migration to Iran, particularly for Shi'a Muslims and ethnic Hazzars, have been viewed as a "rite of passage" and method to become a man by proving one's manhood through the struggle of migration and living apart from one's family (Monsutti, 2007). Because of Iran's limitations on legal Afghan migration to Iran, refugees and migrants without funds or contacts have been forced into human-smuggling networks (Monsutti, 2007). Therefore, these difficult journeys and experiences of suffering were part of the process of proving one's masculinity.

Young men choose to leave Afghanistan for reasons other than fleeing conflict, such as economic opportunity and to increase their personal autonomy and social networks beyond that of their home and family (Monsutti, 2007, 2008). Therefore, migration to Iran without family was a method for "young Afghans to build both their adulthood and masculinity and to become recognized as a full man" (Monsutti, 2007, p. 184). For Afghan women, migration to Iran often adjusted their understanding of gender roles and relations and women who stayed in Afghanistan often took on previously forbidden tasks (such as agricultural labor) normally conducted exclusively by men.

Inter-national Marriages and Migration

The influx of Afghan immigrants to Iran has mainly consisted of men looking for work. Inter-national marriages between Iranians and Afghans further exemplify gendered inequalities between citizens and immigrants. By Iranian law, it is legal for Afghan men to marry women of different nationalities (in fact, these men increase their social status sometimes by doing so), but if an Iranian woman decides to marry a man of another nationality without first consulting the Iranian Foreign Ministry and having the marriage approved, then the marriage is deemed illegitimate (Abbasi-Shavazi and Kraly, 2017; Abbasi-Shavazi and Sadeghi, 2014, 2016). The explanation behind this legal prioritization of male over female citizens rests on the premise that male presence in the household is to provide and protect the family, which, in the eyes of the government, provides him with more freedom to marry (Zahedi, 2007). Conversely, women do not have equal citizenship with regard to their offspring; therefore, the nationality of her husband, according to the government, must be Iranian in order for her/their children to be granted Iranian citizenship. Thus, the children of an Iranian woman and Afghan man will not be granted citizenship. Conversely, the children of an Iranian man and Afghan woman will automatically be granted citizenship.

According to Iran's Ministry of Foreign Relations, over 32,000 children and more than 1 million people are estimated as undocumented based primarily on their father's lack of

Iranian citizenship. Despite these gendered differences, the number of marriages between Iranian women to Afghan men remains high, especially at border regions/provinces, such as Razavi-Khorasan, northern portions of Sistan and Baluchistan, and southern portions of Kerman, and Tehran. These inter-national marriages continue to increase, while the majority of Afghan-Iranian marriages remain between Iranian men and Afghan women. The Iranian government granted an amendment to the state of marriage law(s) passed in Iran in 2006 stating that children of Iranian mothers may apply for citizenship upon turning 18 and/or qualify for legal residency. However, in order to receive full citizenship, the marriage of the parents must be recognized by the Iranian state, and out of about 40,000 illegitimate Afghan/Iranian marriages in Iran, only 14,000 of these marriages are deemed legitimate. It remains likely that the Iranian government will try to alter these amendments and laws, even though discriminating against both Iranian women and their children violates the UN's International Covenant on Civil and Political Rights (in terms of women and children) and the Convention on the Rights of the Child, which specifically notes that children may not be discriminated against due to their parents' nationalities. Despite the violation of international conventions, it is expected that Iranian immigration laws will become increasingly harsh.

Differences in religious beliefs can be another cause of unrest between Iranian and Afghan populations in Iran. Although both populations speak relatively similar languages, over 90 percent of both the Iranian and Afghan populations are Muslims; while the majority of Iranians are Shi'a and the majority of Afghans are Sunni Muslims. This difference in religion along with discriminatory tendencies that stem from a nationalist perspective certainly increase the chance for conflicts to arise, especially when the Afghan immigrant is not Shi'a. Despite these challenges, Afghan immigrants (especially women) can potentially use marriage as an intimately geopolitical tool of assimilation and ensuring their children retain citizenship (see Smith, 2012). Racial differences between Afghans and Iranians remain pronounced and another way of situating Afghans as "other" in Iran (Abbasi-Shavazi et al., 2005; Yarbakhsh, 2015). In sum, Afghan immigrants to Iran illustrate social, economic, and demographic challenges as well as opportunities for policy-relevant social demographic research. By way of comparison, the following section provides an overview of gendered migration from Afghanistan to Pakistan.

GENDERED AFGHAN MIGRATION TO PAKISTAN

Pakistan has hosted Afghan refugees since the Soviet invasion of Afghanistan in late 1979. The Pakistan government received a significant amount of humanitarian and development assistance from the US and other agencies to help attend to the influx of refugees fleeing Afghanistan. Afghan refugee camps were set up along the border areas, particularly in Peshawar and Quetta, Pakistan. Pashtun-Afghans were in many cases able to connect with kinship networks in Pakistan, as many Pashtuns live on the Pakistani side of the Afghanistan-Pakistan border, which was originally formed in 1893 between British diplomat, Henry Mortimer Durand and Abdur Rahman, the Amir of Afghanistan. This border, known as the Durand Line, split the Pashtun-dominated areas. After the partition of India and Pakistan (1947) the Durand Line continued as the border between Pakistan and Afghanistan. The Pashtuns remain in the Federally Administered Tribal Area (FATA) in Pakistan, while few recognize the international border as legitimate.

In the 1980s, refugee camps in Pakistan were highly politicized through the provisioning of aid/assistance programs. For example, Afghans were expected to affiliate with one of the mujahideen groups in the camps. Additionally, camp configuration and leadership significantly influenced gender roles and relations. The influence of extremist interpretations of Islam in some camps reinforced conservative and strict gender norms, which limited women's mobility outside their homes as well as expecting specific dress codes for women and men. Simultaneously, the Revolutionary Association of the Women of Afghanistan (RAWA), an Afghan-feminist political organization, established various modes of resistance against the Soviet occupation, the extremist mujahideen groups, and the Taliban, while operating in both Afghanistan and Pakistan. Their influence culminated with developing significant influence and power within one of the refugee camps in Peshawar, Pakistan (Fluri, 2009).

RAWA's influence on this refugee camp included operating orphanages, schools, and literacy programs as well as providing a health clinic for residents. Camp authority and leadership was devised through two leadership councils, one council being all-women and the other all-men, and both councils included representatives from the different ethnic groups in the camp. While refugee displacement in marked by hardship and suffering, this camp provided opportunities that were not previously available for many residents. These opportunities included living with/near a diverse array of ethnic groups as well education and health care. For RAWA, the camp provided a space for them to both envision and experience (on a small scale) a version of their feminist-nationalist beliefs because of their influence and participation in the management of the camp (Fluri, 2008). Additionally, RAWA has had a large number of male supporters who assist with their political and social work within refugee areas and in Afghanistan.

RAWA's control over the camp included the ability to exclude or remove individuals from the camp. The threat of banishment from the camp was used as a method to ensure social control and cohesion within the camp. The influence of this organization was only experienced in one refugee camp; while in other camps, young men and boys were recruited by different groups as mujahideen or Taliban soldiers. RAWA's influence and ability to create a feminist enclave in the midst of extensive and conservative patriarchal control under the banner of Islam illustrates the diversity of social and political thought among Afghan refugees. Additionally, in several camps international assistance organizations were actively forming various women-focused or women-led NGOs. Many of these organizations, such as the Afghan Women's Network, continue to operate in Afghanistan today.

Iran and Pakistan illustrate the disparate approaches to immigration and diverse experiences of Afghan migrants. Afghan migration to both countries has been marked by cyclical processes of back-and-forth migration rather than permanent residency or citizenship in either country, despite long-term stays or desire to remain in a particular country. In addition to refugee and migrant experiences in Pakistan and Iran, many Afghans have migrated outside the region to countries in Europe, North America, and Australia. The following section focuses on different forms of circular and cyclical migration for economic opportunity and the recent special immigrant visa programs sponsored by the US.

CIRCULAR MIGRATIONS, ECONOMIC OPPORTUNITY, AND GENDER

Marsden's (2016) research on Afghan traders examines "globalization from below" as translocal practices of economic exchange across Eurasia. His research dispels stereotypes and myths about Afghan traders as limited to illicit trade in narcotics and precious stones connected to funding insurgent political factions (such as the Taliban). He further reminds readers that Afghan traders have a long history of being connected to the political economics of South Asia, Central Asia, and Russia. Afghan traders are predominantly male who draw upon extensive networks, flexibility, savvy knowledge, and ability to work within disparate social, cultural, religious, and economic structures. However, the migration of Afghans to Europe and the US during the Soviet occupation (1980s) and civil war (1992–96) led to a significant brain drain from Afghanistan and employment concentration in specific industries (Hanifi, 2000). Knowledge transfer among Afghans in the diaspora is often complicated by competition among different identity-based groups. However, the current generation of Afghan-Americans who grew up in the US have not been as stymied by communal divisions compared to their parents' generation and many remain interested in contributing to economic development in Afghanistan (Hanifi, 2000).

Gender, Special Immigrant Visas, and Circular Migration

In the US, the National Defense Authorization Act of 2006 authorized 50 Special Immigrant Visas (SIVs) annually to Afghan and Iraqi interpreters and translators working for the US military or who meet other specific requirements. This provision was amended to allow 500 per year in 2007 and 2009 only. This program was sought after by some Afghans who worked for the US military or on US military bases in Afghanistan. The program allowed for much easier immigration procedures to the US including the ability to bring immediate family members, and expedited procedures for receiving work permits known as "green cards" (i.e., within 45 days of arrival). Some Afghans who received SIVs and green cards to work in the US returned to Afghanistan because they were able to work for different aid/development organizations as *international* rather than *local* workers. Local Afghan salaries within the aid/development community, while providing much better income than other forms of work, remain a fraction of international salaries (Fluri and Lehr, 2017). Many Afghans who have migrated to the US with SIVs found it difficult to find well-paid employment, and therefore returned to Afghanistan to work as temporary employees in the aid/development sector.

For some, returning to Afghanistan to work within the international aid/development sector provided them with more resources than they were able to obtain working in the US, where their skill sets (as translators, interpreters, or assistants in international organizations) were not transferable to comparable jobs or salaries in the US. While both men and women on SIVs have returned to Afghanistan to work, Afghan women have found short-term transitions (i.e., working in Afghanistan for six months or a year and then returning to the US) much more lucrative. Because there are a limited number of Afghan women with (1) the skill sets required of international organizations and (2) permission from families to work in international spaces; Afghan women are able to garner higher wages and more flexible work schedules than many of their male counterparts

(Fluri and Lehr, 2017). Returning to Afghanistan to work as part of the international aid/development mission includes sending remittances to one's family members living in the US as well as Afghanistan. Similar to Marsden's discussion of Afghans as business savvy through trade networks, the use of SIVs and US green cards exemplifies the savvy use of spatial and economic opportunities tied to geographic displacement and replacement in the hierarchy of income and work within existing international aid/development structures in Afghanistan.

Elite Afghans with English-language skills and the ability to navigate the international community in Kabul comprise the majority of individuals participating in this type of circular migration. However, because of the difficulties finding comparable employment in the US, returning to Afghanistan becomes a viable method to secure needed income, albeit a temporally limited option. Gendered experiences of migration have also varied significantly based on socio-political contexts within host countries. As Rostami-Povey (2007) argues, Afghan women in the US (and UK) have more access to citizenship rights than Afghan women refugees in Pakistan and Iran. Afghan female migrants to the US are often of a higher socioeconomic class and therefore able to financially and spatially connect to social and familial networks as well as resource-provisioning organizations in the US. Conversely, Afghan women refugees/migrants in Pakistan and Iran take advantage of spatial shifts to effectively challenge and break down masculine regimes of control as compared to Afghan female migrants in the US. Afghan women in the US have experienced a continual struggle between western values and Afghan/Muslim values and have found precious little space to articulate their gender rights within their communities. Additionally, due to Islamophobia, they have been "forced to defend their Islamic identity," which made it more difficult for them to be viewed as visibly liberated "modern" women within their host countries (Rostami-Povey, 2007, p. 261).

Afghan patterns of gendered circular and cyclical migration toward economic opportunity and in flight from conflict illustrate disparate experiences, of difficulty, opportunity, challenge, and change (van Houte et al., 2015). Spatial disruptions can have a rippling impact on gender roles and relations, leading to changes in gendered divisions of labor, as well as changes in authority and influence based on gender. Conversely, migration can further entrench unequal gender roles and make it difficult for women to articulate gender-based rights, when struggling with other identity-based issues such as race, nationality, and religious affiliation.

CONCLUSION

This chapter provides an overview of the various phases of migration from Afghanistan to neighboring countries, Iran and Pakistan, and circular migrations of Afghans for economic opportunity and trading in South and Central Asia, as well as in and out of the US. The gendering of migration patterns illustrates multiple influences on gender roles and relations. In some cases, refugee camps provided a space for articulating a feminist-nationalist ideology and framework for a civil city, such as RAWA's camp management style in Pakistan. In other experiences, boys and young men were recruited from refugee camps (mostly in Pakistan) to join disparate mujahideen groups in the 1980s and the 1990s and recruitment into the Taliban. During the Soviet occupation of Afghanistan, Afghan refugees in Pakistan were often required to affiliate with one of several mujahideen groups to receive assistance. Thus, exchanging political affiliation for humanitarian aid and economic resources.

Refugee spaces in Iran and Pakistan have been seen as plausible options for different Afghan groups based on religious and language affiliation. For example, Afghans that speak Dari and are Shi'a Muslims found Iran a much easier and more inviting place of refuge, even after the Iranian government placed more restrictions (i.e., limiting the number of refugees and amount of time they could legally stay within the country). Many Pashto-speaking Afghans (Pashtuns) found affinity among existing kinship and social networks in Pakistan, because an international border had divided the Pashtun territory since the late nineteenth century. Therefore, more Pashtuns and Sunni Muslims of various ethnicity or language groups also sought refuge in Pakistan. The geographic proximity of different areas of Afghanistan (eastern Afghanistan bordering Pakistan and western Afghanistan bordering Iran) has been another deciding/driving factor for Afghans who migrated to these two countries, despite language or religious affiliation.

More recently, Afghans who worked for the US military or on military bases in Afghanistan were able to qualify for SIVs. The SIVs provided a quicker path to legal immigrant status in the US and the ability to receive a green card in the US. While these visas provided opportunities for Afghans to immigrate to the US, particularly individuals under threat because of their work with the US military, some have found it difficult to adjust to the US or to find work comparable to their skill sets and employment options in Afghanistan. In response, some individuals with SIVs and US green cards have returned to Afghanistan to work within the aid/development community and earn international salaries, which are significantly higher than local Afghan salaries. These circular migrations include sending remittances both from Afghanistan to the US and from the US to Afghanistan.

Gender roles and relations have been altered by these multiple and diverse experiences of migration. Interestingly, Afghan women in the US tend to come from elite families with more resources and therefore are better situated financially and politically. Conversely, these women often find it more difficult to assimilate because their actions are much more scrutinized and they are caught between expressing their Muslim identity in the face of Islamaphobia and challenging patriarchal structures without appearing to be "western." Women of lower socioeconomic status have experienced changes to gender roles, such as participating in work that had previously been exclusively gendered male (i.e., agricultural labor). With the loss of male labor due to migration, women have taken on male-gendered labor and other tasks, such as expressions of authority. Additionally, women's experience of migration includes new influences that often challenge or change their understanding of gender roles and relations. These new influences range significantly by location and the sociocultural and political context of the new location. For example, Afghan female refugees in Iran experienced social norms that encouraged women's education and participation in public life within an Islamic framework as well as Islamic feminist articulations of women's rights.

As this chapter has shown, critical geographies of migration that engage with feminist and embodied analyses are necessary to further our understanding of intersectional identities (gender, race, ethnicity, language, class, and religions). Additionally, comprehensive and complicated analyses of intersectional identities must attend to sociocultural and political contexts within disparate geographic places to understand how they shape the multiple and shifting experiences of migration during various phases of displacement, migration, and resettlement.

REFERENCES

Abbasi-Shavazi, M.J. and Kraly, E.P. (2017), Forced and refugee migration in Asia. In Z. Zhao and A. Hayes (eds), *Handbook of Asian Demography* (pp. 331–50). New York: Routledge.

Abbasi-Shavazi, M.J. and Sadeghi, R. (2014), Socio-cultural adaptation of second-generation Afghans in Iran. *International Migration*, **53**(6), 89–110.

Abbasi-Shavazi, M.J. and Sadeghi, R. (2016), Integration of Afghans in Iran: patterns, levels and policy implications. *Migration Policy and Practice*, **VI**(3), 22–9.

Abbasi-Shavazi, M., Glazebrook, D., Jamshidiha, G., Mahmoudian, H., and Sadeghi, R. (2005), *Return to Afghanistan? A Study of Afghans Living in Islamic Republic of Iran*. Tehran: University of Tehran Press.

Adelkhah, F. and Olszewska, Z. (2007), The Iranian Afghans. *Iranian Studies*, **40**(2), 137–65.

Bush, L. (2001), *Radio Address by Mrs. Bush*. Retrieved from http://www.presidency.ucsb.edu/ws/?pid=24992 (last accessed May 5, 2018).

Edwards, D.B. (2002), *Before Taliban: Genealogies of the Afghan Jihad*. Berkeley, CA: University of California Press.

Fluri, J.L. (2008), Feminist-nation building in Afghanistan: an examination of the Revolutionary Association of the Women of Afghanistan. *Feminist Review*, **89**, 34–54.

Fluri, J.L. (2009), Geopolitics of gender and violence "from below." *Political Geography*, **28**(4), 259–65.

Fluri, J.L. and Lehr, R. (2017), *The Carpetbaggers of Kabul and Other American-Afghan Entanglements: Intimate Development and the Currency of Gender and Grief*. Athens, GA: University of Georgia Press.

Hanifi, M.J. (2000), Anthropology and the representation of recent migrations from Afghanistan. In E.M. Godziak and D.J. Shandy (eds), *Rethinking Refuge and Displacement: Selected Papers on Refugees and Immigrants*, Vol. VIII (pp. 291–321). Arlington, VA: American Anthropological Association.

Jazayery, L. (2002), The migration–development nexus: Afghanistan case study. *International Migration*, **40**(5), 231–54.

Marsden, M. (2016), *Trading Worlds: Afghan Merchants Modern Frontiers*. Oxford: Oxford University Press.

Monsutti, A. (2007), Migration as a rite of passage: young Afghans building masculinity and adulthood in Iran. *Iranian Studies*, **40**(2), 167–85.

Monsutti, A. (2008), Afghan migratory strategies and the three solutions to the refugee problem. *Refugee Survey Quarterly*, **27**(1), 58–73.

Mountz, A. (2010), *Seeking Asylum: Human Struggle and Bureaucracy at the Border*. Minneapolis, MN: Minnesota University Press.

Nojumi, N. (2002), *The Rise of the Taliban in Afghanistan*. New York: Palgrave Macmillan.

Rajaee, B. (2000), The politics of refugee policy in post-revolutionary Iran. *Middle East Journal*, **54**(4), 828–60.

Rostami-Povey, E. (2007), Afghan refugees in Iran, Pakistan, the U.K., and the U.S. and life after return: a comparative gender analysis. *Iranian Studies*, **40**(2), 241–61.

Rubin, B.R. (2002), *The Fragmentation of Afghanistan: State Formation and Collapse in the International System*. New Haven, CT: Yale University Press.

Smith, S. (2012), Intimate geopolitics: religion, marriage, and reproductive bodies in Leh, Ladakh. *Annals of the Association of American Geographers*, **102**(6), 1511–28.

van Houte, M., Siegel, M., and Davids, T. (2015), Return to Afghanistan: migration as reinforcement of socio-economic stratification. *Population, Space and Place*, **21**(8), 692–703.

Wickramasekara, P., Sehgal, J., Mehran, F., Noroozi, L. and Eisazadeh, S. (2006), Afghan households in Iran: Profile and Impact Final Report, United Nations High Commissioner for Refugees (UNHCR), International Migration Programme International Labour Office, Geneva Switzerland.

Williams, B.G. (2014), Afghanistan after the Soviets: from jihad to tribalism. *Small Wars & Insurgencies*, **25**(5–6), 924–56.

Yarbakhsh, E. (2015), Iranian hospitality and Afghan refugees in the city of Shiraz. *Anthropology of the Middle East*, **10**(2), 101–18.

Zahedi, A. (2007), Contested meaning of the veil and political ideologies of Iranian regimes. *Journal of Middle East Women's Studies*, **3**(3), 75–98.

PART III

BORDERS, VIOLENCE AND THE EXTERNALIZATION OF CONTROL

11. The geography of migrant death: violence on the US-Mexico border
Jeremy Slack and Daniel E. Martínez

INTRODUCTION

Around the world the act of migration has become increasingly deadly. Conflicts, economic deprivation, and even climate instability have led to more and more people migrating each year. Areas of intense conflict such as Syria have drawn international attention as tens of thousands of people cross the Mediterranean in rickety small boats hoping to arrive on European soil and request asylum (Fargues and Bonfanti, 2014). Combined with the migrations from Somalia, Sudan, and other North African countries, the International Organization for Migration (IOM) estimates that over 5,000 migrants died crossing the Mediterranean in 2016 (IOM, 2017). In the Bay of Bengal, the Rohingya continue to escape from Myanmar, but perish at sea as they are rejected from Thailand, Malaysia, and Australia (Brough et al., 2012; Jones, 2016; Kiragu et al., 2011; Missbach and Komnas, 2016). Even along the US-Mexico border where we work, scholars are woefully unable to accurately estimate the number of fatalities along the 2,000-mile border that spans deserts, mountains, and grassland. While critical geographers have criticized the drive to quantify death (Hyndman, 2007), there are important benefits to counting and especially identifying the dead. This work provides answers and relief to the families of missing and deceased migrants, something that has long-term ramifications for the ambiguity of their loss (Boss, 2009; Reineke, 2016).

US-Mexico border scholars' efforts to understand, explain, and quantify migrant deaths have been taking place for nearly two decades (Cornelius, 2001; Eschbach et al., 1999). However, there are significant limitations on officials' ability to effectively determine how many people die attempting to migrate each year as well as the total number of migrant deaths that have occurred along the US-Mexico border across time.

This chapter focuses on migrant deaths along the US-Mexico border. We highlight the need to expand the understanding of the linkages between mobility and death both empirically and conceptually by broadening the notion of death. We begin this chapter by discussing a broader framework for how to understand death. We then present recent data on migrant death estimates in Southern Arizona, before exploring the complicated overlap between Mexico's cartel violence and migrant deaths. We ask: Why is death so intertwined with movement and (im)mobility? Why does the clear linkage between increased enforcement, hardened borders, and restricted mobility that kills people fail to elicit outrage or even changes to immigration management? Much of this chapter is devoted to presenting questions to which we do not have answers as well as discussing what future work could do to address the empirical challenges of studying death along the border.

THEORY

Understanding the role of death in the geography of migration is not only an empirical challenge, but a conceptual one as well. Scholars have endlessly critiqued research that purely focuses on counting the dead. Although we emphasize that the process of quantification has important, concrete benefits, we agree that scholars must move the discussion beyond a focus on these quantitative measures. This includes the study of absence, disappearance, and mourning, each of which are factors that shape the acceptability and reception of death. Studying the social stigma produced through disappearance and death must coincide with efforts to quantify migrant deaths. The use of a feminist geopolitical perspective can help us connect the geopolitical factors that govern migration and enforcement to the myriad ways different people live with and experience mobility controls (Hyndman, 2004; Massaro and Williams, 2013; Williams and Massaro, 2013). Moreover, this perspective also helps expand the understanding of the social conditions that make death acceptable and normalized (or at least all too easy to ignore), as is the case with undocumented migrants in the Arizona desert. To accomplish this task, we draw on the concept of "social death" from Lisa Marie Cacho (2012). She examines the ways that bodies are policed, categorized, and excluded through the racial apparatus of the state, leading certain groups of people (e.g., undocumented immigrants) to be categorized as undeserving. These narratives come in many forms, but particularly prevalent is the attitude that those who break the law – by crossing into the United States without authorization – do not deserve protections and sympathy. In other words, unauthorized migrants who perish along the US-Mexico border while attempting to enter the country are complicit in their own deaths because they violated immigration law, as are those who may have assisted them to evade detection.

This process of criminalizing people for immigration violations and then leveraging this as a justification to ignore the loss of life has reached new heights. For instance, in July 2017 a semi-truck of 38 would-be migrants was found in a Wal-Mart parking lot in San Antonio when one of the occupants asked an employee for water. When authorities arrived on the scene, eight people had already died inside the vehicle, and another two perished shortly thereafter. San Antonio Police chief William McManus stated, "We're looking at a human trafficking crime here this evening," but followed up by stating that the victims would be taken into custody by Immigration and Customs Enforcement where they would be investigated, and most likely deported (Smith et al., 2017). The discourse of human trafficking, echoed by immigration officials and Texas Governor Greg Abbot, was used to trigger a moral panic and place the blame of migrant death squarely on individuals who were attempting to help people circumvent the immigration controls at the border. This is a common tactic (Sanchez, 2014; Spener, 2009; Vogt, 2016) that has been largely effective in shifting the responsibility of migrant deaths away from immigration policies and inter-related structural factors (Martínez et al., 2013; Martínez et al., 2014) to the individual level. In short, it has become a strategy used to justify and normalize death. And yet, when it comes to the victims, the protections of the state are non-existent. All suspected victims of human trafficking should be screened for T-visa eligibility, which was created in 2000 as part of an initiative to encourage people to testify against human traffickers. However, since their creation, T-visas have been vastly underutilized. For instance, US Citizenship and Immigration Services (USCIS) received a total of 1,848 T-visa applications in fiscal year 2016, 1,737 of which were approved, well under the cap of 5,000 (USCIS, 2017). However, a total of 6,228 T-visa applications were still awaiting a decision as of that year (USCIS, 2017). In comparison, Immigration and Customs Enforcement arrested 1,952 people for human trafficking as part of the Homeland Security Investigations program in 2016 alone, with over 7,000 arrests since 2010 (ICE, 2017). Since multiple agencies arrest people for human trafficking, it is particularly shocking that one agency arrests more people for trafficking than the total number of people granted relief in that same period. It is easy to conclude that alleged victims of trafficking clearly face a much higher degree of scrutiny than those arrested.

Migrant death, in this case, is the direct consequence of the US government's immigration enforcement regime and the limited legal pathways into the United States, among other factors (Martínez et al., 2013; Martínez et al., 2014). However, by blaming the human smugglers, who are often migrants themselves,[1] it becomes morally acceptable for people to die, all the while making a push for more of the same draconian policies of enforcement that lead to these deaths in the first place. This is essentially an effort to negate the structural violence that causes people to die on the border. Drawing from Galtung's concept of structural violence (1964), scholars have explored how poverty, economic conditions and immigration enforcement drive people to risk their lives along the border (Martínez et al., 2014; Nevins, 2007; Nevins and Aizeki, 2008). Scholars have even linked indigenous heritage to a higher likelihood that their bodies will go unidentified (Hughes et al., 2017). This is not to say that human smugglers are always honest or trustworthy individuals, however, they are the product of the enforcement along the border, especially tactics that have pushed people into dangerous, remote, desert areas (Dunn, 1996; Nevins, 2002), and not the root cause of death.

This process of demonizing a convenient scapegoat is not unique to the United States and has become the hallmark of death and disappearance in Mexico's last decade of hyper-violence (Gibler, 2011). To die in Mexico is to be guilty, to be less than human and stigmatized. Scholars have explored this notion of the guilty victim in rich detail as related to the femicides in Ciudad Juárez (Agnew, 2015; Wright, 2011), expanding on notions of how the actions of victims become the object of the investigation, rather than searching for those who committed these acts of violence. This stigma, however, does not stay just with the victims but transfers to their family and loved ones, which creates impediments to searching for the truth. This, combined with the very real danger of searching for answers in Mexico, has led to a chilling effect leading people to not report missing loved ones or to search for answers regarding their murders. In 2017, according to the National Registry of Disappeared Persons there were 30,942 missing people (*desaparecidos*) in Mexico (Rodríguez, 2017). To further complicate this matter is the known presence of migrant massacres in the states of Tamaulipas and Nuevo Leon, as well as other areas, pointing to a convergence of migration-related deaths and those blamed on drug-related violence.

Furthermore, as the United States continues to become more polarized, the process of searching for answers related to a loved one's death during migration may also lead to more silence and reluctance to step out of the shadows due to some family members' precarious immigration status. A January 2017 executive order signed by Donald Trump

---

[1]   Not in the San Antonio case.

that aims to charge the families of undocumented child migrants with human smuggling will have devastating effects and keep families separated for longer, if not forever. If families become worried that a social tie to someone who has died crossing the border could result in charges against them if they are citizens, or a deportation if they are not citizens, they may stem their search for loved ones and their participation in activities that could provide closure to their loss.

Geographers must engage with the politics of mourning and loss, particularly as they relate to the ambiguity of disappearance and the lack of finality that occurs without a physical body (Reineke, 2016). For Boss, "ambiguous loss" results in a number of negative factors including depression and an inability to process the death (e.g., there is no end to the loss) and a distancing from one's social group because people do not know how to treat someone with a missing relative (e.g., no words, not a widow, orphan, and so on) (Boss, 2009, 2010). This inability to physically locate and find where and how death occurs is in and of itself one of the key challenges for developing a fully fledged study of the geography of death and migration.

This brings us back to the importance of empirical studies of death and migration. We certainly should not reduce this loss of life to a number that rises and falls, only garnering attention as it reaches new heights of lethality, like the much criticized *ejecutometro* ("execution meter") in Mexico. However, each bit of information gathered, each individual identified, and each family notified is an important step, not only in the healing process, but also in the quest for change. Therefore, we cannot discount the importance of quantifying death, but we should note its challenges; challenges that magnify with the differing contexts of migrations around the world, but that produce shared solutions that are necessary around the world. In the following sections, we explore some of these challenges as they relate to understanding and quantifying the link between death and mobility along the US-Mexico border.

Migrant Deaths: Evidence from the Arizona-Sonora Border

Some scholars have cautioned against enumerating migrant deaths at the expense of focusing on the structural factors that have led to these largely preventable fatalities as well as the social conditions that have allowed them to become normalized. We echo these concerns. However, we also believe that quantifying and tracking migrant deaths along the border and across time is of upmost importance for advancing discussions of human rights, failed immigration policy, and border research. Collecting reliable and valid estimates of migrant deaths along the US-Mexico border also helps shed light on the relationships between migrant deaths, macro-level structural transformations, and the shifting geography of death.

The true number of migrant deaths along the US-Mexico border across time is unknown, as estimates only consist of cases that come to the attention of US authorities. Nevertheless, sources suggest that such deaths have numbered well into several thousands (see Reineke and Martínez, 2014). Numerous factors make locating, recovering, and identifying migrant remains a challenge, including the remote terrain and environmental conditions in which migrants perish, the immigration status of the deceased's family members, and variation in practices and procedures across jurisdictions that are tasked with recovering migrant remains (Rubio-Goldsmith et al., 2014).

While there is no standardized and centralized database tracking migrant deaths along the US-Mexico border over time (Rubio-Goldsmith et al., 2014), the US Border Patrol estimates that 6,915 migrants perished while attempting to enter the United States between fiscal year 1998 and 2016 (CBP, 2017), which is likely a conservative estimate (see Rubio-Goldsmith et al., 2006; Soto and Martínez, 2018). Nevertheless, scholars have attempted to enumerate migrant deaths in various regions of the border for nearly two decades. According to some scholars, migrant deaths along the US-Mexico border have occurred in relatively high numbers since at least 1985 (Eschbach et al., 2003). Rather, what has shifted has been the geography of migrant death. Prior research has empirically demonstrated that migrant deaths increased in certain areas along the US-Mexico border as a direct consequence of heightened border enforcement efforts. Increased border enforcement effectively funneled unauthorized migration away from traditional urban crossing points (e.g., El Paso-Juarez and San Diego-Tijuana) into remote regions of the border (e.g., southern Arizona and South Texas) where migrants have succumbed to the elements (Cornelius, 2001; Eschbach et al., 1999; Eschbach et al., 2003; Martínez et al., 2013; Martínez et al., 2014; Reineke and Martínez, 2014; Rubio-Goldsmith et al., 2006; Slack et al., 2016; Soto and Martínez, 2018). Others have also called attention to the roles that neo-liberal reform and the inability of the United States to pass comprehensive immigration reform, among other factors, play in increasing and perpetuating migrant deaths (Nevins, 2007; Nevins and Aizeki, 2008; Martínez et al., 2014).

The Pima County Office of the Medical Examiner (PCOME), located in Tucson, Arizona, has made a concerted effort to investigate and identify undocumented border crosser (UBC) deaths in southern Arizona for nearly the past two decades (Anderson, 2008; Anderson and Parks, 2008) and is undoubtedly the leading institution in the country conducting this type of work. Drawing on data from medical investigator reports from the PCOME, Figure 11.1 illustrates annual deaths coded as UBCs (i.e., the solid bars) as well as the approximate UBC death rate standardized to 100,000 US Border Patrol apprehensions (i.e., the dashed trend line) in southern Arizona between fiscal year 1990 and 2016. As noted, there was a sharp increase in UBC deaths in southern Arizona in the early 2000s, which coincided with increased border enforcement efforts in the region, with the remains of more than 2,700 migrants being recovered in southern Arizona alone since 1990.

Despite notable decreases in unauthorized migration through southern Arizona, as suggested by the precipitous drop in US Border Patrol apprehensions since the mid-2000s, migrants continue to perish in high numbers in the region. As such, the migrant death rate in southern Arizona reached all-time highs in fiscal year 2015 and 2016. This suggests that migrants who continue to cross through southern Arizona are crossing for longer periods of time and through more remote areas of the region. In fact, recent geospatial analyses drawing on PCOME records have demonstrated that migrants are being pushed further west of Nogales, Sonora, into the Tohono O'odham Nation as they attempt to avoid detection by US authorities (Giordano and Spradley, 2017; Soto and Martínez, 2018).

All too often the humanity of the dead is lost in aggregate statistics and of which we must not lose sight. As we count the dead, we must constantly remind ourselves and others that each case represents a person – someone's mother, father, child, and so on; each with their own hopes, dreams, and desires for a better future. Acknowledging the deceased's

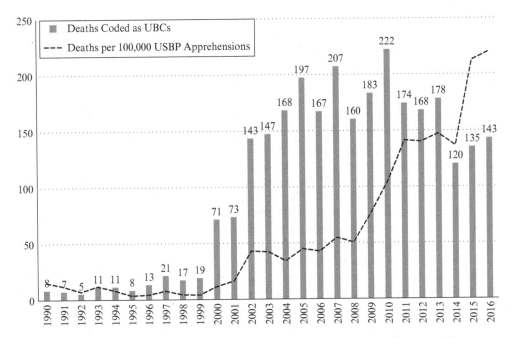

*Figure 11.1   Pima County Office of the Medical Examiner deaths coded as UBCs,
FY 1990–2016 (N = 2,776)*

humanity is especially important for understanding the long-lasting social-psychological ramifications of losing a loved one during the migration process that reverberates throughout immigrant communities across the United States and Latin American, often resulting in a sense of "ambiguous loss" (Boss, 2009, 2010; Reineke, 2016). And yet, if we do not count the dead, we are unable to fully comprehend the magnitude of the humanitarian crisis and mass disaster playing out across the borderlands. Moreover, the counting process is required if we hope to increase identification rates among the dead. Careful record-keeping, forensic analyses, and years of searching will be required if we hope to tie the tragedy of the border to the families with unanswered questions about their loved ones. While aggregate statistics are problematic in that they reduce human life to a number, meticulous counting is the first step in returning people's remains to their loved ones as well as in making death have meaning for the living.

Entanglements of Violence: Mobility, Disappearance, and Armed Conflict

Juanito described the bodies that came out of the vat of acid as looking like "dirt." "It was as if they were salt," he explained. The residue was thrown out and spread onto nearby fields. A deportee and victim of kidnapping by the infamous Zetas drug cartel, Juanito recounted his horrific experience of being detained in San Fernando, Tamaulipas, where the infamous San Fernando massacre took place. When asked how many people were killed in the six months that he was held on the ranch he replied, "Maybe a hundred? No, I believe it was many more. Yeah . . . two-hundred, or less, I don't know," he said. "One or two daily. Imagine it! It was a lot." Another kidnapped migrant explained how his captors "cut out a young Nicaraguan guy's eye and two of his fingers because he didn't pay. He bled to death in two days." These stories became increasingly common during fieldwork and often were told by individuals who were able to escape, giving us a limited view of the true scope of violence against migrants. While migrant kidnapping has received attention in Mexico (CNDH, 2011), limited scholarly work has addressed the reasons behind kidnapping a relatively poor group of people. We have previously argued that kidnapping is often about labor, controlling a workforce and using it as a way to recruit potential cartel members (Slack, 2016; Slack and Campbell, 2016). However, this leaves us to question how to address these deaths.

How do we separate those that die as a result of Mexico's drug conflict and those that die during the migration process? The brutality experienced by Central Americans, as well as deportees is well known and well documented, meaning that among those who go missing along the migrant trail, many are presumed dead at the hands of drug cartels, but now the challenges of identifying clandestine migrants is compounded with identifying the dead in what is essentially a conflict zone.

For all of the challenges of locating, documenting, and identifying the dead in the Arizona desert, the problem is multiplied in a context of armed conflict in Mexico. Attempting to locate, count, and identify the dead without the aid of an uncooperative state whose major response to violence has been to deny that there is a problem is even more challenging. Add to this the fact that drug cartels and other organized criminal groups actively want to obscure the identities of the dead as well as those who committed the crime. This is generally done by dissolving bodies in acid, burning the remains, or simply burying people in unmarked mass graves scattered throughout the country. Generally, this has been a grueling process, one that has led to people being threatened and killed. Few of the missing have been located or identified.

Justice in Mexico, based at the University of San Diego, notes in a 2017 report on the violence that mass graves such as those found in and around San Fernando mark a significant change in patterns of violence (Heinle et al., 2017). By targeting migrants and travelers for profit and killing non-combatants, criminal organizations have moved away from the use of violence to send a message, as is often the case with the high profile, body dumps and banners known as *narco-mantas* (Campbell, 2014). These tactics signal a much more covert approach to killing. In addition, these killings serve to further blur the lines between migration and deaths from armed conflict. Once people are abducted, they are inducted into the geography of death through torture, giving them the option of "freedom" if they agree to kill on behalf of the cartels or work as drug traffickers (Slack, 2016). This is not an escape at all; in fact, individuals are now intimately bound to the drug conflict. Abduction is a way to recruit people into the deadly conflict. Many participants in the so-called drug war were in fact coerced, made to participate by threats on their lives or their loved ones. Therefore, many who die are labeled as gang members, when in fact the process of becoming a gang member involves significant violence and coercion.

In 2017 over 250 skulls were found in the coastal state of Veracruz in what is perhaps the largest mass grave to date (Kahn, 2017). A group of mothers, dedicated to searching for their disappeared loved ones, stumbled upon the mass grave accidentally. None of the bodies identified belonged to the people for which they were searching. This is the tragic paradox of searches for the missing: it is almost impossible to find a specific individual due to the prevalence of unidentified dead scattered throughout the country. The same happened after the disappearance of 43 students in Guerrero. After they were shot by police and the military while traveling on a bus, they were taken and have not been found (GIEI, 2015). Efforts to locate the remains of the missing students in Guerrero have only unearthed clandestine graves (known colloquially as *narco-fosas*) that were unrelated to this specific massacre.

Because searches for the missing often result in discovering additional unidentified bodies in Mexico, the state has been decidedly unsupportive of these efforts. While it is difficult for loved ones of people who disappear to report this violence, the challenge is compounded when people are engaging in migration. Migration itself makes it even more difficult to count the missing simply because of the unanswered question: from where are they missing? Common retorts from authorities that migrants are simply leaving their old life behind, abandoning wives, husbands, parents, or children, only increase doubt, grief, and the ambiguity of their loss (Boss, 2010). (Im)mobility therefore has a distinct link with violence and death. Bodies in transit can easily be abducted, extorted, and killed with impunity. Once dislocated from the geographies of support that exist in a community where one has friends, family, or business associates, it is increasingly easy to make someone disappear. Compound this with the fact that movement related to undocumented migration is "illegal" and those individuals, already invested in breaking a law and remaining hidden, can go missing for weeks or months without anyone noticing. Scholars must be attentive to this link between movement and violence, as dislocated or "illegalized" bodies are increasingly targeted.

CONCLUSION

There is a need to focus explicitly on movement, violence, and death. Geographers in particular are poised to explore these spatial relationships. Understanding unconventional forms of armed conflict and how this violence forms a unique topology, whereupon some people are placed in extreme danger (e.g., targets of genocide, perceived enemies, or migrants who are exposed to dangerous physical environments, kidnapped, ransomed, killed, or recruited into transnational organized crime groups), while others can travel unharmed (e.g., wealthy foreign tourists in vacation destinations). Spaces of violence and death become highly topological as we factor in policing, enforcement, and military operations that target specific individuals such as young brown and black males. In fact, the intensity of the conflict as related to young men has led to a decrease in life expectancy for males aged 15–50 throughout Mexico (Aburto et al., 2016), leading to calls to address *juvenicidio* or youth-focused violence.

On the global scale, we must bear in mind that each of these tragedies is not occurring in isolation, nor within a sending-/receiving-country binary. The phenomena that drive people to risk so much in order to escape violence, reunite with loved ones, or seek out new economic opportunities operate at a global level and are largely interconnected. As scholars, we must step beyond the constraints confining our work and build connections that help construct theory applicable to a global level. Through our research along the US-Mexico border, we can easily forget the broad range of political, physical, and historical contexts of other borders that created similar, yet shared tragedies across the globe.

While scholars have begun to deploy geographical tools to address death in terms of the holocaust (Beorn et al., 2009) and issues such as the decay of bodies in the desert (Spradley et al., 2012), much conceptual work remains. Doing so requires serious attention to the ground-up approach of feminist geopolitics that forces us to recognize the relationships between race, gender, and sexuality that can influence death and violence for specific populations. This will help create a deeper understanding of the linkages between (im)mobility and death, as well as develop a greater empirical base of knowledge about what is actually happening to migrants as they attempt to traverse dangerous territories, all with the hopes of securing a better life for themselves and their families.

REFERENCES

Aburto, Jose, Beltrán-Sánchez, Hiram, García-Guerrero, Victor and Canudas-Romo, Vladimir (2016) Homicides in Mexico reversed life expectancy gains for men and slowed them for women, 2000–10. *Health Affairs* **35**: 88–95.

Agnew, Heather (2015) Reframing "femicide": making room for the balloon effect of drug war violence in studying female homicides in Mexico and Central America. *Territory, Politics, Governance* **3**: 428–45.

Anderson, Bruce (2008) Identifying the dead: methods utilized by the Pima County (Arizona) Office of the Medical Examiner for undocumented border crossers: 2001–2006. *Journal of Forensic Sciences* **53**: 8–15.

Anderson, Bruce and Parks, Bruce (2008) Symposium on border crossing deaths: introduction. *Journal of Forensic Sciences* **53**: 6–7.

Beorn, Waitman, Cole, Tim, Gigliotti, Simone et al. (2009) Geographies of the Holocaust. *Geographical Review* **99**: 563–74.

Boss, Pauline (2009) *Ambiguous Loss: Learning to Live with Unresolved Grief.* Cambridge, MA: Harvard University Press.

Boss, Pauline (2010) The trauma and complicated grief of ambiguous loss. *Pastoral Psychology* **59**: 137–45.

Brough, Mark, Schweitzer, Robert, Shakespeare-Finch, Jane, Vromans, Lyn and King, Julie (2012) Unpacking the micro–macro nexus: narratives of suffering and hope among refugees from Burma recently settled in Australia. *Journal of Refugee Studies* **26**: 207–25.

Cacho, Lisa Marie (2012) *Social Death: Racialized Rightlessness and the Criminalization of the Unprotected.* New York: SUNY Press.

Campbell, Howard (2014) Narco-propaganda in the Mexican "drug war": an anthropological perspective. *Latin American Perspectives* **41**: 60–77.

CBP (2017) Southwest Border deaths by fiscal year. In *Protection*, USCaB (ed.). Washington, DC: Department of Homeland Security. Retrieved from https://www.cbp.gov/sites/default/files/assets/documents/2017-Dec/BP%20Southwest%20Border%20Sector%20Deaths%20FY1998%20-%20FY2017.pdf.

CNDH (2011) Informe Especial Sobre el Secuestro de Migrantes en Mexico. In *Humanos*, CNdID (ed.), pp. 1–49. Mexico, DF: CNDH.

Cornelius, Wayne (2001) Death at the border: efficacy and unintended consequences of US immigration control policy. *Population and Development Review* **27**: 661.

Dunn, Timothy (1996) *The Militarization of the U.S.-Mexico Border, 1978–1992: Low-intensity Conflict Doctrine Comes Home.* Austin, TX: CMAS Books, University of Texas at Austin.

Eschbach, Karl, Hagan, Jacqueline, Rodriguez, Nestor, Hernandez-Leon, R. and Bailey, S. (1999) Death at the border. *International Migration Review* **33**: 430–54.

Eschbach, Karl, Hagan, Jacqueline and Rodriguez, Nestor (2003) Deaths during undocumented migration: trends and policy implications in the new era of homeland security. *In Defense of the Alien* **26**: 37.

Fargues, Philippe and Bonfanti, Sara (2014) When the best option is a leaky boat: why migrants risk their lives crossing the Mediterranean and what Europe is doing about it. Migration Policy Centre; Policy Briefs; pp. 1–16. Retrieved from http://hdl.handle.net/1814/33271.

Galtung, Johan (1964) A structural theory of aggression. *Journal of Peace Research* **1**: 95–119.

Gibler, John (2011) *To Die in Mexico: Dispatches from Inside the Drug War.* San Francisco, CA: City Lights Books.

GIEI (2015) Informe Ayotzinapa: investigación y primeras conclusiones de las desapariciones y homicidios de los normalistas de Ayotzinapa. In *Independientes*, GIdE (ed.), pp. 1–497. Mexico, DF: GIEI.

Giordano, Alberto and Spradley, Katherine (2017) Migrant deaths at the Arizona–Mexico border: spatial trends of a mass disaster. *Forensic Science International* **280**: 200–212.

Heinle, Kimberly, Rodriguez Ferreira, Octavio, Shirk, David (2017) Drug violence in Mexico data analysis through 2016. Justice in Mexico. University of San Diego. March, 2016. 60 pages.

Hughes, Cris, Algee-Hewitt, Bridget, Reineke, Robin, Clausing, Elizabeth and Anderson, Bruce (2017) Temporal patterns of Mexican migrant genetic ancestry: implications for identification. *American Anthropologist* **119**: 193–208.

Hyndman, Jennifer (2004) The (geo) politics of mobility. In *Mapping Women, Making Politics: Feminist Perspectives on Political Geography*, pp. 169–84. New York: Routledge.

Hyndman, Jennifer (2007) Feminist geopolitics revisited: body counts in Iraq. *The Professional Geographer* **59**: 35–46.

ICE (2017) ICE arrests nearly 2,000 human traffickers in 2016, identifies over 400 victims across the US. Washington, DC: Department of Homeland Security.

IOM (2017) The Missing Migrants Project. In *Centre*, IGMdA (ed.). Geneva: International Organization for Migration. Retrieved from https://missingmigrants.iom.int/.

Jones, Reece (2016) *Violent Borders: Refugees and the Right to Move*. London: Verso.

Kahn, Carrie (2017) More than 250 bodies found in mass grave in Mexico. National Public Radio, Washington, DC.

Kiragu, Esther, Rosi, Angela and Morris, Tim (2011) States of denial: a review of UNHCR's response to the protracted situation of stateless Rohingya refugees in Bangladesh. Policy Development and Evaluation Service, UNHCR. Retrieved from http://www.unhcr. org/4ee754c19. pdf.

Martínez, Daniel E., Reineke, Robin, Rubio-Goldsmith, Raquel, Anderson, Bruce, Hess, Gregory and Parks, Bruce (2013) A continued humanitarian crisis at the border: undocumented border crosser deaths recorded by the Pima County Office of the Medical Examiner, 1990–2012. Report. Binational Migration Institute. University of Arizona. Tucson, Arizona.

Martínez, Daniel, Reineke, Robin, Rubio-Goldsmith, Raquel and Parks, Bruce (2014) Structural violence and migrant deaths in southern Arizona: data from the Pima County Office of the Medical Examiner, 1990–2013. *Journal on Migration and Human Security* **2**: 257–86.

Massaro, Vanessa and Williams, Jill (2013) Feminist geopolitics. *Geography Compass* **7**: 567–77.

Missbach, Antje and Komnas, Ham (2016) Detaining asylum seekers and refugees in Indonesia. In *Detaining the Immigrant Other: Global and Transnational Issues*, p. 91. New York: Oxford University Press.

Nevins, Joseph (2002) *Operation Gatekeeper: The Rise of the "Illegal Alien" and the Making of the U.S.-Mexico Boundary*. New York: Routledge.

Nevins, Joseph (2007) Dying for a cup of coffee? Migrant deaths in the US-Mexico border region in a neoliberal age. *Geopolitics* **12**: 228–47.

Nevins, Joseph and Aizeki, Mizue (2008) *Dying to Live: A Story of U.S. Immigration in an Age of Global Apartheid*. San Francisco, CA: Open Media/City Lights Books.

Reineke, Róbin (2016) *Naming the Dead: Identification and Ambiguity along the US-Mexico Border*. Tucson, AZ: University of Arizona.

Reineke, Robin and Martínez, Daniel (2014) Migrant deaths in the Americas (United States and Mexico). In *Fatal Journeys: Tracking Lives Lost during Migration*, pp. 45–83. Geneva, Switzerland: International Organization of Migration. Retrieved from https://publications.iom.int/system/files/pdf/fataljourneys_coun tingtheuncounted.pdf.

Rubio-Goldsmith, Raquel, McCormick, Melissa, Martínez, Daniel and Duarte, Inez (2006) *The "Funnel Effect" & Recovered Bodies of Unauthorized Migrants Processed by the Pima County Office of the Medical Examiner, 1990–2005*. Tucson, AZ: Binational Migration Institute, University of Arizona.

Rubio-Goldsmith, Raquel, O'Leary, Anna and Soto, Gabriela (2014) *Protocol Development for the Standardization of Identification and Examination of UBC Bodies along the U.S. Mexico Border: A Best Practices Manual*. Tucson, AZ: Binational Migration Institute, University of Arizona.

Rodríguez, Josue (2017) Reportan oficialmente más de 30 mil personas desaparecidas en Mexico. *Vanguardia*. Piedras Negras, Coahuila.

Sanchez, Gabriela (2014) *Human Smuggling and Border Crossings*. London: Routledge.

Slack, Jeremy (2016) Captive bodies: migrant kidnapping and deportation in Mexico. *Area* **48**: 271–7.

Slack, Jeremy and Campbell, Howard (2016) On Narco-coyotaje: illicit regimes and their impacts on the US-Mexico border. *Antipode* **48**: 1380–99.

Slack, Jeremy, Martínez, Daniel, Lee, Alison and Whiteford, Scott (2016) The geography of border militarization: violence, death and health in Mexico and the United States. *Journal of Latin American Geography* **15**: 7–32.

Smith, Saphora, Chirbas, Kurt, Muse, Dynast and Silva, Daniella (2017) Truck driver in custody after 9 suspected migrants are found dead in parking lot. NBC News, San Antonio, TX.

Soto, Gabriela and Martínez, Daniel (2018) The geography of migrant death: implications for policy and forensic science. *Sociopolitics of Migrant Death and Repatriation: Perspectives from Forensic Science*. In Latham, K. and O'Daniel, A. (eds), pp. 67–82. Cham, Switzerland: Springer.

Spener, David (2009) *Clandestine Crossings: Migrants and Coyotes on the Texas-Mexico Border*. Ithaca, NY: Cornell University Press.

Spradley, Katherine, Hamilton, Michelle and Giordano, Alberto (2012) Spatial patterning of vulture scavenged human remains. *Forensic Science International* **219**: 57–63.

USCIS (2017) Number of Form I-914, Application for T Nonimmigrant Status, by Fiscal Year, Quarter, and Case Status 2008–2017. In *Services*, USCaI (ed.). Washington, DC: Department of Homeland Security. Retrieved from https://www.uscis.gov/sites/default/files/USCIS/Resources/Reports%20and%20Studies/Immigration%20 Forms%20Data/Victims/I914t_visastatistics_fy2016_qtr1.pdf.

Vogt, Wendy (2016) Stuck in the middle with you: the intimate labours of mobility and smuggling along Mexico's migrant route. *Geopolitics* **21**: 366–86.

Williams, Jill and Massaro, Vanessa (2013) Feminist geopolitics: unpacking (in) security, animating social change. *Geopolitics* **18**: 751–8.

Wright, Melissa (2011) Necropolitics, narcopolitics, and femicide: gendered violence on the Mexico-U.S. border. *Signs* **36**: 707–31.

12. *'Ceci n'est pas la migration'*: countering the cunning cartopolitics of the Frontex migration map

Henk van Houtum and Rodrigo Bueno Lacy

THE FRONTEX MAP AND ITS DISCONTENTS

Figure 12.1 is a migration map. However, it is not just any map. It is the map used by the European Border and Coast Guard Agency – better known as Frontex – in what they suggestively refer to as their quarterly 'risk analysis' to depict the 'threats' that the European Union (EU) faces along its external borders. In isolation, this map might not look like much more than an obscure image confined to one of many technical risk analyses by an equally murky EU border-control agency. However, seen as part of the assemblage of narratives, practices and images that render its visualization meaningful – that is, its semiotic dimension – we will argue that this map puts together a telling discursive mosaic. For, rather than mere images, political maps of this sort are of unparalleled import: they stand as cultural testimonies that allow us to peek into the naked worldview of their makers (Wintle 1999, 2009; Brotton 2013; Bueno Lacy and Van Houtum 2015).

The striking power wielded by this map becomes manifest once we realize that it is by no means a stand-alone exception. Throughout the years, the repetition of its cartographic structure across all kinds of institutional documents has turned its visual composition into the 'normal' cartographic representation of undocumented migration in the EU. And as Foucault argued, it is repetition and hegemony which are the decisive patterns that give a discourse its political sway (Foucault 1981). Variations of either this map – which largely preserve the characteristic elements of its visual arrangement – or the narrative geography that codes its message have found their way into European societies through media (e.g., Lyman 2015; Reimann 2015; Alameda and Gutiérrez Garrido 2016; Booth 2016; The Economist 2016; Beauchamp 2017), education (Wigen 2005), academia (Van Reekum and Schinkel 2016) and non-governmental organizations (NGOs) (Canadian Red Cross 2015).

In this chapter we argue against this Frontex map. Its provenance, manufacture and visual composition make its message pass as thought-through, objective and dispassionate and its recommendations look like impartial, reasonable and inevitable. Yet, under closer examination this map amounts to blatant cartographic malpractice, tendentious science and ruinous policymaking for the EU. In other words, this is the kind of 'science' society needs to be defended against (Feyerabend 1975).

In what follows we distinguish three fundamental flaws of this influential Frontex map – which we deem to be conscious. These 'three myths,' if you will, make up the basic layout of the map: the grid, the arrows and the frame. We will also discuss the distortions that these myths instill in the general perception of undocumented migration across the EU and how they influence its political debate on EU's borders and Europeanness.

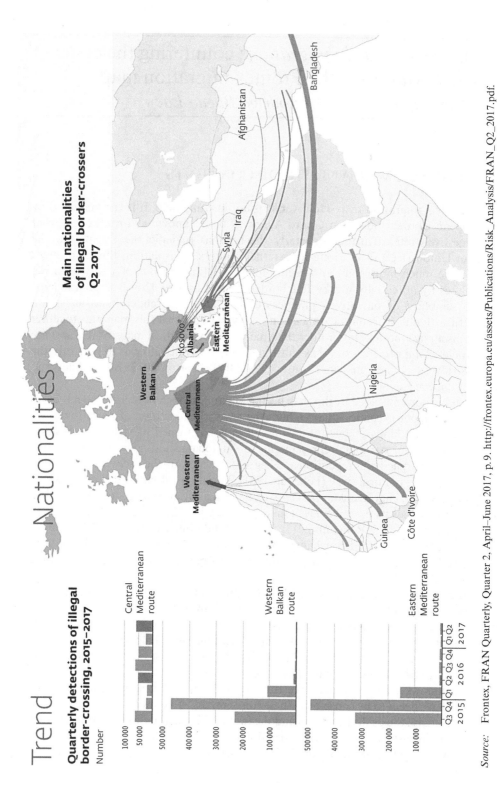

Source: Frontex, FRAN Quarterly, Quarter 2, April–June 2017, p. 9. http://frontex.europa.eu/assets/Publications/Risk_Analysis/FRAN_Q2_2017.pdf.

Figure 12.1 *Undocumented migration to the European Union according to Frontex*

THE GRID

Let us start with the less obvious yet arguably not less important underlying cartographic infrastructure of this map: the grid of nation states. By using this fixed territorial order to represent migration, the Frontex map is predicated on the assumption inherent to its checkered background: namely, that the world *is, can* and *should be seen* as composed of neatly distinguishable compartments; all demarcated by the same thin lines representing their national borders, as if they were containers (Agnew 1994). Although the national grid constitutes a taken-for-granted backdrop shared by all kinds of cartography – from school primers to Google Maps (Farman 2010, pp. 877–8) – its borders are more than mere drawings on an illustration of the world: they are the visual repercussion of a pervasive normative system of statecraft.

These lines symbolize the foundation of the nation state: a political technology that has strived to render territory, its inhabitants and their interactions into readable, measurable and malleable information (Scott 1998). The national grid misleadingly appears to neutrally depict nation states as immobile realities, which provides a subtle but effective legitimization of the spurious national history that mystifies their nature as timeless and uncontested (Renan 1882, p. 37; Hobsbawm 1990, p. 12). What this cartographically legitimized anachronism thereby does is naturalize and normalize the boundaries of nation states while promoting the perception that nations are what their states claim them to be: essential and anciently bound to the territorial boundaries that contain them today (see, e.g., Harley 1989; Ó Tuathail 1996; Walby 2003; Wimmer and Schiller 2003; Parker and Vaughan-Williams et al. 2009, p. 586; Brotton 2013, pp. 289–326; Branch 2014).

Visually, the logic of the national grid operates through its simultaneous erasure of people. We see the boxes of each nation state conspicuously devoid of their populations. A depiction of the world based on this visual premise engages with its spectators in a dehumanizing way, suggesting that the world is a two-dimensional plane consisting only of territorial enclosures owned by state apparatuses. In this world without inhabitants, people are labeled, assumed or merely suggested by the territories in which they are boxed. The deletion of people conceals their movement and the myriad ways in which their bodies and cultural interactions have always defied borders at a ceaseless pace. This anachronic essentialization of the nation state makes the Frontex map (as well as any other map based on the national grid) a surreptitious legitimization of a national biopolitics that, by design, tends to create regimes of political control over foreign bodies trying to permeate its delineated markers. The national grid's normalization of nativity requires the implicit condemnation of the non-native. If people are *natural* inhabitants only in the country where they were born (i.e., natives), then it follows that migrants – a politically constructed category – are *unnatural* intruders in other countries. In the case of the Frontex map, the only people represented are those who apparently confront the 'natural b/order' of the national grid – making them by default an exception and an abnormality (Van Houtum and Van Naerssen 2002; Van Houtum 2010a). Although all other movements of people happening within and across national territories – be it of citizens, tourists, students, commuters or business travelers – greatly outnumber the travels of undocumented migrants, they are all left out of the picture.

This fear of foreigners is aggravated by the Frontex map's emphasis on undocumented migrants, which suggests that their particular bodies and the difference they carry with them (in language, appearance and behavior) is not only a potential threat but an allegedly illegal, even criminal offense to the 'organic' national state – that is, the 'purity' of the nation state's history and people (Kristof 1960, pp. 21–8; Foucault 1978–79 [2004]; Bashford 2004).

In fact, the discrimination of undocumented migrants does not begin at the borders of the EU but already in their home countries, where they have to ask for permission – that is, a visa – to travel to the EU. The EU works with a positive and negative Schengen list. All individuals holding passports identifying them as what the EU considers to be the 'wrong place of birth' make up the negative Schengen list – a total of 135 countries out of 195 – for whom the chances of getting a visa to the EU are near zero (Van Houtum 2010b). This constitutes a clear discrimination on the basis of the accident of birth, forbidden by law in all countries of the EU and a violation of Article 1 of the Universal Declaration of Human Rights, stating that 'all human beings are born free and equal in dignity and rights' (UN 1948), yet this has become standard practice along the external borders of the EU. Contrastingly, those born in one of the countries on the positive list, which are dominantly highly industrialized societies and are apparently seen as less different than 'us,' can travel without much effort to the EU in the comfort of a plane. The paradox is that undocumented migrants fleeing countries on the negative list can apply for regular asylum only irregularly, that is, illicitly and without being allowed to take the official, direct and safe modes of transport. Hence, the toughest border is not the iron of the barbed wire or the concrete of the fences that make up 'Fortress Europe' but this oxymoronic paper border of the EU's visa regime (Van Houtum and Lucassen 2016).

The near absence of legal migration channels for refugees has created a billion-euro smuggling industry (Huysmans 2006; Van Houtum 2010b; The Migrants' Files 2015; Jansen 2016). It has led to a shocking fatality rate among undocumented migrants traveling to the EU, making its external border the deadliest on the planet (Van Houtum 2010b). The apartheid regime of the paper fortress is further defended by a second layer of defense: the iron border. Over time a highly militarized EU borderscape of fences, border guards and detention camps have been put in place to further immobilize undocumented travelers (Figure 12.2). What is more, ghastly policies like the extrajudicial detainment and maltreatment of undocumented migrants are not regarded as extreme anymore but rather as the new normal, acceptable, even necessary policies advocated no longer by marginal extremists but by 'decent,' 'rational,' 'normal' governments across the EU (Van Houtum and Bueno Lacy 2017).

The machine's bludgeoning border guards, unsanitary overcrowded facilities and impoverishing laws – that deprive refugees of the means to work for their own sustenance – force upon undocumented migrants the kind of attributes that the nationalist and xenophobic biopolitical regime most dreads: filth, poverty, violence and overall social inadaptability. The consequence is that the most dehumanizing metaphors to qualify their movement have become seemingly unremarkable: everyday, undocumented migrants have become compared to floods, fluxes, tsunamis, insect plagues, swarms and invasions (Van Houtum and Lucassen 2016). And so the apartheid of the paper border regime that the EU itself has created, coupled with strong iron borders, has not only made it practically impossible for many refugees to enter regularly and safely, but also reinforced racist prejudices and legitimized the idea that undocumented migrants should be seen as outlaws and criminals (Van Houtum 2010b; Gorodzeisky and Semyonov 2015; De Genova 2017).

Source: https://www.theguardian.com/world/2017/aug/08/eu-refugees-serbia-afghanistan-taliban.

Figure 12.2   EU's migrant cages

The media also plays a central role: although cameras zooming into the procession of deprived refugees – who have left everything behind and traveled an unhospitable territory using vulnerable modes of travel like poorly equipped and overcrowded boats – might breed empathy, they also make their material, legal and physical weakness seem undeniable, thus buttressing the biopolitical regime that justifies taking away their dignity and competence on the basis of their inferiority (Pupavac 2008; Esses et al. 2013).

The images of refugee detention camps and fortress-like borders – like the one shown in Figure 12.2 – illustrate the teleological mechanisms of this system. They make undocumented migrants look like a species from a different civilization and in doing so validates their animal-like representation by those who want to keep them at bay. If images of people languishing behind fences or in cages come to seem acceptable for an increasingly large proportion of voters across the EU it is because a long process of dehumanization has already taken place. In sum, the movement of African and Muslim/ Arab undocumented migrants – the only people represented on the Frontex map as a risk – has been increasingly curtailed through all sorts of direct (i.e., paper borders, iron fences, incarceration) or indirect forms of b/ordering and othering (e.g., the EU's deal with Turkey or Libya). The humiliation and abasement of the dark-skinned, poor and exploited along the EU's borders has become an accepted policy to handle human beings defined by their belonging to what has been constructed in EUropean discourse as an undesirable geographical provenance. And it is this dehumanizing b/ordering and othering regime that the Frontex map through its uncritical cartography of a nationalistic biopolitics co-opts and thereby normalizes.

THE ARROWS

Apart from the essentialistic antagonism between *normal fixity* and unwanted *abnormal mobility* that it promotes, a second flaw of the Frontex map is, we would argue, its use of menacing arrows. In the semiotics of maps, the arrow has become the unchallenged symbol to represent movement because of its undisputed navigational practicality: it depicts information about the initiation, route and destination of movement, a path that is followed in order to get from A to B. The value of this knowledge spans everything from a recreational convenience to an indispensable necessity for those undertaking any sort of spatial journey: from a tourist trying to find her way through an unfamiliar city to a container ship plowing its way across the world's oceans.

However, an arrow has also another, more clandestine and less scrutinized existence: it can turn into one of the most forceful symbolical devices when its use is extrapolated from the purely navigational to the political. The way in which arrows are used in political cartography steps beyond strictly navigational purposes and ventures into the realm of metaphor and hyperbole. When arrows are politically used to depict risks, as is the case in the Frontex map, they make the transit of people seeking shelter or work look as dangerous as incoming armed forces – particularly when the former have been construed as a metaphor of the latter.

The effect of 'encirclement' that the arrows produce on the Frontex map has been a much favored visual proposition used to forecast a desperate situation: the impending demise of the EU. Here, as in propagandistic military maps, arrows are being used to symbolize an imminent threat. The use of arrows in this particular visual layout paints such a hopeless situation that it calls upon the viewer to support either a resolute military response or any other measure, regardless of how extreme it might be, to defend the existence of a continent and its civilization.

A famous map relying on the technique of encirclement is 'The Iron Ring around Germany' (Figure 12.3). Published in 1931, this German map justifies the rearmament of Germany and the invasion of its neighboring countries. The 'war power' of each country is represented as a solid block around Germany. This map shows a passive, defenseless Germany which, in contrast to the millions of soldiers from the countries threatening it, has only a barely visible and comparatively insignificant army of only a hundred thousand men.

To give credence to this map is to believe that Germany is under an imminent existential threat. Germany's demise seems inevitable unless something is quickly done. As a German of the time, to see this map is to feel aggravated by the armament limitations imposed by the Versailles Treaty and to wonder why Germany is still respecting an agreement which is so evidently unjust, visibly threatening the very existence of the German nation. This map's message is that the countries surrounding Germany are its enemies, that they are ready to attack and that Germany is alone and defenseless. The subtle but unequivocal recommendation is the breach of the Versailles Treaty and perhaps even the support of any policies necessary to face the threat posed by the surrounding armies – be it rearmament, war or perhaps even a crackdown on political enemies. It is a map calling for the militarization of Germany on the grounds of an illusory engulfing threat.

We may feel inclined to think that maps such as this belong to a more unscrupulous world and that this kind of propaganda cartography is not done anymore. However, we argue that the Frontex map relies on similar techniques of cartographic propaganda. The

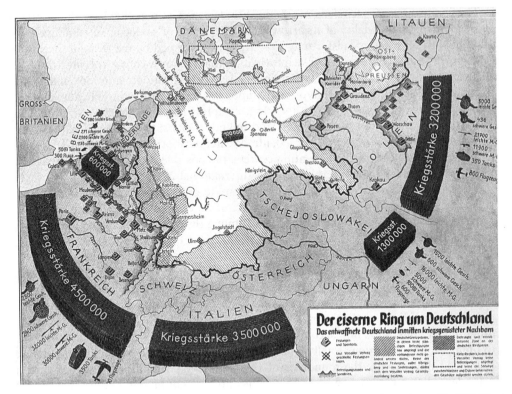

Source: J.J. Weber (ed.) (1931) Der Eiserne Ring um Deutschland. Leipzig: Illustrirte Zeitung, Nr. 4523 (19 November). https://www.abebooks.de/servlet/BookDetailsPL?bi=22392516875&searchurl=kn%3DGem%25E 4lde%26pt%3Dmag%26sortby%3D1&cm_sp=snippet-_-srp1-_-title14.

Figure 12.3   An epitomic invasion map

sneakiness of propaganda maps is that they appear to provide their audiences with nothing but raw information which viewers then can use to contrive sophisticated geopolitical analyses and draw astute conclusions about how to deal with geopolitical issues like undocumented migration. These maps flatter the viewer's judiciousness by making him believe that he can look at a world of insurmountable complexity right in the eye and defy it with a clever geopolitical maneuver. Yet, the most beautiful trick the devil ever played was to convince you he did not exist:[1] the analysis and conclusions have already been anticipated by the mapmaker, who has provided a carefully selected amount of spatial information and geopolitical symbolism. The visual composition of propaganda maps is seductive: they are embellished and ordered in such a way as to lead all viewers to the same conclusion while letting them take pride in believing that it's their own trail of thought which took them there.

---

[1]   Paraphrasing Charles Baudelaire: 'Mes chers frères, n'oubliez jamais, quand vous entendrez vanter le progrès des lumières, que la plus belle des ruses du Diable est de vous persuader qu'il n'existe pas!', a phrase in his poem 'Le joueur généreux' (1869). https://fr.wikisource.org/wiki/Le_Joueur_g%C3%A9n%C3%A9reux.

The impression of encirclement on the Frontex map is magnified by the strongly misleading unidirectionality of its arrows. The pilgrimage of undocumented migrants is fraught with a variety of misfortunes that are entirely denied by the straight lines with which their route is represented. The information that an arrow conveys about a tourist's place of origin, traveling route, destination as well as motivations, emotions, intentions and overall ease of mobility cannot be extrapolated to the distressing phenomenon of undocumented migration. Straight lines do not capture stops that might last months or years sleeping rough in makeshift tents and unknown cities; the perpetual paranoia of being found and imprisoned or deported; life-threatening journeys through the desert; the languishment in overcrowded detention centers; the possible endurance of rape, slavery and overall corporeal abuse (e.g., Amnesty International 2016; Kemp 2017). Thus, the arrows' smooth continuity and straightness promote geographical and temporal distortions that misrepresent the harrowing experience of undocumented migration. We get no sense at all of undocumented migrants being among the most vulnerable and materially insecure people in the world. On the contrary, it is the EU who is portrayed as being at risk.

Rather than a straight and unbroken line the movement of undocumented migrants is in practice of a more zigzagging nature – and could easily be represented as such – that includes long periods of waiting and immobility (Van Houtum 2012). What is more, rather than unidirectional arrows it would be more accurate to visualize circularity in order to take emigration into account – which for many countries is of a comparable size to immigration yet remains totally ignored in the political debate on immigration in the EU – and thus capture the roundness of the migratory phenomenon. Furthermore, a color degradation in the arrows could show the difficulties of migrants' journeys, perhaps even indicating the level of abuse that they fall prey to along certain paths. In short, there is an abundance of creative choices to represent the migratory phenomenon more accurately and honestly and thus to inform a more scientific policymaking in the configuration of the EU's border regime.

An enlightening example of a map without the misleading use of arrows is a map made by Doctors Without Borders (MSF for its abbreviation in French), an NGO that provides medical care across the world to people in need. Rather than a world map compartmentalized by the national grid, MSF provides a diagrammatic map intended to chart the fortunes and misfortunes of the odyssey that Syrian refugees undergo when attempting to travel to the EU (Figure 12.4). Their map takes the board of the popular game 'Snakes and Ladders' as an inspiration: snakes take players on an unpleasant trip and ladders on a lucky one. In the case of Syrian refugees, snakes trace the vicissitudes that make their journey more perilous and ladders the paths and circumstances that make it easier. The contrast with the Frontex map is not merely of structure (a diagrammatic map rather than a world's projection) but ideological. In sharp contrast to the Frontex map, which represents the routes of undocumented migrants into the EU with the ambition to create a border regime more efficient at stopping them, the map made by MSF takes the perspective of migrants and the many threats they face along the way in order to protect them. Differently put, unlike the Frontex map, which centers on the national grid and represents refugees as a threat to *national security* – and the racial prejudices that accompany national preconceptions – the MSF map is centered on the plight of refugees and thus on an approach concerned with *human security*. The ideo-

Source: Doctors Without Borders. https://www.doctorswithoutborders.ca/node/2759.

Figure 12.4   *'This is not a game'*

logical difference distinguishes a hypocritical supranational organization that makes up a struggle with human trafficking – a perverse distortion of refugees' predicament – in order to criminalize the kind of migration that it has an obligation to protect (Refugee Convention 1951) from an NGO that is truly concerned with the wellbeing of Syrian refugees.

THE FRAME

The third and final strikingly flawed element that we wish to draw attention to is the frame of the map. The choice to highlight the EU on a Frontex map is of course not illogical.[2] Yet, as is often the case with models – such as maps – what is left out is as important as what is represented. The Frontex map fails to deliver any kind of global – let alone historical – comparative perspective that may allow us to see that the undocumented migrants coming to the EU actually represent a minority of the overall global migration numbers. According to the United Nations Population Fund (UNFPA), only 3.3 percent of the world's population lives outside their country of birth and this has remained unchanged for decades (more than 96 percent of mankind is hence not a migrant).[3] Of these 247.5 million people, there are approximately 20 million immigrants from non-EU countries residing in the EU (about 3.7 percent of the EU's total population).[4] Of these immigrants living in the EU, between 547,335 (Sabbati and Poptcheva 2015, p. 3) and 3.8 million are 'irregular migrants' (IOM 2018) – a controversial figure given the stealthy nature of the sort of migration that it tries to measure. This means that undocumented migrants make up only between 0.1 and 0.7 percent of the EU's total population.

According to recent figures, there are around 50 million undocumented migrants worldwide (IOM 2018), which means that even if we assume the highest estimate of undocumented migrants in the EU, they amount to only 7.6 percent of the world's total. The implication is, unlike that which the Frontex map so boldly suggests, more than 90 percent of all undocumented travelers in the world do not go to the EU at all. Most of them go to neighboring countries, close to their country of birth. The conclusion to which these numbers lead us paints a remarkably different picture than the one offered by the Frontex map: not only does the EU receive a small fraction of the total global population of asylum seekers and undocumented migrants but their numbers do not amount to a considerable demographic pressure for the EU by any measurement.

And yet, what we see on the Frontex map, from the very bottom of Africa and the farthest corners of Asia, is a multitude of whopping arrows traveling unimpeded across

---

[2]   That being said, to equate the EU with the continent of Europe, including Switzerland or Norway, for example, and excluding the EU's Overseas Countries and Territories, is a common and consciously made mistake (see Van Houtum and Boedeltje 2008). For a more complete territorial representation of the EU see: https://en.wikipedia.org/wiki/Special_member_state_territories_and_the_European_Union#/media/File:EU_OCT_and_OMR_map_en.png.

[3]   Website of the United Nations Population Fund: http://www.unfpa.org/migration/.

[4]   Eurostat's website: People in the EU – statistics on origin of residents: http://ec.europa.eu/eurostat/statistics-explained/index.php/People_in_the_EU_%E2%80%93_statistics_on_origin_of_residents#Foreign-born_residents_from_countries_outside_the_EU.

the Afro-Asian landmasses to reach the EU. Their sheer length and profusion suggest that vast populations of entire continents are coordinately moving into the EU in one single motion that converges at three bottlenecks along its external borders. Although most arrows seem to have specific countries as their point of origin, it is not very clear how rigorous this might be. The source of one arrow is lost beyond the margins of the map, leaving the onlooker to assume that some of this migration harks back to 'somewhere in the far east' and thus implying that what matters about this map is not the specificity of its details but its broader message: the arrows and the migratory movements they refer to might simply come from everywhere around the world, and especially the world of less affluent Muslims and Africans, with the EU as their sole destination.

The misleading framing is further magnified by the convergence of all the migratory movements in the truly gigantic arrowheads piercing into Spain, Italy and the Balkans. Their size is so exaggerated that it looks as if the number of incoming undocumented people were as large as the entire Iberian Peninsula, France, Germany or Britain. Compare the Frontex map's message to the number of yearly tourists visiting Europe (Van Houtum and Boedeltje 2009). France alone receives over 80 million tourists a year (UNWTO 2017, p. 6): what kind of thick arrowheads would that number warrant using the scale of the Frontex map?

Apart from the evident exaggeration in the size of the arrowheads, the colors chosen in the frame also exert a powerful narrative touch. Color has been shown to 'activate different motivations and consequently enhance performances on different types of cognitive tasks' (Mehta and Zhu 2009, p. 1226) – that is, tasks that require a great deal of mental activity such as decision and policymaking. On the Frontex map, most arrows are a shade of red, a color associated across cultures with abnormality, danger, warning, sexual promiscuity, anger and fear (e.g., Hupka et al. 1997, p. 166; Elliot et al. 2007; Gerend and Sias 2009; Feltman and Elliot 2011).

Contrast the color of the intimidating crimson arrows of undocumented refugees with the appeasing blue of the EU, a color 'often associated with openness, peace, and tranquility (e.g., ocean and sky)' (Mehta and Zu 2009, p. 1226), telling the viewer in no uncertain terms that foreboding flows of threatening undocumented migrants are overrunning the peaceful, open and vulnerable EU. It creates a much revealing contrast between the agency of undocumented migrants and the docility and inactivity of the EU. As if the EU had neither responsibility nor leverage in the global geopolitics – let alone the colonial history – that produce these migratory movements. For instance, the role that the EU had in aggravating the causes of these arrivals in spite of its military adventurism in Afghanistan and Libya or its indolence in Syria is completely neglected (Bueno Lacy et al. 2016). The visa regime of the EU that we previously discussed and which discriminates on the basis of where one is born is completely omitted too, even though it makes it impossible for more than two-thirds of the world to travel to the EU legally, hence provoking undocumented travels on board boats and other means, for both migrants looking for better lives and those fleeing war (Van Houtum 2010b). In short, what the map's frame of undocumented migration into the EU completely dismisses is that the misery of people seeking refuge in one of the most prosperous regions of the world does not pose a massive security threat to be averted, but rather constitutes a relatively humble challenge for which its emergence and persistence the EU is itself partly responsible.

OVERVIEW: THE CARTOPOLITICS OF THE FRONTEX MAP

This overview of the three flaws that we have critiqued on the Frontex map should allow us to regard this cartographic artifact as somewhat of a Rorschach test. Whether the Frontex map shows purposeful ideology or subconscious prejudice is unclear. Either way, the viewer is ultimately exposed to a frame and visual composition in which a threatening invasion of migrants is taking over a defenseless EU. The trope of danger against innocence, poor Africans and Muslims against Christians, red versus blue. This is the classical dichotomy on which usually the worst kind of ethnocentric violence is constructed – 'friend vs foe' (Schmitt 1932). Although this is not a new discourse, it is a biopolitical discourse whose presence is troubling to recognize in the official cartography of the EU. The cartographic replication of this inherently discriminatory trope in the Frontex map should by no means be regarded as a small symbolic affront to European society and the EU project. Regardless of how unintentional the map's iconography might be or how unaware onlookers might be about its discursive heritage, these accidents do not make the map's potentially unintended message less striking nor its geopolitical implications less meaningful.

We have previously referred to this intertwining of cartography and geopolitics as *cartopolitics* (Van Houtum 2012, 2013; Bueno Lacy and Van Houtum 2015): a political discourse that relies on cartography to b/order geography and thus to b/order history, culture and people through the geographical imaginations that maps arouse. By manufacturing perceptions of all-encompassing geographical scale, cartographic artifacts implant in people's heads a mediated reality. This is a world people assume to know and are confident to act upon even though the only contact they might ever have had with it is through the indirect experience of representations someone else has made available to them – through school textbooks, newspapers, television, literature, the internet and its social media, movies or other informational channels.

'Men have already learned to distrust words and figures, but they have not yet learned to distrust maps' (Kristof 1960, p. 45), perhaps because unlike language and mathematics, the semiotics of visual language belong to a specialized realm with which most people are unfamiliar. With the exception of people who by profession are inclined to become acutely aware of the power of representations – like art historians, visual artists and filmmakers – most people tend to be unaware that seeing is as much a learning process as speaking (Berger 1972). As for the Frontex cartographers and EU policymakers behind the 'invasion map' that we have discussed here, what their depiction of undocumented migration into the EU reveals is a set of discourses so antithetical to the ethos of the EU one could perhaps even call it *Euroskeptic*.

These discourses advocate the long-held prejudices and ideologies of a xenophobic pedigree that we have discussed here and which are being taken up by the surge of anti-EU movements brewing all throughout the EU. These discursive streams run through the history of European expansionism or what colloquially though inaccurately is called 'the West': a history of racist imperialism that keeps exerting a powerful pressure on the steering wheel of Europe's history (Mishra 2017). What the iconography of Frontex's invasion cartography seems to proclaim so shamelessly are discourses that we assume both Frontex and EU policymakers would find uncomfortable to admit in spoken or written words. However, we suspect that widespread iconographic and, particularly, cartographic illiteracy is what allows these maps to go unchallenged. Perhaps this ignorance

Source: http://www.dagelijksestandaard.nl/2017/02/nieuwe-campagnespot-pvv-is-een-schitterende-patriotti
sche-ode-aan-nederland.

Figure 12.5   *The Frontex map as part of the discourse of the EU's xenophobic and*
Euroskeptic political spectrum

is where maps derive their power from and what makes their study an indispensable yet
undeveloped endeavor.

Given the pervasiveness of the anti-immigrant discourse crystallized in the Frontex
map, it should not come as a surprise to see one of the most extreme nationalists and
EUropskeptics, Geert Wilders – leader of the Freedom Party (PVV) in the Netherlands –
borrowing the exact same cartopolitical technique as Frontex to advance the Islamophobic
and Euroskeptic platform of his political party (Figure 12.5). The same as the Frontex
map, Wilders' map features straight and menacing red arrows of migrants from all over
the world encircling a pure, vulnerable, blue Europe.

This symmetry between official EUropean and extreme nationalistic, anti-EU cartography should sound a shrieking alarm bell among EU policymakers and the EU's
mapmakers: this calls for 'an examination of the history – and stubborn persistence – of
racist imperialism' in Europe (Mishra 2017) and the symbols and overall iconography on
which it relies (Bueno Lacy and Van Houtum 2015). Discourses of this sort infiltrate the
cartography, symbols and overall political myth on which the EU is based (Bottici 2007).
Our caveat is humble and simple: even though the EU might argue that it feels it is unable
to create a better border management regime for undocumented migrants due to political
constraints, at the very least it should try to avoid taking the side of the very authoritarian
and discriminatory Euroskeptics that thrive on promoting its demise. An easy front for
this discursive resistance to start making a first stand would be the Frontex maps.

CONCLUSION: *CECI N'EST PAS LA MIGRATION*

The Frontex map presents itself as a neutral and objective truth on the basis of which
border policies along the EU's external borders can be formulated. Yet, its effect is

precisely the opposite. Through Frontex, the EU has crafted a map whose representation of undocumented migration legitimizes its border policies by inventing a cartopolitical truth that casts a more becoming light upon border policies that under closer examination reveal themselves to be heinous. As we have argued, the arrangement of cartographic and iconographic choices – for example, scale, focus, projection, arrows, colors, borders, legends, title and overall visual signs[5] – on the Frontex map create an image of undocumented migration that bears little resemblance with the phenomenon itself.

This invasion map illustrates some of the worst iconographic deficiencies with which mainstream cartography visualizes the movement of undocumented people as well as the main unsubstantiated narrative it promotes. In a nutshell, the overall message of this map is a nativist diagnosis about 'non-European' immigration into the EU and a subtle but violent recommendation to fix it. This is not a trivial matter. The relevance of this particular map is that, unfortunately, it does not represent a rarity but the norm, not only in cartography but in the larger discourse and 'spectacle industry' that undocumented migration to the EU has become (De Genova 2011; Jones 2016).

The map not only misinterprets or misrepresents but it wildly exaggerates and criminalizes migration. This is the mechanism through which the EU is excusing the rapid increase of international pacts that outsource the violation of international refugee law to more unscrupulous authoritarian regimes, thereby not selling out its own values – particularly the respect for the rule of law and human rights – but also exposing itself to blackmail by these very regimes that do not share them (Van Houtum and Lucassen 2016; Zoeteweij and Turhan 2017). This is how both the modern slavery that is being configured along the migratory routes of North Africa and the increasingly populated graveyard at the bottom of the Mediterranean Sea are being justified. And this is how the multiplication of spaces of exception that run against the liberal-democratic principles of the EU is being excused (Agamben 2005; De Genova and Peutz 2010; Van Houtum and Bueno Lacy 2017). The EU and its Member States are trying to conceal their humanitarian irresponsibility and overall mismanagement of EUrope's borders behind the travesty of a patronizing high ground: that it would be better for undocumented migrants if they would not take the dangerous journey to begin with; and that smugglers are to blame for undocumented migration. As if the flight undertaken by undocumented migrants was much of a choice or less of a right and as if the smuggling of migrants was not an industry propelled by the very border regime that the EU has put in place.

There is a farcical oddity in all this. By misrepresenting what undocumented migration entails and by omitting the role that the EU plays in the larger geopolitical landscape into which this migratory movement is embedded, invasion maps like those used by Frontex and the discourses that they carry with them contribute to make the lives of both undocumented migrants and EU citizens more precarious (Verhofstadt 2016; Bilgic and Pace 2017). The border policies that this map tacitly advocates run against the postwar project of European integration itself, which was conceived precisely to avert the perpetration of the atrocities that the Frontex map implicitly sanctions (Van der Ploeg 2006, p. 178; Van Houtum and Pijpers 2007; De Haas 2008; De Giorgi 2010; The Economist 2017). And so, the foolishness of this improbably sophisticated yet auto-immune border regime, this

---

[5]   For the sake of brevity in this chapter categorized as grid, arrows and frame.

border disorder (Bueno Lacy and Van Houtum 2013), is that no one wins from it: neither undocumented migrants nor the EU.

The surrealist painter René Magritte famously titled one of his paintings: *ceci n'est pas une pipe* ('This is not a pipe'). The apparent contradiction between the representation that it showed (a pipe) and the painting's title (this is not a pipe) was meant to confront the viewer with a seemingly trivial yet widely unacknowledged unawareness: the shape of a pipe painted with oil on a canvas creates a deceptive fantasy about the tangible object it represents. Real only because it so closely resembles what we assume it represents. Our unawareness about the detachment between representations and the objects they refer to prevents us from even questioning the possibility that there might be not only a slight difference between an image and the thing it represents, but an entire disconnection, perhaps a purposeful distortion and even a complete lie. The Frontex map is just like that pipe. To believe that it truly and unambiguously represents migration or sensible policies to address it is a lie made and conveyed by its makers. A 'surreality' made political. However, compared to Magritte's pipe, Frontex's invasion map exerts real life-and-death consequences. Moreover, the treachery of images that so concerned and fascinated Magritte has already been acknowledged by some policies: if the regal insignia on cigarette packages – and their appealing suggestions of glamour and wealth – are being countered these days with gruesome visual warnings about the perniciousness of their contents' lethal impact on health, why not temper this violent cartography with a similar caution? This is our 'Margrittean warning' – if you will. While the Frontex map is intended as a depiction of a 'risk analysis,' the biggest risk it entails is its failure to represent the repercussions for the EU of the discourses it promotes and the policies it recommends. *Ceci n'est pas la migration.*[6]

REFERENCES

Agamben G. (2005) *State of Exception*. Chicago, IL: University of Chicago Press.

Agnew J. (1994) The territorial trap: the geographical assumptions of international relations theory. *Review of International Political Economy* **1**(1): 53–80.

Alameda D. and Gutiérrez Garrido O. (2016) Ruta de los migrantes hacia la UE. *El País* (19 July). Available at: https://elpais.com/elpais/2015/08/26/media/1440588850_385429.html.

Amnesty International (2016) Refugees and migrants fleeing sexual violence, abuse and exploitation in Libya. Available at: https://www.amnesty.org/en/latest/news/2016/07/refugees-and-migrants-fleeing-sexual-violence-abuse-and-exploitation-in-libya/.

Bashford A. (2004) *Imperial Hygiene: A Critical History of Colonialism, Nationalism and Public Health*. New York: Palgrave Macmillan.

Beauchamp Z. (2017) 9 maps and charts that explain the global refugee crisis. *Vox*. Available at: https://www.vox.com/world/2017/1/30/14432500/refugee-crisis-trump-muslim-ban-maps-charts.

Berger J. (1972) *Ways of Seeing – Episode One*. BBC 2. Available at: https://www.youtube.com/watch?v=0pDE4VX_9Kk&t=256s.

Bilgic A. and Pace M. (2017) The European Union and refugees. A struggle over the fate of Europe. *Global Affairs* **3**(1), pp. 89–97.

Boedeltje F. and Houtum, H. V. (2008) The Abduction of Europe: A Plea for Less 'Unionism' and More Europe. *Tijdschrift Voor Economische En Sociale Geografie*, **99**(3), 361–5. https://doi.org/10.1111/j.1467-96 63.2008.00467.x.

Booth W. (2016) Greece was once the fast lane to Europe for refugees. Now it's a grim waiting room. *Washington Post*. Available at: https://www.washingtonpost.com/world/europe/greece-was-once-the-fast-lane-

---

6   This chapter is a modified version of an essay submitted earlier to an international journal.

to-europe-for-refugees-now-its-a-grim-waiting-room/2016/07/07/b35b0c50-3892-11e6-af02-1df55f0c77ff_story. html?utm_term=.6ea180778983.

Bottici C. (2007). *A Philosophy of Political Myth*. New York: Cambridge University Press.

Branch J. (2014) *The Cartographic State*. Cambridge: Cambridge University Press.

Bueno Lacy R. and Van Houtum H. (2013) Europe's border disorder. *E-International Relations*. Available at: http://www.e-ir.info/2013/12/05/europes-border-disorder/.

Brotton J. (2013) *A History of the World in Twelve Maps*. New York: Viking.

Bueno Lacy R. and Van Houtum H. (2015) Lies, damned lies & maps: the EU's cartopolitical invention of Europe. *Journal of Contemporary European Studies* **23**(4): 477–99.

Bueno Lacy R., Raaphorst K. and Van Houtum H. (2016) Recycling violence, how maps about terrorism fail to round up the argument. Available at: https://compasstocartopolitics.wordpress.com/2016/06/17/recyc ling-violence-how-maps-about-terrorism-fail-to-round-up-the-argument/.

Canadian Red Cross (2015) Refugee crisis: how and why we're helping. Available at: http://www.redcross.ca/ blog/2015/9/refugee-crisis--how-and-why-we-re-helping.

De Genova N. (2011) Spectacle of terror, spectacle of security. In: S. Feldman, C. Geisler and G.A. Menon (eds). *Accumulating Insecurity: Violence and Dispossession in the Making of Everyday Life*. Athens, GA and London: University of Georgia Press, pp. 141–65.

De Genova N. (2017) The 'migrant crisis' as racial crisis: do black lives matter in Europe? *Ethnic and Racial Studies* **41**(10): 1765–82.

De Genova N. and Peutz N. (2010) *The Deportation Regime: Sovereignty, Space, and the Freedom of Movement*. Durham, NC: Duke University Press.

De Giorgi A. (2010) Immigration control, post-Fordism, and less eligibility. *Punishment & Society* **12**(2): 147–67.

De Haas H. (2008) The myth of invasion: the inconvenient realities of African migration to Europe. *Third World Quarterly* **29**(7): 1305–22.

Elliot A.J., Maier M.A., Moller A.C., Friedman R. and Meinhardt J. (2007) Color and psychological function- ing: the effect of red on performance attainment. *Journal of Experimental Psychology* **136**(1): 154–68.

Esses V.M., Medianu S. and Lawson A.S. (2013) Uncertainty, threat, and the role of the media in promoting the dehumanization of immigrants and refugees. *Journal of Social Issues* **69**(3): 518–36.

Farman J. (2010) Mapping the digital empire: Google Earth and the process of postmodern cartography. *New Media & Society* **12**(6): 869–88.

Feltman R. and Elliot A.J. (2011) The influence of red on perceptions of relative dominance and threat in a competitive context. *Journal of Sport & Exercise Psychology* **33**: 308–14.

Feyerabend P. (1975) How to defend society against science. *Radical Philosophy* **11**(1): 3–9.

Foucault M. (1978–79) *Naissance de la biopolitique. Cours au collège de France*. Seuil: Gallimard. Reprinted in 2004.

Foucault M. (1981) *L'Ordre du Discours*. Paris: Gallimard.

Gerend M.A. and Sias T. (2009) Message framing and color priming: how subtle threat cues affect persuasion. *Journal of Experimental Social Psychology* **45**: 999–1002.

Gorodzeisky A. and Semyonov M. (2015) Not only competitive threat but also racial prejudice: sources of anti- immigrant attitudes in European societies. *International Journal of Public Opinion Research* **28**(3): 331–54.

Harley, J.B. (1989) Deconstructing the map. *Cartographica* **26**(2): 1–20.

Hobsbawm E. (1990) *Nations and Nationalism since 1780: Programme, Myth, Reality*. Cambridge: Cambridge University Press.

Hupka R.B., Zaleski Z., Otto J., Reidl L. and Tarabrina N.V. (1997) The colors of anger, envy, fear, and jealousy: a cross-cultural study. *Journal of Cross-cultural Psychology* **28**(2): 156–71.

Huysmans J. (2006) *The Politics of Insecurity. Fear, Migration and Asylum in the EU*. London: Routledge.

IOM (2018) Global migration indicators: Insights from the Global Migration Data Portal. Available at: https:// publications.iom.int/system/files/pdf/global_migration_indicators_2018.pdf.

Jansen B. (2016) Access denied: An analysis of the discourse constituting the Common Visa Policy of the Schengen Area (Master's thesis). Available at: http://theses.ubn.ru.nl/bitstream/handle/123456789/3438/ Master%20Thesis%20Final%20Digital.pdf?sequence=1.

Jones R. (2016) *Violent Borders: Refugees and the Right to Move*. London: Verso.

Kemp R. (2017) Libya's migrant hell. Sky UK. Available at: https://www.youtube.com/watch?v=fcDKtLav6WE.

Kristof L. (1960) The origins and evolution of geopolitics. *Journal of Conflict Resolution* **4**(1): 15–51.

Lyman R. (2015) Route of migrants into Europe shifts toward Balkans. *New York Times* (18 July). Available at: https://www.nytimes.com/2015/07/19/world/europe/route-of-migrants-into-europe-shifts-toward-balkans.html.

Mehta R. and Zhu R.J. (2009) Blue or red? Exploring the effect of color on cognitive task performances. *Science* **323**(5918): 1226–9.

Mishra P. (2017) How colonial violence came home: the ugly truth of the First World War. *Guardian* (10 November). Available at: https://www.theguardian.com/news/2017/nov/10/how-colonial-violence-came-ho me-the-ugly-truth-of-the-first-world-war.

Ó Tuathail G. (1996) *Critical Geopolitics*. London: Routledge.

Parker N. and Vaughan-Williams N. et al. (2009) Lines in the sand? Towards an agenda for critical border studies. *Geopolitics* **14**(3): 582–7.

Pupavac V. (2008) Refugee advocacy, traumatic representations and political disenchantment. *Government and Opposition* **43**(2): 270–92.

Reimann A. (2015) Wer sind die Flüchtlinge? Woher kommen sie? *Die Spiegel Online*. Available at: http://www.spiegel.de/politik/ausland/fluechtlinge-im-mittelmeer-fakten-zu-den-bootsfluechtlingen-a-1029512.html.

Renan E. (1882) *Qu'est-ce qu'une nation?* Available at: http://classiques.uqac.ca/classiques/renan_ernest/qu_est_ce_une_nation/renan_quest_ce_une_nation.pdf.

Sabbati G. and Poptcheva E.M. (2015) Irregular immigration in the EU: facts and figures. *European Parliament Research Service* PE 554.202, p. 4. Available at: http://www.europarl.europa.eu/RegData/etudes/BRIE/2015/554202/EPRS_BRI(2015)554202_EN.pdf.

Schmitt C. (1932). *Der Begriff des politischen*. München: Duncker u. Humboldt.

Scott J.C. (1998) *Seeing Like a State*. New Haven, CT and London: Yale University Press.

The Economist (2016) Migration to Europe: travelling in hope. *The Economist* (22 October). Available at: https://www.economist.com/news/international/21709019-flow-africans-libya-italy-now-europes-worst-migration-crisis-travelling.

The Economist (2017) A world of free movement would be $78 trillion richer. *The Economist* (13 July). Available at: https://www.economist.com/news/world-if/21724907-yes-it-would-be-disruptive-potential-gains-are-so-vast-objectors-could-be-bribed.

The Migrants' Files (2015) *The Money Trails*. Available at: http://www.themigrantsfiles.com/.

UN (1948) Universal Declaration of Human Rights. Available at: http://www.un.org/en/universal-declaration-human-rights/.

UN General Assembly (1951), *Convention Relating to the Status of Refugees* (28 July), United Nations, Treaty Series, vol. 189, p. 137. Available at: https://www.refworld.org/docid/3be01b964.html (accessed 11 January 2019).

UNWTO (2017) *UNWTO Tourism Highlights 2017 Edition*. Available at: https://www.e-unwto.org/doi/pdf/10.18111/9789284419029.

Van der Ploeg I. (2006) Borderline identities: the enrollment of bodies in the technological reconstruction of borders. In: T Monaham (ed.), *Surveillance and Security: Technological Politics and Power in Everyday Life*. New York: Routledge, pp. 177–93.

Van Houtum H. (2010a) Waiting before the law: Kafka on the border. *Social and Legal Studies* **19**(3): 285–97.

Van Houtum H. (2010b) Human blacklisting, the global apartheid of the EU's external border regime. *Environment and Planning: D, Society and Space* **28**: 957–76.

Van Houtum H. (2012) Remapping borders. In: T.M. Wilson and D. Hastings (eds), *Companion to Border Studies*. Chichester, UK: John Wiley & Sons, pp. 405–18.

Van Houtum H. (2013) Van Atlas naar Hermes. *Geografie* **3**: 96–9.

Van Houtum H. and Boedeltje F. (2009) Europe's shame: death at the borders of the EU. *Antipode* **41**(2): 226–30.

Van Houtum H. and Bueno Lacy R. (2017) The political extreme as the new normal: the cases of Brexit, the French state of emergency and Dutch Islamophobia. *Fennia: International Journal of Geography* **195**(1): 85–101.

Van Houtum, H. and Lucassen L. (2016) *Voorbij Fort Europa: een nieuwe visie op migratie*. Amsterdam: Atlas Contact.

Van Houtum H. and Pijpers R. (2007) The European Union as a gated community: the two-faced border and immigration regime of the EU. *Antipode* **39**(2): 291–309.

Van Houtum H. and Van Naerssen T. (2002) Bordering, ordering and othering. *Tijdschrift voor economische en sociale geografie* **93**(2): 125–36.

Van Reekum R. and Schinkel W. (2016) Drawing lines, enacting migration: visual prostheses of bordering Europe. *Public Culture* **29**(1): 27–51.

Verhofstadt G. (2016) This Turkish deal is illegal and betrays Europe's values. *Guardian* (10 March). Available at: https://www.theguardian.com/commentisfree/2016/mar/10/refugee-crisis-turkey-deal-europe-values.

Walby S. (2003) The myth of the nation-state: theorizing society and polities in a global era. *Sociology* **37**(3): 529–46.

Wigen K. (2005) Cartographies of connection: ocean maps as metaphors for inter-area history. In: H. Schissler and Y.N. Soysal (eds), *The Nation, Europe and the World*. New York: Berghahn Books, pp. 211–27.

Wimmer A. and Schiller N.G. (2003) Methodological nationalism, the social sciences, and the study of migration: an essay in historical epistemology. *The International Migration Review* **37**(3): 576–610.

Wintle M. (1999) Renaissance maps and the construction of the idea of Europe. *Journal of Historical Geography* **25**(2): 137–65.

Wintle M. (2009) *The Image of Europe: Visualizing Europe in Cartography and Iconography Throughout the Ages*. New York: Cambridge University Press.

Zoeteweij M.H. and Turhan O. (2017) Above the law – beneath contempt: the end of the EU-Turkey deal? *Swiss Review of International and European Law* **27**(2): 151–66.

13. From preventive to repressive: the changing use of development and humanitarianism to control migration
Michael Collyer

INTRODUCTION

Since the 1970s, efforts by wealthy states to control unwanted migration have faced a particular set of geopolitical challenges. These arise largely from the fact that a state's humanitarian obligations may be triggered by a request for assistance by a non-citizen on or even at the edge of state territory. In response to mounting costs of meeting these obligations and perceptions of widespread public opposition to the use of public money to do so, state institutions have devoted significant resources to ensuring that migrants do not have the opportunity to ask for help. As a result, migration control policies have been focused not only at preventing territorial access but at preventing any contact with state territory at all. Migration controls beyond state territory targeting those who may (or may not) be planning on travelling to the state in question have become a central element in the migration control strategies of all wealthy states. This approach has been widely labelled the 'externalization' of migration control, resulting in the effective movement of state borders away from state territory. Yet states' monopolization of legitimate violence only applies to state territory so the capacity for extra-territorial coercive action is limited. The nature of this geopolitical challenge is therefore for states to exert coercive force on individuals who have not yet reached the territory of the state.

States have responded to this challenge in three ways. These map onto what López-Sala (2015) refers to as repressive, coercive and preventive dissuasion of migration. First, legitimate (i.e., state sanctioned) violence against unwanted migrants on state territory has increased, principally through extended practices of detention and deportation. This includes activities that López-Sala labels 'repressive dissuasion', which occurs once migrants have arrived on the territory of an intended destination country. Such practices frequently challenge understandings of legitimacy, when violence becomes fatal, where it strays into neighbouring state territory or both. Second, there are a range of policies, labelled 'coercive dissuasion' that are intended to intercept migrants once they have left but before they have reached the territory of their intended destination. This includes surveillance and interception, often through the privatization of migration control. Going back at least several decades, states have outsourced extra-territorial migration control to the market by imposing fines or even custodial sentences on companies and individuals found to be transporting migrants without the correct authorization.[1] They have also

---

[1] In some cases these practices go back much further, although they only applied to a limited number of migrants. In the UK such provisions may be traced to the 1905 Alien's Act, although they were limited to passengers travelling steerage class, that is, only those passengers too poor to afford a cabin.

contracted private security companies to carry out many migration control functions. Finally, 'preventive dissuasion' aims to counter the decision to leave in the first place. This inevitably involves some form of international cooperation in support of migration control objectives, persuading or cajoling other states to take a role. This may involve information campaigns promoting 'safe' migration or opportunities for legal migration. It is also where López-Sala includes Official Development Assistance (ODA).

The actors involved in repressive, coercive and preventive forms of dissuasion differ and with it the levels of violence involved. Repressive dissuasion takes place on state territory by state agents and increasingly involves both direct and indirect violence. Coercive dissuasion may involve state agents operating beyond state territory such as maritime patrols in international waters or visa delivery officers working from consulates, but often this is carried out by commercial interests working for or with state institutions. Finally, preventive forms of dissuasion inevitably take place on the territory of other states and may be carried out by independent actors, such as development professionals or employees of the state concerned. This means it is the least violent form of dissuasion. Where ODA is used with the intention of preventing migration it is most frequently considered in this context. Even here it is often controversial and rarely successful. Nevertheless, it has become increasingly common in most major donor countries in recent years. This chapter explores this process. The central argument is that the expansion of development as a tool of migration control is associated with a shift from preventive to other, more violent forms of dissuasion.

Development has been used as a tool of migration control by wealthy states for more than 40 years. This has typically stemmed from an understanding of migration as a problem caused by underdevelopment. Efforts to incentivize voluntary departure of migrants from France in the early 1970s with the promise of individual financial assistance mark a beginning of the use of development justifications for migration control objectives. Yet Assisted Voluntary Return (AVR) programmes continue to have very mixed results. More generally, the evidence that economic development increases rather than reduces migration is now well established and extremely robust.

Despite this wealth of evidence, interest in the instrumental use of ODA as a way of fixing potential migrants in place and reducing international migration continues. Three clear trends characterize the development of policy in this area since 2010. First, as states have become increasingly concerned about rising numbers of spontaneous arrivals, officials have been increasingly willing to overlook or question the evidence that development does not reduce migration in search of a simple way of addressing the 'root causes' of migration. This relates to a second trend in the use of ODA funds to cover things which would not generally be viewed as development. This includes domestic expenditure in donor's own countries which, while still recognized as ODA, has increased to such an extent that it undermines the credibility of the aid system (Parker, 2017). Finally, this broader set of activities which are being classified as ODA appears to apply to the migration sector as well. The use of development as a tool for migration control has always involved a degree of coercion of states expected to implement new migration control programmes but this is now being passed on to the activities focused at potential migrants too. In terms of López-Sala's analysis of the Spanish situation, migration is moving from a tool of preventive dissuasion to one of both coercive and repressive dissuasion.

THE (RE)TURN TO DEVELOPMENT AS PREVENTIVE MIGRATION CONTROL

Migration and development now describes a vast industry, encompassing everything from regular global intergovernmental meetings through the Global Forum on Migration and Development to grassroots non-governmental organizations (NGOs) and migrants' home town associations. Since 2003, the World Bank has been producing regular updates on migrants' financial transfers and the International Organization for Migration (IOM) has initiated projects, conferences and publications. This amounts to a powerful normative agenda that continues to reinforce knowledge production (Geiger and Pécoud, 2013). This agenda can be effectively summarized in the notion of the 'triple win scenario', referring to the aim that in certain circumstances international migration can be beneficial for migrants' countries of origin, countries of destination and migrants themselves. A faith that there is at least a potential alignment of the complex and typically irreconcilable trade-offs inherent in the formation of migration policy that may result in this magical, mutually beneficial set of outcomes has become what Gamlen has described as 'international policy orthodoxy' (Gamlen, 2010, p. 415).

More critical analysis of this orthodoxy has highlighted how enthusiasm for policy engagement with migration and development has fluctuated considerably since it was first articulated in the 1950s. Key contributions to this analysis have developed an intellectual history of the migration development debate (de Haas, 2012; Gamlen, 2014). A key critique is that the core concepts are highly varied and extremely complex but are vastly oversimplified by the orthodox perspective. As Raghuram argues, 'Almost all theorisations of this link [between migration and development] assume migration to be something that can be contained, regulated or influenced, development as normatively good' (Raghuram, 2009, p. 104). The genealogical approach of this critical analysis reveals how attitudes to migration have historically been informed by attitudes to development. Bakewell (2008) traces these attitudes to colonialist approaches to development, which assumed mobility of certain groups of people violated a natural order of stability. This sedentarist view saw underdevelopment as the cause of migration, and by a process of circular logic, migration became an indication of underdevelopment. The bulk of evidence of this relationship suggests that the opposite is more likely to be the case.

The finding that development may result in migration was first highlighted in the 1990s and labelled the 'migration hump' by Martin (1993). On the basis of projections of migration between Mexico and the US, following the North American Free Trade Agreement (NAFTA), he identified a model characterized by a bell-shaped curve describing how, at relatively low levels of economic development, increases in per capita income resulted in increased migration. This undermined the notion that underdevelopment is a 'root cause' of migration. Evidence for the positive impact economic development may have on migration continues to accumulate, though even to phrase this as a relationship between two discrete processes is a misunderstanding; as Ronald Skeldon argued, 'migration *is* development' (Skeldon, 1997). 'In contrast to received knowledge, social and economic development, whether a result of economic integration and aid or not, tends to stimulate rather than reduce migration in the short to medium run' (de Haas, 2007, p. 837). Most recently, Michael Clemens produced the most comprehensive data analysis yet in support of the positive impact that economic development has on migration (Clemens, 2014).

Based on analysis of census data, Clemens demonstrated that migration continues to increase until medium income levels when international migration starts to slow and then decline. Finally, high income countries have levels of international migration equivalent to low income countries, though the explanation for this is very different. As disposable incomes increase, not only do households have resources to access international migration, they have resources for education or internet access which open them to the world and highlight the potential benefits to be gained from migration. Using development to counter migration will not work.

Policy makers have been receptive to these debates, although the extent of genuine change is unclear. In 2006, Benita Ferrero-Waldner, then European Commissioner for External Relations and European Neighbourhood Policy, announced a new orientation in the European Union (EU) approach to migration and development. She referred to this as 'a policy more in keeping with today's world. It takes us away from "more development for less migration" to "better managing migration for more development"' (Ferrero-Waldner, 2006). Of course, the difference between 'less migration' and 'better managed migration' may be purely rhetorical and certainly for most European policy makers 'less migration' is the very definition of better management. This change of emphasis has resulted in support for collective efforts by migrants and others which has led to clear achievements ranging from reductions in money transfer fees to recognizing the value of migrants' contributions. Yet it is important to highlight when development or humanitarian action is being justified as a way of preventing migration. Not only does this appear to be a misuse of money that should go to making people's lives better, but it will inevitably be unsuccessful, at least in the short term. It will therefore result in increased public opposition to both migration and development. In her analysis of the Spanish response to unwanted migration López-Sala (2015) gives this strategy the effective name 'preventive dissuasion'.

Such preventive dissuasion, the use of development and humanitarian funding in the belief that it will discourage international migration, does appear to be increasing. This is despite the rhetoric which appears to take account of the weight of evidence that it won't work. As de Haas has argued, 'development intentions often seem to camouflage a hidden agenda of voluntarily or forcibly returning irregular immigrants or rejected asylum seekers' (de Haas, 2012, p. 20). In some areas of policy, such as AVR programmes, such an agenda is barely camouflaged since they are explicitly advertised in terms of development support, yet development is not a significant outcome (Collyer, 2017). Similarly, as larger numbers of people have been arriving spontaneously in some wealthy countries over the past few years the rhetoric that the priority should be development, as in Ferrero-Waldner's speech, is also being forgotten. Soon after she was appointed the UK's Secretary of State of International Development, Priti Patel wrote an article in the *Daily Mail*, a tabloid newspaper known for its anti-immigrant views, in which she argued, 'I want to use our aid budget to directly address the great global challenges that affect the UK – like creating jobs in poorer countries so as to reduce the pressure for mass migration to Europe' (Patel, 2016). Such statements, returning to the discredited notion that migration is a result of underdevelopment, have become more common as policy makers have struggled to identify meaningful responses to the increased spontaneous arrivals witnessed particularly since 2015. These attempt to re-evaluate the impact of development as preventive dissuasion, but they also go further than this, using development aid in much more deliberately coercive ways.

BEYOND PREVENTIVE CONTROL: DEVELOPMENT AND HUMANITARIAN AID AS COERCIVE DISSUASION

There is perhaps an element of wishful thinking that a single, simple response will help address one of the most pressing and intractable of contemporary international challenges, certainly in Europe. Yet there are limits to the explanation that policy makers are naive or forgetful or optimistic or stubborn in their refusal to accept the established consensus that development will not stop migration. Any reasoned analysis must credit politicians with more strategic foresight and it is likely that a vain hope of influencing one of the root causes of migration is not the only reason for the growing popularity of migration and development discussions. This is where the use of development begins to go beyond preventive dissuasion. López-Sala's analysis of this process focuses on the relationship between Spain, as a potential destination, and potential migrants. Yet the challenge of the extra-territorial context of identifying *potential* migrants, that is, those individuals who have not yet migrated, is that the state's capacity to act coercively is severely limited. Rather than acting directly on the lives of potential migrants, wealthy states are able to recruit allies to act directly on their behalf. The most willing recruits are almost certainly private companies, though even here the relationship with the state may be necessarily coercive, as in the case of carrier sanctions legislation. Other widely used intermediaries are international organizations, such as IOM, or NGOs. Other sovereign states are probably the most challenging since it is not obviously in their interests.

The growing concern of wealthier states to exert greater control over migration does not sit easily with the development priorities of poorer states. The United Nations Development Programme's (UNDP) *Human Development Report 2009* argued that 'Large gains to human development can be achieved by lowering the barriers to movement and improving the treatment of movers' (UNDP, 2009, p. 3). Yet the discussion of migration and development provides a compromise position. As Geiger and Pécoud argue in the introduction to their special issue of *Population, Space and Place*, 'Western states' efforts to steer the behaviour of sending and transit regions need apparently consensual issues to establish a common ground with governments in less-development regions' (Geiger and Pécoud, 2013, p. 373). In short, migration and development allows for the discussion of apparently contradictory policy goals. These discussions may occur in the context of bilateral relations, but migration and development is surprisingly absent from formal intergovernmental agreements – witness the complete absence of migration from the Millennium Development Goals and the insignificant recognition of migration amongst the far more numerous Sustainable Development Goals. Discussions of migration and development are far more effective at developing a normative framework for international action, which sets the context for subsequent formal action. The growing number of Regional Consultative Processes (RCPs) provide the ideal forum for these discussions.

Migration and development has come to dominate global discussions of migration to such an extent that there are two global processes established to discuss the issue and it has figured significantly in a third, in addition to a huge range of regional process. At the global level, the Global Forum on Migration and Development has met annually since 2007. This arose from the UN High Level Dialogue on Migration and Development, which convenes meetings less regularly; 2006 and 2013 have been the two held so far, but it is still active. The international Dialogue on Migration has been held annually since 2001, coordinated by

IOM. It has followed a different theme annually, though did not focus exclusively on migration and development until 2014 (IOM, 2017). IOM lists another 17 RCPs that take place at an intra-regional level and a further 15 at a regional level. Of these, five are exclusively focused on migration and development, although the theme is discussed regularly in all 32 processes, covering all continents. Very few states have no involvement at all in RCPs and many are involved in several. In the absence of clear policy outcomes, RCPs contribute to the evolution of global norms in this area. The notion of 'migration management' itself is a result of informal, multilateral discussions in the 1980s and 1990s (Oelgemoller, 2011). Much of migration management involves a normative process of discourse development that legitimates longer term changes of practice (Cohen, 2005). A recent example is the insistence on the description of legal migration as 'safe' migration such that unwanted or illegal migration is gradually viewed as unsafe. Unwanted migration can therefore be prevented, not in the interests of states, but in the interests of migrants themselves and a formerly repressive action is transformed into a humanitarian one.

The chief advantage of RCPs for states is the informal, non-binding nature of discussions. This supports normative developments, since such developments cannot be legislated. It also allows much more coercive actions between states to be presented as partnerships. Yet the outcomes of these negotiations are a result of the highly asymmetric relationship between wealthier states of assumed destination and poorer states of origin. The Cotonou Agreement, signed in 2000 between the EU and 79 states from Africa, the Caribbean and the Pacific (ACP) is a prominent example of this asymmetry. The agreement covers cooperation in the fields of development, politics and trade and delivers substantial financial support from the world's wealthiest trading bloc to a selection of the poorest countries in the world. The controversy associated with the agreement surrounds Article 13, the 'migration article' which, in the original 2000 text committed ACP countries to agree bilateral readmission agreements with the EU. The relevant text (Article 13, 5ci) captures the formal equality between the EU Member States, on the one hand, and the ACP, on the other, that is central to the agreement. The text is worded to commit EU states to readmit their nationals found to be illegally resident on the territory of ACP states on an equal basis to ACP states which must readmit their nationals from EU Member States.[2]

The contrast between formal equality and underlying asymmetry of power relations characterizes these kind of readmission agreements between wealthy Western nations and poorer African ones (Pina Delgado, 2010). The explicit conditionality of agreements like the 2000 Cotonou Agreement introduces a much more coercive element into the use of development support as a tool for migration control. The relationship is no longer a direct one between donors and potential migrants, but an indirect one between states. Wealthy states use their greater leverage in international relations to ensure that poorer states have little choice but to cooperate in their migration control objectives. Indeed, in most contexts the objective of keeping migrants away from the territory would not be possible if it were not for the engagement of neighbouring states in these significantly coerced border control practices.

---

[2] The Cotonou Agreement was signed in 2000, entered into force in 2003 and has been regularly amended since then, most recently on 12 July 2016. See http://eur-lex.europa.eu/legal-content/EN/TXT/PDF/?uri=CELEX:02000A1215(01)-20170101&from=EN (accessed 2 May 2018).

The levels of direct and indirect violence necessary to police these borders would not be seen as acceptable by large sections of the electorates of liberal democracies if it were not for a powerful legitimizing discourse. In this context, the broader development project is supplemented by a more urgent set of justifications for humanitarian action. This is what Walters (2011) refers to as the 'humanitarian border' which 'reproduces key elements of a humanitarian script in which intervention is mobilized as an act of charity and protection' (Walters, 2011, p. 145). This is an inevitable consequence of the 'safe migration' discursive project. Yet the discursive deployment of humanitarianism also blurs the line between policing and humanitarian actions (Pallister-Wilkins, 2015). International migration has clear implications for humanitarianism, just as it does for development. Yet the use of either development or humanitarianism as a form of preventive, coercive or repressive dissuasion of migration begins to undermine the altruistic ideals on which the legitimacy of those activities is founded. The following section turns to a case study of recent developments in the EU.

EXTERNALIZING MIGRATION CONTROL IN EUROPEAN UNION HUMANITARIAN AND DEVELOPMENT POLICY

A small minority of the world's refugees, asylum seekers and migrants reach Europe. This is still the case even since the rise in spontaneous arrivals from 2015 provoked a dramatization of migration associated with ubiquitous 'crisis' narratives (Crawley et al., 2016). The failure of the EU response to these arrivals became classified as first a European and then a global 'migration crisis'. This process illustrates the dominance of European countries in driving the global migration agenda. Yet this is also influenced by the complexity of the political context in the EU, summarized by four considerations that only enhance the geopolitical challenges faced by EU Member States. First, the EU can be reached from a wide range of countries facing long-standing political instability and economic crisis. Second, the relationship with these countries often overlays complex post-colonial ties. Third, political integration within the EU is ongoing, including ambitious plans to continue harmonization of asylum and migration policies, although this is occurring in a broader legitimacy crisis of EU institutions. Finally, migration and asylum has a particular salience due to the influence or even governmental participation of prominent anti-migrant populist political parties across the continent. All of these considerations make the EU a particularly relevant case study and this is facilitated by the generally transparent approach that the EU maintains to most data, including financial arrangements.

The complexity and delicacy of negotiations around migration in the EU and between the EU and key partners is reflected in the intensive involvement in RCPs. The EU itself is of course a particularly advanced regional migration arrangement. The EU's approach to its external border and to externalization initially arises not from any prior desire to pool border controls, but as a consequence of the single market-driven logic of free movement. Yet perhaps because of the EU's own experience of intra-regional informal discussions, the EU is a particularly enthusiastic instigator of RCPs. The EU is a key partner in 12 of the 25 RCPs considered by Harns (2013) in a global review of RCPs. This does not include the EU Horn of Africa Migration Route Initiative, the Khartoum Process, established in 2016. Overall, then, the EU is involved in 13, or half of all consultative processes that are ongoing at a global level. All of these 13 involve development to some extent and three are exclusively focused on development: the Tripoli Process (Joint Africa-EU Declaration on Migration and Development), the Rabat Process (Euro-African Dialogue on Migration and Development) and the ACP-EU Dialogue on Migration. All three of these focus on relations with Africa and 13 African countries are involved in all three RCPs.[3] These processes typically involve one or more high level meetings a year and continual exchanges of practice and information, so this represents a particularly dense network of relations around migration and development, especially for those countries involved in all three.

All elements of the EU's global engagement around migration are set out in the Global Approach to Migration and Mobility (GAMM). There is no indication that the multiplicity of forms of engagement through RCPs is driven by any clearly thought out externalization strategy beyond the overarching framework set out in the GAMM (Collyer, 2016). Although many individual Member States pursue bilateral negotiations around migration, the framework for these negotiations is set by the European Commission, which has been able to engage in binding agreements in this area since the entry into force of the Treaty of Amsterdam, in 2004. The original structure of the GAMM involved three areas of policy: regulating and expanding legal migration, restricting illegal migration and migration and development. The key policy priorities of countries of origin mostly fall under the 'legal migration' theme which cover very limited opportunities for the expansion of mobility and visa liberalization initiatives. In contrast, the most obvious priorities of the EU are considered in discussions of illegal migration. This includes areas such as readmission, where there is little inherent policy incentives for cooperation from countries of origin. The 'migration and development' theme is, as observers such as Geiger and Pécoud (2013) suggest, an 'issue linkage' which encourages discussion of other areas of policy where interests of key partners remain conflicting or even completely opposed.

The migration and development theme is therefore a key site of international engagement where explicit differences may be discussed and resolved or perhaps more frequently avoided. It has evolved considerably since the GAMM was first outlined in 2005. The most recent iterations appeared in 2015, first in the European Agenda on Migration, in May (EC, 2015) and second as the Joint Valletta Action Plan (JVAP) in November 2015. The May document sticks fairly closely to the GAMM principles, but by the Valletta conference in November the emphasis had shifted much more clearly towards development. The conference announced a new EU Emergency Trust Fund for 'addressing root causes or irregular migration and displaced persons in Africa' (Valletta Summit, 2015, p. 1). Rather than offering a further structure, it attempts to bring together existing migration policy processes in this area, using the administrative capacities of the Rabat and Khartoum Processes and the ACP-EU Migration Dialogue.

The Valletta Action Plan is organized around five 'priority domains'. These are in order: 1. 'Development benefits of migration and addressing root causes of irregular migration and forced displacement'; 2. Legal migration and mobility; 3. Protection and asylum; 4. Prevention of and fight against irregular migration, migrant smuggling and trafficking in human beings; 5. Return, readmission and reintegration. Of these five, the first, third

---

[3]   The 13 countries that are involved in the Tripoli Process, the Rabat Process and the ACP-EU Migration Dialogue are Benin, Burkina Faso, Cote d'Ivoire, Ghana, Gambia, Guinea, Guinea-Bissau, Liberia, Mali, Niger, Nigeria, Sierra Leone and Togo.

and fifth priority domains cover what fell under the 'migration and development' pillar of the original GAMM, highlighting the expansion of this topic. This is reflected in the budgets allocated to these sections. The 2017 follow-up to the Valletta Action Plan, held under the Maltese Presidency of the European Union, resulted in a series of commitments from Member States and the EU institutions under each of the domains.[4] The total was over 8.5 billion euros, a very substantial budget which reflects the priority given to these initiatives. Although this is partly based on projections of expenditure until 2020, that will not necessarily be adhered to, it also draws on commitments since 2015, so some of this is historical financial data, which is much more certain.

The key information relating to my argument here is that the three JVAP domains relating to migration and development account for over 95 per cent of all these commitments and the first domain alone focusing on the 'development benefits of migration' accounts for over 70 per cent (JVAP, 2017a). Development has clearly gained a new priority, under the JVAP, even a dominance, in migration policy making. When the overviews of the 732 individual projects are considered, there are plenty of examples where development aid appears to be fulfilling purposes not directly related to reducing migration: the biggest single commitment (half a billion euros from the UK government) is directed at improving conditions in refugee camps in South Sudan, although there is no evidence at the moment that onward migration from these camps to Europe is significant. Nevertheless, 'addressing root causes of irregular migration' is one of the stated objectives of this domain and there are also plenty of examples where development aid is directly linked to 'preventive dissuasion'. Yet it is also clear that development aid is going beyond this, not only as a preventive measure to stop people even thinking of leaving but in coercive ways to directly address the issue of migration and repressive ways, to make things more difficult once they have left too. This is a new development. Much of the focus of these projects appears to depart considerably from activities traditionally associated with development, introducing a much clearer security focus into development finance. This supports related discussions around the 'humanitarian border' (Pallister-Wilkins, 2015) and the securitization of development (Nyberg-Sørensen, 2012) but also fits with concerns around the expansion of the definition of development (Parker, 2017).

Preventive dissuasion is based on the assumption that migration is a result of underdevelopment. As discussed earlier, this assumption has been regularly and repeatedly discredited over the last 20 years. Yet the focus on 'root causes' repeats the idea that development can be used to prevent migration. There are many examples of this approach in the policies funded under the JVAP. In Mali, the new Politique Nationale de Promotion des Investissements du Mali includes direct support for the Malian agricultural sector (JVAP, 2017b, p. 11). In Senegal, the Community Agricultural Areas Development Project (PRODAC) 'contributes to the reduction of social insecurity in rural areas by promoting the agricultural entrepreneurship of young people by putting at their disposal land for their agricultural exploitation' (JVAP, 2017b, p.14). Finally, the Tunisian government is concerned with reducing graduate unemployment, through draft law No. 70/2016 on structural measures to support employment opportunities and the integration of young people into the labour market (JVAP, 2017b, p. 15). These are all excellent initiatives,

---

[4]   Details of these commitments are provided in two documents of project summaries, running to several hundred pages, that form the basis for this analysis (JVAP, 2017a, 2017b).

worth doing for their own sake and there are plenty more similar examples listed. The problem arises when they are framed as a way of addressing the root causes of migration and financed through development funding of the EU as a way of doing so. Although in the short term this may be viewed as a good argument to channel additional funds to important development projects, in the long term this undermines public support in Europe for both development funding and reinforces opposition to migration.

This opposition drives public support for the wider use of development finance outlined in the JVAP documents. It is clear from this document that development is not simply being used to provide a valid alternative to migration but to actively oppose individual migration projects, where they may involve any form of irregular movement. In López-Sala's useful (2015) analysis, this may be both coercive, interrupting migration before departure for the EU, or repressive, active involvement in the prevention of movement. In terms of coercive activities, there is a clear connection between migration, development and security. In Nigeria, the Abuja Declaration on the Treatment of Violent Extremist Offenders, of 16 April 2016 (JVAP, 2017b, p. 12) is no doubt an important initiative, but it has little apparent connection to either migration or development. Similarly, the 'reinforcement of the operational capacities of the gendarmerie deployed in the extreme north of Cameroon' (JVAP, 2017a, p. 27) may be a necessary activity, but to have received 135,000 euros from the French government and to be listed as a use of development aid to address the root causes of migration begins to undermine the purposes of development. This is connected to Cameroon's Presidential decree No. 2016/373 relating to conditions of entry, residence and departure of aliens in Cameroon, which supports the development of biometric identification documents in Cameroon and is listed under domain 5 ('return, readmission and reintegration') (JVAP, 2017b, p. 27).

These activities border on the repressive, yet they are clearly designed to stop or discourage migrants some way before they reach Europe. The EU's most important allies in preventing migrants reaching European territory are the immediate neighbours, particularly in North Africa, so it is the activities planned in this area which raise greatest interest. The revision of the Moroccan immigration law 02/03, which was widely criticized as a simple transposition of EU priorities into Moroccan law, is proposed through the draft law 95-14. Morocco has developed a particularly progressive approach to migration recently, so this is likely to be a positive development but once again, the framing of a new immigration law in Morocco as a way of addressing 'root causes' of migration to Europe is questionable. A final example is the cooperation agreement signed between Germany and Egypt in July 2016 which 'solidifies cooperation in preventing all types of crimes, including terrorism and corruption, as well reinforcing airport security and stemming illegal immigration. The agreement includes also the exchange of information, technical training and expertise between Egypt and Germany' (JVAP, 2017b, p. 10).

CONCLUSION: THE FUTURE OF EXTRA-TERRITORIAL MIGRATION CONTROL

The return to the use of development as a preventive measure to reduce migration is now widespread. It is fundamental to discussions of addressing root causes of migration, which have expanded considerably in recent years. These discussions are central to global processes on migration and development and relate to almost all of the 32 regional and intra-regional consultative processes on migration. Yet there is considerable evidence, going back more than two decades, that migration is not caused by underdevelopment and in many cases the reverse is the case. As individuals in the poorest countries gain resources to improve education and develop livelihoods for the majority of the population beyond subsistence levels, migration, including international migration, is almost certain to increase. Migration is integral to the development process, not something that can be instrumentally separated from it. In many cases important projects are being funded with this justification. The explicit linkage to development may help to justify projects which would not be funded otherwise. This may meet some short-term goals, but in the longer term, it is bad for the development process and bad for the development industry. Development projects justified by opposition to migration are likely to fail and undermine public trust in the development process itself. In some contexts, well-targeted support may provide alternatives to migration for those who want them, but this is likely to be in middle income countries, such as the Tunisian example considered above, which are not development priorities.

This chapter has also identified a tendency to use development in ways that go beyond preventive dissuasion into coercive and repressive activities (López-Sala, 2015) which are nonetheless justified in terms of development. The most recent and most influential initiative of EU funding in this area, the Joint Valletta Action Plan, provides details of more than 8.5 billion euros of funding under its key priorities, the most substantial of which involves addressing 'root causes' of migration. This clearly involves preventive activities, but also provides substantial support for activities in the security domain, highlighting the connections between security and development (Nyberg-Sørensen, 2012) and for direct policing activities. As development is defined in increasingly broad terms, it is important to be attentive to this expansion of activities, which use the benevolent language of development to justify expenditure on much more repressive activities. This discursive shifting is an important element in a range of activities associated with 'managing' migration, down to use of the language of management itself. Critical research has a vital role to play in this process.

REFERENCES

Bakewell, O. (2008), '"Keeping them in their place": the ambivalent relationship between development and migration in Africa', *Third World Quarterly* **29**(7): 1341–58.
Clemens, M.A. (2014), 'Does development reduce migration?', in R.E.B Lucas (ed.), *International Handbook on Migration and Economic Development*, Cheltenham, UK and Northampton, MA, USA: Edward Elgar, pp. 152–85.
Cohen, S. (2005), *Deportation is Freedom! The Orwellian World of Immigration Controls*, London: Jessica Kingsley.
Collyer, M. (2016), 'Geopolitics as a migration governance strategy: European Union bilateral relations with Southern Mediterranean countries', *Journal of Ethnic and Migration Studies* **42**(4): 606–24.
Collyer, M. (2017), 'Paying to go: deportability as development', in S. Khosravi (ed.), *After Deportation: Ethnographic Perspectives*, London: Palgrave, pp. 105–25.
Crawley, H., Düvell, F., Jones, K., McMahon, S. and Sigona, N. (2016), *Destination Europe? Understanding the Dynamics and Drivers of Mediterranean Migration in 2015*, MEDMIG Final Report, available at http://www.medmig.info/research-brief-destination-europe.pdf (accessed 1 July 2017).
de Haas, H. (2007), 'Turning the tide? Why development will not stop migration', *Development and Change* **38**(5): 819–41.

de Haas, H. (2012), 'The migration and development pendulum: a critical view on research and policy', *International Migration* **50**(3): 8–25.

EC (European Commission) (2015), Communication from the Commission to the European Parliament, the Council, the European Economic and Social Committee and the Committee of the Regions, A European Agenda on Migration. COM(2015) 240 final, Brussels: European Commission.

Ferrero-Waldner, B. (2006), Introductory speech at Conference on Reinforcing the Area of Freedom, Security, Prosperity and Justice of the EU and its Neighbouring Countries, Brussels, 24 January, available at http://europa.eu/rapid/press-release_SPEECH-06-30_en.htm?locale=EN (accessed 1 July 2017).

Gamlen, A. (2010), 'The new migration and development optimism: a review of the 2009 Human Development Report', *Global Governance* **16**: 415–22.

Gamlen, A. (2014), 'The new migration-and-development pessimism', *Progress in Human Geography* **38**(4): 581–97.

Geiger, M. and Pécoud, A. (2013), 'Migration, development and the "migration and development nexus"', *Population, Space and Place* **19**(4): 369–74.

Harns, C. (2013), 'Regional inter-state consultation mechanisms on migration: approaches, recent activities and implications for global governance of migration', IOM Migration Research Series no. 45.

IOM (2017), International Dialogue on Migration, available at https://www.iom.int/idm (accessed 1 July 2017).

JVAP (Joint Valletta Action Plan) (2017a), 'Mapping of responses to Joint Valletta Action Plan', Table 1. Programmes.

JVAP (Joint Valletta Action Plan) (2017b), 'Mapping of responses to Joint Valletta Action Plan', Table 2. Policies and Legislation.

López-Sala, A. (2015), 'Exploring dissuasion as a (geo)political instrument in irregular migration control at the southern Spanish maritime border', *Geopolitics* **20**(3): 513–34.

Martin, P.L. (1993), 'Trade and migration: the case of NAFTA', *Asian and Pacific Migration Journal* **2**(3): 329–67.

Nyberg-Sørensen, N. (2012), 'Revisiting the migration-development nexus: from social networks and remittances to markets for migration control', *International Migration* **50**(3): 61–76.

Oelgemoller, C. (2011), '"Transit" and "suspension": migration management or the metamorphosis of asylum-seekers into "illegal" immigrants', *Journal of Ethnic and Migration Studies* **37**(3): 407–24.

Pallister-Wilkins, P. (2015), 'The humanitarian politics of European border policing: Frontext and border police in Evros', *International Political Sociology* **9**(1): 53–69.

Parker, B. (2017), 'Aid credibility at stake as donors haggle over reporting rules', IRIN, 21 July, available at http://www.irinnews.org/investigations/2017/07/21/aid-credibility-stake-donors-haggle-over-reporting-rules (accessed 21 July 2017).

Patel, P. (2016), 'My fury at our wasted foreign aid', *Daily Mail*, 13 September, available at http://www.dailymail.co.uk/news/article-3788162/My-fury-wasted-foreign-aid-International-development-secretary-Priti-Patel-ple dges-major-overhaul-12billion-budget.html#ixzz4oXqeqZbc (accessed 1 July 2017).

Pina Delgado, J. (2010), 'The current scheme to manage migration between Europe and Cape Verde: promotor of development or tool for border closure', *Population, Space and Place* **19**(4): 404–14.

Raghuram, P. (2009), 'Which migration? What development? Unsettling the edifice of migration and development', *Population, Space and Place* **15**(2): 103–17.

Skeldon, R. (1997), *Migration and Development: A Global Perspective*, London: Longman.

United Nations Development Programme (UNDP) (2009), *Human Development Report 2009. Overcoming Barriers: Human Mobility and Development*, New York, UNDP.

Valletta Summit (2015), 'Valletta Summit 2015 Action Plan', available at https://www.consilium.europa.eu/media/21839/action_plan_en.pdf (accessed 2 May 2018).

Walters, W. (2011), 'Foucault and frontiers: notes on the birth of the humanitarian border', in Ulrich Bröckling, Susanne Krasmann and Thomas Lemke (eds), *Governmentality: Current Issues and Future Challenges*, New York: Routledge, pp. 138–64.

14. Military-humanitarianism
Glenda Garelli and Martina Tazzioli

THE SPACES OF MILITARY-HUMANITARIANISM

Military-humanitarianism has long become a key migration management tool (Garelli and Tazzioli, 2017, 2018a; Loyd et al., 2016; Pallister-Wilkins, 2015, 2017; Williams, 2015). This has contributed to framing migration crises as situations to forcefully intervene on and performing operations of migration containment in the name of saving migrants. Military-humanitarianism in fact describes two intertwined processes: the deployment of military forces for performing humanitarian tasks (e.g., rescuing migrants at sea) and the militarization of humanitarian work (e.g., the use of military technologies by non-governmental organizations (NGOs) working in situations of humanitarian crisis).

In this chapter we are interested in accounting for the geographies of military-humanitarianism: the spaces through which it operates and, in turn, changes; and the spatial transformations it has undergone in the Mediterranean "of" migrants. In other words, our focus is on military-humanitarianism as a spatial process, where neither the "military" nor the "humanitarian" predicaments of this mode of intervention are taken at face value.

We start from two recent scenes of military-humanitarianism in the Mediterranean Sea in order to both situate this flexible technology for migration control in the context we are speaking from, historically and politically, while at the same time, clarifying our methodological approach to it.

CRIMINALIZING ACTS OF SOLIDARITY THROUGH MILITARY-HUMANITARIANISM

At the end of July 2017, the Italian government approved a "Code of Conduct"[1] to regulate the action of independent organizations engaged in search and rescue operations in the Mediterranean Sea, de facto mandating the militarization of humanitarian actors engaged in preventing border-deaths at the Mediterranean frontier of the European Union (EU).

In 2014, in fact, the Mediterranean Sea started to be actively patrolled by humanitarian fleets. While the mobilization of non-state actors to support refugees fleeing by sea dates back to the late 1970s with the Vietnamese boatpeople crisis, and continued throughout the 1980s and 1990s – most prominently with the German Cap Anamur missions – the 2014 mobilization in the Mediterranean Sea was unprecedented in terms of forces deployed. In this context NGOs,[2] independent actors,[3] and philanthropists[4] enlisted their

---

[1] http://www.interno.gov.it/sites/default/files/allegati/codice_condotta_ong.pdf (accessed October 23, 2018).
[2] Doctors without Borders, Save the Children, SOS Mediterranee.
[3] Sea-Eye, Sea-Watch, Jugend-Rettet, Arms Pro-Activa.
[4] Migrant Offshore Aid Station (MOAS).

own fleets and deployed their means to detect boats in distress and assist with rescue operations (Cusumano, 2017; Cuttitta, 2018; Stierl, 2018). An under-estimate of the lives rescued through these activities speaks of about 84,300 people (Zandonini, 2017).

This is the context where Italy, with the support of the EU, intervened, and mandated that all non-state actors engaged in Search and Rescue (SAR) operations in the Mediterranean have, among other things, to militarize their humanitarian actions by accepting the presence of armed police on board their vessels, in breach of the humanitarian and pacifist mandate of some of these organizations. Doctors without Borders,[5] Sea Watch,[6] and Jugend Rettet[7] refused to sign the Code, claiming that their ability to provide humanitarian support was contingent on two factors that signing the Code would force them to dissolve: first, the neutrality with respect to state powers; second, their non-militaristic approach and equipment. As a consequence of their rebellion to the Code, these organizations' boats were denied access to Italian ports, and Jugend Rettet was put on trial with the allegation that the organization collaborated with Libyan smugglers in organizing migrant journeys.

As we argued elsewhere (Garelli and Tazzioli, 2018b), the Code of Conduct has to be read in relation to the criminalization of acts of solidarity with migrants (Fassin, 2017; Fekete, 2009; Tazzioli, 2018) that European countries and the EU as a whole have been forcefully engaged with in the past few years, claiming that individual citizens' and organizations' solidarity actions were in fact a sort of humanitarian smuggling, breaking – albeit for humanitarian purposes – the 2002 EU Directive which prevents and penalizes "the facilitation of unauthorized entry, transit and residence" of undocumented migrants.

MILITARY-HUMANITARIANISM, MIGRATION CONTAINMENT, AND MIGRANT BODIES AT SEA

In May 2015 the EU launched its first warfare intervention in the field of migration, with Eunavfor Med Operation Sophia, a naval operation deployed for disrupting smugglers' operations in the Central Mediterranean. While the militaries have long been involved in Mediterranean scene of migration as they acted in compliance with the international obligation to assist seafarers in distress, this was the first EU warfare operation specifically aimed at intervening on the logistics of migration. In fact, the EU naval operation aimed at disrupting the "business model"[8] of smuggling networks by identifying, capturing, and disposing of vessels used for ferrying migrants to Europe.

The humanitarian predicament of the EU warfare against smugglers was underlined from the outset as the mission was presented as a military intervention aimed at protecting migrants from smugglers and to "reduce the loss of lives at sea." While the Libyan smuggling industry's abuses against migrants and predatory economy have been widely documented (e.g., United Nations, 2017), it remains that smugglers are in fact the only

---

[5]   http://www.msf.org/en/article/qa-why-msf-didn%E2%80%99t-sign-code-conduct-search-and-rescue (accessed October 23, 2018).

[6]   https://sea-watch.org/en/nonsensical-dishonest-illegal-the-code-of-conduct/ (accessed October 23, 2018).

[7]   https://jugendrettet.org/en/ (accessed October 23, 2018).

[8]   https://eeas.europa.eu/sites/eeas/files/eunavfor_med_-_mission_01_june_2017_en.pdf (accessed October 23, 2018).

passage available for people fleeing violence and destitution at home, when EU visa policies make it practically impossible for refugees to legally access Europe, resettlement programs serve less than 1 percent of the entire refugee population, and the EU relocation programs for refugees are at a dramatic standstill.

In this context, the disruption of the Libyan smuggling industry corresponds to a migration containment agenda: blocking the central Mediterranean route to Europe. So far this military-humanitarian intervention has resulted in dramatic consequences for the people trying to access a safe country out of Libya. The presence of Operation Sophia off the Libyan coast, in fact, while initially producing an effect of deterrence on Libyan smuggling networks, soon prompted them to find new approaches to their business and migrant journeys to Europe through Libya which simply became more dangerous and expensive as a result.[9]

Retaining our focus on military-humanitarianism as a migration management technology, which we approach through a spatial analysis, two important elements should be underlined. First, military-humanitarianism is a forceful migration containment tool in a situation of intersecting crises. The first crisis we are referring to is the humanitarian and political crisis people are fleeing from as they reach Libyan smugglers, ostensibly qualifying them as potential asylum seekers in Europe. The second crisis we are referring to is the political crisis of Europe, unwilling to respond to this situation with a politics of refuge and instead showing its litigious face as states opt out of the "burden sharing" mandate to collectively help with the refugee crisis at the borders of Europe. In this context, a hunt against smugglers to protect refugees against their abuses conveniently performs the blockage of refugees in Libya against their desire to seek refuge in Europe, hence performing a containment effect on migration flows across the Mediterranean. It also provides a humanitarian backing to the warfare enlisted against "the logistics of migrant journeys" (Garelli and Tazzioli, 2017, 2018a). In other words, military-humanitarianism allows state powers to enlist a *politics of refugees' spatial containment* away from Europe and in a place where their lives will certainly be at risk, if not of a possible shipwreck en route to refuge, of certain abuses in a country like Libya.

Second, we also want to zoom in and look at the human geography of this intervention from the vantage point of refugees themselves, at the elemental scale of their individual bodies. In his published conversation with Etienne Balibar, Nicholas De Genova suggested that "we should consider that the most elementary space is that of the body itself" and, he continues, "[we should] think about the mobility of bodies across the Mediterranean, the distribution of bodies across the Mediterranean" (Balibar and De Genova, 2018, p. 752). From this vantage point, military-humanitarianism looks like a flexible technology that allows state powers to zoom in and out of the body of refugees according to the political need of the moment. So, for instance, when the Italian military-humanitarian Operation Mare Nostrum was established, its biopolitical goal was the humanitarization of the shipwrecked refugee to be rescued from the waters (Basaran, 2015) – and eventually abandoned to various forms of destitution

---

[9] In order to minimize the economic loss resulting from their vessels' seizure by Eunavfor Med, Libyan smugglers changed the logistics of crossing, and increasingly used cheaper and more dangerous inflatable boats rather than wooden vessels. See https://publications.parliament.uk/pa/ld201516/ldselect/ldeucom/144/144.pdf (accessed October 23, 2018).

on land in Italy (Pinelli, 2018). With Operation Sophia the biopolitics of military-humanitarianism fences up and intervenes against the logistics of refugees' arrivals in Europe: refugees' bodies become, on the one hand, something to protect the EU from, to keep off shore, off the European shores, through the military-humanitarian warfare against the smugglers ferrying them there; and, on the other hand, bodies to be protected from smugglers' abuses.

In both cases – the criminalization of acts of solidarity and the containment of refugees' bodies away from Europe – military-humanitarianism is a tool that allows migration management to turn to a "securitarian offensive" through military means and under the humanitarian banner.

THE SPATIAL REROUTING OF MILITARY-HUMANITARIANISM

The humanitarian government of migrations is depicted as an EU-led practice, in spatial or in substantial terms. Indeed, even in the case of humanitarian refugee assistance in non-European countries, most of the time European agencies play a major role in coordinating and monitoring local organizations. Similarly, military-humanitarianism tends to be narrated in the media as a mode of intervention put into place and coordinated by Western states. More precisely, military-humanitarianism in the field of refugee management is highly geographically connoted, as it is seen as a South-to-North practice. In this regard, the Italian Mare Nostrum Operation has been a case in point: between October 2013 and December 2014, migrants in distress at sea used to be rescued very close to Libyan waters and then ferried to Italy (Tazzioli, 2015). The "Navy-taxi," as many detractors called Mare Nostrum, was entirely managed by Italy and, moreover, after being taken out of the sea, migrants disembarked on the Northern shore of the Mediterranean. Such spatial orientation – from South-to-North – of the "humanitarian border" (Walters, 2011) actually discloses the main predicaments of the politics of protection: that is, refugees should be protected from "rogue states" (Derrida, 2004) and Western countries are the only true holders of humanitarian criteria. In other words, both human rights and humanitarianism are predicated upon a Euro-centered geography. However, such a narrative appears to be quite misleading today, in light of the undergoing transformations and reshaping of military-humanitarianism in the Mediterranean. Furthermore, and beyond geopolitical considerations, we contend that it is part of a critical account of military-humanitarianism to disengage from a Eurocentric gaze on it, projecting on the Southern shore of the Mediterranean.

The transformations that have recently occurred in military-humanitarianism have showed that, far from being totally driven by the EU, third-countries, such as Turkey and Libya, are decisive actors on the Mediterranean chessboard and pursue their own economic and geopolitical interests (Cassarino, 2014, 2016, 2017). Yet, accounting for the active role played by third-countries in containing and managing migrants in the Mediterranean region does not simply involve widening the geographical focus nor to think of military-humanitarian practices as ways of acting that travel from the Northern to the Southern shore of the Mediterranean. Rather, it entails mapping the different nuances of migration governmentality and the different modes in which the *biopolitics* of *rescuing and letting drown* is played out.

The argument that we want to push forward is twofold. First, through the recent bilateral agreement between Italy and Libya, there has been a substantial spatial rerouting of military-humanitarianism; or better, the implementation of the bilateral agreement has accelerated and made visible the agreements and arrangements that have been put into place over the last three years through political negotiations. Second, military-humanitarianism has been redefined through the blueprint of the *war on smugglers*. Relatedly, as we will illustrate later in this section, the unconditional humanitarian goal of saving migrant lives at sea has become subordinated to what we call *containment through rescue*.

It is important to clarify that the fight against migrant smugglers does not represent a new entry in the EU political agenda; even when Mare Nostrum was in place, curbing the "illegal" economy of migrant crossing was officially considered a political priority along with the duty of rescuing migrants in distress at sea. However, we want to suggest that the war on smugglers has recently gained center stage in the Mediterranean geopolitical scenario. More importantly, it is not only on a quantitative level but also on a qualitative one that the declared fight against smugglers has impacted on military-humanitarian operations. Indeed, since the launch of the EU naval operation Sophia in May 2015, the prioritization of the fight against smuggling networks has reshaped the modus operandi of rescue vessels and, at the same time, the biopolitical predicaments that sustain military-humanitarianism (Garelli and Tazzioli, 2017, 2018a).

By speaking of a spatial reorientation of military-humanitarianism we refer to landing places where migrants rescued at sea are taken. If during Mare Nostrum migrants were transferred to European member states, the implementation of the Italian-Libyan bilateral agreement has officially set forth what in practice was already enacted on the sly: migrants are intercepted and rescued by the Libyan Coast Guard and pushed back to Libya.

Such a spatial rerouting of military-humanitarianism shows us, in fact, an essential transformation in the effects of rescue practices: *being rescued* finally equates with *being captured*; people are fished out of the water but are not put into safety. Migrants are taken back to Libya, the "transit" country they reached to flee war, persecution, and destitution at home. On a more technical level, *rescue* and *interception* activities are conflated and the boundaries between the two get blurred, both on a legal dimension and on a practical one (Heller and Pezzani, 2015). Indeed, migrants in danger in the Mediterranean Sea are, however, heading towards Europe, so by being rescued by the Libyan Coast Guard, they are actually hampered from reaching the European shores. Instead, by sending SOS calls to the Italian Coast Guard and demanding to be rescued, migrants were de facto ferried to Europe.

Gregoire Chamayou's analysis on manhunts helps capture the ambivalences of the biopolitics of rescuing and letting drown: indeed, this latter is not only about saving or not saving migrants at sea but also, in a more proactive way, about pointing to human targets. With manhunting, Chamayou explains, "the combat zone tends to be reduced to the body of the enemy, which must then, according to the principle of distinction, be the only space that is targeted; but, on the other hand, it is believed that this mobile micro-space can be targeted wherever it happens to be" (Chamayou, 2011). Yet, who is the target of the humanitarian migrant-hunt in the Mediterranean? Actually, it is not only the migrant in distress at sea, who in fact is rescued and captured at the same time; rather, migrants and smugglers are both, on paper, the prey of military-humanitarianism.

Hence, what is left of humanitarianism? Humanitarian interventions get split from a politics of protection, which are apt to bring migrants to safety, and recognizing them as refugees (Cuttitta, 2018; Sciurba and Furri, 2018): humanitarianism is relegated to a biopolitics of rescuing and letting drown, which consists of simply fishing out (or not) migrants from the sea. This would mean in fact corroborating the image of a "good humanitarianism," free of articulations/entanglements with security and military modes of intervention. Rather, we point to the fading away of the refugee at sea as the emblematic figure of humanitarianism, a figure that turns out to be superseded by the battle against smuggling networks.

We do not see military-humanitarianism as an antinomic couplet in which we need to rescue one of the two terms against the other: on the contrary, military-humanitarianism, in all its variations and specific enactments, constitutes a logics and a mode of governmentality characterized by the use of humanitarian reasons and measures in military operations and/or the deployment of military actors and technologies for performing humanitarian tasks. Nonetheless, military-humanitarianism should not be seen as the mere juxtaposition of military and humanitarian measures and rationales, nor as a coherent "sovereign machine of governmentality" (Mezzadra and Neilson, 2013).

The multiple entanglements between military and humanitarian approaches, actors and techniques have in fact generated transformations in the way of conceiving and enacting humanitarianism. While humanitarianism is traditionally conceived as the set of measures implemented for "alleviating human suffering" (Barnett, 2011), military-humanitarian operations deployed in the Mediterranean for saving migrants reshape humanitarianism as a politics of rescue, that is, as fishing people out of the sea. Related to that, the central role played by military tactics and actors in saving migrants makes blatant the ambivalent effect of rescue: upon being rescued at sea, migrants are de facto captured, taken back to Libya, or transferred to the Hotspots in Italy and in Greece. In brief, the biopolitics of rescuing and letting drown, played both by military actors (such as the Navy) and humanitarian organizations (such as Doctors Without Borders and independent SAR vessels) narrows the focus to the sea-scenario. The geographies of military-humanitarianism at sea correspond to the scene of rescue and are ultimately defined by the contested boundaries of jurisdiction, competence, and non-responsibility that crisscross the Mediterranean – formed by national waters, contiguous waters, and SAR areas.

Therefore, a thorough critical appraisal of military-humanitarianism requires, instead, engaging in a spatial-temporal stretching of the analysis beyond the space of the sea. This consists of exploring the functioning and the effects of military-humanitarian measures according to a temporal and a spatial "after" with respect to the sequel of interception-rescue-capture in the Mediterranean. Similarly, we contend that what is left out of the picture, in critical analyses on military-humanitarianism, are what can be called the "geographies of ungreviability" (Tazzioli, 2018). Indeed, the recent multiplication of bilateral agreements between EU member states and African countries has moved back deadly frontiers from the Mediterranean Sea to the Libyan and Niger desert. As a consequence of this type of agreement, migrants who do not die at sea but who manage to arrive in Libya are kept in detention in the Libyan prisons.

The function of Libya as a spatial linchpin and pressure valve for Mediterranean migrations is certainly not new. In fact, the crucial role played by Colonel Gaddafi in managing migrations until 2011, and in using migrants as human bombs as a form of pressure on European states, is well known. Soon after the fall of Gaddafi in February 2011, Libya was initially depicted by the EU as a rogue state at the limits of ungovernability, in particular due to the lack of a unique central government. However, at the same time, both the EU and the United Nations started to consider Libya as a country that needed help in its way towards democracy and sovereignty. Even though there are currently three separate governments in the country, the task of supporting Libya towards sovereignty is at the core of the EU political agenda. However, the meaning of containment has visibly changed over the last three years. Under Gaddafi, the regime was engaged with temporarily containing migrants in Libya in exchange for Italian investments in the country, while smugglers were engaged in organizing complex logistics of migrant crossing. In the past three years the situation has radically changed and now the smuggling and state economy is focused on attempts to contain migrants in Libya (Morone, 2016).

The construction of the Libyan space of migration containment directly involves European agencies, such as Frontex, and international agencies, such as the International Organization for Migration (IOM) and the United Nations High Commissioner for Refugees (UNHCR). UNHCR in fact was sent away from Libya by Gaddafi in 2010 and is now back supporting Libyan authorities despite the country never having signed the 1951 Geneva Convention on refugee protection. Both IOM and UNHCR currently operate in the country contributing to what can be called the twofold system of *detentive hosting* and *humanitarized detention* that rescued migrants are subjected to. Indeed, after being rescued and captured by the Libyan Coast Guard and taken back to Libya, migrants are transferred from Libyan port to detention centers and prisons where they are blackmailed. As shown by journalist investigations, the same smuggling networks that the EU officially wants to dismantle do actually work in complicity with Libyan state authorities and, indirectly, with the European organizations that are on the ground. In particular, Italy has unofficially signed on the sly agreements with Libyan militias to stop migrants' departures from the country, thus financing directly the smuggling networks that it condemns (Harchaoui and Herbert, 2017; Michael, 2017; New York Times Editorial Board, 2017).

The underlying negotiations between the Italian government and Libyan militias show that Italy's and the EU's goal is not to tackle the migrant smuggling networks, as an "illicit" economy but, rather, to undermine migrants' "logistics of crossing" (Garelli and Tazzioli, 2017, 2018a). While, on the one hand, the war against smugglers has gained center stage in the EU political agenda and at the level of public media, on the other hand, the deal with Libyan smugglers to stop migrants from leaving the country tells us that the actual targets of military-humanitarianism are migrants.

With the deployment of European and international agencies in Libya, military-humanitarianism and border enforcement cooperation finally overlap: UNHCR, Frontex, and IOM are assisting Libyan authorities by providing technical equipment, training activities, and personnel deployed at the ports to improve migrants' registrations and in detention centers for strengthening the government's "humanitarian capacity". The EU's intervention and support to Libyan detentive hosting can be seen as bestowing on Libya migration containment measures and, at the same time, as a path towards the externalization of the asylum. Yet, we contend that such a view reiterates the Eurocentric narrative which sees Libya as Europe's puppet, erasing in this way both Libya's political and economic interests as well as the (relative) autonomy and specificity of the Libyan economy of migration.

The political tenet of the EU-Libya strategy of migration containment consists in depicting Libya as a "safe country": the same space that under Gaddafi and soon after his fall was considered a hell for migrants is now presented by European agencies as a country which is on the road towards humanitarianism, heading to match international human rights standards. Such an alleged transition of Libya towards safety and human rights starkly contrasts with direct testimonies about violence and blackmailing that migrants are subjected to. The humanitarized detention has been illustrated by the Italian Minister of Foreign Affairs, Angelino Alfano, who argued that "in Libya there won't be concentration camps anymore, but humanitarian camps." Hence, among the many variations of military-humanitarianism, we come to grips with the humanitarization of the inhuman which takes place through the articulation of military and humanitarian actors in Libya. Looking at the Libyan context of migration containment, the threshold of the inhuman appears as the limit-point of military-humanitarianism and that remains fundamentally undertheorized given the taken-for-granted image of the refugee at sea to be saved as the subject par excellence of humanitarianism.

CONCLUSION: THE MILITARIZATION OF HUMANITARIAN RESCUE

The reshaping of military-humanitarianism also concerns humanitarian actors and the humanitarian logics as such. The implementation of the Code of Conduct for NGOs in Italy has formally sanctioned the duty for NGOs involved in SAR activities to be equipped with security and military measures/assets. Armed judiciary policemen are requested to be on board NGOs' vessels and, more broadly, SAR activities are put under direct control of the Italian Coast Guard. Yet, in order to escape the humanitarian narrative that sees humanitarian and military actors as in opposition to each other, it is important to notice that some independent actors were already equipped with military and security technologies. This is the case of the Migrant Offshore Aid Station (MOAS), the first non-governmental actor that deployed a rescue vessel in the Mediterranean in 2014: since the beginning, MOAS used drones for detecting migrants at sea and accepted exchange of data with Frontex.

The increasing militarization of NGOs' activities has been actualized through a *spatial shrinking* of the operation range. Libya's decision on August 10, 2017 to implement a SAR zone came out of the blue and, in fact, is not recognized by the International Maritime Organization (IMO) yet – so, it is still unofficial and the result of an arbitrary sovereign act. A SAR zone officially designates a state's zone of competence – and thus of legal responsibility – in SAR operations and in coordinating vessels, even from other countries, that come across boats in distress. Instead, by activating its SAR zone, Libya has declared its jurisdiction – and not competence – on that area, hampering NGOs from entering there in order to do SAR. Thus, in the place of improving and granting safer rescue operations, paradoxically Libya's establishment of a SAR zone has worked in keeping humanitarian actors out of the scene.

The official bulletin of migrants rescued and captured by the Libyan Coast Guard is quite discontinuous: some days Italian or Libyan authorities communicate the approximate number of migrants saved and then taken back to Libya, but the absence of data and official dispatches is more frequent. According to IOM, 13,148 migrants were saved, or captured, in Libyan waters in 2017. In fact, the gap between effective migrant departures, number of people saved and returned, and of unreported shipwrecks has hardly been closed. The politics of migration containment at sea is in fact played out by states from the Northern and the Southern shore of the Mediterranean and by producing gray zones of jurisdiction at sea, and holes of traceable events.

The partial lack of statistics and numbers regarding migrants rescued and returned by the Libyan Coast Guard actually also depends on the fact that migrants are not allowed to leave. Indeed, as the Italian Coordinator of Doctors Without Borders put it, "even more than intercepting migrants at sea and returning them to Libya, Libyan authorities together with the militias do not allow migrants to leave, and the smuggling economy itself is partially blocked for the moment." Indeed, the reported number of migrants rescued and returned by the Libyan Coast Guard in August 2017 was half the number in July – 608 between August 7 and August 21, 1,298 between July 21 and August 6 – revealing a substantial drop in departures.

Consequently, military-humanitarianism has partially shifted from the scene of the sea towards measures of detentive hosting and humanitarian-ized detention on the mainland. This does not mean that the biopolitics of rescuing and letting drown has come to an end. Despite that the scene of rescue has been shrunk, some NGOs continue to conduct SAR activities in the Mediterranean and military vessels both from the European naval operation Eunavfor and from the Italian Navy and Coast Guard patrol and do rescue operations. Yet, what we want to suggest is that from an almost exclusive focus on the scene of the sea, military-humanitarianism has been re-crafted as a politics aiming at not letting migrants leave. In this way, humanitarianism itself is substantially reshaped: protection becomes synonymous with containment, insofar as keeping them in Libya is presented as a strategy for not letting them die at sea.

A critical appraisal of military-humanitarianism entails, however, bringing issues related to the biopolitical economy of migrations into focus. More precisely, we refer to the modes of value extraction from the commodification of migrant bodies that are run in parallel to (and that in part sustain) the military-humanitarian management of migration in Libyan jurisdiction (at sea and on land).

We want to conclude by pointing to future research paths that should take into account the different forms of capitalization over migrants that are at stake in the humanitarian and military government of refugees. In particular, we contend that further research should critically engage with the nexus between forced mobility and commodification of migrant bodies. Over the last decade there has been a proliferation of journalist reports and academic work on migration and contemporary forms of slavery, referring not only to trafficking but also to migrants being blackmailed and sold from one militia to another. Yet, such a literature conflates slavery and migrants being subjected to violence and forced to be sold in order to come to Europe. In this regard, we suggest shifting attention from slavery as such towards the capitalization over migrants' desire to move on the part of European states and third-countries, as well as of smuggling groups.

A critical migration geography approach should further investigate the emergence of new economic spaces and of spatial economies related to the military-humanitarian government of migrations. Migration geography analyses could contribute to desta-bilize the Eurocentric view on military-humanitarianism, not by simply inverting the gaze, from South to North, but by bringing into focus the mobile spaces of governmentality that emerge, between the sea and the land, from practices of humanitarian containment.

REFERENCES

Balibar, E. and N. De Genova (2018), "Mediterranean struggles for movement and the European government of bodies: an interview with", *Antipode*, **50**, 748–62. doi:10.1111/anti.12347.

Barnett, Michael (2011), *Empire of Humanity: A History of Humanitarianism*, Ithaca, NY: Cornell University Press.

Basaran, T. (2015), "The saved and the drowned: governing indifference in the name of security", *Security Dialogue*, **46**(3), 205–20.

Cassarino, J.-P. (2014), "Channelled policy transfers: EU-Tunisia interactions on migration matters", *European Journal of Migration and Law*, **16**(1), 97–123.

Cassarino, J.-P. (2016), "Réadmission des migrants: les faux-semblants des partenariats euro-africains", *Politique étrangère*, **1**, 25–37.

Cassarino, J.-P. (2017), "Approaching borders and frontiers in North Africa", *International Affairs*, **93**(4), 883–96.

Chamayou, G. (2011), "The manhunt doctrine", *Radical Philosophy*, **169**(Sept/Oct), accessed October 23, 2018 at https://www.radicalphilosophy.com/commentary/the-manhunt-doctrine.

Cusumano, E. (2017), "The sea as humanitarian space. Non-governmental search and rescue dilemmas on the Central Mediterranean migratory route", *Mediterranean Politics*, **23**, 3, 387–94.

Cuttitta, P. (2018), "Repoliticization through search and rescue? Humanitarian NGOs and migration management in the Central Mediterranean", *Geopolitics*, **23**(3), 632–60.

Derrida, J. (2004), "The last of the rogue states: The 'democracy to come,' opening in two turns", *South Atlantic Quarterly*, **103**(2–3), 323–41.

Fassin, E. (2017), "Le procès politique de la solidarité (3/4): les ONG en Méditerranée", *Mediapart*, accessed November 29, 2017 at https://blogs.mediapart.fr/eric-fassin/blog/170817/le-proces-politique-de-la-solidarite-34-les-ong-en-mediterranee.

Fekete, L. (2009), "Europe: crimes of solidarity", *Race & Class*, **50**(4), 83–97.

Garelli, G. and M. Tazzioli (2017), "Warfare on the logistics of migrant movement", *Open Democracy*, June 16, 2016, accessed November 29, 2017 at https://www.opendemocracy.net/mediterranean-journeys-in-hope/glenda-garelli-martina-tazzioli/warfare-on-logistics-of-migrant-movem.

Garelli, G. and M. Tazzioli (2018a), "The biopolitical warfare on migrants: EU Naval Force and NATO operations in the Mediterranean", *Critical Military Studies*, **4**(2), 181–200.

Garelli, G. and M. Tazzioli (2018b), "The humanitarian war against migrant smugglers at sea", *Antipode*, **50**(3), 685–703.

Harchaoui, J. and M. Herbert (2017), "Italy claims it's found a solution to Europe's migration problem. Here's why Italy is wrong", *Washington Post*, September 26, accessed November 29, 2017 at https://www.washingtonpost.com/news/monkey-cage/wp/2017/09/25/italy-claims-its-found-a-solution-to-europes-migrant-problem-heres-why-italys-wrong/?utm_term=.9292007829db.

Heller, C. and L. Pezzani (2015), "'Sharing the burden of rescue': illegalised boat migration, the shipping industry and the costs of rescue in the Central Mediterranean", *Post for the Border Criminologies Themed Blog Series on the Industry of Illegality organised by Ruben Andersson*, 2.

Loyd, J.M., E. Mitchell-Eaton, and A. Mountz (2016), "The militarization of islands and migration: tracing human mobility through US bases in the Caribbean and the Pacific", *Political Geography*, **53**, 65–75. doi:10.1016/j.polgeo.2015.11.006.

Mezzadra, S. and B. Neilson (2013), *Border as Method. Or the Multiplication of Labour*, Durham, NC: Duke University Press.

Michael, M. (2017), "Backed by Italy, Libya enlists militias to stop migrants", Associated Press, August 29, accessed November 29, 2017 at https://www.apnews.com/9e808574a4d04eb38fa8c688d110a23d/.

Morone, A.M. (2016), "The African migratory factor in the Libyan transition", in *North African Societies after the Arab Spring: Between Democracy and Islamic Awakening*, Cambridge: Cambridge Scholars Publishing, pp. 156–80.

New York Times Editorial Board (2017), "Italy's dodgy deal on migrants", *New York Times*, September 25, accessed November 29, 2017 at https://www.nytimes.com/2017/09/25/opinion/migrants-italy-europe.html.

Pallister-Wilkins, P. (2015), "The humanitarian politics of European border policing: Frontex and border police in Evros", *International Political Sociology*, **9**(1), 53–69.

Pallister-Wilkins, P. (2017), "Humanitarian borderwork", in *Border Politics*, New York: Springer International Publishing, pp. 85–103.

Pinelli, B. (2018), "Control and abandonment: the power of surveillance on refugees in Italy, during and after the Mare Nostrum operation", *Antipode*, **50**(3), 725–47.

Sciurba, A. and F. Furri (2018), "Human rights beyond humanitarianism: the radical challenge to the right to asylum in the Mediterranean zone", *Antipode*, **50**(3), 763–82.

Stierl, M. (2018), "A fleet of Mediterranean border humanitarians", *Antipode*, **50**(3), 704–24.

Tazzioli, M. (2015), "The desultory politics of mobility and the humanitarian-military border in the Mediterranean. Mare Nostrum beyond the sea", *REMHU Revista Interdisciplinar de Mobilidad Humana*, **23**, 44–60.

Tazzioli, M. (2018), "Crimes of solidarity. Migration and containment through rescue", *Radical Philosophy*, 2.01, accessed October 23, 2018 at https://www.radicalphilosophy.com/commentary/crimes-of-solidarity.

United Nations (2017), *Final report of the Panel of Experts on Libya established pursuant to resolution 1973* (2011) (S/2017/466), June 1, accessed November 29, 2017 at https://reliefweb.int/report/libya/final-report-panel-experts-libya-established-pursuant-resolution-1973-2011-s2017466.

Walters, William (2011), "Foucault and frontiers: notes on the birth of the humanitarian border", in Ulrich Bröckling, S. Krasmann, and T. Lemke (eds), *Governmentality: Current issues and Future Challenges*, Abingdon: Routledge, pp. 138–64.

Williams, J.M. (2015), "From humanitarian exceptionalism to contingent care. Care and enforcement at the humanitarian border", *Political Geography*, **47**, 11–20.

Zandonini, G. (2017), "How the humanitarian NGOs operate at sea", *Openmigration*, May 22, accessed November 29, 2017 at http://openmigration.org/en/analyses/how-the-humanitarian-ngos-operate-at-sea/.

15. Genealogies of contention in concentric circles: remote migration control and its Eurocentric geographical imaginaries
Maribel Casas-Cortes and Sebastian Cobarrubias

INTRODUCTION

The evocative statement "We did not cross the border, the border crossed us" has become a staple among pro-migration activism beyond the US/Mexico context where it was originally stated.[1] While counter-intuitive, it points to the historical and ongoing contingent movement of borderlines. It also speaks about the ingrained discriminatory character of a border mindset that believes that one's very self can be permanently marked as a border crosser, and thus becoming an inappropriate and usually undesired other.[2] Indeed, the message conveyed by "the border crossed us" uniquely captures current migratory policies. Both the imagining and the enforcing of migration control are intended to "cross" – as in traverse through – certain populations. This crossing *by* borders is conducted through the containment, classification and segregation of those considered unwanted migrants.

As such, borders do carry on their own crossing practices ranging from high-tech infrastructures for the tracking and interception of some human movements *at and beyond* the borderline, all the way to the bordering of bodies *at and inside* the borderline through processes of racialized profiling, incarceration and deportation. The verb form and play on words of "B/Ordering" as developed by critical migration scholars of the Nijmegen School relates well with this notion of borders themselves actively crossing over people. This piece embraces their understanding of borders as complex filters that classify populations under an apartheid logic through the triple function of bordering, ordering and *othering* (Van Houtum and Van Naerssen 2002; Van Houtum et al. 2005). Now, such a twist on borders, not as passive lines to be crossed but as institutional practices actively b/ordering populations, do not only take place at the territorial limits of countries. In fact, the act of arranging people into hierarchies of mobility, along with its corresponding entitlements and lack thereof, is becoming a ubiquitous process wherever one might be.

---

[1]   The origin of this slogan comes from Mexican migrants in the US Southwest expressing the fact that much of the Western US was once part of Mexico. Texas, New Mexico, Arizona and California were seized by the US in the Mexican-American war of 1846–48. Pointing to the irony of labeling Mexican citizens in the US Southwest as foreigners and illegal trespassers, the expression has been attributed to everyone from writer Jose Antonio Burciaga, actress Eva Longoria to the band Aztlan Underground. It is widely popular because it communicates the notion that geopolitical borders are imposed on peoples that have lived in those places prior to those dividing lines.

[2]   Besides being used for immigrant rights, the slogan has resonated among Indigenous movements, Palestinian solidarity groups, anti-colonial and racial justice struggles, all working against institutional racism and practices of exclusion.

The spatial proliferation of such bordering practices – when migration control is carried out across unexpected places regardless of geographical location in reference to a national borderline – is possible due to a double process. The borderline has moved both inwards and outwards of the territorial state's outer limits. This chapter focuses on the second process, that is, the displacement of borderzones further away from apparent destination countries. In fact, these destination countries carry out practices of migration control thousands of kilometers away from their own traditionally claimed borderlines, and request collaboration from third countries to patrol suspected migratory movements. This phenomenon is referred to as "border externalization," both among policy circles and scholarly literature.

This form of borderwork from a distance, by which responsibilities conventionally assumed to be exclusive to a given state are delegated to third parties and carried out extra-territorially, has become standard migration policy in a variety of cases. This is the case of the European Union (EU) and its member states, whose migration control practices increasingly take place beyond their borderlines. The targeting of supposedly migrants' places of origin and transit has become the main policy objective. In order to trace and interfere in migratory journeys, a spectrum of means is carried out ranging from one-on-one interviews, aid plans and development interventions to paramilitary deployments. Far from sporadic or marginal, outsourcing the management of migration flows is indeed proliferating. In fact, border cooperation has become an expected modus operandi in international relations, transforming practices of migration control at the levels of legality, diplomacy and enforcement. This transnational process of border externalization has been underway in the Southern contours of the Mediterranean and Sub-Saharan Africa increasingly since the EU started to implement its *Global Approach to Migration* in 2005 and its Migratory Routes Strategy.

When approaching border externalization, authors have developed a rich spatial vocabulary to understand its geographical shifts and geopolitical effects. From the first engagements with this process as remote border control (Zolberg 2003), police at a distance (Bigo and Guild 2005), shifting out (Lavenex 2006) or re-scaling (Samers 2004) to the later readings of border externalization in terms of bio-political re-territorialization (Vaughan-Williams 2008); spatial stretching and itinerancy (Casas-Cortes et al. 2012); off-shoring and outsourcing (Bialasiewicz 2012); shifts in state sovereignty (Mountz and Hiemstra 2014); a networked and multi-scalar regime (Raeymaekers 2014). All of those conceptualizations are pointing to a spatial re-location and multiplication of bordering – as in its triple function of contention, classification and discrimination – beyond the geographical limits of the nation-state. Thus interdisciplinary debates on extra-territoriality and bio-political power have been pertinent in the geographical understanding of border externalization (Parker and Vaughan-Williams 2012; Gaibazzi et al. 2016; Zaiotti 2016).

This chapter in particular contributes to a genealogy of border externalization by identifying a rather Eurocentric ideological core at work underneath the neutral sounding policies of border externalization. We contend that despite being informed and fueled by circles of professionalism and expertise, current border externalization is inserted into a previous contention logic based on exclusionary thinking and abusive practices on the ground.[3]

GENEALOGIES OF CONTENTION: THE WORLD DIVIDED INTO CONCENTRIC CIRCLES

According to the entry of the New Keywords on Migration, border externalization refers to the practices of migration control that involve acting beyond territorial lines in coordination with adjacent and non-adjacent countries (New Keywords Collective 2014). The origins of outsourcing border control – and the concurrent tendencies to evade the law and constantly extend geo-juridical boundaries – have roots in the US interdiction of Haitian refugees in the early 1980s and have spread, especially among the EU and Australia. For the EU, border externalization is neither new nor anecdotal. It has characterized the EU's strategy for containing migratory flows since the 1990s. Nonetheless, in our own research we have attempted to follow and describe the development of spatial frameworks that facilitated the birth of such bordering practices far from territorial limits of destination countries. In this pursuit we encountered an old proposal to approach inward migration to the EU rich in geographical thinking. By engaging the geographical imaginary that immediately precedes and sustain the bulk of the EU's extra-territorial border operations, a controversial vision of human mobility becomes explicit. This geographic imaginary is fraught with, literally, Euro-concentric tensions, ordering global populations into designated circles: including a first ring of territories entitled to free movement; a second and third ring of territories where movement is relatively allowed; and a fourth ring where it is seemingly prohibited to move. While seen as greatly problematic initially, this uneven division of mobilities and hierarchical designation of territories has been slowly normalized. We point to the influential legacy of the EU draft strategy paper on asylum and migration and contend that the geographical imaginary and the contention logic displayed by this document is underpinning current externalized forms of migration control.

While working on the archaeologies of the current EU migration regime, an official document proposing to divide the world into concentric circles caught our attention: "The EU Strategy Paper on Asylum and Migration" by the Council of the European Union (1998a). This document has been analysed sporadically by authors tracing the history of the EU's inclusion of migration policy into its foreign policy (Boswell 2003; Lindström 2005; Sterkx 2008; Chou 2009; Barbero 2010). We started to take it seriously since encountering the work by Belguendouz (2005, 2009). In his critique of the role of migration policy in the relations between North Africa (especially Morocco) and the EU, Belguendouz argues about the document's foundational importance to understand the current EU border regime. During the Austrian presidency of the EU in 1998, this historical official document was distributed to different branches of the EU Council (it was addressed specifically to the K4 committee of Interior Ministries). An initial draft was leaked to press and non-governmental organizations (NGOs) alerting the public as to its

---

[3]   This chapter is based on a multi-sited research project funded by the National Science Foundation (Grant BCS-1023543). We focus on the EU's strategy of migration routes management in North and West Africa, looking at border cooperation projects between so-called destination-transit-origin countries.

controversial nature. This 1998 document classifies worldwide territories and populations therein into four concentric circles. It evokes a geographical vision of how mobility should be distributed in the world, implying that everyone, in a sense, belongs and should remain in their circle with little exception.

This proposed document, with a heavily geographical vision of managing mobility into Europe, scandalized many, including several EU governments, due to what was perceived as an unnecessarily restrictive and discriminatory approach to migration at that time. Yet, while the policy itself was officially voted down in 1998, many of its ideas were further pursued outside the EU framework by an intergovernmental network: the High Level Working Group (HLWG) on migration. This desired geographical imaginary of control and contention of human flows worldwide is surely not fully achieved on the ground. While EU-funded plans and projects are tried – such as the Frontex-led *Hera* operation, the Spain-led series within the *Seahorse Project*, the ongoing EU *Sophia* operation and Italy's *Mare Sicuro* in the central Mediterranean – there are different levels of success and failure. As such, this 1998 vision of migration control based on concentric circles is not a representation of the EU border regime as it actually exists or existed. Rather, we point to how its designation of worldwide territories beyond the EU in terms of their role in an imagined global migration system have, for the most part, remained intact.

The "Strategy Paper on Asylum and Migration" of 1998 proposes four concentric circles to encompass the entire globe, and they classify countries as either: (1) desirable destinations and zones of mobility; (2) countries of transit adjacent to the EU; (3) countries of transit further away; or (4) sources of undesirable population flows. Quite remarkably, this EU document acknowledges the very existence of a "fortress Europe" policy concept. Indeed, the paper proposes that "a model of concentric circles of migration policy could replace that of "fortress Europe" (Council of the European Union 1998a: point 60) in reducing migratory pressure, and, more specifically, tightening border control. According to this model, all states of the world would be assigned to one of "four concentric circles." We have visualized those four concentric circles cartographically for the sake of clarity and in order to graphically show the geographical imaginary behind current policies (Figure 15.1).

The first circle is formed by the EU member states capable of fulfilling Schengen standards of control, and other countries which "do not cause emigration" but have become "target countries on account of their advanced economic and political situation" (Council of the European Union 1998a: points 60 and 116).

The second circle would consist of "transit countries" which no longer generate emigration but which "on account of a relatively stable internal economic and political situation accept only very limited control procedures and responsibility for migration policy." This second circle would comprise the neighbor countries of the Schengen/EU territory, that is, the associated states and "perhaps also the Mediterranean area." These countries' systems of control should gradually be brought into line with the first circle standards (1998a: points 60 and 118).

The third and fourth circle would contain the countries of emigration. The third circle would be formed of countries of both emigration and transit, that is, the CIS area (former Soviet Union), Turkey and North Africa. These countries would be required to "concentrate primarily on transit checks and combatting facilitator [migrant smuggler] networks." The fourth (outermost) circle would consist of countries of emigration apparently deemed somewhat beyond the reach of European "political muscle" (mention is made of

1 EU member states / Schengen zone

As the integration of the European Union proceeded, the twenty-odd members of the EU pooled their sovereignty together and created a zone of free movement for goods, capital and people called the Schengen zone. The zone allows you to move, work and study freely in any of its member countries. Considered one of the success stories of the EU, Schengen has come under increasing critique since the so-called financial and refugee crises.

2 European Neighbourhood Partner ship

EU candidate countries are potential members of the EU, and must meet Schengen criteria. They are considered countries of transit until membership. Countries of the European Neighbourhood Policy (ENP). These countries which are adjacent to the European Union are offered a chance to participate in the EU's Single Market and regulatory frameworks, but in exchange are asked to manage and police any undocumented migration passing through their territories, potentially on it's way to the EU. Integration to EU structures is made conditional on their cooperation in border security.

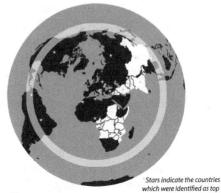

Stars indicate the countries which were identified as top sources of illegal entries in 2016

3 Transit Zone

The transit zone includes many of the ENP countries (which have stronger trade links with the EU), along with other countries, which are seen from the EU as needing to police migrants that are 'transiting' through their countries on the way to the EU. Countries of the third circle are considered to be points of transit for migrants on their way to the first circle. These countries are not offered integration into EU Markets and frameworks.

4 Source Countries

The countries of the 4th circle are seen as migration "source" countries, briefly referred to in the 1998 strategy as "the Middle East, China, and black Africa". The EU approach towards these countries includes border security as in the transit countries but is complimented by programs that encourage people to "stay in their circle". These projects of "dissuasion" can include development projects; PR campaigns on the dangers of irregular migration as well as signing agreements to allow for rapid deportation of these countries' nationals form the EU.

Countries highlighted on this map are those considered part of the "fourth circle" for EU purposes, but as the stars indicate, not all countries which actually make up the top sources of undocumented migrants to the EU are treated as part of the fourth circle by EU policy.

Source: Council of the European Union (1998a).

Figure 15.1   Visualization of concentric circles by MCC, SC and Tim Stallman "the Middle East," China and "black Africa"). These countries are to be encouraged to "eliminate push factors" of migration (1998a: points 60 and 119).[4]

A reward would follow if a country meets the obligations arising from its assignment to a particular circle. "For example, the second circle must meet Schengen standards as a precondition for EU membership; for the third circle, intensified economic cooperation is linked to the fulfillment of their obligations; and the fourth circle, the extent of development aid can be assessed on that basis" (1998a: point 61; Fortress Europe Circular Letter 1998).

EURO CONCENTRIC VISION OF MOBILITY

Such a geographical imaginary literally puts the EU in the center, dictating who should move and who should not move around the world. It also assumes several major dynamics of migration that empirically are very questionable. In the first place, the document implies that everybody intends to get to circle 1, thus ignoring movement within and across circles, especially South to South migrations. Secondly, the document suggests that no one gets out of the EU, and that there is no migratory movement from circle 1 to circles 2, 3 or 4.[5] Thirdly, there is an implication that the EU should be able to designate, or at least heavily influence, which country is in which circle and who can move where.

These maps of the 1998 document and its emphasis on externalization help to make taken for granted assumptions of migratory policies explicit, and in particular point to the Eurocentric basis of externalization. This realization helps to frame single case-studies of border externalization projects (whether more focused on police cooperation projects, legal migration or development initiatives) into a shared implicit spatial reference. Individual border cooperation projects are underpinned by an underlying geographical imaginary where the entire world is b/ordered according to Europe. Distinct regions of the world are assigned particular roles both for governments and how they should carry border control as well as for their populations, in terms of how and where they should migrate.

At the time, this document was firmly contested since its language was not politically correct and went beyond an assumed tradition of cosmopolitan openness towards migration and the welcoming of refugees. The text called upon the EU to show "political muscle" in preventing refugee and migrant fluxes, enumerating possible foreign policy actions ranging from economic pressure to military intervention against refugee

---

[4] Immediately after this strategy paper (1998a) was voted down during the Austria presidency, another EU Council document serving as a brief on the issue of migration and asylum to the incoming German presidency of the EU makes suggestions as to how the strategy on concentric circles could be followed up on. The language and goals of this new document build on that contention logic, for instance: an initial list of countries was to be produced "with action plans comprising measures which can be taken *against* such countries," the goal being to "*reduce* this influx" of asylum seekers and migrants (Council of the European Union 1998b, emphasis added). Despite more recent attention to human rights in the EU's border apparatus, the initial architecture of its externalized borders saw transit and origin countries as targets, legitimating all means under the primary goal of "reducing influx."

[5] As a side note, this omission has been noted in some recent critiques of the lack of vision of emigration policy by Southern European countries, where Southern European emigrants are traveling to countries that were once assumed to be "origins" of migration not destinations (Mavrodi and Moutselos 2016).

and migrant generating states. Controversy arose among human rights associations and certain member states, but especially among non-EU states that criticized the role they would be assigned as border guards for Europe. Border externalization by EU countries though pre-dates the 1998 document. Early attempts to encourage border cooperation with non-EU states can be traced at least as early as 1992 with the formation of the Budapest Process between Central and Eastern European countries, individual EU member states and European Free Trade Association (EFTA) countries; and to 1991 in the case of a request by EU member state interior ministries to the government of Morocco to cooperate in border enforcement. Still, we signal how the Austrian document becomes a point of inflection in the building of a specific geographical imaginary that facilitates a border externalization strategy that can be applied in multiple regions according to its internal logic. Thus, the Austrian document does not constitute the "origin" of future externalization projects, but it is an important landmark for researchers identifying the geographical and ideological underpinnings of current contention politics ingrained in border externalization processes. Many of the provisions regarding migration control, especially those related to the collaboration with and intervention in third states, have materialized or been attempted. The approach of border control envisioned in that document, with its distinct circles of permissible and impermissible human movement surrounding a growing EU, began to rear its head with the adoption of the "External Dimension" of Migration Policy at the Tampere summit of 1999 and more explicitly with the approval of the Global Approach to Migration (2005).

Iterations of distinct externalized spatialities begin to emerge in different EU and member state strategies. The adoption of the European Neighbourhood Policy (ENP) in 2005, as a successor in many respects of the Euro-Med process that began in 1995, explicitly adopts the vision of a "Ring of Friends," of cooperative adjacent states to the EU, which would fulfill requirements around migration management and border control according to EU requests in exchange for a preferential relationship with the bloc. This buffer zone spatiality was overlaid with a distinct spatial imaginary of borders with the adoption of the Global Approach to Migration. In this policy framework the focus is less on entire regions and countries and more on migrant *routes*.

THINKING IN ROUTES: THE EMERGENCE AND SPREAD OF A MIGRATION POLICY CONCEPT AND BORDER PRACTICE

While the policy itself was voted down in 1998, slowly but surely, this vision became the organizing framework for EU policy on migration management. It is a vision where everyone, in a sense, belongs and should remain in its circle with little exception. This understanding of mobility is based on designating the members of specific territories and populations as having different entitlements to move. By doing this, the focus shifts from border crossings at national limits to a more "global" method of migration control. It becomes necessary to pay attention to the points of origin and transit of those flows from places labeled as undesired sources of mobility. This vision of migration control was made explicit and officially approved through the *Global Approach to Migration and Mobility* framework in 2005 with its Routes Strategy connecting points of origin, transit and destination.[6] Both were reinvigorated in 2015 after the Arab Spring uprisings around the Mediterranean.

"The Migration Routes Strategy"

Building on a vision of the world divided into concentric circles of uneven mobilities, a distinct way of imagining migration control emerges: thinking in terms of routes. Besides reinforcing surveillance technology at literal border lines, the goal of tracking and cutting routes spread among EU migration policy circles, expert security actors and border authorities. We observed that this thinking in terms of routes has been possible in great part thanks to a series of maps and cartographic representations of human flows, most of them assumed to originate in Africa and Asia and imagined to move always towards EUrope. This series of cartographic iterations of routes, technologically slick and expert-looking maps, conform to a migration mapping matrix. These maps crystallized and further support the EU's Strategy of Migration Routes.

The conventional understanding of migration control is that each nation-state is in charge of its own borders at its territorial lines and ports, and manages visas in national embassies abroad. Yet this approach is considered incomplete within EU migration policy circles, which believes that "efficient migration management" entails going beyond the place and time of the entry point. Thus, it is necessary to establish transnational cooperation in order to locate *where the migrant is* in her or his process of moving towards an assumed destination point in Europe, and to collaborate with the border authorities of other countries to intercept irregular migrant flows.

The shifting itineraries of migrants (though defined by the EU, member states, and collaborating institutions not by migrants themselves) become the object of migration management policy, and thus the attempt to map and define the spaces of routes becomes the political goal. It is in the creation and implementation of these partial and multiple spatial imaginaries of mobility control that our research intervenes attempting to understand how "routes" – with their endless iterations – are defined, mapped and zeroed in on as objects of policy (Casas-Cortes et al. 2015).

Cutting the Routes: The Mapping Migration Matrix

The objective is to trace and manage the journey, which is how the *route* has become a migration management concept and strategy. Since 2003, the International Centre for Migration Policy Development has visualized migrant routes, with the intent of managing them. Their i-Map project, a regularly updated online cartography, has become a reference point for border management from a distance. The map does not trace border walls or empirically represent individual journeys; rather, it focuses on clustering flows into distinct routes that can be managed as shared itineraries with clear points of origin, transit

---

[6]   While the Global Approach to Migration (GAM) was initially considered a new policy framework that was less repressive in its approach to migration, there is an important linear genealogy from the 1998 Austrian document to the GAM. It is under the section "Global Approach" in the Austrian strategy paper that reference to the concentric circles is first made, and where the terms "origin, transit and destination" countries appear. The GAM's principal contribution then is to articulate a "routes strategy" that connects work across countries in different "circles."

and destination. Initially, the European Commission designated four main routes traversing the African continent: the West African/Atlantic Route, the Western Mediterranean Route, the Central Mediterranean Route, and the East African/Horn of Africa Route.[7] More recent iterations of i-Map show how the representation and naming of routes evolve according to perceived transformations of migrant itineraries.[8] The i-Map's visual work has inspired similar routes mapping projects by institutions relevant to the EU's border regime such as Frontex or the International Organization for Migration (IOM).[9]

In visualizing targets as fluctuating routes, these maps do not provide a straightforward empirical representation of the exact numbers of people moving through the routes, nor are the directionality of the routes accurate, as Europe is often assumed to be the sole destination. Such maps – which are widely disseminated among border authorities and migration experts as well as by the media – produce, spread and normalize a particularly restrictive way of thinking about migration control.

Normalizing and even legitimizing the tracking and the management of movement along a migrant route gives rise to controversial border practices. For instance, since 2006, Spanish border authorities have deployed to Senegalese and Mauritanian territorial waters, and inland borders thousands of miles away from the territorial borders of Spain, where they aid in patrolling potential migrant boats (fishing boats retooled for possible migration) or overland transit migrants through satellite technologies, military vessels, aircraft and the construction of border posts (Casas-Cortes et al. 2016). Recent Migration Compacts between EU and African Union (AU) countries have followed the EU-AU Valletta summit of 2014, which have allowed political relationships, training, equipment and funds to flow to specific transit or origin countries such as Eritrea, Niger, and governing entities in Libya, in some cases allowing states with dubious human rights records to emphasize their international cooperation with migration policy goals (Prestianni 2016).

While we do not think that the routes strategy developed in a linear fashion from the Austrian document on concentric circles of migration control, we suggest that such regional migration control strategies develop out of a very particular geographical, and geopolitical imaginary. Rather than a case by case, or ad hoc approach towards externalization, the concentric circles represent a macro-regional approach that allows for controversial statements that pertain to its vision of each circle. The specifics of particular transit countries or routes that traverse more than one circle fit into its overall narrative, one that reminds readers of classical grand geopolitical concepts such as *Heartland Theory* or *Lebensraum*. The EU as the center of the circles and its differing influence in each circle entail a multi-tiered strategy over borders and migration based on a political influence that appears to "fade out" as one moves away from the center. It is an imaginary with a global reach, but where according to its own logic, different strategies of migration management should be employed in the different macro-regions (the circles).

Yet, as with any grandiose geopolitical fantasy of near global reach, the possibility of

---

[7] See parts of the initial version of i-Map called "Interactive Map on Migration" at http://www.imap-migration.org/index.php?id=1130.

[8] See animation of routes at http://www.imap-migration.org/index.php?id=471.

[9] See Frontex: http://frontex.europa.eu/trends-and-routes/migratory-routes-map/ and IOM: http://migration.iom.int/europe/ (last accessed September 29, 2018).

this geographical imaginary to hold is tepid. The horizons opened early on during the Arab Spring (Tazzioli 2015), the Eurozone crisis and ensuing emigration from Southern Europe, developments in intra-regional migration, especially within Africa, or the growth of new migration destination centers (such as China, see Bodomo 2010; Castillo 2016) demonstrate that a straightforward reading of the EU's centrality in migration streams misses out on the turbulence of migration (Papastergiadis 2000). Migration management strategies based on simplistic geographic understanding and hierarchical thinking over populations will likely lead to errors and abuses in reading and interfering with migrant journeys. In fact, in its own internal review of the migration routes strategy, auditors of EU policy have noted the lack of attention to dynamics such as South-South migration or intra-African migration with regard to EU-Africa relations, and that these lead to inappropriate policy decisions (Picard et al. 2009).

CURRENT CONFIGURATIONS OF CONTENTIOUS POLITICS

The vision of concentric circles presented itself as a way to go beyond the Fortress Europe model. Thus, in understanding the implementation of its near global spatialization of the border, we should not necessarily look for concentric border walls. Instead, its implementation required a distinct notion and practice of borderwork.

The geopolitical imaginary of concentric circles gives rise to a picture of where the border is and how it works that is not straightforward. A series of simultaneous traits might be instructive. In order to further visualize and understand the shifts brought by border externalization policies, a series of simultaneous traits might be instructive: (1) borders are conceived to be on the move; (2) borders actively profile and classify people regardless of territorial limits; and (3) borders need a multi-layered architecture of institutional and extra-institutional actors. Building on the debates in critical border and migration studies, we propose the triple notion of "Itinerant B/Ordering Assemblages." The first term in this triptych refers to the constant itinerancy of migration control practices. That is, when borderwork, besides constituting walls, also expands to become a series of mobile checkpoints and fleeting infrastructures. The second term points to the ongoing suspicion and classification of inappropriate mobilities. Borders are de facto bio-politically ordering individuals and populations into different levels of "illegality" before any unauthorized act of border crossing. The third term addresses the multi-layer coalescence of a series of actors, territories and devices attempting to control certain migratory flows. Borders are enacted through a series of ad hoc assemblages – both hard and soft – at times succeeding and at times failing in their goals. More ethnographic work is needed in order to further locate the infrastructures and dissect the inner workings of such assemblages.

For instance, Ruben Andersson (2014) provides a thorough illustration on the difficulty and elusiveness in identifying "where" the externalized border is. Andersson's work includes an ethnographic "following" of different points, moments or spaces of the externalized "Euro/African Borderlands." He demonstrates in various instances that the "EU border" in its externalized sense only comes into being when a person or group is scripted (or profiled) as the "illegal/irregular migrant" that this border is eagerly searching for. In his exploration of the cooperation of West African security forces in policing the EU's external borders Andersson shows how the "irregular migrant" is a vague figure to identify. He shows how potential candidates for migration must be profiled by their "look" and "behaviors." These include hanging out in groups by fishing beaches and carrying full backpacks (Andersson 2014, pp. 101–2). There is no "EU border" abroad until those police forces profile potential candidates as "migrants."

Further research can illuminate the re-configurations of bordering far away from conventional borderlines. As such, the emerging spaces of illegality are constructed in ways that target border crossing far and before any border is crossed, making someone *illegal* at the very moment and place where she or he decides to migrate. The EU's current practices of remote border control are indeed normalizing a geographical imaginary of illegality beyond the borderline, taking bordering work to a worldwide scale. Processes of border externalization deepen this repurposing of borders for not only containing territories but also intercepting human mobility and classifying populations. As such, the displacement of migration control based on exclusionary genealogies of contention and Eurocentric geographical imaginaries confirm the forceful critiques by Indigenous, anti-colonial and migrant movements of borders as institutions of ingrained racism: "You call it illegal trespassing, I call it White Power" (graffiti in border wall, Arizona). When speaking of the externalization of migration policy, the insights provided by the popular slogan "the border crossed us" definitely resonate. Both in its insinuation that borders actively move and in its message that b/ordering is fraught with a racist politics of othering.

In search of compelling narratives that support a critical yet easy to understand view of the unfolding border regime, we wonder if this cartography conveying a mega-vision of dividing the world in circles might help in reworking assumptions about the neutrality of migration control policies. When visualizing this geographical imaginary of four concentric circles into a series of maps, an explicit counter narrative about migration emerges that questions the status quo. In contrast to the normalized opinion fueled by experts and political authorities that points to the dangers of irregular migration or "too much" migration, the problem is not about trouble-makers from the poor countries in the South fleeing in massive exodus towards the US and the EU. This view, where migration is "changing the face of the world" in unsustainable ways, is exemplified in its legitimized version in Paul Collier's volume *Exodus*, justifying restrictive solutions towards migrants and refugees. In contrast, giving attention to this dusty EU policy document helps to put taken-for granted assumptions about migration control upside down: the problem does not lay with those moving. Rather, our concern should be with the imposition of a top-down plan to manage and even dictate human mobility worldwide.

While talk around Trump's discriminatory approach towards migration and the deadly management of refugee flows in the Mediterranean is on the rise, could it be useful to start mobilizing a narrative around "the border empire strikes back"? A narrative which not only signals the violence and human rights abuses that can occur in the day-to-day carrying out of border policy, but which names and targets the vision of a border as crossing over people, in a sense like a *war on mobility* in the way there is a war on drugs. Is it time to seriously rethink practical forms of resistance and disobedience that delegitimize the very foundations of current border regimes rather than pointing out their abuses? This way of framing the problematic character of current migration management is inspired in a text message sent by a Sub-Saharan migrant while trying to swim the 15 kilometers of seawaters between the African to the European continent through the Strait of Gibraltar. A few decades ago a regular ID would have been enough to enjoy safe travel by ferry to get to Southern Spain but now he and many others are prohibited to embark on the South-to-North route. During his illegalized and otherwise simple international move is when he wrote: "There is an ongoing war on migrants." Indeed, borders are at constant war because of their exclusionary and discriminatory foundations.

REFERENCES

Andersson, Ruben (2014), *Illegality, Inc.: Clandestine Migration and the Business of Bordering Europe*, Oakland, CA: University of California Press.

Barbero, Iker (2010), "Las transformaciones del estado y del derecho ante el control de la inmigración", *Cuadernos del Observatorio Vasco de Inmigración*, **3**, Ikuspegi, Observatorio Vasco de la Inmigracion. Accessed September 29, 2018 at http://gruporuptura.org/wp-content/uploads/2015/01/ikuspegui.pdf.

Belguendouz, Abdelkrim (2005), "Expansion et Sous-Traitance Des Logiques d'enfermement de l'Union Européenne: L'exemple Du Maroc", *Cultures et Conflits*, **57**, 155–219.

Belguendouz, Abdelkrim (2009), "Le Maroc et la migration irrégulière : Une analyse sociopolitique", *CARIM, Notes d'analyse et de synthèse – Série sur la migration irrégulière module socio-politique*. Accessed October 1, 2017 at http://cadmus.eui.eu//handle/1814/10799.

Bialasiewicz, Luiza (2012), "Off-shoring and Out-sourcing the Borders of Europe: Libya and EU Border Work in the Mediterranean", *Geopolitics*, **17** (4), 843–66.

Bigo, Didier and Elspeth Guild (2005), *Controlling Frontiers: Free Movement into and Within Europe*, Aldershot, UK and Burlington, VT: Ashgate.

Bodomo, Adams (2010), "The African Trading Community in Guangzhou: An Emerging Bridge for Africa – China Relations", *The China Quarterly*, **203**, 693–707.

Boswell, Christina (2003), "The External Dimension of EU Immigration and Asylum Policy", *International Affairs*, **79** (3), 619–38.

Casas-Cortes, Maribel, Sebastian Cobarrubias, and John Pickles (2012), "Se Estiran Las Fronteras Más Allá de Los Territorios de Soberanía?" *Geopolítica(s). Revista de Estudios Sobre Espacio y Poder*, **2** (1), 71–90.

Casas-Cortes, Maribel, Sebastian Cobarrubias, and John Pickles (2015), "Riding Routes and Itinerant Borders: Autonomy of Migration and Border Externalization", *Antipode*, **47** (4), 894–914.

Casas-Cortes, Maribel, Sebastian Cobarrubias, and John Pickles (2016), ""Good Neighbours Make Good Fences': Seahorse Operations, Border Externalization and Extra-territoriality", *European Urban and Regional Studies*, **23** (3), 231–51.

Castillo, Roberto (2016), "'Homing' Guangzhou: Emplacement, Belonging and Precarity among Africans in China", *International Journal of Cultural Studies*, **19** (3), 287–306.

Chou, Meng-Hsuan (2009), "The European Security Agenda and the 'External Dimension' of EU Asylum and Migration Cooperation", *Perspectives on European Politics and Society*, **10** (4), 541–59.

Collier, Paul (2015), *Exodus: How Migration is Changing Our World*. Oxford University Press.

Council of the European Union (1998a), "Strategy Paper on Immigration and Asylum Policy, from the Austrian Council Presidency to the K4 Committee", July 1, 9809/98 CK4 27, ASIM 170, limite. (Note: This refers to the initial leaked draft. Subsequent drafts have the following codification: 9809/1/98, Rev 1 Limite, CK4 27, ASIM 170; and 9809/2/98, Rev 2 Limite, CK4 27, ASIM 170.)

Council of the European Union (1998b), "Strategy on Migration and Asylum Policy, from the Incoming German Presidency", 1465/98 Limite ASIM 260.

Fortress Europe Circular Letter (1998), "EU Strategy Paper on Asylum and Immigration: Show of 'Political Muscle'?", *FECL* 56. Accessed October 1, 2017 at http://www.fecl.org/circular/5601.htm.

Gaibazzi, Paolo, Stephan Dünnwald, and Alice Bellagamba (2016), *EurAfrican Borders and Migration Management: Political Cultures, Contested Spaces, and Ordinary Lives*, New York: Palgrave Macmillan.

Lavenex, Sandra (2006), "Shifting Up and Out: The Foreign Policy of European Immigration Control", *West European Politics*, **29** (2), 329–50.

Lindstrøm, Channe (2005), "European Union Policy on Asylum and Immigration. Addressing the Root Causes of Forced Migration: A Justice and Home Affairs Policy of Freedom, Security and Justice?" *Social Policy & Administration*, **39** (6), 587–605.

Mavrodi, Georgia and Michalis Moutselos (2016), "Immobility in Times of Crisis? The Case of Greece", in

Jean-Michel Lafleur and Mikolaj Stanek (eds), *South-North Migration of EU Citizens in Times of Crisis*, New York: Springer Berlin Heidelberg, pp. 33–48.

Mountz, Alison and Nancy Hiemstra (2014), "Chaos and Crisis: Dissecting the Spatiotemporal Logics of Contemporary Migrations and State Practices", *Annals of the Association of American Geographers*, **104** (2), 382–90.

New Keywords Collective (2014), "New Keywords: Migration and Borders", *Cultural Studies*, **29** (1), 55–87.

Papastergiadis, Nikos (2000), *The Turbulence of Migration: Globalization, Deterritorialization and Hybridity*, Cambridge and Malden, MA: Polity Press in Blackwell Publishers.

Parker, Noel and Nick Vaughan-Williams (2012), "Critical Border Studies: Broadening and Deepening the 'Lines in the Sand' Agenda", *Geopolitics*, **17** (4), 727–33.

Picard, E., A. Charpin, L. Aiolfi, and A. Simoni (2009), "Evaluation of the AENEAS Programme, 2004–2006", IBF International Consulting and BAa Consultors.

Prestianni, Sara (2016), "Steps in the Process of Externalisation of Border Controls to Africa, from the Valletta Summit to Today", ARCI Immigrazioni. Accessed October 1, 2017 at http://www.integrationarci.it/wp-content/uploads/2016/06/analysisdoc_externalisation_ARCI_ENG.pdf.

Raeymaekers, Timothy (2014), "Introduction: Europe's Bleeding Border and the Mediterranean as a Relational Space", *ACME: An International Journal for Critical Geographies*, **13** (2), 163–72.

Samers, Michael (2004), "An Emerging Geopolitics of 'Illegal' Immigration in the European Union", *European Journal of Migration and Law*, **6** (1), 27–45.

Sterkx, Steven (2008), "The External Dimension of EU Asylum and Migration Policy: Expanding Fortress Europe?" in Jan Orbie (ed.), *Europe's Global Role: External Policies of the European Union*, London and New York: Routledge, pp. 117–38.

Tazzioli, Martina (2015), *Spaces of Governmentality: Autonomous Migration and the Arab Uprisings*, London and New York: Rowman & Littlefield International.

Van Houtum, Henk and Ton Van Naerssen (2002), "Bordering, Ordering and Othering", *Tijdschrift Voor Economische En Sociale Geografie*, **93** (2), 125–36.

Van Houtum, Henk, Olivier Thomas Kramsch, and Wolfgang Zierhofer (2005), *Bordering Space*, Aldershot, UK and Burlington, VT: Ashgate.

Vaughan-Williams, Nick (2008), "Borderwork Beyond Inside/Outside? Frontex, the Citizen-detective and the War on Terror", *Space and Polity*, **12** (1), 63–79.

Zaiotti, Ruben (2016), "Mapping Remote Control: The Externalization of Migration Management in the 21st Century", in Ruben Zaiotti (ed.), *Externalizing Migration Management: Europe, North America and the Spread of "Remote Control" Practices*, London and New York: Routledge, pp. 3–30.

Zolberg, Aristide (2003), "The Archeology of 'Remote Control'", in Andreas Fahrmeir, Olivier Faron, and Patrick Weil (eds), *Migration Control in the North Atlantic World: The Evolution of State Practices in Europe and the United States*, New York: Berghahn Books, pp. 195–223.

16. Renationalization and spaces of migration: the European border regime after 2015

Bernd Kasparek and Matthias Schmidt-Sembdner

INTRODUCTION

In the morning hours of July 4, 2017, the news spread that Austria intended to close the Austrian-Italian border at Brenner Pass "rapidly." The Austrian Foreign Minister Hans Peter Doskozil declared that 750 soldiers had already been concentrated for a supportive deployment at the border in the district of Tyrol and that they could start their service within 72 hours. In addition, "heavy equipment" had been relocated to the district for a possible mission at the Italian-Austrian border, including four Pandur wheeled tanks (Guardian, 2017).

The Brenner Pass, which is often designated to be the needle eye of the Alps, is regarded to be one of the most significant border crossing points between Italy and Austria, and it constitutes one of the main North-South arteries within the European Union (EU). For migrants wanting to leave Italy to go North and to live in another European country, it is the most obvious passage. But the massive militarization of the border, as it was considered – and even previously pursued – by Doskozil, wouldn't mean an abrupt closure of a highly frequented European transit point. Rather, since Austria presented plans for a new "border management" (ORF, 2016) at the Brenner Pass in April 2016, the use of the Brenner Route had been made more difficult for migrants, a strategy which clearly functioned as a bargaining chip of the Austrian government in the debates about the so-called "refugee crisis." The concentration of Austrian troops in Tyrol constituted the strongest indication for a continued escalation of the conflict by the Austrian government.

The military deployment never materialized, it was but a simple threatening gesture. However, it was fiercely reminiscent of the Italian-French border conflict at Ventimiglia in 2011, which was one of the first episodes – lasting a mere 17 hours (Cuttitta et al., 2011) – in what we have dubbed the crisis of Schengen (Kasparek and Tsianos, 2014), finally resulting in the momentous migrations of 2015 and the temporary breakdown of migration control within the EU (Hess and Kasparek, 2017). We do not and cannot claim to know if the episode sketched out above will be part of a similar genealogy concerning the European border and migration regime. What we aim for in this chapter is to take this episode and use its connections to other events and the involvements of a multiplicity of actors in order to reconstruct a particular passage of the European border regime, namely, the heterogeneous attempts to restabilize control on the so-called Central Mediterranean Route, stretching from Libya across the Mediterranean to Italy, and onwards to Germany via Austria.

We emphasize the heterogeneity of these attempts because we argue that methodologically, a focus and perspective on the conflicts inherent in the European border regime gives us an analytical edge. Not only does it allow us to consider the conflictive relationship between migration and its government, the central characteristic of the border, but also to deconstruct the portrayal of border control and its policies as a monolithic and homogeneous apparatus of control: in the case of the Brenner Pass, the unilateral announcement of the impeding militarized closure of the border between Italy and Austria by the latter not only met protests from Italy, but also from the European Commission, which has been pursuing its "Roadmap back to Schengen" (European Commission, 2016), that is, a return to a functioning Schengen area without internal border controls for the better part of the previous two years.

The chapter is organized as follows. First, we will sketch out the theoretical and methodological underpinnings of what we call Ethnographic Border and Migration Regime Analysis, that is, our approach to the multiplicity of actors, situational alliances and conflicts within the multiscalar European border regime. Second, we will highlight the dynamics which are playing a key role in the larger context of the Austrian border management. Because the measures of Doskozil – and this is hardly a coincidence – took place in the middle of a heated political debate about the refugee situation along the Central Mediterranean route to Italy, we start with the juridification of the Mediterranean Sea and with the politics of externalization. Because it is not possible to separate the closure of an internal border of the Schengen area from the discussion about the dysfunctionality of the European Dublin system, we briefly analyse the collapse of the Dublin system as a next step. This is followed by an analysis of the subsequent renationalization of migration policy in Europe, of which the Brenner Pass is just one of many examples. Thirdly, in our conclusion, we will discuss the space-making character of migration and its government with reference to the material offered before.

A THEORETICAL APPROACH TO THE EUROPEAN BORDER REGIME

It is a common denominator of border studies to emphasize the transformation of the border from a demarcation line surrounding national territory to a ubiquitous, techno-social, de-territorialized apparatus or regime producing geographically stretched border spaces described as "border zones," "borderlands" or "borderscapes." At the same time, these concepts include the idea of mobile, fluid, selective and differentiated border situations. Étienne Balibar proposes to approach the question "What is a border?" by taking into account three main characteristics he observes, that is, their "overdetermined," "polysemic" and "heterogeneous" characters (Balibar, 2002, pp. 78ff.). More recent interventions on precisely this question, such as Johnson et al. (2011), Casas-Cortes et al. (2015) and Jones et al. (2017), demonstrate the continued pertinence of this question, not only in itself, but also in connection with the issues of migration, citizenship and sovereignty that Balibar had already explored. More specific analyses of recent transformations of what is the border include categories such as "mobile borders" (Kuster and Tsianos, 2013) or "networked borders" (Rumford, 2006; Walters and Haahr, 2004).

This shift not only induced a geographical refocusing away from the level of the (nation) state, but also a methodological reorientation with a focus on bordering processes and practices, on doing border, "rather than [on] the border per se" (Newman, 2006; van Houtum and van Naerssen, 2002). The border is now being conceptualized as an effect of a multiplicity of agents and practices, as becomes clear in the concept of "border work" (Rumford, 2008). The concept of border work in particular draws attention to the everyday micropractices of a wide range of actors. Following this perspective, "to border" is to be understood as a performative act. Drawing on Judith Butler's notion of performativity, Mark Salter points to the fact that "sovereignty, like gender, has no essence, and must continually be articulated and rearticulated in terms of 'stylized repetition of acts' of sovereignty" (Johnson et al., 2011, p. 66).

All these recent practice-oriented conceptualizations indeed understand the border as an effect of a multitude of actors and practices – human and non-human alike. However, many of these constructivist approaches still ignore the constitutive power of migration, or once again conceptualize migrants as structurally powerless and as "victims." The dominant focus of border studies, especially those following the classical securitization approach looking at the function of the border as a barrier or filter – to exclude people – also seems mostly to lead to an epistemological exclusion of the agency of migrants.

By contrast, in their recently published volume *Border as Method*, Sandro Mezzadra and Brett Neilson (2013) define borders as "social institutions, which are marked by tensions between practices of border reinforcement and border crossing" (p. 3). Here, they employ the notion of borderscapes indicating the decisive role migration plays in co-constituting the border.

This has many aspects in common with our approach labeled "ethnographic border regime analysis" as a methodology to theorize the border from the perspective of the autonomy of migration (Kasparek, 2016a; Papadopoulos et al., 2008; Transit Migration Forschungsgruppe, 2007). This approach allows us to look at the border regime[1] as a space of conflict and contestation between the various actors trying to govern the border and the movements of migration – without minimizing the border regime's brutality. These conceptualizations represent a methodological and theoretical attempt not only to think about the relationship between migration movements and control regimes in a different way than in the classical sociological way of object-structure, but also to conceive of migration differently than has previously been the dominant practice in the cultural and social sciences – namely, not thinking about it in the sense of a "deviation" from the paradigm of the sedentary way of life in the modern nation state, or as a functionalist variable of economic processes and rationalities. Instead, this theoretical and methodological approach represents an attempt to conceptualize migration both historically and also structurally as an act of "flight" and as "imperceptible" forms of resistance, in the sense of withdrawal and escape from miserable, exploitative conditions of existence (Boutang, 2007; Kasparek and Schmidt-Sembdner, 2017; Papadopoulos et al., 2008). This draws attention to migration as a co-constitutive factor of the border, with the forces of the movements of migration challenging and reshaping the border every single day. This perspective of putting migration central to the analytical endeavor points to the intrinsic structural fragility of the border regime. Crisis in this respect is not reducible to a temporary anomaly or emergency situation, but instead must be seen as a central structural condition for borders.

---

[1]   We employ the concept of "regime" in a Foucauldian sense to indicate the multiple levels and dimensions at play constituting the "border" as a dynamic and somehow contingent apparatus based on laws and regulations, institutions, technical devices, moral beliefs and representations, discourses, actors and practices (Casas-Cortes et al., 2015; Transit Migration Forschungsgruppe, 2007).

The EU can be regarded as a paradigmatic laboratory of the border transformations described above. With the Schengen agreement of 1985, the European project had heralded the creation of a continental border regime, with the newly created notion of an "external border" as the pivotal mechanism and space for migration control. However, the specific characteristic of Europeanization – that is, the becoming of the European Union as a political body – by slowly transferring sovereign national powers to Brussels and building on, rather than outright replacing, national policies, is the reason why the EU can be regarded as paradigmatic, as all relevant political scales, actors, institutions and legal frameworks are multiplied, and not easily ordered into a hierarchy.

If there is one central rationale at the core of the European border regime, it is driven by what Lahav and Guiraudon have called the fundamental "control dilemma" (2000). Culminating in the creation of the EU internal market, this dilemma refers to the question of how to reconcile a neoliberal economic paradigm of a – preferably global – free circulation of goods, services and capital with a continued biopolitical will to control the movements of people. In regards to the border regime, the main practical answer to the control dilemma was, according to Lahav and Guiraudon (2000), to move border controls "away from the border and outside the states," leading to the described new specialization and geographical expansion of the border. In addition, there existed a techno-scientific vision of a "smart," invisible yet selective border that itself is able to distinguish between bona fide travelers and unwanted migrants (Commission of the European Communities, 2008).

To this end, broadly speaking four paradigms were enacted within the European border regime. First, to the outside, a paradigm of "remote control" and externalization (Bialasiewicz, 2012; Hess and Tsianos, 2007; Lavenex, 2004; Zolberg, 2006). Second, as already indicated, a paradigm of a fortified, yet smart external border through technology, digitalization and biometrization (Broeders, 2007; Dijstelbloem and Meijer, 2011; Kuster and Tsianos, 2013). These outward facing strategies were complemented by a third one, namely, an internal regime steeped in the institution of asylum and put into practice through the Dublin/Eurodac regulations, aiming at the immobilization of migrant populations within the European territory (Borri and Fontanari, 2016; Kasparek, 2016a; Picozza, 2017a, 2017b; Schuster, 2011). Finally, fourth, especially in recent years, we can observe an increasing humanitarization of the border (Cuttitta, 2014; Pallister-Wilkins, 2015; Schmidt, 2015; Walters, 2011), which has accelerated in the context of the growing number of shipwrecks and subsequent deaths in the Mediterranean in recent years. All these disparate trends characterizing the European border regime of the last decade are at play in the conflict at the Brenner Pass.

CONNECTING THE CONFLICT AT BRENNER WITH THE REGIME'S TENSIONS

The ongoing crisis of the European border regime cannot be understood without analysing it in a double relationship with the social and democratic uprisings that started in North Africa in 2011. While the uprisings had already strongly destabilized the Euro-Mediterranean border regime as established in the years before 2011, their more long-term consequence was destabilization of the EU itself.

Prior to the Arab Spring, the European border regime stretching towards Africa was built heavily on the externalization paradigm. Through diverse processes such as the Barcelona Process, initiated as far back as 1995, or the Rabat Process of 2006 and the Mediterranean Transit Migration Dialogue, dating back to 2007, many North and West African countries were to some degree involved in the EU's migration and border management project. Its different components were usually driven by EU member states, with the backing and support of Brussels.

Externalization and Juridification in the Central Mediterranean

Throughout the first decade of the twenty-first century, Italy had sought an agreement with Libya, in which the latter would stop the departure of migrants towards the former, and would readmit migrants from there. Under the 2008 Italian-Libyan friendship treaty, a secret protocol created the conditions for the externalization of migration control. Soon after it entered into effect in May 2009, Italy commenced pushback operations towards Libya outside of Italian territorial waters (Bialasiewicz, 2012; Heimeshoff et al., 2014).

With the outbreak of the Libyan civil war in February 2011 and the subsequent North Atlantic Treaty Organization (NATO) intervention, Italian-Libyan cooperation ended. By the end of 2011, the externalized border regime in the Mediterranean had significant gaps. The number of migrants crossing the Mediterranean by boat started to rise sharply, and has continued to do so ever since, despite ongoing efforts and attempts by the EU and member states to reestablish cooperation with the different Northern African regimes, such as the military-led governments of Egypt or Libya (Heller and Pezzani, 2016).

A legal development dating back to 2009 created further obstacles to the return to the previous status quo. After the commencement of the Italian pushback operations towards Libya, a group of migrants subjected to the practice sued the Italian state at the European Court of Human Rights (ECHR) in a case that became famous as *Hirsi Jamaa and Others v. Italy* (ECHR, 2012). Since Libya could not be considered a *Safe Third Country* for refugees, the Court ruled that the Italian pushback operations constituted a violation of the Geneva Convention's non-refoulement principle. This specific case had deep implications for the practices of the European migration and border regime. While not an unsurpassable obstacle to externalization, the ECHR's verdict created a legal limit to such measures.

These developments at the very Southern border of the EU soon led to repercussions in the North, as more and more refugees and migrants from Italy sought their way towards Northern European cities, crossing the border at the Brenner Pass. But the actual volatility of the European migration and border regime was brought into sharp focus with the tragedies that occurred in October 2013 at Lampedusa. Within the space of a few days, two shipwrecks resulted in the deaths of nearly 500 people. While these were not the first, nor the last, they captured the attention of the European public in an unprecedented manner. The legitimacy of restrictive border controls was severely called into question not only by a liberal public but also by prominent members of the European Commission, such as Home Affairs Commissioner Cecilia Malmström, and the President of the Commission, José Manuel Barroso (Kasparek, 2015; Ticktin, 2015).

Even though there was a decisive discursive shift towards a humanitarian rationale that prioritized the saving of lives at sea on the EU level, no policy shift was discernible in the immediate aftermath. The Italian government's decision to initiate the Mare Nostrum operation proved to be more decisive, as, for the first time, a national government reframed its border policies, putting the saving of lives before the securing of borders (Cuttitta, 2014). However, the increased arrival of migrants placed more stress on the Dublin system and registration practices in Italy slowed down severely. EU pressure to replace Mare Nostrum with a mission to police the borders led to its substitution with Frontex's Operation Triton, which again reprioritized secure borders over the lives of humans. This turn was itself short-lived as another tragedy struck in April 2015. Costing nearly 800 people their lives at sea, the disaster put the humanitarian rationale squarely back on the table and underlined once more that the EU border regime needed to take a decisive step if it wanted to stay on top of developments. After a near decade-long effort to seal the migratory route across the Mediterranean, juridification, humanitarianism and the failure of externalization foiled this strategy, and a major access path to Europe remained open.

Crashing Dublin

Despite the European efforts to externalize the control of migratory movements, the Central Mediterranean route remains one of the most frequented pathways for migrants to reach Europe. For that reason, Italy consistently becomes the spotlight of the political debates about the handling of forced migration to Europe. In the last years, news about rising numbers of migrants reaching the Italian island of Lampedusa or Sicily consistently led to discussions about the distribution of asylum seekers in Europe, about the national responsibility of asylum procedures and about the prevention and control of so-called "secondary migration" within Europe, of which movement along the Brenner Pass is but one example. The threat of increased border controls at the Brenner Pass from which our analysis started was a direct result of the failure of enacting a European scheme against these secondary migrations, thus resulting in Austria seeking a national solution, effectively renationalizing migration policies along that route. In order to contextualize this extraordinary move, we recapitulate the genealogy of this European scheme, symbolized by Schengen and Dublin.

The former, that is, the various Schengen agreements and their incorporation into EU law, are well understood and analysed (Huysmans, 2000; Walters, 2002). Briefly, Schengen established a European area without internal border controls, a precondition for freedom of movement within, but went hand in hand with the creation of the European external border and more so-called compensatory measures. Alongside emerged the so-called Dublin system, which established extra rules and procedures for the movements of asylum seekers and non-European migrants within this new area, to exclude them from the regime of freedom of movement and curtail "secondary migration."

The Dublin system is supposed to determine the responsible state for processing an asylum application in Europe. In order to do so, a plurality of hierarchically and definite criteria has been created. In practice, the "country of the first entry" into the EU has turned out to be the central criterion, thus forcing asylum seekers to seek asylum in the country they entered first (Meyerhöfer et al., 2014) and also obliging them to remain in that country. The principle is intended to prevent the so-called "secondary migration" and multiple asylum applications in different member states (Buckel, 2013). However, to make the criterion of the "country of the first entry" powerful, the EU needed an instrument to determine the pathways of migration. For that reason, the creation of the first EU-wide database for fingerprints named Eurodac was decided in the year 2003. In the years 2005 to 2007 the database began to function efficiently. From this time on, the registration of asylum seekers in other national asylum systems, and thus the responsible state, could be verified through comparing fingerprints with Eurodac. This finally enabled Dublin deportations within the EU, enforcing the Dublin system's rationale. In effect, the member states situated at the European external border are primarily responsible for the overwhelming majority of asylum claims.

This is especially the case for Italy. While this circumstance already points out a fundamental problem with the Dublin system, namely, the missing structural balance in the European politics of distribution (Kasparek, 2016a), it has been, above all, the resistant practices of migrants, the struggles of the movements of migration, which scuppered the Dublin system step by step. Quite different from the proposition of the EU, the system produced a highly mobile and simultaneously excluded population in Europe. Unsurprisingly, migrants refused to be subdued by this system and moved to places they believed to be better. The biographies of numerous migrants have been characterized by regular deportations. But over time, they successfully destabilized the Dublin system due to a variety of tactics. Different courts stayed deportation orders allowing migrants to claim their right to stay. Two judgments by the ECHR are noteworthy in this respect, namely, *M.S.S. v. Belgium and Greece* in 2011 (ECHR, 2011) and *Tarakhel v. Switzerland* in 2014 (ECHR, 2014), the former wholly excluding Greece from the Dublin system, and the latter enforcing strict social standards for the deportation of families with children under Dublin.

Albeit the two judgments of the ECHR were milestones for the collapse of the Dublin system, we need to consider the resistant practices and particularly the tenacity of migrants to elude the administrative measures for the executions of deportations. Resistance to deportations, manipulating fingerprints, seeking refuge in churches and simply trying again and again in yet another country rendered the intricate Dublin bureaucracy ineffective. The final blow to the Dublin system came in September 2015 through the action of the migrants stranded at Budapest Keleti train station in Hungary. An internal document of the German Federal Office for Migration and Refugees advising a temporary suspension of Dublin for Syrian refugees surfaced. Even though immediately contradicted by the German government, the rumor that Germany was to open its borders for Syrians was out, the "March of Hope" to the Austrian border was underway, and soon the rumor had been transformed – through the actions of migrants – into a fact. By the end of 2015, the Dublin system was in serious disarray, with grave consequences for the cohesion of European and national migration policies.

National Solutions Within the Schengen Area

These multiplicities of tensions within the European border regime can be acutely felt in the small village of Brenner/Brennero. Located directly on the border between Austria and Italy, the main part of the village is in Italy, although in the predominantly German-speaking autonomous province of Southern Tyrol. Through Schengen, the border which cuts close to the center of the village has been nearly invisibilized, and the concrete remaining border installations appeared more of a historic curiosity than anything else. It is fair to describe the village of Brenner/Brennero as a prototypical European site. Of the millions of people transiting the highway close to the village, few ever stop, or even notice it. The largest building in the village is an outlet mall, where visitors stop to pick up skiing gear or the latest in functional climbing or hiking gear, emphasizing the transnational flow of goods within the internal market of the EU. Mobility has a concrete materiality in the village, not only because of the transitory nature of shopping in the outlet mall, but also because of the highway, seamlessly connecting Germany, Austria and Italy for travelers and transport alike, as well as because of the train station situated on the Italian side, where the "Eurocity" train stops every other hour, connecting the Italian city of Verona with Munich in the south of Germany.

Over the last years though, this European idyll changed. Today, the train station has transformed from a site of transnational mobility epitomized by the Eurocity train into a site of control. On the platform where the Eurocity train stops, there is a constant police and military presence, usually around 20 uniformed officers, conducting checks in the trains and on the platform, pulling migrants travelling North out of the train and stopping them from entering the Northbound trains. On the Austrian side of the border, construction works have been conducted so that fences can be erected within days, and also on the Austrian side, the construction of a parallel train station just a few hundred meters away – but across the border – is under way, so that Austrian police, who have no mandate in Italy, will be enabled to carry out checks on the Eurocity train. In Brenner/Brennero itself, the presence of the Italian military is visible. Intercepted migrants are forced out of the train station, or even onto Southbound trains.

This transformation is directly linked with the inability of the European border regime to control its Southern borders. The increased arrival of migrants in Italy's South is propagating northwards, which turns the village of Brenner/Brennero into a site of interest for Austria and Germany, as it is the last possible location to check and control migrants before they leave Italy. By November 2014 – before the migrations of 2015 – trilateral police cooperation for the train route from Verona to Munich via Brenner/Brennero had been installed in ministerial consultation between Austria, Germany and Italy. A trinational police patrol, with officers of the three involved countries, started to operate at the train stations and in the trains between Verona and Brennero. In the beginning, the registration of migrants, including their fingerprints, was of prime importance for this police patrol. The installation of the trilateral police patrol can be read as a kind of German and Austrian measure to discipline the Italian authorities: Italy should attend to its duty to fingerprint migrants under Dublin rules.

In our analysis, the summer of migration (Kasparek and Speer, 2015) marks precisely the turning point towards renationalization. Before the temporary collapse of the European border regime, the peculiar transnational police cooperation at hand was an effort to stabilize the European system of internal mobility control for non-European migrants. But in the aftermath of the summer of migration, various EU member states analysed the European system of migration control as paralysed, and started to distrust their neighboring countries, and in the case of Austria and Germany suspecting that Italy pursued a covert policy of letting, or even encouraging migrants to travel North.

And indeed, for a long time, migrants knew how to use the relative porosity of the border at the Brenner Pass: until the increase of controls in April 2016, it was quite possible to leave Italy to the North by trains. Occasionally, trains remained unchecked, the presence of the police at the train station was not yet as excessive as the levels reached in 2017. There existed an Italian policy of registering slowly and looking away, a prototypical situational alliance, or tacit complicity of the Italian state with migration, which however was rooted in the structural imbalance caused by the Dublin system's "country of first entry" rule. The aim of facilitating movement towards the North was shared, the motive, however, was not.

From 2015 on, as exemplified by the smoldering conflict around the Brenner border, various EU member states started to pursue migration policies aimed at national interests, abandoning the notion of a European government of migration. Poland, Hungary and Slovakia, for example, refused to receive asylum seekers redistributed under a European scheme. Germany reintroduced border controls at its Southern border as early as September 2015, causing a domino effect along the Balkan Route which led to its subsequent demise in March 2016.

Austria turned its attention to its border crossing points with Italy. Having been confronted with the situation to be the extended part of the Balkan Route, Austria, as well as its European partners, expected a shifting of the migration paths away from the Balkan Route to the Central Mediterranean route. Germany and Austria, which were already putting pressure on Italy to stop secondary movements, pushed Italy to an ever finer woven net of control alongside the Brenner Route. Austria also presented its new "border management" in April 2016: the construction of a fence, amongst other measures, should allow for the Brenner Pass to be blocked within 72 hours. Although this plan has so far never been activated completely, the endeavor of the Austrian government has not remained without after-effects. Even though the Italian Minister of the Interior, Angelino Alfano, characterized the planned closure of the border as to be "against every logic, against reason and against history" (ORF, 2016), at the same time Italy increased its control density from Verona to the Brenner Pass, deploying its army and various police units. However, with steadily high numbers of migrants arriving in Italy's South, this was not enough for Austria, leading to the threat cited in the introduction to this chapter.

From April 2016 onwards, Austria's threat of an impending closure of the Brenner Pass was looming. From Verona to Brenner, Italian police officers and soldiers were positioned at the train stations, the international train connections were controlled without exception. This particular mobile control practice was organized along the route: Italian officials patrol the Brennero train station, some minutes later Austrian police patrol all train compartments. German federal police enter the train shortly before the border to Germany and repeat this control procedure, leaving the train in Rosenheim in Southern Bavaria. It is hardly surprising, then, that migrants started to take new paths to leave Italy. Shortly after the massive increase of controls, there were first indications that from now on migrants would use international freight trains to cross the border. By summer 2017, this very risky form of crossing the border was apparently normalized: hardly a week going by without a press release of the German federal police stating that again, migrants were found on such trains (Bundespolizeidirektion München, 2017).

Migration and Space-making

In our description of the dense mesh of interests, legislations and rationalities on the various scales reaching from the municipal up to the European level, the current policies of the European Commission have been missing. Often described as the guardian of the European treaties, it should be assumed that the Commission was adamantly opposed to the reintroduction of national border controls, a direct contradiction of the Schengen agreements. But in the aftermath of the Arab Spring in 2011, the Schengen border code had already been changed to allow for the temporary reintroduction of internal border controls in the event of "mass migration." To this end, it is not surprising that the Commission did support the border controls which in the end led to the collapse of the Balkan corridor, and gave recurring extensions of original deadlines.

In reference to the European migration and border regime, the Commission pursues a different strategy. In the so-called hotspot approach, first sketched out in the Commission's European Agenda on Migration in May 2015 (European Commission, 2015), the Commission advocated for an intensification of an intervention of European agencies, such as the European Border and Coast Guard Agency Frontex, the European Asylum Support Office (EASO), Europol and Eurojust in sections of the external border designated as hotspots of irregular migration. This intervention aims at the registration and identification of asylum seekers, again with the top priority of registering their fingerprints with the Eurodac database, and a subsequent redistribution of persons likely to be recognized as refugees into other European countries. Clearly, this strategy also aims at stabilizing the existing frameworks of Schengen and Dublin, namely, to increase the control density at the external border and to ensure the functionality of the Dublin system.

While only the registration part of the hotspot approach is working efficiently, the relocations, that is, the transfer to other EU member states are severely lagging. One can, however, see how the Commission's aim to preserve or to reestablish a smooth and homogeneous European space is contained within this approach. The movements of migration within the EU, and its various efforts to control and to impede them, have created a peculiar political space, stretching from Libya across the Mediterranean to Southern Italy, and onwards to the Alps, Austria and Germany. Similar to the political space spanned by the Balkan Route in 2015 (Kasparek, 2016b), this space was never formally constituted nor institutionalized, and its precise shape is ever shifting, mostly determined by the fluid and ever-changing movements of migration.

It is this space-making character of migration that is the extraordinary aspect of our reconstruction of the conflict at the Brenner Pass. Stretching across national borders – an intrinsic characteristic of migration itself – but not encompassing the entirety of the EU, this space was not immediately governable by the member states involved, as this space overlaps with national sovereignties, international legal norms, European legislation, national interests, and finally a multiplicity of actors whose interests are not always aligned, or who might be at odds at how to achieve a common aim. While the involved nation states were ready to fall back to politics that worked in the era of nation states, that is, either a policy of beggar-thy-neighbor or going-it-alone, the Commission, in an attempt to preserve the European project, followed the policies that have long been at the core of the EU's territorial project: intensification of border controls in order to homogenize the inner. For clearly, the hotspot approach aims to achieve both. Registration and identification is biometric bordering, while redistribution is meant to be the end of autonomous secondary movements within the EU. If this policy prevails, and if it will indeed manage to destroy the peculiar political space spanned by the migrations to Europe, remains to be seen.

REFERENCES

Balibar, E. (2002). What is a border? In *Politics and the Other Scene* (pp. 75–86). London: Verso.

Bialasiewicz, L. (2012). Off-shoring and out-sourcing the borders of Europe: Libya and EU border work in the Mediterranean. *Geopolitics*, **17**(4), 843–66. Accessed 28 September 2017 at http://www.tandfonline.com/doi/abs/10.1080/14650045.2012.660579.

Borri, G. and Fontanari, E. (2016). Lampedusa in Berlin: (Im)Mobilität innerhalb des europäischen Grenzregimes. *Peripherie*, **35**, 138–9. Accessed 28 September 2017 at http://www.budrich-journals.de/index.php/peripherie/article/view/22409.

Boutang, Y.M. (2007). Europa, Autonomie der Migration, Biopolitik. In *Empire und die biopolitische Wende* (pp. 169–78). Frankfurt am Main: Campus. Accessed 28 September 2017 at http://www.academia.edu/download/31229080/3._Biopolitische_Wende_book.pdf#page=165.

Broeders, D. (2007). The new digital borders of Europe, EU databases and the surveillance of irregular migrants. *International Sociology*, **22**(1), 71–92.

Buckel, S. (2013). *"Welcome to Europe". Die Grenzen des europäischen Migrationsrechts.* Bielefeld: Transcript.

Bundespolizeidirektion München (2017, March 28). Migranten mit Güterzug über Grenze – Lebensgefährliche Fahrt endet am Rosenheimer Bahnhof. Accessed 28 September 2017 at http://www.presseportal.de/blaulicht/pm/64017/3597222.

Casas-Cortes, M., Cobarrubias, S., De Genova, N. et al. (2015). New keywords: migration and borders. *Cultural Studies*, **29**(1), 55–87. Accessed 28 September 2017 at http://www.tandfonline.com/doi/abs/10.1080/0950238 6.2014.891630.

Commission of the European Communities (2008). *Preparing the Next Steps in Border Management in the European Union.* Communication from the Commission to the European Parliament, the Council, the European Economic and Social Committee and the Committee of the Regions No. COM(2008) 69 final. Brussels.

Cuttitta, P. (2014). From the Cap Anamur to Mare Nostrum. Humanitarianism and migration controls at the EU's maritime borders. CLEER Working Papers.

Cuttitta, P., Dietrich, H., Kasparek, B., Speer, M., and Tsianos, V. (2011). Die Grenze demokratisieren. *Kritische Justiz*, **3**, 244–52.

Dijstelbloem, H. and Meijer, A. (eds) (2011). *Migration and the New Technological Borders of Europe.* London: Palgrave Macmillan. Accessed 28 September 2017 at http://link.springer.com/10.1057/9780230299382.

ECHR. *M.S.S. v. Belgium and Greece*, No. 30696/09 (January 21, 2011). European Court of Human Rights.

ECHR. *Hirsi Jamaa and Others v. Italy*, No. 27765/09 (February 23, 2012). European Court of Human Rights.

ECHR. *Tarakhel v. Switzerland*, No. 29217/12 (November 4, 2014). European Court of Human Rights.

European Commission (2015). *A European Agenda on Migration.* Communication from the Commission to the European Parliament, the Council, the European Economic and Social Committee and the Committee of the Regions No. COM(2015) 240 final. Brussels.

European Commission (2016). *Back to Schengen – a Roadmap.* Communication from the Commission to the European Parliament, the European Council and the Council No. COM(2016) 120 final.

Guardian (2017, July 4). Austrian troops to stop migrants crossing border with Italy. *Guardian: World News.* Accessed 28 September 2017 at http://www.theguardian.com/world/2017/jul/04/austrian-troops-to-stop-migrants-crossing-border-with-italy.

Heimeshoff, L.-M., Hess, S., Kron, S., Schwenken, H., and Trzeciak, M. (2014). *Grenzregime II: Migration – Kontrolle – Wissen. Transnationale Perspektiven* (1st edn). Berlin: Assoziation A.

Heller, C. and Pezzani, L. (2016). Ebbing and flowing: The EU's shifting practices of (non-)assistance and bordering in a time of crisis. *Near Futures Online*, issue no. 1 (March). Online only, accessed 28 September 2017 at http://nearfuturesonline.org/ebbing-and-flowing-the-eus-shifting-practices-of-non-assistance-and-bordering-in-a-time-of-crisis/.

Hess, S. and Kasparek, B. (2017). De- and restabilising Schengen. The European border regime after the summer of migration. *Cuadernos Europeos de Deusto*, **56**/2017, 47–77.

Hess, S. and Tsianos, V. (2007). Europeanizing Transnationalism! Provincializing Europe! – Konturen eines neuen Grenzregimes. In *Turbulente Ränder* (p. 24). Bielefeld: Transcript.

Huysmans, J. (2000). The European Union and the securitization of migration. *JCMS: Journal of Common Market Studies*, **38**(5), 751–77. Accessed 28 September 2017 at http://onlinelibrary.wiley.com/doi/10.1111/1468-5965.00263/abstract.

Johnson, C., Jones, R., Paasi, A. et al. (2011). Interventions on rethinking "the border" in border studies. *Political Geography*, **30**(2), 61–9. Accessed 28 September 2017 at https://doi.org/10.1016/j.polgeo.2011.01.002.

Jones, R., Johnson, C., Brown, W. et al. (2017). Interventions on the state of sovereignty at the border. *Political Geography*, **59**, 1–10. Accessed 28 September 2017 at https://doi.org/10.1016/j.polgeo.2017.02.006.

Kasparek, B. (2015). Was war Mare Nostrum? Dokumentation einer Debatte um die italienische Marineoperation. *Movements. Journal Für Kritische Migrations- und Grenzregimeforschung*, **1**(1). Accessed 28 September 2017 at http://movements-journal.org/issues/01.grenzregime/11.kasparek--mare-nostrum-debatte.html.

Kasparek, B. (2016a). Complementing Schengen: the Dublin system and the European border and migration regime. In H. Bauder and C. Matheis (eds), *Migration Policy and Practice* (pp. 59–78). New York: Palgrave Macmillan. Accessed 28 September 2017 at https://doi.org/10.1057/9781137503817_4.

Kasparek, B. (2016b). Routes, corridors, and spaces of exception: governing migration and Europe. *Near Futures Online*. Accessed 28 September 2017 at http://nearfuturesonline.org/routes-corridors-and-spaces-of-exception-governing-migration-and-europe/.

Kasparek, B. and Schmidt-Sembdner, M. (2017). Towards Democracy. Die Bewegung der Migration und die Demokratisierung des europäischen Projekts. In M. Candeias and A. Demirovic (eds), *Europe – What's Left? Die Europäische Union zwischen Zerfall, Autoritarismus und demokratischer Erneuerung* (pp. 175–91). Münster: Westfälisches Dampfboot.

Kasparek, B. and Speer, M. (2015). Of hope. Hungary and the long summer of migration. Accessed 28 September 2017 at http://bordermonitoring.eu/ungarn/2015/09/of-hope-en/.

Kasparek, B. and Tsianos, V.S. (2014). Whatever works! Kontinuität und Krise des Schengener Systems. In L.-M. Heimeshoff, S. Hess, S. Kron, H. Schwenken, and M. Trzeciak (eds), *Grenzregime II. Migration, Kontrolle, Wissen, Transnationale Perspektiven* (pp. 41–57). Berlin: Assoziation A.

Kuster, B. and Tsianos, V.S. (2013). Erase them! Eurodac and digital deportability. *Eipcp. Europäisches Institut Für Progressive Kulturpolitik*. Accessed 28 September 2017 at http://eipcp.net/transversal/0313/kuster-tsianos/en.

Lahav, G. and Guiraudon, V. (2000). Comparative perspectives on border control: away from the border and outside the state. In *The Wall Around the West. State Borders and Immigration Controls in North America and Europe* (pp. 55–77). Lanham, Boulder, New York, Oxford: Rowman & Littlefield Publishers, Inc.

Lavenex, S. (2004). EU external governance in "wider Europe". *Journal of European Public Policy*, **11**(4), 680–700. Accessed 28 September 2017 at http://www.tandfonline.com/doi/abs/10.1080/1350176042000248098.

Meyerhöfer, A., Hartl, U., Lorenz, D., Neumann, S., and Oeser, A. (2014). Dublin II kippen! In Forschungsgruppe Staatsprojekt Europa (ed.), *Kämpfe um Migrationspolitik. Theorie, Methode und Analysen kritischer Europaforschung* (pp. 151–68). Bielefeld: Transcript.

Mezzadra, S. and Neilson, B. (2013). *Border as Method, or, the Multiplication of Labor*. Durham, NC: Duke University Press.

Newman, D. (2006). The lines that continue to separate us: borders in our "borderless" world. *Progress in Human Geography*, **30**(2), 143–61. Accessed 28 September 2017 at http://journals.sagepub.com/doi/abs/10.1191/0309132506ph599xx.

ORF (2016, April 28). Italien wehrt sich gegen "Brenner-Mauer". Accessed 28 September 2017 at from http://orf.at/stories/2336985/2336984/.

Pallister-Wilkins, P. (2015). The humanitarian politics of European border policing: Frontex and border police in Evros. *International Political Sociology*, **9**(1), 53–69. Accessed 28 September 2017 at http://onlinelibrary.wiley.com/doi/10.1111/ips.12076/full.

Papadopoulos, D., Stephenson, N., and Tsianos, V. (2008). *Escape Routes: Control and Subversion in the Twenty-first Century*. London: Pluto Press.

Picozza, F. (2017a). Dublin on the move. *Movements. Journal Für Kritische Migrations- und Grenzregimeforschung*, **3**(1). Accessed 28 September 2017 at http://movements-journal.org/issues/04.bewegungen/05.picozza--dublin-on-the-move.html.

Picozza, F. (2017b). Dubliners: unthinking displacement, illegality and refugeeness within Europe's geographies of asylum. In N. De Genova (ed.), *The Borders of "Europe": Autonomy of Migration, Tactics of Bordering* (pp. 233–54). Durham, NC: Duke University Press.

Rumford, C. (2006). Theorizing borders. *European Journal of Social Theory*, **9**(2), 155–69.

Rumford, C. (2008). Introduction: citizens and borderwork in Europe. *Space and Polity*, **12**(1), 1–12. Accessed 28 September 2017 at https://doi.org/10.1080/13562570801969333.

Schmidt, M. (2015). Zwischen Moral und Skandal. Humanitarismus und Menschenrechte in der Migrations- und Grenzpolitik Marokkos. *Movements. Journal Für Kritische Migrations- Und Grenzregimeforschung*, **1**(1). Accessed 28 September 2017 at http://movements-journal.org/issues/01.grenzregime/16.schmidt--moral-skandal-marokko-humanitarismus-menschenrechte.html.

Schuster, L. (2011). Dublin II and Eurodac: examining the (un)intendend(?) consequences. *Gender, Place & Culture: A Journal of Feminist Geography*, **18**(3), 401–16.

Ticktin, M. (2015). The problem with humanitarian borders. Accessed 28 September 2017 at http://www.public seminar.org/2015/09/the-problem-with-humanitarian-borders/.

Transit Migration Forschungsgruppe (2007). *Turbulente Ränder: Neue Perspektiven auf Migration an den Grenzen Europas*. Bielefeld: Transcript.

van Houtum, H. and van Naerssen, T. (2002). Bordering, ordering and othering. *Tijdschrift Voor Economische En Sociale Geografie*, **93**(2), 125–36. Accessed 28 September 2017 at http://onlinelibrary.wiley.com/doi/10.1111/1467-9663.00189/abstract.

Walters, W. (2002). Mapping Schengenland: denaturalizing the border. *Environment and Planning D: Society and Space*, **20**(5), 561–80.

Walters, W. (2011). Foucault and frontiers: notes on the birth of the humanitarian border. *Governmentality: Current Issues and Future Challenges*, 138–64. Accessed 28 September 2017 at http://www.academia.edu/download/25286013/FoucaultandFrontiers.pdf.

Walters, W. and Haahr, J.H. (2004). *Governing Europe: Discourse, Governmentality and European Integration*. London: Routledge.

Zolberg, A.R. (2006). Managing a world on the move. *Population and Development Review*, **32**(S1), 222–53. Accessed 28 September 2017 at http://onlinelibrary.wiley.com/doi/10.1111/j.1728-4457.2006.tb00009.x/full.

PART IV

CAMPS, DETENTION AND PRISONS

17. Informal migrant camps

Thom Davies, Arshad Isakjee and Surindar Dhesi

INTRODUCTION: THINKING BEYOND FORMAL CAMPS

Within human geography, despite useful research into official refugee and migrant camps (see Minca, 2005, 2015a; Ramadan, 2013; Feldman, 2015; Oesch, 2017), geographers have largely overlooked the makeshift spatiality of informal encampments and the vital role they play in critical geographies of migration. At its simplest, people on the move need places to shelter, sleep and rest, as they negotiate borders and unfamiliar territory. Due to the biopolitical exclusion experienced by 'irregular' migrants, however, formal provision and shelter is often deliberately suppressed by state actors, or exchanged for the immobilizing threat of biometric surveillance (Dhesi et al., 2017). As critical scholars of migration have argued, the political technology of formal reception centres and official migrant camps are crucial components of predatory border regimes, and can curtail onward movements (Kitagawa, 2011; Davies et al., 2017). Rather than being spaces of sanctuary, formal refugee and migrant encampments are often threatening spaces for people on the move, not least due to the carceral role they play in deportation and refoulement (Mountz et al., 2013). For this reason (among many others), *informal* migrant camps – in all their ephemeral, makeshift and shifting spatialities – are important sites of clandestine mobility.

This chapter confronts the informal camp as a vital space of contemporary migration, discussing it in relation to more formal settings and theorizing the role of political inaction in their spatial politics. The chapter starts by highlighting different formations of the informal camp; from adjunct encampments near formal refugee sites; to urban squats in transit cities; to the widespread prevalence of 'jungles' as important spatial formations for people on the move. Placing this varied 'constellation of camps' (Davies and Isakjee, 2015, p.93) within the wider European context, we conclude with a detailed discussion of one such informal camp: the Calais 'jungle' in northern France. We agree with Martin (2015, p.9), that 'campscapes' are significant spaces for political geographers, yet suggest a more sustained analysis of camp informality is needed to recognize the important role that unofficial camps play in processes of displacement and migration. We suggest that geographers look beyond the confines of formal camps to appreciate the wider role that encampments play in migration processes and the contested production of 'bare life' (Agamben, 1998).

Within Europe the camp itself is a re-emergent phenomenon, with the dark shadow of the concentration camp still firmly embedded in collective-political memory. The new informal camp in Europe – a far less deadly spatial technology – stems not merely from political action but also inaction. Their very formations betray the reluctance of European countries to provide adequate hospitality for some of the most vulnerable displaced populations. Makeshift camps become poignant manifestations of the global inequalities assigned by race and citizenship (Isakjee, 2016; Davies and Isakjee, 2018), reproducing migrant populations as either those whose lives require protection, or alternatively, those whose very presence represents threats to protect against (Vaughan-Williams, 2015b, p. 3). Furthermore, their spectacle as black spaces on a white European landscape provide a spatialized and graphic symbol of global racial segregation. Informal settlements are by no means exclusive to the Global North (see Darling, 2017; Sanyal, 2017). In fact, it is the European-ness of this ongoing spectacle that is significant: the European Union (EU) is one of the wealthiest regions in the world, making the biopolitical exclusion and health inequity embodied in these makeshift spaces of vital importance to critical scholars of migration. Informal migrant camps are therefore prominent yet overlooked sites of everyday geopolitics; visible avatars of global inequality.

Europe hosts an archipelago of informal migrant camps. They can be found along well-travelled migration routes across the continent, stretching from the Greek islands of Lesvos, Chios and Kos, to Thessaloniki on the Aegean coast, and Idomeni on the Greece-Macedonia border. Informal camps have emerged where mobility is curtailed; from the southern reaches of Italy in Lampedusa, to Ventimiglia on the Italy-France border. Railway stations too can become sites of informal encampment, among them Železnička station in Belgrade and Keleti station in Budapest, which became de facto camps for undocumented migrants in 2015. The urban metropolises of Rome, Milan, Athens and Paris have also seen camps spring up along train tracks, under bridges and in disused buildings. Informal camps also exist in more bucolic settings: in Šid on the Serbian-Croatian border, for example, and on the northern edge of the Schengen Zone, dotted along the highways of Northern France, and near the port-towns of Calais and Dunkirk. Small and large, camouflaged and visible, informal camps are here to stay. Their uncertain politics and shifting spatialities play a fundamental role in the experience of forced migration for thousands of people on the move.

SEEING LIKE A CAMP

For refugees and undocumented migrants, formal camps present a tension between hospitality and constriction. As Katz suggests, they are designed 'to assist them but also to control them' (2016, p. 17). In this sense, official camps can be linked to broader Foucauldian attempts to reduce individuals into populations, with camps inhabiting 'the biopolitics of otherness' (Fassin, 2001, p. 3). Borrowing from Scott's work on 'seeing like a state' (1998), we might contend that 'seeing like a camp' involves the compartmentalization of life into bounded and controllable legal orders. As a political technology, formal camps work to categorize people into docile or governable bodies (Minca, 2015a). At best, they offer material security to undocumented migrants and aid them through the complex processes of asylum. At worst, however, formal camps become spaces of detention, conduits of exile, and expose inhabitants to carceral regimes with the ever-present threat of being made *homo sacer* (Agamben, 1998). Formal migrant encampments attempt to do this through biometric surveillance, with fingerprinting, recorded interviews or 'screening', and photographic identification being a prerequisite for access. Informal camps, however, rely less on information *gathering*, and more on a politicized form of 'agnotology' (Proctor and Schiebinger, 2008). Indeed, informal camps are often predicated on remaining officially unnoticed by the state, and beyond its official gaze. In some cases, they may be hidden in plain sight, such as urban squats in transit cities which go largely ignored despite their visibility. More often, however, undocumented migrants may choose to set up informal encampments in places that are peripheral and unused (Sanyal, 2017), as they come into contact with bottlenecks in migration pathways.

Before long, however, informal camps usually become visible to state authorities and apparatus; yet it is in the state's interest not to formally recognize their existence, for to do so would be to acknowledge a responsibility for their vulnerable inhabitants. Consequently, informal camps can become spaces of deliberate ignorance, or *agnopolitics*; reliant on sovereign power strategically 'turning a blind eye' to the existence of irregular migrants and their specific needs (Davies et al., 2017; Stel, 2016). In this sense, makeshift camps are not so much an active political technology but rather a passive *void* into which subaltern groups are allowed to fill. Seen in this way, informal camps can be understood as 'the product of inattention' (Proctor and Schiebinger, 2008, p. 7), where strategic ignorance allows states to ignore, un-recognize and coerce undocumented migrants, through a hands-off or violently inactive response.

Spatially, informal camps may be large or small. They range from a few improvised shelters at the sides of roads and railways, to a sprawling *campopolis* – equipped with makeshift community centres, schools, and their own vibrant communities and ad hoc infrastructures (Mould, 2017; de Vries and Guild, 2018; Freedman, 2018). Simply put, 'where there is an enforced restriction of movement, camps will form' (Katz, 2016, p. 19). However, it is not just the spatial formation of informal camps that makes them stark spaces of exclusion, but also their temporal vulnerability. Throughout the modern era, camps have proven themselves to be extremely 'durable' spatial and political formations (Picker and Pasquetti, 2015, p. 681), yet all camps share the characteristic of being – at least nominally – temporary. As Bülent Diken and Carsten Laustsen remind us: 'the camp is, first of all, a temporary site, a spatially defined location that exists only for a limited period' (2004, p. 17). Indeed, long-standing refugee camps for Palestinian exiles in Jordan, for example, *rely* on remaining politically 'temporary' as a means of continual resistance to Israeli occupation (Oesch, 2017). Yet the idea of temporal vulnerability is most acutely felt with informal migrant camps, which are prone to waves of state-enforced destruction and what we call 'campicide' (inter alia Coward, 2008). Unlike the concrete fixity of formal encampments that emerge through slower processes of regulation, planning and active biopolitical governance, the spatiality of informal camps are constantly shifting, disappearing and re-emerging. Informal camps are fleeting spaces, suspended in constant cycles of demolition and construction. The 'lifespan' of informal camps is generally much shorter than formal migrant spaces, with makeshift encampments vulnerable to violent demolition and the urbicidal whim of the state.

It is important to appreciate that formal-informal distinctions cannot be understood as a binary. The idea that informality operates as a spectrum has become an established position within the informal economies literature (Smith and Stenning, 2006; Morris and Polese, 2013, p. 23). More broadly, geographers have pointed to the way that formal and informal structures are coexistent, relational and often symbiotic (Round et al., 2008; Davies and Polese, 2015). The same can be said for the geographies of the informal camp, which operate heterogeneously and occasionally in close association with formal structures. Formality and informality, then, can exist both as a continuum as well as in parallel (Davies, 2015). Informal settlements have been described as 'grey' spaces (Sanyal,

2017, p. 118), owing to their liminality and uncertain legitimacy as political constructions. Furthermore, critical scholars of migration have discussed a *blurring* between official and unofficial camps (Doraï, 2010; Sanyal, 2014; Marinaro, 2017). One such irregular space of migrant habitation that highlights the close association between formal and informal space is what we have called the 'adjunct camp'.

ADJUNCT ENCAMPMENTS

Adjunct camps are an unofficial add-on to formal migration encampments, often forming a symbiotic relationship with formalized refugee settlements. They occasionally form on the periphery of formal migrant spaces, such as official refugee reception centres on the Greek island of Lesvos. In such cases there is a dynamic interplay between the two geographies of the camp. As critical migration scholars have revealed, such spaces of 'self-settlement' (Bakewell, 2014) or 'counter-camps' (Minca, 2015b, p. 90) are sites of liminality and in-betweenness. Adjunct camps are fringe spaces offering temporary respite from the bureaucratic threat of formal camp surveillance. They also offer more freedom of mobility to attempt further clandestine border crossings. At the same time, they also allow access to non-governmental organizations, legal aid and activists who work in and around formal migration centres. In addition, such adjunct camps benefit from their proximity to important facilities such as drinking water and, occasionally, sources of Wi-Fi.

In some cases, such as with overcrowded refugee centres on the borders of the EU, women and children are prioritized accommodation, meaning male family members are forced to live in these adjunct spaces. Around the edges of official camps, beyond the materiality of barbed wire and identity checks, makeshift food stalls and road-side cafe's sometimes spring up as part of these adjunct camps, sustaining an informal economy that works hand-in-glove with the official camp. Such slippages between formal and informal campscapes turn these adjunct camps into 'hybrid spaces' (Sanyal, 2017, p. 120) whereby informal and formal mechanisms spill out, coexist and overlap. Often made from salvaged wood, tarpaulin or donated tents, the materiality of adjunct camps is often improvised and in contrast to the prefabricated 'permanence' of formal refugee spaces. A second articulation of the informal camp, which makes use of existing infrastructure independently from formal migrant encampments, is the urban squat.

URBAN SQUATS

Sometimes referred to by migrants as a *kharaba*, from the Arabic for a vacant or dilapidated house (Calais Migrant Solidarity, 2016, p. 56), urban migrant squats make use of empty spaces in transit cities. Their materiality is highly varied, from reclaimed buildings and derelict infrastructure that breathe new life into places and processes of 'ruination' (Mah, 2012); to camps that form under bridges, such as those at La Chapelle in Paris; to the use of parks and brownfield zones, as was the case in central Belgrade, until their clearance in 2016. The spatial politics of squatting is by no means the preserve of undocumented migrants, and in fact there have been some interesting alliances between squatter-activists and people on the move. For example, the 'Lampedusa in Hamburg' campaign in Germany, carried out by refugees reclaiming urban space (Borgstede, 2016), or the Calais Migrant Solidarity movement who have been squatting as part of their Open Border strategies in Northern France since 2009. However, unlike squatter-activists who 'squat in places in order to oppose oppression, injustice, and lack of autonomy' (Mudu and Chattopadhyay, 2016, p. 1), undocumented migrants generally inhabit urban squats for more practical reasons.

Cities offer important resources for undocumented migrants and refugees, including informal work, transport options for onwards migration and a vital link to home countries through money transfer shops. Cities also offer something less tangible for marginalized migrants, namely, the opportunity of escaping 'the stigma of refugeeness' (Sanyal, 2014, p. 560) by disappearing into the throng of the city. Geographers have argued that there is a 'new geopolitics of refuge emerging in our cities' (Rokem et al., 2017, p. 257), yet living in urban areas, including squats, also presents an increased danger of predatory border regimes. As Darling (2017, p. 183) argues, 'the city is situated as a strategic location for the enforcement of border control "within" the nation-state', and therefore urban squats – perhaps more so than other types of informal encampment – are vulnerable to these punitive forces.

Such squats are not only vulnerable to biopolitical strategies of exclusion, but also to the persistence of neoliberal forces that threaten all 'quasi-urban' spaces (Darling, 2017, p. 181). For example, the urban squat known as the 'Barracks' in Belgrade – at one time the largest informal camp in the Balkans – was demolished in early 2017 to make way for an exclusive redevelopment project on the banks of the Danube. This informal camp, squeezed into old warehouses and train yards, was just metres from the central bus and train station in the Serbian capital. It informally housed over 1,000 irregular migrants who were taking the 'Balkan route' through to the EU, primarily via Hungary and Croatia. Yet it was not demolished due to its inadequacy as a space of refuge, nor for its poor sanitation or inability to cope with freezing temperatures. Rather, local authorities destroyed the camp to allow the construction of offices, hotels and condominiums in a €3.5 billion 'Belgrade Waterfront' construction project, funded by gulf petrodollars (Wright, 2015; Obradovic-Wochnik, 2018). Urban squats such as the Barracks are important spaces for critical migration studies, and fit into a growing body of scholarship that focuses on the camp-city nexus (see Agier, 2002; Sanyal, 2012, 2017; Bulley, 2014; Martin, 2015; Ehrkamp, 2016; Darling, 2017; Mould, 2017).

JUNGLE CAMPS

A third important articulation of informal migrant camps are 'jungles'. Made infamous by the Calais jungle discussed later, jungles refer to improvised encampments often found on waste ground in more rural or semi-urban settings. The term is often used by undocumented migrants to describe makeshift spaces designed to provide temporary shelter whilst trapped at pinch-points on migration routes; their materiality consisting of plastic sheeting, pallets, tarpaulin, wood, donated tents and a myriad of other gathered and repurposed materials. They are inherently heterogeneous assemblages, shifting and changing with the ebb and flow of marginalized people on the move.

In a western context in particular, the word 'jungle' has troubling, racialized connotations, stretching back to racist descriptions of indigenous peoples living in colonized lands (Mills, 1997). Just as the 'idea of the "urban jungle" encourages racialized containment through separated territories in modern life' (Underhill, 2016, p. 399), the term 'jungle' to describe informal camps is equally problematic. The racialization of this term, and its widespread use to describe informal camps, should alert critical geographers to the neocolonial spectacle of many aspects of contemporary border regimes, as well as the 'zoopolitical' way migrants are animalized (Vaughan-Williams, 2015a).

Yet the etymology of the term jungle is perhaps more nuanced. 'Jungle' in fact originates from Sanskrit, one of the oldest Indo-European languages, meaning 'wilderness', 'wasteland' or 'forest'. Today in Pashto and Urdu, languages spoken by many undocumented migrants in Europe, *dzhangal* is frequently used to describe both the wilderness through which migrants are forced to travel and the informal spaces in which they set up camp. As Harrison reminds us, historically 'forests lie "beyond" the law, or better, they figure as places of the outlaw' (2009, p. 63). Within European folkloric imagination, the forest has always been a space of resistance outside of legal protection. From tales of *Eustace the Monk* in France; to *Kobus van der Schlossen* in Holland, and of course *Robin Hood* in England; forests and exile run in tandem. Contemporary migrant jungles carry on this motif of the forest as a space of the politically outcast. In this way, jungle camps offer a specific rendering of *homo sacer*: a place where bare lives not only inhabit a space of exile, but also exhibit the tenacity, agency and ingenuity to carve out their own space and perform small acts of resistance. Contemporary jungle camps have been discussed in terms of political expression, refusal and 'volunteer humanitarianism' (Sandri, 2017); their very makeshift thrown-togetherness – constructed by undocumented migrants themselves – has led some to position jungles as key sites of political possibility (Rygiel, 2011; Mould, 2017). Yet any optimism about jungle camps should not ignore the wider structural violence that these places also reproduce.

Informal Camps in Calais

The tripartite of makeshift encampments described above are just a few different formations of informal migrant camps. To gauge specifically how the (non-)governance of the informal camp leads to structural violence, we draw upon research conducted in the Calais informal refugee camp which existed in Northern France between April 2015 and October 2016.

Like all informal migrant camps, their spatiality can be directly linked to geopolitical decisions. The policy-related origins of the camp can be meaningfully traced back to the construction of the Schengen Zone itself. By 2001, 15 European nations agreed to remove border controls within the heart of the EU. By 2007, this had been extended to cover a further 11 EU countries, with a population exceeding 450 million. There is an irony to the dismantling of borders in this way: the establishment of free movement of people also creates new zones of profound immobility. The Schengen Area is often construed as a space of free movement within, but protected by, hard external borders, constructing what is often referred to as 'Fortress Europe' (Albrecht, 2002). Yet both on the Schengen Zone's periphery and along popular routes of travel within lie migration pinch-points; towns, villages and liminal spaces that are relatively easy to reach on either side of the new Schengen border – but difficult to cross without the correct documentation or passports.

Calais represents one such 'hotspot' (Painter et al., 2017; Mitchell and Sparke, 2018) for migrants and refugees who intend to reach the UK. The UK opted out of the Schengen Area, and this policy decision together with the material presence of the English Channel created a pinch-point in Calais, on the coast of France and a mere 21 miles away from the UK. Evidence of migrant populations living informally and destitute in Calais can be traced back to the late 1990s (Schuster, 2003). By 2001, a semi-formalized camp, partially supported by state provision had been established, reaching a population of up to 3,000 people (UNHCR, cited in Reinisch, 2015, p. 521). During the summer of that year and at the height of refugee migrations from the Balkans, the French and British authorities closed down the official Sangatte camp whilst also agreeing to formally accept the asylum applications of at least 1,600 inhabitants of that camp (Schuster, 2003, p. 519). This agreement was furthered by an enhanced series of border security protocols crystallized in the broader Le Touquet defence treaty in 2003, which effectively moved the British border to Northern France. The migrant population of Calais declined substantially after the deconstruction of the Sangatte camp in Calais.

However, what is striking about informal camps of this kind is that they exist in constant cycles of construction and destruction. Camps appear through policy interventions, they can grow via inaction, and then are demolished if their spectacle becomes a political liability. So it is with Calais. As formal refugee facilities no longer existed, a steady stream of undocumented migrants continued to encamp forested areas and wilderness around the town of Calais; the majority of whom intended to reach the UK by smuggling into cargo lorries travelling through the port. These areas began to be known as Calais' 'jungles'.

Politically, the presence of migrants undermined the notion of French and indeed British sovereignty; their ability to control their borders and the territory of the state. It is for this reason that in 2014, the governments of both the UK and of France announced a joint plan, funded by £12 million from the UK, for extra security in the port of Calais together with enhanced fencing of the port area (Ibrahim and Howarth, 2018). The dire conditions in which migrants had been living were well known at this point, but ultimately the cold security logics of border control policy trumped any humanitarian imperative for focused state action. Both the Le Touquet treaty and the security pact of 2014 also demonstrate the geopolitical nature of informal camps: they may be spaces of abandonment and desertion on a local scale, but their cyclical existences are regulated to various degrees by international treaties and agreements.

Beyond the perceived threats to sovereign space, the visible spectacle of informal camps also threatens something more intangible, yet crucial: the very identity of the liberal, developed, European state. The presence of impoverished, legally immobile, vulnerable populations from former French and British colonies unsettle the illusions of liberalism, equality and liberty trumpeted loudly by the very constitution of the French state. The divisions produced by capitalism and (post)colonialism are routinely obscured by distance, but arriving in the heart of a French town, the abject informal camp is an unsettling, disturbing presence. Its spectre disturbs the physical boundaries that would normally curtail ethical challenges or resistance to the inequalities produced by global capitalism (Harvey, 2006). When informal migrant camps become visible, their very *being*, alongside a suburb of the world's fifth largest economy shines a piercing light onto these disparities.

The 'New Jungle' in Calais

As sporadic and sustained armed conflicts continued in countries such as Sudan, Syria, Iraq and Afghanistan – and human rights continued to be infringed in Eritrea – the informal population of Calais began to grow more sharply from 2013. The populations at this point lived in multiple small sites including several close to and within the town centre of Calais itself. As local opposition to the rising population of the camp grew, on the 29 March 2015 authorities began to forcibly clear migrants from the multiple, smaller informal camps and urban squats throughout the town. Migrants were corralled and forced to move to a new site, roughly comprising half a square kilometre of derelict land a little over two miles from the centre of the small town. In this space, the population initially numbered 1,500 – but rose to 3,000 within three months (Davies et al., 2017, p. 3). By the end of 2015, the number was estimated at 5,000; 16 months after the camp was first 'established' it housed over 9,000 people.

The forcible movement of migrants was underpinned by calculated inaction. The squalid material and health conditions migrants were exposed to were characterized by inaction so stark that we construe it as a form of violence. During the camp's existence a third-sector organization funded by the French government provided one meal a day – and no more – to a proportion of the camp's population. But even this resource did not stretch to feed a meal a day to half of the inhabitants on site. Those without the independent means to buy food relied on very limited provision by grassroots charities. In one corner of the camp in July 2015, we found approximately 40 migrants who had survived eating boiled pasta for weeks as they had gradually made their way through Italy and into France, before being stuck in Calais. They reported being hungry and constipated. Others spoke of falling asleep whilst being hungry – and when food was received through charitable organizations, it was often rationed so as to last longer. With the French state perfectly able to feed these migrants if they had wanted to, hunger was therefore being used as a political tool to discourage migrants from being in Calais at all.

Inaction underpinned the ways in which the health and hygiene of migrants would be limited to the same ends. Upon moving refugees to the site of what became the informal camp, just four small shacks with rudimentary holes dug in the ground acted as toilets for over a thousand people (Davies and Isakjee, 2015). By July 2015, 20 working toilets existed in the camp during our fieldwork visit. This equates to one toilet per 75 people on site. In comparison, a formal refugee camp is expected to provide one toilet per family, and as a bare minimum one per 20 people (UNHCR, 2007). The result was that people had to resort to urinating and defecating out in the open ground, alongside the shacks and tents – the actual living spaces – which littered the site. Combined with the complete lack of facilities for safe storage of food or water, and with no way to safely prepare food, infections and illness became rife in the camp. Rats, cockroaches and other vermin were also located in the camp, which present significant health risks (Porusia et al., 2017). An environmental health survey we conducted found infectious levels of pathogens such as *E. coli* and *K. pneumoniae*, among others, on swabs taken from a host of cooking surfaces, door handles and pieces of cutlery (Dhesi et al., 2015, 2017). Without adequate sanitation facilities, through what public health scientists call the 'fecal-oral route', these infections caused diarrhoea, vomiting and other gastrointestinal problems for many of those living in the 'jungle'. Furthermore, the complete absence of adequate facilities for washing bedding and clothing, together with a shortage of opportunities to shower resulted in as many as 20 per cent of the camp's population suffering with the indignity of scabies.

The hunger, the scabies, the gastrointestinal illnesses: each of these is a physical and biological manifestation of wholesale abandonment by a state which comfortably has the means and technologies with which to alleviate this suffering – but not the will (Dhesi et al., 2017). As we have discussed in detail elsewhere (see Davies et al., 2017), we can understand the deliberate withholding of provision as a form of necropolitics. Mbembe (2003, p. 35) used the concept of necropolitics to describe the spectacle of suffering which can result from an enhanced, more brutal form of biopolitics. Necropolitical actions at their most stark can lead to the loss of life of swathes of populations – a contemporarily paradigmatic example would be the suspension of rescue operations for migrants at sea which has also seen humanitarian impulses set aside as Europe seeks to securitize its maritime border (see Tazzioli, 2016; Stierl, 2017). However, necropolitics for Mbembe can also entail the permanent wounding of individuals, kept alive but in a state of injury (see Davies, 2018). By October 2016, when the Calais camp was finally dismantled, many migrants in Calais lived in the camp for almost the entirety of its 18-month existence, suffering from an array of physical and mental health ailments associated with the semi-carceral, abject state in which they lived. The living conditions of the migrants in its iniquity was a direct result of a type of governance and domination which bares the hallmarks of necropolitics. The calculated ignorance states demonstrate in denying basic health standards in these spaces makes clear how 'inactivity – as well as political actions – can be wielded as a means of control, coercion and power' (Davies et al., 2017, p. 19). Thus, these camps, in all their state-sanctioned squalor, emphasize the disposability of undocumented migrants as non-citizens.

CONCLUSION

With much academic and media focus still on boats, arrivals and the externalized borders of the EU, informal camps are a reminder that the ongoing emergency for people on the move is 'a more-than-maritime crisis' (Davies and Isakjee, 2015, p. 93); it extends beyond the sea and beyond the barbed wire of official migrant processing centres. Informal camps exist along migration routes as important spaces of flows for irregular migrants – but they are also vital spaces of interrogation for critical geographers. It is only through exploring these spaces that we can begin to understand the lived mobile experience of migrants as they seek to cross nation-state borders. Their conceptual significance is heightened when one reflects on the tangible public health consequences of state inaction with regards to provision in such spaces – and this opens up space for scholars of migration studies to incorporate experts and academics from fields of health studies, legal studies, engineering and architecture, all of whom have a role to play in analysing the embodied impact of camp-life – but also in advocating or indeed co-constructing and designing new ways in which socially just policies for irregular migrants might be made possible.

Informal camps within more developed contexts assume deeper significance still. Camps such as those that have existed in Northern France and elsewhere become linch-pins of debates around the legitimacy and rights of those residing within. Their management or concealment become matters of governance – and for activists they become sites of resistance and solidarity. The willingness of contemporary governments to abandon their marginalized inhabitants, mark makeshift camps as pre-eminent sites of biopolitical exclusion and structural racism. They are the material residue of global inequality and exist at the sharp end of geopolitics. Makeshift camps discussed here are both a reaction to and extension of the violence of contemporary borders. Their shifting and mutating form belies their political entrenchment: they may be bulldozed, moved or dismantled by state actors, but until the wider political landscape changes, informal migrant camps are here to stay.

REFERENCES

Agamben, G., 1998. *Homo sacer: Sovereign Power and Bare Life*. Stanford, CA: Stanford University Press.
Agier, M., 2002. Between war and city: towards an urban anthropology of refugee camps. *Ethnography*, **3**(3), 317–41.
Albrecht, H.-J., 2002. Fortress Europe? – Controlling illegal immigration. *European Journal of Crime, Criminal Law and Criminal Justice*, **10**(1), 1–22.
Bakewell, O., 2014. Encampment and self-settlement. In Fiddian-Qasmiyeh, E., Loescher, G., and Long, K. (eds), *The Oxford Handbook of Refugee and Forced Migration Studies*, Oxford: Oxford University Press, pp. 127–38.
Borgstede, S., 2016. 'We are here to stay': reflections on the struggle of the refugee group 'Lampedusa in Hamburg' and the solidarity campaign, 2013–2015. In Mudu, P. and Chattopadhyay, S. (eds), *Migration, Squatting and Radical Autonomy: Resistance and Destabilization of Racist Regulatory Policies and B/Ordering Mechanisms*, London: Routledge, pp. 162–79.
Bulley, D., 2014. Inside the tent: community and government in refugee camps. *Security Dialogue*, **45**, 63–80.
Calais Migrant Solidarity, 2016. Trapped on the border: a brief history of solidarity squatting practices in Calais. In Mudu, P. and Chattopadhyay, S. (eds), *Migration, Squatting and Radical Autonomy: Resistance and Destabilization of Racist Regulatory Policies and B/Ordering Mechanisms*, London: Routledge, pp. 54–64.
Coward, M., 2008. *Urbicide: The Politics of Urban Destruction*. London: Routledge.
Darling, J., 2017. Forced migration and the city: irregularity, informality, and the politics of presence. *Progress in Human Geography*, **41**(2), 78–198.
Davies, T., 2015. Nuclear borders: informally negotiating the Chernobyl Exclusion Zone. In Morris J. and Polese A. (eds), *Informal Economies in Post-socialist Spaces*, London: Palgrave Macmillan, pp. 225–44.
Davies, T., 2018. Toxic space and time: slow violence, necropolitics, and petrochemical pollution. *Annals of the American Association of Geographers*, 1–17.
Davies, T. and Isakjee, A., 2015. Geography, migration and abandonment in the Calais refugee camp. *Political Geography*, **49**, 93–5.
Davies, T. and Isakjee, A. 2018. Ruins of Empire: race and the postcolonial geographies of European migrant camps. *Geoforum*.
Davies, T. and Polese, A., 2015. Informality and survival in Ukraine's nuclear landscape: living with the risks of Chernobyl. *Journal of Eurasian Studies*, **6**(1), 34–45.
Davies, T., Isakjee, A., and Dhesi, S., 2017. Violent inaction: the necropolitical experience of refugees in Europe. *Antipode*, **49**(5), 1–22.
Dhesi, S., Isakjee A., and Davies T., 2015. An environmental health assessment of the new migrant camp in Calais. University of Birmingham.
Dhesi, S., Isakjee A., and Davies T., 2017. Public health in the Calais refugee camp: environment, health and exclusion. *Critical Public Health*, **28**(2), 1–13.
Diken, B. and Laustsen, C.B., 2004. *The Culture of Exception: Sociology Facing the Camp*. London: Routledge.
Doraï, M.K., 2010. Palestinian refugee camps in Lebanon. Migration, mobility and the urbanization process. In Hanafi, S. and Knudsen, A. (eds), *Palestinian Refugees. Identity, Space and Place in the Levant*, Routledge Studies on the Arab-Israeli Conflict, New York: Routledge, pp. 67–80.
Ehrkamp, P., 2016. Geographies of migration I: Refugees. *Progress in Human Geography*, **41**(6), 813–22. doi/10.1177/0309132516663061.
Fassin, D., 2001. The biopolitics of otherness. Undocumented foreigners and racial discrimination in French public debate. *Anthropology Today*, 17(1), 3–7.
Feldman, I., 2015. What is a camp? Legitimate refugee lives in spaces of long-term displacement. *Geoforum*, **66**, 244–52.

Freedman, J., 2018. 'After Calais': creating and managing (in) security for refugees in Europe. *French Politics*, 1–19.

Harrison, R.P., 2009. *Forests: The Shadow of Civilization*. Chicago, IL: University of Chicago Press.

Harvey, D., 2006. *Spaces of Global Capitalism*. Verso.

Ibrahim, Y. and Howarth, A., 2018. *Calais and its Border Politics: From Control to Demolition*. London: Routledge.

Isakjee, A., 2016. Dissonant belongings: the evolving spatial identities of young Muslim men in the UK. *Environment and Planning A*, **48**(7), 1337–53.

Katz, I., 2016. A network of camps on the way to Europe. *Forced Migration Review*, **51**, 17–19.

Kitagawa, S., 2011. Geographies of migration across and beyond Europe: the camp and the road of movements. In Bialasiewicz, A. (ed.), *Europe in the World: EU Geopolitics and the Making of European Space*, London: Ashgate, pp. 201–22.

Mah, A., 2012. *Industrial Ruination, Community, and Place: Landscapes and Legacies of Urban Decline*. Toronto: University of Toronto Press.

Marinaro, Clough, 2017. The informal faces of the (neo-) ghetto: state confinement, formalization and multidimensional informalities in Italy's Roma camps. *International Sociology*, **32**(4), 545–62.

Martin, D., 2015. From spaces of exception to 'campscapes': Palestinian refugee camps and informal settlements in Beirut. *Political Geography*, **44**, 9–18.

Mbembe, A., 2003. Necropolitics. *Public Culture*, **15**, 11–40.

Mills, C.W., 1997. *The Racial Contract*. Ithaca, NY: Cornell University Press.

Minca, C., 2005. The return of the camp. *Progress in Human Geography*, **29**(4), 405–12.

Minca, C., 2015a. Geographies of the camp. *Political Geography*, **49**, 74–83.

Minca, C., 2015b. Counter-camps and other spatialities. *Political Geography*, **49**(9), 90–92.

Mitchell, K. and Sparke, M., 2018. Hotspot geopolitics versus geosocial solidarity: Contending constructions of safe space for migrants in Europe. *Environment and Planning D: Society and Space*, 1–21.

Morris, J. and Polese, A. (eds), 2013. *The Informal Post-socialist Economy: Embedded Practices and Livelihoods*, Vol. 50. London and New York: Routledge.

Mould, O., 2017. The Calais jungle: a slum of London's making. *City*, **25**(3), 393–409.

Mountz, A., Coddington, K., Catania, R.T., and Loyd, J.M., 2013. Conceptualizing detention: mobility, containment, bordering, and exclusion. *Progress in Human Geography*, **37**(4), 522–41.

Mudu, P. and Chattopadhyay, S. (eds), 2016. *Migration, Squatting and Radical Autonomy*. London: Routledge.

Obradovic-Wochnik, J., 2018. Urban geographies of refugee journeys: biopolitics, neoliberalism and contestation over public space in Belgrade. *Political Geography*, **67**, 65–75.

Oesch, L., 2017. The refugee camp as a space of multiple ambiguities and subjectivities. *Political Geography*, **60**, 110–20.

Painter, J., Papada, E., Papoutsi, A., and Vradis, A., 2017. Hotspot politics – or, when the EU state gets real. *Political Geography*, **60**, 259–60.

Picker, G. and Pasquetti, S., 2015. Durable camps: the state, the urban, the everyday. Introduction. *City*, **19**(5), 681–8.

Porusia, M., Poynter, A., Dhesi, S., and Lynch, Z., 2017. The bait preference of American cockroach (*Periplaneta americana*): field and laboratory strains. *Advanced Science Letters*, **23**(4), 3558–61.

Proctor, R. and Schiebinger, L.L. (eds), 2008. *Agnotology: The Making and Unmaking of Ignorance*. Stanford, CA: Stanford University Press.

Ramadan, A., 2013. Spatialising the refugee camp. *Transactions of the Institute of British Geographers*, **38**(1), 65–77.

Reinisch, J., 2015. 'Forever temporary': migrants in Calais, then and now. *The Political Quarterly*, **86**(4), 515–22.

Rokem, J., Fregonese, S., Ramadan, A. et al., 2017. Interventions in urban geopolitics. *Political Geography*, **61**, 253–62.

Round, J., Williams, C.C., and Rodgers, P., 2008. Everyday tactics and spaces of power: the role of informal economies in post-Soviet Ukraine. *Social & Cultural Geography*, **9**(2), 171–85.

Rygiel, K., 2011. Bordering solidarities: migrant activism and the politics of movement and camps at Calais. *Citizenship Studies*, **15**(1), 1–19.

Sandri, E., 2017. 'Volunteer Humanitarianism': volunteers and humanitarian aid in the Jungle refugee camp of Calais. *Journal of Ethnic and Migration Studies*, **44**(1), 65–80.

Sanyal, R., 2012. Refugees and the city: an urban discussion. *Geography Compass*, **6**(11), 633–44.

Sanyal, R., 2014. Urbanizing refuge: interrogating spaces of displacement. *International Journal of Urban and Regional Research*, **38**(2), 558–72.

Sanyal, R., 2017. A no-camp policy: interrogating informal settlements in Lebanon. *Geoforum*, **84**, 117–25.

Schuster, L., 2003. Asylum seekers: Sangatte and the tunnel. *Parliamentary Affairs*, **56**(3), 506–22.

Scott, J.C., 1998. *Seeing Like a State: How Certain Schemes to Improve the Human Condition Have Failed*. New York: Yale University Press.

Smith, A. and Stenning, A., 2006. Beyond household economies: articulations and spaces of economic practice in postsocialism. *Progress in Human Geography*, **30**(2), 190–213.

Stel, N., 2016. The agnotology of eviction in South Lebanon's Palestinian gatherings: how institutional ambiguity and deliberate ignorance shape sensitive spaces. *Antipode*, **48**(5), 1400–1419.

Stierl, M., 2017. A fleet of Mediterranean border humanitarians. *Antipode*, **50**(3), 704–24.

Tazzioli, M., 2016. Border displacements. Challenging the politics of rescue between Mare Nostrum and Triton. *Migration Studies*, **4**(1), 1–19.

Underhill, S.M., 2016. Urban jungle, Ferguson: rhetorical homology and institutional critique. *Quarterly Journal of Speech*, **102**(4), 396–417.

UNHCR, 2007. *Handbook for Emergencies*, 3rd edn. Geneva: United Nations High Commissioner for Refugees.

Vaughan-Williams, N., 2015a. 'We are not animals!' Humanitarian border security and zoopolitical spaces in Europe. *Political Geography*, **45**, 1–10.

Vaughan-Williams, N., 2015b. *Europe's Border Crisis: Biopolitical Security and Beyond*. Oxford: Oxford University Press.

de Vries, L.A. and Guild, E., 2018. Seeking refuge in Europe: spaces of transit and the violence of migration management. *Journal of Ethnic and Migration Studies*, Special Issue, 1–11.

Wright, H., 2015. Belgrade Waterfront: an unlikely place for Gulf petrodollars to settle. *Guardian*. https://www.theguardian.com/cities/2015/dec/10/belgrade-waterfront-gulf-petrodollars-exclusive-waterside-development.

18. Fractures in Australia's Asia-Pacific border continuum: deterrence, detention and the production of illegality
Kate Coddington

INTRODUCTION

In a 2014 speech to the Biometrics Institute Asia-Pacific Conference in Sydney, Australia, Minister for Immigration and Border Protection, Scott Morrison, described his administration's project of constructing what he called a "border continuum" (Morrison, 2014). The Australian border, according to Morrison, is a "national asset, holding critical economic, social and strategic value for our nation". Establishing a "border continuum" would preserve what Morrison called the "integrity of identity", "protecting Australia against the threat of illegitimate movements across the border" (Morrison, 2014). In order to maintain the border continuum, Morrison's Liberal party envisioned a border protection agency devoted to everything from customs control, port management, and the deterrence and apprehension of irregular migrants under a single point of highly militarized control called the "Australian Border Force", which was later established in July 2015 (Morrison, 2014). Although the Australian Border Force represents a new agency devoted to border protection (in a country known for changing the name, and mission, of the border enforcement agency multiple times over the past few governments), it envisions a similar all-encompassing, "everywhere" border regime that has been the vision behind Australia's restrictive policies towards refugees over the past two decades.

The border continuum represents part of the fragmentation of "the border" that scholars have documented in recent years; as Jones et al. (2017, p. 4) notes, contemporary enforcement regimes are known for "dislocating linear border functions and pushing them both outward into other states' territories and inward into national societies". Enforcement practices extend outward, into extraterritorial spaces and with the involvement of third-party actors including both states and non-governmental organizations, even as they extend into the space of the nation-state. Such visions of a "total" border rely on logics of anticipation. Geography has become a key method for this anticipatory border policing: as Mountz (2010) writes, the spatiality of the nation-state may itself be a weapon against irregular migrants. This is especially true for the island nation of Australia, where the Australian Border Force represents the latest iteration of the "most comprehensive exclusion of asylum seekers among Western states" (Tazreiter, 2015, p. 102).

Yet while the border continuum may appear to be a spatially expansive, functionally all-encompassing regulatory regime, it is also fallible. Indeed, as Perera (2007, p. 224) describes, such "borderscapes" involve the simultaneous expansion and contraction of political spaces as well as "the new geographies, spatial identities and territorial claims and counterclaims" that arise. Making a similar point, Burridge et al. (2017, p. 245) describe border regimes more along the lines of nets or webs – spatially expansive, but containing gaps, holes, and loops: "the *apparent* diffusion of bordering practices should not be mistaken for an effective, global border enforcement complex" (original emphasis). I argue here that while the reach of Australia's border continuum appears extensive and the practices encompassed within it actively shrink refugees' access to asylum, it too contains fissures. While these fractures within Australia's border continuum do not radically change the outcomes for refugees, they do make visible potential opportunities for change. This chapter proceeds as follows. I first describe three central components of the border continuum limiting access to refugee protection: *deterrence*, including projects ranging from regional collaborations to policing Indian Ocean maritime spaces, militarized interdiction practices intercepting or even towing back asylum seeker vessels and advertising campaigns attempting to dissuade refugees from seeking asylum; *detention*, including Australia's range of on- and offshore immigration facilities as well as detention sites on Nauru and Manus Island, Papua New Guinea; and the *production of illegality*, which includes hostile rhetoric directed at refugees as well as increasingly restrictive legal regimes that criminalize migrants. Next, I explore where these elements of the border continuum break down – the fractures that reveal the fundamental instability of the enforcement regime. Finally, I conclude by considering the effectiveness of fractures in the border continuum: Do the fissures revealed open new spaces of political transformation? Or is Australia's relentless targeting of refugees spreading throughout the region?

MAPPING THE CONTINUUM

Deterrence

Morrison's border continuum relies on a range of deterrence activities, from enforcement collaborations across the Indian Ocean region to detention, interdiction, and media campaigns. The following subsection will detail the on-and offshore detention practices; this subsection will focus on other deterrence measures. Together, as Hodge (2015, p. 125) notes, these practices build on long-standing neo-colonial relationships throughout the region and "constitute attempts by the coalition government to control the contingency of circulation".

Attempts to anticipate and prevent the arrival of asylum seekers by boat have dominated Australian refugee policies since 2001, when the arrival of the *M.V. Tampa* was politicized as a "crisis" for the nation during the election campaign of Prime Minister Howard. Indeed, any type of anticipatory deterrence strategy is "always-already a regional engagement" simply due to Australia's island geography (Chambers, 2015, p. 421). During the Labour administration from 2007 to 2013, the government attempted a variety of strategic alliances with Indian Ocean neighbours. In July 2013, with the election of the Coalition government, the government released a pamphlet describing the arrival of asylum seekers by boat as a "national emergency" and announced a militarized programme of deterrence activities called "Operation Sovereign Borders" (OSB) to tackle the crisis (Chambers, 2015). OSB includes joint migration policing efforts with Indonesia, Malaysia, and Sri Lanka to disrupt smuggling activities, military operations to interdict and turn back asylum seeker vessels, and the reduction of resettlement places for refugees

(Fleay and Hartley, 2016). OSB also expands upon Australia's communications strategies since 2009 to discourage asylum seekers from attempting to travel by boat. Overseas public information campaigns have argued, as, for instance, in the 2014 "No way" campaign, that "you will not make Australia home". Australia has budgeted AUD$39.9 million on such campaigns from 2015 to 2019 (Watkins, 2017).

OSB expands on Australia's existing relationships with Indonesia. As the primary departure country for asylum seeker vessels bound for Australia, Indonesia had been the target of "anti-people smuggling" campaigns since 2009 in the numerous coastal villages in Java from which asylum seekers would depart. Under pressure from Australia, Indonesia expanded its migration detention capacities and criminalized irregular migration. Under OSB, migrants were unable to quickly transit through Indonesia, and Hargrave et al. (2016) document that refugee numbers in 2016 (officially estimated at nearly 14,000) were up 30 percent from 2013 levels. Migrants have been voluntarily turning themselves into detention facilities because of the difficulties obtaining work or food for subsistence. In exchange for the crackdown on migrants and the continued participation in the 2000 bilateral regional cooperation agreement on migration governance between Indonesia, Australia, and the International Organization for Migration, Indonesia receives large-scale bilateral aid from Australia.

As I will detail in the following subsection, OSB also included renewed relationships with Nauru and Papua New Guinea (PNG) for the detention and resettlement of refugees. Nauru and Manus Island (PNG) had been sites of migrant detention in the early 2000s, after the implementation of Prime Minister Howard's 2001 "Pacific Solution". In 2013, the Rudd government turned again to these Pacific Island nations to detain all asylum seekers who arrived by boat in Australia (or were interdicted near Australian waters), but this time the arrangement with Nauru and PNG went beyond simply short-term detention to including claims processing and long-term settlement (Warbrooke, 2014). Without consulting the governments of Nauru and PNG, Australia expanded their obligations regarding the detained refugees to include human rights and non-refoulement responsibilities (Warbrooke, 2014). Australia signed a Regional Resettlement Agreement with PNG in July 2013, entirely funded by Australia, as well as a Memorandum of Understanding (MOU) with Nauru on 3 August 2013 for the temporary resettlement of refugees with successful claims before their permanent resettlement in Cambodia (Asylum Insight, 2014, 2017a). While Nauru signed the Refugee Convention in 2011, it and PNG have been criticized by international observers for the unsafe and inhumane conditions refugees experience (Asylum Insight, 2014).

Like in Indonesia, Australia has used development and aid as leverage for achieving these regional arrangements, promising AUD$1.1 billion to build and operate the Manus Island detention facility, with an accompanying package of AUD$420 million in aid and AUD$18 million for "law and order" cooperation (Grewcock, 2014, p. 75). PNG has also received extensive funding from Australia for capacity building projects in border enforcement, IT border management, and surveillance (Taylor, 2010) and the Australian aid packages also fund development of universities, a new hospital, infrastructure upgrades, and the deployment of Australian police to PNG (Giannacopoulos, 2013). Nauru, similarly, received AUD$27.1 million in development assistance from Australia in 2014–15 (Dickson, 2015). Yet the bargain comes with consequences for the poor states of PNG and Nauru: Warbrooke (2014) documents increasing resentment, stress on resources like food and water, increased prices for services (e.g., rent), and problems from Australians who work in the detention facilities, such as the case of the off-duty G4S security guard who harassed people travelling near Lombrum Naval Base (PNG). While the development of detention centres is framed in terms of new skilled employment for the island nations, private contractors primarily employ Australians who are paid far more than their island counterparts (Dickson, 2015). Resettlement possibilities for migrants detained on these islands have become so remote that Australia forged a one-off 2016 agreement with the US Obama administration to resettle up to 1,250 refugees in the US. Officials deny that the arrangement is part of a swap deal, but at around the same time, Australia announced it would resettle Central American refugees from Costa Rica. Although the agreement was characterized as a "dumb deal" by the incoming US Trump administration, US officials promised it would go ahead as planned (Asylum Insight, 2017b).

OSB has also included increased efforts to interdict and, in many cases, turn back asylum seeker vessels journeying to Australia. As I describe elsewhere (Coddington, 2018), Australian strategies have included paying smugglers to return boats to Indonesia, forcibly towing asylum seeker vessels towards Indonesia, and transferring asylum seekers to purpose-purchased lifeboats in order to tow them back to Indonesian waters. Between the end of September 2013 and December 2013 the Coalition government interdicted 22 boats and detained 1,151 people, as well as paid one boat captain AUD$32,000 to turn back (Asylum Insight, 2016a). By August 2015, 20 boats had been turned back under OSB (Refugee Council of Australia, 2016a). This method of "people dumping", as Chambers (2015, p. 421) characterizes it, is both illegal under international law and ineffective as a deterrence strategy (Doherty, 2017a). Tow-backs in particular demonstrate how "the vulnerability of national sovereignty is addressed by *operationally* recognizing the vulnerability of boat arrivals – in a way that does not discursively recognize their vulnerability", Chambers argues (2015, p. 427, original emphasis).

Detention

Detention of asylum seekers arriving by boat has been a cornerstone of Australian border enforcement practices since the 1990s. Since the early 2000s, Australia has employed both onshore and offshore detention for asylum seekers, and currently (2017) has onshore detention facilities in a range of locations, "offshore" detention on Christmas Island and contracts detention facilities on Nauru and Manus Island, PNG. In addition, customs vessels intercepting asylum seekers arriving by boat have become de facto floating detention facilities for asylum seekers (Dickson, 2015, p. 447). Australia has been widely critiqued for the inhumane conditions and mental and physical health impacts on asylum seekers in detention: Doherty (2016b, p. 2) writes that "detention centres are designed to damage people, and that illnesses, injuries, and deaths are the predictable, expected outcomes of the regime. Detention damages people because it is supposed to."

Incidents of physical and sexual violence dominate conditions especially at the Nauru and Manus Island sites, where jurisdiction over Australia-funded detention is legally blurred. Detention centres represent "zones that are neither of PNG or Nauru, nor detached from them; neither of Australia, nor free from Australia's authoritative jurisdiction" (Dickson, 2015, p. 444). In October 2015, the *Guardian* published a cache of 2,116 incident reports leaked from the Nauru facilities, documenting reports of 66 instances of sexual assault and assault on children, 30 instances of self-harm involving children and 159 instances of threatened self-harm involving children, in addition to many other incidents involving adults over a 19-month period (Asylum Insight, 2016c). Yasaman, a refugee on Nauru, relayed her experience in the detention centre, saying:

> My memories in Nauru are eating away at my soul like leprosy. I feel I am devalued and humiliated. Every day I see people harming themselves and I feel powerless to help them. Whenever I hear any noises from a crowd I automatically think someone has killed themselves again. I can't get used to this nightmare. (Vasefi, 2017, p. 1)

Conditions at Manus Island had been particularly appalling: detainees face high rates of self-harm, repeated suicide attempts, regular violent and sexual assaults, and the regular use of armed police to deal with non-compliant detainees, which led to the death of asylum seeker Reza Barati in February 2014 (Doherty et al., 2017). As in other detention facilities, guards are issued with cut-down knives in order to rescue refugees who hang themselves. The *Guardian* also documented a year-long campaign by contractors Broadspectrum and Wilson Security to make conditions on Manus Island inhospitable enough to force refugees to leave the centre, including the downgrading of conditions for those not formally granted refugee status, frequent forced deportations, and a widespread culture of bullying including the reported threats by Australia security staff instructing PNG officers to beat asylum seekers (Doherty et al., 2017, p. 4).

In April 2016 the Papua New Guinea Supreme Court ruled that detention of asylum seekers on Manus Island was illegal and unconstitutional. In response, the centre was "opened" for free movement in May 2016, partially closed later that month, and as of November 2017 has closed entirely, leaving about 600 asylum seekers who feared for their safety if moved in squalid conditions. The closure of the detention centre has not improved conditions for asylum seekers, Perera and Pugliese (2017, p. 2) write, as the detention centre was not closed but reverted back to its original capacity as a naval base: "the detainees have, through this legal sleight-of-hand, been *moved to nowhere*" (original emphasis). On the naval base, refugees continue to face assaults and threats from the local Manus Island population, and in 2017 International Health and Medical Services, the medical contractor, was removed for practising without proper licensing, leaving only skeleton medical care on the island (Doherty and Davidson, 2017).

Yet detention has become extremely profitable, not just because of the exchange of aid and development funds as noted above, but also for the contractors who operate the facilities. Broadspectrum (formerly Transfield Services) operates catering, maintenance, garrison, and welfare services in both Manus Island and Nauru, and earned over AUD$1.5 billion between 2012 and 2015. SERCO, who operates onshore facilities as well as the detention centre on Christmas Island, had its five-year contract renewed in 2014 for over AUD$1 billion as well (Asylum Insight, 2016b). Contractors depend on high levels of secrecy in order to carry out detention operations. Reporters and independent authorities are banned inside both Nauru and Manus Island detention facilities, and Nauru raised the visa fee for journalists from AUD$200 to AUD$8,000 to discourage reporting on the issue (Dickson, 2015). Jurisdictional ambiguities help to obscure detention practices: for instance, the Australian Human Rights Commission would not travel to Nauru or Manus Island because they determined they could not exercise their power of inquiry outside Australia (Dickson, 2015, p. 443). Reports about conditions on both islands generally come from leaked documents and people who have breached non-disclosure agreements (Hargrave et al., 2016), and since the 2014 Border Force legislation these whistleblowers can face a two-year prison term for sharing information.

While island detention continues to be the focus of government policy, refugees also face extended time in onshore facilities as well: as of 31 January 2017, 1,351 people were in onshore detention facilities around the country, and their stay in detention averaged 493 days, representing an increase of nearly 150 percent since 2013 (Refugee Council of Australia, 2017b). The decrease in overall numbers has prompted the government to announce that it plans to close centres in Darwin, Sydney, Melbourne, and Perth (Gregory, 2016) but people continue to languish for ever-longer periods in detention. As Fleay and Hoffman (2014, p. 19) write, "despair is once again the result" of detention policies in Australia, between the lengthy stays onshore and the proliferation of dangerous and desperate conditions offshore.

Construction of Illegality

The final element in Australia's border continuum involves the construction of asylum seekers as "illegal migrants" within Australia, involving both hostile rhetoric against asylum seekers as well as tightening legal restrictions around access to protection. Since the early 2000s, the Australian government and media sources have portrayed asylum seekers as threats to Australian sovereignty; images of floods, waves or tides suggest boat arrivals are not "genuine" refugees. Asylum seekers continue to be dehumanized through labels such as queue jumpers, people traffickers, boat people or illegal immigrants. The militarization of border enforcement helps suggest a causal link between migration and illegality. Indeed, in 2015 the Australian government spent AUD$10 million to rename the immigration agency the "Australian Border Force", including designing new airport signs and military-style uniforms, overriding opposition from department insiders "unhappy at the 'militarization' of the new regime" (Hasham, 2015, p. 3). Similarly, practices of detention rationalize and normalize processes of criminalization of migrants in public discourse. Members of the public may come to believe that migrants must be criminals if they are detained like criminals. Chambers (2015) notes these tendencies are amplified by the preponderance of Australian mass media sources owned by Rupert Murdoch, whose conservative politics dominate editorial pages.

New legal tactics have also limited refugees' access to protection. People who come by boat after 13 August 2012 are required to "fast track" their asylum applications, limiting opportunities for appeal (Refugee Council of Australia, 2017a). The Australian government also returned to granting Temporary Protection Visas rather than permanent protection for refugees, and by 2016 over 21,200 Temporary Protection Visas or Safe Haven Enterprise Visas had been granted, providing only temporary protection for forced migrants to Australia (Refugee Council of Australia, 2016b). New codes of conduct apply to asylum seekers living in the community, who risk detention or cancellation for breaching Australian laws or exhibiting anti-social behaviour (Hodge, 2015). The Refugee Council of Australia documented 281 potential breaches of the code of conduct in 2016 though no cancellation of visas, and advocates argue that "This new code of conduct is just more shock and awe to try and frighten people" (Kerr, quoted in Barlow, 2013). In May 2017, the immigration minister announced a deadline of 1 October 2017 for all asylum seekers who had arrived by sea between August 2012 and January 2014, the so-called "legacy caseload", to apply for temporary protection or be removed from Australia. Many of the over 7,000 asylum seekers who have yet to apply have been waiting for months for legal assistance, or were previously banned from applying. Advocates criticized the deadline as arbitrary, and the Executive Director of Refugee Legal, David Manne, stated that "it simply can't be met. And the government well and truly knows that" (quoted in Doherty, 2017b, p. 1). The deadline represents the latest in a series of legal manoeuvres to tighten restrictions on asylum claims, producing illegal migrants through limiting their access to protection and legal status.

LITTLE FAILURES IN THE BORDER CONTINUUM

Morrison's "border continuum" gives the impression of an all-encompassing border regime, stretching from pre-emptive surveillance and cooperation with regional allies to interdiction, detention and the ratcheting down of asylum prospects through ever-tightening legal access to protection, what Coleman (2007, p. 64) describes as the "border – and border enforcement – is increasingly everywhere". Yet while the Australian border regime is spatially expansive, there are also cracks in the facade of the all-encompassing continuum: little failures riddle Australian attempts to secure the border. In this section, I will discuss three moments of failure: first, the deterrence attempts that sometimes fail to connect; second, the regional partners who resist cooperation; and finally, the activism in and beyond detention that reasserts the humanity of asylum seekers even as they are portrayed as "illegal".

Deterrence messaging is a core component of the Australian border continuum, and media campaigns in print and online media testify to the harsh treatment of asylum seekers with slogans such as "No way by boat: you will not make Australia home". Yet Fleay et al. (2016) note that the forms of deterrence messaging purchased by the Australian government do not map on to the methods through which asylum seekers receive information. Indeed, their study of asylum seekers travelling by boat revealed that social media and word of mouth dominated asylum seekers' access to media and most never even accessed the venues where Australian media campaigns are concentrated. As one asylum seeker noted, "I never looked at Internet. I didn't know about Internet until I got out of detention" (Fleay et al., 2016, p. 66). New media technologies have also given asylum seekers the ability to testify and document secretive border enforcement practices, and Whitlock (2015, p. 254) describes how the recording and dissemination of videos documenting asylum seeker tow-backs refuted official denials of the practice and became sites of "microactivism". As I write elsewhere (Coddington, 2018), the circulation of these videos embodied the highly abstract, remote, and secretive practices of border enforcement on the high seas, although they did not fundamentally change Australian public opinion about the rightness of the government's actions. The efforts by the Australian government to militarize OSB through uniforms and collaboration with the armed forces have also raised concerns, even amongst parties assumed to agree: the Australian Defence Association has argued that the militarization of humanitarian aid is a "dubious" matter because OSB directs the military to report to the immigration minister, placing military operations outside military chains of command (Wadham, 2014, p. 2).

The 2016 ruling by the Papua New Guinea High Court declaring the Manus Island detention centre illegal represents one way in which Australia's regional partnerships have frayed under the demands of the border enforcement regime. Aspects of cooperation with Indonesia have also eroded under pressure from Australia. For Indonesia, border protection, especially along Indonesia's less populated northern borders, has been traditionally erratic and difficult to conduct, and the government assumed that most asylum seekers arriving in Indonesia were using it as a transit point and not a final destination (Missbach, 2014). Yet under pressure from Australia, Indonesia began detaining asylum seekers in the 2000s, and by 2013 had 13 detention centres across the archipelago plus arrangements with the International Organization for Migration (IOM) and Jesuit Refugee Services to provide subsistence to refugees waiting for resettlement in the village of Cisarua on Java. Australian interventions in Indonesia border enforcement have also occurred at the grassroots level: Australian intelligence has been permitted to sabotage asylum seeker boats, and an Australian-funded IOM campaign has distributed posters, films, and radio announcements advertising the dangers of cooperating with migrants or people smugglers (Missbach, 2014). Australia has paid coastal residents to report migrant boat trips, with local watchmen in Java earning AUD$50 per month, and residents of inland areas paid to report to local police who were reimbursed by the IOM for their enforcement efforts (Missbach, 2014). Yet the paid watchmen campaign has not been entirely successful, reflecting national-scale uneasiness at the prospect of close cooperation on immigration issues with Australia. At a federal level, Indonesia has been unwilling to publicly align itself too closely with Australian migration policies, fearing that they would appear to be Australia's "lackeys" (Missbach, 2014, p. 234). Indeed, after Australia towed asylum seeker boats into Indonesian waters and Australian security organizations were revealed to have spied on Indonesian leaders in the fall of 2013, Indonesia formally suspended cooperation between Australian and Indonesian police forces, who had been sharing intelligence about asylum seekers. At a local level, overburdened police find migrant policing unrewarding and pointless, as many migrants are using Indonesia as a transit country (Missbach, 2014). The Indonesian coastline is simply too vast to permit paying local residents everywhere to watch for migrant traffic, and without financial incentives people are unwilling to expend the effort.

Activism both inside and outside of detention has also countered the efforts by the Australian government to produce asylum seekers as illegal migrants, asserting instead the humanity of people seeking protection. For instance, the February 2016 decision by the High Court that Australia was not responsible for the conditions of detention on Nauru left the fate of 267 asylum seekers in Australia in limbo: these asylum seekers had either been transferred to Australia from Nauru for medical treatment, or their mothers had been transferred from Nauru and gave birth to them in Australia. With the ruling, the 267 were now legally permitted to be returned to Nauru, prompting a passionate Twitter campaign #LetThemStay, which raised the profile of the asylum seekers, especially the 37 babies, prompting rallies and efforts by state and local leaders to call for their release in Australia (Doherty, 2016a). Less heartening are the continued desperate protests, from self-harm to cases of self-immolation, such as the 2016 death of Iranian refugee Omid Masoumali, who set himself alight to protest conditions on Nauru, that make visible the violence of Australia's "border continuum". These acts forcibly claim recognition of asylum seekers as human beings, as "worthy of grief if lost" (Hodge, 2015, p. 131;

Coddington et al., 2012). The power of such forms of resistance is documented by the efforts within detention centres to minimize such risky behaviours by detainees. In July 2014, for instance, the news media in Australia received a leaked memorandum from SERCO, the company contracted to manage Australia's onshore immigration detention network titled "Enhancements to the Immigration Detention Operating Model". The memorandum, dated 21 February 2014, offers insight into how SERCO understands the impact of such violent assertions to humanity. Despite an array of predictive models and risk calculations, SERCO acknowledges that "the current detainee risk assessment tools have been shown to be an unsuccessful predictor of future behaviour" and unpredictable demands for recognition continue to fray at the attempts to fully "secure" detention facilities (SERCO, 2014, p. 6).

CONCLUSIONS

Despite the appearance of an all-encompassing border continuum dominated by militarized deterrence strategies, harsh detention practices, and rhetoric and legal tactics designed to construct asylum seekers as "illegal" migrants, Australian border enforcement is in fact riddled with small fissures. Deterrence messaging does not connect with intended audiences, migrants have used new media technologies to chip away at the government's attempts at secrecy, and the militarization of border enforcement has raised eyebrows even amongst supposed allies. Regional partnerships fray, and activism both inside and outside of detention reasserts the humanity of asylum seekers even as Australian rhetoric reinforces their dehumanization. Failures in the border continuum resist the notion of an "everywhere" border, suggesting instead that border governance is dominated by inconsistencies, contradictions, and human error. A vision of the border continuum not dominated by overarching logics and technological control but instead populated by fallible people prone to misunderstandings and open to difference makes for a compelling version of border governance that opens possible avenues for resistance and alternative political claims. Yet do these failures matter?

Increasingly, Australian policies are becoming a model for regional border enforcement. Hargrave et al. (2016, p. 10) quote one regional representative from an international organization as stating that "Australia has certainly set a very bad example for countries in the region." They trace increased Australian funding of border infrastructure, training, and intelligence sharing throughout the region as having profound consequences for neighbouring countries (Hargrave et al., 2016). Narratives of "illegal migration" rather than asylum seekers in need of protection dominate regional agreements such as the Bali Process on People Smuggling, Trafficking on Persons and Related Transnational Crime, which substitute for more effective protection policies as there are currently no real frameworks to have refugee rights recognized in the Asia-Pacific (Dickson, 2015). Such narratives and Australian pressure have increased practices of criminalization of refugee, including the use of detention (e.g., Indonesia's Immigration Law No. 6 of 2011). The practice of turning back asylum vessels has emboldened neighbouring countries, and Thailand, Indonesia, and Malaysia have all attempted to force asylum seeker vessels away from their coastlines. For instance, in June 2016 Indonesian authorities attempted to force a boat carrying 453 Sri Lankan Tamils back to sea, before eventually allowing passengers to disembark (Hargrave et al., 2016). During the 2015 Andaman Sea refugee crisis, when asked about possible help from Australia, the Australian Prime Minister replied "nope, nope, nope", arguing that assisting refugees stranded aboard drifting vessels in the Andaman Sea would "encourage people to get on boats" (Taylor, 2015, p. 2). Australia's categorical unwillingness to protect refugees in the region prompts other countries to do the same.

Yet even as Australia's practices of limiting access to protection spread throughout the region, they are accompanied by paradoxical rhetoric arguing that these very same strategies "save lives". As Prime Minister Tony Abbott told European countries in 2015, "The only way you can stop the deaths is, in fact, to stop the boats" (Dearden, 2015). Australia has dominated transnational discourses that connect increasingly securitized and violent border enforcement practices to humanitarian logics, but as Little and Vaughan-Williams (2016) argue, such arguments construct migrants not as subjects with political agency, but nevertheless connected to wider social relations: "biological" rather than "biographical" lives. Increasing the precariousness of asylum seekers under the rhetoric of "saving lives" is performed to "secure citizen lives", Hodge (2015, p. 123) argues. Such performances require ever-increasing degrees of suffering. The former chief immigration psychiatrist employed by SERCO, the contractor operating onshore detention in Australia, spoke out against practices within the detention system, arguing that treatments were delayed, patient information misused, and statistics about detainee mental health that could "result in controversy or threaten the application of policies of deterrence" were erased as purposeful elements of the detention system (Marr and Laughland, 2014). He said, "You can't mitigate the harm because the system is designed to create a negative mental state. It's designed to produce suffering" (Marr and Laughland, 2014). Despite the failures of the border continuum, the Australian enforcement regime that is "designed to produce suffering" continues to endanger the lives of asylum seekers across the Asia-Pacific.

REFERENCES

Asylum Insight (2014), Nauru arrangement. Accessed 24 May 2017 at http://www.asyluminsight.com/nauru-arr angement.

Asylum Insight (2016a), Boat turnbacks. Accessed 24 May 2017 at http://www.asyluminsight.com/boat-turn backs.

Asylum Insight (2016b), Private contractors at onshore and offshore processing center. Accessed 24 May 2017 at http://www.asyluminsight.com/private-contractors.

Asylum Insight (2016c), The Nauru files. Accessed 24 May 2017 at http://www.asyluminsight.com/nauru-files.

Asylum Insight (2017a), Papua New Guinea arrangement. Accessed 24 May 2017 at http://www.asyluminsight. com/papua-new-guinea-arrangement.

Asylum Insight (2017b), United States resettlement deal. Accessed 24 May 2017 at http://www.asyluminsight. com/united-states-resettlement-of-refugees-on-nauru-and-manus-island#.

Barlow, K. (2013), Asylum seekers required to follow government's new code of conduct, *ABC News*. Accessed 9 November 2017 at http://www.abc.net.au/news/2013-12-16/an-asylum-seekers-required-to-follow-code-of-conduct/5160118.

Burridge, A., N. Gill, A. Kocher, and L. Martin (2017), Polymorphic borders, *Territory, Politics, Governance*, **5**(3), 239–51.

Chambers, P. (2015), The embrace of border security: maritime jurisdiction, national sovereignty, and the geopolitics of Operation Sovereign Borders, *Geopolitics*, **20**(2), 404–37.

Coddington, K. (2018) Settler colonial territorial imaginaries: maritime mobilities and the "tow-backs" of asylum seekers. In K. Peters, P. Steinberg, and E. Stratford (eds), *Territory Beyond Terra*, London: Rowman & Littlefield International, pp. 185–202.

Coddington, K., R.T. Catania, J. Loyd, E. Mitchell-Eaton, and A. Mountz (2012), Embodied possibilities, sovereign geographies and island detention: negotiating the "right to have rights" on Guam, Lampedusa and Christmas Island, *Shima: The International Journal of Research into Islands*, **6**(2), 27–48.

Coleman, M. (2007), Immigration geopolitics beyond the Mexico-US border, *Antipode*, **38**(1), 54–75.

Dearden, L. (2015), Tony Abbott tells Europe to "stop the boats" like Australia as migrant crisis continues, *Independent*, Europe, 1.

Dickson, A. (2015), Distancing asylum seekers from the state: Australia's evolving political geography of immigration and border control, *Australian Geographer*, **46**(4), 437–54.

Doherty, B. (2016a), "Let them stay": backlash in Australia against plans to send asylum seekers to detention camps, *Guardian*, Australia News.

Doherty, B. (2016b), Australia's offshore detention damages asylum seekers because it's supposed to, *Guardian*, Australia News, 1–2.

Doherty, B. (2017a), Asylum seeker boat turnbacks illegal and don't deter people, report finds, *Guardian*, World News.

Doherty, B. (2017b), Deadline for asylum seekers in Australia impossible to meet, lawyers say, *Guardian*, Australia News.

Doherty, B. and H. Davidson (2017), Manus healthcare provider forced to leave for practicing unlicensed, *Guardian*, Australia News.

Doherty, B., N. Evershed, and B. Boochani (2017), Self-harm, suicide, and assaults: brutality on Manus revealed, *Guardian*, Australia News, 1–5.

Fleay, C. and L. Hartley (2016), Limited resettlement and ongoing uncertainty: responses to and experiences of people seeking asylum in Australia and Indonesia, *Cosmopolitan Civil Societies Journal*, **8**(2), 5086.

Fleay, C. and S. Hoffman (2014), Despair as a governing strategy: Australia and the offshore processing of asylum seekers on Nauru, *Refugee Survey Quarterly*, **33**(2), 1–19.

Fleay, C., J. Cokley, A. Dodd, L. Briskman, and L. Schwartz (2016), Missing the boat: Australia and asylum seeker deterrence messaging, *International Migration*, **54**(4), 60–73.

Giannacopoulos, M. (2013), Offshore hospitality: law, asylum, and colonization, *Law Text Culture*, **17**, 163–83.

Gregory, K. (2016), NT Chief Minister disappointed with plan to close Darwin's Wickham Point Detention Center, *ABC News*. Accessed 9 November 2017 at http://www.abc.net.au/news/2016-05-04/disappointment-over-plan-to-close-darwin-detention-centre/7384416.

Grewcock, M. (2014), Australian border policing: regional 'solutions' and neocolonialism, *Race & Class*, **55**(3), 71–8.

Hargrave, K., S. Pantuliano, and A. Idris (2016), Closing borders: the ripple effects of Australian and European refugee policy: case studies from Indonesia, Kenya and Jordan, HPG Working Paper, September.

Hasham, N. (2015), $10 million splurge to rename Australian Border Force, *Sydney Morning Herald*. Accessed 9 November 2017 at http://www.smh.com.au/federal-politics/political-news/10-million-splurge-to-rename-australian-border-force-20150825-gj7rz2.html.

Hodge, P. (2015), A grievable life? The criminalization and securing of asylum seeker bodies in the "violent frames" of Australia's Operation Sovereign Borders, *Geoforum*, **58**, 122–31.

Jones, R., C. Johnson, W. Brown, E. Gilbert et al. (2017), Interventions on the state of sovereignty at the border, *Political Geography*, **59**, 1–10.

Little, A. and N. Vaughan-Williams (2016), Stopping boats, saving lives, securing subjects: humanitarian borders in Europe and Australia, *European Journal of International Relations*, **23**(3), 533–56.

Marr, D. and O. Laughland (2014), Australia's detention regime sets out to make asylum seekers suffer, says chief immigration psychiatrist, *Guardian*, Australia, World News.

Missbach, A. (2014), Doors and fences: controlling Indonesia's porous borders and policing asylum seekers, *Singapore Journal of Tropical Geography*, **35**(2), 228–44.

Morrison, S. (2014), Creating stronger borders with smarter borders, Keynote address to the Biometrics Institute Asia Pacific Conference, Sydney, Australia, 28 May.

Mountz, A. (2010), *Seeking Asylum: Human Smuggling and Bureaucracy at the Border*, Minneapolis, MN: University of Minnesota Press.

Perera, S. (2007), A Pacific zone? (In)security, sovereignty, and stories of the Pacific borderscape. In P.K. Rajaram and C. Grundy-Warr (eds), *Borderscapes: Hidden Geographies and Politics at Territory's Edge*, Minnesota, MN: University of Minnesota Press, pp. 201–30.

Perera, S. and J. Pugliese (2017), Arrested lives: the move to nowhere. Accessed 24 May 2017 at http://research ersagainstpacificblacksites.org/.

Refugee Council of Australia (2016a), Operation Sovereign Borders and offshore processing statistics. Accessed 24 May 2017 at http://www.refugeecouncil.org.au.

Refugee Council of Australia (2016b), What we learnt from Senate estimates – and what we didn't. Accessed 24 May 2017 at http://www.refugeecouncil.org.au.

Refugee Council of Australia (2017a), "Fast Tracking" statistics. Accessed 24 May 2017 at http://www.refugee council.org.au.

Refugee Council of Australia (2017b), Statistics on people in Australia's onshore detention system. Accessed 24 May 2017 at http://www.refugeecouncil.org.au.

SERCO (2014), Enhancements to the Immigration Detention Operating Model, 21 February. Sydney: SERCO ASIA-PACIFIC.

Taylor, S. (2010), The impact of Australian-PNG management cooperation on refugee protection, *Local-Global: Identity, Security, Community*, **8**, 76–99.

Taylor, S. (2015), Australia and the southeast Asia refugee crisis, *The Diplomat*, 31 July. Accessed 9 November 2017 at https://thediplomat.com/2015/07/australia-and-the-southeast-asia-refugee-crisis/.

Tazreiter, C. (2015), Lifeboat politics in the Pacific: affect and the ripples and shimmers of a migrant saturated future, *Emotion, Space and Society*, **16**, 99–107.

Vasefi, S. (2017), Women of Nauru: seeing my sons in a school uniform is my only dream, *Guardian*, Comment is free, 1–5. Accessed 9 November 2017 at https://www.theguardian.com/commentisfree/2017/feb/17/women-of-nauru-seeing-my-sons-in-a-school-uniform-is-my-only-dream.

Wadham, B. (2014), Operation Sovereign Borders: dignified silence or diminishing democracy? *The Conversation*, 8 January. Accessed 9 November 2017 at https://theconversation.com/operation-sovereign-borders-dignified-silence-or-diminishing-democracy-21294.

Warbrooke, A. (2014), Australia's "Pacific Solution:" issues for the Pacific Islands, *Asia & the Pacific Policy Studies*, **1**(2), 337–48.

Watkins, J. (2017), Australia's irregular migration information campaign: border externalization, spatial imaginaries, and extraterritorial subjugation, *Territory, Politics, Governance*, **5**(3), 282–303.

Whitlock, G. (2015), The hospitality of cyberspace: mobilizing asylum seeker testimony online, *Biography*, **38**(2), 245–66.

19. Carceral mobility and flexible territoriality in immigration enforcement
Lauren Martin

INTRODUCTION

Detention and deportation remain critical forms of confinement and forced mobility. In fact, close attention to the mobilities of detention has opened up some exciting rethinking around carceral mobilities. Mountz et al. (2013) argue that "detention can be conceptualized as a series of processes" (p. 3), in particular, intertwined logics of bordering/exclusion and mobility/containment. A recent series of essays on European hotspots has shown that hotspots work to contain by mediating the ability to move; they filter, sort, categorize, and give access to further mobility between Greek and Italian islands and the mainland (Martin and Tazzioli, 2016). As Nick Gill (2009) has shown, transfers are used to penalize detained migrants for political actions and prevent detained people from forming bonds with other detainees, service organizations, or case workers. Moran et al. (2012) call this "disciplined mobility," and they argue that transfers and intrafacility transportation is a key part of the subjectification process for those who are confined. Jenn Turner and Kimberley Peters' (2017) recently published edited volume includes a collection of essays that explore how mobility constitutes carceral space, rather than being excluded from it. For Kate Coddington, it is the mobility of carceral logics themselves that include but exceed detention centers:

> in each case, the carceral spaces built upon carceral logics involved more than simply spaces of imprisonment and detention, but expanded the reach of the carceral far into people's everyday lives . . . Their mobility allows for the expansion of these carceral spaces into new areas of people's everyday lives, resulting in increasing levels of confinement, containment, and enclosure. (Coddington, 2017, pp. 27, 18)

To capture these meta-institutional geographies, Gill et al. (2018) argue that we should understand "the relations between people's, objects' and practices' journeys and the more-than-institutional systems of capital and value-creation that drive them" as "carceral circuits." "Such an approach," they write, "foregrounds connections over discrete and compartmentalized ways of understanding incarceration, providing a corrective to the popular institutionalist perception of the 'sealed off' nature of carceral places" (Gill et al., 2018). Geographers have come to understand immigration detention, then, as an assemblage of practices, discourses, and material infrastructures that are connected to wider institutional, financial, legal, and geopolitical networks.

In this chapter, I focus on the US immigration detention system to review a series of spatial practices of migration control. In particular, I trace the growing linkages between criminal justice and immigration enforcement systems, forced mobility between detention centers, alternative to detention, and externalization. Taken together, these practices show

how detention is linked up with other spatial practices to "widen the net" of detention and deportation in the United States. While I focus on the United States, I make reference to global examples, as practices and policies travel through training and technology. These different spatial practices of migration control demonstrate the "flexible territoriality" (Novak, 2011) of immigration policing.

BUILDING THE PRISON-DETENTION-DEPORTATION PIPELINE

As of 2007, the United States imprisoned 2.39 million people in federal and state prisons and county jails, up from 1.29 million in 1992; per capita, the rate of incarceration rose from 501 to 758 per 100,000 residents (International Center for Prison Studies, 2010). The US immigration detention system grew even more dramatically over the same period. In 1994, 6,785 detention beds were used for noncitizens in civil immigration proceedings, which grew to 9,011 beds in 1996, to 19,485 beds in 2000, and to the current capacity of 34,000 beds (Detention Watch Network, 2017). Counterintuitively, crime rates have been steady or dropping since 1980, but new approaches to mandatory sentencing and "three strikes" laws limited judges' discretion to grant shorter sentences, probation, drug treatment, or house arrest to those convicted of drug and other nonviolent offenses. This process swelled the prisoner population and resulted in the long-term removal of men of color from their communities (Alexander, 2012; Gilmore, 2007). The 1996 Illegal Immigration Reform and Immigrant Responsibility Act (IIRIRA) limited immigration judges' discretion in similar ways. Thus, the criminal justice and immigration systems have long shared legal tactics that privilege automatic imprisonment individualized judicial rulings.

There are important local and regional differences in the development of mass incarceration, however. Ruth Gilmore (2007) describes California's prison-building boom in the 1980s and 1990s, where the prisoner population grew 500 percent between 1982 and 2000. For Gilmore, this penchant for prisons extended and intensified racial and ethnic hierarchies – and in relation to anti-racist organizing. In Texas, a similar trend unfolded, but where California's expanded system remained publicly owned, Texas' expansion relied heavily upon *private* prison corporations to build and operate its new prisons. When incarceration rates leveled off in the early 2000s, speculative private prison building (building before contracts to house prisoners were obtained) resulted in the overproduction of prison space across the country. In many cases, these small-town prisons were built with public financing but were to be managed and operated by private companies (Perkinson, 2010). Sitting empty, they produced significant financial burdens on already struggling towns, and created pressures for new prisoners or detainees (Bonds, 2012). For companies that owned facilities, this shift left companies like the Corrections Corporation of America on the verge of bankruptcy in 2003. This surplus prison space was put to use as immigration detention.

The creation of the Department of Homeland Security (DHS) reorganized 26 federal agencies bringing immigration, border, and citizenship administrations under a security-driven agency. Post-9/11 emphases on security opened up high levels of funding for immigration, border, and counter-terrorism, allowing both Customs and Border Patrol

(CBP) and Immigration and Customs Enforcement (ICE) to dramatically increase staffing and infrastructure. As stated above, IIRIRA limited judicial discretion over immigration decisions, and it did so by mandating detention for noncitizens (documented or undocumented) with records of "aggravated felonies." In addition, IIRIRA expanded the range of deportable offenses. For some, this punitive approach to immigration indicates a "criminalization of immigration," and the use of detention and deportation as a form of social control (Coleman, 2007; De Genova, 2002). As Teresa Miller (2003) has noted, however, the coupling of expanded administrative powers and the limitation of judicial discretion was common in the criminal justice system as well. Parole boards, for example, decide how long prisoners will serve and decisions cannot be appealed to judges. For Miller, this expanded space of administrative decision-making, outside the court system, constitutes an "immigrationization of criminal justice." That is, legal techniques developed in the immigration and criminal justice fields have been transferred to the other, in most cases rolling back rights and protections for the incarcerated.

In 2004 and 2005, the then-new ICE agencies changed mandatory detention rules so that anyone caught within two weeks of arrival and 100 miles of the US-Mexico border could be processed through the Expedited Removal (ER) program. As of this writing (summer 2017), the Trump Administration is considering a further expansion of Expedited Removal to noncitizens apprehended anywhere in the United States (Boyce, 2017). Prior to 2004, ER was reserved for undocumented border-crossers arrested at a port of entry. Expedited Removal processing triggers mandatory detention and authorizes ICE officers to issue deportation orders without giving people access to an immigration judge. Expanding Expedited Removal's territorial and temporal scope drew new groups of migrants into the detention system, and created the demand for more beds. ICE met this demand by contracting with private prison companies with empty facilities and county jails with empty beds. At its peak, the immigration detention system included 300 facilities, 240 of which were mixed population jails and prisons, where immigration detainees were housed alongside pre-trial and convicted prisoners (Schriro, 2009, p. 10). In some cases, counties charged ICE above daily cost, using immigration detainees to fund jails and other county services. Since then, ICE has reduced detention to around 250 facilities, but has introduced two important policy changes that have broadened interior enforcement.

The Secure Communities program, or SComm, required police officers in almost all counties in the United States to run noncitizens' fingerprints through immigration databases (US ICE, 2012); after nationwide contestation, ICE replaced SComm with a nearly identical program called the Priority Enforcement Program (PEP) in 2014. Local law enforcement collects fingerprints and submits them to FBI fingerprint databases to search for a match, and PEP works alongside this process. If ICE finds a match, it requests that the local jail hold the person in question until ICE can speak to them. Where some local law enforcement refused to participate in SComm (or were pressured to by immigration rights organizations), PEP is mandatory. If ICE does perform the interview, the person may leave through bond or parole procedures. If the person is charged, tried, and convicted for the original arrest, then she or he serves time and is later transferred to an immigration detention center to begin deportation proceedings. If the person is not charged (in which case she or he would normally return to the community), ICE may still detain her or him with an immigration-related offense or initiate deportation proceedings.

ICE has claimed that it used a priority system for detention and deportation to focus on violent offenders (US ICE, 2010), but implementation varied a great deal (Transactions Records Access Clearinghouse, 2013). The Trump Administration has ended the prioritization process, resulting in deportation of long-term residents with no criminal record (Stillman, 2017). Thus, SComm uses the other policing practices to funnel noncitizens into the immigration detention system, expanding the points of contact between ICE and noncitizens in everyday life. More importantly, it normalizes the link between criminality and immigration enforcement as a matter of procedure.

At the same time that Expedited Removal was expanded to "close loopholes" of who could be detained and where, ICE also explicitly criminalized immigration violations. Operation Streamline is a program of automatic prosecution of unauthorized border-crossers along the US-Mexico boundary. The program was initiated in 2005 as part of a wider effort to detain "Other than Mexicans" or (OTMs) caught crossing the border without authorization who could not be immediately returned to their countries of origin. (Mexicans caught at the border were immediately returned to Mexico.) These migrants were most often released upon recognizance, a policy dubiously referred to as "Catch and Release" (see Martin, 2012a on broader efforts to detain OTMs). Prior to Operation Streamline, the US Attorney's Office retained discretion to prosecute (or not) unauthorized border-crossers, and reserved federal criminal prosecution for repeat offenders and those with significant criminal records. Streamline, however, *requires* federal prosecutors to charge and try unauthorized noncitizens for migration-related violations in federal criminal courts (Borderlands Autonomous Collective, 2012, p. 190).

Operation Streamline "closes the loophole" available to OTMs in two ways. First, the program moves migrants that do not qualify for IIRIRA's mandatory detention to the federal criminal justice system, where they will be confined in the pre-trial custody system (many of them not having the resources for bond). Second, *criminal* prosecutions and prison terms place noncitizens in IIRIRA's "aggravated felony" category, making them not only deportable, but subject to mandatory detention upon completing their sentences. For those charged with "reentry of deported alien" (08 USC 1326), conviction triggers a ten-year ban on entering the United States. The consequences of this shift have been clear. The total federal court caseload has risen 31.8 percent since 2008, and immigration-related charges now comprise around 57 percent of all prosecutions in the federal courts. DHS, which includes ICE and CBP, refers 64 percent of all federal prosecutions across the country (Transactions Records Access Clearinghouse, 2013). As many critics have noted, the quick increase in caseloads has led to serious concerns over the process itself, as immigrants are charged, tried, and sentenced in groups of up to 80 people (Lydgate, 2010).

While some noncitizens enter the federal prison system for long-term sentences, the majority are incarcerated in Criminal Alien Requirement facilities that hold exclusively noncitizens. Much of this dedicated bedspace has been provided by private prison companies. These facilities do not provide services or family support equal to the rest of the federal prison system, and noncitizens are categorically excluded from minimum-security facilities and drug rehabilitation (Robertson et al., 2012). Thus, the apparent advantages of the criminal justice system over the civil immigration system (such as the right to a lawyer and due process protections) are systematically eroded for noncitizens in the federal criminal justice system.

The criminalization of immigration is not, then, solely symbolic, rather the civil immigration system and criminal justice systems have intersected in specific ways. In particular, the two systems share legal techniques, such as expanded administrative discretion to detain and release, facilities, and databases. And yet, federal criminal prosecution of immigration-related violations has led not to the incorporation of immigration into that system, but to the creation of a separate set of procedures and facilities *within the criminal justice system.* Operation Streamline uses highly questionable "due process" to classify noncitizens as aggravated felons, funneling them into mandatory detention and, subsequently, deportation. Without becoming one system, immigration and criminal justice procedures have been linked in strategic ways. Here, I want to focus on the spatial practices of detention, in particular, to highlight the ways in which the spatiality of confinement is deployed to policy transboundary mobility.

DISCIPLINED MOBILITY IN DETENTION

US immigration detention centers are secure facilities. Detainee mobility is highly constrained within the centers, and visitation is closely regulated. Detained noncitizen adults receive different colored uniforms that sort them into facilities' low, medium, and high security zones. Movement between areas of the detention center is highly controlled. In facilities that have multiple security levels, detainees of different security levels must remain in their cells while other groups move through the facility for visitation, meals, or transport. This means that detainees often spend long periods confined to their cells during the day, regardless of their security level. Solitary confinement is widely used to both "protect" vulnerable people, such as gay, lesbian, and transgender people, and to discipline political organizers within detention centers. A few centers for low-risk detainees have relatively freer internal mobility inside the centers (such as the Berks County Family Care Shelter, T. Don Hutto Detention Center, and the Karnes Family Detention Center), because of legal restrictions on holding children and asylum-seekers in penal conditions. In these cases, however, zones of less-restricted mobility are nested within securitized boundaries that are fenced and patrolled (Martin, 2012b). In their internal spatial orderings, immigration detention centers operate very much like their counterparts in the criminal justice system. A key difference, however, is that immigration detention is indefinite in the United States. This sense of indeterminacy has dramatic effects on detained persons' mental health, as well as their families.

Long-distance transfers have also been common. In 2007 and 2008, ICE transferred over 50 percent of detained adults at least once, and over 20 percent twice or more (Transactions Records Access Clearinghouse, 2009). Detainees are often transferred without notice, and until the Online Detainee Locator System was implemented in 2010, it was common to lose track of detainees for days after their transfer (Hiemstra, 2012). Moreover, visitation policies have been set by detention center operators, and the identification requirements, hours, dress codes, and other regulations vary widely between facilities. For detainees in county jails, visitation follows the facility policy, and visitors often speak to detained noncitizens through plexiglass barriers. Detained migrants and their families experience these visits as criminalizing, and in some cases detainees prefer their families not to visit (Martin, 2011, 2012a). The association of detention with prisons and criminality creates a powerful series of "collateral effects" (Moran, 2013) on family members in the United States and abroad and on government agents and non-governmental service organizations (Gill, 2009), as described above.

EXPANDING DETENTION

Families have been detained by the US government before, but not as a permanent deterrence policy. Detention of noncitizen families with minor children was implemented in March 2001 at the Berks County Family Shelter Care Center (Berks hereafter) near Reading, Pennsylvania, a location close enough to house families arriving on the East Coast. The facility was built as Berks Heim (German for *home*), a nursing home for indigent elderly people in the county. When a new elderly care facility was built in the late 1990s, the county looked for ways to use the building. Berks County already contracted with then-Immigration and Naturalization Services (INS) to hold noncitizen detainees in the county jail. County officials charged far more for detainee beds than it paid for county prisoners, allowing it to support further county operations. A family detention facility, however, had to meet the standards of care for minors laid out in a 1997 lawsuit, *Flores v. Meese*, including state licensing and oversight. Because INS detention facilities were modeled on prisons, rather than residential centers, the INS faced a contradiction between court-mandated conditions for children and the actually existing conditions of its own facilities. Berks filled a gap, allowing the INS to detain some families without violating children's entitlements. With these procedures in place, the county detained a maximum of 94 people, primarily asylum-seeking families arriving without identity documentation. A *pre*-9/11 policy, family detention remained a small-scale practice in relation to the 24,000 adult detention beds in use at the time.

The terrorist attacks of 9/11 heightened concerns over cross-border migration, and in 2003, the Department of Homeland Security was founded. DHS absorbed and reorganized 27 agencies, immigration, citizenship, and border enforcement among them (Martin and Simon, 2008). In 2004 and 2005, DHS expanded Expedited Removal, a provision in immigration legislation allowing summary deportation, from ports of entry to areas between ports of entry and maritime areas. In other words, DHS changed how it applied legislative categories and, in doing so, made a much larger set of noncitizens subject to mandatory detention, also required by immigration legislation. At the time, expanding detainability reasserted the contradiction between immigration detention conditions and children's protections: families who had not been subject to mandatory detention before now fell into that category. Now subject to mandatory detention, ICE officers' discretion to release families with Notices to Appear in immigration court was limited. To address this gap in detention capacity, and also to deter more families from attempting entry, ICE opened the T. Don Hutto Family Detention Center (Hutto hereafter) in Taylor, Texas, for families in 2006.

Hutto is a 512-bed former medium-security prison, owned and operated by the Corrections Corporation of America (CCA). Conditions were not significantly changed for the new population of families, and so local lawyers sued DHS for violating *Flores v. Meese*, using Berks as an example of how family detention might be done in compliance with existing regulations. DHS and the plaintiffs settled, and a federal magistrate oversaw the facility for two years, ultimately reporting that despite significant improvements,

Hutto remained too prison-like for families. The Obama Administration decided to release Hutto's families in 2009, filling the empty beds with adult women. From 2009 to 2014, ICE returned to issuing Notice to Appear documents to families, and Berks was once again the only family detention facility. Billed as the opening salvo of a broad reform to immigration detention nationwide, the Obama Administration was still careful to maintain its *discretion* to detain families.

In 2013 and 2014, however, CBP and ICE faced a steady and sizeable increase in arriving unaccompanied children and families. While billed as a "migration crisis," entries by children and families increased over months. Concerned about reports that people smugglers told children and families that the United States would not detain them, ICE and federal officials began a media campaign to keep migrants at home. This included public advertisements and education about the dangers of crossing (Arnold, 2014), and a blanket detention and deportation policy for children and families arriving at the US-Mexico border (Doty, 2017; Preston, 2014a). Beginning in June 2014, ICE detained families at a converted 672-bed border patrol training facility in Artesia, New Mexico. Artesia is 200 miles from the nearest city, and the facility was closed to visitors for over a month, including human rights representatives and lawyers. Policies on communication, legal orientations, and basic child welfare practices changed frequently (Manning, 2015; Detention Watch Network, 2014). Artesia was shuttered in December 2014 after a class action lawsuit charging due process violation (Preston, 2014b). In the meantime, ICE had contracted with Karnes County, who subcontracted to GEO Group, for a 532-bed family detention center. Shortly following this expansion, ICE contracted with Dilley County, who subcontracted to CCA, for a 2,400-bed family detention facility in South Texas. Thus, family detention's historical geography of how immigration agencies can expand and contract detention for different groups at different times, using administrative and prosecutorial discretion to implement different spatial practices to control mobility (see also Williams, 2017).

"ALTERNATIVES TO DETENTION"

In addition to secured facilities, ICE retains custody over more than 17,000 noncitizens through Alternatives to Detention (ATD) programs, which include a combination of electronic monitoring (GPS ankle bracelet), in-person and phone reporting, unannounced visits from immigration staff, curfews, and court appearance requirements. ICE contracts with BI Incorporated, owned by the private prison company GEO Group, which also operates detention centers (American Civil Liberties Union, 2014), to run two Intensive Supervision Appearance Programs (ISAP). "Full-service ISAP" includes case management, in which BI caseworkers give noncitizens information about local services. As critics have pointed out, they do not provide sufficient individual needs analysis, nor do they connect noncitizens with service organizations themselves (see Lutheran Immigrant and Refugee Services, 2012, p. 31). "Technology-assisted ISAP" utilizes BI's electronic monitors, while ICE retains direct supervision of noncitizens. Notably, migrants are eligible for full-service ISAP if they live within 50–85 miles of 30 ICE offices, while technology-assisted ISAP is available at all ICE offices.

These ATD programs allow noncitizens to avoid confinement, but restrict mobility within their communities (Martin, 2012b). For example, ankle monitors must be charged and this requires ATD participants to sit near an electrical socket for periods of time each day. The bracelets are difficult to shower with, and pregnant women find them painful when their ankles swell. Others have reported stigmatization in their neighborhood because the monitors are the same type as those used in the criminal justice system. The existence of the monitor implies criminality, despite the fact that ICE uses them with populations who cannot be detained in secure facilities. Furthermore, ICE uses ATD programs for noncitizens that are ineligible for detention, such as mothers with dependent children and asylum-seekers, drawing *more* noncitizens into ICE custody rather than replacing detention beds (Lutheran Immigrant and Refugee Services, 2012). ATD programs have, in effect, widened ICE surveillance over noncitizens in their own communities.

EXTERNALIZATION

While criminalization of immigration violations has linked criminal justice and immigration systems in new ways, the United States is one of many countries externalizing immigration and asylum processing. While Zolberg (2008) argues that embassies and visa regulations have long worked as "remote control" of potential immigrants, formal bi-lateral and regional agreements have proliferated in recent years. In response to the "child migrant crisis" of 2014, the United States partnered with Mexico to stop Central American migrants from reaching the US-Mexico border. Subsequently, the number of asylum-seekers apprehended in Mexico rose in proportion to the US decrease in apprehensions of asylum-seekers (Dominguez-Villegas and Rieteg, 2015). This follows on from a decade of regional expansion of immigration enforcement in Central America and the Caribbean that seeks to preempt migration to the United States and "push the border outward" (Coleman, 2007). These practices work alongside airline carrier sanctions that outsource document and visa checking directly to international airlines, so that airline employees make determinations on documentation status abroad (Lahav, 1998; Scholten, 2015). While this chapter has focused on the US example, the European Union (EU) has institutionalized externalized border and migration controls through the European Neighbourhood Policy, which ties border control harmonization to development aid in Eastern Europe and North Africa (Casas-Cortes et al., 2015a). Crucially, the intertwined internalization of immigration enforcement (Coleman, 2007) and externalization of border controls demand foregrounding migrant movements and struggles in research in order to problematize states' spatial practices, rather than those of migrants (Casas-Cortes et al., 2015b).

CONCLUSION

Detention is a spatial strategy of enclosure, of bringing mobile bodies to rest, but detention is also a mobility strategy (Turner and Peters, 2017). It remobilizes people in various ways; it places their integration or acceptance into the arriving country. It performs state power in a spectacular way. It closes off relationships with local communities and services in some cases, and facilitates them in others. Remote detention facilities house people far from services they might mobilize on their own (Loyd and Mountz, 2014).

By detailing the legal maneuvers used to expand and intermingle criminal justice and immigration enforcement in the United States, I have outlined a series of practices used to expand the purview of enforcement and the role of detention in controlling migrant mobility. Detention, electronic monitoring, externalization, and expanded categories of high-risk migrants characterize responses to migration "crises" around the world (Crawley, 2016), but the specificities of national legislation and judicial precedent make comparative research challenging. What is clear, however, is a global tendency to restrict access to the territorial spaces of asylum and authorized entry while expanding spaces of policing and monitoring (Basaran, 2011; Mountz, 2011). Asylum processes in the EU, for example, adjudicate between deportable and admittable subjects, differentiating between detainable and non-detainable people (Tazzioli, 2017). Blanket reports on "safe countries" for repatriation override individual determinations, in many cases, so that geopolitical conflict direction bears on individuals' ability to seek refuge. Thus, incarceration needs to be understood in relation to a broader assemblage of spatial practices that police human mobility. I close by arguing that the specific territoriality of asylum and the asymmetrical lack of mobility rights allows states to become increasingly creative in their policing responses and migrants to become increasingly precarious in their journeys. We can see three deployments of spatial enclosures, whether it is called residential or quarantine: detention as deterrence; detention as externalization; and carceral infrastructure as capacity to maintain flexibility.

From this perspective, detention and other enclosure practices work more like Paolo Novak's (2011) concept of "flexible territoriality": the imbrication of networked and hierarchical spatial strategies and the simultaneity of strategic territoriality and territoriality as it actually unfolds. In other words, the territoriality of migration control is not a single kind of sovereign or rights-bound space, but a bordering strategy, deployed to both differentiate various actors and to jockey for authority over how space can be ordered. And so, understood in relation to the geographies of mobility, enforcement, and other enforcement practices, detention is always more than an enclosure. It is part of a larger project of mobility management, in which states seek to channel and refine where and how noncitizens arrive in their territory. Detention is always connected to other border and policing practices, discourses of belonging and exclusion, criminalization, and so on. For states, detention remains valuable, even when rendered legally unfeasible as with family detention, because it allows states to be flexible in the exercise of their authority over mobile people and territorial space.

REFERENCES

Alexander, Michelle (2012), *The New Jim Crow: Mass Incarceration in an Age of Colorblindness*, New York: The New Press.
American Civil Liberties Union (2014), "Alternatives to Immigration Detention: Less Costly and More Humane than Federal Lock-up", accessed November 3, 2017 at https://www.aclu.org/other/aclu-fact-sheet-alternatives-immigration-detention-atd.
Arnold, R. (2014), "Government's warning not deterring all immigrants", KPRC Houston. August 6, accessed September 11, 2015 at http://www.click2houston.com/news/how-are-american-tax-dollars-being-used-for-texas-border-crisis/26968928.
Basaran, Tugba (2011), *Security, Law and Borders: At the Limits of Liberties*, Oxon: Routledge.

Bonds, Anne (2012), "Building Prisons, Building Poverty: Prison Sitings, Dispossession, and Mass Incarceration", in Jenna M. Loyd, Matt Michelson, and Andrew Burridge (eds), *Beyond Walls and Cages: Prisons, Borders, and Global Crisis*, Athens, GA: University of Georgia Press, pp. 129–51.

Borderlands Autonomous Collective (2012), "Resisting the Security-Industrial Complex: Operation Streamline and the Militarization of the Arizona-Mexico Borderlands", in Jenna M. Loyd, Matt Michelson, and Andrew Burridge (eds), *Beyond Walls and Cages: Prisons, Borders, and Global Crisis*, Athens, GA: University of Georgia Press, pp. 190–208.

Boyce, Geoff (2017), "The Border's Temporal Reach and US Immigration Enforcement Under Donald J. Trump", accessed August 11, 2017 at http://societyandspace.org/2017/07/04/the-borders-temporal-reach-and-us-immigration-enforcement-under-donald-j-trump/.

Casas-Cortes, Maribel, Cobarrubias, Sebastion, and Pickles, John (2015a), "Riding Routes and Itinerant Borders: Autonomy of Migration and Border Externalization", *Antipode*, **47**(4), 894–914.

Casas-Cortes, Maribel, Cobarrubias, S., De Genova, N. et al. (2015b), "New Keywords: Migration and Borders", *Cultural Studies*, **29**(1), 55–87.

Coddington, Kate (2017), "Mobile Carceral Logics: Aboriginal Communities and Asylum Seekers Facing Enclosure in Australia's Northern Territory", in Jennifer Turner and Kimberley Peters (eds), *Carceral Mobilities: Interrogating Movement in Incarceration*, London: Taylor & Francis, pp. 17–29.

Coleman, Mat (2007), "A Geopolitics of Engagement: Neoliberalism, the War on Terrorism, and the Reconfiguration of US Immigration Enforcement", *Geopolitics*, **12**(4), 607–34.

Crawley, Heaven (2016), "Managing the Unmanageable? Understanding Europe's Response to the Migration 'Crisis'", *Human Geography*, **9**(2), 13–23.

De Genova, Nicholas (2002), "Migrant 'Illegality' and Deportability in Everyday Life", *Annual Review of Anthropology*, **31**, 419–47.

Detention Watch Network (2014), "Expose & Close: Artesia", accessed August, 11 2017 at http://www.detentionwatchnetwork.org/pressroom/reports/2014/expose-close-artesia.

Detention Watch Network (2017), "Detention 101," accessed August 11, 2017 at https://www.detentionwatchnetwork.org/issues/detention-101.

Dominguez-Villegas, Rodrigo and Rieteg, Victoria (2015), *Migrants Deported from the United States and Mexico to the Northern Triangle: A Statistical and Socioeconomic Profile*, Washington, DC: Migration Policy Institute, accessed August 10, 2017 at http://www.migrationpolicy.org/research/migrants-deported-united-states-and-mexico-northern-triangle-statistical-and-socioeconomic.

Doty, Roxanne (2017), "Families in Detention in the United States", in Philippe Bourbeau (ed.), *Handbook on Migration and Security*, Cheltenham, UK and Northampton, MA, USA: Edward Elgar, pp. 161–74.

Gill, Nick (2009), "Governmental Mobility: The Power Effects of the Movement of Detained Asylum Seekers around Britain's Detention Estate", *Political Geography*, **28**, 186–96.

Gill, Nick, Conlon, Deirdre, Moran, Dominique, and Burridge, Andrew (2018), "Carceral Circuitry: New Directions in Carceral Geography", *Progress in Human Geography*, **42**(2), 183–204.

Gilmore, Ruth Wilson (2007), *Golden Gulag: Prisons, Surplus, Crisis and Opposition in Globalizing California*, Berkeley, CA: University of California Press.

Hiemstra, Nancy (2012), "Geopolitical Reverberations of US Migrant Detention and Deportation: The View from Ecuador", *Geopolitics*, **17**(2), 293–311.

International Center for Prison Studies (2010), *World Prison Brief*.

Lahav, Gallya (1998), "Immigration and the State: The Devolution and Privatisation of Immigration Control in the EU", *Journal of Ethnic and Migration Studies*, **24**(4), 675–94.

Loyd, Jenna and Mountz, Alison (2014), "Transnational Productions of Remoteness: Building Onshore and Offshore Carceral Regimes Across Borders", *Geographica Helvetica*, **69**, 389–98.

Lutheran Immigration and Refugee Services (2012), *Unlocking Liberty: A Way Forward for U.S. Immigration Detention Policy*, Baltimore, Maryland.

Lydgate, Joanna (2010), "Assembly-Line Justice: A Review of Operation Streamline." Policy Brief, The Chief Justice Earl Warren Institute on Race, Ethnicity and Diversity, University of California, Berkeley Law School. Available at: http://www.law.berkeley.edu/files/Operation_Streamline_Policy_Brief.pdf. Accessed 8 October, 2018.

Manning, Stephen (2015), *The Artesia Report*, accessed August 11, 2017 at https://innovationlawlab.org/the-artesia-report/.

Martin, Lauren (2011), "The Geopolitics of Vulnerability: Migrant Families in U.S. Immigrant Family Detention Policy", *Gender, Place, & Culture*, **18**(4), 477–98.

Martin, Lauren (2012a), "'Catch and Remove': Detention, Deterrence, and Discipline in US Noncitizen Family Detention Practice", *Geopolitics*, **17**(2), 312–34.

Martin, Lauren (2012b), "Governing through the Family: Struggles over US Noncitizen Family Detention Policy", *Environment and Planning*, **44**(4), 866–88.

Martin, Lauren and Simon, Stephanie (2008), A Formula for Disaster: The Department of Homeland Security's Virtual Ontology, *Space and Polity*, **12**(3), 281–96.

Martin, Lauren and Tazzioli, Martina (2016), "Governing Mobility through the European Union's Hotspot Centre: A Forum", accessed August 11, 2017 at http://societyandspace.org/2016/11/08/governing-mobility-thr ough-the-european-unions-hotspot-centres-a-forum/.

Miller, Teresa (2003), "Citizenship and Severity: Recent Immigration Reforms and the New Penology", *Georgetown Immigration Law Journal*, **29**, 611–66.

Moran, Dominique (2013), "Carceral Geography and the Spatialities of Prison Visiting: Visitation, Recidivism, and Hyperincarceration", *Environment and Planning D: Society and Space*, **31**(1), 174–90.

Moran, Dominique, Piacentini, Laura, and Pallot, Judith (2012), "Disciplined Mobility and Carceral Geography: Prisoner Transport in Russia", *Transactions of the Institute of British Geographers*, **37**(3), 446–60.

Mountz, Alison (2011), "The Enforcement Archipelago: Detention, Haunting, and Asylum on Islands", *Political Geography*, **30**(3), 118–28.

Mountz, Alison, Coddington, Kate, Catania, R. Tina, Loyd, Jenna M. (2013), "Conceptualizing Detention: Mobility, Containment, Bordering and Exclusion", *Progress in Human Geography*, **37**(4), 522–41.

Novak, Paolo (2011), "The Flexible Territoriality of Borders", *Geopolitics*, **16**(4), 741–67.

Perkinson, Robert (2010), *Texas Tough: The Rise of America's Prison Empire*, New York: Metropolitan Books.

Preston, Julia (2014a), "As U.S. Speeds the Path to Deportation, Distress Fills New Family Detention Centers", *New York Times*, 5 August, accessed August 11, 2017 at https://www.nytimes.com/2014/08/06/us/seeking-to-stop-migrants-from-risking-trip-us-speeds-the-path-to-deportation-for-families.html.

Preston, Julia (2014b), "Detention Center Presented as Deterrent to Border Crossings", *New York Times*, 15 December, accessed August 11, 2017 at https://www.nytimes.com/2014/12/16/us/homeland-security-chief-opens-largest-immigration-detention-center-in-us.html.

Robertson, Alistair Graham, Beaty, Rachel, Atkinson, Jane, and Libal, Bob (2012), *Operation Streamline: Costs and Consequences*, Austin, TX: Grassroots Leadership, Inc., accessed August 11, 2017 at http://grassroots leadership.org/sites/default/files/uploads/GRL_Sept2012_Report-final.pdf.

Scholten, Sophie (2015), *The Privatization of Immigration Control through Carrier Sanctions: The Role of Private Transport Companies in Dutch and British Immigration Control*, Boston: Brill Nijhoff.

Schriro, Dora (2009), *Immigration Detention Overview and Recommendations*, Washington, DC: Immigration and Customs Enforcement, accessed June 20, 2013 at http://www.ice.gov/doclib/about/offices/odpp/pdf/ice-detention-rpt.pdf. 2013.

Stillman, Sarah (2017), "The Mothers Being Deported by Trump", *New Yorker*, 22 July, accessed August 11, 2017 at http://www.newyorker.com/news/news-desk/the-mothers-being-deported-by-trump.

Tazzioli, M. (2017), "The Government of Migrant Mobs: Temporary Divisible Multiplicities in Border Zones", *European Journal of Social Theory*, **20**(4), 473–90. https://doi.org/10.1177/1368431016658894.

Transactions Records Access Clearinghouse (2009), "Huge Increase in Transfers of ICE Detainees", accessed August 11, 2017 at http://trac.syr.edu/immigration/reports/220/.

Transactions Records Access Clearinghouse (2013), "Prosecutions for April 2013", accessed June 20, 2013 at http://trac.syr.edu/tracreports/bulletins/overall/monthlyapr13/fil/.

Turner, Jennifer and Peters, Kim (eds) (2017), *Carceral Mobilities*, London: Routledge.

US ICE (Immigration and Customs Enforcement) (2010), "Civil Immigration Enforcement: Priorities for the Apprehension, Detention, and Removal of Aliens", Memo, June 30, accessed August 11, 2017 at http://www.ice.gov/doclib/detention-reform/pdf/civil_enforcement_priorities.pdf.

US ICE (Immigration and Customs Enforcement) (2012), "Activated Jurisdictions", August 22, accessed August 11, 2017 at https://www.hsdl.org/?abstract&did=682236.

Williams, Jill (2017), "Crisis, Subjectivity, and the Polymorphous Character of Immigrant Family Detention in the United States", *Territory, Politics, Governance*, **5**(3), 269–81.

Zolberg, Aristide (2008), *A Nation by Design: Immigration Policy and the Fashioning of America*, Cambridge, MA: Harvard University Press.

20. The biopolitics of alternatives to immigration detention

Robyn Sampson

INTRODUCTION

> If borders are multiplicities then we need a plurality of concepts to think their different dimensions and changing functions. (Walters, 2006, p. 145)

States and their territorial borders constitute the basic components of any geopolitical map of the world. Like pieces of a jigsaw puzzle, the physical boundaries of individual countries snap together in perfect cohesion, reflecting the limits of domestic government and the cohabitation of neighbouring power regimes. A piecemeal, colourful but ordered globe.

Or so the story goes.

As John Agnew's (1994, 2010) aphorism so effectively captures, such normative constructions constitute a "territorial trap" in which states are conflated with territory. Such essentialist imageries suggest territory is a "container" (Taylor, 1994) which circumscribes sovereign authority and limits the extent of the privileges of citizenship. In such a paradigm, migrants – and irregular and forced migrants in particular – become a threat to the natural order of things as people who have strayed from their native place in the world (Malkki, 1997). It is at this critical juncture between international territorial norms and human migration flows that states step in to restore order to an emerging chaos through border controls (Walters, 2006). Border control and migration management are thus crucial areas in which fundamental concepts regarding states and territory are not only brought to light but also tested as state authority is brought to bear on the lives of individual migrants.

This chapter explores the relationship between states and their territories by investigating one element of contemporary border control policy in depth: an alternative to immigration detention known as "community detention". Community detention is an emerging practice in which immigration detention is applied as a legal status that permits the migrant to reside in the community with freedom of movement while a migration issue is resolved. Such a person is thus physically present but legally absent from the territory. This status has been developed to allow particular bodies – namely, children, survivors of torture, and others experiencing vulnerability – to be placed in less harmful settings. Individuals who are living with detention as their legal status carry the border with them in their daily life in society, as they are legally constructed as being in detention and, consequently, at the border. I argue that this status highlights the ways in which the border is located and negotiated at the scale of the migrant body.

The location of borders on to the bodies of migrants has important ramifications for our conceptualization of the normative relationship between states and territory. Through the chapter, I show that the regulated use of this official non-presence highlights a departure from the traditional territory-sovereignty nexus. I evaluate the power of Giorgio Agamben's (1998, 2005) concept of the exception to explain this form of bordering, drawing from a body of work within feminist and political geography to grapple with the biopolitics of contemporary borders.

In keeping with the arguments in that literature, I use the term *embodied borders* to account for, and highlight, the relocation and negotiation of the border at the scale of the migrant body. I argue that embodied borders are not homogeneous states of exception produced by sovereign authority alone but rather are highly variable forms of differentiation lawfully produced in specific contexts as a result of multiple actors in the political arena. These unruly forms of differentiation combine a mixture of exclusionary and inclusionary measures that are not limited to legal categories but extend to social, economic, and geographic constructs. The nature and experience of borders is thus shown to vary according to the individual migrant and their context.

Borders: Location, Process, Spectacle, or Legal Indistinction

Scholars have long recognized that the work of border control is not contained to those physical sites where state territories abut, but rather involves a multitude of locations within and beyond the territory (Johnson et al., 2011; Mountz, 2013). Through "externalization" a variety of interdiction measures prevent particular migrants from reaching the territory (Davidson, 2003; Lavenex and Uçarer, 2004; Legomsky, 2006; Taylor and Rafferty-Brown, 2010). Meanwhile, internal policing of non-citizens through work place raids, the dispersal of immigration powers to local police, and deportation further disrupt the apparent location of borders at territory's edge (Hedman, 2008; Provine and Varsanyi, 2012).

Such multiplicities have led scholars to debate the best set of terms for the field. Nevins (in Pickering and Weber, 2006, p. 3) differentiates between *boundary* (a strict line of separation), *border* (a zone of gradual division and interaction), and *frontier* (a sparsely controlled zone of contact). Others, such as Berg and Van Houtum (2003), move away from location or site-specific terms, preferring to focus on the processes involved through the concept of *bordering*. Thus, Motomura conceives of the border as "not a fixed location but rather wherever the government performs border functions" (1993, p. 712), although this still tethers borders to the places where these functions occur. Meanwhile, some scholars have focused on the performative elements of borders (Kaiser, 2012; Mainwaring and Silverman, 2017).

The State of Exception and Bare Life

Exclusion is at the heart of border control, and Giorgio Agamben (1998, 2005) attends to this issue by focusing on the role of the exception in the maintenance of sovereign authority. Through the concepts of the state of exception (2005) and *homo sacer* (1998), Agamben provides a set of tools to explore the nature of the exception in contemporary political systems. His principal argument is that the apparatus by which authority is sustained relies on the sovereign power to decide on the exception – on that which is excluded and yet suspended within the political order (1998).

The state of exception (Agamben, 2005) is a lawful period or zone in which the rule of law does not apply but is instead lawfully suspended. This state within the law but devoid of law is traditionally invoked in times of crisis to empower the sovereign or executive arm of government to take the necessary measures to maintain or (re)establish the rule of law, while at the same time bypassing the rule of law. The power of the sovereign to decide on the exception is also used to create a form of (human) life – the figure of *homo sacer* (Agamben, 1998) – that is excluded from political life and yet is suspended within the political structure. Agamben argues that sovereign power relies on its ability to create such "bare life" and ban it from the political sphere while continuing to hold it subject to sovereign powers.

Scholars have applied both the state of exception and *homo sacer* to key exclusionary mechanisms used in the name of border control (Minca, 2015; Mountz, 2013; Salter, 2008). The spatial state of exception – the camp – has been applied to such spaces as immigration detention (Diken, 2004; Rajaram and Grundy-Warr, 2004), refugee camps (Ramadan, 2012), and transit processing centres (Noll, 2003). Similarly, several scholars have agreed with Agamben's interpretation of the refugee as *homo sacer* exemplar (Diken, 2004), while others have applied the concept of bare life to refused asylum seekers (Darling, 2009) and irregular migrants (Doty, 2011; Rajaram and Grundy-Warr, 2004). As Salter claims, "the border is a permanent "state of exception" in that one may claim no rights but is still subject to the law" (2006, p. 169).

Vaughan-Williams agrees, arguing Agamben's theory provides a new conceptualization of bordering in which law, and the limits of sovereign power, are decoupled from territory and are instead framed in terms of the sovereign decision regarding bare life:

> [The exception is] a decision on the status of life that can effectively happen anywhere: a multi-faceted and decentred bio-political apparatus that is as mobile as the subjects it seeks to control ... [B]orders are continually (re)inscribed through bodies in transit that can be categorised into politically qualified life on one hand and bare life on the other. (Vaughan-Williams, 2009b, p. 749)

These authors highlight the ability of Agamben's theory to provide insight on developments in contemporary border regimes that are de-coupled from territory and instead asserted according to the body to be governed.

The Differentiated and Variable Nature of Bare Life

One strand of criticism of Agamben's conceptualizations of bare life is worth highlighting at this point. Several scholars question whether bare life can account for highly differentiated and variable experiences that incorporate exclusionary and inclusionary elements (Belcher et al., 2008; Coddington et al., 2012; Mitchell, 2006; Mountz, 2011; Pratt, 2005; Robins, 2009; Zeveleva, 2017). These concerns focus on Agamben's distinctions between politically qualified life, the bare life of *homo sacer*, and the biological life of *zöe*. While Agamben (2005) argues the demarcation between these life forms is a zone of indistinction by which the sovereign maintains its power, a politically qualified life must be viable in order to apply the theory to real world phenomena (Connolly, 2004).

This is further complicated if bare life is not purely a legal standing, but one that also takes into account the power that stems from social, economic, and political realms. Darling (2009), for one, extends the concept of exception to *social* exclusion, arguing that the enforced destitution of migrants can be read as a form of exception. Lemke is another author who believes that legal status is a poor litmus test when it comes to identifying exception:

> The analysis of biopolitics cannot be limited to those without legal rights, such as the refugee or asylum seeker, but must encompass all those who are confronted with social processes of exclusion – even if they may be formally enjoying full political rights. (Lemke, 2005, p. 10)

This weakness is particularly evident when constructs such as gender and race are brought to bear on an analysis of the nature and experience of bordering. Feminist and poststructuralist scholars have worked to understand the impact of individual and localized particularities on the exercise of sovereign power (Amoore, 2006; Belcher et al., 2008; Mountz, 2011; Pratt, 2005). As Mitchell argues, "An awareness of the *embodiment of exceptionalism* forms the crucial distinction between the conceptualizations of feminist and poststructuralist scholars and those of Agamben" (2006, p. 97, original emphasis). Whether the exception can account for the differentiated and contradictory elements of both inclusion and abandonment will be explored further in this chapter.

DETENTION AS A LEGAL STATUS: THE DEVELOPMENT OF "COMMUNITY DETENTION"

This section analyses a subtle yet significant development in border control identified during research undertaken on alternatives to immigration detention. The research aimed to identify and describe community-based alternatives to immigration detention and consisted of an online survey of 88 participants in 28 countries; in-depth interviews with 57 participants in nine countries; and eight site visits. A detailed description of the methods, and the findings from which these three case studies are drawn, is available elsewhere (Sampson et al., 2015).

A number of the alternatives to detention identified rely upon a new interpretation and application of immigration detention as a legal status: three of these are described below. In these cases, individuals are legally considered to be detained but are living in circumstances in which they are allowed to move about in their local area of residence. Immigration authorities retain significant power over an individual while at the same time enabling the person to live in a less restrictive environment.

In 2008, Belgium developed an alternative to detention for families with minors who had been refused at all levels and were required to depart the country. The legal status of the families in this programme is of being in detention. This means the family is not legally on Belgium territory but, rather than being held in a (closed) detention facility, they have the *status* of being "in detention". This status is carried with them when they leave the accommodation facility, such as when they go to the local supermarket to buy food or when the children go to school. The development of this new use of detention as a status appears to stem from a bureaucratic issue. The initial pilot project for this programme was developed and operated by the department responsible for removals and deportations. A separate department is responsible for the reception and accommodation of asylum seekers. It was reported that the reception department was unwilling to allow their facilities to be used to house people facing deportation or return, as it fell outside their mandate. This meant the removal department was required to "detain" these families in order to establish the authority to house them. Since opening, the programme was expanded to include families who are refused permission to enter Belgium at the border. Like people detained on arrival in facilities at the border, these families have not legally entered the territory for the purposes of migration and are bureaucratically considered to be in a transit zone.

A similar example is found in Hong Kong. Asylum seekers, torture claimants, and other migrants can be released from immigration detention on their "own recognizance". On the recognizance form, authorities must indicate one of two possibilities: that the individual named is detained under section 27, 32 or 34 of the Immigration Ordinance, or that the individual named is liable to be detained under section 27, 32 or 34 of the Immigration Ordinance and is not now so detained. The form goes on to state the amount of surety required and any reporting requirements. Interviewees confirmed that people are regularly released on recognizance with an on-going legal status of being detained. Such recognizance papers therefore provide documentation demonstrating the person is allowed to be in the community while also retaining the legal status of being detained pending removal.

A third example can be found in Australia. "Community detention" (formally referred to as a residence determination or community placement) was introduced in 2005 as an avenue to allow vulnerable groups to live outside of immigration detention facilities in the community without requiring an escort. This enabled the government to maintain a mandatory detention policy while responding to on-going criticism of systemic failings. Community detention does not give a person any lawful status in Australia; instead, the person remains administratively in detention while living amongst the wider community. Individuals in this programme have conditions such as regular reporting and/or residence at a specified address. The decision to award this status is a non-compellable ministerial power, and is only granted to those assessed as low risk. Because individuals released through this avenue are legally still "in detention", the government remains responsible for meeting their basic needs.

In each of these three examples, individuals are living with the exceptional legal status of detention despite not being physically confined. A number of other types of status confer a similar form of permitted non-presence on the territory. Several countries have introduced measures that ensure a person remains legally categorized as being able to be deported, but is protected from that deportation until a certain period or outcome is negotiated. For example, the Netherlands introduced a programme for former unaccompanied minors who had lost or "grown out of" the protection afforded to them while under the age of 18. The programme issues the young people with identification cards that do not provide formal legal status but which nevertheless protects them from detention and deportation. While these young people are technically irregular migrants with no legal rights by virtue of the expiry of their prior status, they are nevertheless protected from certain state actions. In a similar manner, a letter of attestation by the United Nations High Commissioner for Refugees (UNHCR) for refugees and asylum seekers in Indonesia is not a form of legal status but rather prevents their detention and deportation as irregular migrants by Indonesian authorities by permitting their continued (and yet "illegal") presence on the territory.

In the United Kingdom, Sawyer and Turpin (2005) identify a similar form of officially regulated non-status. "Temporary admission" grants no clear substantive status and deems that the person has not entered the United Kingdom. As they note:

> The nature of temporary admission is particularly intriguing in that it leaves the person concerned in a legal position that is difficult to explain save in the negative. Unlike forms of temporary protection, it grants no clear substantive status . . . Accordingly, whilst that person may be physically present, legally they are not here. (Sawyer and Turpin, 2005, p. 696)

The lack of regular status maintains the person's vulnerability to the power of the state, such as the risk of detention during signing-in to meet reporting requirements (Burridge, forthcoming), reflected in the experience of "everyday deportability" (De Genova, 2002).

PART I: DETERRITORALIZATION

Individuals who are living with detention as their legal status carry the border with them in their daily life in society, as they are legally constructed as being in detention and, consequently, at the border. The shift in territorial borders to the scale of the individual body has previously been flagged (Amoore, 2006; Coutin, 2010; Mountz, 2013). Alongside the development of functionally mobile borders, spatially mobile borders and temporally mobile borders, Weber notes:

> the possibility of fully *personalised borders* where the border is defined, not by a fixed geographical location, nor with reference to the location of border control activities, but is equated with the location of officially sanctioned border crossers, who legally *embody* the border. (Weber, 2006, p. 24, emphasis in the original)

Weber came to this idea through the work of Guild (2000, quoted in Weber, 2006) who had identified a development in UK border policy in which migrants who had applied for a visa before travelling to the United Kingdom were considered to have legally entered the territory at the point the visa was issued by a consular official overseas. "For the purposes of United Kingdom immigration law, the holder of a valid entry visa was henceforth to be considered, not just entry cleared, but actually legally present in the United Kingdom" (Weber, 2006, p. 35). This was designed to improve the flow of (desirable) passengers through immigration control points at congested international airports. Thus, "[t]he UK border for persons has become entirely personal to the individual and unrelated to the physical territory over which the UK is sovereign" (Weber, 2006, p. 35).

An individual with a valid visa can therefore be *legally present but physically absent* from the territory while, in a similar but contradictory move identified in the field work, those with detention as a legal status are deemed *legally absent despite being physically present* on the territory. This latter status is in some ways not unusual, in the sense that irregular migrants are often physically present on the territory without legal permission. The substantive difference to such clandestine migrants, however, is the regulated use of this official non-entity by authorities as an integrated aspect of border control.

 These developments in bordering lead me to agree with those scholars who believe the inside/outside dichotomy associated with territorial boundaries fails to capture the complex ways in which the work of bordering as an aspect of statecraft is not tied to the physical spaces of territory (Basaran, 2008; Coutin, 2010). As flagged in the opening paragraphs of this chapter, the conventional paradigm of the state relies on overlapping legal and spatial constructs, whereby borders mark the physical boundaries of the territory and this corresponds directly to the limits of sovereign authority (Agnew, 1994; Walker, 1993). The application of the exceptional legal status of "community detention" exposes the deterritori-alized relationship between migrant and sovereign, as the exercise of power by the sovereign in the name of border control is separated from the physical and legal confines of territory.

PART II: DIFFERENTIATION AND PROTECTION

The decision to categorize an individual as "detained", thereby creating a legally countable but politically unviable non-presence, resonates strongly with the sovereign decision on bare life. Persons detained in such a way are excluded from political recognition in the community on the territory and are held in the sway of the sovereign powers – in this case, through the authority of immigration officials. As shown, the programmes in Belgium, Australia, and Hong Kong create legally eviscerated beings who are, nevertheless, officially permitted to engage in society through social, economic, and geographic means. Their lived experience of "detention" differs greatly from those who are excluded through confinement.

However, two elements of this phenomenon are not easily captured by the theory of the exception. The first is the variable experience of those living with the exceptional status of a detainee. While a person's *legal status* is consistent across confinement in detention facilities and "community detention", non-legal elements created a highly differentiated experience. Agamben's theory struggles to allow for economic, social, and geographical systems that integrate a person in to legal systems. For example, "detainees" who become victims of crime in the community can access the legal protections of the judicial systems that stem from that violation.

The second is the use of the exception to provide an element of protection. This is an intriguing aspect of community detention: that a form of (legal) exclusion is being used to provide (limited) protection and (provisional) inclusion. Importantly, constructs such as age, gender, and health status modify this exclusionary power, with children, women, and the seriously ill more likely to be placed in "community detention", and adult men travelling alone incarcerated in detention facilities. Through recognition of selected rights, access to some basic government-funded services, and participation in the community of the nation, I argue fulfils some of the rights of these migrants and includes them, to an extent, in the political community.

The use of exclusion to provide some form of limited protection can be seen in several other examples, including in the "hotspots" established to respond to the large number of people crossing the borders of Europe in the past five years. Such sites provide some freedom of movement and supports but limited access to the protections of legal status (European Council on Refugees and Exiles, 2016). An important correlation to this research can also be found in Kenworthy's (2012) work on an exceptional space being used to protect a group of undocumented migrants with mental health issues in the United States. This group remains confined in a state psychiatric centre because they are ineligible for community support programmes required to safely release them. As Kenworthy notes, "the institution could provide a crucial, albeit flimsy, layer of protection from economic, legal, and medical abandonment" (2012, p. 130). Confinement in this space of exception thus offers a form of protection from destitution, from the withdrawal of mental health services, and from potential deportation.

EMBODIED BORDERS

This research showed that migrants experience a highly variable and overlapping mixture of legal, political, economic, social, and spatial positionings that do not map directly onto a legal distinction between those who belong and those who are abandoned by the state. My findings coincide with the views of those authors who argue that bare life is not a uniform status but is, rather, highly differentiated (Belcher et al., 2008; Coddington et al., 2012; Mitchell, 2006; Mountz, 2011; Pratt, 2005; Robins, 2009; Shewly, 2013; Zeveleva, 2017). As Lemke argues:

> [Agamben] cannot analyse how inside "bare life" hierarchisations and evaluations become possible . . . because his attention is fixed on the establishment of a border . . . In fact, the "camp" is by no means a homogeneous zone where differences collapse but a site where differences are produced. (Lemke, 2005, p. 8)

The sovereign decision regarding bare life is therefore not dichotomous but finely graded, as Landau and Monson (2008) also contend: "[T]here is considerable variation in the broadcast and recognition of state authority . . . [including] locally derived gradations, modes and configurations in the state's monopoly over territorial control" (p. 334). The theoretical construct of the exception has the potential to falter at this critical point due to its lack of nuance.

Vaughan-Williams believes such criticism is unwarranted if bare life is seen as an indeterminate status produced by sovereign power for its own purposes. As he argues:

> If bare life is treated as precisely *an indistinct form of subjectivity* that is produced immanently by sovereign power for sovereign power then the undecidability of the figure of *homo sacer* is brought into relief. This move allows for a differentiated approach to the production of subjectivities under biopolitical conditions because it does not fix bare life as some sort of given that pre-exists sovereign power. (Vaughan-Williams, 2009a, p. 107, emphasis in the original)

Vaughan-Williams's point is valid to an extent. However, I find his defence hard to reconcile with the exception, which rests so heavily on the decision of the sovereign on the exception for delimiting the boundaries of political community. If a politically qualified life is not distinct from *homo sacer*, then the power of the theory to illuminate the particular experiences of detainees and other exceptional beings is lost. I have tackled this issue by shifting the lens of analysis away from the sovereign decision on the exception and towards the points of connection between the sovereign and *homo sacer*, the state and the irregular migrant. Inverting Agamben's theoretical focus in this way reaches a more intricate interpretation which can accommodate the seemingly contradictory elements of migration management found in this research.

CONCLUSION

This chapter has explored an area of contemporary borders that has not previously been analysed: an alternative to detention in which a person is legally categorized as a detainee but living with freedom of movement amongst the host society. This emerging practice maintains the legal basis of state power over a person's body, while limiting the person's exposure to the harms of confinement and deprivation of liberty. The use of such "community detention" is not a unified policy applied to all migrants, but is rather a strategy used for particular – especially vulnerable – migrant bodies.

This new form of bordering provides important insights into the location and nature of contemporary borders. Traditional definitions of the state portray the spatial bounds of territory as the limit of government authority. However, by disentangling the boundaries of sovereign authority from the "territorial trap" (Agnew, 1994, 2010), I have found that borders are located and negotiated according to the population to be controlled. In doing this, I reassert the disruption of the fundamental relationship between sovereign authority and territory. As Mountz propounds, "If sovereignty ever operated in such a way, it no longer does" (2013, p. 831).

It is hard to imagine a map that represents state borders as a collection of individual bodies rather than as a line tracing the boundaries of territory. However, that is exactly what contemporary bordering practices require. Unlike the colourful, piecemeal but stable and ordered world map described in the opening lines of this chapter, a representation of state borders as embodied borders – or a map that traces the bodies of migrants living under border control measures – would result in a chaotic spray of pixelated dots constantly on the move. These individuals would be found not only along the line of traditional territorial boundaries, but in a variety of locations both within and beyond territory's edge. State borders would thus be represented as a dispersed, disaggregated, and unstable collection of elements that intermingle with, and overlap, those of other states. While each individual within this would be one small element, sites of significance in which many bordered bodies converge could well become apparent in unexpected ways. Cartographers certainly have their work cut out for them.

ACKNOWLEDGEMENTS

The chapter comes out of a research partnership with the International Detention Coalition, which obtained financial support for the project from the Myer Foundation, the Oak Foundation, and the Open Society. Robyn Sampson was financially supported by an award from La Trobe University. I would like to thank Gwenda Tavan and Sandy Gifford for their comments on an earlier draft of this work.

REFERENCES

Agamben, Giorgio (1998), *Homo Sacer: Sovereign Power and Bare Life*, trans. D. Heller-Roazen, Stanford, CA: Stanford University Press.

Agamben, Giorgio (2005), *State of Exception*, trans. K. Attell, Chicago, IL and London: University of Chicago Press.

Agnew, John (1994), "The territorial trap: the geographical assumptions of international relations theory", *Review of International Political Economy*, **1** (1), 53–80.

Agnew, John (2010), "Still trapped in territory?", *Geopolitics*, **15** (4), 779–84.

Amoore, Louise (2006), "Biometric borders: governing mobilities in the war on terror", *Political Geography*, **25** (3), 336–51.

Basaran, Tugba (2008), "Security, law, borders: spaces of exclusion", *International Political Sociology*, **2** (4), 339–54.

Belcher, Oliver, Lauren Martin, Anna Secor, Stephanie Simon and Tommy Wilson (2008), "Everywhere and nowhere: the exception and the topological challenge to geography", *Antipode*, **40** (4), 499–503.

Berg, Eiki and Hank Van Houtum (2003), "Prologue. A border is not a border: writing and reading borders in space", in Eiki Berg and Hank Van Houtum (eds), *Routing Borders between Territories, Discourses and Practices*, Burlington, VT: Ashgate, pp. 1–10.

Burridge, Andrew (forthcoming), "'Signing on' with the UK Home Office: reporting as a site of anxiety, detention and solidarity", in Reece Jones (ed.), *Open Borders: In Defense of Free Movement*, Athens, GA: University of Georgia Press.

Coddington, Kate, R. Tina Catania, Jennifer Loyd, Emily Mitchell-Eaton and Alison Mountz (2012), "Embodied possibilities, sovereign geographies and island detention: negotiating the 'right to have rights' on Guam, Lampedusa and Christmas Island", *Shima: The International Journal of Research into Island Cultures*, **6** (2), 27–48.

Connolly, William E. (2004), "The complexity of sovereignty", in Jenny Edkins, Véronique Pin-Fat and Michael J. Shapiro (eds), *Sovereign Lives: Power in Global Politics*, New York: Routledge, pp. 23–40.

Coutin, Susan Bibler (2010), "Confined within: national territories as zones of confinement", *Political Geography*, **29** (4), 200–208.

Darling, Jonathan (2009), "Becoming bare life: asylum, hospitality, and the politics of encampment", *Environment and Planning D: Society and Space*, **27** (4), 649–65.

Davidson, Robert A. (2003), "Spaces of immigration 'prevention': interdiction and the nonplace", *Diacritics*, **33** (3/4), 2.

De Genova, Nicholas P. (2002), "Migrant 'illegality' and deportability in everyday life", *Annual Review of Anthropology*, **31**, 419–47.

Diken, Bülent (2004), "From refugee camps to gated communities: biopolitics and the end of the city", *Citizenship Studies*, **8** (1), 83–106.

Doty, Roxanne L. (2011), "Bare life: border-crossing deaths and spaces of moral alibi", *Environment and Planning D: Society and Space*, **29** (4), 599–612.

European Council on Refugees and Exiles (2016), *The Implementation of the Hotspots in Italy and Greece – A Study*, Amsterdam: Dutch Council for Refugees.

Hedman, Eva-Lotta E. (2008), "Refuge, governmentality and citizenship: capturing 'illegal migrants' in Malaysia and Thailand", *Government and Opposition*, **43** (2), 358–83.

Johnson, Corey, Reece Jones, Anssi Paasi et al. (2011), "Interventions on rethinking 'the border' in border studies", *Political Geography*, **30** (2), 61–9.

Kaiser, Robert (2012), "Performativity and the eventfulness of bordering practices", in Thomas Wilson and Hastings Donnan (eds), *A Companion to Border Studies*, Chichester: Wiley-Blackwell, pp. 522–37.

Kenworthy, Nora (2012), "Asylum's asylum: undocumented immigrants, belonging, and the space of exception at a state psychiatric center", *Human Organization*, **71** (2), 123–34.

Landau, Loren B. and Tamlyn Monson (2008), "Displacement, estrangement and sovereignty: reconfiguring state power in urban South Africa", *Government and Opposition*, **43** (2), 315–36.

Lavenex, Sandra and Emek M. Uçarer (2004), "The external dimension of Europeanization", *Cooperation and Conflict*, **39** (4), 417–43.

Legomsky, Stephen H. (2006), "The USA and the Caribbean interdiction program", *International Journal of Refugee Law*, **18** (3–4), 677–95.

Lemke, Thomas (2005), "'A zone of indistinction' – a critique of Giorgio Agamben's concept of biopolitics", *Outlines. Critical Practice Studies*, **7** (1), 3–13.

Mainwaring, Cetta and Stephanie J. Silverman (2017), "Detention-as-spectacle", *International Political Sociology*, **11** (1), 21–38.

Malkki, Liisa H. (1997), "National geographic: the rooting of peoples and the territorialization of national identity among scholars and refugees", *Cultural Anthropology*, **7** (1), 24–44.

Minca, Claudio (2015), "Geographies of the camp", *Political Geography*, **49**, 74–83.

Mitchell, Katharyne (2006), "Geographies of identity: the new exceptionalism", *Progress in Human Geography*, **30** (1), 95–106.

Motomura, Hiroshi (1993), "Haitian asylum seekers: interdiction and immigrants' rights", *Cornell International Law Journal*, **26**, 698–717.

Mountz, Alison (2011), "The enforcement archipelago: detention, haunting, and asylum on islands", *Political Geography*, **30** (3), 118–28.

Mountz, Alison (2013), "Political geography I: reconfiguring geographies of sovereignty", *Progress in Human Geography*, **37** (6), 829–41.

Noll, Gregor (2003), "Visions of the exceptional: legal and theoretical issues raised by transit processing centres and protection zones", *European Journal of Migration and Law*, **5** (3), 303–41.

Pickering, Sharon and Leanne Weber (2006), *Borders, Mobility and Technologies of Control*, Dordrecht: Springer Netherlands.

Pratt, Geraldine (2005), "Abandoned women and spaces of the exception", *Antipode*, **37** (5), 1052–78.
Provine, Doris M. and Monica W. Varsanyi (2012), "Scaled down: perspectives on state and local creation and enforcement of immigration law", *Law & Policy*, **34** (2), 105–12.
Rajaram, Prem Kumar and Carl Grundy-Warr (2004), "The irregular migrant as homo sacer: migration and detention in Australia, Malaysia, and Thailand", *International Migration*, **42** (1), 33–64.
Ramadan, Adam (2012), "Spatialising the refugee camp", *Transactions of the Institute of British Geographers*, **38** (1), 65–77.
Robins, Steven (2009), "Humanitarian aid beyond 'bare survival': social movement responses to xenophobic violence in South Africa", *American Ethnologist*, **36** (4), 637–50.
Salter, Mark B. (2006), "The global visa regime and the political technologies of the international self: borders, bodies, biopolitics", *Alternatives: Global, Local, Political*, **31** (2), 167–89.
Salter, Mark B. (2008), "When the exception becomes the rule: borders, sovereignty, and citizenship", *Citizenship Studies*, **12** (4), 365–80.
Sampson, Robyn, Vivienne Chew, Grant Mitchell, and Lucy Bowring (2015), *There are Alternatives: A Handbook for Preventing Unnecessary Immigration Detention (Revised)*, Melbourne: International Detention Coalition. Available at: http://idcoalition.org/publication/there-are-alternatives-revised-edition/.
Sawyer, Caroline and Philip Turpin (2005), "Neither here nor there: temporary admission to the UK", *International Journal of Refugee Law*, **17** (4), 688–728.
Shewly, Hosna J. (2013), "Abandoned spaces and bare life in the enclaves of the India-Bangladesh border", *Political Geography*, **32**, 23–31.
Taylor, Peter (1994), "The state as container: territoriality in the modern world-system", *Progress in Human Geography*, **18** (2), 151–62.
Taylor, Savitri and Brynna Rafferty-Brown (2010), "Waiting for life to begin: the plight of asylum seekers caught by Australia's Indonesian solution", *International Journal of Refugee Law*, **22** (4), 558–92.
Vaughan-Williams, Nick (2009a), *Border Politics: The Limits of Sovereign Power*, Edinburgh: Edinburgh University Press.
Vaughan-Williams, Nick (2009b), "The generalised bio-political border? Re-conceptualising the limits of sovereign power", *Review of International Studies*, **35** (4), 729–49.
Walker, Rob B.J. (1993), *Inside/Outside: International Relations as Political Theory*, Cambridge: Cambridge University Press.
Walters, William (2006), "Rethinking borders beyond the state 1", *Comparative European Politics*, **4** (2/3), 141–59.
Weber, Leanne (2006), "The shifting frontiers of migration control", in Sharon Pickering and Leanne Weber (eds), *Borders, Mobility and Technologies of Control*, Dordrecht: Springer Netherlands, pp. 21–43.
Zeveleva, Olga (2017), "Biopolitics, borders, and refugee camps: exercising sovereign power over nonmembers of the state", *Nationalities Papers*, **45** (1), 41–60.

PART V

TRANSNATIONALISM AND DIASPORA

21. Home and diaspora
Alison Blunt and Jayani Bonnerjee

Ideas and experiences of home and diaspora are closely bound up together over a range of spatial and temporal scales and over emotional, imaginative and material terrains. The lived experiences and spatial imaginaries of people living in diaspora often revolve around ideas about home through, for example, 'the relationships between home and homeland, the existence of multiple homes, diverse home-making practices, and the intersections of home, memory, identity and belonging' (Blunt and Dowling, 2006, p. 199). The changing dynamics of home are widely understood to shape experiences of transnational migration (Ahmed et al., 2003; Al-Ali and Koser, 2002; Boccagni, 2017; Ralph and Staeheli, 2011) but to have a particular resonance in the more specific context of diaspora. For Paul Gilroy, for example, the qualities of diaspora represent 'a historical and experiential rift between the locations of residence and the locations of belonging' (2000, p. 124): a disjuncture between 'here' and 'there'. This chapter explores the ways in which such a 'rift' between diasporic 'residence' and 'belonging' – and between 'here' and 'there' – are both articulated and challenged through a focus on home. We begin by examining the contested relationships between 'homeland' and diaspora before turning to diasporic home-making on a domestic scale. We then draw on our own research (together with Noah Hysler-Rubin and Shompa Lahiri) to explore the city as a site of diasporic belonging and attachment that relates to but differs from ideas of diaspora in relation to 'homeland' and domestic home-making. Throughout, we argue that home and diaspora, and the connections between them, involve processes and practices of dwelling and mobility that unsettle not only fixed assumptions about place, but also about identity, ethnicity, culture and community (Bonnerjee et al., 2012; Kalra et al., 2005).

'HOMELAND' AND DIASPORA

Experiences, memories and ideas about a 'homeland' are widely understood to be significant for people living in diaspora, signalling the importance of another place prior to resettlement and its influence across subsequent generations. As Bronwen Walter explains, 'Diaspora involves feeling "at home" in the area of settlement while retaining significant identification outside it' (2000, p. 206). This 'significant identification' is often articulated as an attachment to a homeland that – usually on a national scale – may be remembered, lost, imagined or yet to be achieved (Blunt and Dowling, 2006; for more on homeland belongings, see Abdelhady, 2008; Hage, 1996). The contrast between diasporic 'roots' and 'routes' revolves around the relationships between home, homeland and diaspora (Clifford, 1997). While 'roots' implies an originary homeland, 'routes' suggests mobile and multiple journeys over time and space, unsettling a single and identifiable homeland as a place of departure and potential return. In this section we consider the mobilization of diasporic connections to a 'homeland', outlining the tensions between the transnational dispersal of the former alongside the territorial – and often national – origins of the latter.

According to Elizabeth Mavroudi and Anastasia Christou (2016, p. 3), a 'diasporic approach' to understanding the connections between 'here' and 'there' is mobilized by 'the ethnic, national, and/or religious ties that those in diaspora share with one another and with the homeland', with particular attention given to the ways in which such 'ties' 'are used to 'help' the homeland through the various intellectual, scientific, and academic skills that those in diaspora are seen to possess'. Homeland politics and development are two key, and often connected, areas that mobilize connections between 'here' and 'there' in diaspora (for more on diaspora and development, see Walton-Roberts, Crush and Chikanda, Chapter 23 in this volume). For Werbner, 'diasporas are deeply implicated both ideologically and materially in the nationalist projects of their homelands' (2000, p. 5), but in varied and complex ways, and with particular resonances for Palestinian, Tibetan, Kurdish and other stateless diasporas (Baser, 2016; Mavroudi, 2010; McConnell, 2016). The homeland, for example, is central to ideas about 'diaspora nationalism', and for Gal et al. (2010) is both influenced by but clearly distinguished from the 'host country' whereby the similarities and differences between them inform 'the nature and the intensity of the attachment to the homeland' (p. xv). Through his focus on the '*subjective* experience of nationalism', Khachig Tölölyan (2010) questions the pre-eminence of the 'homeland' in diaspora politics by contrasting an older form of 'exilic nationalism' with a 'new diasporic transnationalism' (p. 28). While the latter for Tölölyan 'continues to be marked by a commitment to the survival and security of the homeland', the homeland – distinguished from what he terms the 'hostland' – is no longer 'the unchallenged center of national identity' (p. 36) but might rather be one node of significance in a wider network. Whether in recognizing the 'variety of diasporas and their range of attachment to the homeland' (Gal et al., 2010, p. xv) or in seeking to move 'beyond the homeland' (Tölölyan, 2010), the very idea of a 'homeland' in contrast to a 'host country' or 'hostland' contrasts not only with other research on multiple, co-existing homes but also with the possibility of being at home – rather than 'hosted' – in diaspora (Blunt and Dowling, 2006).

Another key area where ideas about a 'homeland' articulate diasporic connections between 'here' and 'there' revolves around return, whether on a permanent or tempo-rary basis. As Avtar Brah (1996) explains, some (but not all) diaspora spaces are fash-ioned in relation to experiences, memories and ideas about a homeland. The 'homing desire' for some (but not all) people living in diaspora space is to return. For Brah, 'the concept of diaspora offers a critique of discourses of fixed origins while taking account of a homing desire, as distinct from a desire for a "homeland." This distinction is important not least because not all diasporas sustain an ideology of "return"' (Brah, 1996, p. 16). While an 'ideology' or 'myth' of return has been widely critiqued, a grow-ing body of work has studied different experiences of return in practice (Bolognani, 2007, 2016). Part of this work has explored the ways in which ideas and attachments to a 'homeland' might be bound up with particular places and landscapes on a range of scales that sometimes – but not always – include a national sense of belonging. In her classic study of return visits between Perth in Western Australia and the village of San Fior in northeastern Italy, Loretta Baldassar (2001) vividly describes the idea of *campanilismo* – 'bell-towerism' (p. 110). This term refers to local identity, and 'is a useful conceptual tool in the comprehension of both the migrants' attachment to their home town and their ethnic identification in the host country' (p. 323). Such attachments and identities are rooted but not limited to a particular home town, as they can 'expand or contract along provincial, regional or national lines depending on the context' (p. 323). Also drawing out different scales of attachment and grounded identifications in diaspora, David Timothy Duval focuses on return visits by Caribbean migrants in Toronto, describing them as 'one manifestation of the numerous social conduits between former homelands and new homelands' (2005, p. 249). And yet, as he shows, the connections between different 'homelands' may be experienced most strongly on a range of scales smaller than the nation: 'Some may feel nationalistic ties, while others may identify, first and foremost, with a smaller unit of association – a village, district, part of town, or a family home and neighbourhood' (2005, p. 254).

Just as in homeland politics, research on homeland returns often revolves around an assumption of ethnic affinity. Some studies reveal the ways in which ethnic identities come to be unsettled on return (including Christou and King, 2006; Kibria, 2002; Potter and Phillips, 2006), but most identify prior links between an assumed ethnicity and attachments to a 'homeland'. Takeyuki Tsuda (2009), for example, refers to '*ethnic* return migration' to denote 'later-generation descendants of diasporic peoples who "return" to their countries of ancestral origin after living outside their ethnic homelands for generations' (p. 1). Tsuda draws clear links between ethnicity, diaspora and the 'homeland', although recognizes that some migrants might 'find themselves becoming ethnic minorities because of their cultural differences' (p. 11). Other research on the second generation living in diaspora reveals the multiple negotiations between 'here' and 'there' in everyday life. Claire Dwyer, for example, explores the hybridity of diasporic home-making through her research on British Muslim schoolgirls whose parents had been born in Pakistan, and who describe themselves as British Asian or British Pakistani (2002). Rather than view home or identity as fixed and static, Dwyer shows both to be dynamic whereby 'In the process of *making home* in Britain, other places are also *made home* as identities are made, re-made and negotiated . . . [T]he evocation of Pakistan as "home" suggests not a return to a mythical or lost "homeland" or roots but instead a symbolic process of making home' (Dwyer, 2002, p. 197, emphases in original). Unsettling clear distinctions between 'here' and 'there', the young women in Dwyer's research 'negotiate belongings to several different homes at one and the same time' (p. 198). Such multiple and negotiated belongings can be difficult, particularly across different generations, as shown by Diane Wolf (2002) in her research on 'emotional transnationalism' for second-generation Filipino students in the United States. The students interviewed by Wolf described their attachment to their parents' homeland: 'despite place of birth, and whether or not they had lived in or visited the Philippines, the students, in their references to "home," always meant the greater Home across the ocean' (Wolf, 2002, p. 263). As Wolf found, everyday life for second-generation Filipinos in the United States was shaped by their parents' perception of the moral superiority of the Philippines as 'Home':

> While this may offer the security of a source of identity, it also creates tensions, confusion, and contradictory messages that . . . can lead to intense alienation and despair among some. The son who is told, 'Just because you live here in America, don't be influenced by everything you see, because you are Filipino and should know who you are and where you come from,' is being told to differentiate between home and Home. (Wolf, 2002, p. 285)

DIASPORIC HOME-MAKING

Home on a domestic scale is also important in both articulating and challenging distinctions between 'here' and 'there' in diaspora. On subjects including domestic architecture, material culture and practice, research on diasporic home-making reveals it to be expansive rather than bounded, often rooted in but stretching far beyond the scale of a domestic dwelling. Just as both home and diaspora are dynamic and in process rather than fixed and static, so too is diasporic home-making, challenging not only a distinction between home as 'sedenterist' and diaspora as 'mobile' (Boccagni, 2017; Ralph and Staeheli, 2011), but also between 'homeland' and 'hostland' in diaspora. The materialities of diasporic home-making are closely bound up with imaginative and emotional geographies of both home and diaspora and shaped by different identities and power relations over multi-layered spatial and temporal scales (Blunt and Dowling, 2006). As Joanna Long writes in her analysis of diasporic dwelling, 'Home is thus an interplay of the house and the world, the intimate and the global, the material and the symbolic' (Long, 2013, p. 335).

The built form of a dwelling and the ways in which it may be understood and experienced as home is one example of the ways in which diasporic identities can not only take material form on a domestic scale but also travel over diaspora space. For affluent migrants from Hong Kong who moved to Vancouver from the 1980s as investor and entrepreneur immigrants, for example, the construction of new, large (and so-called 'monster') houses changed the landscape aesthetics of old, elite neighbourhoods such as Shaughnessy Heights. Taking a hybrid form that incorporated traditional values alongside modernity (Ley, 1995), Katharyne Mitchell explains that 'The newly constructed houses contrasted vividly – in form, structure, scale, aesthetic and urban sensibility – with the historicist styles of the existing residential architecture in its picturesque suburban streetscapes' (2004, p. 145). The new form of such houses prompted bitter debates in the media and planning committees about residence and belonging not only in this particular neighbourhood but also in the wider Canadian nation. For Mitchell, 'the Hong Kong economic migrants quite literally brought contemporary, often paradoxical forces of dispersion, dwelling and diaspora "home" to the heretofore protected spaces of suburban Shaughnessy Heights' (2004, p. 143).

In contrast, poor housing conditions mean that diasporic home-making takes different forms for less wealthy migrants. In her research on recent Bangladeshi migrants living in high-rise blocks in Toronto, for example, Sutama Ghosh (2014) explores the ways in which these often poorly kept spaces changed from 'regimented functional spaces into their own social, sacred and economic spaces' (p. 2015), fostering a form of belonging understood as *para* (Bengali for 'neighbourhood'; also see Bonnerjee, 2012) in a previously unhomely context. Similarly identifying new locations and spaces of diasporic home-making, Pierette Hodagneu-Sotelo (2017) studies the ways in which inner-city community gardens became significant for Latino/a residents in New York. While recognizing conflicts around, for example, governance and funding, such gardens have come to serve as 'surrogate homes for marginalized, undocumented migrant workers who have experienced a double dislocation, displacement, from their countries of origin and incorporation into crowded substandard apartments' (p. 15).

The construction of new homes in places of origin provides tangible evidence of connections between 'here' and 'there' and an important context for the investment of migrant remittances. Studying both 'immigrant' and 'emigrant' houses for Ecuadorians living in northern Italy, for example, Paolo Boccagni (2014) explains that building new homes in Ecuador was a priority for many migrants. And yet, as he writes, 'Remittance houses ... were a striking indicator of ambivalent and inflated views about migrants' homecomings' (p. 288), and were visited at best once a year from Italy. Vividly describing the poor conditions of many of the homes he visited in Italy, Boccagni describes such 'dual housing' as both an opportunity and a cost (p. 289; also see Dalokoglou, 2010; Levin and Fincher, 2010; Van der Horst, 2010).

The locatedness and mobility of domestic material culture also reflects diasporic connections not only between 'here' and 'there' but also between the past and present. Such connections are not one way or linear, as shown by Ruba Salih's study of domestic material culture for Moroccan women living in Italy (2002). Understanding home as a site reflecting 'double belonging' and 'plural identity' (p. 56), Salih describes images and objects within the homes of Moroccans living in Italy:

> Typical cheap, popular Italian furniture is displayed together with objects recalling the Moroccan and Muslim world such as covers for sofas, pictures showing Quranic writings on the walls and, in some cases, calendars arriving from France with dates of Islamic celebrations and feasts or posters of Moroccan women wearing the traditional dress of different areas of Morocco. (Salih, 2002, p. 56)

Not only does domestic material culture connect homes in Italy to other places, but it also travels beyond the domestic sphere, particularly on annual return visits to Morocco. As Salih writes, 'To feel "at home" in Morocco women need to bring with them those things that constitute and represent their "other home" in Italy. Through these commodities women display what they have become and affirm their identities contextually that signal the[ir] Moroccan and Muslim belonging' (p. 65). The display, use and mobility of objects and images within diasporic homes is also bound up with memories of past homes, as shown by Divya Tolia-Kelly's research on South Asian women from South Asia and East Africa living in London (2004). As Tolia-Kelly explains, visual and material cultures shape 'new textures of home' in London that 'are shot through with memory of "other" spaces of being' (Tolia-Kelly, 2004, p. 676). As such, they serve as 'prismatic devices which import "other" landscapes into the British one, and thereby shift notions of Britishness, and British domestic landscapes' (p. 678).

Like wider studies of home, research on diasporic home-making has often focused on the gendered nature of domestic work and other gender politics of home. Bronwen Walter situates her research on 'placement' and 'displacement' for women in the Irish diaspora in the United Kingdom and United States as part of a wider process of 'feminising the diaspora' (2000, p. 11), and explores the ways in which diasporic homes can be sites of both containment and liberation for women. As a wide range of research has also shown, migrant domestic workers – most of whom are women – often live and work in the homes of their employers and are vulnerable to abuse or exploitation. Revealing the ways in which home on a domestic scale is bound up with wider economic and social processes on a global scale, this research is an important reminder that home can be a site of alienation and exclusion as well as inclusion and belonging. Stretching home beyond the domestic scale to explore new sites and practices of belonging, Lisa Law (2001) vividly conveys the ways in which Filipina domestic workers come together to create 'little Manila' in central

Hong Kong every Sunday. As she writes, 'Statue Square and its environs become a home from home for migrant women, a place of remembering and forgetting, and a lively place full of laughter, songs and home cooking' (Law, 2001, p. 266; also see Boccagni and Brighenti, 2017 for more on migrant home-making and 'domesticity, commonality and publicness', and Blunt and Sheringham, 2018 on home-city geographies).

DIASPORA CITIES

The city is a space where key questions around ideas of home in the context of diaspora are reconfigured. As an intermediary scale between the nation (homeland) and the domestic, and also often representing the actual site of departure and resettlement, the city offers an analytical frame for both home and diaspora. Research over the past 15 years has questioned the predominance of the idea of nation in defining a diaspora as well as a sense of home. Michael Peter Smith's (2001) idea of 'transnational urbanism', for example, focuses on everyday practices of migrants in the city, and highlights the importance of urban space in enabling and maintaining transnational connections (also see Conradson and Latham, 2005). Zooming in further on the idea of locality, Katherine Brickell and Ayona Datta (2011) explore translocal geographies of mobile lives. They define translocality as '"groundedness" during movement, including those everyday movements that are not necessarily transnational' (p. 4). Indeed, this duality of mobility and fixity in both ideas of home and diaspora pose a conceptual challenge. As Ralph and Staeheli (2011) note, 'the challenge, therefore, is not only to examine migrants' articulations of mobile/grounded homes, but at the same time to interrogate the ways in which various power geometries influence such complex registers of home' (p. 520). Other research has highlighted the significance of focusing on the city to identify such power geometries. Kevin Robins (2001), for example, urges us to think 'through the city' as it offers a more productive way to understand contemporary cultural interactions (p. 77). Robins argues that 'The nation . . . is a space of identification and identity, whilst the city is an existential and experiential space' (p. 87), which offers 'important possibilities for cultural unsettling and transformation' (p. 89). More recently, Natalie Oswin and Brenda Yeoh (2010) have introduced the idea of Singapore as a 'mobile city' to explore the multiple connections that shape urban space. Similarly, for Glick Schiller and Çağlar (2009), analysis of the 'city scale' is vital for understanding migrant incorporation, particularly in terms of 'the varying positionings of cities within global fields of power and the different roles migrants play within the reconstitution of specific cities' (p. 178).

Taking inspiration from such emphases on the urban, our own research has argued for a conceptualization of the city through its diasporas and imagining the city as home (Blunt and Bonnerjee, 2013). Focusing on four minority communities from Calcutta (Anglo-Indian, Brahmo, Chinese and Jewish) and their migration to London, Toronto and towns in Israel, the 'Diaspora Cities' research highlights the importance of a diasporic focus to analyse connections within and between cities (see Blunt and Bonnerjee, 2013; Bonnerjee, 2012; Lahiri, 2010, 2011). Two key arguments are put forward in this research. First, in contrast to the imagination of the nation as homeland, it conceptualizes the city as home. In doing so, we explore contexts of urban memory, emotions and attachment, and in particular emphasize the importance of the city as a space of belonging for minority communities. Second, we explore how cities themselves are connected through their diasporas, not simply via processes of transnationalism, but also through ways in which ideas of home travel. In this section, we draw on examples from our research to explore connections between ideas of home and diaspora. While research on home in the context of diaspora has principally alluded to ideas of homeland and also home-making practices, the focus on the city, we argue, unsettles notions of ethnicity, identity, community and culture that are used to theorize diaspora. We bring in our research on Calcutta's Anglo-Indian and Chinese communities to complicate ideas of homeland, home-making practices and return journeys home.

As two of Calcutta's significant minorities that made the city home during colonial times, the migration trajectories of the Anglo-Indian and Chinese communities have shaped their connection to the city. Anglo-Indians form a community of mixed descent that has a prominent history in Calcutta and imagined themselves a part of an imperial diaspora (Blunt, 2005). The city's Chinese community has its origins in the southern provinces of China, mainly Guangtong and Fujian (Liang, 2007), with the Cantonese and Hakka sub-groups thus making up most of Calcutta's Chinese population. Both of these communities live/d in neighbourhoods around central Calcutta with which they identify and which evoke a deep sense of nostalgia in diaspora (Bonnerjee, 2012). Both communities have migrated out of Calcutta at important political moments – India's Independence in 1947 and the Sino-Indian border conflict in 1962 – and continue to emigrate. Our research followed them to London and Toronto, two cities where they have migrated in large numbers. We explore connections across these cities in imagining, making and returning home for these two communities.

City as Home

'Where is home?' is an often asked question to people living in diaspora, the answer to which is never simple. Complex histories of 'roots' and 'routes' (Clifford, 1997) shape an imagination of home that can be located in different places simultaneously. At the same time, the idea of homeland holds a powerful connotation in the context of politics and belonging. For minority communities, such as the Anglo-Indian and Chinese, the nation becomes a problematic space to express a sense of belonging. Brenda, a young Chinese woman, who migrated to Toronto in the 1990s, described her dilemma in the following manner:

> Now it is Toronto, but there's always the sense that I was raised in Calcutta . . . more and more I live in Toronto it becomes home. But because you are in Toronto, they ask – 'where are you from originally'? It's always like, oh yeah . . . yes . . . but . . . and then you say you are from Calcutta. The funny thing is you never say India, always Calcutta . . . because you always want to distinguish in your mind that you are not from Bombay or Delhi . . . and the point is if the question comes from someone with an Indian background, and you say you are from India, they look almost shocked, so you always have to qualify and say that you are from Calcutta.

In Toronto, the Calcutta Chinese community is part of both a wider Chinese and Indian diaspora, and this necessitates an articulation of a city-specific identity. Although nation-focused identities come to the fore, for example, in expressing a sense of connection to the Indian diaspora through consumption of Indian food in restaurants and watching Bollywood films, the emotional sense of belonging is expressed through the city. As Bradley, an Anglo-Indian who migrated to London in the 1970s, explains:

> Home is here . . . heart is there . . . how do you leave your children . . . grandchildren . . . this [London] has got to be home. The heart is always there . . .

The city as a familial space also comes through in the narratives of the Chinese community who make an annual pilgrimage to the tomb of Yong Atchew, the first Chinese to have arrived in Bengal according to popular stories. Located in the southern suburb of Calcutta, Achhipur is the destination for this pilgrimage and reflects the importance of ancestor worship amongst the Chinese community in shaping a 'clan' identity as well as marking a territory for this clan. Drawing on Laura Bear's (2007) work that describes the railway colony as a representation of Anglo-Indian *desh*, a Bengali word denoting a place of origin and nation as homeland, we put forward the idea of the city as *desh* (Blunt and Bonnerjee, 2013).

Making Home in the City

Besides narratives of belonging, home-making practices of the Anglo-Indian and Chinese communities also point to the significance of the city in a diasporic context. 'Jade', one of the short stories in *The Palm Leaf Fan* written by Kwai-Yun Li, follows the life of the central character across her different homes in Calcutta and Toronto, and charts a route that many Calcutta Chinese women have taken, negotiating the promise of a better life in Toronto and arranged marriage, as families are keen to find suitors amongst young Chinese men settled in Toronto. The story flits between the crowded setting of 14/1 Chattawalla Gully in Calcutta where Jade lives with her extended family; 5 Trafford Road, Markham, Toronto, where she and her husband share a three-bedroom house with her parents-in-law and four brothers-in-law; and 17 Pioneer Road, Scarborough, a one-roomed basement apartment where a pregnant Jade moves in with her husband and two children. The story reveals several aspects of the 'homing desire' of the Calcutta Chinese diaspora in Toronto as well as the cartographies of home for the community (Brah, 1996). It offers readers a glimpse into the patriarchal nature of the Chinese (particularly Hakka) community in Calcutta and into the home-life of Hakka women in central Calcutta. It also highlights issues around sharing home-space and owning a home in Toronto. For both Anglo-Indian and Chinese communities, owning a home in Calcutta was usually not the norm. Hence, narratives around home-making in London and Toronto often revolved around the importance of owning a home. Lawrence, an Anglo-Indian settled in Toronto, explained this urge to own a house in similar terms. He said, 'people ask me why am I so materialistic, but I think, I have never had a home, now I have a home'. Although the experience that Anglo-Indians went through in relocating their home from Calcutta to London and Toronto was unsettling in terms of domesticity and also a wider unease about embodied identities (Blunt, 2005), having English as their first language made the transition easier compared to some groups within the Calcutta Chinese community. For some members of the Hakka Chinese community, the inability to speak English compelled them to work in factories doing manual work (Oxfeld, 1993, p. 254). Many could only afford to live in government assisted housing like St. Jamestown (Oxfeld, 1993, p. 254). Talking about St. Jamestown, a housing estate in east Toronto which was the destination of many Chinese Calcuttans, Mei Ling mentioned that those who lived there were generally 'looked down upon'. She explained that 'you start in St. Jamestown and then when you save enough money, you buy somewhere else'. Owning and having a home in Toronto revolves around familial relationships for the Chinese community. When asked whether it was common for the Calcutta Chinese community to live in St. Jamestown when they first moved to Toronto, Mei Ling answered:

> For the new immigrants . . . it means they have no relatives. For those who come through sponsorship by brother or sister or uncle, they move into the home and help pay the mortgage . . . that is very common.

Yet, as Mei Ling further explained, the issue of a house was a lot more than carrying over familial relationships, even extended ones, from Calcutta. It also opened up a divide within the community between those who can own a house and those who cannot. Talking about how, for those who are unable to speak English, the hold of the community continued, Mei Ling said:

> Some of them would really prefer to be in Calcutta . . . especially those who work in factories. Because if you look at some, they have these huge houses, these mega-houses in Markham and there are these people who live in government housing or in basement apartments. They are seeing the other side . . . because they are in factory jobs, it means they don't speak much English . . . they cannot break out of the community, so they have to stay within the community. They are in a disadvantaged position, so people look down upon them . . . that is why cars and houses are so important.

As Mei Ling shows, memories of home in the city and the city as home across diaspora intersect to create complex connections between home as a site of dwelling in the city, issues around ownership of home and spaces of difference within communities.

Returning Home

Return visits to the city and narratives around return also shape the idea of city as home. In recent times, restrictions imposed on the Chinese community in the aftermath of the 1962 Sino-Indian conflict have been relaxed, and some have opted to pay a visit back 'home' to China. While there is a wider identification with Chinese culture, going back home for the community has meant visiting the particular province and village/town of origin with existing family links. For the Calcutta Chinese community that has migrated to Toronto, returning home, however, means returning to Calcutta. During Chinese New Year, for example, a sizeable number come back to be with family, and to pay their respects at the tombs of ancestors. The notion of returning to one's 'roots' is also an emotional affair for many Anglo-Indians. For several people the return is a one-off visit, and involves visiting their old homes, neighbourhoods and familiar haunts (Blunt et al., 2012). However, returning home is not straightforward. Nostalgia and reality clash and often lead to disappointment. Return visits are journeys to re-capture the past, yet at the same time these visits also shatter memories. Belinda's comment captures this sentiment aptly:

> My feelings for Calcutta are nostalgic . . . it is actually very hard to separate the two. When I talk about back home, I am really talking about Calcutta . . . but when I went back, I couldn't find

my home in Calcutta, because things weren't the same . . . some ties are never severed, but the places I knew are all so different.

Many Anglo-Indian and Chinese Calcuttans, on their return to the city, expressed dismay at the way the city had developed. Many rued the loss and decline of places that they fondly remembered. In re-encountering memories of the city, Anglo-Indian and Chinese Calcuttans see the city through the past, but also set up a difference between their past lives in Calcutta and their lives today in London and Toronto. Emigration from Calcutta has also fractured the communities through class differences. While exceptions exist on both sides of the migration divide, a number of Anglo-Indians, for example, who remained in Calcutta, depend on charity of community associations and individuals in London and Toronto and elsewhere in the wider diaspora. Such disjunctures make return journeys a complex and layered process (Blunt et al., 2012).

CONCLUSIONS

Ideas of home and diaspora inform and are influenced by critical geographies of migration in significant ways. In this chapter, we have explored these connections through three broad contexts. First, we have outlined how the notion of homeland is often evoked in questions of home across diaspora. Noting that the nation usually defines a sense of homeland, we have analysed diasporic engagement with the homeland through politics, belonging and return. Second, we have explored practices of home-making and how it finds expression through built forms and domestic material culture. Finally, through the context of our own research on 'diaspora cities', we have argued that the city is an important space to interrogate and unpack ideas of both home and diaspora. Focusing on experiences of Anglo-Indian and Chinese communities from Calcutta and their diasporic lives in London and Toronto, we have explained that ideas of the city as home, home-making practices in diaspora and returning home are complicated through the intersections of urban space and community identity, and raise questions around fixed notions of ethnicity, culture and community. Our focus on a community of mixed descent (Anglo-Indian) and another with multiple migration journeys (Chinese) also highlights the multi-scalarity of home and diaspora and the connections between them.

REFERENCES

Abdelhady, D. (2008), 'Representing the homeland: Lebanese diasporic notions of home and return in a global context', *Cultural Dynamics*, **20**, 53–72.
Ahmed, S., Castañeda, C., Fortier, A.-M., and Sheller, M. (eds) (2003), *Uprootings/Regroundings: Questions of Home and Migration*, Oxford: Berg.
Al-Ali, N. and Koser, K. (eds) (2002), *New Approaches to Migration? Transnational Communities and the Transformation of Home*, London and New York: Routledge.
Baldassar, L. (2001), *Visits Home: Migration Experiences between Italy and Australia*, Melbourne: Melbourne University Press.
Baser, B. (2016), 'KOMKAR: the unheard voice in the Kurdish diaspora', in A. Christou and E. Mavroudi (eds), *Dismantling Diasporas: Rethinking the Geographies of Diasporic Identity, Connection and Development*, London: Routledge, pp.113–28.

Bear, L. (2007), *Lines of the Nation: Indian Railway Workers, Bureaucracy and the Intimate Historical Self*, New York: Columbia University Press.

Blunt, A. (2005), *Anglo-Indian Women and the Spatial Politics of Home*, Oxford: Blackwell.

Blunt, A. and Bonnerjee, J. (2013), 'Home, city and diaspora: Anglo-Indian and Chinese attachments to Calcutta', *Global Networks*, **13**, 220–40.

Blunt, A. and Dowling, R. (2006), *Home*, London: Routledge.

Blunt, A. and Sheringham, O. (2018), 'Home-city geographies: urban dwelling and mobility', *Progress in Human Geography*, available at https://doi.org/10.1177%2F0309132518786590 (accessed 13 November 2018).

Blunt, A., Bonnerjee, J., and Hysler-Rubin, N. (2012), 'Diasporic returns to the city: Anglo-Indian and Jewish visits to Calcutta', *South Asian Diaspora*, **4**, 25–43.

Boccagni, P. (2014), 'What's in a (migrant) house? Changing domestic spaces, the negotiation of belonging and home-making in Ecuadorian migration', *Housing, Theory and Society*, **31**, 277–93.

Boccagni, P. (2017), *Migration and the Search for Home: Mapping Domestic Space in Migrants' Everyday Lives*, New York: Palgrave Macmillan.

Boccagni, P. and Brighenti, A.M. (2017), 'Immigrants and home in the making: thresholds of domesticity, communality and publicness', *Journal of Housing and the Built Environment*, **32**, 1–11.

Bolognani, M. (2007), 'The myth of return: dismissal, survival or revival? A Bradford example of transnationalism as a political instrument', *Journal of Ethnic and Migration Studies*, **33**, 59–76.

Bolognani, M. (2016), 'From myth of return to return phantasy', *Identities*, **23**, 193–209.

Bonnerjee, J. (2012), 'Dias-*para*: neighbourhood, memory and the city', *South Asian Diaspora*, **4**, 5–23.

Bonnerjee, J., Blunt, A., McIlwaine, C., and Periera, C. (2012), 'Connected communities: diaspora and transnationality', available at http://geog.qmul.ac.uk/media/geography/images/staff/Connected-Communities--Diaspora-and-Transnationality.pdf (accessed 15 January 2018).

Brah, A. (1996), *Cartographies of Diaspora: Contesting Identities*, London: Routledge.

Brickell, K. and Datta, A. (2011), *Translocal Geographies: Space, Places and Connections*, London: Routledge.

Christou, A. and King, R. (2006), 'Migrants encounter migrants in the city: the changing context of "home" for second-generation Greek-American return migrants', *International Journal of Urban and Regional Research*, **30**, 816–35.

Clifford, J. (1997), *Routes: Travel and Translation in the Late Twentieth Century*, Cambridge, MA: Harvard University Press.

Conradson, D. and Latham, A. (eds) (2005), 'Transnational urbanism: everyday practices and mobilities', Special issue, *Journal of Ethnic and Migration Studies*, **31** (2), 227–413.

Dalokoglou, D. (2010), 'Migrating-remitting-"building"-dwelling: house-making as a "proxy" presence in postsocialist Albania', *Journal of the Royal Anthropological Institute*, **16**, 761–77.

Duval, D.T. (2005), 'Expressions of migrant mobilities among Caribbean migrants in Toronto, Canada', in R.B. Potter, D. Conway, and J. Phillips (eds), *The Experience of Return Migration: Caribbean Perspectives*, Aldershot: Ashgate, pp. 245–61.

Dwyer, C. (2002), '"Where are you from?" Young British Muslim women and the making of "home"', in A. Blunt and C. McEwan (eds), *Postcolonial Geographies*, London: Continuum, pp. 184–99.

Gal, A., Leoussi, A.S., and Smith, A.D. (2010), 'Introduction', in A. Gal, A.S. Leoussi, and A.D. Smith (eds), *The Call of the Homeland: Diaspora Nationalisms, Past and Present*, Leiden: Brill, pp. xv–xxv.

Ghosh, S. (2014), 'The production of vertical neighbourhoods: an analysis of Bangladeshi residential spaces in Toronto', *International Journal of Urban and Regional Research*, **30**, 2008–24.

Gilroy, P. (2000), *Between Camps*, London: Allen Lane.

Glick Schiller, N. and Çağlar, A. (2009), 'Towards a comparative theory of locality in migration studies: migrant incorporation and the city scale', *Journal of Ethnic and Migration Studies*, **35** (2), 177–202.

Hage, G. (1996), 'The spatial imaginary of national practices: dwelling-domesticating/being-exterminating', *Environment and Planning D: Society and Space*, **14**, 463–86.

Hodagneu-Sotelo, P. (2017), 'At home in inner-city immigrant community gardens', *Journal of Housing and the Built Environment*, **32**, 13–18.

Kalra, V., Kaur, R., and Hutnyk, J. (2005), *Diaspora and Hybridity*, London: Sage.

Kibria, N. (2002), 'Of blood, belonging and homeland trips: transnationalism and identity among second-generation Chinese and Korean Americans', in P. Levitt and M.C. Waters (eds), *The Changing Face of Home: The Transnational Lives of the Second Generation*, New York: Russell Sage Foundation, pp. 295–311.

Lahiri, S. (2010), 'At home in the city, at home in the world: cosmopolitanism and urban belonging in Kolkata', *Contemporary South Asia*, **18**, 191–204.

Lahiri, S. (2011), 'Remembering the city: translocality and the senses', *Social and Cultural Geography*, **12**, 855–69.

Law, L. (2001), 'Home cooking: Filipino women and geographies of the senses in Hong Kong', *Ecumene*, **8**, 264–83.

Levin, I. and Fincher, R. (2010), 'Tangible transnational links in the houses of Italian immigrants in Melbourne', *Global Networks*, **10**, 401–23.

Ley, D. (1995), 'Between Europe and Asia: the case of the missing sequoias', *Ecumene*, **2**, 185–210.

Liang, J. (2007), 'Migration patterns and occupational specialisations of the Kolkata Chinese: an insider's story', *China Report*, **43** (4), 397–410.

Long, J. (2013), 'Diasporic dwelling: the poetics of domestic space', *Gender, Place and Culture*, **20**, 329–45.

Mavroudi, E. (2010), 'Contesting identities, differences and a unified Palestinian community', *Environment and Planning D: Society and Space*, **28**, 239–53.

Mavroudi, E. and Christou, A. (2016), 'Introduction', in A. Christou and E. Mavroudi (eds), *Dismantling Diasporas: Rethinking the Geographies of Diasporic Identity, Connection and Development*, London: Routledge, pp. 1–14.

McConnell, F. (2016), 'Reconfiguring diaspora identities and homeland connections: the Tibetan "Lhakar" movement', in A. Christou and E. Mavroudi (eds), *Dismantling Diasporas: Rethinking the Geographies of Diasporic Identity, Connection and Development*, London: Routledge, pp. 99–112.

Mitchell, K. (2004), 'Conflicting landscapes of dwelling and democracy in Canada', in S. Cairns (ed.), *Drifting: Architecture and Migrancy*, London: Routledge, pp. 142–64.

Oswin, N. and Yeoh, B. (2010), 'Introduction: mobile city Singapore', *Mobilities*, **5** (2), 167–75.

Oxfeld, E. (1993), *Blood, Sweat and Mahjong – Family and Enterprise in an Overseas Chinese Community*, Ithaca, NY: Cornell University Press.

Potter, R.B. and Phillips, J. (2006), 'Both black and symbolically white: the "Bajan-Brit" return migrant as post-colonial hybrid', *Ethnic and Racial Studies*, **29**, 901–27.

Ralph, D. and Staeheli, L. (2011) 'Home and migration: mobilities, belongings and identities', *Geography Compass*, **5**, 517–30.

Robins, K. (2001), 'Becoming anybody: thinking against the nation and through the city', *City*, **5**, 77–90.

Salih, R. (2002), 'Shifting meanings of "home": consumption and identity in Moroccan women's transnational practices between Italy and Morocco', in N. Al-Ali and K. Koser (eds), *New Approaches to Migration? Transnational Communities and the Transformation of Home*, London: Routledge, pp. 51–67.

Smith, M.P. (2001), *Transnational Urbanism: Locating Globalisation*, Oxford: Blackwell.

Tolia-Kelly, D. (2004), 'Materializing post-colonial geographies: examining the textural landscapes of migration in the South Asian home', *Geoforum*, **35**, 675–88.

Tölölyan, K. (2010), 'Beyond the homeland: from exile nationalism to diasporic transnationalism', in A. Gal., A.S. Leoussi, and A.D. Smith (eds), *The Call of the Homeland: Diaspora Nationalisms, Past and Present*, Leiden: Brill, pp. 27–46.

Tsuda, T. (2009), 'Introduction: diasporic return and migration studies', in T. Tsuda (ed.), *Diasporic Homecomings: Ethnic Return Migration in Comparative Perspectives*, Stanford, CA: Stanford University Press, pp. 1–18.

Van der Horst, H. (2010), 'Dwellings in transnational lives: a biographical perspective on "Turkish-Dutch" houses in Turkey', *Journal of Ethnic and Migration Studies*, **36**, 1175–92.

Walter, B. (2000), *Outsiders Inside: Whiteness, Place and Irish Women*, London: Routledge.

Werbner, P. (2000), 'Introduction: the materiality of diaspora between aesthetic and "real" politics', *Diaspora*, **9**, 5–20.

Wolf, D. (2002), 'There's no place like "home": emotional transnationalism and the struggles of second-generation Filipinos', in P. Levitt and M.C. Waters (eds), *The Changing Face of Home: The Transnational Lives of the Second Generation*, New York: Russell Sage Foundation, pp. 255–94.

22. Revisiting diaspora as process: timespace, performative diasporas?
Elizabeth Mavroudi

INTRODUCTION

There are tensions between the roots and routes of diaspora, on the one hand stressing fluid, hybrid lives and identities 'on the move' whilst, on the other, the constant striving for connectedness with, and belonging to, the homeland (Clifford 1997; Mavroudi 2007a). These dynamic boundary (de)constructions (Brubaker 2005) can be empowering, but also problematic for those in diaspora and serve as a reminder that we need to pay attention to the potential challenges of living, feeling and belonging in diaspora through time and space.

Conceptualising diasporas as process rather than a static group or community tries to address such tensions, and accounts for these evolving, myriad and often difficult relationships across and within boundaries (Mavroudi 2007a, 2007b, 2008a, 2010). Being in diaspora often requires flexibility, creativity, adaptivity as notions of home and belonging can be more complex to articulate. Diasporic identities may be constructed in more essentialised, ethno-national, fixed ways for strategic, emotional reasons (Mavroudi 2007b). However, the reality of diasporic lives and identities is often in-between, hybrid and ambivalent. Diasporic identities, lives, spaces, times and connections with host country/homeland are complex, dynamic, grounded, gendered, historicised and contextualised. By viewing diaspora as an ongoing, active process, those in diaspora are imbued with agency; they are neither static beings blindly following primordial attachments and territorialisation nor untethered post-modern nomads, freely swaying in the winds of uncontrolled globalisation and cross-border connections. It is a way of unravelling, dissecting and following such complex cross-border connections, stressing the need to ask critical questions about the nature, intensity, reality and repercussions of such linkages without resorting to easy or simplistic assumptions. It also potentially allows for the recognition of the messiness and arbitrary, confusing, hard-to-explain or rationalise actions, feelings and experiences of those in diaspora.

This chapter builds upon these themes by focusing on two cross-cutting and inter-linking themes as a means of further fleshing out and engaging with the notion of diaspora as process: diasporas and timespace and linkages between diasporas, mobilities and non-representational theory or diasporas as performed and negotiated. In doing so, the chapter will also seek to highlight the important role that geographers can play in debating such issues, and in making theoretical contributions to conceptualising diaspora.

DEBATING THE MEANINGS OF DIASPORA

Despite the many uses of the word diaspora, there are arguably three main ways in which diasporas can be conceptualised (Brubaker 2005; Mavroudi 2007a). Firstly, diasporas can be seen in more 'static' ways, as defined, dispersed, and displaced communities or entities held together by common traditions, histories, ethnicities, nations and religions that centre around a homeland (Cohen 1997; Sheffer 1999); the Jewish diaspora is often perceived to be such an archetypal diaspora. Secondly, diasporas can be understood as imagined, constructed and fluid in the sense that diasporic lives and identities are perceived to be 'on the move', transgressing and moving beyond boundaries, borders and the nation-state, exemplified by ideas such as Yeoh and Huang's (2000, p. 415) 'diaspora as a journey' idea: 'not unidirectional, or even circular, but often ridden with disruptions, detours, and multi-destinations'. Therefore, on the one hand, traditional definitions of diaspora centre on the creation of boundaries (of identity, community and the nation-state); the focus is on roots and the homeland. On the other hand, postmodern conceptualisations of diaspora are based on ideas of fluidity, movement, routes and the destabilisation of (potentially) homogenising boundaries (of, for example, identity, community and the nation-state). Here, identities are seen as fluid, flexible, malleable, and as constantly 'in-the-making' (Hall 1999; Papastergiadis 2004). Those in diaspora may be involved in connections, flows and networks, creating hybrid, 'diasporic spaces' (Brah 1996) of potentially flexible citizens across national borders (Ong 1999), who hold plural identities negotiated differently through time and space (Dwyer 1999; Burdsey 2006; Kalra et al. 2006; Blunt 2007). This suggests that diasporas operate beyond nation-state borders, challenging the nation-state with post-national attachments and belonging (Soysal 1998). However, at the same time, diasporas are grounded in places, and nations and nation-states continue to influence those in diaspora (Wimmer and Glick Schiller 2002; Kalra et al. 2006).

Therefore, as Werbner (2002, p. 120) has noted: 'diasporas, it seems, are both ethnic-parochial and cosmopolitan'. This leads to the third way of conceptualising diasporas, which tries to incorporate the approaches above; it stresses the need to account for plural, dynamic, malleable diasporic identities and belonging. However, at the same time, it aims to ground such identities and lives and bring to the fore the potential realities of power struggles, strategic essentialisms, tensions and ambivalences of those in diaspora as they negotiate identity, politics and cross-border connections. It is this which diaspora as process attempts to do.

Scholars have addressed the tensions between these different approaches as a roots and routes debate (Gilroy 1993), and as the need to engage with boundedness and unboundedness or boundary erosion and creation (Brubaker 2005). Gilroy (1993), in his work on black populations on both sides of the Atlantic, used the 'Black Atlantic' as a single, complex unit of analysis and in doing so, rallied against ethnic absolutism and purity of cultures. He viewed cultural identities as based around continuity and rupture, sameness and difference; their 'double consciousness' meant that Black African slaves were seen as agents, as racialised, victimised, oppressed but also with elements of control and creativity. However, he also distanced himself from hybridity and purely celebratory accounts of diaspora routes and critiqued them for being potentially elitist. He therefore stressed the need to account for both the roots and routes of the Black Atlantic diaspora (Gilroy 1993). Similarly, Clifford's work (1997, p. 269) pays attention to the 'here' and 'there' of diaspora, highlighting that 'there is not necessarily a single place or an exclusivist nation'. Cultures and identities are therefore seen as mixed and plural and 'on the move', yet his approach is also based very much in grounded everyday lives and practices. The idea of roots and routes being important therefore helps to account for the ambivalence and potential tensions those in diaspora feel in relation to both.

More recently, but very much based on such ideas, diasporas have been conceptualised as incomplete and 'becoming' (Morawska 2011) and as a process (Houston and Wright 2003), potentially struggling to belong (Mavroudi 2010; Christou 2011; Hopkins et al. 2012) and be political (Yeh 2007; Mavroudi 2008a, 2008b; Demir 2015; McConnell 2015). Houston and Wright (2003, p. 219), for example, have written about the Tibetan diasporas, referring to the ways in which the diaspora is constantly in the making: '[this] elucidates the continual creation of composite Tibetan refugee identities and spaces'. Those in diaspora can feel torn between: spaces and networks centred on the homeland, loyalties to ethnic, national or religious group-based identities in the host country or homeland, on the one hand, and, on the other, personal negotiations of their own complex, individual identities and the messiness, difficulties and ambivalences of living and feeling between here and there.

Defining who does and does not belong to a diaspora has become a customary exercise, particularly in more traditional understandings which privilege ethno-national, religious and territorial connections amongst those in the diaspora and with the homeland. Yet, defining who belongs to a diaspora needs to take emotion into account (Mavroudi and Christou 2015) and to acknowledge that 'not all biographically-connected individuals wish to be part of a country's diaspora, whilst others may feel connected to more than one diasporic community' (Jöns et al. 2015, p. 125). We need to pay attention to such issues and the fact that flexible, inclusive, open-ended notions of diaspora are needed as those in diaspora grapple with issues such as identity, belonging, mobility, development and politics whilst being positioned and juxtaposed between here and there.

Diaspora as process is a notion which attempts to capture such ideas and issues. Rather than seek to close or box in, categorise, attribute characteristics to those in diaspora, the notion of process is more open and inclusive. It allows for those who may wish to stress certain group similarities and make comparisons and generalisations but it also always highlights the difficulties in doing so, and the importance of the idea that there is no one way to feel and be in diaspora. In other words, we need to pay attention to the emotional and embodied individuals who make up diasporas, as well as the ways in which they negotiate, work (or struggle) together, the ways they connect, and disconnect with each other and across borders, and the intricate, myriad, plural ways to be and belong.

Geographers stress the importance of recognising differences over time and space and the impacts that diaspora can have on the state and issues such as gender, class and power relations. Geographical analyses of diaspora also enable the exploration of the process of constructing 'sameness' or collective 'diasporic consciousness', as well as difference. As Werbner (2004, p. 896) succinctly notes:

> Diasporic communities create arenas for debate and celebration. As mobilised groups, they are cultural, economic, political and social formations in process ... This means that diasporas are culturally and politically reflexive and experimental; they encompass internal arguments of identity about who 'we' are and where we are going. Diasporas are full of division and dissent. At the same time they recognise collective responsibilities, not only to the home country but to co-ethnics in far-flung places.

Diaspora needs to be a broad, open-ended notion that is able to take into account, as Werbner notes, the cultural, economic, political and social 'formations in process'; such an approach which recognises the complexities and the disjointed potential merging of such factors is useful.

What arguably makes such negotiations more complex is time and space and the ways in which such identities, lives, feelings, perceptions and actions are constantly and actively performed and re-constituted in specific, but connected places. Although space, place and time often form part of discussions on diaspora, there is arguably a need for further conceptualisation and research which brings them to the fore even more, and in more innovative ways. Blunt (2005, p. 10) has argued: 'while geography is clearly central to understanding diaspora both in theory and practice, ideas about diaspora also raise questions about space and place'. This stresses the need to further explore the contribution that geographers have made, and can make, particularly in relation to notions of space, time and place. Carter (2005, pp. 55, 56) also points out that 'the diaspora literature has failed . . . to fully explore this transformation of space, beyond re-stating that diaspora consciousness opens up a rift between location and identity' and that, as a result, there has been an 'inadequate treatment' of territory and of politics. There is, therefore, ample work for geographers to do in this respect. However, they also have a role to play in examining the complex dynamics and tensions that arise as those in diaspora negotiate a juxtaposition of the here and there, past and present, colonial and postcolonial, which constitute messy times and spaces that would appear to defy simplistic categorisation and representation. It is for such reasons that it is arguably useful for geographers working on diaspora to engage with non-representational theory, and more specifically, the idea of performative timespace.

DIASPORA AS PROCESS IN PERFORMATIVE TIMESPACE

Early work on timespace in geography can be traced to Hägerstrand's (1970) time-geography diagrams which viewed the world, and of how individuals moved in places, in visual, embodied, connected but also ordered and constrained ways. As a philosophical approach it challenged geographers to think more critically about the relationships between space and time so that the two were inter-related but not completely collapsed. His 'space-time path' stressed that time continuously affects spatial movements and that people, and their desired 'projects' and activities are important processes within this even as they may be constrained (Hägerstrand 1982). Despite criticisms (see Lenntorp 1999), his work continues to have significance, primarily because of the way he deals with time and space as non-dualistic and connected (Thrift and Pred 1981; May and Thrift 2001). His work has been important in the writing of Alan Pred (1984), Nigel Thrift (1996) and Doreen Massey (2005), amongst others, and it has been used in feminist research (Kwan 1999) although Kwan also stressed the importance of using rich ethnographic data as well as the GIS-based approach used in the paper. More recently, Carling (2017) has used migration history charts to visually present the trajectories of interviewees and their family members and which are based on detailed qualitative data. Like Carling, whose work focuses on transnational migration, many contemporary uses of timespace in geography have moved beyond Hägerstrand's understanding of space as finite, and absolute.

Lenntorp (1999) stressed how time-geography continues to have salience in, and can strengthen geographical analyses and beyond, and in relation to different themes and issues but primarily in theory-building, which is what this chapter attempts to do. Schwanen and Kwan (2012) have also argued that the ways in which the geographies of difference and inequality are played out have not been adequately theorised from a spatio-temporal perspective. This means that the geographies of marginalisation and exclusion still require more research and analysis in relation to time and space. It also serves as a reminder that the critical geographies of migration and diaspora need to explore and unravel the complex ways migrants and those in diaspora might be marginalised, excluded and disempowered through conjunctions and juxtapositions of time *and* space and as a result of intersections of race, class, gender and so forth. Viewing migration and diaspora through the lens of timespace can help in this respect. However, Merriman (2012) sounds a word of caution in how timespace has been used in foundational and a priori ways in geography, particularly by scholars such as Thrift and Massey. In other words, he suggests that time and space have themselves become used in primordial, normative ways and this closes off the possibility of examining space and time separately as well as together.

As a potential way forward, Page et al. (2017) ask how the exploration and recognition of the differences between space and time can become a practical project, whilst at the same time acknowledging that time and space cannot be treated separately. They argue that language could be used as a helpful metaphor whereby time and space are seen as different languages, which exist and make sense separately, but can also be viewed together, relationally, through a process of partial translation where there are similarities and differences. Such an approach echoes other work in transnational migration and diaspora studies which stresses the provisional nature of diaspora as process, and the ways in which time, space and place are used and negotiated by those in diaspora (Mavroudi 2007b) in what Nagel (2002) called the politics of 'sameness' and 'difference'. By explicitly utilising a timespace approach, migration and diaspora scholars may usefully pay attention to space and time in more critical, innovative, untethered ways but without throwing away time and space as separate concepts and realities. In doing so, there is a commitment to seeing diaspora as 'becoming', on the move, enabled but also as potentially constrained through timespace. If, in turn, we see diaspora as an active process, in which doing, feeling, experiencing and performing occurs in particular places, times and spaces but in open-ended, flexible, non-static ways, we can then start to discuss the potential relevance of performative timespace (Mavroudi 2017).

The notion of timespace stresses that what we see and perceive is not isolated or separate but takes place in motion, in everyday time, and thus connectedness is paramount (Mavroudi 2017). As a result, we are constantly sensing and experiencing in and through timespace, not separately from it: it forms part of our everyday lives in tangible and intangible ways (Crang 2001, p. 196). However, in timespace, space and time can become potentially disrupted and juxtaposed, rendering experience a sensory, embodied one which is both in tune but also out of sync with one's daily life, rhythms, memories, emotions and past experiences and knowledges and so forth. For scholars exploring the lives and identities of those in diaspora, such an approach may offer useful insights into the complex ways feelings of displacement, exile, rupture, disconnectedness and difference jar and jostle with belonging, connectedness and shared consciousness. In addition, it provides a way to help make sense of such experiences and feelings in a more holistic manner, linking material and immaterial worlds, in order to examine them in and through timespace. This might then enable the opening up and partial revealing of different, unseen, unknown and hidden aspects of such lives and identities 'on the move'. In a timespace approach, times and spaces are slippery, both merging and separate, connected and disconnected as those in diaspora are constrained and enabled by their grounded, embodied, historicised, gendered materialities and emotionalities. This is a performative way of viewing the world, one which refuses to be pigeon-holed by concrete representations: it is non-representational in that the active 'doing' and experiencing is constant, elusive and uncontainable by conventional representations. The concern is very much with the 'doing' in everyday life, the actual practices that constitute continuous moments of performance (Lorimer 2007, p. 96).

Geographers engaging with the notion of performance stress the need to see everyday life as a series of continuous actions and practices that are materialised, unique, connected and unquantifiable in the sense that they are moments in timespace that are elusive yet practiced and experienced in particular ways. Representations are seen as limiting because they attempt to state and describe and, as a result, close off alternative and creative understandings and experiences of space, place and time (Thrift and Dewsbury 2000). Therefore, performance and non-representation are seen as ongoing processes which are difficult to pin down, but which form part of daily life (Thrift 2008). As Nash (2000, p. 657) points out: 'the value of ideas of performance and practice is their challenge to forms of interpretation which focus on the representation of meaning in visual or literary texts or use textual analysis to understand the world'.

However, as Tolia-Kelly (2006, p. 213) stresses, we need to be aware of what is 'occluded in the writing on affect' and that bodies are subject to power relations and geometrics that make it difficult for people to act. She, like Nash (2000), has warned against non-representational writing that is ahistorical, universalistic and ethnocentric. Jones (2011) has also pointed out that it ignores the past, and memories, focusing too much on the present and the 'doing'. Such critiques rightly highlight the need to consider that the processes of power and control within different spaces, times and scales are important as struggles occur over representation, negotiation and performance of difference. Such power relations and historical, gendered, classed, racialised contexts and positionalities need to be addressed in the geographies of diaspora. Therefore, non-representational theory has been found to be apolitical and lacking, with its focus on practice and the near obsession of methods which celebrate the mobile, the rhythmic and the performative as opposed to a grounded politics of place:

> We acknowledge the validity of NRT [non-representational theory] as a philosophical intervention but deplore its increasing use as method in empirical research. In the work of many (but not all) proponents of NRT we see not an opening of the entrenched battle lines of what constitutes the political but rather, through the elision of geographical methods which elicit social interrelations and historical patterns, an inversion of politics – the extension of a mode of thought that we believe to be profoundly depoliticizing. (Mitchell and Elwood 2012, p. 789)

Such critique reminds us of the importance of both research methods and analysis which pay attention to the ways in which people might be, and are, political, and the limitations to potential empowerment and political action. For diaspora studies, which itself has been critiqued for not focusing enough on the political (Carter 2005) and linked to this, the national (Dirlik 2006) as well as the historical (Dirlik 2002), there is a need for conceptualisations which are inclusive enough to both gather a wide range of experiences, identities and practices. However, they also need to be powerful and robust enough to stand up to theoretical scrutiny rather than become fixated on matters such as definitions of diaspora, the description and analysis of diasporic identities, lives, politics, cultures and practices as either ethno-national or hybrid-plural, or as performative or representational.

Borrowing ideas from performative, non-representational theory, and using the notion of timespace allows research on the geographies of diaspora to go further, and to push the limits of our analysis and conceptualisation. To do this, there is scope for exploring how and why people represent *and* perform and how they may be limited and empowered by both. As Laurier and Philo (2006, p. 355) point out, we can engage with representation as well as performance; in other words, despite the criticism representation has received, it is still possible to 'accept representation as one of many possible expressive practices, one correlate of which is greatly to expand our understanding of the terrain of representation *beyond* the word, spoken, or written'. Researching representations still remains important, in order to come to terms with how constructions of identity, for example, are created and maintained in potentially static and singular ways. One could further argue that the politics of representation has the potential to liberate peoples who choose to represent themselves in certain (potentially essentialised) and unified ways to get messages across.

By viewing diasporic lives, bodies, feelings and experiences as performative, one can arguably deconstruct representations more readily, as embodiments, emotions and acts that are fluid, yet also contextualised within a changing environment. Diaspora as process can therefore be conceptualised as a notion which allows for the analysis of active, performative, mobile timespace materialities and dynamic practices and the ways in which migrants and those in diaspora might use representations in more static or strategic ways for specific reasons. According to non-representational theory, authenticity itself is problematic, but also redundant. There may continue to be claims to authenticity and truth by those in diaspora but one could argue that these form part of the endless performances of everyday life, in which people feel that politicisation and the state may dictate a need for 'authentic' practices, places and representations. Place, although continuously claimed, sought for, memorialised and so forth, needs to be seen as one part of performance and is incorporated into timespace. If identities are to be seen as in-the-making, we need to critique attempts to define them and be open to attempts that allow flexible and open-ended identities that are positioned and grounded. In this way, place continues to be important, but it is not static anymore because it is dependent on, and forms part of, connections and mobilities. It is not inert and passive, but is part of life-worlds, timespace and performances.

Mobility, and being 'on the move' conjures up dynamic temporality, and the focus in performative research and non-representational theory is often on movement: 'however, a research agenda addressing such mobilities need not embrace them as a supposed form of freedom or liberation from space and place' (Sheller and Urry 2006, p. 210). Indeed, the notion of timespace incorporates and necessitates mobility. The world is one which is seemingly in motion and our perceptions, bodies and consciousness are too, even as they are constantly connected to but also jolting against and juxtaposed with other times and spaces in messy ways. In doing so, at particular moments, time and space are fractured or disrupted as a result of what we see, perceive and experience. Through such performance, which is linked to the everyday, what those in diaspora experience becomes part of their everyday lives, bodies, emotions, pasts and presents, reminiscent of 'the serenity of the Greek kairos: what we might call the temporal opportunities of everyday life' (Maffesoli 1998, p. 268). Here, the notion of 'kairos' conjures up ever-changing weather, the constant process of weathering in the landscape, as well as being in and part of time and space, and located in place, with particular, but also dynamic, patterns and rhythms.

Non-representational theory and a focus on mobilities may, methodologically, have profound limitations because of the focus on temporality and the moment, rather than on representation and the outcomes of such representational processes. However, as Cresswell (2010) outlines, in relation to mobilities, examining movement does not have to come at the expense of history, immobility, politics or representation. In addition, the use of non-representational theory as a way to think more critically about timespace for those in diaspora might arguably be welcome, not as a means to ignore context, or the materialities of factors such as race, gender, history, place or politics, or to ignore the communal at the expense of the individual. Rather, in its treatment and elevation of timespace, it allows us the potential to think more creatively and expansively about the ways in which those in diaspora engage with their identities and lives in and through timespace in more complex ways. By honing in on being and becoming, on the now, on the present, it allows us to think through the intimate connections between time, space and place and stresses the realities of how people actually live and feel in mobile, dynamic ways. People's lives and identities are not suspended in time and space vacuums, with each neatly separated out for us to examine as scholars. We need ways of researching lives, identities, feelings and embodied practices which are more in tune with the complexities of lives on the move, in multiple places, across borders, times and spaces. It is, perhaps, an extension of Massey's relational and political sense of place: 'it is in the terms of engagement among these intersecting trajectories that lie the politics, the productivity, the questions, the expectations, the potential for surprise' (Massey 2003, p. 118).

CONCLUDING THOUGHTS: DIASPORAS AS PROCESS IN-BETWEEN REPRESENTATION AND PERFORMANCE?

Rather than unbridled adherence to non-representational theory, the linking of diaspora with timespace allows us to potentially take some of the more positive aspects of non-representational theory – the focus on the temporal, embodied and the performative – with the groundedness and connectedness of timespace imagined in more holistic ways: that timespace is not just a celebration of the here and now and all that encompasses, but also stretches to include other times and spaces. It is an inclusive notion, one which incorporates what is present, but can also account for what is missing, what is occluded, and the power relations which cross-cut and may be hidden. Because it pays attention to both time and space simultaneously, it also opens up deeper articulations of place and what it means to be and feel and inhabit that place as a specific, gendered, racialised, embodied individual, who experiences timespace on their own but also in relation to others. In doing so, different, creative ways to be political and to make connections through timespace such as through social media, in and across generations may be found.

For diaspora, it potentially enables a more critical and nuanced exploration of the (dis)connections between people and place, locating their grounded lives, identities, feelings and practices in and through timespace, in active, dynamic ways. Through such diaspora as process, it may then be possible to examine both the politics of representation, of struggle, of identity, as well as the fluid ways those in diaspora might be political as they perform and negotiate and practice their lives and identities in embodied and emotional ways. As such, viewing their lives through a timespace non-representational lens does not mean their politics, or ways to be political within and across borders are ignored or negated. It is precisely as a result of the focus on active, dynamic, intimate, intricate timespace juxtapositions of here, there, past, future, them, us, within individual, but also shared diasporic lives that may allow us to discover surprising new ways to be and feel in diaspora. This, in turn, also means that we might need to borrow some of the research methods used by non-representational theorists and by those focusing on mobilities, in order to try and further make sense of the complex, and border and boundary crossing mobilities (and stasis) in diasporic lives and identities. This is not a substitute for the already excellent research on diasporas which use more traditional research methods. Rather, it is a call for geographers (and non-geographers) to be open to innovative or different methods (using and analysing, for example, social media, new forms of mapping and GIS, visual and virtual analysis, participatory action research, mobile ethnographies, timespace diaries and so forth) when it comes to analysing diaspora (im)mobilities in this age of globalisation and technological connection. As Sheller and Urry (2006, p. 222) aptly note in relation to what they call the new mobilities paradigm but which is also relevant for diaspora studies:

> New mobilities are bringing into being new surprising combinations of presence and absence as the new century chaotically unfolds. Methods and theories will need to be ever on the move to keep up with these new forms of mobilities, new systems of scheduling and monitoring, and new pervasive modes of mobilised social inclusion/exclusion.

In addition, it is also a plea for geographers to engage more deeply with the complex ways in which those in diaspora live, feel and operate in mobile timespace, by focusing on the everyday, on how the here and the now connects with there, and the past in simultaneous, potentially political ways. In doing so, it recognises the constraining structures and enabling opportunities faced by those in diaspora by situating, placing and tracing individuals, with their own power assemblages, within multiple contexts, networks and timespaces.

REFERENCES

Blunt, A. (2005), *Domicile and Diaspora: Anglo-Indian Women and the Spatial Politics of Home*, Oxford: Blackwell.

Blunt, A. (2007), 'Cultural geographies of migration: mobility, transnationality and diaspora', *Progress in Human Geography* **31**, 684–94.

Brah, A. (1996), *Cartographies of Diaspora*, London: Routledge.

Brubaker, R. (2005), 'The "diaspora" diaspora', *Ethnic and Racial Studies* **28** (1), 1–19.

Burdsey, D. (2006), '"If I ever play football, Dad, can I play for England or India?" British Asians, sport and diasporic national identities', *Sociology* **40**, 11–28.

Carling, J. (2017), 'On conjunctures in transnational lives: linear time, relative mobility and individual experience', in E. Mavroudi, B. Page and A. Christou (eds), *Timespace and International Migration*, Cheltenham, UK and Northampton, MA, USA: Edward Elgar.

Carter, S. (2005), 'The geopolitics of diaspora', *Area* **37** (1), 54–63.

Christou, A. (2011), 'Narrating lives in (e)motion: embodiment, belongingness and displacement in diasporic spaces of home and return', *Emotion, Space and Society* **4**, 249–57.

Clifford, J. (1997), *Routes: Travel and Translation in the Late Twentieth Century*, Cambridge, MA: Harvard University Press.

Cohen, R. (1997), *Global Diasporas*, London: UCL Press.

Crang, M. (2001), 'Rhythms of the city: temporalised space and motion', in Jon May and Nigel Thrift (eds), *Timespace: Geographies of Temporality*, London: Routledge, pp. 187–207.

Cresswell, T. (2010), 'Towards a politics of mobility', *Environment and Planning D: Society and Space* **28**, 17–31.

Demir, I. (2015), 'Battlespace diaspora: how the Kurds of Turkey revive, contruct and translate the Kurdish struggle in London', in A. Christou and E. Mavroudi (eds), *Dismantling Diasporas: Rethinking the Geographies of Diasporic Identity, Connection and Development*, Farnham: Ashgate, pp. 71–85.

Dirlik, A. (2002), 'Literature/identity: transnationalism, narrative and representation', *Review of Education, Pedagogy, and Cultural Studies* **24** (3), 209–34.

Dirlik, A. (2006), 'Intimate others: [private] nations and diaspora in an age of globalisation', *Inter-Asia Cultural Studies* **5**, 491–502.

Dwyer, C. (1999), 'Contradictions of community: questions of identity for young British Muslim women', *Environment and Planning A* **31**, 53–68.

Gilroy, P. (1993), *The Black Atlantic: Modernity and Double Consciousness*, London: Routledge.

Hägerstrand, T. (1970), 'What about people in regional science?', *Papers in Regional Science* **24** (1), 7–24.

Hägerstrand, T. (1982), 'Diorama, path and project', *Tijdschrift Voor Economische En Sociale Geografie* **73** (6), 323–39.

Hall, S. (1999), 'Cultural identity and diaspora', in Steven Vertovec and Robin Cohen (eds), *Migration, Diasporas and Transnationalism*, Cheltenham, UK and Northampton, MA, USA: Edward Elgar, pp. 299–314.

Hopkins, P., Kwan, M. and Aitchison, C. (2012), *Geographies of Muslim Identities: Diaspora, Gender and Belonging*, Farnham, Ashgate.

Houston, S. and Wright, R. (2003), 'Making and remaking Tibetan diasporic identities', *Social and Cultural Geography* **4** (2), 217–32.

Jones, O. (2011), 'Geography, memory and non-representational geographies', *Geography Compass* **5**, 875–85.

Jöns, H., Mavroudi, E. and Heffernan, M. (2015), 'Mobilising the elective diaspora: German-American academic exchanges in the postwar period', *Transactions of the Institute of British Geographers* **40**, 113–27.

Kalra, V.S., Kaur, R. and Hutnyk, J. (2006), *Diaspora and Hybridity*, London: Sage.

Kwan, M. (1999), 'Gender and individual access to urban opportunities: a study using space-time measures', *Professional Geographer* **51** (2), 210–27.

Laurier, E. and Philo, C. (2006), 'Possible geographies: a passing encounter in a café', *Area* **38** (4), 353–63.

Lenntorp, B. (1999), 'Time-geography: at the end of its beginning', *GeoJournal* **48**, 155–8.

Lorimer, H. (2007), 'Cultural geography: worldly shapes, differently arranged', *Progress in Human Geography* **31** (1), 89–100.

McConnell, F. (2015), 'Reconfiguring diaspora identities and homeland connections: the Tibetan "Lhakar" Movement', in A. Christou and E. Mavroudi (eds), *Dismantling Diasporas: Rethinking the Geographies of Diasporic Identity, Connection and Development*, Farnham: Ashgate, pp. 99–113.

Maffesoli, M. (1998), 'Presentism – or the value of the cycle', *Cultural Values* **2** (2–3), 261–9.

Massey, D. (2003), 'Some times of space', in Susan May (ed.), *Olafur Eliasson – The Weather Project, Exhibition Catalogue*, London: Tate Publishing, pp. 107–18.

Massey, D. (2005), *For Space*, London: Sage.

Mavroudi, E. (2007a), 'Diaspora as process: (de)constructing boundaries', *Geography Compass* **1**, 467–79.

Mavroudi, E. (2007b), 'Learning to be Palestinian in Athens: constructing diasporic national identities', *Global Networks* **7**, 392–412.

Mavroudi, E. (2008a), 'Palestinians and pragmatic citizenship: negotiating relationships between citizenship and national identity in diaspora', *Geoforum* **39**, 307–18.

Mavroudi, E. (2008b), 'Palestinians in diaspora, empowerment and informal political space', *Political Geography* **27**, 57–73.

Mavroudi, E. (2010), 'Contesting identities, differences and a unified Palestinian community', *Environment and Planning D: Society and Space* **28**, 239–53.

Mavroudi, E. (2017), 'The timespace of identity and belonging: female migrants in Greece', in E. Mavroudi, B. Page and A. Christou (eds), *Timespace and International Migration*, Cheltenham, UK and Northampton, MA, USA: Edward Elgar, pp. 119–32.

Mavroudi, E. and A. Christou (2015), 'Introduction', in A. Christou and E. Mavroudi (eds), *Dismantling Diasporas: Rethinking the Geographies of Diasporic Identity, Connection and Development*, Farnham: Ashgate, pp. 1–15.

May, J. and Thift, N. (eds) (2001), *TimeSpace: Geographies of Temporality*, London and New York: Routledge.

Merriman, P. (2012), 'Human geography without time-space', *Transactions of the Institute of British Geographers* **37**, 13–27.

Mitchell, K. and Elwood, S. (2012), 'Mapping children's politics: the promise of articulation and the limits of nonrepresentational theory', *Environment and Planning D: Society and Space* **30**, 788–804.

Morawska, E. (2011), '"Diaspora" diasporas' representations of their homelands: exploring the polymorphs', *Ethnic and Racial Studies* **34** (6), 1029–48.

Nagel, C. (2002), 'Constructing difference and sameness: the politics of assimilation in London's Arab communities', *Ethnic and Racial Studies* **26** (2), 258–87.

Nash, C. (2000), 'Performativity in practice: some recent work in cultural geography', *Progress in Human Geography* **24** (4), 653–64.

Ong, A. (1999), *Flexible Citizenship: The Cultural Logics of Transnationality*, London and Durham, NC: Duke University Press.

Page, B., Christou, A. and Mavroudi, E. (2017), 'Introduction: from time to timespace and forward to time again in migration studies', in E. Mavroudi, B. Page and A. Christou (eds), *Timespace and International Migration*, Cheltenham, UK and Northampton, MA, USA: Edward Elgar, pp. 1–17.

Papastergiadis, N. (2004), *The Turbulence of Migration*, London: Polity Press.

Pred, A. (1984), 'Place as historically contingent process: structuration and the time-geography of becoming places', *Annals of the Association of American Geographers* **74** (2), 279–97.

Schwanen, T. and Kwan, M. (2012), 'Critical space–time geographies', *Environment and Planning A* **44**, 2043–8.

Sheffer, G. (1999), 'The emergence of new ethno-national diasporas', in Steven Vertovec and Robin Cohen (eds), *Migration, Diasporas and Transnationalism*, Cheltenham, UK and Northampton, MA, USA: Edward Elgar, pp. 396–419.

Sheller, M. and Urry, J. (2006), 'The new mobilities paradigm', *Environment and Planning A* **38**, 207–26.

Soysal, Y. (1998), 'Towards a postnational model of membership', in G. Shafir (ed.), *The Citizenship Debates: A Reader*, Minneapolis, MN: University of Minnesota Press, pp. 189–221.

Thrift, N. (1996), *Spatial Formations*, London: Sage.

Thrift, N. (2008), *Non-representational Theory: Space, Politics, Affect*, Abingdon: Routledge.

Thrift, N. and Dewsbury, J.D. (2000), 'Dead geographies and how to make them live', *Environment and Planning D: Society and Space* **18**, 411–32.

Thrift, N. and Pred, A. (1981), 'Time-geography: a new beginning', *Progress in Human Geography* **5**, 277–86.

Tolia-Kelly, D. (2006), 'Affect – an ethnocentric encounter? Exploring the "universalistic" imperative of emotional/affective geographies', *Area* **28**, 213–17.

Werbner, P. (2002), 'The place which is diaspora: citizenship, religion and gender in the making of chaordic transnationalism', *Journal of Ethnic and Migration Studies* **28** (1), 119–33.

Werbner, P. (2004), 'Theorising complex diasporas: purity and hybridity in the South Asian public sphere in Britain', *Journal of Ethnic and Migration Studies* **30** (5), 895–911.

Wimmer, A. and Glick Schiller, N. (2002), 'Methodological nationalism and beyond: nation-state building, migration and the social sciences', *Global Networks* **2** (4), 301–34.

Yeh, E.T. (2007), 'Exile meets homeland: politics, performance, and authenticity in the Tibetan diaspora', *Environment and Planning D: Society and Space* **25**, 648–67.

Yeoh, B. and Huang, S. (2000), 'Home and away: foreign domestic workers and negotiations of diasporic identity in Singapore', *Women's Studies', International Forum* **23** (4), 413–29.

23. Diasporas and development
Margaret Walton-Roberts, Jonathan Crush and Abel Chikanda

INTRODUCTION

Population mobility is a major international policy issue in the twenty-first century (Castles and Miller 2009; UNDP 2009). The United Nations Department of Economic and Social Affairs (UNDESA 2016) estimates that over 244 million people are international migrants. The emergent literature on international migration has heralded a new agent in the migration-development nexus: migrant diasporas (Faist and Fauser 2011). Diasporas consist of international migrant communities who create networks and connections with the home country and other parts of the world and are increasingly seen as key development resources for the Global South (Bakewell 2009; Chikanda et al. 2016; Cohen 1997). International migration and diaspora formation are important global processes, but they have not been subjected to an international regime framework to the same degree as practices such as trade, financial exchange, human rights, security and the internet. In this chapter we chart how diasporas are increasingly viewed as development resources, and suggest some key issues researchers should critically examine in their analysis of this reality.

VIEWING DIASPORAS AS DEVELOPMENT AGENTS

During the last decade there has been a lively policy debate promoting migration as a vital part of development for the Global South and North (Iskander 2010; Kuznetsov 2006). Diaspora-based remittances have surged in recent years, becoming as large as foreign direct investment (FDI) and outpacing overseas development assistance (ODA) and portfolio investment (Ratha and Mohapatra 2009; World Bank 2013). In 2016, remittances sent to the Global South were estimated at US$429 billion, nearly three times the size of ODA flows to developing countries (Ratha et al. 2017). In the early 2000s the range of voices engaged in promoting diasporas as a development agent expanded to include a wide array of multilateral, state and non-state actors (Pellerin and Mullings 2013; Simmons 2008). Sending states also focused on formal representations for, and inclusion of, their diasporic populations in national development agendas (Kapur 2010; Orozco and Lapointe 2004; Sidel 2007).

Today, migrant mobility is a core feature of globalization, but public and political responses to this mobility are varied (Hatton 2014). Despite the variable perception of immigration, initiatives to engage with diasporas for development purposes are at the centre of emerging global migration governance frameworks (Gamlen 2008, 2014a), making diasporas and their perceived development role particularly important to assess. Migration-development debates are actively promoted in forums such as the

Global Forum for Migration and Development (GFMD), which has repeatedly raised the question of diaspora contributions and promoted the inclusion of migration in the post-2015 development agenda (Omelaniuk 2012, 2016). Alongside this policy embrace of diasporas as development agents there has been a significant critical scholarly debate about the role diasporas can and should play in development (Chikanda et al. 2016; de Haas 2010). However, little attention has been paid to the socio-spatial dimensions of diaspora engagement in development and the need to view the phenomenon through a critical geography lens.

Diasporas are constructed in official discourses in ways that deny certain socio-spatial realities about contemporary human mobility. For example, the inter-governmental Africa Union (AU) has designated the African diaspora as the 'sixth region' of Africa (Ogom 2009), but the AU definition excludes those who have moved to other countries in the Global South, and disregards the important contribution to development made by South-South diasporas (Chikanda and Crush 2014; Crush 2011). Global North governments are encouraging diaspora engagement with the South; the United States Agency for International Development's (USAID) Global Diaspora Alliance and the Global Diaspora Forum are prime examples of such initiatives, but these are mostly to promote trade and investment to the benefit of the Global North. Many governments in the Global South are also reaching out to their diasporas (de Haas 2006; Hugo 2006; Mercer et al. 2008; Nurse 2006), leading the International Organization for Migration (IOM) and the Migration Policy Institute to launch the first 'diaspora engagement toolkit' for governments and other stakeholders (Agunias and Newland 2012). Notwithstanding the role of diasporas as being so important in terms of new approaches to the development and migration agenda, there has been relatively little interest in the socio-spatial complexities that now accompany global migration. In this chapter we bring this contemporary reality of human mobility to light by emphasizing how the locus of diaspora research must increasingly shift to a focus on diasporas in the Global South as a corrective to the dominance of North-based diaspora studies evident in the literature (Bakewell 2009; Crush 2011).

Despite these agendas to create state to diaspora connections, their development potential may sometimes be invisible to states, and in many cases the private sector plays a more important role in engagement (Leclerc and Meyer 2007). Diasporic philanthropy likewise increases individual and civil society participation in development (Belay 2013). Even supranational organizations appear more organized in their diasporic engagement than states, as evidenced in the Joint Migration and Development Initiative (JMDI) and the World Bank's 'Knowledge for Development' Program (Kuznetsov 2006). Despite this range of formal diaspora-development initiatives there are several challenges and cautions associated with the growing policy interest in the development role of diasporas (Gamlen 2014b), especially the potential for diaspora-led development activity to reproduce entrenched systems of social and spatial inequality (Mullings 2012; Walton-Roberts 2004), and the potential for new forms of neoliberal governance to download state responsibilities to migrant groups (Pellerin and Mullings 2013; Raghuram 2009).

In this chapter, we offer three broad critical geography approaches to the idea of diasporas as development agents: *policy, place* and *people*. In each of these we elaborate the social-spatial complexities that need to be highlighted by further identifying four cross-cutting factors related to the development role of diasporas.

POLICY: TRANSFERS, GOVERNANCE AND DISCOURSE

The rapidity with which the 'business case' for diaspora-induced development has circulated through multilateral forums suggests we can view this process as a transnational 'fast-policy' regime:

> Policy flows have themselves been (neo)liberalized, as emergent patterns of reform are ever more closely reflecting, while at the same time remaking, the inherited pattern and priorities of multi-jurisdictional experimentation. In this context, processes of policy norm formation are assuming radically dispersed and nonlinear characteristics, as proto-orthodoxies are propelled, often by the preemptive conclusions of evaluation science, between sites of simultaneous reinvention. New modalities of transnational social policy programming are effectively being 'co-formed' in locations across the Global North and South. (Peck and Theodore 2010, p. 207)

These hegemonic forms of policy model creep from one national context to the other via multilateral agencies such as the World Bank and UN agencies (de Haas 2006; Pellerin and Mullings 2013). Under this new post-Washington Consensus model, diaspora engagement (more specifically highly skilled migrant engagement and the remittances they send) is seen as a key development strategy for Global South nations (Kuznetsov 2006; Pellerin and Mullings 2013).

Unlike other cross-boundary issues such as finance, trade and the environment, global migration is more clearly manifested at the state-to-state level, rather than with effective global agreement (Betts 2011; Gamlen 2013; Koser 2010; Newland 2010). Yet in order to understand the current enthusiasm for the idea of diaspora-led development, we must understand that state diaspora engagement policy is emerging in a landscape of global policy transfer and peer to peer learning, which Gamlen (2014a) terms 'diaspora governance'. Pécoud (2015) has also examined international organizations' interest in migration and development and sees it as evidence of an 'international migration narrative', where 'solutions' are presented to 'problems' of migration without acknowledging the political contexts that frame these issues. That political context is the singular obsession with the state as the preeminent scale of migration research, and this needs to be countered by considering how these emerging 'global' migration governance frameworks relate to diaspora populations and their activities. An appropriate research framework on this cross-cutting issue is a comparative analysis of how 'diaspora governance' (Gamlen 2014a) or 'international migration narratives' (Pécoud 2015) percolate across national systems and the intended and unintended consequences they have on development agendas and community development elsewhere. Few existing studies examine diaspora-development and governance issues from such a cross-national and international perspective (Gamlen 2014a).

When the assumption of diasporic homogeneity is present it can facilitate policy agendas that maximize the 'payoff' from migration through well-worn agendas of entrepreneurialism and philanthropy. These individualistic policy solutions overshadow serious policy debate regarding the facilitation of migration and the protection of migrant rights globally. Caution regarding the assumption of diasporic homogeneity is evident in the work of geographers, who clearly highlight spatial and social differences and distinctions and the ways in which these inform how migrants position themselves in relation to state development trajectories in the sending nation (Chikanda et al. 2016; Mullings

2012; Raghuram 2009; Walton-Roberts 2014). For example, Pellerin and Mullings (2013), focusing on the World Bank's Africa Diaspora Program, caution researchers to critically assess the assumptions embedded in such strategies, arguing that the idea of migrants' shouldering the burden of economic and social transformation is imbued with neoliberal thinking. Such concerns are also evident in the policy focus on volunteerism and entrepreneurship highlighted in many diaspora and development initiatives. For example, the US State Department and the USAID-led IdEA (International diaspora Engagement Alliance) project cites five themes: entrepreneurship, innovation, volunteerism, philanthropy and diplomacy. This suggests a form of individualized activism rather than state responsibility for development, be it in the migrant sending or the receiving state.

There are increasing numbers of studies at the national scale – ranging from Afghanistan (Kuschminder 2014) to Zimbabwe (McGregor 2014; McGregor and Pasura 2010) – highlighting and questioning how diaspora strategies and subjectivities are being put to work on multiple agendas of development, innovation, diplomacy, training and governance. The hegemonic tendency of these framings is also being critically assessed across various transnational, comparative contexts in the Global North (Larner 2007) and South (Pellerin and Mullings 2013). But these policy ideas have still become embedded in the toolbox of economic development and international political leverage that states can exploit. Such growing policy orthodoxy is clearly a warning for critical scholars, and raises a number of issues that demand more attention.

PLACE

Sovereign state engagement with diaspora groups challenges geopolitical thinking that is based on a binary between the territorially bounded nation state and globally dispersed diaspora communities (Sidel 2007; Walton-Roberts 2004). As Lavie and Swedenburg (1996, p. 14) argue:

> The phenomena of diasporas calls for re-imagining the 'areas' of area studies and developing units of analysis that enable us to understand the dynamics of transnational cultural and economic processes, as well as to challenge the conceptual limits imposed by national and ethnic/racial boundaries.

Gamlen (2008) suggests that several states (both more and less developed) have created 'diaspora mechanisms' that incorporate overseas migrant communities into their national agendas and planning. Rather than an aberration, this extra-territorial policy framing is increasingly seen as a normal part of national policy making. Gamlen's argument rests on a differentiation of the state (as an institutional complex), from territory (a geographically bounded area governed by an institutional complex). This allows for the state as institutional complex to engage with extra-territorial populations. One of the most obvious ways this is achieved is through elections, with over 115 countries in the world having some kind of provision that permits overseas citizens to vote. These processes can become highly contentious, both in terms of the political influence of the diaspora in the home nation as well as the reception of political campaigning aimed at the diaspora overseas, as the recent Turkish referendum on constitutional change attests (Başer 2017).

There are inherent tensions embedded within many diaspora communities that are denied if they are viewed as a homogeneous extension of a singular homeland. Consider, for example, the complex politics of Tamil, Sikh, Burmese, Tibetan, Armenian and Kurd diasporas. When the complex geopolitics of diaspora communities is actually taken into account by states, it can quickly result in the excessive securitization of diaspora communities with their engagement in long-distance nationalism often being viewed as a threat to national security. Furthermore, the issue of 'security' can be differentially felt according to age, gender, race, class, religion, region, nationality and so on; both sending and receiving states might then engage only certain 'acceptable' sections of the diaspora, such that only elite or certain generational viewpoints become prioritized. So, security certificates are demanded of racialized and othered members of diaspora communities and trade and investment are promoted for diaspora elites (Rygiel and Walton-Roberts 2015). Such contradictory engagements may align with periods of fiscal liberalization, so that diaspora engagement becomes one of the options states can pursue to expand financial investment (Kapur 2010; Walton-Roberts 2004).

PEOPLE: CHANGE FOR WHOM BY WHOM?

Financial instruments such as diaspora bonds are discursively constructed by institutions such as the World Bank as embedding certain kinds of territorial loyalty from a highly de-territorialized collective. In practice, diasporas with financial means interact with the state and create the context for the reproduction of advantage for themselves and disadvantage for others. Mullings (2012, p. 411) highlights this outcome in the case of skilled migrants and entrepreneurs in the Jamaican diaspora:

> To the extent that state governmental projects aimed at opening up economies to global markets reflect the individual and collective interests of elite groups, then the spaces of development created through state–diaspora partnership are prone to reproducing the patterns of inequality created between those who are able to successfully compete in free markets and those who cannot.

This echoes Burgess's (2009) concern in the Latin American context, which asks if remittances can be both the product of and solution to neoliberal processes of inequality. When the political economy of remittances and diaspora-led development schemes are taken into account, what we often find are processes that reproduce already existing inequalities. This reproduction of socio-spatial inequality through diaspora activity is evident in Jamaica (Mullings 2012), India (Walton-Roberts 2004) and Ethiopia (Chacko and Gebre 2013). Inequality within the diaspora itself also exists based on distinctions between elite/non-elite groups and those with secure or insecure status in their places of residence (McGregor and Pasura 2010). The reality that migration and remittances create new forms of uneven development is becoming increasingly evident (Guarnizo 2003; Williams 2009). In addition, focusing too heavily on diasporas as a development magic bullet can marginalize poor regions and families that have few links into migrant networks and channels of diaspora resources. Research needs to assess if diaspora-led interventions are equitable and sustainable in specific regional contexts, and to consider the wider political economy of international migration and state development interests (Iskander 2010).

Government diaspora strategies that emphasize volunteerism, philanthropy and entrepreneurialism tend to individualize (or spatially concentrate) potential rewards while leaving the burden of risk and poor development as more collectively felt. Too heavy a focus on the sending region also overlooks how migrants are subjected to a lack of protection in the receiving country; here the very basic issues of migrant status insecurity contradict the bold claims diaspora development advocates have articulated over the past decade. Trump's America is now a space where immigrants in general and undocumented migrants in particular are under attack, and migrant remittances are viewed as resources open to plunder to further securitize state borders (Klein 2016). It is impossible to see how the diaspora-development dialogue can yield positive results for migrants or their home communities under such conditions.

We have offered these three themes of policy, place and people to frame our understanding of the development-diaspora interface. Based on this we suggest that researchers need to pay more attention to: (a) how policy frames diasporas in national contexts (when the issues are global) and the deep contradictions embedded in the analysis of development under ever expanding securitization; (b) how a homogenized view of diasporas can be resisted by contextualizing their activities through issues of place; and (c) how people are also differentially placed (both migrants and non-migrants) in terms of how they can advance and benefit from diaspora-development processes. Building on these three themes we now turn to present four cross-cutting issues that we argue need to frame research in this field.

CROSS-CUTTING ISSUES

Diasporas and the New Economy

With the current world trend toward knowledge-based economies, the demand for higher education, specialised knowledge, and a more highly skilled workforce is growing. Highly skilled migration is a dominant characteristic of high-income countries' immigration policy (Docquier and Rapoport 2012); several research themes emerge from this reality. First, scientific diasporas, networks of emigrated scientists and engineers involved in the circulation of knowledge via transnational cooperative links with their home country, are playing an increasingly important role in national innovation agendas (Tejada and Bolay 2010). Countries of origin that take advantage of their overseas skilled diasporas are seen as pursuing 'the diaspora option' (Meyer 2001). There is an important need to identify and compare the role played by diasporas in innovative technology transfer, knowledge spill-overs and scientific cooperation (Agunias and Newland 2012; CODEV-EPFL et al. 2013; Lowell and Gerova 2004). Skilled diaspora professionals are also contributing through connections with sending region universities (Tettey 2016), who then become key resources in university efforts to create global knowledge networks (Larner 2015).

The transnational practices of scientific diasporas are only possible when adequate scientific and technological infrastructure are in place, meaning that certain policies determine the state's ability to benefit from their scientific diasporas (Tejada et al. 2013). The issue of state and scientific diaspora interaction in terms of infrastructure development demands comparative analysis, and this might usefully be explored by mapping scientific diaspora communities' academic interactions. Research in this area has shown how states can use their diasporas as a network to find international partners, with variable success. Hofman and Kramer (2015), for example, argue for a key development role for South African health care professionals in the diaspora. In contrast, Crush et al. (2012) show how the South African medical diaspora in Canada is profoundly disengaged and antagonistic to the idea of contributing to South African development. Similarly, Ho and Boyle (2015) provide a case study of the Singaporean state's mixed efforts to engage its overseas diaspora. There are methodological challenges in assessing the role of diasporas in global knowledge flows, but innovative approaches have been developed to track the mobility of scientists through publications, career paths and international collaborators (Meyer et al. 2016; Tejada et al. 2014). This research signals the growing importance of agendas that connect science, innovation and technological change with the reality of an increasingly global, skilled and mobile migrant population.

Diasporas and Information and Communication Technology (ICT)

Brazil, India, Indonesia and Mexico comprise four of the top five countries globally with the greatest number of Facebook users, showing that Southern countries are connected through digital media (UNDP 2013). ICTs play an increasingly important role in the transnational diasporic exchanges, types of connections used, and the influence of these tools on social change (Parham 2004). Researchers need to engage in comparative work to show how ICTs have enabled the formation of innovative and expansive global networks and how these might reinforce transnational linkages (Brinkerhoff 2009; Tettey 2009). There is a growing literature on how labour migrants rely on ICTs and mobile transfer systems for remittance sending (Hennebry 2008), and for the articulation of political interests (Alonso and Oiarzabal 2010; Keles 2015; Mano and Willems 2010). Migrants and their offspring also establish themselves as transnational diasporic communities through ICTs; consider, for example, the innovative NFB High Rise Digital Citizenship Project[1] which reveals how a rapidly urbanizing world is also increasingly transnationally connected through everyday social digital interactions and exchanges. Diaspora communities are central to our understanding of the socio-economic and political consequences of living in an increasingly technologically connected world.

Identity/Gender/Intersectionality

We certainly need more critical inquiry about issues of identity and intersectionality within diaspora groups. Regional, ethnic, religious, class and even alumni associations often coalesce around the diaspora long before governments begin targeting their financial and political potential. Likewise, gender is a neglected aspect of diaspora scholarship that demands greater consideration, especially when we consider that women carry the transnational double burden in terms of family and nation (Kunz 2011; Oza 2006). Immigration regulations and diaspora engagement efforts are often gender-blind, which can cause uneven outcomes for men and women and skew development efforts. Further, women are often ignored in the diaspora policies of governments and private actors. This

---

[1]   http://highrise.nfb.ca/about/ (accessed October 8, 2018).

is significant because, as the evidence shows, immigrant women make up an increasing share of diaspora populations, and tend to remit greater proportions of their earnings than male counterparts (Hennebry et al. 2017).

The role of immigrant and second generation youth is another vital, yet relatively ignored, element of diaspora engagement. The kinds of ties maintained by countries of origin to children and subsequent generations in the diaspora are yet to be fully understood (Berg 2009). With large numbers of diaspora youth and a steadily expanding cohort of second and third generations in settlement countries, their active participation would considerably extend engagement (Dlamini and Anucha 2009). Likewise, if the diaspora's ties to their places of origin are to be understood as 'sustained' and long term rather than 'severed' over time, as some early research suggests (Lee 2011), then the involvement of successive generations is crucial. Diaspora youth may not engage identically as their parents or grandparents, but this does not imply that their transnational practices will be absent or insignificant (Levitt and Waters 2002).

Other aspects of identity which strongly influence diaspora outcomes and relationships include ethno-cultural, religion, caste, class and kinship (Chikanda et al. 2016; Kurien 2002). Class issues are often ignored, and the increasing focus on high skilled groups overlooks the diasporic connections and potential of marginal groups (CODEV-EPFL et al. 2013). Large-scale emigration produced by fraught colonial histories and political and economic instability in the postcolonial period underscore the complicated and ambivalent relationship between immigrants and origin countries based on social and political identities (Chikanda et al. 2016; Crush et al. 2013). This results in cases where not all emigrants identify themselves as diaspora communities, or align themselves with sending countries (Crush 2011).

Marginalization

By pinning their hopes on diasporas for development, states and international organizations are in danger of losing sight of the negative development consequences of migration. There are several strands to this type of analysis, but we suggest three.

Current remittance governance is narrowly focused on two issues: restrictive financial regulations and policies to combat terrorism financing and money laundering at the global level; and policy initiatives to increase the flow of remittances and channel them to formal banking systems (El Qorchi et al. 2003). Research rarely addresses the costs associated with securing and sending remittances (e.g., international student tuition, visas and permits, remittance transfer fees, travel) (Hennebry 2008; Moniruzzaman and Walton-Roberts 2018). These costs exact a significant drag on development potential since remittances are increasingly becoming one of the most economically viable options for the financial inclusion of a large number of people for whom remittance transfer is their only formal financial transaction, and thus contributing to wider financial development (Giuliano and Ruiz-Arranz 2009). However, improved financial inclusion cannot be achieved through laissez-faire practices, since the state is the most influential actor in enabling market friendly institutional environments for financial development (World Bank 2013). Second, diasporic mobility is differentially structured by state policies, and this must be foregrounded in research on the potential of diasporas. States generate mobile classes of persons who can access their territories based on wealth, lineage and economic output, while tightly restricting access for less skilled labour, which ensures an 'immobile class' who retain fewer rights (Castles 2011; Rygiel and Walton-Roberts 2015). Third, diaspora networks reproduce access for certain communities through social factors such as class, caste, gender, religion (Kurien 2002). Scholars must understand how diaspora groups reproduce these exclusions, and what factors excluded groups use to break in or break off in terms of securing access to overseas opportunities.

CONCLUSION

Migrant diasporas are increasingly perceived as key development resources in responding to persistent global challenges of poverty, under-development and inequality (Bakewell 2011; Lowell and Gerova 2004). Historically, diasporas were seen as truncating full immigrant integration, but under conditions of globalization diasporas are now seen as 'national reserves' working with 'creative states' to create new policies for development. Diaspora-based remittances have surged in recent years and become as large as FDI and outpaced ODA and portfolio investment (Ratha and Mohapatra 2009).

Using the three broad themes of policy, place and people, we have identified some key critical approaches that researchers can develop to analyse how diasporas inform broader development agendas, and how those development agendas themselves present a certain type of framing. We need to examine how the formal policy interest in diasporas as development agents exists in a context of policy learning and transfer between states and international organizations that shapes diaspora engagement practices in both positive and negative ways. Researchers must consider if diaspora-led development is sustainable, especially since migrant remittances may trap the benefits of migration to specific social and regional groups. We also highlight four cross-cutting factors that we consider are increasingly important to the analysis of diasporic formation, organization and influence: diasporas and the new economy, the role of ICTs, identity and the overlooked question of marginalization.

The range of voices now engaged in promoting diasporas as development agents has expanded to include a wide array of actors. This is accompanied by increasing numbers of sending states that are creating mechanisms to promote the formal representation and inclusion of their diasporic populations, while at the same time states are enhancing border and other forms of securitization. We consider these tendencies as vital reasons for migration scholars to critically examine and engage with the research and policy agenda of diasporas and development from a socio-spatial perspective.

REFERENCES

Agunias, D.R. and Newland, K. (2012), *Developing a Road Map for Engaging Diasporas in Development. A Handbook for Policymakers and Practitioners in Home and Host Countries*, Geneva and Washington. DC: International Organization for Migration and Migration Policy Institute.
Alonso, A. and Oiarzabal, P.J. (eds) (2010), *Diasporas in the New Media Age: Identity, Politics and Community*, Reno, NE: University of Nevada Press.
Bakewell, O. (2009), *Which Diaspora for Whose Development? Some Critical Questions about Roles of African Diaspora Organizations as Development Actors*, Copenhagen: Danish Institute for International Studies.

Bakewell, O. (2011), 'Migration and development in sub-Saharan Africa', in N. Phillips (ed.), *Migration in the Global Political Economy*, Boulder, CO: Lynne Rienner Publishers, pp. 121–42.

Başer, B. (2017), 'The Turkish diaspora and the constitutional referendum', *Independent Turkey*, April 22, accessed July 7, 2017 at http://independentturkey.org/the-turkish-diaspora-and-the-constitutional-referendu m/#YFgHiJdOKWXsEidA.99.

Belay, S. (2013), *Diaspora Volunteers and International Development*, Ottawa: Association for Higher Education and Development and CUSO.

Berg, M.L. (2009), 'Between cosmopolitanism and the national slot: Cuba's diasporic children of the revolution', *Identities: Global Studies in Culture and Power*, **16**(2), 129–56.

Betts, A. (2011), *Global Migration Governance*, Oxford: Oxford University Press.

Brinkerhoff, J. (2009), *Digital Diasporas: Identity and Transnational Engagement*, Cambridge: Cambridge University Press.

Burgess, K. (2009), 'Neoliberal reform and migrant remittances: symptom or solution?' in John Burdick, Philip Oxhorn and Kenneth Roberts (eds), *Beyond Neoliberalism in Latin America? Societies and Politics at the Crossroads*, New York: Palgrave Macmillan, pp. 177–95.

Castles, S. (2011), 'Bringing human rights into the migration and development debate', *Global Policy*, **2**(3), 248–58.

Castles, S. and Miller, M.J. (2009), *The Age of Migration: International Population Movements in the Modern World*, Basingstoke: Palgrave Macmillan.

Chacko, E. and Gebre, P.H. (2013), 'Leveraging the diaspora for development: lessons from Ethiopia', *GeoJournal*, **78**(3), 495–505.

Chikanda, A. and Crush, J. (2014), 'Diasporas of the South', in R. Anich, J. Crush, S. Melde and J. Oucho (eds), *A New Perspective on Human Mobility in the South*, New York: Springer, pp. 65–88.

Chikanda, A., Crush, J. and Walton-Roberts, M. (2016), 'Introduction: disaggregating diasporas', in A. Chikanda, J. Crush, and M. Walton-Roberts (eds), *Diasporas, Development and Governance*, Heidelberg and New York: Springer, pp. 1–8.

CODEV-EPFL, IDSK, JNU and ILO (2013), *Migration, Scientific Diasporas and Development: Impact of Skilled Return Migration on Development in India. Final Research Report*, accessed July 7, 2017 at http:// infoscience.epfl.ch/record/188059/files/Migration_ScientificDiasporas_Development.pdf.

Cohen, R. (1997), *Global Diasporas: An Introduction*, London: UCL Press.

Crush, J. (2011), 'Diasporas of the South: situating the African diaspora in Africa', in S. Plaza and D. Ratha (eds), *Diaspora for Development in Africa*, Washington, DC: World Bank, pp. 55–77.

Crush, J., Chikanda, A. and Pendleton, W. (2012), 'The disengagement of the South African medical diaspora in Canada', *Journal of Southern African Studies*, **38**, 27–49.

Crush, J., Chikanda, A., Pendleton, W. et al. (2013), *Divided Diasporas: Southern Africans in Canada*, Waterloo: Southern African Migration Program and Center for International Governance Innovation.

de Haas, H. (2006), *Engaging Diasporas. How Governments and Development Agencies Can Support Diasporas Involvement in the Development of Origin Countries*, Oxford: University of Oxford, International Migration Institute.

de Haas, H. (2010), 'Migration and development: a theoretical perspective', *International Migration Review*, **44**(1), 227–64.

Dlamini, S.N. and Anucha, U. (2009), 'Trans-nationalism, social identities and African youth in the Canadian diaspora', *Social Identities*, **15**(2), 227–42.

Docquier, F. and Rapoport, H. (2012), 'Quantifying the impact of highly skilled emigration on developing countries', in T. Boeri, H. Brücker, F. Docquier and H. Rapoport (eds), *Brain Drain and Brain Gain: The Global Competition to Attract High-skilled Migrants*, Oxford: Oxford University Press, pp. 209–89.

El Qorchi, M., Maimbo, S.M. and Wilson, J.F. (2003), *Informal Funds Transfer Systems: An Analysis of the Informal Hawala System*, Washington, DC: International Monetary Fund.

Faist, T. and Fauser, M. (2011), 'The migration-development nexus: toward a transnational perspective', in T. Faist, M. Fauser and P. Kivisto (eds), *The Migration-Development Nexus*, Basingstoke: Palgrave Macmillan, pp. 1–26.

Gamlen, A. (2008), 'The emigration state and the modern geopolitical imagination', *Political Geography*, **27**(8), 840–56.

Gamlen, A. (2013), 'Creating and destroying diaspora strategies: New Zealand's emigration policies re-examined', *Transactions of the Institute of British Geographers*, **38**(2), 238–53.

Gamlen, A. (2014a), 'Diaspora institutions and diaspora governance', *International Migration Review*, **48**(s1), 180–217.

Gamlen, A. (2014b), 'The new migration-and-development pessimism', *Progress in Human Geography*, **38**(4), 581–97.

Giuliano, P. and Ruiz-Arranz, M. (2009), 'Remittances, financial development, and growth', *Journal of Development Economics*, **90**(1), 144–52.

Guarnizo, L.E. (2003), 'The economics of transnational living', *International Migration Review*, **37**(3), 666–99.

Hatton, T.J. (2014), 'Public opinion on immigration: has the recession changed minds?' CEPR Discussion Paper No. DP10008 (June), available at SSRN: https://ssrn.com/abstract=2501460.

Hennebry, J.L. (2008), 'Bienvenidos a Canadá? Globalization and the migration industry surrounding temporary agricultural migration in Canada', *Canadian Studies in Population*, **35**(2), 339–56.

Hennebry, J., Holliday, J. and Moniruzzaman, M. (2017), *At What Cost? Women Migrant Workers, Remittances and Development*, United Nations Entity for Gender Equality and the Empowerment of Women (UN Women), accessed July 7, 2017 at http://www.unwomen.org/en/digital-library/publications/2017/2/women-migrant-workers-remittances-and-development.

Ho, E. and Boyle, M. (2015), 'Migration-as-development repackaged? The globalizing imperative of the Singaporean state's diaspora strategies', *Singapore Journal of Tropical Geography*, **36**(2), 164–82.

Hofman, K. and Kramer, B. (2015), 'Human resources for research: building bridges through the diaspora', *Global Health Action*, **8**(1), 29559.

Hugo, G. (2006), 'An Australian diaspora?' *International Migration*, **44**(1), 105–33.

Iskander, N. (2010), *Creative State: Forty Years of Migration and Development Policy in Morocco and Mexico*, Ithaca, NY: Cornell University Press.

Kapur, D. (2010), *Diaspora, Development, and Democracy: The Domestic Impact of International Migration from India*, Princeton, NJ: Princeton University Press.

Keles, J. (2015), 'Diaspora, the internet and social capital', in L. Ryan, U. Erel and A. D'Angelo (eds), *Migrant Capital: Migration, Diasporas and Citizenship*, Basingstoke: Palgrave Macmillan, pp. 102–16.

Klein, A. (2016), 'Donald Trump's plan to build a wall is really dangerous', *Brookings*, April 17, accessed July 7. 2017 at https://www.brookings.edu/opinions/donald-trumps-plan-to-build-a-wall-is-really-dangerous/.

Koser, K. (2010), 'International migration and global governance', *Global Governance*, **16**, 301–15.

Kunz, R. (2011), *The Political Economy of Global Remittances: Gender, Governmentality and Neoliberalism*, London and New York: Routledge.

Kurien, P.A. (2002), *Kaleidoscopic Ethnicity: International Migration and the Reconstruction of Community Identities in India*, New Brunswick, NJ: Rutgers University Press.

Kuschminder, K. (2014), 'Knowledge transfer and capacity building through the temporary return of qualified nationals to Afghanistan', *International Migration*, **52**(5), 191–207.

Kuznetsov, Y. (2006), 'Leveraging diasporas of talent: toward a new policy agenda', in Y. Kuznetsov (ed.), *Diaspora Networks and the International Migration of Skills: How Countries Can Draw on their Talent Abroad*, Washington, DC: World Bank, pp. 221–37.

Larner, W. (2007), 'Expatriate experts and globalising governmentalities: the New Zealand diaspora strategy', *Transactions of the Institute of British Geographers*, **32**, 331–45.

Larner, W. (2015), 'Globalising knowledge networks: universities, diaspora strategies, and academic intermediaries', *Geoforum*, **59**, 197–205.

Lavie, S. and Swedenburg, T. (1996), 'Introduction: displacement, diaspora, and geographies of identity', in S. Lavie and T. Swedenburg (eds), *Displacement, Diaspora and Geographies of Identity*, Durham, NC: Duke University Press, pp. 1–26.

Leclerc, E. and Meyer, J.-B. (2007), 'Knowledge diasporas for development: a shrinking space for scepticism', *Asian Population Studies*, **3**(2), 153–68.

Lee, H. (2011), 'Rethinking transnationalism through the second generation', *The Australian Journal of Anthropology*, **22**(3), 295–313.

Levitt, P. and Waters, M. (2002), *The Changing Face of Home: The Transnational Lives of Second Generation*, New York: Russell Sage Foundation.

Lowell, L. and Gerova, S.G. (2004), *Diasporas and Economic Development: State of Knowledge*, Washington, DC: Georgetown University, Institute for the Study of International Migration.

Mano, W. and Willems, W. (2010), 'Debating "Zimbabweanness" in diasporic internet forums', in J. McGregor and R. Primorac (eds), *Zimbabwe's New Diaspora*, New York and Oxford: Berghahn Books, pp. 183–201.

McGregor, J. (2014), 'Sentimentality or speculation? Diaspora investment, crisis economies and urban transformation', *Geoforum*, **56**, 172–81.

McGregor, J. and Pasura, D. (2010), 'Diasporic repositioning and the politics of re-engagement: developmentalising Zimbabwe's diaspora?' *The Round Table*, **99**(411), 687–703.

Mercer, C., Page, B. and Evans, M. (2008), *Development and the African Diaspora: Place and the Politics of Home*, London: Zed Books.

Meyer, J.-B. (2001), 'Network approach versus brain drain: lessons from the diaspora', *International Migration*, **39**(5), 91–110.

Meyer, J.-B., Wang Maio, F. and Zhao, Y. (2016), 'Visualizing the diaspora: new options', in A. Chikanda, J. Crush and M. Walton-Roberts (eds), *Diasporas, Development and Governance*, Heidelberg and New York: Springer, pp. 205–20.

Moniruzzaman, M. and Walton-Roberts, M. (2018), 'Migration, debt and resource backwash: how sustainable is Bangladesh-Gulf circular migration?' *Migration and Development*, **7**(1), 85–103.

Mullings, B. (2012), 'Governmentality, diaspora assemblages and the ongoing challenge of "development"', *Antipode*, **44**, 406–27.

Newland, K. (2010), 'The governance of international migration: mechanisms, processes, and institutions', *Global Governance*, **16**, 331–43.

Nurse, K. (2006), 'Migration, diaspora and development in the Caribbean', Policy Paper Focal FPP-04-6, Ottawa: Canadian Foundation for the Americas (FOCAL).

Ogom, R.O. (2009), 'The African Union, African diasporas and the quest for development: in search of the missing link', *African Journal of Political Science and International Relations*, **3**(4), 165.

Omelaniuk, I. (ed.) (2012), *Global Perspectives on Migration and Development: GFMD Puerto Vallarta and Beyond*, New York: Springer.

Omelaniuk, I. (2016), 'The Global Forum on Migration and Development and diaspora engagement', in A. Chikanda, J. Crush and M. Walton-Roberts (eds), *Diasporas, Development and Governance*, Heidelberg and New York: Springer, pp. 19–32.

Orozco, M. and Lapointe, M. (2004), 'Mexican hometown associations and development opportunities', *Journal of International Affairs*, **57**(2), 1–21.

Oza, R. (2006), *The Making of Neoliberal India: Nationalism, Gender and the Paradoxes of Globalization*, New York: Routledge.

Parham, A.A. (2004), 'Diaspora, community and communication: internet use in transnational Haiti', *Global Networks*, **4**(2), 199–217.

Peck, J. and Theodore, N. (2010), 'Recombinant workfare, across the Americas: transnationalizing "fast" social policy', *Geoforum*, **41**(2), 195–208.

Pécoud, Antoine (2015), *Depoliticising Migration: Global Governance and International Migration Narratives*, London: Palgrave Macmillan, pp. 95–123.

Pellerin, H. and Mullings, B. (2013), 'The "diaspora option", migration and the changing political economy of development', *Review of International Political Economy*, **20**(1), 89–120.

Raghuram, P. (2009), 'Which migration, which development? Unsettling the edifice of migration and development', *Population, Space and Place*, **15**, 103–17.

Ratha, D. and Mohapatra, S. (2009), 'Revised outlook for remittance flows 2009–2011: remittances expected to fall by 5 to 8 percent in 2009', *Growth*, **25**, 30.

Ratha, D., Plaza, S., Schuettler, K., Seshan, G., Wyss, H. and Yameogo, N.D. (2017), 'Migration and remittances: recent developments and outlook', *Migration and Development Brief* no. 27, Washington, DC: KNOMAD.

Rygiel, K. and Walton-Roberts, M. (2015), 'Post-national and multiple citizenships', in R. Howard-Hassmann and M. Walton-Roberts (eds), *The Human Right to Citizenship: A Slippery Concept*, Philadelphia, PA: University of Pennsylvania Press, pp. 220–22.

Sidel, M. (2007), 'Focusing on the state: government responses to diaspora giving and implications for equity', in B.J. Merz, L.C. Chen and P.F. Geithne (eds), *Diasporas and Development*, Cambridge, MA: Global Equity Initiative, Harvard University, pp. 25–54.

Simmons, A. (2008), 'Why international banks became interested in migrant remittances: a critical reflection on globalisation, ideology and international migration', in C. Gabriel and H. Pellerin (eds), *Governing International Labour Migration: Current Issues, Challenges and Dilemmas*, London and New York: Routledge, pp. 60–77.

Tejada, G. and Bolay, J.C. (eds) (2010), *Scientific Diasporas as Development Partners: Skilled Migrants from Colombia, India and South Africa in Switzerland: Empirical Evidence and Policy Responses*, Bern: Peter Lang AG.

Tejada, G., Varzari, V. and Porcescu, S. (2013), 'Scientific diasporas, transnationalism and home country development: evidence from a study of skilled Moldovans abroad', *Journal of South East European and Black Sea Studies*, **13**(2), 157–73.

Tejada, G., Hercog, M., Kuptsch, C. and Bolay, J.C. (2014), 'The link with a home country: a comparative analysis of host country environments for diaspora engagement', in S. Sahoo and B.K. Pattanaik (eds), *Global Diasporas and Development: Socio-economic, Cultural, and Policy Perspectives*, New Delhi: Springer, pp. 39–68.

Tettey, W. (2009), 'Transnationalism, the African diaspora, and the deterritorialized politics of the Internet', in O. Mudhai, W. Tettey and F. Banda (eds), *African Media and the Digital Public Sphere*, New York: Palgrave Macmillan, pp. 143–63.

Tettey, W. (2016), 'Regenerating scholarly capacity through diaspora engagement: the case of a Ghana diaspora knowledge network', in A. Chikanda, J. Crush and M. Walton-Roberts (eds), *Diasporas, Development and Governance*, Heidelberg and New York: Springer, pp. 171–86.

UNDESA (United Nations Department of Social and Economic Affairs) (2016), *International Migration Report 2015, Highlights*, New York: United Nations.

UNDP (United Nations Development Programme) (2009), *Human Development Report 2009: Overcoming Barriers: Human Mobility and Development*, New York: UNDP.

UNDP (United Nations Development Programme) (2013), *Human Development Report 2013. The Rise of the South: Human Progress in a Diverse World*, accessed July 7, 2017 at http://www.undp.org/content/dam/philippines/docs/HDR/HDR2013%20Report%20English.pdf.

Walton-Roberts, M. (2004), 'Globalization, national autonomy and non-resident Indians', *Contemporary South Asia*, **13**(1), 53–69.

Walton-Roberts, M. (2014), 'Diasporas and divergent development in Kerala and Punjab: querying the migration-development discourse', in S. Sahoo and B.K. Pattanaik (eds), *Global Diasporas and Development: Socio-economic, Cultural, and Policy Perspectives*, New York: Springer, pp. 69–86.

Williams, A.M. (2009), 'International migration, uneven regional development and polarization', *European Urban and Regional Studies*, **16**(3), 309–22.

World Bank (2013), 'Migration and remittance flows: recent trends and outlook, 2013–2016', accessed October 8, 2018 at https://siteresources.worldbank.org/INTPROSPECTS/Resources/334934-1288990760745/Migration andDevelopmentBrief21.pdf.

24. Approximating citizenship: affective practices of Chinese diasporic descendants in Myanmar
Elaine Lynn-Ee Ho

INTRODUCTION

Citizenship is regarded as a social compact between a nation-state and the people it governs, and an institution that signifies the political status and identity of those considered the citizens of a nation-state. Since the turn of the millennium, an 'emotional turn' within Geography (see Anderson and Smith, 2001; Davidson and Milligan, 2004) has impacted how researchers approach the study of citizenship. Such researchers consider citizenship as not only a political-legal category and a set of social-cultural relations (see Painter and Philo, 1995), but also experiential, embodied, relational and constituted through the emotions in everyday lives and places (e.g., Ho, 2009; Faria, 2014; Askins, 2016; Jackson, 2016). Transnational migration features prominently in such analyses of citizenship; movement across borders compels reconsideration of what citizenship means to both citizens and migrants alike, such as when citizens move abroad and become immigrants in another country, or when migrants arrive in a nation-state and reside alongside citizens. Such movements result in changing cultural backdrops and prompt encounters with difference that produce emotional responses towards citizenship and citizenship formation. Migration biographies and the emotions they engender persist into later generations (see Levitt and Waters, 2002), impacting the extent to which diasporic descendants experience citizenship inclusion or exclusion in the country they consider their natal land (i.e., the country where their migrant parents or earlier generations settled).

This chapter reviews the extant literature on citizenship and belonging, showing how such research informs analyses of why the emotions matter for understanding citizenship more fully. While many researchers have studied the emotions that contribute to activism or visible political action (e.g., Bosco, 2007; Griffiths, 2014) it is critical to also consider in what ways and under what circumstances do emotions towards transnational migration and citizenship translate into less visible but no less important expressions of political subjectivity in everyday life (Thawnghmung, 2011; Häkli and Kallio, 2014). Through an empirical example of Chinese diasporic descendants in Myanmar (Burma), the chapter directs attention to emotions that motivate what Susan Coutin (2013, p. 117) refers to as 'citizenship approximations' to describe movement between 'informal and unrecognized or unreal forms of membership [that] may approach and resemble but never fully replicate formal and recognized versions [of citizenship]' (Coutin, 2013, p. 115).

The chapter argues that the Burmese-Chinese approximate citizenship by practising compliance to dominant norms for securing their community's safety in a political context that has discriminated against them during different historical junctures. Buddhism is the state religion in Myanmar and notions of 'merit-making' (Schober, 2005, p. 118) take on special importance for the Burmese-Chinese. I argue that their monetary and material donations to monks and temples signify not only cultural values, such as respect and piety, but also function as valued forms of capital (Bourdieu, 1990; Kelly and Lusis, 2006; Holt, 2008) and affective practices (Wetherell, 2012) that produce habitus and gives expression to their political subjectivity. The emotions constitute a habitus that functions as a backdrop in which the Burmese-Chinese deploy various forms of economic, social and cultural capital to express their political subjectivity in Myanmar. I further extend the analysis of emotions, habitus and citizenship approximation to a transnational context by considering the links the Burmese-Chinese continue to foster with China, such as through lineage networks that symbolise forms of cultural and social capital[1] (e.g., social ties and language competencies) which they use to generate new economic opportunities in post-reform Myanmar. However, the various forms of capital they accrue through their transnational links affect their social locations within Myanmar too.

Chinese diasporic descendants in Myanmar are referred to as Burmese-Chinese (translated from *miandianhuaren* in Mandarin). In Myanmar they are known as *tayout* and their ethnicity and family histories identify them as descendants of migrants (i.e., non-indigenous persons). As Chinese diasporic descendants, they maintain long-standing cultural and economic ties with China, the ancestral land. But as descendants of migrants in Myanmar, they were not eligible for any form of legal citizenship until the citizenship laws were partially changed in 1982. As subjects located in transnational social fields, the political contexts of both Myanmar and China impact their quest for recognition and belonging. Although the social locations of the Burmese-Chinese may be unique, their emotional negotiations are revealing of the citizenship approximations that researchers should examine in order to study the 'grey spaces' (Yiftachel, 2009) that exist between formal and informal political membership. The analyses in this chapter extend such arguments to consider how the emotional subjectivities of the Burmese-Chinese prompt them to deploy spatial strategies to preserve their culture and identity as ethnic minorities in Myanmar (also see Ho and Chua, 2016).

From 2012 to 2013, I conducted ethnography in the homes, schools, religious spaces, workplaces and other sites associated with Chinese populations in Yangon, Mandalay and Lashio. To deepen understanding of the historical and political context, I carried out 18 semi-structured interviews with Burmese-Chinese community leaders. The interviews were conducted in Mandarin but were not recorded at the request of the respondents and I took detailed field notes instead. An interpreter was on standby to translate Burmese words the respondents had difficulty expressing. Given the small number of Burmese-Chinese associations in Myanmar, the linguistic or regional affiliations of the respondents will not be revealed so as to protect their identities.

The next section reviews the relevant literature on emotions and citizenship. This sets the context for the third section which discusses the ethnic hatred reflected in laws and actions enacted against the Burmese-Chinese. The fourth section considers the emotional subjectivities that deter them from rights assertion. Instead, they engage in acts of

---

[1]   Following Bourdieu's (1986, 1990) conceptualisation of social and cultural capital, social capital refers to the social networks and relationships that can reproduce privilege or disadvantage depending on whether a person possesses such resources, while cultural capital can be understood as the embodied aspects of a person's cultural or social standing such as observed through attire, accent, comportment or ethnicity (see Kelly and Lusis, 2006; Holt, 2008).

approximating citizenship for safety and to sustain their cultural community. The fifth section examines the emotional negotiations of the Burmese-Chinese in a transnational context. The chapter concludes by reiterating the importance of studying the emotions to draw out a range of political subjectivities towards citizenship meaning and practice.

EMOTIONS AND CITIZENSHIP APPROXIMATIONS

Citizenship and belonging are often discussed in conjunction, but can one have citizenship status and not experience belonging? Is it possible to feel a sense of belonging to a nation-state despite being only partially recognised as a citizen of that country? How is the quest for recognition experienced? Earlier research has drawn attention to the emotional representations of citizenship (Ho, 2009; Erdal, 2014; Jackson, 2016). Researchers who study emotional representations bring focus to how belonging is couched in emotional metaphors that symbolise and invoke feelings towards the nation. Such emotional representations of citizenship may include homeland, home, family, safety and roots (see Ho, 2008, 2009; Jackson, 2016). Another approach has been to consider how emotional subjectivities shape people's attitudes towards citizenship and political relations (see Ho, 2009; Walsh, 2012; Wood, 2013). Wright (2010) and other scholars have usefully signalled how emotions drive social justice activism that seeks to achieve more egalitarian relations (e.g., Bosco, 2007; Griffiths, 2014). I contribute to such analyses by arguing that just as important are the emotional negotiations that bring about what Coutin (2013) describes as 'citizenship approximations' wherein individuals whose social positions fall between a formal citizenship regime and a shadow regime move cautiously between the two positions to secure safety and gains. For Coutin (2013), approximations refer to the gap or 'breach' between the formal status of citizenship and the deep yet incomplete connections that a person bears to the country in question. She analyses such 'membership in the breach' in terms of 'law in action' and 'law in the books', whereas I want to ask 'what do the emotions tell us about "membership in the breach"'?

Put differently, what do the emotions tell us about citizenship as experienced when compared to citizenship as legal status? Emotions are an expression of power relations but also function as tools to (re)calibrate power relations in the lives of individuals and the social context they inhabit (Heaney, 2011). Drawing on Holt et al.'s (2013) analysis of the emotions and habitus, I argue that the emotional subjectivities and mores of the Burmese-Chinese towards their citizenship status in Myanmar reproduce a form of habitus that functions as a backdrop to their citizenship experiences. Sociologist Pierre Bourdieu (1990) developed the theory of habitus to examine the connections between economic, cultural and social processes by studying people's practices (Kelly and Lusis, 2006, p. 831). Habitus, as Kelly and Lusis (2006, p. 833) explain, 'provides the context in which capitals of various forms (economic, social, cultural) are valued and given meaning'. Crucially, for Holt et al. (2013), Bourdieu's theory of habitus neglects the emotional relations that contribute to the acquisition of social and cultural capital, and the production of habitus that helps explain why individuals and social groups accept their social positions. They argue that 'emotions are at the heart of the operation of social and cultural capital and the embodiment of habitus' (Holt et al., 2013, p. 34). Such a focus on emotions and habitus provides new ways of understanding how and why the Burmese-Chinese deploy various forms of capital to subtly negotiate the unequal power relations they experience in Myanmar.

This chapter suggests that emotional negotiations towards 'membership in the breach' (Coutin, 2013, p. 113) produce practices of moving between formal/informal membership and legality/illegality that are akin to approximating citizenship. Such practices mimic citizenship to garner recognition or secure protection, but they never fully replicate formal and recognised versions of citizenship. The case of the Burmese-Chinese, as persons who lack the privilege of living under the protection of citizenship law in Myanmar, is instructive in this respect. Coutin (2013, p. 117) explains that 'approximation can result in membership or disqualification'. Sadiq's (2009) research on undocumented migrants in India and Malaysia provide telling examples of how unrecognised individuals can gain full membership and rights akin to citizenship by obtaining fraudulent documents. But their actions also threaten the national security and sovereignty of the states where they settle illegally, which leaves them vulnerable to punitive action and expulsion by those states. Similarly, the Burmese-Chinese discussed in this chapter stop short of mobilising for rights assertion to minimise the risk of disqualification from membership in a political context where their status is uncertain.

Emotional negotiations towards citizenship is arguably heightened through migration, whether experienced first-hand (both migrant and non-migrant populations experiencing change) or through migration biographies that linger across decades. Faria (2014), for example, discusses the strong feelings of attachment expressed by Sudanese migrants she had interviewed and their aspirations for the next generation to maintain long-distance intimacy to the homeland. Ongoing transnational practices passed down from generation to generation can sustain the emotional negotiations of diasporic descendants. Their family histories of migration remain with them in the country where their parents or earlier generations have settled, which they consider their natal land. Whether through personal mobility or inhabiting transnational social locations, diasporic descendants remain embedded between the ancestral land and the country of settlement (Levitt and Waters, 2002). The next section contextualises the social and political circumstances of the Burmese-Chinese in Myanmar, examining the politics of hatred reflected through laws and actions enacted against the Burmese-Chinese.

BURMESE-CHINESE IN MYANMAR

The Burmese-Chinese comprise about 3 per cent of the population in Myanmar. They are considered 'immigrants' because their ancestors moved to Myanmar from Yunnan province in China as caravan traders during dynastic times or as refugees and nationalist supporters escaping the communist takeover of China after 1949 (see Chang, 2014). Others came to Myanmar as merchants from coastal provinces in China or via Southeast Asia during the late eighteenth and early nineteenth centuries (Roberts, 2016). On account of their immigrant backgrounds they are classified separately from the officially recognised 'races' in Myanmar which stratifies the population by lineage and period of settlement. As Chinese diasporic descendants, the Burmese-Chinese are not eligible to become full 'Burma citizens' (there are exceptions but few). In 1982 new categories of 'Associate Citizen' and 'Naturalised Citizens' were created (ILO, n.d.). This enabled the

Burmese-Chinese to secure citizenship status but as a form of membership that gives them partial recognition and rights only. The status of 'Associate Citizen' is granted to the children of mixed marriages where one parent is a Burma citizen, as well as to individuals who had lived in Myanmar for five consecutive years, or to individuals who lived in Myanmar for eight out of the ten years prior to independence. Associate Citizens cannot serve in political office. The category of 'Naturalised Citizen' is applied to the offspring of immigrants who arrived in Myanmar during the period of British colonial rule. Before these citizenship categories, the Burmese-Chinese only had identity cards attesting to their status as long-term 'foreigners' in Myanmar. Even with the new citizenship categories created, those bearing such statuses are considered second-class citizens with limited political rights in Myanmar. As foreign nationals, they did not qualify for a Myanmar passport so to travel they carry an official document verifying their place of birth and right to travel. Their Family Registration Certificate (FRC) cards had to be left with the immigration office prior to departure (Ho and Chua, 2016).

Roberts (2016) argues that the Burmese-Chinese had to negotiate multiple forces during different time periods in order to secure their status in Myanmar. They navigate the assimilation pressures of living in a society where Burman identity is prioritised, and in relation to the different power brokers in political, economic and social life. The ethnic segregation found in Myanmar today was started under British colonialism, but under U Nu and later Ne Win, the political leadership encouraged Burman nationalism and laws to justify unequal treatment towards ethnic groups like the Chinese. Before the 1982 changes allowing them to acquire Associate or Naturalised Citizen status, the Burmese-Chinese were categorised as 'foreign nationals' in Myanmar, which excluded them from professional qualifications in law, medicine and accountancy. This exclusion directed more Burmese-Chinese to business and property ownership. They accrued substantive economic capital as a result of these activities, but their economic dominance also incurred the resentment of Burman nationalists. The Enterprise Nationalisation Law introduced in 1963 by General Ne Win impacted the Chinese to a greater extent than the rest of the population (Tong, 2011). On the pretext of nationalisation, the military government confiscated Chinese businesses, property and land on which Chinese schools were sited. Laws and policy directives such as the 1908 Unlawful Associations Act and the military junta's Law No. 6/88 (1988) restricting associational activity were used to intimidate social groups seen to be culturally different from norms encouraged under Burman nationalism.

Underlying the laws and policies legitimising exclusion and subordination is the ethnic hatred expressed by Burman nationalists who seek to preserve the purity or homogeneity of the nation despite the racial difference contained within its territory. Ahmed (2004, p. 139) argues that 'if community binds others together through the demand that others become like us, then the narrative of love converts swiftly into hatred for "unlike others"'. Attitudes of Burmese supremacy and hate for the ethnic minority Chinese of immigrant ancestry manifested visibly during the 1967 anti-Chinese riots in Central and Lower Burma. The anti-Chinese riots were reportedly triggered by successive incidents in which Chinese students wore pro-communist insignia to schools despite regulations prohibiting such acts. Roberts (2016) reports that in Rangoon a mob of Burmese people protested the actions of the Chinese students and it culminated in deaths, injury and the destruction of Chinese neighbourhoods. As Amin (2012, p. 5) observes, public feelings of empathy or aversion towards the stranger are 'instantiations of a slew of personal and collective labelling conventions – inherited, learnt, absorbed and practised – that flow into that moment of encounter, but that are regulated by cognitive and sensory judgements stimulated by the specifics of the occasion'. The Burmese-Chinese were isolated targets as a result of their ethnicity, economic dominance in society, and links with China, which at that time was feverishly extending communist ideology to the region.

Emotions of hate and violence are expressions of perceived power imbalances by the perpetuators and such emotions manifest as tangible action meant to put the subjects of hate in their place on the lowest rung of the social hierarchy in that society. As Nayak (2011, p. 556) puts it, 'it is through these emotional and affective registers that the sheer weightiness of race can be felt'. Through a combination of laws, policies, institutional norms, embodied practices and relations, such acts of hate congeal into 'feeling rules' (Hochschild, 1983, p. 56) which subjects of hate come to recognise and navigate emotionally and behaviourally in their daily lives. As Hochschild explains, feeling rules establish a sense of entitlement or obligation that governs emotional exchanges. She adds that feeling rules can be established by observing external reactions towards social exchanges and the emotions undergirding such encounters. As I will discuss in the next section, the community leaders whom I met during fieldwork in Myanmar regularly deflected discussion of ethnic hatred towards the Burmese-Chinese. Unlike other ethnic groups that have mobilised to protest against unfair treatment by the Burman elite (e.g., the Kachin and Karen), the Burmese-Chinese seek safety by staying under the radar of government scrutiny. Nonetheless, they engage in practices that exhibit their political subjectivity, through what Coutin (2013) describes as 'citizenship approximations'. With their own ethnic or cultural capital devalued, the Burmese-Chinese seek to accumulate other forms of cultural and social capital to secure a place in society and ensure their economic and cultural survival. In doing so, they exhibit a range of emotional subjectivities and practices that speak to acts of citizenship approximations. Emotions function as a type of logic tempering judgements on the best course of action for those who seek safety rather than rights assertion.

EMOTIONAL NEGOTIATIONS AND POLITICAL SUBJECTIVITY

On my first visit to a Chinese temple in Mandalay, the community elders of that temple warmly received me and gestured to me to take a seat in the office. One of them was in his early fifties and another in his eighties. Accompanying me was a Burmese-Chinese respondent who had brought me to the temple where he also volunteers as a youth leader. I explained my research to the elders and they gamely answered my questions, until I asked how the Chinese members of that temple had fared under General Ne Win's nationalisation policies during the 1960s. My question was met with a pregnant pause and then summarily dismissed as the elders signalled that they would like to show me the rest of the temple premises. I was puzzled but I did not probe further so as not to offend my hosts. Subsequently, my friend explained to me that the older generation are guarded about speaking of the discrimination and difficulties they had faced during the period I asked about.

Wetherell (2012, p. 4) introduces the concept of 'affective practice' to capture 'the emotional as it appears in social life', placing emphasis on 'what participants do' as they engage with 'forms of order'. Affective practice encompasses how 'emotions are felt, displayed and managed' in the context of 'expectations as to what people are to feel (feeling rules) and how they are to express those feelings (display rules) in situations' (Boccagni and Baldassar, 2015, p. 75, citing Stets, 2010, p. 265). This section's opening anecdote illustrates the feeling rules that the Burmese-Chinese negotiate in their social milieu. The harsh treatment the Chinese in Myanmar encountered under General Ne Win's nationalisation agenda and the anti-Chinese riots of the 1960s is a topic they deflect in order not to be seen as complaining or ungrateful ethnic minorities, which can invite further trouble if found out by the Burman elites. Anticipating the potential hateful dispositions that can be directed at the Chinese ethnic minority, the Burmese-Chinese emotionally negotiate feeling rules through other types of affective practices that produce and reproduce the habitus they inhabit. On the one hand, they stoically acknowledge the need to blend into Burman society in public spaces by adopting Burmese speech, wearing the *longyi* and practising Buddhism (as expected by the assimilation policies adopted across successive military governments). On the other hand, their affective practice also entails tactics to preserve their culture in semi-private community space and carve out the survival of their community in other ways.

Emotional subjectivities constitute affective practices that produce the habitus which forms the backdrop for social behaviour. The intangible aspects of the emotions, affective practices and habitus become manifested in visible ways through the organisation of space. For example, fear of recrimination, particularly amongst ethnic minorities whose citizenship status is precarious in Myanmar, prompts such social groups to sanction any behaviour that may be construed as challenging Burman privilege. As reflected in this section's opening anecdote, such fear is expressed in embodied ways (such as by deflecting questions that are considered risky to answer). Fear also has material implications, establishing the physical and social spaces that those who experience fear carve out for their safety. I observe that the emotional subjectivities of the Burmese-Chinese prompt acts of approximating citizenship in everyday life, which may not be as visible as demonstrations and protests, but are no less important for collective cultural survival.

Although all associations can submit procedures for legal registration in Myanmar, under the repressive laws of the former military regime, associational activity that deviated from alleged Burman 'norms' were at risk of being charged under the 1908 Unlawful Associations Act and Law No. 6/88. A new law known as the Association Registration Law was promulgated in 2014 but ethnic minorities such as the Burmese-Chinese remain mindful of capricious changes that have been made to laws and policies in the past, as well as a disjuncture between law that exists on paper and law as practised by enforcement agencies in Myanmar. Believing that it will be difficult to register clan associations (formal social spaces for nurturing ethnic and cultural identity), the Burmese-Chinese use temples as spaces to preserve their cultural practices and religious beliefs instead. Chinese temples are considered culturally acceptable to the mainstream Buddhist population in Myanmar because of similarities in religious beliefs and practices.

Temple spaces function as sites where the Burmese-Chinese conduct Chinese language lessons and celebrate festivals, activities that are not allowed publicly under the law in Myanmar (even though in practice wealthy Chinese families have done so under the patronage of powerful Burman generals or political leaders). To prevent recrimination for celebrating their ethnic identity, they invite prominent monks from the Theravada tradition (practised by Burman Buddhists) to convene religious ceremonies during festivals even though the Chinese practise Mahayana Buddhism. This deliberate practice indicates their respect for Buddhism as the state religion and their willingness to align their community's culture with the cultural norms of the Burman majority in Myanmar (signalling integration). Following the religious ceremony, the host (i.e., the Burmese-Chinese) would normally give a generous donation to the monks (or their temple) who participated in the ceremony. Such rituals signal reciprocal relations and build longer-term social ties. In these ways, the Burmese-Chinese deploy economic capital to secure social capital (social connections with prominent religious leaders) and cultural capital (alignment with Burman cultural norms) for the protection of their community in a political context where protection under citizenship law is uncertain. As Häkli and Kallio (2014, p. 181) argue, 'political agency is not restricted to participation in social movements or institutional political processes but, rather, it refers to a variety of individual and collective, official and mundane, rational and affective, and human and non-human ways of acting, affecting and impacting politically'. Such expressions of political agency can be described as quiet encroachment (Bayat, 1997) through circumventing the law (i.e., patterns of compliance) and subverting the law (i.e., actions contrary to the intention of the law) (see Ho and Chua, 2016).

Collectively and across generations, feeling rules and circumventing or subverting tactics become an 'emotion norm' for the Burmese-Chinese, a template they deploy as shadow citizens (Chouinard, 2001). The feeling rules, emotional subjectivities and resultant citizenship approximations experienced by the Burmese-Chinese produce a habitus that they negotiate emotionally and behaviourally. In contrast to Holt et al.'s (2013) study affirming the value of emotional support in creating a convivial habitus, the Burmese-Chinese negotiate ethnic hatred, distrust and fear in their everyday lives by using the economic, cultural and social capital they have to approximate citizenship protection and welfare. The Burmese-Chinese are subject to feeling rules of subordination to dominant Burman nationalism. Stoicism and quiet perseverance constitute the affective practices of shadow citizens (Chouinard, 2001, p. 187) like the Burmese-Chinese in this study.

EMOTIONAL DIMENSIONS OF A TRANSNATIONAL HABITUS

In a seminal publication, Levitt and Waters (2002) and the contributors to their edited volume established that the second generation continues to sustain ties with the ancestral land even if they have not lived there before (also see Conway and Potter, 2009). Boccagni and Baldassar (2015, p. 75) critique the literature that assumes immigrants will experience diminishing identification with the homeland with each generation. They argue that if issues of belonging and identity were examined in terms of emotions and emotional processes, then such 'straight-line' theses would be confounded. Kelly and Lusis (2006) introduced the concept of 'transnational habitus' to capture the multiple forms of capital that migrants embody and which link transnational contexts. Building on Holt et al.'s (2013) arguments on emotions and habitus, I focus here on the emotional dimensions of transnational habitus. While the literature on emotional transnationalism (Wolf, 2002; Faria, 2014) foregrounds the long-distance attachments and belonging of migrants and diasporic descendants, I examine the emotional dimensions of transnational habitus in order to make sense of the political subjectivity of the Burmese-Chinese. The emotional dimensions of their transnational habitus, I argue, is characterised by appreciation for the opportunities allowed by their Chinese identity but also wariness of the implications this may have for their life-worlds in Myanmar.

The emotions and emotional processes experienced by the Burmese-Chinese point to lingering ties that they retain with China as Chinese diasporic descendants living in Myanmar. China is regarded not only as a crucible of ancestral culture but also a site of learning, due to its proximity and the accelerated development it experienced after economic reforms in 1979. As an example, I relate here the identity and emotional negotiations of the Burmese-Chinese respondent who had introduced me to the temple elders (see previous section). His family owns a candy factory in Myanmar, which is located in the outskirts of Mandalay. His grandfather migrated from Guangdong province to settle in Myanmar but it was his father who started the family business. He recalled that his father used to prepare the candy by getting the children to assist in manually stirring the candy mixture and wrapping them in paper. During the 1990s, a period when international travel outside of Myanmar was rare, through contacts from the clan association, his father had the opportunity to visit candy factories in China and saw that the businesses there were using mechanisation. At that time, such technology was not easily available in Myanmar.

His father studied the machines he saw in China carefully and by trial and error replicated one such machine when he returned to Myanmar. Consequently, the family business was able to produce candies in larger quantities, extending its reach to markets in other parts of Myanmar. At the factory site, the respondent showed me two machines and explained that one he had bought recently for US$20,000 while the other is the old machine that his father had built all those years ago. Even though his father was deceased, the family decided to retain the machine to remind themselves of their humble beginnings and, by implication, the opportunities afforded through their links to China. Without the visit to China where his father learned about mechanisation, the family fortune would have been different now. Today, the family business continues to purchase candy wrappers from China since the material is sold more cheaply there than in Myanmar. His young children, like those in many other Burmese-Chinese families, continue to learn Mandarin and Chinese customs through their cultural community in Myanmar.

In narrating his family story, the Burmese-Chinese respondent was visibly grateful for the economic opportunities afforded through lineage networks and a cultural habitus he inhabits that allowed him to capitalise on opportunities in China. As Levitt (2009) observes, when the second generation or diasporic descendants are 'brought up in households that are regularly influenced by people, objects, practices and know-how from their ancestral homes, they are socialised into its norms and values and they learn how to negotiate its institutions'. The ability to communicate in Mandarin and Chinese dialects opens doors in China for the Burmese-Chinese who want to capitalise on educational and business opportunities there. For example, the temples run Chinese language classes for children and young adults. The textbooks they use are adopted from China and student exchange programmes are conducted with schools in Yunnan province, China. Families in Myanmar may return to China to conduct rites for their ancestors buried there (*jizu*). Business people develop economic opportunities in China through visits organised by the Chinese embassy in Myanmar and China's *qiaoban* (diaspora-centred government agencies). In turn, the Chinese temples-cum-clan associations in Myanmar regularly host

visiting business and government delegations from China. The emotional transnationalism (Wolf, 2002) they experience, however, is mixed. China is considered an ancestral
land and considerable pride is placed on how the Burmese-Chinese have maintained their
ancestral culture generationally, despite the many hurdles placed by the laws and policies
for assimilating into Burman society.

But the Burmese-Chinese recognise that they are Myanmar nationals and their affective
ties are anchored in Myanmar as the place where their families live and where their memories and futures are based. They do not have legal citizenship status in China and they recall
that the Chinese government did not intervene when the Burmese-Chinese experienced
ethnic persecution during the 1960s. Their prominent economic linkages with China may
in fact jeopardise their safety in Myanmar in two ways: first, by incurring the resentment
of less wealthy Burmans; and second, calling into suspicion whether their loyalties lie with
China or Myanmar. As mentioned in the previous section, the Burmese-Chinese minimise
such risks and secure their place in Myanmar by 'doing good works' such as donating to
temples and serving food to the resident monks to demonstrate their respect and piety.
At one such event that I observed, the family donated alm bowls, robes and other daily
necessities used by the monks. The family hired helpers to prepare vegetarian food for the
monks and they took turns to go from table to table to serve the monks. From a religious
perspective, paying homage to revered monks in this way serves as penance for the sins
they had committed. But such obligatory social exchanges also function as affective
practices that approximate citizenship to secure their membership in a society where they
are considered partial outsiders. The politics of hate and ensuing emotional subjectivities
they experience constitute a habitus in which economic capital is used to secure the cultural
and social capital that allows them to maintain membership in the breach.

CONCLUSION

As descendants of migrants, the Burmese-Chinese in Myanmar experience exclusion
from citizenship. Although other ethnic minorities in Myanmar are subject to Burman
domination as well, the Burmese-Chinese are subject to suspicion also on account of the
transnational ties with China, the larger neighbour to the east of Myanmar. They negotiate ethnic hatred that is manifested through laws, policy directives and actions. Such acts
of hate prompt feeling rules that subjects of hate come to recognise and navigate emotionally and behaviourally in their daily lives. Towards fear of violence and punishment, the
Burmese-Chinese develop stoicism and quiet perseverance for survival and to maintain
their cultural community. Their emotional subjectivities operationalise the deployment
of economic, social and cultural capital for the purpose of securing membership in the
breach, moving between illegality/legality and informal/formal citizenship practices.
Such acts of citizenship approximations direct attention to the emotions that constitute
political subjectivity, even if these are less visible than the emotions that drive collective
mobilisation and activism towards unjust treatment. As Olson (2016, p. 836) observes,
'unresolved or unrecognised emotions could be signalling habits or policies that require
moral movement and attention to things that have, for various reasons, been excluded
from our sensibilities'.

In this chapter I also considered how the emotional subjectivities of the Burmese-

Chinese prompt them to create spaces of safety within Myanmar and deploy spatial strategies to preserve their culture and nurture a sense of community. They use temple spaces, considered legitimate places of worship to the dominant Buddhist population, as a domain for nurturing Chinese language, culture and social networks with co-ethnics in both Myanmar and China. The chapter has noted that the long-distance links they maintain with China represent a resource for accruing economic, cultural and social capital. However, those same transnational ties may also jeopardise their safety in Myanmar where Burman nationalists seek to advance assimilation and preserve national sovereignty in a regional context in which China's influence looms large. The chapter focuses attention on the transnational habitus and affective practices of diasporic descendants as they negotiate inclusion and exclusion in both worlds. It argues for the importance of considering the circumstances and ways in which the emotions towards transnational migration and citizenship translate into less visible but no less important expressions of political subjectivity in everyday life.

REFERENCES

Ahmed, S. (2004), 'Affective economies', *Social Text*, **22** (2), 117–39.

Amin, A. (2012), *Land of Strangers*, Cambridge: Polity Press.

Anderson, K. and S.J. Smith (2001), 'Editorial: emotional geographies', *Transactions of the Institute of British Geographers*, **26** (1), 7–10.

Askins, K. (2016), 'Emotional citizenry: everyday geographies of befriending, belonging and intercultural encounter', *Transactions of the Institute of British Geographers*, **41** (4), 515–27.

Bayat, A. (1997), 'Un-civil society: the politics of the "informal people"', *Third World Quarterly*, **18** (1), 53–72.

Boccagni, P. and L. Baldassar (2015), 'Emotions on the move: mapping the emergent field of emotion and migration', *Emotion, Space and Society*, **16**, 73–80.

Bosco, F.J. (2007), 'Emotions that build networks: geographies of human rights movements in Argentina and beyond', *Tijdschrift voor Economische en Sociale Geografie*, **98** (5), 545–63.

Bourdieu, P. (1986), 'The forms of capital', in John Richardson (ed.), *Handbook of Theory and Research in the Sociology of Education*, New York: Greenwood Press, pp. 280–91.

Bourdieu, P. (1990), *The Logic of Practice*, Stanford, CA: Stanford University Press.

Chang, W.-C. (2014), *Beyond Borders: Stories of Yunnanese Chinese Migrants of Burma*, Ithaca, NY and London: Cornell University Press.

Chouinard, V. (2001), 'Legal peripheries: struggles over disabled Canadians' places in law, society and space', *Canadian Geographer*, **45** (1), 187–92.

Conway, D. and R.B. Potter (2009), 'Return of the next generations: transnational migration and development in the 21st century', in Dennis Conway and Robert B. Potter (eds), *Return Migration of the Next Generations: 21st Century Transnational Mobility*, Farnham, UK and Burlington, VT: Ashgate, pp. 1–16.

Coutin, S. (2013), 'In the breach: citizenship and its approximations', *Indiana Journal of Global Legal Studies*, **20** (1), 109–40.

Davidson, J. and C. Milligan (2004), 'Embodying emotion sensing space: introducing emotional geographies', *Social & Cultural Geography*, **5** (4), 523–32.

Erdal, M.B. (2014), '"This is my home": Pakistani and Polish migrants' return considerations as articulations about "home"', *Comparative Migration Studies*, **2**, 361–83.

Faria, C. (2014), 'I want my children to know Sudan: narrating the long-distance intimacies of diasporic politics', *Annals of the Association of American Geographers*, **104** (5), 1052–67.

Griffiths, M. (2014), 'The affective spaces of global civil society and why they matter', *Emotion, Space and Society*, **11**, 89–95.

Häkli, J. and K.P. Kallio (2014), 'The global as a field: children's rights advocacy as a transnational practice', *Environment and Planning D: Society and Space*, **32** (2), 180–200.

Heaney, J.G. (2011), 'Emotions and power: reconciling conceptual twins', *Journal of Political Power*, **4** (2), 259–77.

Ho, E.L.E. (2008), '"Flexible citizenship" or familial ties that bind? Singaporean transmigrants in London', *International Migration*, **46**, 146–75.

Ho, E.L.E. (2009), 'Constituting citizenship through the emotions: Singaporean transmigrants in London', *Annals of the Association of American Geographers*, **99** (4), 788–804.

Ho, E.L.E. and L.J. Chua (2016), 'Law and "race" in the citizenship spaces of Myanmar: spatial strategies and the political subjectivity of the Burmese Chinese', *Ethnic and Racial Studies*, **39** (5), 896–916.

Hochschild, A.R. (1983), *The Managed Heart: Commercialization of Human Feeling*, Berkeley, CA: University of California Press.

Holt, L. (2008), 'Embodied social capital and geographic perspectives: performing the habitus', *Progress in Human Geography*, **32**, 227–46.

Holt, L., S. Bowlby and J. Lea (2013), 'Emotions and the habitus: young people with socio-emotional differences (re)producing social, emotional and cultural capital in family and leisure space-times', *Emotion, Space and Society*, **9**, 33–41.

ILO (International Labour Organization) (n.d.), 'Burma Citizenship Law', accessed 26 June 2017 at http://www.ilo.org/dyn/natlex/docs/ELECTRONIC/87413/99608/. . ./MMR87413.pdf.

Jackson, L. (2016), 'Intimate citizenship? Rethinking the politics and experience of citizenship as emotional in Wales and Singapore', *Gender, Place & Culture*, **23** (6), 817–33.

Kelly, P. and T. Lusis (2006), 'Migration and the transnational habitus: evidence from Canada and the Philippines', *Environment and Planning A*, **38** (5), 831–47.

Levitt, P. (2009), 'Roots and routes: understanding the lives of the second generation transnationally', *Journal of Ethnic and Migration Studies*, **35**, 1225–42.

Levitt, P. and M.C. Waters (eds) (2002), *The Changing Face of Home: the Transnational Lives of the Second Generation*, New York: Russell Sage Foundation.

Nayak, A. (2011), 'Geography, race and emotions: social and cultural intersections', *Social & Cultural Geography*, **12** (6), 548–62.

Olson, E. (2016), 'Geography and ethics II: emotions and morality', *Progress in Human Geography*, **40** (6), 830–38.

Painter, J. and C. Philo (1995), 'Spaces of citizenship: an introduction', *Political Geography*, **14**, 107–20.

Roberts, J.L. (2016), *Mapping Chinese Rangoon: Place and Nation Among the Sino-Burmese*, Seattle, WA and London: University of Washington Press.

Sadiq, K. (2009), *Paper Citizens: How Illegal Immigrants Acquire Citizenship in Developing Countries*, New York: Oxford University Press.

Schober, J. (2005) 'Buddhist visions of moral authority and modernity in Myanmar', in M. Skidmore (ed.), *Burma at the Turn of the Twenty-first Century*, Honolulu: University of Hawai'i Press, pp. 113–32.

Stets, J. (2010), 'Future directions in the sociology of emotions', *Emotion Review*, **2** (3), 265–8.

Thawnghmung, A.M. (2011), 'The politics of everyday life in twenty-first century Myanmar', *Journal of Asian Studies*, **70** (3), 641–56.

Tong, C.K. (2011), *Identity and Ethnic Relations in Southeast Asia*, London: Springer.

Walsh, K. (2012), 'Emotion and migration: British transnationals in Dubai', *Environment and Planning D: Society and Space*, **30**, 43–59.

Wetherell, M. (2012), *Affect and Emotion: A New Social Science Understanding*, London: Sage.

Wolf, D.L. (2002), 'There's no place like "home": emotional transnationalism and the struggles of second-generation Filipinos', in P. Levitt and M.C. Waters (eds), *The Changing Face of Home: The Transnational Lives of the Second Generation*, New York: Russell Sage Foundation, pp. 255–94.

Wood, B.E. (2013), 'Young people's emotional geographies of citizenship participation: spatial and relational insights', *Emotion, Space and Society*, **9**, 50–58.

Wright, M.W. (2010), 'Geography and gender: feminism and a feeling of justice', *Progress in Human Geography*, **34** (6), 818–27.

Yiftachel, O. (2009), 'Critical theory and "gray space": mobilization of the colonized', *City*, **13** (2), 246–63.

25. Geographies of the next generation: outcomes for the children of immigrants through a spatial lens
Philip Kelly and Cindy Maharaj

INTRODUCTION

Immigration is an intergenerational process. By this, we mean that when immigrant parents find themselves marginalized in social and economic terms, the impacts of such marginalization do not end there, but are often reproduced among their children. These forms of marginalization in the first generation may be related to racism, labor market access, language barriers or precarious immigration status. While experiences of racism may be reproduced across generations, there is generally an assumption that other barriers to social mobility will not affect the next generation. Indeed, for many immigrant parents, it is precisely this hope of a better future for their children that fortifies them to withstand the indignities of marginalization. There is a powerful sense in many immigrant families that the next generation, fully educated and socialized in the place of settlement, will have all the advantages of a native-born member of that society.

For some, this does indeed seem to be the trajectory that is followed. In the United States, for example, second generation adults (those born to at least one immigrant parent) have a median household income that is significantly higher than the first generation and is roughly the same as the median for all American households (Pew Research Center, 2013). Rates of poverty and home ownership also improve significantly and converge with a national average. The rate of post-secondary graduation significantly exceeds the national average (36 per cent for the second generation, 31 per cent nationally) (Pew Research Center, 2013). Similar statistical stories can be told in other contexts with extensive programs for permanent immigrant settlement, including Canada, the United Kingdom and Australia (Boyd, 2009; Picot and Hou, 2011a, 2011b; Reitz et al., 2011).

There are, however, complexities hiding within such sweeping statistical portraits. There is a great deal of unevenness in the educational and employment outcomes of the next generation. In Canada, for example, various racialized groups see quite different levels of intergenerational social mobility. If graduation with a university degree is taken as a proxy for successful outcomes, there is considerable variation among groups. Kelly (2014, p. 15) uses 2011 data to show that among 25–29 year-olds who were childhood immigrants to Canada and who self-identify as Chinese or Korean women (using Canada's 'visible minority' categories for racialized groups), over 60 per cent held a university degree. Among Black, Filipino, Latin American and Southeast Asian groups, the rate was less than 30 per cent. This kind of disparity raises many questions, especially in the case of the Filipino community, where the parental generation is among the most highly educated of all immigrant groups. Clearly, then, there is more to intergenerational reproduction among immigrant families than the simple good news story of upward mobility would imply.

The disparity of outcomes is, furthermore, an issue of increasing concern as the second generation is expanding in both size and diversity in many immigrant-receiving countries. To take Canada as an example, even in a single decade between 2006 and 2016 there was a clear increase in the size and diversity of the second generation. In 2006, 18.7 per cent of 15–24 year-olds were members of the second generation and 14.9 per cent were first generation immigrants. By 2016, the second generation had grown to 21.9 per cent of this age cohort, and first generation immigrants were a further 17.9 per cent. In just ten years, then, the proportion of young people in this age cohort who were immigrants or the children of immigrants went from 33.6 per cent to 39.8 per cent. The profile of this group was also becoming more diverse. In 2006, 38.3 per cent of the second generation were members of racialized groups (termed 'visible minorities' as noted above). By 2016, this figure was 55.2 per cent – the largest being South Asian, Black, Chinese and Filipino (all data calculated from Statistics Canada, 2006, 2016). Similar patterns are evident in the United States as well. The second generation there is projected to increase from 24.5 per cent of the total population in 2012 to 36.9 per cent by 2050 (Pew Research Center, 2013).

THEORIZING NEXT GENERATION OUTCOMES

The American experience has dominated the debate over the educational and economic outcomes of the children of immigrants, but there is also an expanding literature in Europe, Canada and elsewhere (Crul and Vermeulen, 2003; Picot and Hou 2011a, 2011b; Reitz et al., 2011; Thomson and Crul, 2007). While early studies had assumed that the children of immigrants would gradually assimilate (i.e., converge with the mainstream in cultural and economic terms), the 1990s saw the development of theories that envisioned the possibility of downward mobility across generations. The most influential of these has been segmented assimilation theory, associated with sociologist Alejandro Portes and his collaborators (Portes, 1996; Portes and Fernandez-Kelly, 2008; Portes and Rumbaut, 2001; Portes and Zhou, 1993; Portes et al., 2009). They argue that major differences in the characteristics and circumstances of contemporary immigrant populations translate into the diverse outcomes experienced by their offspring.

The segmented assimilation framework points out various barriers to successful adaptation and mobility in the United States, including racial prejudice (the next generation being increasingly non-white), a labor market that provides fewer good jobs, and proliferating symptoms of social marginalization such as gangs and drugs that provide an alternative route out of school. The key question then is: how do some young people overcome these barriers while others do not? The segmented assimilation approach suggests three causal factors. The first is human capital – are the first generation educated professionals or are they unskilled (although the former may end up doing the latter kinds of work)? The second factor involves modes of incorporation – what is the context of reception in terms of treatment by the state (legal status), the attitude of the public at large (receptive, neutral, hostile) and the characteristics of the pre-existing co-ethnic community? The latter context is important since a very strong co-ethnic community may help counter the negative effects of a more hostile public or state. The pre-existing history of a particular group may also shape the reception of future arrivals. A third factor is family structure – to what extent do families stay together, and can they provide support, guidance and discipline for young people (support that can also be reinforced by a strong co-ethnic community)? Segmented assimilation theory also addresses the link between socio-economic mobility and ethnic identity (Rumbaut, 1996). The model suggests that the best outcomes are enjoyed by those who can move easily and comfortably between parental and mainstream cultures.

The outcomes for children might then be (1) stagnation or downward assimilation into subordinate manual or unskilled jobs or into 'deviant lifestyles' with a strong sense of social marginalization based on race; (2) mostly upward assimilation into the mainstream but with some blockages and ceilings based on race; or (3) upward assimilation and biculturalism, in which young people can work equally in multiple cultural registers. The combination of factors at play in any given case will determine which of these trajectories is followed. Low parental education may not hold back the success of the next generation if their parents have been incorporated positively and if they have stable family structure around them. Poor incorporation because of racial prejudice or spatial segregation might in turn be overcome by parents' high (but often unrecognized) human capital. The key point, then, is that there are different segments that define the trajectory of assimilation and social mobility – unlike a more benign interpretation of assimilation that sees it as a linear and ultimately universal process: the 'second-generation advantage' (Kasinitz et al., 2008; Waters et al., 2010; and in the Canadian context Abada et al., 2009; Picot and Hou, 2011a, 2011b).

Critics of the segmented assimilation approach have pointed out that the 'main-stream' of society, towards which the children of immigrants are supposedly moving when assimilation is successful, is itself moving (Alba and Nee, 2009). In particular, attitudes and legal frameworks in relation to diversity are quite different than in previous generations (Farley and Alba, 2002). The model also fails to acknowledge the role of peer groups, even as extensive empirical evidence indicates the importance of this factor (Ali and Fokkema, 2015).

Although these studies have been attentive to variations across different urban contexts, there is a need for a more complete geography of next generation outcomes. It is possible to identify a range of spatialities that constitute and shape the social and economic outcomes of the next generation. In this chapter, we seek to clarify the spatialities of next generation outcomes, with a particular focus on some of those spatialities that may provide critical perspectives on barriers to intergenerational social mobility. First, we look at the ways in which specific place-based experiences, and representations of place, shape intergenerational outcomes. In particular, geographical research has highlighted the role of school-based streaming into particular pathways or the attenuation of aspirations. Neighborhoods have also been seen as significant place-based shapers of trajectories and ambitions among youth from immigrant families. More broadly, research suggests that urban contexts at the scale of metropolitan regions offer quite different opportunities and life chances to the children of immigrants.

A second type of spatiality comes in the form of territory. The boundary-making effects of territory are seldom more apparent than in immigration processes and these in turn impact the outcomes of the next generation. Perhaps most clearly, a territorial boundary that excludes and renders some people 'illegal' will have a profound impact on parents' labor market integration and by extension the economic circumstances and rights of the family. Or, a selective territorial boundary that allows one family member to migrate, while others must follow later, will also impact the experiences of children. Finally, the ability of parents to practice certain kinds of employment is shaped by professional regulatory systems administered territorially in places of settlement.

A third spatiality is the transnational context of immigrants and their families. The next generation children of immigrants may never have set foot in their ancestral homeland, and yet it might exert a profound influence on their life course. The transnational financial commitments of their parents may affect their ability to fund post-secondary education; and there is evidence that ancestral homelands play an increasing role in the labor market and political engagements, as well as the ethnic identity, of the next generation. But a critical transnational lens also problematizes the bounded spaces, scales and temporalities through which immigrant experiences are often understood. It opens up a critical perspective on the roots of migration and the ways in which racialized identities have been formulated over time.

It is worth pointing out that the themes we address in this chapter will find varying levels of relevance in different contexts. Here we draw examples from the places and communities with which we are most familiar – hence there is a bias towards North American contexts. We should also note that in much of our discussion we will merge various categories into the phrase 'the next generation'. Conventionally, the second generation comprises those who were born in a country to which at least one of their parents were immigrants. Those who immigrate to a country as young children (usually defined as 12 years old or younger) are referred to as the 1.5 generation. There are significant differences in the experiences of these two groups, especially if the 1.5 generation arrived towards the upper end of the age range. Space precludes us from delving into these differences, so for the most part we settle for the 'next generation'.

GEOGRAPHIES OF THE NEXT GENERATION

In this section we will address each of our spatialities in turn: place, territory and transnationalism.

Place

A growing body of geographical literature has explored how place-based experiences shape the educational aspirations of next generation youth (Basu, 2011; Holloway et al., 2010). Other than the home, schools are primary places of socialization. From a very young age, children interact with significant members of school institutions such as teachers and academic counsellors who help prepare students to make critical career decisions (Basu, 2011; Kelly, 2015). During the upper years, especially in high school, students' career paths can be shaped through support in the course selection process and by learning about post-secondary opportunities. However, guidance and support can be a highly racialized and gendered process. It is not unusual for racialized and ethnic minority students to be guided into segmented sectors of work and to pursue careers associated with cultural stereotypes (James, 2012). James (2012) notes, for example, the stereotyping of African Canadian males in the Canadian school system and comments that black youth are often respected for athletic prowess, rather than their academic capabilities.

Just as stigmatization in schools can hinder the opportunities for youth, classroom policies can also play a role in educational trajectories. A clear example can be seen in Farrales's (2017) study of educational aspirations among Filipino students in Vancouver. By charting the first-hand experiences of Filipino youth, she shows that school-based streaming programs, such as English as a Second Language (ESL), hinder, stall and discourage these youths from completing high school. Students who migrate to Canada from the Philippines must 'prove' their English competency, despite being taught in English in their home country. The curriculum and structure of ESL programs for these students can often be repetitive, leaving many students concerned that they will never be fully integrated into 'regular' course work. Further frustrations are felt by Filipino youth in ESL programs because credits are not given for having completed the program. The outcome is that graduation is deferred for many young people and in some cases students drop out or delay their education (see also Farrales and Pratt, 2012; and for the case of Chinese students in Canada, Kobayashi and Preston, 2014).

Our second place-based spatiality is the neighborhood. Poor educational and employment outcomes of low-income youth have been tied to the social and cultural dimensions of neighborhoods. Much of the traditional literature on the neighborhood effect links socio-economic inequality to the demographic of inner city neighborhoods, the presence of violence, high concentrations of single-parent households and welfare recipients. Alternative perspectives have been offered by Bauder (2002) who shifts the focus away from analysing the pathology of neighborhood residents to the external practices that shape neighborhood-based outcomes. For example, the stigmatization of inner city areas as 'cultural wastelands' has meant that employers reject job applications from neighborhoods associated with the poor. Bauder (2002) suggests that another dimension of neighborhood stigmatization can be seen by looking at the interactions between children and the staff of neighborhood institutions. Some youth have faced stigmatization from individuals working in community centers, schools, libraries and local shop owners 'based on the cultural label associated with their neighborhood of residence' (p. 88). Discrimination in work-based opportunities, coupled with the lack of support from key community leaders, further hinders the mobility of ethnic minority youth.

Our third form of place-based influence on next generation outcomes concerns the broader differences between urban regions, even within the same country. Goodwin-White (2008), for example, looks at different ethnic minority groups in Los Angeles and New York, finding that in Los Angeles, US-born Hispanics see greater opportunities than in New York, or in the country as a whole. She points out that attention needs to be paid to a variety of factors that shape outcomes in specific urban settings. These factors include the local structure of the urban labor market in terms of inequality, wage levels and changing sectoral composition (i.e., the types of industries in which people are employed). We also need to look at the ways in which race has historically stratified the labor market in specific places. Urban regions may also differ in terms of their levels of unionization and civil society activism – consider, for example, the significant impact of the Justice for Janitors campaign in Los Angeles (Aguiar and Ryan, 2009). Variations in government programs at the urban scale may also make a difference, including welfare programs, crackdowns on undocumented labor and the regulation of housing markets. Overall, then, there are many place-based variables at work that seem to make a difference to next generation outcomes at an urban scale. Making a similar point, Ellis and Almgren

(2009) note that opportunities for next generation youth require equal access to labor markets, educational resources, high levels of electoral participation and labor unions.

Territory

Territory 'delimits the spatial scope and limits of sovereignty, jurisdiction, administration, and citizenship' (Delaney, 2009, p. 196) and is often applied to the scale of the national state. Territory can, however, operate through other scales and institutions, most notably through the power of subnational jurisdictions and other spaces over which power is exercised by public or private institutions (university campuses, shopping malls, industrial estates and so on). Broadly speaking, then, territory can be thought of as the 'spatialization of power of various kinds' (Delaney, 2009, p. 196). Here we will focus on the territorial power of the state, which is exercised over migrants in several ways, all of which may have profound implications for the life chances and outcomes of their children.

Territories necessarily involve the creation and enforcement of borders, which start with decisions about who may legally enter and remain within a territory (Anderson, 2013; Goldring and Landolt, 2013). When migrants enter, or stay, without legal recognition from the state, the impact on their children can be profound. This has been at the root of the 'Dreamer' movement in the United States, which takes its name from the federal DREAM (Development, Relief and Education for Alien Minors) Act, introduced into the US Congress in August 2001 but then abandoned after 9/11 (Milkman, 2016). The Act sought to provide a path to permanent residency for those who had entered the United States illegally as minors (usually accompanying their parents). The Obama administration implemented a Deferred Action for Childhood Arrivals (DACA) program that delayed deportation and granted a work permit – a program that the Trump administration is in the process of dismantling. Around 800,000 individuals were enrolled in the DACA program in 2017, indicating the sheer scale of the phenomenon.

While a state decides who can enter and live legally within its territorial jurisdiction, immigration policy also dictates whether family members can accompany a migrant. Canada's Live-in Caregiver Program (LCP) is one example of an immigration program that requires participants to work for several years before they can apply for permanent residency. The LCP was created by Canada's federal government in 1993 and provided a supply of migrant care labor – in part to compensate for the lack of a national child care policy or adequate in-home care for the elderly or disabled. The LCP required participants to complete at least 24 months or 3,900 hours (within a four-year period) of full-time work as caregivers before they qualified to apply for permanent residency (Pratt, 2012). Living in the employer's home was also mandatory until 2014 when significant changes were introduced to the program. There are, however, significant time lags between each of these stages, with the Canadian government taking about four years to process applications for permanent residency. Most of those entering the LCP are women from the Philippines, where public and private institutions train, recruit and deploy care workers to countries around the world (Rodriguez, 2010).

As a result of enforced family separation and long delays in processing times, the family stability that children need is often sacrificed. Children often feel abandoned by their mothers and many miss their grandmothers who looked after them in the Philippines when their mothers were in Canada (Pratt, 2012). Long-term family separation also often harms marital relations. Several studies have documented the effects of family separation on the educational outcomes of Filipino-Canadian youth. Pratt et al. (2008) found that recently arrived Filipino youth in Vancouver tended to have lower grades and higher drop-out rates in high school. They attribute these patterns to family separation under the LCP and the resulting family conflict, the shock of downward social mobility as children arrive to find that their lifestyles will be very different than in the Philippines, and the intensity of labor market participation required of mothers who have been deskilled (see also de Leon, 2009; Farrales and Pratt, 2012; Pratt, 2012). Kelly (2014) and Austria et al. (2018) find a similar set of processes at play in the Toronto region, noting also that the restrictions associated with the LCP led to significantly lower academic achievement among the children of caregivers. Austria et al. conclude that there is 'a clear relationship between the precarity of status and disrupted family life that the program requires, the precarity of employment that often results, and the outcomes and experiences of children in the school system' (2018, p. 72).

A third effect of territorial power is often the determination of what kinds of work immigrants are able to undertake. Even where parents have been selected for immigration based on their skills, education and experience, they may still find themselves unable to practice their profession and therefore languishing at the precarious margins of the labor market. Many professions are regulated at national or subnational levels and it is these regulatory bodies that determine who is qualified to practice. Lawyers, for example, are regulated by bar societies at the scale of individual states in the United States and provinces in Canada. In some cases, professionals can practice in other countries – the European Union provides a single market for legal services, for example – but in general access to professions is restricted to those recognized by territorial regulatory bodies. This gives extensive gatekeeping powers to professional licensing bodies and the ability to exclude newcomers from practicing (Chatterjee, 2015; Sharma, 2006).

Girard and Bauder (2007) provide a case study of the regulatory body for professional engineers in the Canadian province of Ontario. They use Pierre Bourdieu's (1986) notion of institutional cultural capital to suggest that the capital held by immigrants in the form of foreign credentials is devalued by the Canadian regulator. Girard and Bauder also suggest that the testing processes applied by the regulatory body seek conformity to a culturally specific way of practicing the profession. Here they draw upon Bourdieu's concept of 'habitus' as a set of tacit codes, traits and requirements that constitute the unwritten 'rules of the game'. Put another way, these requirements seek a 'cultural fit' that is hard to achieve for immigrants trained in other contexts. In this way, the barriers to entry go beyond the assessment of technical skills and also encompass teamwork, leadership, communication and presentation skills. Thus, '[u]ntil candidates internalize the habitus of the engineering profession in the form of Canada-specific professional practices and "ethics", they will not be licensed as a professional engineer regardless of how well they understand and can apply the scientific principles of engineering' (Girard and Bauder, 2007, p. 47).

The impact of exclusionary practices for first generation immigrants is felt in the second generation. The reduced earning power of immigrant parents due to their devalued professional credentials has a variety of implications for their children (Austria et al., 2018; Kelly et al., 2012). First, the income levels of families with deprofessionalized parents means that post-secondary education is a more difficult financial proposition. Second, youth in immigrant communities have fewer networks and role models to guide them into remunerative professional careers. Third, youth have more difficulty in seeing themselves and imagining their future in professional occupations in which their parents' generation is underrepresented. In all of these ways, both material and intangible, parental deprofessionalization, driven in part by the territorial power of regulatory bodies to define who is worthy of professional recognition, can resonate into the lives of the next generation.

Transnationalism

There is increasing interest in the ways in which the lives of the 1.5 and second generation are not constituted in quite the same way as the 3+ generations. Lives are lived transnationally.

First, and most prosaically, financial commitments to relatives left behind may play a significant role in the families of next generation youth. The obligation to support the living expenses, tuition fees, medical bills and business investments of family members 'back home' may represent a significant drain on a household's financial resources. This, in turn, deepens the need for young people to focus on working rather than extended post-secondary studies, and places constraints on a family's capacity to pay for post-secondary education. The impact of this kind of obligation is illustrated in Kelly's (2014, p. 20) study of Filipino youth in Toronto, where one respondent described the support sent by her parents for the university education of a relative in the Philippines, while she settled for a shorter community college program:

> . . . I even question my mom – I'm like, 'Why are you supporting people?' She actually supports someone, like, sends them to school, right, she's supporting one of my cousins to go to school. I'm like, 'How can you support them and yet not support my education?' Like, I had to work for my education. I'm like, 'That's kinda weird.' I'm like, 'I am your child, after all.' But you know their reasoning is it's easy for you to earn money here, unlike in the Philippines where you need to have connections to get the good jobs. (Focus group participant, 2013)

Transnational connections with the homeland can also play a tangible role in the life course of next generation youth. There is increasing attention, for example, to the phenomenon of homeland tourism, employment and activism among next generation youth (Foner, 2009; Levitt, 2009; Levitt and Waters, 2002; Wessendorf, 2013). There is also an acknowledgment that for the next generation the ancestral homeland has significance as a source of hyphenated identity formation. This involves the role of the homeland as part of a process of 'ethnification' in which identity is developed relationally in the context of a 'host' society in which they are a minority (Haller and Landolt, 2005). Haikkola (2011, p. 1202), for example, argues that the 'transnational field of relations that children have been incorporated into forms a significant context for their everyday lives'. The idea of the homeland and its connotations can be as important as any tangible connection with the place. Levitt and Waters (2002, p. 24) therefore describe the homeland as a 'place of desire that one returns to in one's imagination'. A yearning to explore the homeland may be manifested in the form of visits, volunteering, pursuing a career, as well as political activism and solidarity missions (Garrido, 2011; Pratt et al., 2008).

A third form of transnationalism is, at the same time, perhaps both the most intangible and the most impactful. The lives of next generation youth are transnational not just because of family visits, financial remittances or communications linkages. They are also transnational because of the prior connections (and connotations) that tie their family's places of origin and settlement. As Espiritu (2003) points out in relation to the American context, 'contemporary immigrants from the Philippines, South Vietnam, South Korea, Cambodia, and Laos come from countries that have been deeply disrupted by US colonialism, war, and neocolonialism' (p. 11). For this reason, she argues for a 'critical transnational approach' to understanding the experiences of immigrants and the generations that follow:

> From an America-centric perspective, the stories of Filipino and Mexican migration begin when the migrants arrive on US soil. Thus told, the differences in their socioeconomic profiles become 'interiorized'; that is, they become differences in natural abilities, unmediated by global politics and power. But when recounted from a critical transnational perspective, the stories of Filipino and Mexican migration must begin with US military, economic, and market intervention in the Philippines and Mexico, respectively. It is the history of the US exercise of global power in Asia and Latin America – and not of the immigrants' abilities and values – that shape the terms on which these groups enter and become integrated into the United States. (Espiritu, 2003, p. 13)

This presents a rich line of thinking that highlights several points. First, that colonial and neocolonial exploitation, and the class relations and political systems that were thereby created and sustained, are often the root causes of migration from source countries. Most migration is economic migration in search of better opportunities, but the lack of opportunities in the 'homeland' is a direct result of unequal colonial and neocolonial power. The same argument could quite easily be made in relation to the migrations that reflect the imperial reach of other contemporary migration destinations, notably the United Kingdom and France (Gilroy, 1987; Samers, 1997, 1998). A second point is that the racial hierarchies created and entrenched by colonialism inform the racialized subjectivities that migrants and their children occupy. As Espiritu (2003, p. 6) points out, 'immigrant lives are shaped not only by the social location of their group within the host country but also by the position of their home country within the global racial order'. Importantly, it is the implied superiority of whiteness, established by colonialism, that continues to render racialized youth as 'other' within societies where whiteness is taken as the norm. This point is equally applicable to settler colonies such as Canada, Australia and New Zealand as it is to the colonial heartlands themselves. More broadly, these points highlight the fact that a transnational space – historical and contemporary – is always part of the story when understanding the lives of next generation youth.

CONCLUSION

Much of this chapter has related to specific communities and contexts, with a weighting towards those that are most familiar to us. The illustrative examples, however, are less important than the broader point concerning the development of a critical geographical perspective on the socio-economic outcomes of the children of immigrants.

We suggest that a geographical focus on the spatialities of intergenerational social mobility is essential. We have delineated three sets of spatialities. The first concerns the ways in which specific places shape youth outcomes in terms of education and employment.

Schools represent key sites where the pathways and aspirations of immigrant and next generation youth are shaped, while neighborhoods can be both stigmatizing and confining. The broader urban context can also create some strikingly different outcomes for the children of immigrants. In all of these ways, then, the specificity of social relations within places, and the representation of spaces, are integral to understanding youth outcomes. A second fundamental form of spatiality is the territorial power of states to determine legal residency, to enforce family separation during the immigration process, and to shape access to privileged segments of the labor market. All of these processes have direct impacts on the economic resources available to immigrant families, relations within families, and the legal status of childhood immigrants. Third, viewing next generation outcomes within the frame of a transnational spatiality allows us to think about the social processes that link life in one place with life in another. The mobility of both people and remittance capital between countries reminds us of the need to think outside of contained spaces in understanding the processes that might shape next generation outcomes. Moreover, taking a critical transnational perspective emphasizes the ways in which historical and contemporary relations of power shape the racialized hierarchies into which the next generation is born.

These forms of spatiality are not necessarily novel – many are already being explored by geographers and others. They are also far from exhaustive – there are many other ways in which a spatial perspective can be applied. We have, for example, deliberately avoided the home as a place in which intergenerational mobility is shaped. There would be good reasons for thinking carefully about the home as a place, but at the same time it is easy to slip into a pathologizing tendency that blames parents for the outcomes seen by their children. We believe that a critical perspective needs to look beyond such arguments, and thus beyond the space of the home, to examine systemic processes. The key point, though, is that geographers need to approach the question of next generation outcomes with a lens that draws attention to how spatialities are constitutive of intergenerational mobility and immobility.

REFERENCES

Abada, T., F. Hou and B. Ram (2009), 'Ethnic differences in educational attainment among the children of Canadian immigrants', *Canadian Journal of Sociology*, **34** (1), 1–28.

Aguiar, L. and S. Ryan (2009), 'The geographies of the Justice for Janitors', *Geoforum*, **40** (6), 949–58.

Alba, R. and V. Nee (2009), *Remaking the American Mainstream: Assimilation and Contemporary Immigration*, Cambridge, MA: Harvard University Press.

Ali, S. and T. Fokkema (2015), 'The importance of peers: assimilation patterns among second-generation Turkish immigrants in Western Europe', *Journal of Ethnic and Migration Studies*, **41** (2), 260–83.

Anderson, B.L. (2013), *Us and Them? The Dangerous Politics of Immigration Control*, Oxford: Oxford University Press.

Austria, J., P.F. Kelly and D. Wells (2018), 'Precarious students and families in Halton, Ontario: linking citizenship, employment and Filipino student success', in W. Lewchuk, S. Procyk and J. Shields (eds), *Precarious Employment: Causes, Consequences and Remedies*, Winnipeg: Fernwood, pp. 57–73

Basu, R. (2011), 'Multiculturalism through multilingualism in schools: emerging places of "integration" in Toronto', *Annals of the Association of American Geographers*, **101** (6), 1307–30.

Bauder, H. (2002), 'Neighbourhood effects and cultural exclusion', *Urban Studies*, **39** (1), 85–93.

Bourdieu, P. (1986), 'The forms of capital', in J.G. Richardson (ed.), *Handbook of Theory and Research for the Sociology of Education*, New York: Greenwood Press, pp. 241–58.

Boyd, M. (2009), 'Social origins and the educational and occupational achievements of the 1.5 and second generations', *Canadian Review of Sociology-Revue Canadienne De Sociologie*, **46** (4), 339–69.

Chatterjee, S. (2015), 'Skills to build the nation: the ideology of "Canadian experience" and nationalism in global knowledge regime', *Ethnicities*, **15** (4), 544–67.

Crul, M. and H. Vermeulen (2003), 'The second generation in Europe', *International Migration Review*, **37** (4), 965–86.

de Leon, C. (2009), 'Post-reunification reconciliation among PINAY domestic workers and adult daughters in Canada', *Canadian Woman Studies*, **27** (1), 68–7.

Delaney, D. (2009), 'Territory and territoriality', in R. Kitchin and N. Thrift (eds), *International Encyclopedia of Human Geography*, Amsterdam: Elsevier, pp. 196–208.

Ellis, M. and G. Almgren (2009), 'Local contexts of immigrant and second-generation integration in the United States', *Journal of Ethnic and Migration Studies*, **35** (7), 1059–76.

Espiritu, Y.L. (2003), *Home Bound: Filipino American Lives across Cultures, Communities, and Countries*, Berkeley: University of California Press.

Farley, R. and R. Alba (2002), 'The new second generation in the United States', *International Migration Review*, **36** (3), 669–701.

Farrales, M. (2017), 'Delayed, deferred and dropped out: geographies of Filipino-Canadian high school students', *Children's Geographies*, **15** (2), 207–23.

Farrales, M. and G. Pratt (2012), 'Stalled development of immigrant Filipino youths: migration, suspended ambitions and the ESL classroom', Working Paper Series, Metropolis British Columbia, Vancouver.

Foner, N. (2009), *Across Generations: Immigrant Families in America*, New York: SUNY Press.

Garrido, M. (2011), 'Home is another country: ethnic identification in Philippine homeland tours', *Qualitative Sociology*, **34** (1), 177–99.

Gilroy, P. (1987), *There Ain't No Black in the Union Jack: The Cultural Politics of Race and Nation*, London: Hutchinson.

Girard, E.R. and H. Bauder (2007), 'Assimilation and exclusion of foreign trained engineers in Canada: inside a professional regulatory organization', *Antipode*, **39** (1), 35–53.

Goldring, L. and P. Landolt (2013), *Producing and Negotiating Non-citizenship: Precarious Legal Status in Canada*, Toronto: University of Toronto Press.

Goodwin-White, J. (2008), 'Placing progress: contextual inequality and immigrant incorporation in the United States', *Economic Geography*, **84** (3), 303–32.

Haikkola, L. (2011), 'Making connections: second-generation children and the transnational field of relations', *Journal of Ethnic and Migration Studies*, **37** (8), 1201–17.

Haller, W. and P. Landolt (2005), 'The transnational dimensions of identity formation: adult children of immigrants in Miami', *Ethnic and Racial Studies*, **28** (6), 1182–214.

Holloway, S.L., P. Hubbard, H. Jöns and H. Pimlott-Wilson (2010), 'Geographies of education and the significance of children, youth and families', *Progress in Human Geography*, **34** (5), 583–600.

James, C.E. (2012), 'Students "at risk": stereotyping and the schooling of black boys', *Urban Education*, **47** (2), 464–94.

Kasinitz, P., J.H. Mollenkopf, M.C. Waters and J. Holdaway (2008), *Inheriting the City: The Children of Immigrants Come of Age*, New York: Russell Sage Foundation.

Kelly, P.F. (2014), *Understanding Intergenerational Social Mobility: Filipino Youth in Canada*, Montreal: Institute for Research on Public Policy.

Kelly, P.F. (2015), 'Transnationalism, emotion and second-generation social mobility in the Filipino–Canadian diaspora', *Singapore Journal of Tropical Geography*, **36** (3), 280–99.

Kelly. P.F., M. Garcia, E. Esguerra, Community Alliance for Social Justice (2012), 'Filipino immigrants in the Toronto labour market: towards a qualitative understanding of deprofessionalization', in R.S. Coloma, B. McElhinny, E. Tungohan, J.P. Catungal and L. Davidson (eds), *Filipinos in Canada: Disturbing Invisibility*, Toronto: University of Toronto Press, pp. 68–88.

Kobayashi, A. and V. Preston (2014), 'Being CBC: the ambivalent identities and belonging of Canadian-born children of immigrants', *Annals of the Association of American Geographers*, **104** (2), 234–42.

Levitt, P. (2009), 'Roots and routes: understanding the lives of the second generation transnationally', *Journal of Ethnic and Migration Studies*, **35** (7), 1225–42.

Levitt, P. and M.C. Waters (eds) (2002), *The Changing Face of Home: The Transnational Lives of the Second Generation*, New York: Russell Sage Foundation.

Milkman, R. (2016), 'A new political generation: millennials and the post-2008 wave of protest', *American Sociological Review*, **82** (1), 1–31.

Pew Research Center (2013), *Second-generation Americans: A Portrait of the Adult Children of Immigrants*, Washington, DC: Pew Research Center.

Picot, G. and F. Hou (2011a), *Preparing for Success in Canada and the United States: The Determinants of Educational Attainment among the Children of Immigrants*, Research Paper Series, Statistics Canada, Ottawa: Statistics Canada Analytical Studies Branch.

Picot, G. and F. Hou (2011b), *Seeking Success in Canada and the United States: The Determinants of Labour*

Market Outcomes among the Children of Immigrants, Research Paper Series, Statistics Canada, Ottawa: Statistics Canada Analytical Studies Branch.

Portes, A. (1996), *The New Second Generation*, New York: Russell Sage Foundation.

Portes, A. and P. Fernandez-Kelly (2008), 'No margin for error: educational and occupational achievement among disadvantaged children of immigrants', *Annals of the American Academy of Political and Social Science*, **620**, 12–36.

Portes, A. and R.G. Rumbaut (2001), *Legacies: The Story of the Immigrant Second Generation*, Berkeley, CA: University of California Press.

Portes, A. and M. Zhou (1993), 'The new 2nd-generation – segmented assimilation and its variants', *Annals of the American Academy of Political and Social Science*, **530**, 74–96.

Portes, A., P. Fernandez-Kelly and W. Haller (2009), 'The adaptation of the immigrant second generation in America: a theoretical overview and recent evidence', *Journal of Ethnic and Migration Studies*, **35** (7), 1077–104.

Pratt, G. (2012), *Families Apart: Migrant Mothers and the Conflicts of Labor and Love*, Minneapolis, MN: University of Minnesota Press.

Pratt, G., Philippine Women Centre of BC and Ugnayan ng Kabataang Pilipino sa Canada (2008), 'Deskilling across the generations: reunification among transnational Filipino families in Vancouver', Metropolis British Columbia Working Paper Series 08-06, Metropolis British Columbia Centre of Excellence for Research on Immigration and Diversity, Vancouver.

Reitz, J.G., H. Zhang and N. Hawkins (2011), 'Comparisons of the success of racial minority immigrant offspring in the United States, Canada and Australia', *Social Science Research*, **40** (4), 1051–66.

Rodriguez, R.M. (2010), *Migrants for Export: How the Philippine State Brokers Labor to the World*, Minneapolis, MN: University of Minnesota Press.

Rumbaut, R. (1996), 'The crucible within: ethnic identity, self-esteem, and segmented assimilation among children of immigrants', in A. Portes (ed.), *The New Second Generation*, New York: Russell Sage Foundation, pp. 119–70.

Samers, M. (1997), 'The production of diaspora: Algerian emigration from colonialism to neo-colonialism (1840–1970)', *Antipode*, **29** (1), 32–64.

Samers, M. (1998), 'Immigration, "ethnic minorities", and "social exclusion" in the European Union: a critical perspective', *Geoforum*, **29** (2), 123–44.

Sharma, N.R. (2006), *Home Economics: Nationalism and the Making of "Migrant Workers" in Canada*, Toronto: University of Toronto Press.

Statistics Canada (2006), Census of Population, Statistics Canada Catalogue no. 97-562-XCB2006010.

Statistics Canada (2016), Census of Population, Statistics Canada Catalogue no. 98-400-X2016190.

Thomson, M. and M. Crul (2007), 'The second generation in Europe and the United States: how is the transatlantic debate relevant for further research on the European second generation?', *Journal of Ethnic and Migration Studies*, **33** (7), 1025–41.

Waters, M.C., V.C. Tran, P. Kasinitz and J.H. Mollenkopf (2010), 'Segmented assimilation revisited: types of acculturation and socioeconomic mobility in young adulthood', *Ethnic and Racial Studies*, **33** (7), 1168–93.

Wessendorf, S. (2013), *Second-generation Transnationalism and Roots Migration: Cross-border Lives*, Farnham, Surrey: Ashgate.

26. Social media and Rwandan migration: a moral epistemology of return

Saskia Kok and Richard Rogers

INTRODUCTION

The Rwandan repatriation debate is timely and poignant. When the United Nations High Commissioner for Refugees (UNHCR) announced that the refugee status of Rwandan refugees who fled the country between 1959 and December 1998 would cease to exist in 2013 (UNHCR, 2011, 2013), many non-governmental organizations (NGOs) and refugee rights groups expressed concern regarding the premature invocation of the clause, asserting it could lead to coercive pressure to return and *refoulement* (AI, 2004; HRW, 2010). After a period of debate to reconsider UNHCR's recommendation for the invocation of the cessation clause, the date was extended several times, and ultimately pushed back and implemented in December 2017 (MIDIMAR, 2016; Tumwebaze, 2018; UNHCR, 2016). In a bid to aid the return process, and support income generating opportunities of returned Rwandan refugees, UNHCR in collaboration with the Government of Rwanda has implemented large-scale voluntary repatriation programs, which include the provision of reintegration packages before the end of the cessation clause. Despite repeated attempts to repatriate Rwandan refugees, a considerable number has been hesitant to return (IRIN, 2013).

In a long-standing effort to promote unity and reconciliation in Rwanda (Buckley-Zistel, 2006b; Longman, 2017), the Government of Rwanda, as well as other host countries, have long lobbied for this declaration, claiming that the country has been peaceful and safe to accept returnees (O'Connor, 2013). Voluntary repatriation, together with resettlement and local integration, are the durable solutions UNHCR advocates to ensure the safety and dignity of refugees. These approaches are key components of the refugee regime and are considered instrumental in accessing either protection or rights as they promise an end to the suffering of refugees (Black and Koser, 1999), which is mainly achieved through the re-establishment of a protective link between a (forced) migrant and the nation-state (Long, 2009). Nonetheless, increasingly, international organizations and scholarly research have called for the limits of repatriation to be addressed, highlighting the need to consider the long-term process of sustainable repatriation, which contrasts with the continued pressure by states to ensure refugee return (Long, 2009; UNHCR, 2008). Refugees often have an ambiguous feeling towards their homeland, and mostly consider repatriation as a return in terms of geographic placement as opposed to a return to one's 'home' (Black and Koser, 1999; Hammond, 1999; Long, 2009). As such, the process of repatriation as organized by governments and the international community has arguably overlooked those who speak for the majority of refugees (Harrell-Bond, 1989; Pottier, 1996).

In short, in an organized process of reconciling the Rwandan state, voluntary repatriation has been a viable option of the Government of Rwanda to embrace all members of society – both within Rwanda as well as abroad. Whilst the efforts to construct a collective identity and unite Rwanda, amongst others through a process of 'de-ethnicization', has been identified in scholarly literature (Buckley-Zistel, 2006b; Melvin, 2010; Moss, 2014), the success of its construction online, among the diaspora in social media, is understudied. To what extent can social media research, through publicly available data made available on Facebook, be utilized to study the resonance of Rwanda's reconstruction, reconciliation and engagement?

CONNECTED MIGRATION

Scholars have increasingly recognized that the analysis of migrant networks, both online and in the field, is crucial for understanding the dynamics of contemporary migration (Kissau and Hunger, 2010; Tilly, 1990; Vertovec, 2008). Studies have shown how social media may facilitate the process of migration by enhancing and sustaining social ties and transnational communities (Adamson and Kumar, 2014; Diminescu, 2008; Glick Schiller et al., 1995), or how the online circulation of voice, video, text and pictures may affect the process of social integration and political participation in the country of destination (Komito, 2011). It has been said that the rise of social media and availability of digital technology have made available specific enabling affordances that can help to give voice to individuals or (migrant) communities through information circulation, or the promotion of inter-group relations by way of collective action (Bennett and Segerberg, 2012; Soriano, 2013). The rise of the *connected* migrant (Diminescu, 2008), through mobility and connectivity, has thus enabled a shift in thinking from treating the migrant as 'uprooted' to one that emphazises mobilization and 'presence at a distance' (Diminescu, 2012). Whilst these strands of research are important for advancing the burgeoning field of migration in relation to digital technology, scant research exists with regard to how social media platforms may function as repositories for migrant data, and particularly how these data collections may be employed for social and political inference.

Whilst the emergence of the connected migrant and availability of tools and methods to repurpose digital data for social research (Rogers, 2013) provide the field of migration ample opportunity for social empiricism, these developments also raise numerous questions with regard to the use of digital data for understanding the social world. To what extent can clicks, likes and shares (in a social media platform such as Facebook) serve as a means to study behaviour such as content circulation within migrant communities? That is, how may social media analysis be made meaningful for migration studies? What forms of social knowledge does one obtain whilst doing research with (publicly available) platform data? We take these questions in turn to illustrate how social media data may be used to study connected migration, and how migration research may benefit from relying on digital data for studying social and political inference.

This study is based on a cross-disciplinary approach, drawing mainly on scholarly literature from media and migration studies. We examine the online engagement of the Rwandan diaspora on Facebook, questioning the potential of social media to either give voice to or silence (parts of) the diasporic community, together with the kinds of divides that may be identified. From a methodological perspective, we join scholars who have illustrated how social media data can be extracted and mapped, and used as productive repositories for migrant data (Crush et al., 2011; Diminescu, 2008; Kissau and Hunger, 2010). We employ digital methods for corpus building and analysis in a three-step process: web data capture, data enrichment and network analysis, and visualization (Kok and Rogers, 2017; Rogers, 2013), and focus specifically on building a corpus of Rwandan diaspora organizations on the web and on Facebook. Through an online network and content analysis, we thus examine the ways in which the web and digital technology may aid or silence diasporic engagement, but also how these repositories of data can be used as a source of study. In the Rwandan diaspora in North America and Europe, in geographically demarcated sets of Facebook pages, we have found a government-dominated narrative that is characterized by Rwanda's promotion of reconciliation and national unity which, as we argue, not only influences our knowledge of Rwanda's nation-building initiative, but also constrains and empowers alternative diasporic identities and views on return. As a result, we contend that the examination of digital data benefits the advancement of our understanding of migration practices, but also shows how online research may reflect a particular response bias. In the case of Rwanda, a specific construction of the social world emerges where predominantly a narrative of Rwandan unification prevails, and the critical diaspora voice is absent (which one may expect to find online).

The process of voluntary repatriation and return organized by the Government of Rwanda has arguably (re)constituted refugees residing in the diaspora both as citizens and members of the nation (O'Connor, 2013). In doing so, the government has been particularly successful in marshalling diasporic content on social media, staging its diaspora as 'agents of change'. This guiding narrative of Rwandan identity, afforded by social media and driven by the Government of Rwanda as well as its diaspora, influences what those gathering information may come to know about Rwandan matters of concern, including those considering return. As such, our findings are contiguous with previous research arguing that the government's nation-building discourse of national unity and de-ethnicization is counterproductive, for it denies an alternative space of differences, and 'silences criticism and legitimates grievances' by fabricating unity without reconciliation (Buckley-Zistel, 2006a, p. 102; Moss, 2014).

As a result of the study's findings, we propose a normative approach we call the 'moral epistemology of return', which seeks to specify how displacement and return is conceived, politicized and mediated with social media. By 'moral epistemology of return' we mean how one comes to know about the opportunities and consequences of repatriation to one's homeland, together with the concerns associated with not knowing about issues pertaining to return. Through the engagement of the Rwandan diaspora on social media spaces (on Facebook) that organize discussions and information surrounding the situation in the homeland, a meta-narrative of Rwandan unification and nation building prevails, putting on display a depoliticized process of repatriation driven by the government. Drawing upon Roy's (2004) notion of the 'preferably unheard' and also Long's (2008) observations concerning the politicized process of repatriation, we argue that the meta-narrative of the 'successful Rwandan diaspora' thus restricts the space available for alternative voices to be heard (both online and in the field). Ultimately, we do not argue that digital data is not suitable for empirical migrant research, but rather that future research needs to recognize these competing positionalities between how digital data can be used as proxy for social and political inference, and how a government-organized diasporic discourse influences epistemological and moral considerations of return.

ENABLING AFFORDANCES OF SOCIAL MEDIA

The one-time, perceived success of political liberalization in various countries in the Middle East, such as the 'Arab Spring' in Egypt (2011) or the 'Jasmine Revolution' in Tunisia (2010), is a major cause of the widespread debate of how social media could be viewed as a bearer of democratic affordances. Social media is said to give power to event organisers by enabling the circulation of information, promoting inter-group relations through the power of collective (and connective) action, weakening the ability of political regimes to exercise control of flows of information across borders, and promoting social and economic development (Bennett and Segerberg, 2012; Soriano, 2013). Hence, whilst the connection between digital technology and political change is complex and often times circumstantial, scholars and policy-makers have highlighted the potential of digital technology in shaping political mobilization. These views have been contested and fine-tuned by scholars from a wide range of related disciplines over the past decade, and remain the subject of debate (Castells, 2008; Dahlgren, 2005; Goldberg, 2011; Habermas, 1991, 1992, 2006; Papacharissi, 2002). Digital technology, through online platforms such as Facebook and Twitter, could be utilized to form groups and create social interaction, something that previously more often was facilitated in institutionalized settings (Shirky, 2008). Through communal 'cognitive surplus' (Shirky, 2010), groups would be able to produce significant results by sharing and coordinating efforts.

Critics have argued against the liberating potential of the internet, or the fallacy of so-called 'internet-centrism', claiming that it is these utopian views that strengthen the hand of authoritarian governments which surveil the traces the enthusiastic mobilizations leave behind online (Morozov, 2012). Even if people are engaged in political activism through social media, the low costs associated with online communication have made this type of activism too easy and thus overestimate commitment (Karpf, 2010; Morozov, 2009; White, 2010). The relationships on which so-called slacktivism are based are only existent on a micro-level, serving the feel-good factor of participants (Gladwell, 2010), which ultimately results in a decline of political engagement. As White (2010) argues, 'as the novelty of online activism wears off, millions of formerly socially engaged individuals who trusted digital organizations are coming away believing in the impotence of all forms of activism'.

When it comes to political conversation and interaction, some argue that social media platforms may in fact increase group polarization and isolation, as well as ideological segregation (McPherson et al., 2001; Pariser, 2011; Sunstein, 2001). The principle of homophily is seen as a determining factor surrounding (online) behaviour and how people structure their social interaction around socially similar individuals (Yardi and Boyd, 2010). Classic analyses of the liberal and conservative blogospheres in the United States found a divided community structure with limited interaction between liberal and conservative groups (Adamic and Glance, 2005), illustrating how social interaction can be seen as both a cause and effect of selection, in that online encounters affect and shift patterns of activities towards similar social behaviour (Crandall et al., 2008). The latter is in keeping with previous lines of research examining Noelle-Neuman's 'spiral of silence' (1974) on Facebook, whereby it is shown that people are less likely to speak openly about their political or policy-related issues when they feel their point of view or beliefs are in the minority (Hampton et al., 2014).

Furthermore, classic debates within media and migration studies emphasize the unequal opportunities in information access, termed the 'digital divide', whereby (low-skilled) migrants appear as a disadvantaged group owing to their lack of language skills, education or income (Benitez, 2006; Harlow and Guo, 2014; Ono and Zavodny, 2008). Additional demographic factors are shown to contribute to a lack of information access such as age, gender, disability, community type and ethnicity (Hargittai, 2010; Hoffman and Novak, 1998; Howard et al., 2001; Smith et al., 2009). It is argued that the internet is mostly used for 'capital-enhancing' purposes, especially amongst internet users coming from privilege (DiMaggio and Hargittai, 2001). Although the presence of a digital divide would arguably increase pre-existing qualities in political engagement or conversation, recent studies in transnational migration have shown how digital technology and social media are used to transform migrant networks and facilitate processes of migration (Dekker and Engbersen, 2012).

In the following we take up the Rwandan diaspora's use of social media. We focus on Facebook, the online platform used on a computer as well as smartphone, with a worldwide uptake (nearing 2 billion monthly users, including 1.8 billion mobile ones), with the exception of certain countries (China, Iran and Syria), where it is either routinely censored or unable to operate (Facebook, 2017). Rwandan diaspora populations are in greater numbers in such western countries as Belgium, France, United States, Canada, United Kingdom and the Netherlands (OECD, 2012), as well as in countries neighbouring Rwanda, particularly the Democratic Republic of the Congo, Uganda, Republic of Congo, Zambia and Kenya. For the purposes of this study we chose the countries with the highest Facebook penetration (North America and Europe) (Alexa, 2017). In the empirical analysis, we thus isolate Facebook content geographically, and compare how the diasporic communities engage (post and react) to content. The employed timeframe for the Facebook network analysis was set at January 2012 to June 2014, a 30-month period.

DIGITAL METHODS FOR EXAMINING THE RWANDAN DIASPORA

The empirical potentialities and issues involved in social media analysis have attracted widespread attention in recent years (Rogers, 2013; Tufekci, 2014). A shift in internet research from 'virtual' to 'grounded' approaches has prompted scholars to develop methods and repurpose digital data, or 'traces', for cultural and political research through the use of such web analysis software as the *Issue Crawler* and *Netvizz* for Facebook (Rieder, 2013; Rogers, 2010). The online, and the inherent dynamics captured and analysed through digital methods, has become a baseline against which societal conditions and cultural change can be assessed, also referred to as 'online groundedness' (Rogers, 2009). Scholars have also asserted that new media and digital methods can aid researchers in the study of social or cultural condition, and also with respect to migration (Adamson and Kumar, 2014; Diminescu, 2008; Kissau and Hunger, 2010; Kok and Rogers, 2017). Online platforms are considered to be spaces where diasporic networks are formed, and where migrant data may be extracted and analysed. This research thus aims to join scholars who are examining the broader structural dynamics of 'connected migration', drawing on methodology set out by the e-Diaspora Atlas programme as well as the Digital Methods Initiative.

One of the most prevalent problems pertaining to migration research is the difficulty in estimating scope, certainly online (Kok and Rogers, 2017). Accurate population data of diaspora is limited and ambiguous, with no estimates of the Rwandan diaspora online. As a result, this study relies mostly on inter-governmental and NGO reports as well as scholarly literature that have estimated the size of the Rwanda population abroad (Fahamu Refugee Programme, 2011; OECD, 2012), forming the starting point to an empirical examination of mapping the Rwandan diasporic community online. Subsequently, Rwandan diaspora-related web pages from North American and European countries are sourced through a two-step operation. First, the corresponding local domain search engines (google.be, google.ca, google.fr, google.nl, google.co.uk and google.com) are queried for [Rwandan diaspora], [Rwandan community], [Rwandan diaspora interest group] and similar (using the advanced operator to geo-locate results). Rwandan diaspora URLs are entered into the Issue Crawler, both per country as well as collectively in one mother crawl, whereupon it captures the outlinks of inputted sites, performs co-link analysis and outputs cluster maps (and URL lists ranked by inlink count). The found network suggests that Facebook is the largest node overall as well as in many of the 'national' networks, thereby confirming the importance of the further study of the social media platform.

In a second step, all of the organizations and group names are entered into Facebook search (via Netvizz), and if found, their pages are listed. Keyword searches for [Rwandan diaspora] and similar are also undertaken in Facebook. A total of 22 Rwandan diaspora Facebook pages are found and used as starting points (seeds) to the subsequent network analysis. With Netvizz (and Gephi), an inter-liked page analysis is performed and a network is built, both per country as well as overall. This technique is repeated until a point of saturation is reached, and no more Rwandan diasporic pages are found.

After the corpora are established, a classification scheme is developed based on the Facebook dataset for analysing the network according to the contextualized interpretations of all posts from the period in question. An additional platform-specific content analysis is performed, together with an analysis of the most engaged-with-content on Facebook according to the sums of likes, shares, comments and liked comments, again both per country as well as overall.

NETWORK ANALYSES: GOVERNMENT-DRIVEN DIASPORA

The network analyses of the Rwandan diaspora websites and Facebook groups point towards engagement that is predominantly centred on endorsement and commemoration activities organized by the Government of Rwanda, both on the web as well as on Facebook. Of all organizations present in the hyperlink (inter-actor) network generated by the Issue Crawler, the Rwanda Governmental Diaspora website under the auspices of Rwanda's Ministry of Foreign Affairs receives the most inlinks (after Facebook). A specific emphasis is placed on creating a cohesive community with Rwandan diaspora around the world, in order to foster a 'constructive relationship with their country of origin aiming at the national development of Rwanda' (Diaspora General Directorate, 2012). It has driven what is termed 'statist diaspora building', the products of which could be said to be visible in our findings (Betts and Jones, 2016), and thus arguably influences epistemological understandings of return.

The Issue Crawler analysis points towards a government-organized diaspora network as well as Facebook as the most important node (Figure 26.1). On Facebook, a total of 22 Rwandan diaspora Facebook pages are found through the methodology described above. The pages are used as starting points for the inter-page like analysis. The inter-page network analysis results in a network comprising 529 organizations (actors) (Figure 26.2). The network mostly consists of civic-oriented actors, including communities (65 actors), non-profit organizations (47 actors), governmental organizations (31 actors) and non-governmental organizations (29 actors) (Table 26.1, top 15 categories).[1] When turning to the analysis (Figure 26.2), the network reveals a large cluster revolving mainly around the governmental actors of President Paul Kagame and the Rwanda High Commissioner UK. This cluster is linked to (or liking) their commemoration events (Rwanda Week), Rwandan news, youth as well as diasporic networking sites (Rwandan International Network Association or RINA), which itself promotes other official Rwandan (diasporic and national) activities such as Rwandan Culture Week that is aimed at educating youth about Rwanda's rich cultural heritage.[2] The National Unity and Reconciliation Commission (NURC) has introduced a variety of societal-level interventions, together with frequently organized public meetings and commemoration events, urging Rwandans to reconcile and live together peacefully (Buckley-Zistel, 2006b; Longman, 2017). This main government-organized network found online is flanked by two other cluster types of interest. One is an alternative genocide commemoration cluster, separate from the Government of Rwanda's and the other country clusters, consisting of pages hosted by the US Holocaust Museum, Never Again International – Canada (NAI-C), a youth-focused NGO led by civil society that originated in Winnipeg, as well as the Enough Project, the Washington, DC-based NGO critical of Rwanda's engagement in the ongoing violence across the border in the Democratic Republic of Congo (DRC). The remaining clusters are mainly country-specific and are host land (or integration-related within Canada) rather than oriented to the homeland.

CONTENT ANALYSES: UNITY AND RECONCILIATION

With respect to the content analyses of the Facebook pages (comprising 703 posts over a 30-month period), we sort them according to most-engaged-with content and categorize them through emergent coding. First, the engagement analysis reveals a series of findings complementary to the overall network analysis results from the web and Facebook: there is a clear narrative visible surrounding 'Rwandaness' (Buckley-Zistel, 2006b) with uplifting homeland commemoration events organized by the Government of Rwanda and Rwanda's diaspora community, together with Rwandan business events and beauty pageants. The content most engaged with on the specific country pages also fits the overall pattern. In Belgium, most content is focused almost exclusively on Miss and Mister pageants, which is also the material that dominates the French diasporic pages (Figure

---

[1] The categorization of the pages is done by the page administrators, and is included in the extracted dataset through Netvizz.

[2] The data suggests that the Facebook network does not necessarily follow a power law; there is a distribution of hubs. The graph density, clustering coefficient and connectivity level indicate that the Rwandan network is loosely interconnected, with clear, distinct country clusters.

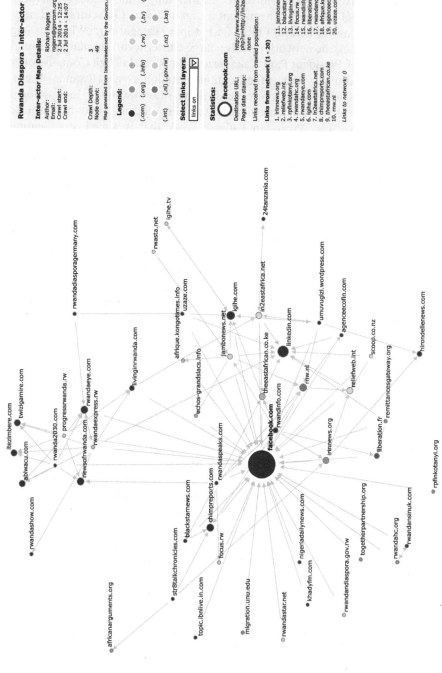

Rwanda Diaspora – Inter-actor

Inter-actor Map Details:

Author: Richard Rogers
Email: rogers@govcom.org
Crawl start: 2 Jul 2014 - 12:25
Crawl end: 2 Jul 2014 - 14:07

Crawl Depth: 3
Node count: 49

Map generated from Issuecrawler.net by the Govcom.org Foundation, Amsterdam.

Legend:

(.com) (.org) (.info) (.rw) (.net) (.tv) (.fr) (.edu)

(.int) (.nl) (.gov.rw) (.nz) (.ke)

Select links layers:

links on ▽

Statistics:

○ facebook.com

Destination URL: http://www.facebook.com/sharer/sharer
php?u=http://in2eastafrica.net/why-...
Page date stamp: none

Links received from crawled population: 11012

Links from network (1 - 20)

1. irinnews.org
2. reliefweb.int
3. rpfinkotanyi.org
4. rwandahc.org
5. rwandaeye.com
6. igihe.com
7. in2eastafrica.net
8. chimpreports.com
9. theeastafrican.co.ke
10. rrw.nl

11. jambonews.net
12. blackstarnews.com
13. livinginrwanda.com
14. focus.rw
15. rwandinfo.com
16. liberation.fr
17. rwandandiaspora.gov.rw
18. afrique.kongotimes.info
19. agenceecofin.com
20. uzaze.com

Links to network: 0

< I >

Source: Issue Crawler data, 2 July 2014.

Figure 26.1   Visual representation of the Rwanda web corpus and its interlinkings

Rwanda Diaspora Facebook inter-page like network

Rwanda   Canada   Belgium   US   France   Transnational   UK   Kenya

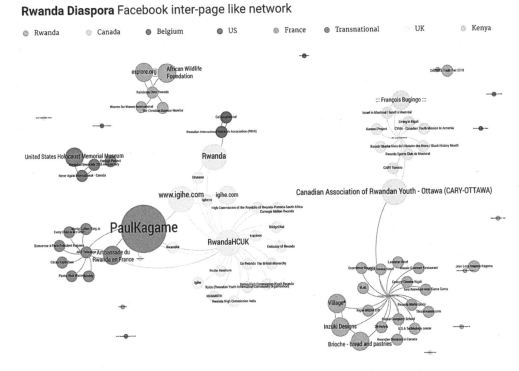

Source: Netvizz data – rendered by Gephi, 4 July 2014.

Figure 26.2 Network graph of the Rwanda Facebook corpus n = 529

26.3). In Canada, most of the engagement is centred around posts focusing on investment forums and Rwanda Week, the annual commemoration event of the 1994 Genocide, designed by President Kagame (Guardian, 2014). The Rwandan diaspora residing in the United States focuses on contacting the homeland (with phone cards), and raising funds for Rwandan exchange students educated abroad and understood to be returning home (Figure 26.4). To sum up, the country diasporic analyses result in content collections that build the case and demonstrate the benefit of returning to Rwanda.

With respect to the content analysis, where the themes are derived from the research findings, the two most dominant ones in the analysis are *Rwanda endorsement* (168 posts, 24 per cent) and *memory and reconciliation* (132 posts, 19 per cent), followed by *community and sociality* (99 posts, 14 per cent), *Rwanda investment and business* (58 posts, 8 per cent), as well as *beauty pageants* (35 posts, 5 per cent) (Table 26.2). The majority of the content is thus specifically centred on endorsing an image of Rwanda of national unity as well as organizing commemoration activities, all of which are of the government's framing (rather than, say, the US Holocaust Museum's or the Enough Project's).

Additional categorization is undertaken concerning their directionality of engagement, where most content is directed towards the homeland (353 posts), followed by the host land (178 posts). As cases in point, several users have repeatedly posted content regarding

Table 26.1   Top 15: classification of Rwanda pages by type of organization (n = 315, 59 per cent of total number of pages)

Categories	Quantity
Community	65
Non-profit organization	47
Governmental organization	31
Non-governmental organization (NGO)	29
Company/business	22
Organization	20
Media/news/publishing	19
Travel/leisure	19
Local business	16
Community organization	11
Website/online	11
Education	9
Magazine	8
Public figure	8
Sports team	7
Total	322

Rwanda's development and the numerous commemoration activities, with one user writing:

> Rwanda Week in Canada is one of our innovative activities and services that will be offered to the community at large . . . from young children to the elderly. Our philosophy is to support survival and growth of our organizations and promote the welfare of our members while giving back to our home country.[3]

These sorts of messages appear to endorse a specific image of Rwanda, as one user wrote with regard to the Rwandan film, *Rising From the Ashes* (2012): 'The fundraising event was attended by the Rwandan High Commissioner, Vincent Karega, who emphasised the importance of the film carrying a positive message to the world about Rwanda and that the country is actively striving for and achieving "peace, stability and rejuvenation".'[4]

It is mainly the absence of critical content, however, that raises questions regarding the kinds of voices present in the diaspora on Facebook, and especially one's capacity to differentiate them from the governmental. For example, one of the three critical posts (of 703) is an article from the *Independent* questioning President Kagame's desire to extend his term in power, through constitutional amendment. The article cites a human rights journalist, who argues that by remaining president, Kagame would avoid facing arrests for war crimes carried out in Eastern Congo since Rwanda supports the rebel groups guarding 'conflict mineral' deposits in the region. Whilst these notes are critical of Rwanda's so-called 'semblance of democracy', which later fell apart when Kagame engineered the

---

[3]   Anonymized user, "Rwandan Diaspora in Canada", *Facebook*, 10 June 2013.
[4]   Anonymized user, "Rwandan Community Abroad", *Facebook*, 4 March 2014.

Rwandan Diaspora - Belgium. Most engaged with content on Facebook

Source: Facebook data by Netvizz, analysed in Gephi and visualized as tree map, 4 July 2014.

Figure 26.3   Most-engaged-with content on Facebook by Belgium-based Rwandan diaspora, January 2012–June 2014

constitutional change he sought (HRW, 2017), the Facebook user who posted the message is quoted saying, 'Could the media be over-analyzing this?',[5] indicating a level of mistrust towards the article's contents.

The country's preferred narrative of redemption and renewal, as illustrated through the numerous commemoration events, societal-level interventions and overall development push, can thus be seen as a driver to transform Rwanda into Africa's success story. It showcases how epistemological considerations of return are influenced and sustained by new media technology, the government as well as its diaspora. Nonetheless, numerous NGOs and human rights organization express distress concerning the ongoing human rights abuses and political instability under Kagame's 'authoritarian' rule (AI, 2015; HRW, 2015, 2017), illustrating the country's perceived 'double reality'. The controversial 2015 constitutional referendum, which would allow President Kagame the right to rule until 2034, attracted widespread criticism from the international community who considered it as a setback for the progress in African governance (McVeigh, 2015). Little

---

[5]   Anonymized user, "Rwandan International Network Association (RINA)", *Facebook*, 13 December 2011.

Rwandan Diaspora - United States. Most engaged with content on Facebook

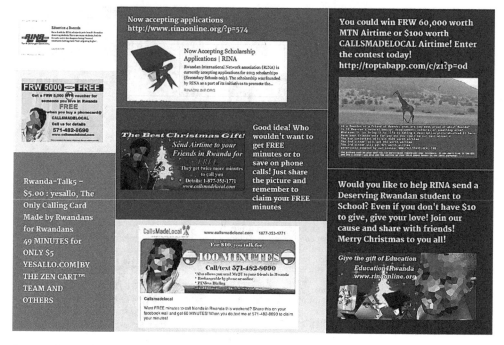

Source: Facebook data by Netvizz, analysed in Gephi and visualized as tree map, 4 July 2014.

Figure 26.4 *Most-engaged-with content on Facebook by US-based Rwandan diaspora, January 2012–June 2014*

opposition to the amendments was raised in Rwanda, except for the Democratic Green Party of Rwanda (DGPR), which has continuously been held out of politics by the regime during recent years (HRW, 2017). Although the Government of Rwanda enacted several media laws in 2014, aimed at increasing freedom of expression and scope for independent journalism (HRW, 2014), most media, print and broadcast media remain dominated by government views, arguably resulting from the government's tight grip on internet censorship, and (being accused of) keeping unlawful detention centres, committing human rights abuses, especially concerning journalists or people in opposition (AI, 2015; Freedom House, 2014; HRW, 2017).

Hence, the NGO country reports highlight the government's effort to construct a collective identity narrative of unity and reconciliation that simultaneously silences criticism or grievances, as well as in the diasporic space online. The meta-narrative emerging from the online network and web content analysis through Facebook – emphasizing a successful and unified Rwanda – is an indication of how the Rwandan community on social media are part of representing a construction of the social world, one imposed by the Government of Rwanda, whereby Facebook functions as a potential staging platform for governmental messaging. From this perspective, returning to one's homeland could thus be seen as a moral plea to contribute to Rwanda's reconstruction.

Table 26.2   Classification of Rwanda diaspora Facebook posts (n = 703)

Categories	Quantity	Percentage
Rwanda endorsement	168	23.9
Memory and reconciliation	132	18.8
Community and sociality	99	14.1
Finance/business/investment	58	8.3
Rebuilding Rwanda	36	5.1
Beauty pageant	35	5.0
Rwandan culture	22	3.1
Airtime/phone cards	21	3.0
Education	20	2.8
Tourism	16	2.3
Sports	16	2.3
International community (support/aid)	16	2.3
Bilateral relations	14	2.0
Children's rights	10	1.4
Justice/genocide	9	1.3
Integration	5	0.7
Protest	4	0.6
Diaspora	4	0.6
Media/news	4	0.6
Military and defence	3	0.4
Criticism/Kagame	3	0.4
Economic growth	2	0.3
Youth	2	0.3
Women participation	2	0.3
Infrastructure	1	0.1
Legal and social help	1	0.1
Total	703	100.0

DISCUSSION: 'A MORAL EPISTEMOLOGY OF RETURN'

Contextualizing voluntary repatriation in relation to Rwanda's unifying efforts to state building reflects a normative acceptance of return to normalcy and stability. Yet critical approaches to the process of repatriation as part of the refugee cycle have highlighted the ambiguous relationship between the nation-state, home and belonging (Black and Koser, 1999; Harrell-Bond, 1989; Long, 2009; Malkki, 1992, 1995, 1996), asserting to reframe the notion of return as re-emplacement to a 'place known in shorthand as home' (Hammond, 1999, p. 227). The depoliticized process of repatriation, whereby successful 'return' is achieved when a refugee has crossed the border into their homeland (Hammond, 1999; Long, 2008), has failed to recognize the root causes of displacement and the remaking of state-citizen bonds, and the inclusion of refugee groups as highly organized political communities (Long, 2008). The recognition of the latter in 'more direct and politicised refugee engagement in displacement resolution offers an opportunity to strengthen both concepts of refugee dignity and the durability of return' (Long, 2008, p. 5). In the case of Rwanda, the absence of political engagement of the diaspora community on social media illustrates a particular one-sidedness of the repatriation process and expressions surrounding return, demonstrating the recognized absence of the critiques of Rwanda's repatriation (O'Connor, 2013). The theoretical and empirical findings of this study thus portray the success of Rwanda's meta-narrative of unification and reconciliation, putting on display a depoliticized process of repatriation, and making other Rwandans (including journalists) into the 'preferably unheard'.

Furthermore, the paradox of successful coming together under authoritarian rule (Moss, 2014; Reyntjens, 2004), whereby Rwanda's success is attributed to incorporating the 'positive diaspora' into its information campaigns (Turner and Kleist, 2013), has disallowed the emergence of any disputing narratives pertaining to the repatriation process (Reyntjens, 2004). As such, the notion of spectacle becomes an important part of Rwanda's sovereignty by staging its diaspora as positive agents of change and national unity (Turner and Kleist, 2013). By illustrating how Facebook is used as a staging platform for governmental messaging, the repatriation issue space is arguably characterized by a spiral of silence as well as homophily. Somewhat akin to the 'spinternet' (Morozov, 2009), in Facebook official discourse from an authoritarian regime could be said to maintain a meta-narrative of unification, whilst at the same time discouraging any alternative voices. In reinforcing the Rwandan meta-narrative of unification, reconciliation and renewal, little space is left for those questioning the wish to return to Rwanda.

When turning to the epistemological considerations of using social media as a proxy for social and political inference, we have proposed a normative approach we call a 'moral epistemology of return', which seeks to specify how forced displacement is conceived, politicized and mediated with social media. It pertains to how knowledge about the opportunities and consequences of repatriation towards one's homeland are constructed. As social media (through Facebook) facilitates discussion and information surrounding the situation in the homeland, a meta-narrative of Rwandan unification prevails, putting on display a particular depoliticization of repatriation, and an absence of critique of the authoritarian rule. A moral epistemology of return thus influences how conceptual understandings to displacement are formed, how the displaced are resourced and con-sulted, and how approaches to forced migration are morally grounded. The Government of Rwanda has been successful in setting out a nation-building initiative that drives the Rwandan repatriation process (Buckley-Zistel, 2006b; O'Connor, 2013). It has attempted to frame the Rwandan diaspora as 'ideal citizens', agents of change, and proponents of Rwandan futurism, which is arguably both empowering as well as it is constraining for those who may wish to stay away.

ACKNOWLEDGMENTS

We would like to express our appreciation to the participants of the 2014 Digital Methods Summer School at the University of Amsterdam, and in particular to Gabriele Colombo and Michiel van der Haagen for their useful commentary and analytical assistance.

REFERENCES

Adamic, L.A. and N. Glance (2005), 'The Political Blogosphere and the 2004 US Election: Divided they Blog', in *Proceedings of the 3rd International Workshop on Link Discovery*, New York: ACM, pp. 1–15.

Adamson, F.B. and P. Kumar (2014), 'Imagined Communities 2.0: Space and Place in Tamil, Sikh and Palestinian On-line Identity Politics', Paper presented at the 55th Annual Meeting of the International Studies Association, Toronto, Canada, 26–29 March.

Alexa (2017), 'Facebook.com Traffic Statistics', Alexa.com, San Francisco.

AI (Amnesty International) (2004), 'Protecting their Rights: Rwandese Refugees in the Great Lakes Region'. Available from: https://www.amnesty.org/en/documents/AFR47/016/2004/en/ (Created 15 December 2004, accessed 26 October 2018).

AI (Amnesty International) (2015), *Amnesty International Report 2014/2015*, London: Amnesty International.

Benitez, J.L. (2006), 'Transnational Dimensions of the Digital Divide among Salvadoran Immigrants in the Washington DC Metropolitan Area', *Global Networks*, **6**(2), 181–99.

Bennett, W.L. and A. Segerberg (2012), 'The Logic of Connective Action: Digital Media and the Personalization of Contentious Politics', *Information, Communication & Society*, **15**(5), 739–68.

Betts, A. and W. Jones (2016), *Mobilising the Diaspora: How Refugees Challenge Authoritarianism*, Cambridge: Cambridge University Press.

Black, R. and K. Koser (1999), 'The End of the Refugee Cycle?', in R. Black and K. Koser (eds), *The End of the Refugee Cycle? Refugee Repatriation and Reconstruction*, Oxford: Berghahn Books, pp. 2–17.

Buckley-Zistel, S. (2006a). Dividing and uniting: The use of citizenship discourses in conflict and reconciliation in Rwanda, *Global Society*, **20**(1), 101–13.

Buckley-Zistel, S. (2006b). Remembering to Forget: Chosen Amnesia as a Strategy for Local Coexistence in Post-genocide Rwanda', *Africa*, **76**(2), 131–50.

Castells, M. (2008), 'The New Public Sphere: Global Civil Society, Communication Networks, and Global Governance', *Annals of the American Academy of Political and Social Science*, **616**(1), 78–93.

Crandall, D., Cosley, D., Huttenlocher, D., Kleinberg, J., and Suri, S. (2008), 'Feedback Effects between Similarity and Social Influence in Online Communities', in *Proceedings of the 14th ACM SIGKDD International Conference on Knowledge Discovery and Data Mining*, New York: ACM, pp. 160–68.

Crush, J., C. Eberhardt, M. Caesar, A. Chikanda, W. Pendleton and A. Hill (2011), 'Social Media, The Internet and Diasporas for Development', SAMP Policy Brief No. 26, International Migration Research Centre, Waterloo, Ontario.

Dahlgren, P. (2005), 'The Internet, Public Spheres, and Political Communication: Dispersion and Deliberation', *Political Communication*, **22**, 147–62.

Dekker, R. and G. Engbersen (2012), 'How Social Media Transform Migrant Networks and Facilitate Migration', Working Paper, International Migration Institute, University of Oxford.

Diaspora General Directorate (2012), 'About Us. Objectives', Republic of Rwanda, accessed 9 December 2017 at http://www.rwandandiaspora.gov.rw/about-us/objectives/.

DiMaggio, P. and E. Hargittai (2001), 'From the "Digital Divide" to "Digital Inequality": Studying Internet Use as Penetration Increases', Working Paper No. 15, Center for Arts and Cultural Policy Studies, Princeton University.

Diminescu, D. (2008), 'The Connected Migrant: An Epistemological Manifesto', *Social Science Information*, **47**, 565–79.

Diminescu, D. (2012), 'Introduction: Digital Methods for the Exploration, Analysis and Mapping of E-diasporas', *Social Science Information*, **51**(4), 451–8.

Facebook (2017), 'Facebook Statistics', Company Info, Facebook News, Menlo Park, CA.

Fahamu Refugee Programme (2011), 'Rwanda: Cessation of Status is Unwarranted: Memorandum of Fact and Law', accessed 14 November 2018 at http://www.refugeelegalaidinformation.org/sites/srlan/files/fileuploads/Memo%20of%20Fact%20and%20Law.pdf.

Freedom House (2014), *Freedom in the World 2014: Rwanda*, Washington, DC: Freedom House.

Gladwell, M. (2010), 'Small Change: Why the Revolution Will Not be Tweeted', *The New Yorker*, 4 October.

Glick Schiller, N., L. Basch and C. Szanton Blanc (1995), 'From Immigrant to Transmigrant: Theorizing Transnational Migration', *Anthropological Quarterly*, **68**(1), 48–63. doi: 10.2307/3317464.

Goldberg, Greg (2011), 'Rethinking the Public/Virtual Sphere: The Problem with Participation', *New Media & Society*, **13**(5), 739–54.

Guardian (2014), 'Rwanda Genocide: 20th Anniversary Brings a Nation Together to Mourn', *Guardian*, World, 7 April, accessed 7 December at https://www.theguardian.com/global-development/2014/apr/07/rwandan-genocide-20th-anniversary-thousands-mourn-stadium.

Habermas, J. (1991), *The Structural Transformation of the Public Sphere*, Cambridge, MA: MIT Press.

Habermas, J. (1992), 'Further Reflections on the Public Sphere', in C. Calhoun (ed.), *Habermas and the Public Sphere*, Cambridge, MA: MIT Press, pp. 411–26.

Habermas, J. (2006), 'Political Communication in Media Society: Does Democracy Still Enjoy an Epistemic Dimension? The Impact of Normative Theory on Empirical Research', *Communication Theory*, **16**, 411–26.

Hammond, L. (1999), 'Examining the Discourse of Repatriation: Towards a More Proactive Theory of Return Migration', in R. Black and K. Koser (eds), *The End of the Refugee Cycle? Refugee Repatriation and Reconstruction*, Oxford: Berghahn Books, pp. 227–44.

Hampton, K.N., H. Rainie, W. Lu, M. Dwyer, I. Shin and K. Purcell (2014), *Social Media and the 'Spiral of Silence'*, Washington, DC: Pew Research Center.

Hargittai, E. (2010), 'Digital Na(t)ives? Variation in Internet Skills and Uses among Members of the "Net Genderation"', *Sociological Inquiry*, **80**(1), 92–113.

Harlow, S. and L. Guo (2014), 'Will the Revolution be Tweeted or Facebooked? Using Digital Communication Tools in Immigrant Activism', *Journal of Computer-Mediated Communication*, **19**(3), 463–78.

Harrell-Bond, B.E. (1989), 'Repatriation: Under What Conditions is it the Most Desirable Solution for Refugees? An Agenda for Research', *African Studies Review*, **32**(1), 41–70.

Hoffman, D.L. and T.P. Novak (1998), 'Bridging the Racial Divide on the Internet', *Science*, **280**(5362), 390–91.

Howard, P., L. Rainie and S. Jones (2001), 'Days and Nights on the Internet: The Impact of a Diffusing Technology', in B. Wellman and C. Haythornthwaite (eds), *The Internet in Everyday Life*, Oxford: Blackwell, pp. 45–73.

HRW (Human Rights Watch) (2010), 'Uganda/Rwanda: Halt Forced Returns of Refugees', Human Rights Watch, New York.

HRW (Human Rights Watch) (2014), 'Rwanda, Events of 2013', Human Rights Watch, New York.

HRW (Human Rights Watch) (2015), 'Rwanda, Events of 2014', Human Rights Watch, New York.

HRW (Human Right Watch) (2017), 'Rwanda, Events of 2016', Human Rights Watch, New York.

IRIN (2013), 'No Consensus on Implementation of Cessation Clause for Rwandan Refugees', Irin News, Geneva, 12 July.

Karpf, D. (2010), 'Online Political Mobilization from the Advocacy Group's Perspective: Looking Beyond Clicktivism', *Policy & Internet*, **2**(4), Article 2.

Kissau, K. and U. Hunger (2010), 'The Internet as a Means of Studying Transnationalism and Diaspora', in R. Baubock and T. Faist (eds), *Diaspora and Transnationalism: Concepts, Theories and Methodology*, Amsterdam: Amsterdam University Press, pp. 245–66.

Kok, S. and R. Rogers (2017), 'Rethinking Migration in the Digital Age: Transglocalization and the Somali Diaspora', *Global Networks*, **17**(1), 23–46.

Komito, L. (2011), 'Social Media and Migration: Virtual Community 2.0', *Journal of the American Society for Information Science and Technology*, **62**(6), 1075–86.

Long, K. (2008), 'State, Nation, Citizen: Rethinking Repatriation', Working Series Paper No. 48, Refugee Studies Centre, Oxford University.

Long, K. (2009), 'Extending Protection? Labour Migration and Durable Solutions for Refugees, New Issues in Refugee Research', Research Paper No. 176, United Nations High Commissioner for Refugees, Geneva.

Longman, T. (2017), *Memory and Justice in Post-Genocide Rwanda*, Cambridge: Cambridge University Press.

Malkki, L. (1992), 'National Geographic: The Rooting of Peoples and the Territorialization of National Identity among Scholars and Refugees', *Cultural Anthropology*, **7**(1), 24–44.

Malkki, L.H. (1995), 'Refugees and Exile: From "Refugee Studies" to the National Order of Things', *Annual Review of Anthropology*, **24**(1), 495–523.

Malkki, L.H. (1996), 'Speechless Emissaries: Refugees, Humanitarianism, and Dehistoricization', *Cultural Anthropology*, **11**(3), 377–404.

McPherson, M., L. Smith-Lovin and J.M. Cook (2001), 'Birds of a Feather: Homophily in Social Networks', *Annual Review of Sociology*, **27**(1), 415–44.

McVeigh, T. (2015), 'Rwanda Votes to Give President Paul Kagame Right to Rule Until 2034', *Guardian*, World, 20 December, accessed 9 December 2017 at https://www.theguardian.com/world/2015/dec/20/rwanda-vote-gives-president-paul-kagame-extended-powers.

Melvin, J. (2010), 'Reconstructing Rwanda: Balancing Human Rights and the Promotion of National Reconciliation', in *Sociology and Human Rights: New Engagements*, Abingdon: Routledge, pp. 130–49.

MIDIMAR (Ministry of Disaster Management and Refugees) (2016), 'Cessation Clause Deadline Closing in', News and Multimedia, Republic of Rwanda, accessed 14 November 2018 at http://midimar.gov.rw/index.php?id=45&tx_ttnews%5Btt_news%5D=119&cHash=519e8ce094f0ace9ab42137757b42f29.

Morozov, E. (2009), 'The Brave New World of Slacktivism', *Foreign Policy*, 19 May.

Morozov, E. (2012), *The Net Delusion: The Dark Side of Internet Freedom*, New York: Public Affairs.

Moss, S.M. (2014), 'Beyond Conflict and Spoilt Identities: How Rwandan Leaders Justify a Single Recategorization Model for Post-conflict Reconciliation', *Journal of Social and Political Psychology*, **2**(1), 435–49.

Noelle-Neumann, E. (1974), 'The Spiral of Silence a Theory of Public Opinion', *Journal of Communication*, **24**(2), 43–51, https://doi.org/10.1111/j.1460-2466.1974.tb00367.x.

O'Connor, K. (2013), 'The Politics of (re)-Constructing and Contesting Rwandan Citizenship', Working Paper Series No. 92, Refugee Studies Centre, Oxford University.

OECD (2012), *Connecting with Emigrants: A Global Profile of Diasporas*, Paris: OECD Publishing.

Ono, H. and M. Zavodny (2008), 'Immigrants, English Ability and the Digital Divide', *Social Forces*, **86**(4), 1455–79.

Papacharissi, Z. (2002), 'The Virtual Sphere: The Internet as a Public Sphere', *New Media & Society*, **4**(1), 9–27.

Pariser, E. (2011), *The Filter Bubble*, New York: Penguin.

Pottier, J. (1996), 'Relief and Repatriation: Views by Rwandan Refugees: Lessons for Humanitarian Aid Workers', *African Affairs*, **95**(380), 403–29.

Reyntjens, F. (2004), 'Rwanda, Ten Years On: From Genocide to Dictatorship', *African Affairs*, **103**, 177–210.

Rieder, B. (2013), 'Studying Facebook via Data Extraction: The Netvizz Application', in *Proceedings of the 5th Annual ACM Web Science Conference*, New York: ACM, pp. 346–55.

Rogers, R. (2009), *The End of the Virtual: Digital Methods*, Amsterdam: Amsterdam University Press.

Rogers, R. (2010), 'Mapping Public Web Space with the Issuecrawler', in C. Brossard and B. Reber (eds), *Digital Cognitive Technologies: Epistemology and the Knowledge Economy*, London: Wiley, pp. 89–99.

Rogers, R. (2013), *Digital Methods*, Cambridge, MA: MIT Press.

Roy, A. (2004), 'Peace & the New Corporate Liberation Theology', 2004 City of Sydney Peace Prize Lecture, CPACS Occasional Paper No. 04/2, Centre for Peace and Conflict Studies, University of Sydney.

Shirky, C. (2008), *Here Comes Everybody*, New York: Penguin.

Shirky, C. (2010), 'The Political Power of Social Media: Technology, the Public Sphere, and Political Change', *Foreign Affairs*, **90**(1), 28–41.

Smith, A., K.L. Schlozman, S. Verba and H. Brady (2009), *The Internet and Civic Engagement*, Washington, DC: Pew Research Center.

Soriano, M.R.T. (2013), 'Internet as a Driver of Political Change: Cyber-pessimists and Cyber Optimists', *Revista del Instituto Español de Estudios Estratégicos*, **1**, 332–52.

Sunstein, C. (2001), *Republic.com*, Princeton, NJ: Princeton University Press.

Tilly, C. (1990), 'Transplanted Networks', in V. Yans-MacLoughlin (ed.), *Immigration Reconsidered*, New York: Oxford University Press, pp. 79–95.

Tufekci, Z. (2014), 'Big Questions for Social Media Big Data: Representativeness, Validity and Other Methodological Pitfalls', in *Proceedings of the 8th International Conference on Weblogs and Social Media, ICWSM 2014*, Palo Alto, CA: AAAI Press, pp. 505–14.

Tumwebaze, P. (2018), 'Rwandans lose refugee status as cessation clause comes into force', *The New Times*, https://www.newtimes.co.rw/section/read/226701 (published on 1 January 2018 and accessed on 26 October 2018).

Turner, S. and N. Kleist (2013), 'Introduction: Agents of Change? Staging and Governing Diasporas and the African State', *African Studies*, **72**(2), 192–206.

UNHCR (2008), 'UNHCR's Role in Support of the Return and Reintegration of Displaced Populations: Policy Framework and Implementation Strategy', UNHCR, Geneva, 11 February, accessed 9 December 2017 at http://www.unhcr.org/excom/standcom/47b06de42/unhcrs-role-support-return-reintegration-displaced-populations-policy-framework.html.

UNHCR (2011), 'Implementation of the Comprehensive Strategy for the Rwandan Refugee Situation, Including UNHCR's Recommendations on the Applicability of the "Ceased Circumstances" Cessation Clauses', 31 December, UNHCR, Geneva.

UNHCR (2013), 'Ending of Refugee Status for Rwandan Approaching', 28 June, UNHCR, Geneva, accessed 9 December 2017 at http://www.unhcr.org/news/briefing/2013/6/51cd7df06/ending-refugee-status-rwandans-approaching.html.

UNHCR (2016), 'UNHCR, African Host Countries Agree on Final Steps to Resolve Rwandan Refugee Situation', 30 September, UNHCR, Geneva, accessed 9 December 2017 at http://www.unhcr.org/news/press/2016/9/57f20dd54/unhcr-african-host-countries-agree-final-steps-resolve-rwandan-refugee.html.

Vertovec, S. (2008), *Transnationalism*, London: Routledge.

White, M (2010), 'Clicktivism is Ruining Leftist Activism', *Guardian*, Opinion, 12 August, accessed 9 December at https://www.theguardian.com/commentisfree/2010/aug/12/clicktivism-ruining-leftist-activism.

Yardi, S. and D. Boyd (2010), 'Dynamic Debates: An Analysis of Group Polarization Over Time on Twitter', *Bulletin of Science, Technology & Society*, **30**(5), 316–27.

PART VI

REFUGEES, ASYLUM, HUMANITARIANISM

27. Contentious subjects: spatial and relational perspectives on refugee mobilizations in Europe
Elias Steinhilper and Ilker Ataç

INTRODUCTION: THE NEGLECTED POLITICS OF REFUGEE SUBJECTIVITY

Political protest by refugees[1] for rights and recognition has proliferated worldwide in the last decade (Nicholls and Uitermark, 2016; Tyler and Marciniak, 2013). Yet, these contentious actions including collective hunger strikes, lip-sewing, long-distance marches and sit-ins have only recently received growing public attention. They contrast with a dominant portrayal of such individuals as either passive, needy and ideally grateful objects of government or civil society humanitarianism (Fassin, 2012; Malkki, 1996) or stigmatized outsiders and intruders in a national order of things (Bigo, 2003; Nicholls, 2013a). In addition, the academic reflection on the issue has started only relatively recently, particularly in critical migration and citizenship studies (Ataç et al., 2015; Isin and Nielsen, 2008; Schwenken, 2006; Tyler and Marciniak, 2014), and far less so in social movement studies (for an overview and critical comments see Ataç et al., 2016; Eggert and Giugni, 2015). According to dominant movement theories, (forced) migrants are unlikely subjects of mobilization due to legal obstacles (including 'deportability'), limited economic and social capital and closed political and discursive opportunities.

The important question for those interested in the political subjectivity of refugees is, hence, to understand how marginalized actors succeed in organizing political action against all evident odds. In this chapter, we sketch out processes of self-organized refugee activism in Germany and Austria and theorize them in the light of recent innovations in social movements studies, critical migration and critical geography. Such a relational and space-sensitive perspective points at specific geographies of control, and the spatial repertoires to overcome them (Ataç, 2016; Nicholls and Uitermark, 2016; Nicholls and Vermeulen, 2012).

SPACES OF CONTROL AND CONTESTATION: A RELATIONAL AND SPATIAL LENS ON POLITICAL PROTEST

At the core of social movement theory lies the expectation that social actors need to control certain resources such as knowledge, money and logistics to transform eruptions of dissent into sustained mobilizations (for an overview see Della Porta and Diani,

---

[1] The term 'refugee' is used in this chapter to refer to individuals, self-identifying as 'refugees'. It does not refer exclusively to those who have been granted official refugee status by the German and Austrian state, including also asylum seekers and individuals with a temporary suspension of deportation ("*Duldung*").

2009). Based on the work of Mark Granovetter (1973), such resources are expected to be embedded as weak and strong ties in social *networks* (Diani and McAdam, 2003; Diani and Mische, 2015). Whereas *weak ties* depict social relations providing access to resources an actor otherwise would not have, *strong ties* refer to emotionally deep ties as reservoirs of trust, which are particularly paramount for 'high-risk activism' (McAdam, 1986).

More recent scholarship has advocated for a dynamic approach and shifted the focus from rather static networks to micro-*interactions* of players with often disparate interests in contentious arenas (Jasper and Duyvendak, 2014). Scholarship on mobilizations of marginalized groups has stressed the need of weakly resourced actors to establish social ties to more powerful pro-beneficiaries with a view to compensating lacking resources (Chabanet and Royall, 2014; Lahusen, 2014; Passy, 2001). Many episodes of (undocumented) migrant protest are indeed frequently mobilizations of migrants and natives often identifying as 'supporters' (Nicholls, 2013b; Siméant, 1998). Such alliances of actors in highly different power positions (e.g., with regard to legal status) have proven to be highly precarious and prone to conflicts concerning paternalism (Cappiali, 2017; Ünsal, 2015). Yet, shared experiences of 'eventful protest' (Della Porta, 2008) can contribute to collective identities and alliances, which are built and negotiated during contentious actions (Monforte and Dufour, 2011).

Building upon this *relational turn* in the study of contentious politics, a group of scholars with a background in critical geography has explored the relational qualities of space and their specific implications for social movements (Nicholls, 2008; Nicholls and Uitermark, 2016; Nicholls and Vermeulen, 2012). They show the unequal distribution of resources across space and point to the role of urban environments as incubators for counterhegemonic political activity due to the concentration of alternative milieus and the accentuation of social problems. Staged in cities, protests – even by marginalized actors – convey a *claim to centrality*, and tend to attract more visibility due to the incubating role of progressive social movements in the urban sphere and the proximity of multiple media outlets. The so-called protest movements of the squares from 2010 onwards (for an overview see Della Porta and Mattoni, 2014) relied heavily on central camps as manifested claims to centrality and spaces of encounter. Moreover, previous scholarship on the *spaces of contention* (Martin and Miller, 2003; Nicholls et al., 2013; Sewell, 2001) stressed that social movements of all kinds require autonomous, *safe spaces*, in which trust and empathetic strong ties can be built up in preparation of and during protest. The importance of such spaces with particular emotional, relational and material qualities has furthermore been demonstrated for the protection and empowerment of marginalized migrants (Mitchell and Sparke, 2018; Mudu and Chattopadhyay, 2017). Consequently, occupations of buildings and tent camps in inner-city areas constitute core elements of a specific repertoire of contention in migrant activism. In a similar vein, mobile actions such as long-distance marches and bus tours (Leitner et al., 2008) have an important role in accessing spaces with advantageous relational qualities, which are unequally distributed. Physical mobility within space and occupation of concrete places are hence intimately related in their function in episodes of contentious politics. Spatial perspectives furthermore underline that space is particularly influential as a moderator for the establishment, quality and sustainability of social ties. In consequence, perspectives rooted in social networks research and human geography are particularly fruitful if applied in conjunction with each other.

Such spatialized strategies have a threefold effect. First, they disrupt exclusive routines and shift attention to groups that are usually invisible at the margins of society. Second, mobile tactics can overcome restrictive local contexts (such as asylum camps or remote villages) and relocate protest to places with more favourable relational qualities, such as access to support milieus. Third, the public practices of protest by marginalized populations constitute by themselves 'acts of citizenship' (Isin and Nielsen, 2008), 'acts of emancipation' (Monforte and Dufour, 2013) or manifestations of 'insurgent citizenship' (Leitner and Strunk, 2014) exceeding the national territorial logic with a focus on civic action: '[T]he appropriation of public space and convening of public forums create new political spaces for deliberation, which are crucial in the formulation of new values and the development of new criteria for citizenship and belonging' (Leitner and Strunk, 2014, p. 354). Given these important spatial foundations and repercussions for political protest, opponents of social movements can and indeed have employed spatialized technologies of power to supress the creation of contentious networks through mobility restrictions or forced dispersal (see also Nicholls and Uitermark, 2016).

EXPLORING THE SPATIALITIES OF REFUGEE ACTIVISM IN AUSTRIA AND GERMANY

Asylum seekers' everyday experiences in both Austria and Germany are fundamentally shaped by their social, political and economic isolation from the society. Despite considerable national and regional differences,[2] both systems of reception remain characterized by widespread collective accommodation in peripheral locations, a system of benefits in kind, considerable obstacles in accessing the job market and education, and in Germany until 2015 the mobility restriction *Residenzpflicht*, obliging asylum seekers and those with a temporary exemption from deportation not to stay within strictly delineated geographic areas (Hinger, 2016; Pieper, 2008; Täubig, 2009). In Austria, with the exception of Vienna, asylum seekers are widely dispersed in the rural periphery, where most of them suffer from eroding socio-economic structures. This exacerbates social and spatial separation and exclusion from the receiving society (Rosenberger and König, 2012). These restrictive spaces, rules and practices lead to a widespread feeling of despair, apathy and isolation among asylum seekers and a de facto segregation from the majority population (Johansson, 2016).

Both the German (Täubig, 2009) and the Austrian (Rosenberger, 2011) asylum system have been qualified as 'organized disintegration'. From the perspective of the asylum seeker, conditions and dispersal policy is shaped by a 'no choice' principle, which is counterproductive for social inclusion since it hinders access to social networks. In addition, refugee voices are rarely heard in the public sphere as they lack the institutional and societal resources of power. At the same time, either stigmatizing or victimizing representations of asylum seekers are widespread in public debates. In Austria, the political and public debate on asylum has, since the 1990s, become confined to a narrow discourse of

---

[2]   Due to the current rapid pace in asylum law reforms in Germany, overviews regularly become outdated. Some orientations, however, provide the following contributions (Müller, 2013; Ndahayo, 2014; Werdermann, 2016). For Austria see AIDA (2017) and Hinterberger (2016).

asylum misuse and exclusion, resulting in the contraction of social rights for asylum seekers (Ataç, 2014). Such patterns of exclusion constitute an ambivalent context for political mobilizations of asylum seekers. While the system itself constantly produces dissent, the isolation from support networks and favourable conditions for surveillance by the state in most cases prevents sparks of protest to transform into sustainable mobilizations (see also Nicholls and Uitermark, 2016). By portraying two contemporary refugee movements which emerged at roughly the same time in Germany and Austria – the *Oranienplatz-Movement in Berlin* and the *Protest Camp Vienna* – we intend to illustrate how a spatial and relational lens contributes to the understanding of their emergence and trajectories.

Both protest movements were characterized by three spatialities: mobility, place and social space. In both movements, a long-distance march, a tent camp in an inner-city location and the occupation of buildings were constitutive for the emergence of the movement and profoundly shaped its respective trajectories. Each of these locations and spatialities entailed specific relational qualities providing access to material resources and spaces to develop trust and a sense of collectivity.

In early 2012, refugee protests erupted in the Southern German city of Wurzburg following the suicide of an Iranian asylum seeker in his room in a refugee camp.[3] Outraged by the death of their friend, refugees in Wurzburg demonstrated in front of the city hall in Wurzburg and demanded improved health care, accelerated asylum procedures, decentralized accommodation of refugees, the abolition of *Residenzpflicht* as well as the right to work (Glöde and Böhlo, 2015). They subsequently set up a camp in the city centre, and some went on hunger strike and sewed their lips to mark their status as voiceless 'non-citizens'. One of the protesters declared: 'In the morning, when asylum seekers wake up, they are scared of being deported. If they want to meet friends, the *Residenzpflicht* prevents them from doing so. Everywhere in their life hurdles exist, built by the state, because we are not meant to be part of society' (cited in Jakob, 2013, authors' translation from German). What started as a spark of protest against the living conditions in one camp quickly spread like a wildfire. Protest camps emerged in other cities, loosely knit together in the 'refugee tent action' campaign (International Refugee Center Berlin, 2015).

The March: Breaking Immobility and Enacting Rights

In September 2012, the different camps joined forces and organized a bus tour and a 600 kilometre protest march to Berlin (Glöde and Böhlo, 2015; Langa, 2015). The activists explicitly intended to upscale their protest and stage at the national level. Relocating their dissent from geographical and social margins of society to the German capital constituted a *claim to centrality*. Moreover, the march had the important function of connecting a highly dispersed population of asylum seekers in the German province and mobilizing new protesters. Both march and bus tour were planned to pass by numerous asylum camps. It was hence a means to attract media attention, but also to empower and reach out to the hidden refugee community. Every stop during the one-month march added nodes

---

[3]   In Germany, refugees have been organizing political protest and established sustainable networks such as the *Voice Refugee Forum* and the *Caravan for the Rights of Refugees and Migrants in Germany* since the 1990s (Jakob, 2016). Yet, these mobilizations remained in a niche receiving neither extensive media coverage nor widespread civil society support. This changed fundamentally with the protest wave starting in 2012.

in a growing contentious network and, hence, contributed to the accumulation of weak ties. Even more important, however, was the internal effect of this spectacular protest, deepening emotional ties among refugees and between refugees and supporters. Indeed, the march was symbolically and practically conceived as an appropriation and prefigurative enactment of rights – an *act of emancipation*. Literally moving forward disrupted the sense of 'being stuck', forcefully immobilized by a, in many cases, lengthy and burdensome administrative procedure. At the former inner German border, the protesters tore up the documents identifying them as asylum seekers and sent them back to the German Agency for Migration and Refugees (BAMF), underlining their determination to resist forced immobilities in the asylum procedure and to prefigure a country allowing (internal) freedom of movement for all.

Also, in Austria, a long-distance foot march was constitutive for the emergence of the refugee protest movement in Austria.[4] In November 2012, around 100 refugees left the main reception centre of Traiskirchen and marched 35 kilometres in one day to Vienna. A rally in solidarity with the refugee protests in Germany two weeks before had prepared the ground for this mobile and highly mediatized protest event. One of the refugees involved had met *no border* activists in the so-called *Subotica jungle* in Serbia, who connected him to other supporters in Vienna. He soon established contact with the antiracist scene in Vienna, involving political activists, lawyers and counsellors. While collecting and sharing information on asylum procedures and rights of asylum seekers, he not only established ties with the local solidarity scene, but also gained trust among the refugees in Traiskirchen (Interview, 15 January 2014). Both were paramount for the organization of the march, which, in turn, kicked-off the refugee protest movement in Austria. During the march, political demands were voiced loudly, with slogans such as 'we want justice' or 'what we want is our rights' (Ataç, 2016).

The Inner-city Tent Camp: Magnet for Weak Ties and Safe Space to Build Trust

After the arrival of the protest march in Berlin, a protest camp was set up on the Oranienplatz square in the neighbourhood of Kreuzberg. This location was not coincidental but strategically used the public image as subversive stronghold and the de facto density of progressive social movement organizations in this part of the city (Lang, 1998; Stehle, 2006). As in Wurzburg, the central location and visibility of the protest resulted in a magnetic effect, attracting hundreds of individual supporters and groups as well as refugees from isolated asylum camps to join the protest movement.

Similarly, in Austria, after the march to the city centre in Vienna, a protest camp was set up in Sigmund-Freud Park. The location of the camp was strategically chosen, as it both guaranteed high public visibility and accessibility through its vicinity to one of the main nodes of public transport leading to important tourist attractions (Votive Church), and a convenient infrastructure (facilities offered by student unions and academics) at

---

[4]   In Austria, until 2012, protest by refugees has remained short-termed and mostly directed against the imminent deportation of individuals. However, six weeks before the protest march started, a two-day rally by refugees from Somalia took place in front of the Austrian parliament. Mobilizations by Austrian citizens in support of refugees to stop the expulsion of asylum seekers have a far longer tradition (Rosenberger and Winkler, 2014).

the nearby University of Vienna. Immediately after its establishment, the camp turned into a social space in which refugees started to establish contacts with other refugees and actors such as members of non-governmental organizations (NGOs), trade unionists and independent individuals who disagreed on moral and/or political grounds with the Austrian asylum policies (Ataç, 2016, p. 641). For many refugees, the protest camp provided the environment to build their first close social relations with other refugees in an autonomous space.

In both Berlin and Vienna, resources necessary to sustain the protest could be mobilized on the spot, as multiple weak ties could be accessed. These camps served as reservoirs for multiple weak ties to civil society organizations, individual supporters and the media: neighbours and associations donated money, tents and food, organized translation and legal support. In relocating the protest, the refugees had rapidly transformed themselves from 'weakly resourced', isolated and dispersed communities into an emerging movement with astonishing resources and means to organize and sustain protest (Jakob, 2016; Mokre, 2015). The refugees did not need to beg for scarce support, but could even choose among various kinds of assistance offered by a multitude of actors.

Due to this magnetic effect and the shift in power relations between refugees and supporters, at the beginning, little energy was needed to reproduce the protest itself. In consequence, countless protest actions such as demonstrations, occupations of embassies and so on could be organized from the protest centre in both cities. As the camp constituted a space of both subsistence and political articulation, it mitigated the obstacle of mobilizing dispersed and financially precarious communities to participate in protest. Given the (initially) supportive environment, the camps became *a safe space of encounter* for an extremely heterogeneous group of refugees and supporters with a plethora of legal status, social backgrounds and ideologies. Numerous activities in the camp were organized to make these spaces safe in material, emotional and relational terms. This was particularly important, given the highly unsafe context combining the risk of eviction of the camp with the precarious status of the people involved. Assemblies were organized translating all interventions into multiple languages. While these processes of developing and negotiating a collective identity did not evolve without fundamental frictions, both camps created the very basis to develop strong ties of trust among refugees and between refugees and supporters. The 'eventful' character of the camp and the collective actions it encouraged deepened a sense of collectivity and solidarity despite diversity. Asked by journalists why some of the protesters in Berlin did not accept the deal offered by the local administration of Kreuzberg to move back into asylum camps and get individual reviews of their asylum claims, one refugee answered: 'We are alone there, we cannot fight together. The authorities can take and deport us easily' (refugee cited in International Refugee Center Berlin, 2015).

Compared to Berlin, the protest camp in Vienna was short-termed. After initial euphoria, the maintenance of the camp became increasingly challenging due to decreasing financial resources as well as the precarious legal status of both the refugees involved and the camp itself. In this period the strong ties among refugees and supporters were vital to keeping up the infrastructure of the camp, compensating decreasing external support. Yet, the increasing police pressure in combination with freezing temperatures and physical exhaustion of supporters and refugees also showed the limits of the Protest Camp Vienna as *a safe space of encounter.* As a result, the activists decided to move into the nearby Votive Church, but intended to maintain the tent camp. However, as a result of the relocation, the protest camp started to lose its status as the centre of the protest movement and was eventually evicted by the police and the camp infrastructure destroyed ten days after the refugees had sought shelter in the church (Ataç, 2016).

The Occupied Building: Space of Protection and Space of Alienation

Two months after the establishment of the Oranienplatz protest camp, in the midst of an icy Berlin winter, refugees and supporters squatted in an abandoned school building in the same neighbourhood, with a view to appropriate a safe space for the winter and extend the advantageous relational qualities of the occupied square. Designed as an 'international refugee centre', the movement, indeed, further expanded in size. One floor of the building was transformed into an 'International Women Space' – a self-organized political space for refugees and migrants (International Refugee Center Berlin, 2015). Yet, the availability of a shelter also attracted hundreds of individuals in need of a place to stay but with various degrees of affinity to the political struggles for rights and recognition. In addition to the multiple controversies in the tent camp (Ünsal, 2015), the closed occupied building posed specific challenges to assure the security and basic functioning of the place, including debates on access restrictions. Over time, the place became overcrowded and increasingly contested, receiving negative media coverage and opposition by the initially supportive district government. While accentuating cleavages and conflicts within the movement on the one hand, the school kept its function as both an important place of shelter and a symbol of the protest on the other hand. In consequence, thousands of political activists and neighbours resisted an eviction of the place in summer 2014 (Danielzik and Bendix, 2016). Since the attention shifted to the newly arriving refugees from the Middle East during the long 'summer of migration' (Hess et al., 2017), visibility and support for the occupied school faded. Its final eviction in January 2018 received comparatively little contestation (Maxwill and Witte, 2018).

In Austria, by taking shelter in the Votive Church in Vienna, the movement gained a new space, which was symbolically characterized by the history of the church's support for the rights of refugees (Jørgensen, 2013). Relocating the protest to a church led to increasing media and public attention, especially in the time before Christmas as it embedded the protest practices into a tradition and moral imaginary of church asylum. The Catholic Church in Austria, as an influential institution, was hence pressured to take a clear stand on the refugees' demands. Over time, refugees were successful in transforming the sacred space into a political space. Waging a hunger strike for over six weeks was decisive in drawing attention to their determination and desperation regarding governmental asylum policies. The shelter in the church in combination with the hunger strike strengthened the social-relational ties among refugees. By turning their body into a tool of resistance, the hunger strike brought the refugees closer to one another, and they increasingly developed a collective identity. On the other side, it also introduced new conflicts: not all supporters were in favour of this form of action and not all refugees could or wanted to take part in the hunger strike. In addition, the authorities of the Votive Church introduced a strict policy of access control, only allowing a limited group of refugees to enter the church. Consequently, despite providing shelter from the harsh weather conditions, the new protest site could not function as an open social space in the way the tent camp did. Instead, it increasingly produced exclusionary effects.

Governing Space, Governing Social Ties

In Berlin, from the very beginning, the incubating effect of the occupied Oranienplatz and the school provoked unease and opposition by the regional government of Berlin, particularly the conservative Senator of the Interior. It was, hence, repeatedly attempted to disperse and discourage the movement by eliminating the two occupied centres of the protest. Over time, dissent proliferated to parts of the neighbourhood and the newly elected district mayor from the Green party. As internal cleavages between and among supporters and refugees grew, due to the absence of short-term success and the increasingly precarious living conditions on the square, both district and senate engaged in a governance of social ties largely avoiding open repression. Particularly, selective incentives were offered to many, yet not all refugees involved, which eventually resulted in the 'Oranienplatz agreement' (Senate of Berlin, 2014) and a subsequent predominantly non-violent dissolution of the protest camp two years after its establishment in April 2014. As part of the so-called 'deal', refugees were offered temporary accommodation in various shelters dispersed throughout the entire city. Despite breaking the promises given in the agreement, the dissolution and dispersal of the protesters effectively fragmented the protest movement. The lack of a central culmination point with favourable conditions to build weak and strong ties was decisive in the fragmentation and retrospectively underlined its importance for the movement (Jakob, 2016).

Compared to Berlin, the protest movement in Vienna was under far more pressure at an early stage. Although politicians of the red-green governed city and civil society organizations, supported the camp, their influence was limited. The camp was evicted very soon after the refugees moved into the church. During their time in the Votive Church, the charity organization Caritas and the Catholic Church suggested to relocate the refugees into a nearby monastery. After ten weeks of shelter in the church, the refugees decided to move to the 'Serviten' monastery, where they were offered the protection of the church until the end of June 2013. The relocation of the protest movement was described by the press release of the protest movement as 'a new stage in the refugee protest' (Refugee Protest Camp Vienna, 2013). The refugees and supporters were hoping to establish a model project of self-organized space where refugees would get support such as legal counselling and collaborative work on their asylum cases in combination with a continuation of their political struggles for legal reform. However, the relocation of the protest was built on a consensus with moderating actors and was not a place chosen by the refugees themselves. As a result, conflicts between refugees, supporters and Caritas arose over house rules, particularly access restrictions. At the end, there were limits to organizing the monastery as a self-organized space.

Moreover, the protest movement was affected by increasing repression. By the end of July 2013, eight protesters were deported directly to Pakistan and Hungary (within the European Union Dublin agreement). A few days later, a police action took place in the monastery during which three refugees were arrested on charges of human smuggling and put in pre-trial detention. The interior ministry and parts of the press accused the respective protesters of having earned millions of euros through smuggling, which was criticized by NGOs and part of the media as an attempt to criminalize the protest movement as a whole.[5] In a final attempt to appropriate a new *safe space*, the protest movement occupied the Academy of Fine Arts in October 2013 in Vienna, which is well known for its liberal policy. However, the dean of the Academy did not allow them to stay in the Academy and instead offered the protest movement the opportunity to use the rooms for meetings and public discussions. After this unsuccessful attempt to appropriate a space of both shelter and political subjectivity, the protest movement lost its momentum and eventually dissolved.

In Berlin, with the dissolution of the protest camp and the de facto eviction of the occupied school, the movement suffered a heavy blow. The arrival of hundreds to thousands of refugees in Germany during the 'long summer of migration' in 2015 furthermore shifted the focus in both public attention and civil society engagement to emergency response, which, in turn, contributed to invisibilize refugee protest (Fleischmann and Steinhilper, 2017). Yet, the movement has not disappeared, but rather gradually entered a phase of restructuration or 'abeyance' (Taylor, 1989). In such periods of disadvantageous contexts, nodes in an increasingly pluri-central movement continue to exist, sustaining networks and collective identity, while (temporarily) adopting a less radical repertoire of contention (Taylor and Crossley, 2013). In Berlin, refugee activists involved in the protest cycle from 2012 have remained engaged in various antiracist groups, regularly participating at protest events, and confidently 'making place' for migrant' political subjectivity in the local immigrant rights movement and the society at large. The mobilizations have hence not only resulted in a momentary rupture of exclusive routines, but also provide relational, material and symbolic resources for future mobilizations of refugees in Germany.

In Vienna, the end of the protest camp was even more consequential. In the absence of autonomous spaces with (temporarily) advantageous relational qualities and in the context of the criminalization of the protest movement, maintaining a self-organized protest movement was not successful. The attempts by the activists to revive the protest movement were not successful. Yet, the protest nevertheless had lasting effects. On an individual basis, an essential number of people received either refugee status or temporary protection. For the migrant solidarity movement more broadly, the most visible and disruptive protest cycle by refugees in Austria has created links and served as a reference point.

CONCLUSION: BREAKING ISOLATION TO BECOME POLITICAL SUBJECTS

Experiences of isolation and exclusion from society have fundamentally shaped the life-worlds of refugees and the contentious strategies they have chosen to overcome spaces of control and disintegration: mobile tactics such as marches and bus tours as well as autonomous camps and occupied buildings are central components of refugees' repertoire of contention across the two national contexts we explored. In both cases,

---

[5]   This was followed by a 43-day trial between March and December 2014, in which eight refugees from the protest camp were accused of human smuggling. At the end of a highly contentious court procedure, eight refugees were convicted, although none of the original charges could be properly proven (Kusche and Schütze, 2017, pp. 112 ff.).

appropriating and accessing spaces with favourable relational qualities was crucial for transforming sparks of protest into sustained mobilizations.

Both movements raised public attention and were able to mobilize asylum seekers and the media by moving from socially and spatially isolated locations into urban centres. In doing so, refugees literally left behind their excluded position and articulated a claim to urban and social centrality. The relocation from the periphery of the asylum camp to the inner-city space broke the routine of refugee invisibility through extensive media coverage and a disruption of the everyday life of citizens.

The long-distance marches in both cases had specific cultural and strategic effects in this regard. First, marches allow refugees and illegalized migrants to formulate claims in public spaces and to regain power over their own lives. The act of marching hence entails an important cultural component as during the marches, political demands are developed and a sense of collective self gradually emerges (Ataç, 2016). Second, the mobile strategy relocated the protest from highly restrictive and disintegrating collective asylum accommodations to places with more favourable relational qualities, for example, the urban centres with strong(er) progressive social movements. In the German case, the march furthermore allowed assembling and mobilizing the highly dispersed refugee population at their respective locations in the German periphery.

Autonomous protest camps, set up subsequently, generated magnetic fields, attracting diverse support milieus from which refugees were previously cut off in the disintegrating asylum system. The refugees, hence, gradually succeeded in compensating for the lack of resources. In addition to constituting reservoirs for weak ties, the protest camps served also as spaces of encounter and trust-building among refugees in which stories and opinions could be shared and a collective identity developed despite tremendous heterogeneity of the actors involved. Plenary assemblies were organized on a daily basis – as extensive deliberative *fora*, translated into various languages. These protest sites furthermore created imaginaries of hope for refugees in isolated camps to join the movement and became laboratories of collective action.

In both cases, the occupation of buildings had ambivalent effects. While providing an important shelter and further visibility, the closed infrastructure also introduced additional challenges with regard to access policies and increasing policing. In Vienna, this ambivalence was particularly accentuated as the occupied church building raised questions of ethics and morality which further widened the solidarity spectrum, yet the protest became less autonomous and gradually lost the autonomous grassroots character it had in the highly inclusive tent camp.

The highly diverging trajectories of the protests in both cities can be partly understood through the different relational qualities of the locations in which the protests unfolded. In Berlin, for a long time the movement received astonishing support in civil society circles, the neighbourhood, the media and even the district administration of Kreuzberg. In Vienna, in contrast, criminalization in public discourse and political pressure on refugees, and a much weaker solidarity scene contributed to a much faster erosion of the converging energies of the camp. Despite these important differences, the appropriation of *safe spaces* with favourable relational qualities were paramount, which became even more evident after their (forced) dissolution. Both in Berlin and Vienna the end of the protest camps fundamentally weakened and fragmented the self-organized movements as weak ties for mobilizing resources and spaces of encounter to develop trust and strong ties were missing.

The absence of a physical safe place has profound effects on precarious movements in both cities, however, does not necessarily eliminate the social spaces and political subjectivities created during eventful protests. Yet, at least in Berlin, the movement has not disappeared but entered a phase of 'abeyance'. Despite decreased public visibility, the movement has managed to sustain important relational and symbolic resources for future mobilizations. In Vienna, social networks and relations were in the absence of the physical spaces quite important for the refugees in their daily socialization.

Given these spatial and relational characteristics of the two refugee protests in Germany and Austria, we argue, they are best understood as seemingly paradoxical *escapes from the asylum system*. The German and Austrian asylum systems are a safe space only in abstract terms – in reality, it has a disintegrating and isolating effect, undermining the creation of support networks and the development of mutual support and trust. In consequence, alternative spaces with more advantageous relational qualities need to be appropriated (through marches and autonomous camps) outside the asylum system to disrupt exclusive routines, attract visibility and develop strong and weak ties, necessary for sustaining political mobilization. And, ultimately, to be recognized as political subjects with rights and voices rather than passive victims or stigmatized outsiders.

REFERENCES

AIDA (2017). *Country Report Austria*. Asylum Information Database, Vienna. Retrieved from http://www.asy lumineurope.org/reports/country/austria/asylum-procedure/procedures/regular-procedure%0D (last accessed 3 October 2018).

Ataç, I. (2014). Die diskursive Konstruktion von Flüchtlingen und Asylpolitik in Österreich seit 2000. In: U. Hunger, R. Pioch, S. Rother (eds), *Deutsche Migrations- und Integrationspolitik im europäischen Vergleich. Jahrbuch Migration 2012/13* (pp. 113–30). Berlin/Münster: Lit-Verlag.

Ataç, I. (2016). 'Refugee Protest Camp Vienna': Making Citizens through Location of the Protest Movement. *Citizenship Studies*, **20**(5), 625–46.

Ataç, I., Kron, S., Schilliger, S., Schwiertz, H., and Stierl, M. (2015). Struggles of Migration as In-/visible Politics. *Movements. Journal Für Kritische Migrations- Und Grenzregimeforschung*, **1**(2), 1–18.

Ataç, I., Rygiel, K., and Stierl, M. (2016). Introduction: The Contentious Politics of Refugee and Migrant Protest and Solidarity Movements: Remaking Citizenship from the Margins. *Citizenship Studies*, **20**(5), 527–44.

Bigo, D. (2003). Migration and Security. In V. Guiraudon and C. Joppke (eds), *Controlling a New Migration World* (pp. 121–49). London: Routledge.

Cappiali, T.M. (2017). 'Whoever Decides for You Without You, S/he is Against You!': Immigrant Activism and the Role of the Left in Political Racialization. *Ethnic and Racial Studies*, **40**(6), 969–987.

Chabanet, D. and Royall, F. (2014). From Social Movement Analsyis to Contentious Politics. In D. Chabanet and F. Royall (eds), *From Silence to Protest: International Perspectives on Weakly Resourced Groups* (pp. 1–18). Farnham: Ashgate.

Danielzik, C.-M. and Bendix, D. (2016). Neighbours Welcome! – Die Willkommenskultur, die Geflüchteten-Bewegung und die Suche nach Gemeinsamkeiten der Kämpfe um rechte. In S. Hess, S. Kron, B. Kasparek, M. Rodatz, M. Schwert, and S. Sontowski (eds), *Grenzregime III: Der lange Sommer der Migration* (pp. 196–206). Berlin: Assoziation A.

Della Porta, D. (2008). Eventful Protest, Global Conflicts. *Distinktion: Scandinavian Journal of Social Theory*, **9**(2), 27–56.

Della Porta, D. and Diani, M. (2009). *Social Movements: An Introduction*. Hoboken, NJ: John Wiley & Sons.

Della Porta, D. and Mattoni, A. (2014). *Spreading Protest: Social Movements in Times of Crisis*. Colchester: ECPR.

Diani, M. and McAdam, D. (eds) (2003). *Social Movements and Networks: Relational Approaches to Collective Action*. Oxford: Oxford University Press.

Diani, M. and Mische, A. (2015). Network Approaches and Social Movements. In D. Della Porta and M. Diani (eds), *The Oxford Handbook of Social Movements* (pp. 306–25). Oxford: Oxford University Press.

Eggert, N. and Giugni, M. (2015). Migration and Social Movements. In D. Della Porta and M. Diani (eds), *The Oxford Handbook of Social Movements* (pp. 159–72). Oxford: Oxford University Press.

Fassin, D. (2012). *Humanitarian Reason: A Moral History of the Present*. Berkeley, CA: University of California Press.

Fleischmann, L. and Steinhilper, E. (2017). The Myth of Apolitical Volunteering for Refugees. German Welcome Culture and a New Dispositif of Helping. *Social Inclusion*, **5**(3), 17–27.

Glöde, H. and Böhlo, B. (2015). Der Marsch der protestierenden Flüchtlinge von Würzburg nach Berlin und ihr Protest bis heute. *Forschungsjournal Soziale Bewegungen*, **28**(4), 75–87.

Granovetter, M.S. (1973). The Strength of Weak Ties. *American Journal of Sociology*, **78**(6), 1360–80.

Hess, S., Kasparek, B., Kron, S., Rodatz, M., Schwertl, M., and Sontowski, S. (2017). *Der lange Sommer der Migration. Grenzregime III*. Berlin and Hamburg: Assoziation A.

Hinger, S. (2016). Asylum in Germany: The Making of the 'Crisis' and the Role of Civil Society. *Human Geography*, **9**(2), 78–88.

Hinterberger, K.F. (2016). Das österreichische Asylgesetzänderungsgesetz 2016. In Marc Bungenberg, Thomas Giegerich, and Torsten Stein (eds), *Asyl und Migration in Europa – rechtliche Herausforderungen und Perspektiven* (pp. 185–206). ZEuS Sonderband 2016. *Zeitschrift Für Europäische Studien* (Special Issue 2016).

International Refugee Center Berlin (2015). *Movement Magazine*. Ed. International Refugee Center. Berlin.

Isin, E.F. and Nielsen, G.M. (2008). *Acts of Citizenship*. London and New York: Zed Books.

Jakob, C. (2013, 28 February). Aufstand der Nichtbürger. *Jungle World*. Berlin. Retrieved from http://jungle-world.com/artikel/2013/09/47223.html (last accessed 3 October 2018).

Jakob, C. (2016). *Die Bleibenden. Wie Flüchtlinge Deutschland seit 20 Jahren verändern*. Berlin: Ch. Links Verlag.

Jasper, J.M. and Duyvendak, J. (2014). *Players and Arenas. The Interactive Dynamics of Protest*. Amsterdam: Amsterdam University Press.

Johansson, S. (2016). *Was wir über Flüchtlinge (nicht) wissen. Der wissenschaftliche Erkenntnisstand zur Lebenssituation von Flüchtlingen in Deutschland*. Berlin: Robert Bosch Stiftung.

Jørgensen, M.B. (2013). Church Asylum – New Strategies, Alliances and Modes of Resistance. *Migration Letters*, **10**(3), 299–312.

Kusche, F. and Schütze, T. (2017). Schmutziges Geschäft oder Helfende Hände? Zur Kriminalisierung von Fluchthilfe. *Journal Für Entwicklungspolitik*, **33**(1), 110–17.

Lahusen, C. (2014). The Localism of Disruptive Actions: The Protest of the Unemployed in Germany. In D. Chabanet and F. Royall (eds), *From Silence to Protest: International Perspectives on Weakly Resourced Groups* (pp. 141–58). Farnham: Ashgate.

Lang, B. (1998). *Mythos Kreuzberg. Ethnographie eines Stadtteils (1961–1995)*. Frankfurt: Campus.

Langa, N. (2015). About the Refugee Movement in Kreuzberg/Berlin. *Movements*, **1**(2), 1–10.

Leitner, H. and Strunk, C. (2014). Spaces of Immigrant Advocacy and Liberal Democratic Citizenship. *Annals of the Association of American Geographers*, **104**(2), 348–56.

Leitner, H., Sheppard, E., and Sziarto, K.M. (2008). The Spatialities of Contentious Politics. *Transactions of the Institute of British Geographers*, **33**(2), 157–72.

Malkki, L. (1996). Speechless Emissaries: Refugees, Humanitarianism, and Dehistoricization. *Cultural Anthropology*, **11**(3), 377–404.

Martin, D.G. and Miller, B. (2003). Space and Contentious Politics. *Mobilization*, **8**(2), 143–56.

Maxwill, P. and Witte, J. (2018, 11 January). Ende einer Besetzung. *Spiegel Online*. Berlin. Retrieved from http://www.spiegel.de/panorama/gesellschaft/berlin-kreuzberg-polizei-raeumt-besetzte-gerhard-hauptmann-schule-a-1187277.html (last accessed 3 October 2018).

McAdam, D. (1986). Recruitment to High-risk Activism: The Case of Freedom Summer. *American Journal of Sociology*, **92**(1), 64.

Mitchell, K. and Sparke, M. (2018). Hotspot Geopolitics versus Geosocial Solidarity: Contending Constructions of Safe Space for Migrants in Europe. *Environment and Planning D: Society and Space*, online first. doi:10.1177/0263775818793647, 1–21.

Mokre, M. (2015). *Solidarität als Übersetzung. Überlegungen zum Refugee Protest Camp Vienna*. Vienna: Transversal Texts.

Monforte, P. and Dufour, P. (2011). Mobilizing in Borderline Citizenship Regimes: A Comparative Analysis of Undocumented Migrants' Collective Actions. *Politics & Society*, **39**(2), 203–32.

Monforte, P. and Dufour, P. (2013). Comparing the Protests of Undocumented Migrants Beyond Contexts: Collective Actions as Acts of Emancipation. *European Political Science Review*, **5**(1), 83–104.

Mudu, P. and Chattopadhyay, S. (2017). *Migration, Squatting and Radical Autonomy*. London and New York: Routledge.

Müller, A. (2013). *The Organisation of Reception Facilities for Asylum Seekers in Germany*. Nürnberg: Bundesamt für Migration und Flüchtlinge. Retrieved from https://www.bamf.de/SharedDocs/Anlagen/EN/Publikationen/EMN/Studien/wp55-emn-organisation-und-aufnahme-asylbewerber.pdf;jsessionid=FB995D17F378AA26FF5585C2070872A5.1_cid368?__blob=publicationFile (last accessed 3 October 2018).

Ndahayo, E. (2014). Asylsuchende in Deutschland – Handlungsmöglichkeiten auf lokaler Ebene. *Migration Und Soziale Arbeit*, **2**, 183–7.

Nicholls, W. (2008). The Urban Question Revisited: The Importance of Cities for Social Movements. *International Journal of Urban and Regional Research*, **32**(4), 841–59.

Nicholls, W. (2013a). Making Undocumented Immigrants into a Legitimate Political Subject: Theoretical Observations from the United States and France. *Theory, Culture & Society*, **30**(3), 82–107.

Nicholls, W. (2013b). *The DREAMers: How the Undocumented Youth Movement Transformed the Immigrant Rights Debate*. Stanford, CA: Stanford University Press.

Nicholls, W. and Uitermark, J. (2016). *Cities and the Immigrant Rights Movement. A Comparison of Activism in the US, France, and the Netherlands*. Hoboken, NJ: Wiley-Blackwell.

Nicholls, W. and Vermeulen, F. (2012). Rights through the City: The Urban Basis of Immigrant Rights Struggles in Amsterdam and Paris. In M.P. Smith and M. McQuarrie (eds), *Remaking Urban Citizenship. Organizations, Institutions, and the Right to the City* (pp. 79–96). New Brunswick, NJ: Transaction.

Nicholls, W., Miller, B., and Beaumont, J. (eds) (2013). *Spaces of Contention: Spatialities and Social Movements* (Vol. 9). Farnham: Ashgate.

Passy, F. (2001). Political Altruism and the Solidarity Movement. An Introduction. In M. Giugni and F. Passy (eds), *Political Altruism? Solidarity Movements in International Perspective* (pp. 3–26). Lanham, MD: Rowman & Littlefield.

Pieper, T. (2008). *Die Gegenwart der Lager. Zur Mikrophysik der Herrschaft in der deutschen Flüchtlingspolitik*. Münster: Westfälisches Dampfboot.

Refugee Protest Camp Vienna (2013). Neue Etappe des Flüchtlingsprotests (New Stage of Refugee Protest). Retrieved from https://refugeecampvienna.noblogs.org/post/2013/03/03/neue-etappe-des-fluchtlingsprotests/ (last accessed 3 October 2018).

Rosenberger, S. (2011). Integration von AsylwerberInnen? Zur Paradoxie individueller Integrationsleistungen und staatlicher Desintegration. In J. Dahlvik, H. Fassmann, W. Sievers (eds), *Migrations- und Integrationsforschung – wissenschaftliche Perspektiven aus Österreich* (pp. 91–106). Göttingen: V&R unipress.

Rosenberger, S. and König, A. (2012). Welcoming the Unwelcome: The Politics of Minimum Reception Standards for Asylum Seekers in Austria. *Journal of Refugee Studies*, **25**(4), 537–54.

Rosenberger, S. and Winkler, J. (2014). Com/passionate Protests – Fighting the Deportation of Asylum Seekers. *Mobilization. An International Quarterly*, **19**(2), 489–510.

Schwenken, H. (2006). *Rechtlos, aber nicht ohne Stimme: politische Mobilisierungen um irreguläre Migration in die Europäische Union*. Bielefeld: Transcript.

Senate of Berlin. (2014). Einigungspapier Oranienplatz. Retrieved from https://www.berlin.de/rbmskzl/_assets/aktuelles/2014/maerz/einigungspapier_oranienplatz.pdf (last accessed 3 October 2018).

Sewell, W. (2001). Space in Contentious Politics. In R. Aminzade, J. Goldstone, D. McAdam, E. Perry, W. Sewell, S. Tarrow, and C. Tilly (eds), *Silence and Voice in the Study of Contentious Politics* (pp. 51–88). Cambridge: Cambridge University Press.

Siméant, J. (1998). *La Cause des sans-papiers*. Paris: Les Presses de Sciences Po.

Stehle, M. (2006). Narrating the Ghetto, Narrating Europe: From Berlin, Kreuzberg to the Banlieus of Paris. *Westminster Papers in Communication and Culture*, **3**(3), 48–70.

Täubig, V. (2009). *Totale Institution Asyl Empirische Befunde zu alltäglichen Lebensführungen in der organisierten Desintegration*. Weinheim: Juventa.

Taylor, V. (1989). Social Movement Continuity: The Women's Movement in Abeyance. *American Political Science Review*, **54**(5), 761–75.

Taylor, V. and Crossley, A.D. (2013). Abeyance. In D.A. Snow, D. Della Porta, B. Klandermans, and D. McAdam (eds), *The Wiley-Blackwell Encyclopedia of Social and Politcal Movements* (pp. 1–2). Hoboken, NJ: Wiley-Blackwell. https://doi.org/10.1002/9781405198431.wbespm001 (last accessed 3 October 2018).

Tyler, I. and Marciniak, K. (2013). Immigrant Protest: An Introduction. *Citizenship Studies*, **17**(2), 143–56.

Tyler, I. and Marciniak, K. (2014). *Immigrant Protest: Politics, Aesthetics, and Everyday Dissent*. Albany, NY: State University of New York Press.

Ünsal, N. (2015). Challenging 'Refugees' and 'Supporters'. Intersectional Power Structures in the Refugee Movement in Berlin. *Movements*, **1**(2), 1–18.

Werdermann, D. (2016). Rechtliche Grundlagen der Teilhabe und Ausgrenzung von Flüchtlingen. *Neue Praxis* (Sonderheft 14), 86–95.

28. Law, presence and refugee claim determination

Nick Gill, Jennifer Allsopp, Andrew Burridge,
*Melanie Griffiths, Natalia Paszkiewicz and Rebecca Rotter**

INTRODUCTION

Under international law, people seeking asylum have to show that they have a well-founded fear of persecution by means of a legal claim for refugee status. In developed Western countries, when a refugee claim is rejected, the individual applicant usually has the right of appeal before an immigration judge.[1]

Josef's asylum appeal[2] was heard in the UK in 2013 under a system known as the 'Detained Fast Track' (DFT), which speedily processed claims while asylum seekers were detained, and typically had rates of appeal success of less than 10 per cent. Josef came into the court room doubled-up in pain and spent the whole hearing bent over the desk, with his head on the table and whispering replies, if he replied at all to the interpreter. Everyone completely ignored the situation – including the judge, the interpreter and the legal representative for the government – until about half-way through the hearing. At this point Josef whispered: 'I cannot speak more. I have severe pain at the moment.' The judge paused the hearing so that Josef could receive medical treatment, although this consisted only of the usher, as the designated first aider, asking what the matter was. Ethnographic notes taken by one of the authors at the time record that Josef looked 'weak and in a really terrible way', that he was 'unaware of what's going on around him', 'not engaging' and 'not looking at anyone or anything'. The judge faced a decision. Should he continue with the hearing in order to get it over with, or should he adjourn to a later date? He asked Josef for his preference. Josef explained that his mind was 'not my own' and, for the second time, said that he would prefer not to continue. The judge nevertheless continued the hearing and rushed through the remaining parts of the case. Josef did whisper a few words, although these were ill-chosen and likely detrimental to his case. It was as though he had no chance whatsoever of winning, so it was more important to finish the charade rather than to stop the proceedings. Josef was not legally represented.

Every year statistics are produced about how many asylum appeals are heard in the UK. The statistics would have implied that Josef enjoyed access to justice since his legal right to an appeal hearing before an immigration judge was upheld. But the important ways in which Josef was absent despite being literally present at his hearing cast doubt over this view. In this instance, the judge made the telling decision to allow the physical presence of Josef's body to stand-in for his effective participation in, and engagement with, the hearing.

* We acknowledge funding from the British Economic and Social Research Council, ES/J023426/1.
[1] This will be discussed in more detail later in the chapter.
[2] 'Josef' is a pseudonym.

In this chapter we outline a set of conceptual resources with which to generate renewed attention among critical geographers to the issues of 'access to' and 'exclusion from' legal justice, with particular attention to legal justice in the context of refugee claims. In order for the formal legal system to work, claimants must be able to access the legal system not just bodily, but also in health-related, psychological and emotional terms, as well as in terms of communicative and material capital. Where these possibilities of access are not in place, as we demonstrate in what follows, various different types of absence arise irrespective of, and sometimes concurrently with, bodily presence. The law's over-emphasis on bodily forms of presence overlooks the multiple forms of presence that are practically required for the law to function. In what follows we demonstrate that thinking about the relationship between law, space and refugee claim determination in terms of multiple forms of absence and presence is an important way to reveal how exclusions from legal justice arise.

In the next section we will examine two currents in academic legal scholarship in order to prepare the way for considering legal exclusions through the lens of absence and presence. We will then advocate for attention to be given to legal absent-presences as an analytical approach, setting out how and why geographers and sociologists have resisted the opposition of absence and presence, and how a typology of different presences might be translated into the legal context. Finally, we explore five types of legal absence – imaginative, material, corporeal, communicative and virtual – drawing on empirical research into the legal process of refugee claim determination in Britain.

RETHINKING LEGAL EXCLUSION

The first current we assess concerns the well-known space-blindness of the academic discipline of law (Blomley, 1994). As Bartel et al. (2013, pp. 339–40) write: 'the academic discipline of law possesses only very basic conceptions of geographic matters such as space, place and human–environment relations. It is often ignorant of geographic influences as well as its own geographic actions and effects.' This said, it is worth pointing out that not all of academic law is space-blind. Traditions of legal anthropology, which are highly sensitive to the influences of social and spatial phenomena over the law and vice versa, are a case in point (see, for instance, Benda-Beckmann et al., 2009; Merry, 1988). Within refugee studies there is also a keen awareness of the spatial unevenness of legal systems of determination by outcome (in Europe see Neumayer, 2005; in America see Ramji-Nogales et al., 2009). What Bartel et al. (2013) are referring to is a still-dominant strand of legal scholarship that is heavily doctrinal in nature, meaning that it is primarily focused on the law as such and employs, mostly implicitly, the classical legal assumption that the law operates independently from social and spatial context. It is this form of space-blindness that they quite rightly view as in need of rectifying. 'Geography needs to be made visible to the law' (Ibid., p. 342), they write.

When it comes to the challenges facing refugees as a particular sort of legal subject, the space-blindness of legal doctrine is all the more consequential. In the European Union (EU) a system called the 'Dublin' system stipulates that an asylum seeker should have their claim for asylum determined at the first safe country they arrive at. If they claim asylum in France, Germany or the UK, for example, and it becomes clear that they have passed through Italy or Greece, then their claim will often be transferred back to these countries. Additionally, in 2016 the EU struck a deal with Turkey that allowed asylum seekers on the Greek islands to be transferred to Turkey for their claims to be processed. Both the Dublin system and the deal have been critiqued because they do not take into account differences in the capacity or political disposition to host refugees between these different countries, national differences in the process by which refugee status is determined, or differences in the grant rate of asylum claims across space (see Guild et al., 2015). In short: they are persistently space-blind.

Although efforts have been made to harmonise refugee determination systems across Europe,[3] there remain significant differences. For instance, while the overall rate at which Syrians were awarded some form of protection in 2015 was 97 per cent in the EU-28, particular countries deviated significantly – including Hungary and Romania, which both awarded some form of positive status in fewer than 60 per cent of cases. In the same year, the refugee recognition rate for Afghans – the second most common nationality of asylum claimants to Europe after Syrians (Eurostat, 2016) – varied from 78 per cent, 83 per cent and 96 per cent in Austria, France and Italy to 16 per cent, 14 per cent and 5 per cent in Hungary, Romania and Bulgaria, respectively.[4] What these differences convey is the importance of thinking critically about spatial variety and difference in the face of the apparent coherence that legal systems attempt to project.

The second current concerns the law's over-emphasis on two types of presence: textual and corporeal. The law's heavy reliance on the written form as a way to present cases and deliver judgments privileges certain cultural subjects. Similarly, the principle that the defendant/appellant should appear in person in court during certain types of proceedings,[5] while laudable in many ways, is built on assumptions of able-bodiedness and capability, and therefore once again privileges certain sorts of subject. In the context of refugee migration these tendencies are particularly regrettable. The text-fetish renders the migrant, who is often unfamiliar with the legal jargon of the reception country even if they are familiar with the language of the reception country more generally, hostage to the activities of a set of intermediaries, from translators, interpreters and transcribers to solicitors and non-governmental organisations (NGOs) who each provide marketed services of 'entextualisation' (Jacquemet, 2009). The body-fetish, for its part, abstracts from the corporeal histories of refugees,[6] which might well dictate their demeanour, their states of mind, their emotions, their abilities, their comfort, and their conformity to local norms of etiquette and comportment. To conclude that a subject is present simply because their body happens to be in a particular location, or because some mediated version of

---

[3]   Notably through the Common European Asylum System's Asylum Procedures Directive introduced in 2005 and recast in 2013.

[4]   The statistics in this paragraph refer to first instance decisions only. Countries that delivered fewer than 100 first instance decisions are discounted. Statistics are taken from Eurostat table migr_asydcfsta, 'First instance decisions on applications by citizenship, age and sex; Annual aggregated data (rounded)'. Available at: http://ec.europa.eu/eurostat/data/database; published 14 September 2016 (accessed 6 January 2017).

[5]   The principle of habeas corpus, for example, is inherited from English common law in the legal systems of the United States, Australia and Canada, and refers to the recourse in law by which a person can report an unlawful detention or imprisonment to a court and require the custodian to present – in person – the detained individual to a judge so that the judge can determine whether the imprisonment is legal. Habeas corpus means, literally, 'that you have the body'.

[6]   Which may include torture as well as the physical consequences of hard journeys.

their narrative appears on a particular page, discounts a vast array of considerations that influence the form of being that is possible at and through legal sites.

Beyond Absence and Presence

Sociologists have critiqued the view that absence and presence are to be understood as coherently opposed antonyms. 'We should be putting the oppositions implied in such pairs behind us', Callon and Law write (2004, p. 5). Modern machines such as individualised screen devices and other immersive technologies produce new spaces 'with people both here and there, present and absent' (Urry, 2004, p. 34), for example, offering the opportunity to 'uncouple' oneself from one's surroundings (Sheller, 2004). As such, co-location in a literal, bodily sense is an increasingly tenuous way to assure functional co-presence (Urry, 2007).

Philosophers too have peered beyond the binary opposition of absence and presence. Lyotard et al. (1988, p. 286), for example, warns against the lack of sophistication of the concept of 'absence' as such. 'That any being whatever may be absent', he writes, 'and this applies all the more strongly to being itself, is in my view an idea that is much too simple, for at least the absence of being is present, being presents itself *in absentia*'. As if to illustrate the point, another philosopher, Sartre (1956), gives the example of his intense experience of the absence of his friend Pierre upon walking into a café at which he expected to meet him. 'His absence fixes the café in its evanescence', Sartre writes (Ibid., pp. 9–10), '. . . Pierre absent haunts this café'.

Cultural geographers have elaborated upon this insight in various ways. Attention has been paid, for example, to the continuing presence of the deceased: absent in a mortal sense but made present through both the traces that they leave behind in material form and the practices of memorialisation undertaken to recall them (Maddrell, 2013; Wylie, 2009; see also Miller and Parrott, 2009). Others have focused on the absent-presences surrounding consumption practices: from the traces of distant factory workers that inhere in the products we use and wear, to the afterlives of discarded property (Mansvelt, 2010). The frame of absent-presence, then, offers a way to reconcile apparently contradictory phenomena. In the case of the law, the way that the concept can transcend and reconcile different ontological conditions may be capable of providing intellectual purchase on the contradictory forms of absent-presence that Josef experienced.

Additionally, a sociological literature culminating in John Urry's theorisation of mobilities (2007) offers a rich understanding of *different forms* of presence as well as movement. These include corporeal, imaginative and virtual modalities, as well as the transmission of presences via the movement of materials or objects, and via 'communicative travel' such as 'telephone, fax, and mobile phone' (Urry, 2004, p. 28). One can be absent or present to varying degrees in terms of both the extent to which one can command these different forms of mobility and the degree to which one is adept at combining them. For Urry (2007) it is therefore possible to be mobile, present and absent in different senses at the same time.

The law relies upon, requires and assumes each of these types of presence to varying degrees, and the protections it promises are often contingent upon them. In the rest of this chapter we outline some of the absent-presences that characterise the asylum appeal system in the UK by considering what happens when these forms of presence are lacking in important respects. We draw on a three-year study of asylum appeal processes that involved observing 100 hearings ethnographically, another 290 with surveys and conducting 70 interviews (35 of which with former appellants) between 2013 and 2016.

LEGAL ABSENT-PRESENCES

In the UK, the Home Office is responsible for the initial processing of applications for asylum. In roughly three-quarters of cases, the Home Office decision is a refusal of asylum. At this point (following a negative decision) asylum applicants can appeal against this decision to an independent tribunal. It is a measure of the importance of this process, and the degree of error[7] inherent to the Home Office's initial decision-making, that over a quarter of appeals are usually allowed each year. During the years of the research, around 19 major tribunal hearing centres were operating.[8] They are dotted around the UK, some in cities and some in peri-urban locations such as out-of-town industrial parks. Each appeal is heard before an immigration judge and usually involves the appellant, their legal representative, the Home Office Presenting Officer (HOPO) (that is, the legal representative acting on behalf of the government), an interpreter if required, witnesses if called, and tribunal ushers (who are 'silent' actors who assist in the smooth running of the process). Following the hearing, the immigration judge must produce a written determination within ten days, either allowing or dismissing the appeal.

For this research access was confined to the public areas of hearing centres. The ushers' and judges' areas were not accessible to us, nor was the paperwork pertaining to cases. We made observations from the public gallery at the back of hearing rooms and we remained as inconspicuous as possible, although when appropriate or requested we provided an explanation of the purposes of the research to the parties present.

Interviewees who had gone through the asylum appeal system were recruited via existing contacts with NGOs and refugee community groups in a research process that was separate from the observations of the hearings. Consent to be interviewed and for the interview material to appear in published work in an anonymised form was collected from the interviewees, but for the purposes of this chapter we follow the methodology of using composite fictional characters (Gough, 2008). That is, the characters are not only pseudonyms, but places, dates and events have been lightly fictionalised, and the correspondence between events and characters has been recombined.

There are at least two reasons why social scientists might choose to use composite fictional characters in research. First, while 'in much everyday speech fiction is equated with falsehood' (Gough, 2008, p. 339), this approach recognises the narrative force of fiction as a means of conveying certain forms of truth. If the assumption is made that academic research is chiefly concerned with documenting facts without distorting them, then it is reasonable to suppose that there is no place for fiction in academic

---

[7]   The term 'error' here adopts the viewpoint that travelling across international borders in search of a better life can legitimately be judged to be right or wrong by anyone other than the traveller. See Gill (2009) and Burridge (2014) for a critique of this view.

[8]   Depending on how they are counted and at what period the count is taken.

work. But academic work, especially ethnographic work that seeks to convey meaning and feelings, is concerned with more than the brute transmission of facts. As such, fictionalisation can be an indispensable strategy towards the fulfilment of academic objectives. Telling the story of the data and the experiences of observation can be central.

In the case of this chapter, however, the use of composite fictional characters is driven by practical considerations about confidentiality. 'Storying' (Piper and Sikes, 2010, p. 568) certain elements of empirical data offers a degree of protection to participants that is difficult to achieve by just altering identifiers (for a discussion of interview anonymisation, see Saunders et al., 2015). Clearly this introduces the need for reader trust of the authors, but it is worth pointing out that other forms of academic work including scientific work in the positivist tradition also requires trust (Piper and Sikes, 2010). In what follows, we occasionally fictionalise the accounts given, but at the same time do not make up anything that directly relates to peoples' experiences. This has been recognised as 'an important strategy for protecting vulnerable participants' (Piper and Sikes, 2010, p. 573).

Imaginative Absence

Many of the asylum appellants interviewed understood themselves as incomplete while attending their asylum hearing, describing the mental health challenges they faced and that were exacerbated by the daunting procedures. Feelings of under-preparedness, of the surreal nature of the hearings, of the unerring feeling that this was a movie and not real life and that they were operating in some sort of dream-like, altered state were common. In other words, although the interviewees were physically present in their hearings, they often felt uncannily absent from them.

This unreality was heightened by the dissonance between the criminalising tone of the proceedings and their self-image as law-abiding individuals. 'I haven't committed a crime, I am not a criminal, why do I have to be tried and convicted?' one of the respondents asked. Others were profoundly suspicious of the legal system, questioning the independence of the judges, especially when judges and government representatives tended to enter the room together, sometimes chatting about the weather and the football at the weekend. Others were confused about the process: 'Is this it?' one of the interviewees recalled thinking just after their hearing, 'I thought this was a practice.'

These experiences underscore how easy it was for the interviewees to be both present and absent from the hearings. Some respondents found the whole experience so distressing that they developed individual tactics of imaginative escape. When the intensity of the cross-examination (at which refugees are often pointedly accused of lying about their cases)[9] became overwhelming respondents described switching off, recalling their homes and their loved ones and purposefully disengaging from the scene at which they found themselves.

---

[9]   Typical examples include 'I put it to you that you are lying to the judge today' and 'But that simply is not true is it, Mr X?'

Material Absence

In order to be recognised as a refugee, not only in the British system but under international law, an asylum seeker must prove that they fulfil the specific definition set out in Article 1(A)2 of the 1951 Geneva Convention, as modified by the accompanying 1967 Protocol, namely, that a refugee is someone who:

> owing to well-founded fear of being persecuted for reasons of race, religion, nationality, membership of a particular social group or political opinion, is outside the country of his nationality and is unable or, owing to such fear, is unwilling to avail himself of the protection of that country.

There are various factors that make the determination of refugee claims according to this criteria troublesome. First, none of these five 'Convention reasons' are precisely defined, either in the Convention itself or in the UNHCR[10] *Handbook* that provides guidance on its application,[11] nor are the key notions of 'well-founded fear' and 'persecution'. Second, since refugee law is an area of administrative rather than criminal law the burden of proof is upon the appellant. Third, refugee claim determination is asking judges to predict the future. With criminal matters the essence of the case is backward-looking: asking who did such-and-such a thing. With refugee determination, the essence of the case is forward-looking. Judges are asked to decide if there is a reasonable degree of likelihood that the appellant will be persecuted if they were returned to their country of origin. There is often a paucity of hard evidence for judges to use to determine cases due to the circumstances of individual flight and exile, and the availability of reliable information about the country of origin, and as a result many will, often by necessity, turn to assessments of appellant's 'credibility': a slippery, elusive and often subjective legal concept, especially in refugee law (Coffey, 2003; Sweeney, 2009).

Under such circumstances whatever material evidence can be gathered to either prove the past experience or future risk of persecution, or to establish the 'credibility' of the appellant, takes on heightened significance. This might include letters, scars, photographs, newspaper reports, memories, testimonials, internet sources, witnesses, medical and expert opinions. The abilities of appellants to collect (and in some cases, such as those concerned with sexual violence, also to disclose) such evidence differ depending on the appellant. The material capital that appellants command to mobilise and integrate such objects into the legal system of decision-making will depend upon their social networks, financial position, mental health, ethnic ties, familial connections, trust in the determination system of the receiving country, and type of claim (is it based on persecution owing to sexual orientation or religion, for example?). Appellants may very well appear in front of a tribunal judge while still lacking or not disclosing crucial material elements of their case: thereby they may be present in a legal sense but materially absent at the same time.

Take, for example, Mabel's case. Mabel was a 17-year-old girl when she experienced

---

[10]　United Nations High Commissioner for Refugees.
[11]　UNHCR (1979, Annexes updated 2011). *Handbook and Guidelines on Procedures and Criteria for Determining Refugee Status.* Available at: http://www.unhcr.org/uk/publications/legal/3d58e13b4/handbook-procedures-criteria-determining-refugee-status-under-1951-convention.html (accessed 31 July 2016). The notions are clarified by case law.

sexual abuse at the hands of government forces in her home country in Africa. After being smuggled to the UK she contacted a solicitor[12] to ask him to represent her case for asylum, but Mabel struggled to disclose the details of her sexual abuse to the solicitor who therefore refused to take her case on. At the time she remembers thinking 'Why is he asking these questions? Why is he asking me about my parents? About my grandfather? Do I have to tell him everything? I don't know why I would meet him for the first time and tell them everything about me, A-Z, inside and out. Why?' After the difficulties she had in disclosing information, Mabel went into her asylum appeal hearing without a legal representative and without having received legal advice, and consequently lost her case.

One way to interpret this experience is to recognise that important aspects of Mabel's experience and life-history were absent from the case that was heard at the time. Several years later, after an extended period of homelessness and destitution, Mabel received psychological support that helped her to disclose important aspects of her case and she was eventually granted asylum by a different judge. This success corroborates the view that important elements of her case were missing the first time around.

The sheer volume of work involved in assembling the materials required for a hearing also makes the outcome a contingent and fragile affair (Latour, 2010). At the beginning of almost all of the hearings observed, the Home Office, the judge and the legal representative for the appellant (where there was one) would check that they had the same paperwork. All too frequently there would be significant problems, with one or other of the parties having lost important files, having forgotten them, not received them, not having had time to read them, not having had them translated, having different versions, having incomplete or spoiled copies, or simply not understanding the significance of the documents before them. The material presence of the appellant was consequently often partial and highly precarious.

Corporeal Absence

Alongside sickness, which can refract and distort an appellant's presence, as Josef's case illustrates, of particular importance to the physical experience of hearings are tiredness and stress. During hearings, some judges offered comfort breaks and others did not (see Gill et al., 2018). Appellants often had to travel a long way and regularly struggled to find the hearing centres, sometimes arriving several hours early 'just in case'. Some hearings began at 10.00 am and others much later in the day. However, appellants did not know when theirs would start until cases were scheduled at the hearing centre on the day of the hearing itself, so would therefore arrive and sometimes be at the centre for an entire day, often with limited food – meaning they entered their hearings hungry and emotionally drained from the anticipation of waiting.

Appellants are often required to make significant journeys, of between one and a half and four hours on public transport, to the peri-urban hearing centres to which their case has been allocated. One unrepresented appellant highlighted the difficulties of getting to his appeal:

---

[12]   The equivalent of an American attorney.

I was a little bit worried about how we could get there. I went on the internet to find a way to get there, but there was not any clear way. I couldn't afford to stay the night in a hotel, so we started my journey in the middle of the night. On the day of the hearing we asked a friend of a friend who had a car if he could take me some of the way. Then, we had heard that the train would be two pounds something to get back, but that was a special offer that had expired. It turned out to be four pounds fifty and we couldn't pay for it, so we got stuck.

Additional sources of stress for some appellants can include the presence of their babies or children in or just outside the hearing room, the nature and tone of the cross-examination by the HOPO, the conduct of judges and the difficulties that the appellant had in understanding the language being used. The consequences of being stressed are often embodied and corporeal, including a rapid heartbeat, a dry mouth, agitation, headaches and low energy levels (Stress Management Health Centre, 2018). Appellants who were stressed sometimes behaved differently in the court: for example, by falling silent,[13] becoming confused, struggling to follow the hearing, or occasionally displaying frustration and anger.

Appellant anger challenged the expectation that they would be passive, expectant, needy and accepting (Sigona, 2014). Appellant body language was often defensive or hostile; sometimes they would tut, choke, laugh and occasionally even shout out in opposition to what was being said. One appellant twice challenged the Home Office representative when faced with particularly intense and long questioning. Afterwards the Home Office representative seemed to think that this had undermined the appellant's case, commenting that 'he lost his legs by his attitude alone'. When faced with the anger of appellants, judges would chide them to 'Stop getting so excited'. The tribunals were 'no place for emotion' one judge explained. Judges had little patience for appellants who 'lost control'. In this sense the law actively suppresses forms of presence while requiring others.

Communicative Absence

Central to a fair hearing is the ability to communicate clearly. In asylum cases communication is especially important as appellants are expected to build narratives to support their claims while maintaining consistency with their previous statements. The key challenges that appellants face in terms of communicating clearly include access to, and quality of legal representation (Burridge and Gill, 2017), adequately qualified, attentive and meticulous interpreters, and a complex set of cultural and linguistic issues that arise when an interpreter is used (Gill et al., 2016). Of comparable importance, however, were the questioning tactics used by the legal representative for the government during the cross-examination, some of which aimed to render the appellant effectively absented from the dialogue that was taking place.

One such tactic included what HOPOs would call 'fishing'. This involved making the appellant go over their story multiple times during cross-examination in the hope of catching them out with an inconsistency. Psychologists have established that inconsistency is not only common when two descriptions are given of the same event at different times, but that inconsistencies in peripheral details in the account are especially likely if the events recalled are traumatic ones (Herlihy and Turner, 2006). This fishing technique can therefore be viewed as a cynical tactic that exploits the trauma of appellants.

---

[13]   See Johnson (2011) for a detailed discussion of the role of silence in asylum hearings.

Another tactic included what we call 'miscommunication', which involved allowing misunderstandings to go uncorrected during a cross-examination in order to give the impression to the judge that the appellant was being unhelpful or evasive. According to this technique, if an appellant does not appear to understand the question, the HOPO would simply repeat it verbatim rather than choose an alternative form of words, but with rising volume and anger.

A third tactic we call 'boxing-in'. Many HOPOs use statements with which the appellant must either agree or disagree, rather than open-ended, exploratory questions. Examples include: 'but you didn't mention it in the first interview, did you?', 'So your mother was in the house, was she?', 'You have no direct experience of living as a Christian in Pakistan. Correct?' The addition of a well-chosen suffix does various things. It can add to the accusatory feel of a conversation, and thereby increase the pressure on the respondent. It also sets an expectation that the appellant will either agree with the statement or disagree with it, thereby constricting the opportunity to provide more detail or correct aspects of the statement that are not accurate, securing a subordinate linguistic role for the appellant. It takes a very assertive appellant to go further than simply agreeing or denying and provide elaboration or explanation. In such ways, these various questioning tactics contested not the grounds of the case as such, but the ability to compete on a level playing field when making the case. In other words, they sought to delete facets of the appellant's communicative presence.

It was often challenging to witness the hearings as researchers. There were frequently no other observers present, meaning that we were prominent in the hearing room even if we were not formally involved in the proceedings. We were required to remain unobtrusive and to watch the proceedings without intervening, which could sometimes feel uncomfortable. Following a particularly heated exchange between an appellant and a judge, for example, in which the judge had berated the appellant for not speaking clearly, the ethnographic diary entry reads:

> Silence and deep shame descends in the room. It feels like we are in school and he's unfairly being singled out as a really naughty child and everyone else is silently allowing this to continue, being complicit in his treatment, out of fear of receiving the same degrading treatment.

As a research team we met frequently and had explicitly discussed our strategy for dealing with a range of situations in the court room. We explained our purposes wherever possible, for example, and honoured any requests for us to leave. We also gave some thought to the risk of vicarious traumatisation before we began the fieldwork, and put in place a strategy for detecting it and dealing with it. This involved meeting frequently, sometimes for joint observations, and sharing our frustrations and insights within the safe space of the research team.

Virtual Absence

Although appellants did not appear via videolink in the asylum appeal hearings observed, it is a pertinent issue for various reasons. Other types of cases, including cases for bail from immigration detention, are routinely heard by judges in the UK via videolink; sometimes witnesses can appear in an asylum appeal via videolink in the UK; other countries use videolink for asylum appeals; and there are aspirations in Britain as elsewhere to hold an increasing number of virtual immigration hearings[14] (alongside an increase in online processes generally) as a way to increase the efficiency of the tribunal system and reduce estates' costs.

Although video enabled hearings might allow a wider pool of expert witnesses, including from source countries, to corroborate appellants' stories, activists have historically been firmly opposed to hearings at which the appellant appears on a screen. This is because it is more difficult for lawyers to communicate with video-linked clients in private before or during the hearing, there are often technical glitches with the equipment and the transmission of voices can compound language difficulties (Bail for Immigration Detainees and the Refugee Council, 2008; see also Gill et al., 2012). While the videolinking of appellants might save them an arduous journey to the court and may be less intimidating than an in-person appearance, they may also find screen-based communication impersonal and therefore struggle to disclose important information about their case. There are also practical safety concerns. Holding an appeal hearing at a tribunal allows the ushers, security staff and judge to be reasonably confident that the appellant is able to speak freely,[15] while it is difficult to be sure about whether an appellant is being coerced by someone off-screen when they are using a videolink. It may also be difficult to ensure the privacy of online procedures, which could have severe ramifications for individuals fleeing malicious government forces. Because of the risks of coercion and concerns over compromised privacy, it may be that the apparent presence of an appellant via videolink conceals important forms of absence.

The question of whether a videolink is sufficient to enable an appellant to participate in a hearing is not only key to whether appellants already in the UK need to attend a physical hearing, it is also central to the issue of deportability from Britain. If video enabled appellant appearances are deemed effective by law, this could easily open the door to the tactic of deporting asylum seekers after an initial negative decision on their claim by the government, and conducting any appeals from their country of origin or country to which they are deported. Indeed, this was the policy (dubbed 'Deport First, Appeal Later') in Britain for certain immigration cases (although not asylum) from 2014 to 2017, until a Supreme Court case ruled in 2017 that video enabled hearings of this sort were not effective (*Kiarie and Byndloss v The Secretary of State for the Home Department* [2017]), citing financial barriers to setting up and accessing the required technology (see also BBC, 2017). It may very well only be a matter of time before this judgment is reconsidered in the light of a large-scale round of investment in Her Majesty's Courts and Tribunals, including their technological capability (Ministry of Justice, 2016). In order to circumvent the objection that deported individuals may not have access to safe videolinking technology in their countries of origin, the option of using British consulates has been mooted, which appears to overlook a host of difficulties in accessing the consulates themselves.

---

[14]   It is helpful to distinguish between video enabled hearings, which involve one or more of the parties, but not all of them, participating via videolink and virtual hearings, in which all parties including the judge participate via videolink and there is no use made of a physical court room.

[15]   Although it should be noted that it is possible for a coercive agent to be sitting in the public area of the physical court.

CONCLUSION

The key point about the absences that we have described in this chapter is that they are concomitant with apparent presences. When a hearing takes place the law necessarily makes a series of assumptions. The appellant is presumed to be partaking in that hearing to the best of their ability. The provisions made to help them communicate are presumed to be effective unless reasons are given during the hearing to the contrary. The evidence before the judge is taken to be the best possible. And the narrative given by the appellant is viewed as a complete and accurate record of events. The problem is that lurking behind each of these assumptions are various forms of absence that lie largely outside the legal frame. These absences are all the more acute in the contexts of migration, trauma and linguistic incomprehension that often characterise the refugee experience.

It is worth bearing in mind the specificities of the British asylum system and hence the research reported here. For example, numerous countries do not have a judicial appeal process, preferring to rely upon administrative forms of review and redress. Some generally carry out appeal processes on paper rather than via a hearing. The publicness of appeals also varies internationally. In Britain first instance appeal decisions are not publicised (they are sent privately to the appellant) while in other countries they are made public. Similarly, there is a great deal of variability internationally in the degree of access that the public, including academic researchers, have to asylum appeal hearings. In many cases asylum appeal procedures are carried out behind closed doors, preventing the sort of scrutiny of the system that we have carried out. In these instances another form of presence – the presence of observers – is erased.

Critical geographers studying migration have an important role to play with regard to legal systems of border control. Conceptually, they must be willing to question commonly employed notions like absence and presence, as a way to keep the law accountable and grounded not in abstractions but in real human experience. Drawing on insights from geographers and others into the increasingly hybridised character of contemporary presence, this chapter has revealed how the eliding of bodily attendance with functional engagement not only overlooks the various ways in which absences coexist with presences in the legal context, but also risks obscuring important ways in which vulnerable asylum seekers are denied access to justice.

Practically, a geographical approach such as this can inform various forms of activism. Evidence from our project is being used to produce introductory videos to the asylum hearings in various languages, for example, as a way to help orientate appellants before the proceedings.[16] Furthermore, evidence from our ethnography informed a High Court case brought by the charity Detention Action in 2015 against the DFT rules that Josef's case was heard under, and which were applied to over 4,000 asylum seekers in Britain in 2013 alone (*Detention Action v First-tier Tribunal (Immigration and Asylum Chamber)* et al. [2015]). Alongside the legal arguments made in the case, our research illustrated the practical difficulties facing appellants trying to gather evidence to support their claim from inside immigration detention within the strict time limits set out by the rules. The

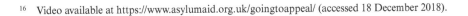

16   Video available at https://www.asylumaid.org.uk/goingtoappeal/ (accessed 18 December 2018).

High Court decided that the rules were unfair and unlawful (BBC, 2015a), a decision that was upheld by the Court of Appeal (BBC, 2015b). This led to the suspension of the entire DFT system (BBC, 2015c), the release of hundreds of detainees (Guardian, 2015), the opportunity for over 10,000 appeals against decisions made under the rules to be mounted (Guardian, 2017), and halting – at least for a while – this particular form of injustice.

REFERENCES

Bail for Immigration Detainees and the Refugee Council (2008), *Immigration Bail Hearings by Videolink: A Monitoring Exercise by Bail for Immigration Detainees and the Refugee Council*, London.

Bartel, R., Graham, N., Jackson, S. et al. (2013), 'Legal geography: an Australian perspective'. *Geographical Research*, **51**(4), 339–53.

BBC (British Broadcasting Corporation) (2015a), 'Fast-track asylum system "unlawful", High Court rules'. Available at http://www.bbc.co.uk/news/uk-33113132 (accessed 30 January 2018).

BBC (British Broadcasting Corporation) (2015b), 'Asylum appeal fast-track system unlawful says Court of Appeal'. Available at http://www.bbc.co.uk/news/uk-33704163 (accessed 30 January 2018).

BBC (British Broadcasting Corporation) (2015c), 'Fast-track asylum appeal system suspended by government'. Available at http://www.bbc.co.uk/news/uk-33371814 (accessed 30 January 2018).

BBC (British Broadcasting Corporation) (2017), 'Deport First, Appeal Later' policy ruled unlawful'. Available at http://www.bbc.co.uk/news/uk-40272323 (accessed 30 January 2018).

Benda-Beckmann, Franz von., Benda-Beckmann, Keebet von and Griffiths, Anne (eds) (2009), *Spatializing Law: An Anthropological Geography of Law in Society*, Farnham, Surrey: Ashgate.

Blomley, Nicholas (1994), *Law, Space and the Geographies of Power*, New York: Guilford Press.

Burridge, A. (2014), '"No Borders" as a critical politics of mobility and migration'. *ACME: An International Journal for Critical Geographies*, **13**(3), 463–70.

Burridge, A. and Gill, N. (2017), 'Conveyor-belt justice: precarity, access to justice and geographies of legal aid in asylum appeals'. *Antipode*, **49**(1), 23–42.

Callon, M. and Law, J. (2004), 'Guest editorial'. *Environment and Planning D: Society and Space*, **22**(1), 3–11.

Coffey, G. (2003), 'The credibility of credibility evidence at the Refugee Review Tribunal'. *International Journal of Refugee Law*, **15**(3), 377–417.

Eurostat (2016), *Asylum Statistics*. Available at http://ec.europa.eu/eurostat/statistics-explained/index.php/Asylum_statistics (accessed 6 January 2017).

Gill, N. (2009), 'Whose "No Borders"? Achieving No Borders for the right reasons'. *Refuge*, **26**(2), 107–20.

Gill, N., Conlon, D., Oeppen, C. and Tyler, I. (2012), 'Networks of asylum support in the UK and USA: A handbook of ideas, strategies and best practice for asylum support groups in a challenging social and economic climate'. Available at https://steedee.files.wordpress.com/2012/03/networks-of-asylum-support-print2.pdf (accessed 31 October 2018).

Gill, N., Rotter, R., Burridge, A., Allsopp, J. and Griffiths, M. (2016), 'Linguistic incomprehension in British asylum appeal hearings'. *Anthropology Today*, **32**(2), 18–21.

Gill, N., Rotter, R., Burridge A. and Allsopp, J. (2018), 'The limits of procedural discretion: unequal treatment and vulnerability in Britain's asylum appeals'. *Social & Legal Studies*, **27**(1), 49–78. DOI: 10.1177/0964663917703178 Open Access. Available at http://journals.sagepub.com/doi/pdf/10.1177/0964663917703178 (accessed 31 October 2018).

Gough, Noel (2008), 'Fictional writing', in L. Given (ed.), *The Sage Encyclopedia of Qualitative Research*, Los Angeles, CA, London, New Delhi and Singapore: Sage, pp. 338–9.

Guardian (2015), 'Court rejects government appeal over fast-track detention of asylum seekers'. Available at https://www.theguardian.com/uk-news/2015/jul/29/court-rejects-government-appeal-fast-track-detention-asylum-seekers-michael-gove (accessed 30 January 2018).

Guardian (2017), 'High Court rules that more than 10,000 asylum seekers treated unfairly'. Available at https://www.theguardian.com/uk-news/2017/jan/20/uk-high-court-rules-10000-asylum-seekers-treated-unfairly-detained-fast-track (accessed 18 December 2018).

Guild, E., Costello, C., Garlick, M., Moreno-Lax, V. and Carrera, S. (2015), 'Enhancing the Common European Asylum System and Alternatives to Dublin' Study for the European Parliament, LIBE Committee, 2015. Available at: SSRN: https://ssrn.com/abstract=2640526.

Herlihy, J. and Turner, S. (2006), 'Should discrepant accounts given by asylum seekers be taken as proof of deceit?' *Torture*, **16**(2), 81–92.

Jacquemet, M. (2009), 'Transcribing refugees: the entextualization of asylum seekers' hearings in a transidiomatic environment'. *Text and Talk*, **29**(5), 525–46.

Johnson, T. (2011), 'On silence, sexuality and skeletons: reconceptualizing narrative in asylum hearings'. *Social and Legal Studies*, **20**(1), 57–78.

Latour, Bruno (2010), *The Making of Law: An Ethnography of the Conseil d'État*, Cambridge: Polity Press.

Lyotard, J.-F., Van Reijen, W. and Veerman, D. (1988), 'An interview with Jean-François Lyotard'. *Theory, Culture and Society*, **5**(2–3), 277–309.

Maddrell, A. (2013), 'Living with the deceased: absence, presence and absence-presence'. *Cultural Geographies*, **20**(4), 501–22.

Mansvelt, J. (2010), 'Geographies of consumption: engaging with absent presences'. *Progress in Human Geography*, **34**(2), 224–33.

Merry, S. (1988), 'Legal pluralism'. *Law and Society Review*, **22**(5), 869–96.

Miller, D. and Parrott, F. (2009), 'Loss and material culture in South London'. *Journal of the Royal Anthropological Institute*, **15**(3), 502–19.

Ministry of Justice (2016), *Transforming Our Justice System: Summary of Reforms and Consultation*. Available at https://consult.justice.gov.uk/digital-communications/transforming-our-courts-and-tribunals/supporting_documents/consultationpaper.pdf (accessed 30 January 2018).

Neumayer, E. (2005), 'Bogus refugees? The determinants of asylum migration to Western Europe'. *International Studies Quarterly*, **49**(3), 389–410.

Piper, H. and Sikes, P. (2010), 'All teachers are vulnerable but especially gay teachers: using composite fictions to protect research participants in pupil–teacher sex-related research'. *Qualitative Inquiry*, **16**(7), 566–74.

Ramji-Nogales, Jaya, Schoenholtz, Andrew and Schrag, Philip (2009), *Refugee Roulette: Disparities in Asylum Adjudication and Proposals for Reform*, New York and London: New York University Press.

Sartre, Jean-Paul (1956), *Being and Nothingness*, trans. H. Barnes, New York: Philosophical Library.

Saunders, B., Kitzinger, J. and Kitzinger, C. (2015), 'Anonymising interview data: Challenges and compromise in practice'. *Qualitative Research*, **15**(5), 616–32.

Sigona, N. (2014), 'The politics of refugee voices: representations, narratives, and memories', in Elena Iddian-Qasmiyeh, Gil Loescher, Katy Long and Nando Sigona (eds), *The Oxford Handbook of Refugee and Forced Migration Studies*, Oxford: Oxford University Press, pp. 369–83.

Sheller, M. (2004), 'Mobile publics: beyond the network perspective'. *Environment and Planning D: Society and Space*, **22**(1), 39–52.

Stress Management Health Centre (2018), https://www.webmd.boots.com/stress-management/physical-stress-symptoms (accessed 30 January 2018).

Sweeney, J.A. (2009), 'Credibility, proof and refugee law'. *International Journal of Refugee Law*, **21**(4), 700–26.

Urry, J. (2004), 'Connections'. *Environment and Planning D: Society and Space*, **22**(1), 27–37.

Urry, J. (2007), *Mobilities*, Cambridge: Policy Press.

Wylie, J. (2009), 'Landscape, absence and the geographies of love'. *Transactions of the Institute of British Geographers*, **34**(3), 275–89.

Cases Cited

Kiarie and Byndloss v The Secretary of State for the Home Department [2017] UKSC 42.

Detention Action v First-tier Tribunal (Immigration and Asylum Chamber), Upper Tribunal (Immigration and Asylum Chamber) and Lord Chancellor [2015] EWHC 1689 (Admin).

29. Im/mobility and humanitarian triage
Polly Pallister-Wilkins

INTRODUCTION

In this chapter I examine the interrelationship between im/mobility and humanitarian triage. Humanitarian interventions in border spaces have increased as the world's borders become more exclusive and violent (Jones et al. 2017). These interventions are undertaken by a range of actors from border police, coast guards and state militaries (Cuttitta 2018; Pallister-Wilkins 2015) and non-state humanitarian actors (Stierl 2018). Elsewhere I have called these interventions 'humanitarian borderwork' (Jones et al. 2017; Pallister-Wilkins 2016a). This humanitarian borderwork not only has an intimate relationship to the border but also to im/mobility. It is this relationship with im/mobility that I want to focus on here. In shifting the gaze from borders – while remaining mindful of their presence – to im/mobility, scholarship on humanitarian work in border settings can more comprehensively grasp the challenges humanitarian actors face and the new ways of working they produce. Work on humanitarianism in border spaces has predominantly focused on how humanitarianism changes borderwork; a shift to focus on mobility allows us to also consider how this work changes humanitarian practice. In so doing, it uncovers humanitarianism's uncomfortable relationship with mobility, dominant rationalities of intervention and the ethics of care. But more than this, it asks humanitarianism in practice – traditionally self-declared as apolitical – to re-examine its relationship with the political structures that produce differentiated and risky regimes of mobility (see Scott-Smith 2016a).

Humanitarianism is predominantly understood as the relief of suffering and the upholding of human dignity through the provision of the necessary conditions for life in 'emergency' situations by non-state, humanitarian organisations (see Barnett 2011). Humanitarian borderwork unsettles this mainstream understanding as state and security actors take up concern for the saving of lives and incorporate these concerns into their everyday practices (Jones et al. 2017; Pallister-Wilkins 2015, 2016a) even as some scholars call attention to the longer running presence of humanitarian logics in the modern liberal state project (Fassin 2012; Feldman and Ticktin 2012; Reid-Henry 2014; Weizman 2012) and European colonial practices (Lester and Dussart 2014). As such, humanitarianism has a particular rationality built around processes of efficiency and restoring the status quo as opposed to proposing and advocating an alternative politics.

Alongside this, mobility has been repeatedly identified as not only a key field of security by Foucauldian inspired scholars (Aradau and Blanke 2010; Pallister-Wilkins 2016b; Rosière and Jones 2012) but one of the key forces of our present (Creswell 2006). However, much of the academic work on mobility and security has focused on the risk of mobility to territorialised states and the populations contained therein, and as a result differentiated regimes of mobility have been enacted to counteract such risks (Jones 2016). Popular depictions present mobile populations as risks to security in the form of the migrant-terrorist or as the bearer of disease (Voelkner 2011). Meanwhile, scholarly work has tended to overlook the risks faced by those who move through these variegated regimes of mobility (Smith 2016). This has led to calls from scholars of feminist geopolitics for a greater focus on the violence faced by those excluded from the privilege of 'safe' travel (see Hyndman 2001, 2004, 2012) and in feminist inspired mobility studies for greater attention to the ways this differentiation is embodied by those excluded because they are considered *a* risk that results perversely in such mobile populations being *at* risk (see Sheller 2013, 2016).

I intend this chapter to be in conversation with these approaches that highlight the ways a focus on risk and how it is experienced at the scale of the human body enable us to unpack how geopolitical processes are experienced unequally between different populations (Massaro and Williams 2013); or the ways attempts to alleviate such risks often function to reproduce hierarchical relations (Fluri 2011; Pallister-Wilkins 2015; Williams 2016) and reproduce subjects with differential mobility capability (Sheller 2013). Through these it is possible to render visible not only the ways processes of im/mobility produce risk at the level of the individual and are experienced differently but also the ways attempts to manage such risks concomitantly work to create hierarchies of power along feminised vectors of vulnerability (Hyndman and Giles 2011; Pallister-Wilkins 2019; Ticktin 2016).

My argument proceeds as follows: First, I discuss traditional modes of humanitarian practice in relation to mobility. I show how mobility has a particular role in humanitarian practice privileging the mobility of humanitarian actors over that of the 'distant suffering strangers' humanitarianism seeks to care for and the traditional need for stasis in the provision of the necessary conditions for life. Second, I discuss triage, a process involving the social sorting of bodies, in relation to humanitarianism, its rationalities and its spatial aspects. Third, I discuss how the im/mobility of migrants unsettles traditional humanitarian practices as they relate to mobility and triage creating ethical problems, reducing what types of humanitarian work is possible while producing new hierarchies of suffering and relief. Here I advance the idea of 'sticky' triage to capture the constitutive role of im/mobility, transport infrastructures and border spaces in humanitarian care giving. I argue that humanitarian borderwork practices a form of triage that is based on the sorting of bodies according to suffering and need. However, this sorting is compromised and complicated by the forces of im/mobility experienced and undertaken by migrant populations. Throughout the chapter I draw on my ongoing research with Médecins Sans Frontières (MSF) and other humanitarian actors and their work with mobile populations.

THE VITAL MOBILITY OF HUMANITARIANS

Mobility in humanitarianism has coalesced and is best articulated by the focus on the mobility of humanitarian practitioners themselves. Here mobility is traditionally understood as relating to the ability of humanitarian practitioners and their objects to move unimpeded and quickly to 'other' places to attend to distant strangers in static spaces and fixed locations such as the refugee camp (Agier 2011; Redfield 2013). The idea of *ingérence* (interference) central to MSF is exactly this mobility; that humanitarian intervention or the right and ability to intervene is inherently mobile and should not and must not, from an ethical standpoint, respect sovereign borders.

As part of this 'vital mobility' (Redfield 2013) mobility and transport infrastructures are considered to have a central role and be 'vital' in humanitarian practice and humanitarians' ability to move to distant places to provide the necessary conditions for life. Here the ability to preserve life is intimately tied to and shaped by the mobility of the life preserving humanitarian practitioners and their 'kit'. For example, Peter Redfield's work on the humanitarian kit has stressed the central role of logistics in enabling humanitarian intervention (2013). The ability to transport much needed life-saving equipment quickly and efficiently is at the heart of much humanitarian practice today. MSF boasts that it can get anything anywhere in the world in 48 hours and jokes that it is in many instances a logistics organisation. Meanwhile, think of the visibility of the Toyota Land Cruiser in humanitarian imaginaries that acts as a visual cue for the mobility of humanitarianism and its ability to go anywhere and overcome any obstacle (Smirl 2015).

However, this seemingly expansive and infinitely mobile humanitarian vision is tempered somewhat by reflections from the everyday practices of humanitarian intervention. Recently, Sean Healy and Sandrine Tiller (2016) have argued about the importance of humanitarian subjects needing to be near a road in order to be accessible to humanitarian intervention. This suggests instead a humanitarianism that is limited and structured by the material constraints of transport infrastructures. Meanwhile, in recognition of the ways traditional transport infrastructures such as roads limit the ability of humanitarians to 'access' those in need, humanitarians have, as is often the case, turned to a technological fix (Read et al. 2016). The turn to technological fixes is a common theme in humanitarianism that seeks to find a 'quick' solution to structural problems considered beyond the scope of (emergency) humanitarianism. One of the new key technological fixes offered in the case of hard-to-reach populations is the 'good drone' (Sandvik and Jumbert 2017). The 'good drone', it is thought, has the potential to access hard-to-reach places and populations and can thus expand the mobility of humanitarian relief efforts through delivering medicines and providing information.

Redfield's work on logistics, Healy and Tiller's work on roads and the work on the 'good drone' focus on mobility as a tool of humanitarian practitioners. Mobility here is a privileged asset giving humanitarians and humanitarianism the ability to act. This tension between the easily assumed mobility of humanitarian practitioners responding to the suffering of distant strangers and the assumed immobility of those strangers not only highlights the variegated regimes of mobility underpinning modern humanitarianism, but also its older colonial and Eurocentric roots, where the power of an enlightened, universal modernity endowed humanitarians with the right and the power for intervention elsewhere. The idea that humanitarian practice is mobile, moving to where those in need are, those 'distant' strangers, contains within it assumptions about who has the right and the ability to move, and what type of activities – in this instance the provision of care and the necessary conditions for life – relate to such movement. And yet this understanding alone is too simplistic in today's highly mobile world where suffering bodies no longer remain 'distant' and fails to capture the complexity of mobility in today's humanitarian response to mobile populations at and across borders. Here mobility is claimed and exercised by those in need and as such this unsettles traditional ways of working and traditional hierarchies between practitioners and subjects of protection. This unsettling has resulted in humanitarian practitioners and approaches more generally having to face the politics of mobility itself and the injustices that emanate from the variegated regimes of mobility and the attended risks such regimes of mobility produce.

TRIAGE AS EMBODIED SORTING

Border scholars are familiar with practices of sorting being carried out on bodies. Categorisation and filtering is one of the primary socio-political roles of the border (Jones 2009). Meanwhile triage is a process that assigns a category to an individual from a larger group to enable categorisation and decision-making (Mitchell 2008, p. 4) and follows similar logics to that of border sorting. However, while border sorting performs acts of inclusion and exclusion emanating from citizenship and mobility, triage is a response to the suffering body (Lacquer 1989) and is designed to rationalise the act of care. Just as the acts of sorting undertaken at the border attempt to sort the mobility of people efficiently so that circulation can be rationalised and the 'dangerous elements cancelled out' (Foucault 2009), triage is the performance of efficient and rational care for suffering bodies. Triage plays a central role in medical humanitarianism but its logics have also come to structure much wider processes of humanitarian management as pre-emptive risk management (Corsellis and Vitale 2005) such as the refugee or internally displaced persons camp where populations are produced through registration, aggregation and calculation (see Bulley 2014; Hoffmann 2017).

Triage, like many elements of humanitarian practice, has a military history. This military history is interesting beyond simply the many aspects of humanitarian practice from logistics, to particular techniques, to specific technology like the drone that come from military advances. It is interesting because of the ways this military history has a specific spatial arrangement and relationship to mobility. A genealogy of triage, while containing specific 'revolutionary' methods such as the introduction of ambulances to move wounded soldiers away from the battlefield, is rooted in fixed sites and locations. The battlefield being a prime example of the place of triage and suggesting a fixed, static location in which processes of category assignation take place in order to determine levels of care. Alongside this, military triage techniques developed the idea of the 'aid station', again a fixed, locatable site where wounded soldiers could be treated according to their needs and the logics of the military that required as many wounded soldiers as possible to be saved in the most efficient manner available. These soldiers were treated in hospitals, located close to the battlefield, and designed to treat those categorised as having a chance of survival. Even with advances in transportation and the introduction of helicopter evacuations extending the mobility of the wounded and the space of intervention, triage itself remained located in the field hospital or aid station (Mitchell 2008, pp. 4–6).

Humanitarian triage shares many of these logics. The mobility and speed of bringing those in need of care to locations where triage can take place is clearly a shared logic, as is the sorting of those most in need of care. Rationalities of efficiency also apply although differ from those employed by the military. While the military is concerned with saving the largest number of 'useful combatant lives' as dictated by the logics of warfare, humanitarianism prioritises, up to a point and within the limits of its capabilities, both in terms of expertise but also in terms of equipment and resources, those most in need. Triage in a humanitarian context then focuses on suffering and the saving of lives based on principles of humanity (Brauman 2012, p. 23). In all these situations triage and subsequent care happens in fixed locations: the aid station, the clinic, the hospital or the wider camp. This is done due to the need for systems of not only care giving and medical care in particular but also wider government for fixity, for the ability to locate and act upon those being governed.

The provision of the necessary conditions for life in sovereign territories is built on vast architectures of bureaucratic knowledge, from population statistics and databases; infrastructures such as sewage systems, housing and hospitals; and expertise including engineers, civil servants and medical practitioners. Humanitarianism is also dependent on particular bureaucratic knowledge, infrastructures and expertise and as a result is most usually practised in territorialised settings such as refugee camps. Triage is a process of sorting that takes place on human bodies in order to administer relief and care. Similar in its spatial practices to the traditional process of border control taking place at fixed locations and times (Pallister-Wilkins 2016b), triage as sorting has traditionally taken place in fixed locations and at definite times. While in border sorting it is the particular spatial logics of the border that determine where and when such sorting takes place, in triage it is the constitutive act of care that has traditionally determined where and when such sorting takes place.

Here the embodied nature of care in triage and humanitarianism more generally is important. While the border undertakes processes of embodied sorting or is said to be biopolitical in a variety of ways (Topak 2014; Vaughan-Williams 2009), the embodied nature of humanitarianism, built as it is around human life, comes to the fore. Thomas W. Lacquer, in his exposition of the role of bodies in the history of humanitarianism, has suggested that humanitarianism 'relies on the personal body, not only as the locus of pain but also as the common bond between those who suffer and those who would help and as the object of the scientific discourse through which the causal links between an evil, a victim, and a benefactor are forged' (1989, p. 177) The body, then, is the site or location and object of care. When dealing with the body, humanitarian practice, most principally in medical humanitarianism, has sought to easily locate, access and thus treat the body. Therefore, humanitarianism makes use of the bed, the ward and the hospital – and in wider instances the camp – as fixed sites of care giving following processes of triage that determine in which beds, wards and hospitals those in need will be treated/receive the necessary conditions for life. These embodied and spatial practices of triage are unsettled by the im/mobility of migrants, in border spaces and along their, often highly complex, journeys. It is to an in-depth discussion of this unsettling that I now turn.

IM/MOBILITY AND STICKY TRIAGE

Migrants and the humanitarian response intended to relieve the risks faced by those excluded from safe forms of passage upsets the way we have come to think about security, risk, mobility and their intersection. As migrants move to seek life, security is not something being performed only by a sovereign life giving and taking actor but it is something being claimed by migrants themselves. Mobility is something active for migrants, it is a terrain infused by agency, structured by power and full of contestation. Mobility is not something that is managed by states alone. Such an argument speaks to

Jennifer Hyndman's recent work (2012) on the geopolitics of migration and mobility that has been keen to caution against seeing mobility as something produced through top-down governance alone while, drawing on the earlier work of Doreen Massey (1993), also being keen to understand how such constraints condition regimes of im/mobility. In my research the claiming of mobility by migrants comes to be oriented around, facilitated by and configured through transport infrastructures. Transport infrastructures and border spaces play a central role in both the risks faced by migrants and the ability for humanitarian actors to relieve suffering.

Mobility here is a field where humanitarianism acts (a field acted upon and in) but it is also a field acted with, used in ways that disturb traditional ways of thinking about the relationship between humanitarianism and mobility. As discussed above, mobility is no longer only a tool of the powerful actor but also of the traditionally weak humanitarian subject, the distant stranger saved and rescued. Different hierarchies of power between humanitarians and migrants determine mobility and importantly the speed of mobility, while humanitarians and their subjects experience mobility in different ways, with humanitarians having access and making use of safe and regular forms of transportation while processes of migrant exclusion sees these safe and regular forms of transportation denied to those without the necessary citizenship or visas.

In turn, as humanitarians seek to respond to the needs of migrants, infrastructures of mobility become spaces of humanitarian triage mapping the intimate relationship between mobility and life, becoming, as Keller Easterling says, a 'point of contact and access' (2014). In this instance overt infrastructures, roads, boats, ports, railways, bus lines and terminals come to be the points of contact between migrants and humanitarians. Here these infrastructures actually do something: they make certain things possible and other things impossible (Easterling 2014). They are spaces of interruption and contact, points that check the mobility of migrants. In this case they make humanitarian intervention possible through providing times and spaces of immobility and the fixity that triage and care giving require.

Through this relationship with transport infrastructures and the way people use them mobility is reconfigured not as something 'fast' dictating the speed of humanitarian intervention but instead as something I want to call 'sticky'. Here I borrow from Tom Scott-Smith's work on the sticky nature of therapeutic foods that rely on stickiness for effectiveness (2016b). If the food flows too fast it fails to administer its life-giving properties. Too slow and it may not administer them fast enough. Triage works in the same way. It requires stickiness because triage is a relationship of power generating differential subject positions. So I borrow shamelessly from Scott-Smith to suggest that the im/mobility, infrastructure and humanitarian intervention relationship we see emerging is a sticky one, one that relies on a sticky form of mobility. Here sticky denotes something important about uneven regimes mobility and the times and spaces of intervention it opens up.

As migrants use transport infrastructures and come into contact with border spaces these transport infrastructures and border spaces come to make possible and condition humanitarian intervention. Sticky humanitarianism in turn is a very limited humanitarianism, a bare form of security provision, an anaemic triage attending to only the quickest, simplest and most basic of needs as complexity requires stasis in humanitarianism, and stasis or getting stuck is an ever present risk faced by migrants on the move where mobility means life. As a result, humanitarians have developed their own mobile infrastructures for dealing with mobile populations and the needs of sticky triage that are constituted through transport infrastructures.

So, not only do we see spaces developing along routes and corridors and in spaces of transit, or the provision of transport itself as a form of intervention, but we also see MSF and the International Committee of the Red Cross (ICRC) use mobile and pop-up clinics to address mobile populations. In other instances, systems of surveillance have been created through the establishment of 'first contact points' and 'transferable patient record cards' that can be carried with people as they make their journeys, rendering their needs legible to those humanitarians and public health agencies they encounter along the way. However, these practices designed to deal with the embodied risks of mobility are not smooth. Humanitarianism's traditional relationship to mobility and established practices of care provision are not only unsettled by the mobility of migrants producing new ways of working. Humanitarian ethics of care are also unsettled by and unsettle regimes of im/mobility and the possible humanitarian responses. The ethical dilemmas of im/mobility and triage are the focus of the following section.

IM/MOBILITY AND THE ETHICS OF TRIAGE

The spatial logics of triage that require fixed spaces and the immobility of the suffering body under care is the result not only of a requirement for stasis in medical practice for ease of treatment but also because of ethical considerations around when treatment and intervention should be undertaken (Redfield 2013). Embodied interventions not only have particular biopolitical logics designed to ensure the necessary conditions for life but they also have a particular ethical genealogy that is best expressed through the role of ethics in medical practice (Lacquer 1989). Medical practitioners, be they engaged in particular humanitarian interventions or not, have ethical concerns that differ from and come into conflict with the demands of migrant populations. As a result, medicine – and by extension humanitarianism as it seeks to care for suffering bodies – has developed particular spatial logics.

Put simply, medical ethics suggest that interventions at the level of individual bodies should only be undertaken when continuity in treatment and care can be secured. These demands come to be expressed in a range of ways, from the reticence to engage in treatments when follow-up care and observation cannot be ensured, to reticence to engage in initial diagnosis due to the responsibility that a diagnosis is also a commitment to treatment and care (Ponthieu and Incerti 2016). If a medical professional or humanitarian practitioner cannot be sure that the possibility for and continuation of treatment is secure then it is often thought better not to diagnose at all. The need for continuity of care in stasis is therefore in conflict with the desire of migrant populations for mobility and to continue their journeys.[1]

In working through the conflicting relationships of humanitarian triage and im/mobility I draw on the work of humanitarian practitioners in what has been termed

---

[1]   These issues were one of the main topics discussed by medical humanitarians during the workshop 'Humanitarian Mobilities' run at the University of Amsterdam on 4 May 2017. Available at: https://www.acces seurope.org/component/jevents/eventdetail/264/8%7C10/humanitarian-mobilities?Itemid=142 (last accessed 3 October, 2018).

the 'migration crisis' (Pallister-Wilkins 2016c) in Europe between 2015 and 2017. I have encountered such work during a number of fieldwork visits and through intensive engagement with humanitarian practitioners working on the Aegean islands, in particular MSF, and this work informs my analysis. MSF's, and other humanitarian practitioners', encounters with migrants at risk from unsafe journeys and exclusive and violent borders have been conditioned by im/mobility and transport infrastructures as discussed above as well as the limits of humanitarian triage. Time, space and resources are always limited in humanitarian practice; however, when addressing mobile, migrant populations during the 'migration crisis' such limits were stark as the desire for migrants to keep moving before borders closed and the spaces of their travel, in this instance, ports, roads, beaches, boats and ports, shrunk the limits further. MSF has always been clear about humanitarian practice being impacted by the 'limitation of means' (MSF 1999), yet the practicing of triage in these instances renders further visible these limitations of means and the particular choices made regarding when and how to intervene.

The means MSF has at its disposal when treating mobile populations also need to take account of the importance of being able to 'move-on' for migrants seeking a secure future. The desire of migrants to keep moving and the respect of humanitarian practitioners to foster this reversed 'vital mobility' is reflected in the types of triage performed. Care takes time as discussed. Even the speediest forms of triage with its forms of embodied sorting according to logics of efficiency need time and space. What then should humanitarian practitioners – medical or not – do when faced with the agency and desires of migrants who do not want to stop for help? Such a conundrum also has to take account of questions of ethics that only work to complicate these tensions between mobility and care. As already mentioned, medical professionals have an obligation to provide follow-up treatment after diagnosis. Therefore, if they offer the time and space of diagnosis then they are ethically obligated to provide follow-up treatment or at the very least to ensure such follow-up treatment is provided. And so it can be argued that initial practices of triage that seek to sort people according to their needs have repercussions far beyond the initial spatio-temporally limited act of sorting.

The need to follow up is exactly why traditional medical intervention as well as many forms of triage require immobility so that patients can be observed, further tests performed, treatment given and, if necessary, referrals made. In the case of mobile populations and the 'migration crisis' these particular spatio-temporal requirements are challenged by the desires of the patients themselves to keep moving. This tension played out repeatedly on the Aegean islands where migrants in need of medical assistance for often chronic, long-term illnesses, would forego treatment or humanitarian medical practitioners would provide only basic public health advice and intervention so as not to become yet another 'barrier' in the way of migrants' mobility. Meanwhile, during search and rescue (SAR) at sea that responds to the risks to life caused by Europe's violent and exclusive border in the Mediterranean, care giving is structured and limited in very particular ways by the limited time and space available and the particular environment of a SAR vessel. The medical and care facilities available on SAR ships is limited, not only by the desire of migrants to keep moving and ethical considerations around diagnosis and treatment but also by the way a boat at sea limits what is possible. SAR vessels are not hospital ships and have very limited treatment facilities. They are designed to save as many lives as possible in the most efficient way and to transport those rescued to port.

They act more like floating triage facilities or ambulances highlighting the limits of providing medical and wider humanitarian care in mobile conditions. What is clear from humanitarianism's intersection with im/mobility is that mobile populations create unique challenges for some of the basic practices underpinning traditional humanitarian work and raise ethical concerns especially in the field of medical humanitarianism. But more than this, the relationship between humanitarianism and im/mobility also works to sort migrants in particular ways according to forms of vulnerability and care needs. As such, what I have called humanitarian borderwork performs acts of sorting, like the border, but along different logics (Jones et al. 2017; Pallister-Wilkins 2016a). This is the focus of the final section.

IM/MOBILITY VULNERABILITY AND SUFFERING

Humanitarian intervention that responds to the suffering caused by violent and exclusive borders is most readily presented as a panacea to such suffering. This is too simplistic in two principle ways. One, it fails to adequately address either the structural causes for such suffering, in this instance the particular border policies enacted by sovereign states, and thus humanitarianism remains a simple sticking plaster for the status quo. Two, it fails to address the performative and productive aspects of this humanitarian intervention. As I have argued in focusing on the practice of triage above, humanitarianism performs acts of sorting on suffering bodies. This sorting has affects, restructuring the border and im/mobility around the vulnerable and suffering body.

The international refugee regime itself is premised partially on the logics of the suffering body, with the idea of harm or fear of harm playing a role in the granting of asylum. However, as human testimony concerning harm or perceptions of future harm have come to be seen as unreliable, and the prominence of political persecution has waned in the post-Communist era (see Weizman 2012), the suffering body itself has come to play a central role in the granting of protection. Miriam Ticktin (2005) and Didier Fassin (2012) have explored how France's asylum and immigration practices have increasingly come to rely on medical evidence of suffering or future suffering in the granting of asylum or permissions to remain in France. Here suffering and vulnerability, or future vulnerability as in cases where people can show they would not be able to access life-saving medical treatment in their countries of origin, have come to structure decisions relating to protection, altering border practices in the process and re-orienting decision-making around vulnerability.

These logics are not only found in decisions around asylum or immigration status, they also impact processes of im/mobility. Within the format of the European Union-Turkey 'deal' that, since 26 March 2016, governs those who arrive in Greece and those who were present in Greece at that time, vulnerability and suffering determines who is allowed to leave the Aegean islands that have become effective prisons (Jones et al. 2017; Mountz 2011; Pallister-Wilkins 2016d). Greek law currently allows for vulnerable people to be exempted from the 'admissibility procedure' governing returns to Turkey and are eligible for transfer to mainland Greece. This is important in the ways suffering comes to structure the immobility of some migrants and the mobility of others. On the Greek mainland, migrants with specific medical needs can more readily access adequate services and await the outcome of their asylum claim (MSF 2017, p. 17). Greek law categorises vulnerable people as belonging to one or more of the following: pregnant women, unaccompanied children, single parents with children, victims of torture, and people with disabilities (HRW 2017).

This is troubling for critical scholars of migration in a number of ways. By privileging suffering and vulnerability as a condition governing mobility, restrictive mobility regimes are not politically challenged, only partially realigned. Privileging vulnerability and suffering as embodied and the need for tangible forms of often embodied 'evidence' for the right to mobility or the right to access particular rights not only maintains exclusivity but also ignores the needs of those who appear 'fine' or those with less obvious forms of trauma such as post-traumatic stress disorder (MSF 2017). Additionally, reassembling the right to mobility around the suffering body shifts the right away from being a universal human right, which it is, to an exclusive one that people have to suffer for.

This is, of course, deeply ethically problematic and suggests that migrants have to effectively hold up their wounds to power in order to be recognised and granted the right to move. Further, this privileging of the vulnerable and suffering body maintains the idea that the migrant is somehow a 'sick body' (Muller 2004) that has been present in dominant discourses around migration and migrants since the end of the Cold War. What critical scholars of migration, humanitarianism and security need to question is why vulnerability and suffering is produced in the first instance. This is not to advocate for a turn away from the 'sick body' or an abdication of a responsibility to care, but a call to ask why that body is sick and how it is intimately related to regimes of im/mobility.

CONCLUSION

In this chapter I have argued for a deeper understanding of the way im/mobility interacts with humanitarian practice. By invoking the practice of triage that aims to sort bodies according to need I have shown how such practices are intimately, bodily, entwined with processes of im/mobility both in the provision of care and in the ability to move itself. This chapter calls for a greater reflection on the risks produced through uneven mobility regimes as well as greater attention to the particular opportunities for care created or foreclosed. It is not intended as a comprehensive review of the ways im/mobility is reshaping humanitarian practices of triage or care giving. Rather, it is intended as a conversation starter for further reflection and research from critical scholars of migration, humanitarianism and security and those feminist political geographers and mobility studies scholars who have called for a greater understanding of the embodied violence of uneven regimes of mobility. Following this, it is important to consider the extent to which triage operating at the level of the human body and considerate of the risks faced by that body is working to remake mobility regimes and migration geographies in more equitable and safe ways, or conversely to reproduce differential forms of mobility and re-inscribing power. But more than this, this chapter is also intended as a jumping off point for humanitarian practice to take seriously the politics of im/mobility in its encounters with those in need of assistance.

REFERENCES

Agier, Michel (2011), *Managing the Undesirables: Refugee Camps and Humanitarian Government*, London: Polity.

Aradau, Claudia and Tobias Blanke (2010), 'Governing Circulation: A Critique of the Biopolitics of Security', in Miguel de Larringa and Marc G. Doucet (eds), *Security and Global Governmentality: Globalization, Governance and the State*, London: Routledge, pp. 43–58.

Barnett, Michael (2011), *Empire of Humanity: A History of Humanitarianism*, Ithaca, NY: Cornell University Press.

Brauman, Rony (2012), *Humanitarian Medicine*, Paris: Crash/Foundation Médecins Sans Frontières.

Bulley, Dan (2014), 'Inside the Tent: Community and Government in Refugee Camps', *Security Dialogue* **45** (1), 63–80.

Corsellis, Tom and Antonella Vitale (2005), *Transitional Settlement: Displaced Population*, Cambridge: University of Cambridge shelterproject and Oxfam GB.

Creswell, Tim (2006), *On the Move: Mobility in the Modern Western World*, London: Routledge.

Cuttitta, Paolo (2018), 'Delocalization, Humanitarianism, and Human Rights: The Mediterranean Border Between Exclusion and Inclusion', *Antipode* **50** (3), 783–803.

Easterling, Keller (2014), *Extrastatecraft: The Power of Infrastructure Space*, London: Verso.

Fassin, Didier (2012), *Humanitarian Reason: A Moral History of the Present*, Berkeley, CA: University of California Press.

Feldman, Ilana and Miriam Ticktin (2012), *In the Name of Humanity: The Government of Threat and Care*, Durham, NC: Duke University Press.

Fluri, Jennifer (2011), 'Amored Peacocks and Proxy Bodies: Gender Geopolitics in Aid/Development Spaces of Afghanistan', *Gender, Place & Culture* **18** (4), 519–36.

Foucault, Michel (2009), *Security, Territory, Population: Lectures at the Collège de France 1977–1978*, New York: Picador.

Healy, Sean and Sandrine Tiller (2016), 'Be Near a Road: Humanitarian Practice and Displaced Persons in North Kivu', *Refugee Survey Quarterly* **35** (2), 56–78.

Hoffmann, Sophia (2017), 'Humanitarian Security in Jordan's Azraq Camp', *Security Dialogue* **48** (2), 97–112.

HRW (2017), *Greece: A Year of Suffering for Asylum Seekers*. Available at: https://www.hrw.org/print/301122 (last accessed 3 October, 2018).

Hyndman, Jennifer (2001), 'Towards a Feminist Geopolitics', *The Canadian Geographer* **45** (2), 210–22.

Hyndman, Jennifer (2004), 'Mind the Gap: Bridging Feminist and Political Geography through Geopolitics', *Political Geography* **23** (3), 307–22.

Hyndman, Jennifer (2012), 'The Geopolitics of Migration and Mobility', *Geopolitics* **12** (2), 243–55.

Hyndman, Jennifer and Wenona Giles (2011), 'Waiting for What? The Feminization of Asylum in Protracted Situations', *Gender, Place & Culture* **18** (3), 361–79.

Jones, Reece (2009), 'Categories, Borders and Boundaries', *Progress in Human Geography* **33** (2), 174–89.

Jones, Reece (2016), *Violent Borders: Refugees and the Right to Move*, London: Verso.

Jones, Reece, Corey Johnson, Wendy Brown et al. (2017), 'Interventions on the State of Sovereignty at the Border', *Political Geography* **59**, 1–10. http://dx.doi.org/10.1016/j.polgeo.2017.02.006.

Lacquer, Thomas W. (1989), 'Bodies, Details, and the Humanitarian Narrative', in Lynn Hunt (ed.), *The New Cultural History*, Berkeley, CA: University of California Press, pp. 176–204.

Lester, Alan and Fae Dussart (2014), *Colonization and the Origins of Humanitarian Government: Protecting Aborigines across the Nineteenth-century British Empire*, Cambridge: Cambridge University Press.

Massaro, Vanessa A. and Jill Williams (2013), 'Feminist Geopolitics', *Geography Compass* **7** (8), 567–77.

Massey, Doreen (1993), 'Power-Geometry and a Progressive Sense of Place', in Jon Bird, Barry Curtis, Tim Putnam, George Robertson and Lisa Tickner (eds), *Mapping the Futures: Local Cultures, Global Change*, New York: Routledge, pp. 59–69.

Mitchell, Glenn W. (2008), 'A Brief History of Triage', *Disaster Medicine and Public Health* **2** (S1), S4–S7.

Mountz, Alison (2011), 'The Enforcement Archipelago: Detention, Haunting and Asylum on Islands', *Political Geography* **30** (3), 118–28.

MSF (1999), Nobel Lecture. Available at: http://www.nobelprize.org/nobel_prizes/peace/laureates/1999/msf-lecture.html (last accessed 3 October 2018).

MSF (2017), *One Year On From the EU-Turkey Deal: Challenging the EU's Alternative Facts*. Available at: http://www.msf.org/sites/msf.org/files/one_year_on_from_the_eu-turkey_deal.pdf (last accessed 3 October 2018).

Muller, Benjamin (2004), 'Globalisation, Security, Paradox: Towards a Refugee Biopolitics', *Refuge* **22** (1), 49–57.

Pallister-Wilkins, Polly (2015), 'The Humanitarian Politics of European Border Policing: Frontex and Border Police in Evros', *International Political Sociology* **9** (1), 53–69.

Pallister-Wilkins, Polly (2016a), 'Humanitarian Borderwork', in Cengiz Günay and Nina Witjes (eds), *Border Politics: Defining Spaces of Governance and Forms of Transgressions*, New York: Springer, pp. 85–103.

Pallister-Wilkins, Polly (2016b), 'How Walls Do Work: Security Barriers as Devices of Interruption and Data Capture', *Security Dialogue* **47** (2), 151–64.

Pallister-Wilkins, Polly (2016c), 'Interrogating the Mediterranean "Migration Crisis"', *Mediterranean Politics* **21** (2), 311–15.

Pallister-Wilkins, Polly (2016d), 'Hotspots and the Politics of Humanitarian Control and Care', *Society & Space.* Available at: http://societyandspace.org/2016/12/06/hotspots-and-the-politics-of-humanitarian-control-and-ca re/ (last accessed 3 October 2018).

Pallister-Wilkins, Polly (2019), 'The Boundaries of Médecins Sans Frontières: Universalist Humanitarianism in Practice', in Reece Jones (ed), *Open Borders: For a Borderless World*, Athens, GA: University of Georgia Press, pp. 158–75.

Ponthieu, Aurélie and Andrea Incerti (2016), 'Continuity of Care for Migrant Populations in Southern Africa', *Refugee Survey Quarterly* **35** (2), 98–115.

Read, Roísín, Bertrand Taithe and Roger Mac Ginty (2016), 'Data Hubris? Humanitarian Information Systems and the Mirage of Technology', *Third World Quarterly* **37** (8), 1314–31.

Redfield, Peter (2013), *Life in Crisis: The Ethical Journey of Doctors Without Borders*, Berkeley, CA: University of California Press.

Reid-Henry, Simon (2014), 'Humanitarianism as Liberal Diagnostic: Humanitarian Reason and the Political Rationalities of the Liberal Will-to-Care', *Transactions of the Institute of British Geographers* **39** (3), 418–31.

Rosière, Stéphane and Reece Jones (2012), 'Teichopolitics: Re-considering Globalisation through the Role of Walls and Fences', *Geopolitics* **17** (1), 217–34.

Sandvik, Kristin Bergtora and Marie Gabrielsen Jumbert (2017), *The Good Drone*, London: Routledge.

Scott-Smith, Tom (2016a), 'Humanitarian Dilemmas in a Mobile World', *Refugee Survey Quarterly* **35** (2), 1–21.

Scott-Smith, Tom (2016b), 'Sticky Technologies: Plumpy'nut, Emergency Feeding, and the Viscosity of Humanitarian Design', Paper presented at the Humanitarian Objects and Designs workshop, University of Oxford, 28–29 July.

Sheller, Mimi (2013), 'The Islanding Effect: Post-disaster Mobility Systems and Humanitarian Logistics in Haiti', *Cultural Geographies* **20** (2), 185–204.

Sheller, Mimi (2016), 'Uneven Mobility Futures: A Foucauldian Approach', *Mobilities* **11** (1), 15–31.

Smirl, Lisa (2015), *Spaces of Aid: How Cars, Compounds, and Hotels Shape Humanitarianism*, London: Zed Books.

Smith, James (2016), 'Thinking Beyond Borders: Reconceptualising Migration to Better Meet the Needs of People in Transit', *International Journal of Public Health* **61**, 521–2.

Stierl, Maurice (2018), 'A Fleet of Mediterranean Border Humanitarians', *Antipode* **50** (3), 704–24.

Ticktin, Miriam (2005), 'Policing and Humanitarianism in France: Immigration and the Turn to Law as State of Exception', *Interventions: International Journal of Postcolonial Studies* **7** (3), 347–68.

Ticktin, Miriam (2016), 'Thinking Beyond Humanitarian Borders', *Social Research* **83** (2), 255–71.

Topak, Özgün E. (2014), 'The Biopolitical Border in Practice: Surveillance and Death at the Greece Turkey Boderzones', *Environment and Planning D: Society and Space*, **32** (5), 815–33.

Vaughan-Williams, Nick (2009), 'The Generalised Bio-political Border? Re-conceptualising the Limits of Sovereign Power', *Review of International Studies* **35** (4), 729–49.

Voelkner, Nadine (2011), 'Managing Pathogenic Circulation: Human Security and the Migrant Health Assemblage in Thailand', *Security Dialogue* **42** (3), 239–59.

Weizman, Eyal (2012), *The Least of All Possible Evils: Humanitarian Violence from Arendt to Gaza*, London: Verso.

Williams, Jill (2016), 'The Safety/Security Nexus and the Humanitarianisation of Border Enforcement', *The Geographical Journal* **182** (1), 27–37.

30. Contradictions and provocations of neoliberal governmentality in the US asylum seeking system
Deirdre Conlon

INTRODUCTION

The figures on forcibly displaced migration and asylum specifically are both dizzying and disturbing. In 2015, according to the United Nations High Commissioner for Refugees (UNHCR) statistics, 65.3 million people were forcibly displaced worldwide. Of these, 3.2 million individuals were asylum seekers (UNHCR, 2016). Over 2 million new asylum applications were registered in 2015 alone; this figure represents a 48 percent increase over 2014 and the highest number of applications ever recorded by the UNHCR (2016). A majority of individuals who seek international protection with a request for refugee status do so in the Global South and developing states, with Turkey, Pakistan, and Lebanon as the top three "hosting countries" in 2015. States in the Global North have also experienced marked increases in asylum applications recently, with Germany, the US, and Sweden in rank order as recipients of new applications in 2015 (UNHCR, 2016).[1] Mid-year trends for 2016, while still indicative, are informative. Globally, over 1 million new asylum applications were registered in the first six months of 2016, which represents a slight increase over the same period in 2015.[2] For the same six-month period, the top three recipient states for applications saw more significant increases. Germany received 387,700 applications, or 87 percent of the total number of applications received for all of 2015 while the US received 112,400 applications, a 44 percent increase over the same period in 2015, and Italy received 49,100 applications, or a 63 percent increase over applications in the first six months of 2015 (UNHCR, 2017).

I open this chapter with an "avalanche of printed numbers" (Hacking, 1982, p. 279) related to asylum for a few reasons. First, and perhaps most obviously, to highlight the scale as well as the shifting geographies of displacement and asylum that are characteristic of forced migration today, and thus to underscore the significance of these issues for critical geographers. Second, while recounting asylum statistics at length I want to acknowledge the human lives and day-to-day realities that constitute these figures and that are readily elided with a focus on enumeration. This links to a third, and, indeed, the primary reason I have initiated discussion of asylum and neoliberal governmentality in the way I have here. Governmentality describes a rationality as well as practices that are used in order to regulate and manage social groups or populations (Foucault, 1991; Gordon, 1991). As I discuss below, governmental processes are often considered alongside neoliberalism and linked to free market logic and characteristics. Calculation

---

[1]   2015 figures are as follows: Germany received 441,900 applications; the US received 172,700 applications; Sweden received 156,400 applications.
[2]   In the first six months of 2015 there were 993,600 new asylum applications globally (UNHCR, 2016).

and statistics related to different populations are key to the workings of governmentality. As such, producing numbers and relaying knowledge about them, as I have done above, imbricates research and scholarship with governmental practice vis-à-vis asylum. At the outset, then, I want to highlight the need for reflection and scrutiny when it comes to knowledge production in critical geographies of migration. This is a key concern, and one that I take up again later in the chapter.

The principal aim of the chapter is to examine some of the ways neoliberal governmentality impinges upon the asylum process. Following Larner (2000) and others I take neoliberal governmentality to refer to the ways individuals and institutions become autonomous and active, "entrepreneurial, enterprising, and innovative" (Larner, 2000, p. 13) subjects that "conform to the norms of the market" (Larner, 2000, p. 12). Of significance here is that individuals are not only free – as in unfettered by the state – to pursue their own interests but said interests are understood and articulated vis-à-vis the market economy. With this, practices such as calculation, cost-benefit analyses, and self-directed entrepreneurialism are taken to be normal ways of thinking and being in the world. There is a wealth of scholarship in geography and allied social sciences that examines migration and mobility using governmentality or neoliberal governmentality as a framework. The array of scholarship includes analyses of governmental technologies of border control and immigration enforcement practices (e.g., Bigo, 2002; De Genova, 2002; Hyndman, 2012; Prokkola, 2013; Burridge et al., 2017); the biopolitical and neoliberal governance of citizenship (e.g., Tyler, 2013; Turner, 2014; Mitchell, 2016); the actors engaged in and effects of systems of migration management including detention, deportation, housing, and "welfare" (e.g., Gill, 2009; Conlon, 2010; Mountz, 2010; Darling, 2011; Mountz et al., 2012; Hiemstra, 2014; Martin, 2016); and humanitarian and resistance practices (e.g., Fassin, 2011; Tazzioli, 2014; Mitchell, 2017; Pascucci, 2017). This is by no means a comprehensive catalog of the breadth of recent work in this area; as Walters (2015) observes, "governmentality themes and concepts are being extended to the analysis of ever more aspects of 'new migration worlds'" (p. 2).

Of late, several scholars have identified the need to further develop this rich work through empirical analyses that can nuance understandings of neoliberal governmentality "on the ground" and, relatedly, that attend to the "complexity and messiness" (Mitchell, 2017, p. 273) and often contradictory articulations of neoliberal governmentality (see also Sparke, 2006; Walters, 2015; Brady and Lippert, 2016; Mitchell, 2016). In this chapter I look at facets of the application and adjudication of asylum claims and at how logics and technologies of neoliberal governmentality operate for actors and institutions that are differently positioned within the asylum system. In particular, I am concerned with elucidating some of the contradictions that unfold in the encounter between neoliberal governmentality and the asylum process. In this system, asylum seekers become recognizable as individual subjects and as a population that is simultaneously disciplined and autonomous. Neoliberal conditions and governance produce a system that, while espousing efficiency, is mired in bureaucracy and produces scarcity. This helps to foster a situation where asylum seekers are encouraged to be active, enterprising – yet compliant – neoliberal individuals. Furthermore, this system generates demand for evidence and expert knowledge, which, in turn, necessitates calculative decisions by professionals, migrant support organizations, and by asylum seekers themselves. By presenting these examples my goals are to highlight some of the ways that neoliberal governmental processes are embedded with the asylum system and, at the same time, to call attention to the "composite, improvised and impure character of governmentality" (Walters, 2015, p. 5).

The chapter develops as follows. First, I provide an outline of the asylum application and adjudication process, which is embedded within an elaborate system of population management. Following this, drawing on my own research and that of my colleagues, I discuss how neoliberal governmentality fosters bureaucracy and inefficiency, which run counter to the usual claims that neoliberalism cuts through these "problems" and provides a more "rational" approach to governance. Then, I examine how evidence and expertise are linked to calculative political and economic processes for asylum seekers as well as support groups. The concluding section reflects on these imbrications and their implications for stymying the asylum system and for critical geographies of migration more broadly.

SEEKING ASYLUM: A PROCEDURAL OVERVIEW

There is a tendency to think of the refugee and asylum systems as part of a long-standing, universally understood apparatus to support individuals who have fled unsafe and intolerable conditions and seek refuge in another state. They are, of course, twentieth-century inventions borne out of the cruelty and violence of the Second World War (UNHCR, n.d.) and intended to manage mass displacement in standardized ways (Malkki, 1995). While the term refugee describes someone who has been forced to flee their home country to escape war or disaster, an asylum seeker is an individual who, unable to return to their country of origin, is seeking sanctuary or protection in another country because of a well-founded fear of persecution in accordance with the 1951 UN Refugee Convention and the 1967 Protocol Relating to the Status of Refugees.

Asylum seeking is deemed problematic for governance for a host of reasons. Among these is the fact that asylum seekers act individually and independently. In policy language they are described as "spontaneous arrivals"; they reach borders or file asylum claims unpredictably and, therefore, are viewed as a difficult population to control or manage. Also, when asylum seekers arrive to a country as part of mixed migration flows that may include economic migrants, they are subjected to scrutiny and skepticism about their motives. These and other factors mean that the asylum system, which, arguably, might have been initially understood to reflect a liberal, cosmopolitan conception of citizenship and state responsibilities in the global era, has morphed into "sustained intensification in the way systems of governing asylum seekers act to exclude them" (Gill, 2016, p. 9).

This chapter analyses some of the ways neoliberal governmental processes operate and impact the asylum system; as such, it is helpful to provide a general overview of procedures involved in pursuing an asylum claim. As immigration enforcement in the US is a focus in my research, this overview is limited to the US. However, in the discussion that follows, I draw from previous work as well as research with and by colleagues in other sites in Europe.[3] States vary on specific aspects of the asylum claims process. For example, timelines for applications, types of welfare and social supports available to asylum seek-

---

[3]   See Malkki (1995) on Eurocentrism in refugee studies broadly and for discussion of Europe as the standardized and globalized model for refugee (as well as asylum) management.

ers, the right to work while awaiting claim adjudication, detention as a mandate, and maximum periods of detention vary from one country to another. Nonetheless, in most asylum procedures in the Global North, individuals who seek asylum must navigate a system that entails initial screening, interview, and adjudication, and that is punctuated by periods of waiting and uncertainty.

In the US, an individual can file an *affirmative* application for asylum when they arrive at a port of entry or within one year of arriving in the state. Alternatively, a *defensive* application may be filed where an individual is apprehended by immigration enforcement authorities, detained, and informed of plans to deport them. In affirmative cases, an asylum seeker submits an application, completes a biometric assessment, and waits for an interview with an asylum officer from the US Citizenship and Immigration Services (USCIS). At the interview, an attorney may accompany the applicant, if she or he has legal representation. Attorneys may also present evidence, including witnesses, on the applicant's behalf. The interview process is described as non-adversarial, it takes place in an administrative, immigration office setting. A second asylum officer reviews the application, and, if necessary, a further internal review by a supervisory officer may be sought. In any case, the asylum officer has the authority to grant or deny an application. If denied, the case can be referred to immigration court in the US Department of Justice, where an immigration judge considers the case.

In defensive applications, a person may be placed in expedited removal proceedings, which means they are detained with plans to deport them. This can occur upon arrival at the border or within an area that extends 100 miles beyond the border, if an individual is picked up by immigration authorities within 14 days of their arrival to the US. Alternatively, Immigration and Customs Enforcement (ICE) may take custody and detain an individual in connection with several interior enforcement programs (see Coleman, 2007; Varsanyi, 2008; Hiemstra, 2010; Nevins, 2010). When apprehended in one of these ways, if an individual indicates that they have a basis for fear of persecution if deported to their country of origin, an asylum officer is required to conduct a "credible fear" screening, which determines whether or not their case should proceed for consideration by a Department of Justice immigration judge. Although the number of asylum seekers who are detained in the US is small compared to the overall population of immigration detainees in the US and relative to other states (Meili, 2014),[4] reports indicate that since 2014 increasing numbers of asylum seekers are being detained at some detention facilities (HRF, 2016a). Once a detained asylum seeker's identity has been verified satisfactorily, she or he becomes eligible for parole and possible release from detention. Conditions for parole typically include reporting requirements and may include payment of a bond as surety for attendance at future appointments related to their case. With increasingly restrictive parole policies implemented in recent years, asylum seekers are now less likely to be considered eligible for or released on parole (HRF, 2009, 2016a).[5] Also noteworthy is that asylum seekers are detained longer than most other migrant detainees, with average periods of detention lasting at least three months (HRF, 2009, p. 6). In contrast

---

[4]   Meili (2014) reports between 2006 and 2010 asylum seekers comprised between 1 and 1.9 percent of the US immigration detention population.

[5]   Citing ICE data, HRF (2009) reports that parole release declined from 66 percent in 2004 to 4.5 percent in 2007.

to affirmative asylum applications, defensive interviews are adversarial. For example, applicants are expected to present evidence to support their claim, witnesses may be called on to provide evidence, and cross-examination by a government attorney is allowed. If a defensive application is denied, it is possible to enter a sequence of appeals for further review.

In 2015, a total of 83,000 applications for asylum were filed in the US. The same year 26,124 people were granted asylum; 68 percent of these claims were granted via the affirmative application process and 32 percent in association with defensive claims (DHS, 2016; Zong and Batalova, 2017). Worth noting is that approval of affirmative applications increased (23 percent over 2014), whereas approval of defensive applications declined (by 6 percent on the previous year) (Mossaud, 2016, p. 7). Also, in recent years, requests for asylum via the defensive process, where an individual is placed in deportation proceedings, have increased significantly. Having presented an overview of the complex procedures associated with seeking asylum, the next section focuses on facets of the asylum screening and interview process, specifically demands to confess and self-present as autonomous actors, and periods of waiting, as examples of neoliberal governmentality within this system.

(IN)EFFICIENCY: BUREAUCRATIC GOVERNANCE AND NEOLIBERAL CAPITAL

There is little that is unfamiliar or unusual about the procedures detailed above. The asylum application process is a bureaucratic process that operates much like other government institutions. It is intended to provide an orderly, dispassionate, evidence-based assessment of asylum claims. Research highlights some of the ways the US immigration enforcement system is enmeshed with "street level bureaucrats" (Lipsky, 1980) who perform the tasks of asylum seeker governance (Hiemstra, 2010; Nevins, 2010). In the UK and focused on asylum specifically, Gill describes bureaucracy as having "inherent tendencies towards depersonalisation" (2016, p. 36). In combination with the neoliberal state, where "an ethos of business" (2016, p. 39) now dominates, this produces an asylum system where concrete, social, and moral distance can flourish in detrimental ways. From ethnographic work in Canada, Mountz "demystifies and deconstructs" (2010, p. 57) a complex immigration system that, on the one hand, projects order and homogeneity; yet, when viewed from the embodied purview of employees, is often frenzied and crisis-ridden.

Also consistent with bureaucracy, the asylum system is supposed to be efficient, yet, in practice, this is not the case. For example, the average wait time from filing an affirmative application to initial interview with an asylum officer is at least two years, while the waiting period for a hearing in immigration court in defensive applications averages three years (HRF, 2016b). During these protracted periods of waiting individuals are encouraged to "participate in a politics of the self" (Larner, 2000, p. 13) whereby they come to understand and conduct themselves simultaneously as asylum seekers in need of protection and as neoliberal, entrepreneurial subjects. In practical terms, this means, for example, that an asylum seeker must be able to demonstrate *and* document fear or trauma, be ready to reveal their past independently and in culturally appropriate ways, and also be willing to get on with life despite radically different and difficult circumstances.

My research with migrant women in Ireland showed how repeated encounters over lengthy periods with actors and institutions of bureaucratic governance worked to produce asylum seeker subjectivity (Conlon, 2010, 2013a). Individuals become visible and legible as asylum seekers through repeated acts of "confession," a practice that Foucault describes as pervasive in governmental society. He notes, confession is "one of the West's most highly valued techniques for producing truth . . . in the most ordinary affairs of everyday life and in the most solemn rites . . . one goes about telling, with the greatest precision, what is most difficult to tell" (Foucault, 1990, p. 59). At every stage of the asylum process, individuals must tell and retell, in other words, confess, private, personal details and histories that account for their fear of persecution. In this process they are rendered legible as asylum seekers. Moreover, as I discuss further on, in this bureaucratic system individuals must assemble reams of evidence and expertise to support the veracity of an asylum claim. Together these demands – to confess and to curate compelling evidence about one's claim – produce neoliberal subjectivity within the context of the asylum process.

At the same time, asylum seekers are also encouraged to demonstrate their suitability for inclusion in neoliberal society, and as potential future "neoliberal citizens" (Mitchell, 2016). My research with Nick Gill (Conlon and Gill, 2013) outlines a range of governmental spaces and technologies – including handbooks and guides, classes in detention, and legal self-representation manuals – where asylum seekers are encouraged to "see themselves as individualized and active subjects responsible for enhancing their own well being" (Larner, 2000, p. 13). In her discussion of "neoliberal citizenship," Mitchell details some of the ways institutions and policies converge around neoliberal imperatives. For instance, securitized immigration policies eschew and replace multiculturalism with the demand that immigrants "evolve and adjust to new circumstances – including both labour market changes and cultural shifts" (Mitchell, 2016, p. 111). From the limited resources and opportunities available to them, it is clear that asylum seekers are among those who are expected to "strategically learn and relearn, train and retrain in order to adapt to a flowing and unstable set of living and working environments" (Mitchell, 2016, p. 112). As they become enmeshed in the asylum system, individuals establish themselves as both asylum seekers and neoliberal subjects who are heroic and resilient; adept with fear, willing to face a traumatic past, and, yet, ready and able to forge ahead as an autonomous "economic-rational-actor" (Lemke, 2001, p. 197, cited in Mitchell, 2016, p. 107).

In turn, these technologies and imperatives may provide information that is useful for sorting individuals who are suitable participants in institutional activities and for inclusion in broader society from those who are not. Again, Mitchell's discussion is instructive here. Discussing securitized immigration policy, she notes that immigrants who do not comply with neoliberal imperatives "become ungovernable subjects [who are] threatening by virtue of their inability to function as *homo economicus* in the neoliberal nation" (Bigo, 2005, cited in Mitchell, 2016, p. 111)

In their encounters with the bureaucratic governmental system and as they wait for their claims to be reviewed, asylum seekers are produced as a population that is subject to internal comparisons and categorizations. Those who do not conform are sanctioned or disciplined. They may be moved from one facility to another, for instance (Conlon and Gill, 2013), or, among detained migrants, disciplinary measures include being excluded from participating in voluntary work programs, which has ramifications for wellbeing, as well as being perceived as coercive (Conlon and Hiemstra, 2016).

There is still another dimension of this bureaucratic system that demands critical attention. This is also where neoliberal capital and the governance of asylum intersect in significant ways. As previously noted, average wait time for applicant interviews with an immigration officer is between two and three years, and, when it comes to all cases pending immigration court hearings, wait time now averages 670 days, or 1.8 years, while some cases are scheduled with a 1,908 day, or a 5.2 year, wait before a hearing (TRAC, 2017). Among the reasons for such protracted periods of waiting for an interview with USCIS asylum officers or a court hearing one has to do with resource allocation and spending. Since the terrorist attacks on September 11, 2001, spending on securitization and border enforcement has expanded tremendously. The 2002 immigration enforcement budget was $7.3 billion, the 2016 budget was over $19 billion, and, at the time of writing, the current administration's budget request for 2018 includes increases of over 20 percent for Customs and Border Protection (CBP) and ICE, which would result in a combined immigration enforcement budget of $24 billion (see Meissner et al., 2013; Jones, 2016; Conlon, 2017; DHS, 2017). Scholars and advocacy groups trace and illuminate the relationships between privatization, government spending, and massive expansion of immigration enforcement (see Fernandes, 2007; Golash-Boza, 2009; Doty and Wheatley, 2013; Hiemstra and Conlon, 2016; Martin, 2016). With this, it is clear that neoliberal capital – characterized by market expansion and accumulation strategies and a shifting, but not a diminished, role for the state – is thoroughly embedded with immigration governance, particularly when it comes to border enforcement and detention.

However, investments have not "trickled down" to USCIS, the division of the Department of Homeland Security (DHS) that conducts credible fear screenings and asylum interviews, and that administers the asylum system more generally. Among the markers of increased border enforcement has been expansion of expedited removal (referenced earlier), which results in more immigrants being likely to end up within the orbit of the DHS and mandatory detention as a requirement pending deportation without a hearing. In addition to greatly increasing the population of migrant detainees and deportations, expedited removal has also produced a sizable increase in defensive asylum requests, with a 221 percent increase in initial defensive asylum receipts received by immigration courts from 2012 to 2016 (EOIR, 2017). As outlined previously, once fear of persecution is indicated in this situation, the bureaucratic asylum process is triggered, which begins with a credible fear screening conducted by a USCIS asylum officer. Human Rights First (2014) reports that referrals for credible fear screenings have increased significantly of late, with 7,917 referrals in 2004 and 36,035 in 2013, or a 355 percent increase in less than a decade. The same report observes "while resources for the immigration enforcement authorities who initiate expedited removal proceedings have soared, there has been no commensurate increase in resources for the portions of expedited removal . . . entrusted to the USCIS Asylum Division" (HRF, 2014, p. 2). Consequently, the asylum office now screens more asylum requests on top of adjudicating affirmative asylum applications. With this we see resources stretched and made scarcer while the system of bureaucratic government and governance explodes. Put differently, the asylum system is one where neoliberal capital begets ever greater labor and bureaucratic demands and, simultaneously, produces ever greater (in)efficiency.

CALCULATING THE VALUE OF EVIDENCE AND EXPERTISE

Amidst this mix of bureaucratic governance and neoliberal capital, there is great pressure to mount an unassailable case in support of an asylum seeker's claim of a well-founded fear of persecution. This means the value of costly legal representation, the significance of an individual's "confession," and the importance of expertise are heightened in the system. This section examines how legal and support organizations become entangled with governmentality and neoliberal ideology, resulting in an asylum system where expertise is scarce and uneven access and inequalities are perpetuated.

Whether an affirmative or defensive application is filed, both the application form and interview require asylum seekers to impart, under oath, evidence related to their claim by providing details about what and when harm, mistreatment or threats occurred, who was responsible, and why the applicant believes harm, mistreatment, or threats occurred (Form i-589[6]). The difficulty of talking about painful experiences that precipitated fleeing the asylum seeker's country of origin is acknowledged and, yet, the imperative to talk, to "confess," is underscored by guidance that indicates "it is very important that you talk about your experience so that the asylum officer can determine whether you qualify for a grant of asylum".[7] As noted before, legal representation is allowed, any number of witnesses can be called, and any amount or type of evidence can be presented in support of a case.[8] In some respects, these provisions might be considered generous, save for fact that asylum seekers are ineligible for court appointed legal representatives, as is the case for needy clients in the criminal justice system. The provisions also suggest that evidence and expert knowledge are desirable, if not a requirement, of the asylum process. Even so, research shows "an increasing number of asylum seekers are attempting to navigate the Immigration Court system without representation" (TRAC, 2016, n.p.), with the number of unrepresented asylum cases decided in immigration courts increasing from 13 percent in 2006 to 20 percent in 2016 (TRAC, 2016). The same report shows that the likelihood of being granted asylum is much higher for individuals with legal representation; this finding is corroborated by the American Bar Association, which observes that "whether a noncitizen is represented is the single most important factor affecting the outcome of an asylum case" (Ardalan, 2015, p. 1015, note 5). The denial rate is 48 percent compared to 90 percent for those with and without legal representation, respectively (TRAC, 2016). In other words, the odds of being granted asylum are five times higher when a legal representative is involved (TRAC, 2016).

What are we to make of this system where evidence and expertise appear to make all the difference? Writing from anthropology, Fassin (2011) provides an incisive analysis that links the degradation of individual asylum seekers to the delegitimization of asylum as an institution, expert knowledge, and what counts as "truth." He notes declining grant rates for asylum claims linked to increasing questioning of asylum seekers' credibility, which drives the demand to produce more and more evidence. At the same time, state and private institutions have greater abilities to produce ever more precise evidence, which, nonetheless,

---

[6] See http://www.uscis.gov.

[7] "Preparing for your asylum interview," http://www.uscis.gov.

[8] An asylum officer can place a reasonable limit on length and subject matter of a witness's statement, any documents submitted as evidence must include a certified English language translation.

is more likely to be rejected. In other words, even though applicants may provide vast quantities of evidence and expertise to help verify an asylum seeker's claim, increasingly this knowledge is deemed invalid as more and more claims are rejected in a political calculus that delegitimizes asylum wholesale. Effectively, this means that experts and support are entwined in knotty ways with governmental technologies in the asylum system.

From another perspective, it is clear that the asylum system involves a political-economic calculus at the level of the individual asylum seeker as well as for representatives and organizations working to support them. First, asylum seekers who have access to financial resources and can afford to pay for an attorney are more likely to be granted asylum. Consequently, it is worth investigating how the asylum system perpetuates socio-economic inequalities that flourish under neoliberal capitalism and reflect a logic of individualized winners and losers in a system governed by market norms. For increasing numbers of asylum seekers and other migrants who are in removal proceedings, they must rely on pro bono support or navigate the system without representation. Organizations that provide legal support are numerous and varied ranging from university law clinics, non-profit support and advocacy groups, and law firms. USCIS provides a list of verified pro bono services for asylum seekers; this resource indicates that asylum seekers are susceptible to exploitation by unscrupulous actors, referred to as "notarios," in a "free choice" market economy.

Organizations that provide legal support or representation are entangled with biopolitical governmentality as part of their calculations and to prepare asylum seekers for their day in court. In my research with support groups in the US and the UK, lawyers spoke about the great weight of asylum seekers demeanor and testimony in court. For instance, when deciding whether to take a case, credibility is a key consideration, as one study participant noted: "when we're evaluating a case [we look at] credibility, do we believe this person and the story they're telling us? Because it's so crucial in asylum cases . . . we're assessing credibility all the time because that's what the judges are doing" (Author interview, 2011a).[9] Another attorney explained how preparing a client for immigration court is a key element of legal support work: "we spend hours together trying to humanize the story . . . I feel we have to be cultural translators as well as advocates . . . on the one hand you want them to be genuine but at the same time you don't want them to be misunderstood" (Author interview, 2011b).

In his work on immigration courts in the UK, Gill has found that factors such as an asylum seeker's attire and gender garner significant differences in judicial procedural discretion (Burridge and Gill, 2017; Gill et al., 2017). These studies indicate that more and more responsibility is placed both on the individual asylum seeker and legal support organizations to be discerning and savvy in presenting asylum claims. To be clear, I am not questioning these support efforts, indeed, the empirical evidence indicates that legal, evidentiary and other forms of migrant support are vital. Rather, following Fassin (2011), I want to emphasize that support organizations are ensnared in the machinations

---

[9]   Interview quotes are from an Economic and Social Research Council (ESRC) project conducted by N. Gill, D. Conlon, I. Tyler, and C. Oeppen (2010–12), "Making asylum seekers legible and visible: an analysis of the dilemmas and strategies of asylum advocacy organisations in the UK and US." Quotes included are: 2011a, Conlon interview w/Legal provider, US115 (May 31, 2011); 2011b, Conlon interview w/Legal/Social Support Provider, US10 (June 27, 2011).

of governmentality. That they may guide comportment or attune accounts in hopes of maximizing positive outcomes for asylum seekers is laudable, indeed, it is necessary. At the same time, as Fassin's analysis indicates, there is also a need for vigilance as to the political ends that various forms of support are used.

There are other calculations involved here that link demands for evidence and expertise to neoliberal capital more explicitly. Access to government sanctioned legal support was restricted in the mid-1990s when Congress eliminated Legal Service Corporation, or legal aid, funds to organizations providing legal representation to asylum seekers and other immigrants (Ardalan, 2015, p. 1010). This shift was tied to the neoliberal ideology that brought about welfare reform in the US, and to a sharpening of distinctions between the deserving and undeserving poor. Among asylum seekers, individuals who are deserving of legal representation are autonomous, entrepreneurial, economic actors who can access support via the free market. As the aforementioned report on increases in the number of asylum seekers without legal support suggests, this appears to be what is happening with resulting unequal access and potentially dangerous consequences for those deemed "undeserving" in this calculus. There is an impact for professionals too as decisions to provide support through the asylum process – whether as a lawyer or expert witness – necessitate calculation of trade-offs in relation to individual time, productivity, and earnings in the labor market vis-à-vis uncompensated work. While professions and professional organizations, such as the American Bar Association, have established standards for pro bono commitments (see Model Rule 6.1), the cost-benefit analyses required align such undertakings with the logic of neoliberal capital, and render law, for example, a private rather than a public good (Luban, 1999).

CONCLUSION: PROVOCATION AS "MESSY" IMPERATIVE

This chapter has identified several ways neoliberal governmentality is articulated in the US asylum system. I have drawn attention to governmental technologies that are awash with bureaucracy and produce asylum seekers as victims of persecution and, yet, autonomous, rational actors at the same time. I have also shown how neoliberal logic and privatization clash with and stymy efficiency in the system. Additionally, I have highlighted how the asylum system demands "confession" along with increasingly precise forms of evidence and expertise. In turn, this begets strategic complicity with technologies of government by asylum support groups. Furthermore, demands for evidence and expertise are linked recursively to political-economic calculations that reproduce inequalities and potentially exacerbate uneven access to justice. What emerges from this specifically grounded account is that neoliberal governmentality is not smooth or cohesive; instead, it is uneven and unstable. The asylum process within the broader neoliberal landscape of US society reveals contradictions at every scale. It seeks to produce asylum seekers as neoliberal subjects who are active and entrepreneurial but, also, compliant and passive. It relies on institutions of governance and technologies of government that embody calculation, and efficiency, for example, yet, simultaneously, undermine these practices and goals.[10]

---

[10] Thanks to Katharyne Mitchell for guidance on this point.

Viewed in this way – as heterogeneous, paradoxical, and unstable (see Walters, 2015) – the asylum process as an example of neoliberal governmentality can be understood as susceptible to challenge and contestation. As I have indicated, advocates and activists navigate this process in complex and often contradictory ways. Indeed, there is growing attention to the remarkably complicated sites and practices of opposition that inhere where neoliberal governmentality and migration collide (see, for example, Tyler, 2013; Tazzioli, 2014).

Attending to these spaces is a theoretical and empirical undertaking with practical implications for researchers. This chapter opened noting reflection and scrutiny as key concerns for critical geographies of migration. Throughout, I have emphasized some of the knotty ways efforts to inject humanity and safeguard justice, as well as initiatives more explicitly aimed at disrupting the asylum system are imbricated with neoliberal governmentality. Two points are worth reiterating here: first, the trajectory and effects of neoliberal governmentality are not inevitable and, second, opposition is, itself, shambolic and contradictory. With this, there is a clear need to be attuned to the instabilities and possible alternative courses of action that arise. In other words, vigilance, questioning, and critique are vital praxes in all engagements with the asylum system specifically, and with the nexus between neoliberal governmentality and migration more broadly. Foucault characterizes such practice as counter-conduct, which describes provocations that are embedded with and emanate from governmental processes (see Cadman, 2010; Conlon, 2013b; Conlon and Gill, 2013). Counter-conduct refers to a willingness to persistently and relentlessly probe and to ask why "govern *like that*, by that, in the name of those principles" (Foucault, 1997, p. 28, original emphasis). In turn, engaging in this practice, or conduct, can set in motion uncertainties vis-à-vis the knowledge we produce and our role and place in the neoliberal governmental asylum system. If we accept that the asylum system is prone to the messy contradictions of neoliberal governmentality, and we take seriously the task of producing critical geographies of migration, then we must practice counter-conduct in every sphere, from the academe to advocacy and activism. In short, to apprehend – in all senses – neoliberal governmentality in the asylum system and in migration processes broadly, provocation is a "messy" imperative.

REFERENCES

Ardalan, S. (2015) "Access to justice for asylum seekers: developing an effective model of holistic asylum representation", *University of Michigan Journal of Law Reform*, **48**(4), 1001–38.

Bigo, D. (2002) "Security and immigration: toward a critique of the governmentality of unease", *Alternatives*, **27**, 63–92.

Brady, M. and Lippert, R. (2016) *Governing Practices: Neoliberalism, Governmentality and the Ethnographic Imaginary*. Toronto: University of Toronto Press.

Burridge, A. and Gill, N. (2017) "Conveyor-belt justice: precarity, access to justice, and uneven geographies of legal aid in UK asylum appeals", *Antipode*, **49**(1), 23–42.

Burridge, A., Gill, N., Kocher, A., and Martin, L. (2017) "Polymorphic borders", *Territory, Politics, Governance*, **5**(3), 239–51.

Cadman, L. (2010) "How (not) to be governed: Foucault, critique, and the political", *Environment and Planning D: Society and Space*, **28**, 539–56.

Coleman, M. (2007) "Immigration and geopolitics beyond the US-Mexico border", *Antipode*, **39**(1), 54–76.

Conlon, D. (2010) "Ties that bind: governmentality, the state, and asylum in contemporary Ireland", *Environment and Planning D: Society and Space*, **28**(1), 95–111.

Conlon, D. (2013a) "Becoming legible and 'legitimized': subjectivation and governmentality among asylum seekers", in G. Jacobs and J. Capetillo (eds), *Migrant Marginality: A Transnational Perspective*. New York: Routledge, pp. 186–204.

Conlon, D. (2013b) "Hungering for freedom: asylum seekers' hunger strikes – rethinking resistance as counter-conduct", in D. Moran, N. Gill, and D. Conlon (eds), *Carceral Spaces: Mobility and Agency in Imprisonment and Migrant Detention*. Farnham, UK: Ashgate, pp. 133–48.

Conlon, D. (2017) "Immigration policy and migrant support organizations in an era of austerity and hope", in D. Brotherton and P. Kretsedemas (eds), *Immigration Policy in the Age of Punishment: Detention, Deportation and Border Control*. Columbia, NY: Columbia University Press, pp. 57–74.

Conlon, D. and Gill, N. (2013) "Gagging orders: asylum seekers and paradoxes of freedom and protest in liberal society", *Citizenship Studies*, **17**(2), 241–59.

Conlon, D. and Hiemstra, N. (eds) (2016) *Intimate Economies of Immigration Detention: Critical Perspectives*. London and New York: Routledge.

Darling, J. (2011) "Domopolitics, governmentality and the regulation of asylum accommodation", *Political Geography*, **30**, 263–71.

De Genova, N. (2002) "Migrant 'illegality' and deportability in everyday life", *Annual Review of Anthropology*, **1**(4), 419–47.

DHS (2016) *2015 Yearbook of Immigration Statistics*. December 15. Washington, DC: Department of Homeland Security. Available at https://www.dhs.gov/immigration-statistics/yearbook/2015/table16 (accessed November 10, 2017).

DHS (2017) "FY 2018 budget in brief". May 23. Washington, DC: Department of Homeland Security. Available at https://www.dhs.gov/sites/default/files/publications/DHS%20FY18%20BIB%20Final.pdf (accessed November 10, 2017).

Doty, R.L. and Wheatley, E.S. (2013) "Private detention and the immigration industrial complex", *International Political Sociology*, **7**(4), 426–43.

EOIR (US Department of Justice, Executive Office for Immigration Review) (2017) *FY 2016 Statistics Yearbook*. March. Office of Planning and Analysis and Statistics, Veterans Affairs.

Fassin, D. (2011) "Policing borders, producing boundaries. The governmentality of immigration in dark times", *Annual Review of Anthropology*, **40**, 213–16.

Fernandes, D. (2007) *Targeted: Homeland Security and the Business of Immigration*. New York: Seven Stories Press.

Foucault, M. (1990) *The History of Sexuality*, vol. 3, *The Care of the Self*. London: Penguin.

Foucault, M. (1991) "Governmentality", in G. Burchell, C. Gordon, and P. Miller (eds), *The Foucault Effect: Studies in Governmentality*. Chicago, IL: University of Chicago Press, pp. 87–104.

Foucault, M. (1997) *The Politics of Truth*. Ed. L. Hochroth and S. Lotringer. Los Angeles, CA: Semiotexte.

Gill, N. (2009) "Governmental mobility: the power effects of the movement of detained asylum seekers around Britain's detention estate", *Political Geography*, **28**, 186–96.

Gill, N. (2016) "Nothing personal", in *Geographies of Governing and Activism in the British Asylum System*. London: Wiley-Blackwell.

Gill, N., Rotter, R., Burridge, A., Allsopp, J. (2017) "The limits of procedural discretion: Unequal treatment and vulnerability in Britain's asylum appeals", *Social and Legal Studies*. doi: 10.1177/10964663917703178.

Golash-Boza, T. (2009) "The immigration industrial complex: why we enforce immigration policies destined to fail", *Sociology Compass*, 3(2), pp. 295–309.

Gordon, C. (1991) "Governmental rationality: an introduction", in G. Burchell, C. Gordon, and P. Miller (eds), *The Foucault Effect: Studies in Governmentality*. Chicago, IL: University of Chicago Press, pp. 1–52.

Hacking, I. (1982) "Biopower and the avalanche of printed numbers", *Humanities in Society*, **5**, 279–95.

Hiemstra, N. (2010) "Immigration 'illegality' as neoliberal governmentality in Leadville, Colorado", *Antipode*, **42**, 74–102.

Hiemstra, N. (2014) "Performing homeland (in)security: employee-detainee relationships within the immigrant detention center", *Environment and Planning D: Society and Space*, **32**, 571–88.

Hiemstra, N. and Conlon, D. (2016) "Captive consumers and coerced labourers: intimate economies and the expanding US detention regime", in D. Conlon and N. Hiemstra (eds), *Intimate Economies of Immigration Detention: Critical Perspectives*. London: Routledge, pp. 123–39.

HRF (Human Rights First) (2009) "U.S. detention of asylum seekers: seeking protection, finding prison". Human Rights First, New York. Available at https://www.humanrightsfirst.org/wp-content/uploads/pdf/090429-RP-hrf-asylum-detention-report.pdf (accessed November 10, 2017).

HRF (Human Rights First) (2014) "Key statistics and findings on asylum protection request at the US-Mexico border". Fact sheet, June 5. Human Rights First, New York. Available at https://www.humanrightsfirst.org/resource/key-statistics-and-findings-asylum-protection-requests-us-mexico-border (accessed November 10, 2017).

HRF (Human Rights First) (2016a) "Detention of asylum seekers in New Jersey". Brief November. Human Rights First, New York. Available at http://www.humanrightsfirst.org/sites/default/files/hrf-detention-asylum-seekers-nj-nov2016.pdf (accessed November 10, 2017).

HRF (Human Rights First) (2016b) "In the balance: Backlogs delay protection in the US asylum and immigration court systems". April 19. Human Rights First, New York. Available at http://www.humanrights first.org/sites/default/files/HRF-In-The-Balance.pdf (accessed November 10, 2017).

Hyndman, J. (2012) "The geopolitics of migration and mobility", *Geopolitics*, **17**(2), 243–55.

Jones, R. (2016) *Violent Borders: Refugees and the Right to Move*. New York: Verso.

Larner, W. (2000) "Neoliberalism, policy, ideology, governmentality", *Studies in Political Economy*, **63**(1), 5–25.

Lipsky, M. (1980) *Street Level Bureaucracy: Dilemmas of the Individual in Public Services*. New York: Russell Sage Foundation.

Luban, D. (1999) "Faculty pro bono and the question of identity", *Journal of Legal Education*, **49**(1), 58–75.

Malkki, L. (1995) "Refugees and exiles: from 'refugee studies' to the national order of things", *Annual Review of Anthropology*, **24**, 495–523.

Martin, L. (2016) "Discretion, contracting, and commodification: privatisation of US immigration detention as a technology of government", in D. Conlon and N. Hiemstra (eds), *Intimate Economies of Immigration Detention: Critical Perspectives*. Abingdon, Oxon: Routledge, pp. 32–50.

Meili, S. (2014) "Comparing the detention of asylum seekers in the UK and the US". June 9. Available at http://bordercriminologies.law.ox.ac.uk/comparing-the-uk-and-the-us/ (accessed November 10, 2017).

Meissner, D., Kerwin, D., Chishti, M., and Bergeron, C. (2013) *Immigration Enforcement in the United States: The Rise of a Formidable Machinery*. Washington, DC: Migration Policy Institute.

Mitchell, K. (2016) "Neoliberalism and citizenship", in S. Springer (ed.), *Handbook of Neoliberalism*. New York: Routledge, pp. 104–15.

Mitchell, K. (2017) "Freedom, faith and humanitarian governance: the spatial politics of church asylum in Europe", *Space and Polity*, **21**(3), 269–88.

Mossaud, N. (2016) *Refugees and Asylees 2015*. Annual flow report, November. Office of Immigration Statistics, Department of Homeland Security, Washington, DC. Available at https://www.dhs.gov/sites/default/files/publications/Refugees_Asylees_2015.pdf (accessed November 10, 2017).

Mountz, A. (2010) *Seeking Asylum: Human Smuggling and Bureaucracy at the Border*. Minnesota, MN: University of Minnesota Press.

Mountz, A., Coddington, K., Catania, R.T., and Loyd, J. (2012) "Conceptualizing detention: mobility, containment, bordering, and exclusion", *Progress in Human Geography*, **37**(4), 522–41.

Nevins, J. (2010) *Operation Gatekeeper and Beyond: The War on Illegals and the Remaking of the US Mexico Boundary* (2nd edn). New York: Routledge.

Pascucci, E. (2017) "Community infrastructures: shelter, self-reliance and polymorphic borders in urban refugee governance", *Territory, Politics, Governance*, **5**(3), 332–45.

Prokkola (2013) "Neoliberalizing border management in Finland and Schengen", *Antipode*, **45**(5), 1318–36.

Sparke, M. (2006) "Political geography: political geographies of globalization (2) – governance", *Progress in Human Geography*, **30**(3), 357–72.

Tazzioli, M. (2014) *Spaces of Governmentality: Autonomous Migration and the Arab Uprisings*. London: Rowman and Littlefield.

TRAC (2016) "Continued rise in asylum denial rates: impact of representation and nationality". December 13. Syracuse, NY. Available at http://trac.syr.edu/immigration/reports/448/ (accessed November 10, 2017).

TRAC (2017) "Despite hiring, immigration court backlog and wait times climb". May 15. Syracuse, NY. Available at http://trac.syr.edu/immigration/reports/468/ (accessed November 10, 2017).

Turner, J. (2014) "The family migration visa in the history of marriage restrictions: postcolonial relations and the UK border", *British Journal of Politics & International Relations*, **17**(4), 623–43.

Tyler, I. (2013) *Revolting Subjects: Social Abjection and Resistance in Neoliberal Britain*. London: Zed Books.

UNHCR (n.d.) "History of UNHCR". Available at http://www.unhcr.org/uk/history-of-unhcr.html (accessed November 10, 2017).

UNHCR (2016) *Global Trends: Forced Displacement in 2015*. Geneva: UNHCR. Available at http://www.unhcr.org/576408cd7.pdf (accessed November 10, 2017).

UNHCR (2017) *Mid-year Trends 2016*. Geneva: UNHCR. Available at http://unhcr.org/statistics (accessed November 10, 2017).

Varsanyi, M. (2008) "Rescaling the 'alien', rescaling personhood: neoliberalism, immigration and the state", *Annals of the Association of American Geographers*, **98**(4), 877–96.

Walters, W. (2015) "Reflections on migration and governmentality", *Movements Journal for Critical Migration and Border Studies*, **1**(1), 1–25.

Zong, J. and Batalova, J. (2017) "Refugees and asylees in the United States". June spotlight. Migration Policy Institute, Washington, DC. Available at http://www.migrationpolicy.org/article/refugees-and-asylees-united-states (accessed November 10, 2017).

31. Counter-mapping, refugees and asylum borders
*Martina Tazzioli and Glenda Garelli**

Migration maps are lively cartographies, which need to be constantly updated with numbers, statistics and figures showing the geographical changes in migrant routes, and the quantitative variations in migrants' composition. Focusing on refugee maps in particular – those produced by international organizations such as the United Nations High Commissioner for Refugees (UNHCR), for instance – it's worth noting that what ends up on the map is both the presence of migrants in a given space and their juridical status. Refugee maps are by far more static, representing the migrant population in a refugee camp or the results of asylum claims. More broadly, both refugee maps and migration maps at large stand out on a pre-given territoriality, formed by a constellation of nation-states: a Westphalian imaginary substantially underpins and informs migration and refugee maps. Yet, as we demonstrate in this chapter, border regimes and migratory movements produce spaces that cannot be contained within the temporal and spatial fixes of the geopolitical map. How to account for the geographies of asylum, those that result from the spatial restrictions imposed on asylum seekers and of refugees' movements and those enacted by them in order to claim a space of refuge? How to bring to the fore spaces of movement and control that are not comprehensible on the geopolitical map of Europe? In short, what does it mean to engage a counter-mapping approach in relation to migration and asylum policies?

The aim of this chapter is to mobilize a counter-mapping approach with respect to the normative geographies of the asylum system, and to first explore what "counter" means in the context of a critical cartography of migration, and then to unpack the main theoretical and political tenets such a methodological perspective mobilizes against. Our take on counter-mapping relies on what we would call a *reflexive cartography*, meaning an analysis that does not consist only in a cartographic practice, but that, rather, interrogates the predicaments and the implications of mapping migration. More precisely, counter-mapping is for us a "reflexive practice", that is, a *methodological approach* that unsettles and unpacks the spatial assumptions upon which migration maps are crafted. Moreover, we also refer to cartographic experimentations that trouble the spatial and temporal fixes of a state-based gaze on migration. In sum, counter-mapping as a method and counter-mapping as a cartographic experimentation intertwine as part of our critical account of the visualizations of migration and refugee issues.

This means engaging in a counter-mapping approach to borders and migration that consists in refusing *the visibilities and temporalities that are performed by the statist gaze that produces migration maps*. By speaking of a state-based visibility on migration – a sort of "seeing like a state" (Scott, 1998) approach to migration – we refer to the fact that migrations are (re)presented and narrated on the map as a visual counterpoint to

* Some of the arguments developed in this chapter were presented by Martina Tazzioli at a conference organized at Duisburg University on April 26, 2017.

the nation-state, while at the same time being grounded in it. That is, migrations are visualized on maps as deviations from what can be called the *territorial norm*, that is, from the primacy of the territory and of a settled subject figure in the Western political tradition. Further, the state's cartographic perspective consists in "translating" some practices of movements into "migration flows," through a process of abstraction, and in reifying some subjects as "migrants." It is important here to clarify that a state-based gaze on migration is not narrowed to state-actors' interventions in the field of migration. More broadly, by a "state-gaze on migration" we refer to the enforcement of the nexus between migration and government; that is, migration is posited as an unquestioned object of government, a phenomenon that requires mobilizing a governmental approach to it. The state-based gaze on migration is characterized not only by a specific spatiality – the territorial norm – but also by a certain temporality through which migrations are "captured" and framed as an object of governmental concern. More precisely, migration maps produced by states or by international agencies are sustained by a sort of *hidden linear temporality*, insofar as they appear deprived of a temporal dimension. In fact, the narrative that sustains institutional migration maps is a South-to-North linear movement that migration routes are supposed to reproduce.

Does counter-mapping in the field of migration consist in a "disobedient gaze" (Heller and Pezzani, 2014)? The argument that we develop in this chapter is that counter-mapping should be put to work in relation to migration governmentality[1] not (only) in terms of *seeing differently* or *seeing more*. In other words, *it is not a question of "gaze" on migration*; it is instead a matter of a particular knowledge production practice that brings to the fore spaces of mobility and control that cannot be grasped within the register of cartographic representation.

By assuming counter-mapping as a method, we shift attention from the question about how to represent (or not to represent) migration towards an interrogation about the effects that mechanisms of control generate on migrant lives and geographies, and about the temporary or constituent spaces opened up by migration movements and border enforcements. This means investigating the spaces of governmentality (contested spaces of control) and spaces of movement that are generated through measures of border enforcement and migration movements and that are not apprehensible on the geopolitical map.

Counter-mapping as method means, first of all, conceiving of counter-mapping as an epistemic approach and not merely as a cartographic perspective. It means referring to an analytical gaze that requires engaging both in a deconstructive move and in a constructive one. The former consists in refusing the temporalities and the visibilities of migration enacted by states. The latter involves bringing to the fore the multiple disjunctions between the spaces and the borders of sovereignty on the one hand, and the spaces of migration mobility and control that are the outcome of migrant movements and "bordering practices" on the other (Parker and Vaugham-Williams, 2012). This resonates with Sandro Mezzadra and Brett Neilson's argument about the heterogeneity of spaces (and times) as a characteristic of contemporary capitalism: they point to a fundamental disjunction between spaces of capital and spaces produced by logistics, and the "traditional" territorial spaces of the state (Mezzadra and Neilson, 2017). Border practices are not

---

[1] Among the many contributions that address governmentality from a spatial perspective see in particular: Hannah (2000), Elden (2007) and Legg (2007).

narrowed here to border controls and border enforcement measures but, rather, include the technical cooperation between the European Union (EU) and third-countries and the virtual circuits of data flows and data exchange activities. These spaces of control remain essentially invisible, and therefore inexistent, on geopolitical maps. Simultaneously, there are migration spaces that remain unaccounted and unperceived, and which result from migrants' movements and presence as long as these exceed and cannot be contained by the government of routes – that is, what Sebastian Cobarrubias and Maribel Casas-Cortes (Casas-Cortes et al., 2015) poignantly named "itinerant borders." This doesn't mean falling into the trap of a "romanticization" (Scheel, 2013) of migration, as a phenomenon that would in itself challenge the "national order of things" (Mallki, 1995) – or, in our case, the cartographic national order of things.

Counter-mapping should not be limited to representing the shifting of geopolitical borders and the displacement of the actual frontiers that migrants are confronted with, for instance, as a result of bilateral cooperation agreements between states or of the EU politics of externalization. Nor is it only a question of drawing attention to the so-called pre-frontiers of Europe, located in the embassies where visa applications are examined. In our view, the theoretical and political stakes of counter-mapping in the field of migration consist in accounting for the mobility of borders and, at once, for their heterogenization. By mobility of borders we do not only mean the displacement of the frontiers. More than that, we refer to the heterogenization of borders – most of which follow and chase after migrants, as is the case with biometric borders. How to counter-map borders that do not conflate with geopolitical boundaries? Furthermore, all these heterogeneous borders are mobile in the sense that in fact they are not fixed and do constantly change place. In this sense, we concur with Tugba Basaran in shifting attention "from territorial geographies to practices of bordering" (Basaran, 2010, p. 32) and in playing with the frictions between geopolitical spaces and the multiplication of legal, digital and administrative spaces on the other. Ultimately, coming to grips with the mobility of borders confronts us with what Bruno Latour and others have called the "navigational interpretation" of maps (Latour et al., 2010, p. 586). However, unlike scholarship that mainly focuses on maps in terms of a politics of knowledge, we contend that in order to account for the actual mobility of borders attention should be focused on the materiality of migrant geographies and on the spaces of control and movement that are connected to these.

WHAT IS THE "COUNTER" IN COUNTER-MAPPING MIGRATION GOVERNMENTALITY?

Reflecting on counter-mapping and migrations entails a radical questioning of critical cartography at large. Indeed, migration allows us to raise fundamental interrogations on cartographic representation: the gist of any critical approach to migration maps revolves around the question of the extent or degree to which it is ethically and politically desirable to even map migrations. In other words, while a critical question has generally been "how to unveil the silences of maps?," if we focus on migration maps and draw from critical cartography literature (e.g., Harley, 1989, 2009; Sparke, 1995) we should instead ask: "what should not be put on the map?," what is politically important to conceal from the public gaze in order to preserve migrants' desire and practices of movement across space?

Second, counter-mapping migration governmentality involves engaging not only with space but also with time. Migrations tend to be represented through temporal fixations – that is, through snapshots. In this way, what is fundamentally missing, and what is erased from the map, is the autonomous temporality of migration (migrants' own lived and enacted temporality in movement), and how this autonomous temporality is obstructed and altered by migration policies and border enforcement practices. Mapping migration needs to rely on the *mobile spaces* that characterize the border regime and, relatedly, on their temporary dimension – as spaces that are generated by the implementation of migration policies, or as migrant spaces of transit and refuge that are suddenly evicted, or as mobile borders that are constantly displaced in order to follow and anticipate migration movements.

We expand here on the theoretical implications of counter-mapping in the field of migration. This involves questioning the gaze mobilized by the academic scholarship that "(however critical) is implicated in a continuous (re-) reification of 'migrants' as a distinct category of human mobility" (De Genova, 2013, p. 250). For instance, looking at the Mediterranean Sea, we see how, in the Mediterranean northern shore's accounts, rescued migrants get depicted and narrated in a way that reiterates the gesture of making migration start in correspondence with the *scene of drown and rescue* or at the moment when migrants enter or land in Europe. Challenging the state-based visibilities of migration entails shifting away from the regime of visibility that is at stake in a governmental gaze on migration. However, it is not merely a question of overcoming some spatial delimitations. Rather, the main point is related to the space-time narrative that implicitly sustains discourses and analyses on migration, and which tends to posit an indefinite (spatial and temporal) "before" where migrants pass through before landing on the European shores.

Migrants are, in some circumstances, the *looked at* and *monitored* subjects par excellence. *To be looked at* and to *be monitored* correspond in fact to two coexisting but distinct mechanisms of visibility for capturing subjects within a gaze. Migrants are looked at insofar as they are objects of processes of racialization, selection and categorization – all processes that feed a political economy of exploitation – despite this often being disjoined from an act of interpellation (Fanon, 2008). They are monitored as a way of governance in which populations can be controlled, detected and mapped.

Migrants are also targeted by a politics of invisibilization making them inexistent to state records and data even if they are spatially present within these states' territories. Two main points ensue from this context. First, challenging the regime of visibility that underpins the government of migration means questioning the gesture of freezing migration into a stable and essentialized category, and hence shifting attention to processes of "migrantization" whereby governmental technologies fix certain categories of people as migrants. The visibility of migration cannot be disconnected from the spaces and times whereby people are labeled and governed as "migrants" through border enforcement policies, state discourses, techniques of control and forms of visualization. Starting from a critical appraisal of governmental visibilities, the goal of a non-cartographic counter-mapping approach does not consist in extending the field of visibility of migration (i.e., making some objects more visible, giving them visibility). Nor does it consist in showing what remains hidden or overshadowed in processes of migration. This type of move would, in fact, contribute to the translation of movements, subjects and conducts into "governable" targets, hence making them intelligible in the terms of power's discourse.

The work of critical geographers is particularly helpful in this regard, as it explains what a counter-mapping gaze means at the level of knowledge production. In *A History of Spaces* John Pickles stresses that counter-mapping must go "beyond the unmasking of the silences in traditional maps to the production of new maps," pointing to what he calls "a de-ontologized cartography" (Pickles, 2004, p. 23) that needs to produce a new openness, bringing to the fore spaces that result from connections and border practices.

In the article "Unfolding mapping practices: a new epistemology for cartography," Robert Kitchin, Justin Gleeson and Martin Dodge advocate for a radical shift from a critical cartography still grounded on maps as fixed and autonomous objects (an ontological dimension) towards an understanding of maps in terms of mapping practices (an ontogenic approach) (Kitchin et al., 2013). Through this move they reconceptualize mapping as something that should not be disconnected from the discursive and non-discursive practices that make a series of lines and dots, a map. This methodological and epistemological move entails questioning the critical cartography literature which has been essentially predicated upon deconstruction – "deconstructing the map" (Harley, 1989). Maps, while critically analysed, remain nonetheless autonomous artifacts characterized by a certain degree of ontological security. Pushing this argument further, they move beyond post-representational map analyses, arguing that what matters is not stressing the irreducible discrepancy between map and territory, but to disjoin the map from the question of representation as such. In "Seeing Red. Baghdad and the event-ful city," Derek Gregory (2010) points to the nexus between spaces of constructed visibility and spaces of intervention (war battlefields), highlighting how a focus on modes of visibility and of visuality allows one to grasp the specific entanglement between biopolitics and geopolitics. Gregory concurs with the challenge of the ontological security of maps – proposed by Kitchen et al. – adding that, however, a shift towards mapping practices requires not a narrow attention to mapping as such, but rather an exploration of the security operations and the biopolitical modes that sustain any regime of visualization.

Producing visibility on what remains under the threshold of knowledge results in the governmentalization of migration to the extent that it does not question the categories and the political mechanisms that sustain the regime of visibility. In "The evidence of experience," Joan Scott provides a critique of the quest for evidence that is at the core of history as a discipline, arguing that "the evidence of experience," as it is produced by analyses that challenge normative history, tends to reproduce "rather than contests given ideological experiences, its categories of representation" (Scott, 1991, p. 778). In this way, she concludes, "the project of making experience visible precludes analysis of the workings of this system and of its historicity; instead, it reproduces its terms" (Scott, 1991, p. 779).

Scott's position entails refusing the categories and the epistemological-political rationales that establish the condition of emergence (i.e., the visibilization) of subjects as migrants. Simultaneously, a counter-mapping gaze consists in unsettling the binary alternative between making visible and letting/making invisible, pointing rather to the constitutive opacity of migration governmentality (Pinelli, 2017).[2] In fact, a counter-mapping approach does not consist in unveiling the secrecy of a state's operations, nor

---

[2]   We conceive of migration governmentality as a field of tensions between techniques of migration control and migration practices and struggles (Mezzadra and Neilson, 2013).

in embracing a neo-positivist approach and proving evidence of the state's violations of the international law.

Counter-mapping as a method takes a distance from an epistemic commitment to fill in the gaps of black holes and grey zones of maps. On the contrary, it starts from the assumption that the struggles over the border regime do not depend on a lack of knowledge but, rather, on the hyper-exposure of states' "warfare on migrants" (Garelli and Tazzioli, 2016a, 2018). Hence, a counter-mapping gaze would engage in undoing and rewriting the modes of discourse and visibility on migration not according to a less-to-more logic – more of visibility, more of knowledge, more of evidence – but by building new and different constellations of political and historical connection.[3]

Contributing to Scott's argument, according to which "making visible the experience of a different group exposes the existence of repressive mechanisms but not their inner working or logics" (Scott, 1991, p. 799), we suggest that it is not so much a question of unveiling human rights violations to which migrants are subjected. Neither is it a matter of making migrants' presence visible. In other words, *counter-mapping* consists in a *rippling gesture* that brings to the fore spaces of control that are neither accounted for, nor represented on geopolitical maps but that are the result of border cooperation practices, virtual spaces of data circulation, or spaces formed by channels of forced mobility. Moreover, a counter-mapping approach to migration and borders engages in highlighting the spaces of mobility opened up by migration movements, thereby bringing attention to the way in which these latter exceed the humanitarian and security captures of the border regime. William Walters has poignantly remarked that "a cartography of deportation is virtually non-existent" (Walters, 2017), arguing for an engagement in mapping practices that chart channels of forced mobility. He writes, "Border studies displays an ingression bias. It is focused much more on the socio-material systems that are dedicated to policing movements towards the territories of the global north than it is with questions of how the removal of people is carried on" (Walters, 2017).

COUNTER-MAPPING ASYLUM'S BORDERS

Building on the theoretical understanding of counter-mapping and migration illustrated above, we turn to questioning the territorial norms and normative predicaments that underpin the asylum regime. Our use of the expression "asylum regime" is meant to resonate with analyses of the border regime that highlight both the heterogeneity of bordering policies and their contested nature – conceiving the politics of migration control as a field of struggle (De Genova, 2016; Mezzadra and Neilson, 2013; Tsianos and Karakayali, 2010). Moreover, by speaking of "asylum regime" we point to the spatial restrictions and the effects of temporal suspension – what can alternatively be called spatial and temporal confinement – generated by the asylum system. The asylum system should not be taken as a monolithic entity but, rather, as a set of national and international laws, measures and policies that are enforced for producing and governing both asylum seekers and

---

[3]   In this sense, such a counter-mapping approach differs from the Forensic perspective, proposed by Eyal Weizman and the Forensic Architecture research group, that aims to prove material evidence of human rights violations (Weizman, 2014).

those whose claim to international protection is rejected. We contend that it is crucial to maintain the two verbs – *to produce* and *to govern* asylum seekers – in order not to essentialize "asylum seekers" or "refugees" as distinct subject-categories that pre-exist the asylum system. In fact, it is the politics of asylum that produces some subjects as refugees (and as asylum seekers), well before managing them as refugees. Relatedly, while it produces asylum seekers, it also illegalizes some migrants. In other words, in order for refugees to exist and to be legally recognized as refugees, many other migrants need to be illegalized and excluded from the channels of protection. Therefore, it is within such a framework that a counter-mapping approach to the asylum's borders should be situated. By engaging in a counter-mapping approach to the asylum regime, we want to critically address and twist two main aspects of it: the normative predicaments of the asylum and its territorial norm. The first point, the normative predicaments, refers to the normative-juridical ground that historically and politically sustains the global politics of asylum. The second point, the territorial norm, consists in the persistence of a strict relationship between refugee status and migrant's country of origin, or better in the dependence of the former on the latter (Garelli and Tazzioli, 2013a, 2013b).

Our counter-mapping approach in relation to the asylum regimes is formed by two simultaneous methodological and theoretical moves. One consists in a non-normative approach to the politics of asylum, challenging the normative ground and the territorial norm of the asylum system, that in fact determine the modes of migrants' spatial and temporal confinement, as well as of the multiple exclusionary partitions that are enacted by national authorities governing refugees and the UNHCR. Our goal consists in assessing the consequences of refugee politics by interrogating how we can disconnect claims to refuge and protection from the juridical institutions of asylum. This does not mean, however, engaging in a naive move which would consider the political history of the asylum system as something that we can get rid of, while still using the same vocabulary. Rather, we want to bring to the fore how certain migrant struggles and claims have, de facto, cracked and exploded the normative and exclusionary terrain of asylum, forcing us to rethink of it not in opposition to but, instead, together with migrants' practices of freedom (De Genova et al., 2018). As we illustrate later in the chapter, migrants' collective refusals against the spatial restrictions imposed by the Dublin Regulation and by the asylum system, as well as against the Relocation Program, unsettle the supposed opposition between practices of freedom on the one hand, and seeking refuge on the other. In this sense, as we will develop in the next section, challenging the normative grounds of asylum does not mean dismissing the juridical level through which refugee status or other forms of temporary protection are granted. Rather, our point is that the existing legal framework can neither accommodate nor match the forced mobility practices of the people who seek asylum in Europe today.

The second related counter-mapping move is a spatial gaze that brings to the fore the convoluted geographies of asylum, that is, the spaces of control and mobility opened up by the implementation of the asylum regime and by migrants' "spatial disobediences." Yet, unlike a "disobedient gaze" (Heller and Pezzani, 2014), this does not aim at appropriating states' technologies for twisting it against them or for proving evidence of human rights violations. On the contrary, it starts from the assumption that border regime struggles do not depend on a lack of knowledge; instead they are connected to the hyper-exposure of states' "warfare on migrants" (Garelli and Tazzioli, 2016a). Hence, a counter-mapping gaze undoes and rewrites migration visibility and it does so not through a sort of crescendo logic (more of visibility, more of knowledge, more of evidence) but by building new and different topologies of political and historical connections. In the specific case of asylum, this consists in undoing the Westphalian-geopolitical cartography that underpins both the academic and non-academic analysis of refugees' mobility and spatial claims. Instead of locating asylum seekers' presence in a given country or analysing how they impact on societies, we advocate for an analysis that takes into account the spaces of refuge and control, as well as the exclusionary channels of asylum that crisscross, or better to say "exceed," the geopolitical map (Mezzadra and Neilson, 2017; Walters, 2017).

THE TERRITORIAL NORM OF ASYLUM

What we call "the territorial norm" of asylum clearly emerged in its consequences on migrants' lives in 2011, with the outbreak of the war in Libya and with the political turmoil of the Arab Uprisings and the geopolitical destabilization of the entire Mediterranean region that followed (Cassarino and Tocci, 2012; Garelli and Tazzioli, 2013a). The arrival of 1 million Libyan war escapees in Tunisia in 2011 was a case in point: while about 600,000 of them were Libyan citizens, the remaining were third-country nationals who had been living in Libya for years as migrants. Once they crossed the Libyan-Tunisian border to escape the war, they were directed to Choucha camp by international organizations, that is, to a refugee camp located in the desert, along the road which connects Tunisia with Libya, ten kilometers away from the border of Ras-Jadir. The camp was opened in February 2011 explicitly to host people fleeing Libya. The asylum claims of most of these people ended up being rejected by the UNHCR. Thus, these people became "illegal" migrants on the Tunisian territory.

This migrant group was denied international protection because their asylum claim was examined on the basis of the country of origin criterion. That is, migrants' asylum request was processed by the UNHCR asking the question "why did you escape your country of birth?," instead of asking why they fled Libya, the country where they have been living for years. Three years later, in 2014, about 400 rejected refugees were still at Choucha camp, persisting in demanding that their asylum claims should be processed considering their forced mobility from Libya due to the war. "We all fled the war in Libya, so no distinction should be made among us. We are all refugees as we had been forced to escape the country where we were living and working."[4] Remaining at Choucha even after the official closure of the camp in June 2013, they subverted the territorial norm of asylum. They in fact replaced the country of origin criterion with the space of migration where they had been living until the war broke out and where their common experience of Libyan war refugees/escapees was produced. Up against the geographies of the asylum regime, they claimed a right to protection predicated on *migration geographies*, that is, on the spaces where they were residing, having moved there years ago and still being there at the time when the war broke out. More than a mere politics of actual presence (in the Tunisian space), they defined themselves as "refugees" on the basis of their histories, patterns and spaces of

---

[4]   Interview with rejected refugees at Choucha refugee camp, August 2014.

migration. Thus, the intertwining of *history* (of migration) and *cartography* (of present spaces of residence) is what determines the counter-geographies of asylum claimed and enacted by rejected refugees at Choucha camp. However, despite their protracted struggle at the camp, the UNHCR did not reopen their cases for consideration. In May 2017 a group of 34 rejected refugees were still living at Choucha camp, which they felt was the only safe place for them in Tunisia.[5]

UNDOING THE ANTINOMY BETWEEN ASYLUM AND FREEDOM

Lampedusa, December 17, 2015: a group of about 250 migrants who had arrived in Lampedusa, between November and early December 2015 and who refused to be finger-printed by the Italian police, organized a march in the streets of the island and a sit-in in front of the main church chanting "No fingerprints. We want freedom. We want to move out of the camp." While they initially resisted identification on an individual basis, over the span of a few weeks this silent individual dissent became a collective concerted refusal. They carried on their collective struggle against identification inside the Lampedusa hotspot until January 6, 2016, when they staged another public protest by remaining for two nights outside the main church on Lampedusa island. At the end of January they were transferred to Sicily in groups of ten, where they were fingerprinted by the use of force (Garelli and Tazzioli, 2016b). Most of them were Eritreans, hence people eligible for the Relocation Scheme, which was launched in the European Migration Agenda in May 2015 and had been conceived as the EU program for transferring "persons who are in need of international protection"[6] from Greece and Italy to other member states. Yet, by refusing to be identified they were at the same time refusing to apply for the Relocation Program. Refusals against the exclusionary channels of the Relocation multiplied in Greece as well. While there are no official statistics of migrants' refusals, our 2016 fieldwork in Greece, as well as non-governmental organizations' and activists' reports indicated that a relevant percentage of people eligible for the Relocation Program decided to move on in an autonomous way. The main reason for these individual and collective refusals were the slowness of the relocation procedures and, most importantly, the impossibility for migrants to choose the EU country of destination. These "outrageous" refusals, as the President of the EU Commission, Claude Juncker, called migrants' rejections, show that "migrants assert their freedom into the process of protection, initiating a discrepant politics of asylum that starts from their actual experiences, extant social relations, desires, aspirations, and political subjectivity" (De Genova et al., 2018, p. 5). In fact, migrants who refuse to apply for the Relocation scheme "enact their freedom to choose where to settle in Europe and thereby stage their refusal of the coercive refuge forcefully mandated by EU agencies" (De Genova et al., 2018, p. 18).

Thus, while migrants are usually depicted by states and non-state actors as deserving

---

[5]   On June 19, 2017, the camp was fully evicted, and the group of 34 rejected refugees was left with no space on the Tunisian territory and in a legal limbo.

[6]   https://ec.europa.eu/home-affairs/sites/homeaffairs/files/what-we-do/policies/european-agenda-migration/ background-information/docs/2_eu_solidarity_a_refugee_relocation_system_en.pdf (accessed October 23, 2018).

protection only insofar as they are considered in a condition of substantial unfreedom – about the place to live and where to move – through these "outrageous refusals" they staged practices of freedom and claims to asylum as non-oppositional terms. To put it differently, migrants' reiterated refusal of the spatial restrictions imposed by the Dublin Regulation and by the Relocation Program undermined the image of the worthy refugee as the subject who cannot but accept protection at any cost. Instead, these people staged the possibility to choose where to go to claim asylum as the non-negotiable condition for seeking asylum in Europe. In this way, they essentially troubled both the image of refugees' political subjectivity and the idea of a politics of free mobility. Their enacted refusals force us to rethink the critique of the border regime and political claims in a way that match with refugees' radical practices of freedom: refuge and possibility of choice cannot but be re-elaborated together. Thinking of mapping as an epistemological posture, this means finding ways to articulate refugees' politics by breaking the visual codes associated with the citizens' political scene and hence developing a counter-cartography of political claims.

MIGRANTS' EUROPE MAP

The second related counter-mapping move in relation to the asylum regime that we mentioned above consists in a cartographic experimentation that strives to account for the spaces of refuge and transit opened up by migrants' practices of movements (why "practices of movements" and not just movements?). While the external frontiers of Europe and internal national borders are extensively marked in our geographical imagination, the temporary spaces of transit and refuge that result from the clash between migrants' movements and border enforcement politics are missing in the geopolitical map of Europe. Our argument is that instead of locating on maps migrants and refugees or of representing their routes, we should gesture towards (advocate) a re-mapping of Europe bringing in the temporary spaces of migration, transit and refuge that have multiplied across the European space. Most of these spaces are informal encampments, built by migrants or by refugees' supporters groups, and that, however, have become also zones of control – such as in the case of Ventimiglia, the Italian city located at the Italian-French border, since France suspended the Schengen agreement in 2015.

Following the multiplication of official and informal encampments and the uneven temporality made of appearances, evictions and recursive re-emergences of these spaces of confinement, the impossibility of a fixed cartography of migrant encampments is blatantly revealed. Moreover, tracing a history of the turbulences of migration camps involves resisting claims to transparency and full visibility, dealing rather with what Ann Laura Stoler has called "symptomatic" spaces (Stoler, 2010, p. 7), that is, spaces that can be grasped only through minor traces left in the archives. In fact, many of the encampments that mushroomed across Europe as a result of border enforcement measures or as spaces of refuge opened up by migrants are not apprehensible through a mapping gaze that aims to unveil hidden places in the name of transparency or to make fully visible what is invisible. On the contrary, by bringing attention to the traces left by these encampments and to the irregular pace of their emergence and disappearance it becomes possible to draw what we call a *minor cartography of vanishing refugees' spaces*. Such a map would be a constitutively opaque and missing cartography, which confront us with the spatial and temporal traces of heterogeneous encampments.

However, by highlighting the fundamentally fleeting dimension of migrant spaces of refuge and confinement we should not conclude the impossibility of an archive of encampments nor the total disappearance of the memory and the existence of places that have been evicted or shut down. Spaces of refuge and transit often crystallize or remain alive in collective memory due to reiterated re-emergence of these spaces, upon eviction or, in the case of institutional camps, after being officially closed. Many of these places blur with the surrounding urban areas and cannot be approached through the lens of extraterritoriality. What we want to suggest is an ethnography of "infamous" vanishing spaces, which brings attention to temporary migration sites that become apprehensible only through "an encounter with power" and as something that is "beside what is usually estimated as worthy of being recounted" (Foucault, 1954, p. 1979).

Re-mapping Europe, as a space of migrant and refugees' temporary spaces, requires navigating through the interstices of the produced opacity of migrant encampments, for grasping the persistence of camps' traces, as spatial landmarks in migrants enacted geographies. Thus, it entails bringing into maps the dimension of temporality, accounting for and keeping alive the temporariness of these spaces. Yet, more than mapping official refugee camps or reception centers, the crafting of refugees' map of Europe involves research on unofficial spaces that have been produced as an effect of migration and border policies, as well as of migrants' practices of movement. Some of these spaces of transit have become places of containment or are places with European cities that have played the twofold role of spaces-refuge and are controlled by the police, and then have been evicted as dwelling places where migrants found a temporary place to stay. Others are self-managed places, like Refugee City Plaza Hotel in Athens, or square and public spaces that had been sites of migrant struggles for some time, such as Orianenplatz in Berlin. This map-archive is an ongoing collective project that we have put in place with a group of researchers and activists based in different European countries, with the goal of keeping a memory archive of refugees' spaces that had been evicted, or "disappeared." Simultaneously, this allows challenging governmental refugees maps that locate refugees in spaces, counting them and visualizing their juridical status.

CONCLUSION: ASYLUM BEYOND ITS NORMATIVE GROUND?

Mobilizing a counter-mapping gaze to the asylum regime involves, as we have illustrated above, engaging both in a cartographic experimentation – re-mapping Europe through the multiple, informal and temporary refugees' spaces – and an epistemological approach, which critiques the normative ground of asylum and tries to rethink the politics of asylum and practices of freedom together. Yet, pointing towards a non-normative approach to asylum does not mean dismissing the level of rights and the legal guarantees of inter- national protection. Rather, as we have shown above, rethinking the politics of asylum should start from actual migrants' spatial disobediences, which posit freedom of choice and movement and seeking refuge as two inseparable claims. In other words, we are not interested in a reconceptualization of the abstract or philosophical terms of asylum but in unsettling its normative assumptions through a material politics that matches with migrants' enacted claims to freedom and refuge – that is, those claims to space and presence that tend to be invisibilized in current discourses about migrant politics.

These tactics would certainly require further strategic engagement with the juridical horizon of rights. Instead of relying on the exclusionary existing legal framework of the asylum regime, we sketch a research agenda and a political practice that would explore new forms of rights, what Michel Foucault defined as "relational right," that is, those rights to be invented and that "permits all possible types of relations to exist and not be prevented" (Foucault, 1997, p. 159). Such a perspective entails refusing to assume the subject of rights and its institutions as the starting point of the analysis. It prompts us instead to begin the analysis from the practices of freedom and the fields of struggles through which rights are negotiated on the ground, strategically claimed and enacted. Indeed, rethinking the politics of asylum from within migrants' struggles for freedom of choice and movement is not merely a question of individual rights to be granted but of a relational right that would restructure the relationship among residents beyond the divide between citizens and non-citizens. Therefore, recalling Edward Said's argument, geography "can also be the art of resistance if there is a counter-map and a counter-strategy" (Said, 1995, p. 27). Similarly, we contend, the politics of asylum can be turned from an exclusionary normative setting into a contested political terrain, as a struggle for refuge through practices of freedom.

REFERENCES

Basaran, T. (2010), *Security, Law and Borders: At the Limits of Liberties.* Abingdon, Oxon: Routledge.

Casas-Cortes, M., S. Cobarrubias, and J. Pickles (2015), "Riding routes and itinerant borders: autonomy of migration and border externalization", *Antipode*, **47** (4), 894–914.

Cassarino, J.P. and N. Tocci (2012), "The European Union's Mediterranean policies after the Arab revolts: from crisis to a new order?" in Lorenzo Firoamonti (ed.), *Regions and Crises: New Challenges for Contemporary Regionalisms.* Basingstoke: Palgrave Macmillan, pp. 105–25.

De Genova, N. (2013), "'We are of the connections': migration, methodological nationalism, and 'militant research'", *Postcolonial Studies*, **16** (3), 250–58.

De Genova, N. (2016), "The crisis of the border regime: towards a Marxist theory of borders. International Socialism", *Post for International Socialism.* Available at http://isj.org.uk/the-crisis-of-the-european-border-regime-towards-a-marxist-theory-of-borde (accessed October 23, 2018).

De Genova, N., G. Garelli, and M. Tazzioli (2018), "The autonomy of migration within the crises", *South Atlantic Quarterly*, **117** (2), 239–65.

Elden, S. (2007), "Governmentality, calculation, territory", *Environment and Planning D: Society and Space*, **25** (3), 562–80.

Fanon, F. (2008), *Black Skin, White Masks.* New York: Grove Press.

Foucault, M. (1954), "Lives of infamous men", *Power*, **3**, 1954–84.

Foucault, M. (1997), "What is critique", in *The Politics of Truth.* Los Angeles, CA: Semiotexte.

Garelli, G. and M. Tazzioli (2013a), "Arab Springs making space: territoriality and moral geographies for asylum seekers in Italy", *Environment and Planning D: Society and Space*, **31** (6), 1004–21.

Garelli, G. and M. Tazzioli (2013b), "Migration discipline hijacked: distances and interruptions of a research militancy", *Postcolonial Studies*, **16** (3), 299–308.

Garelli, G. and M. Tazzioli (2016a), "Warfare on the logistics of migrant movements: EU and NATO military operations in the Mediterranean", *Open Democracy*, June 16, accessed April 20, 2018 at https://www.opendemocracy.net/mediterranean-journeys-in-hope/glenda-garelli-martina-tazzioli/warfare-on-logistics-of-migrant-movem.

Garelli, G. and M. Tazzioli (2016b), "The EU hotspot approach at Lampedusa", *Open Democracy*, February 26, accessed April 20, 2018 at https://www.opendemocracy.net/can-europe-make-it/glenda-garelli-martina-tazzioli/eu-hotspot-approach-at-lampedusa.

Garelli, G. and M. Tazzioli (2018), "The biopolitical warfare on migrants: EU Naval Force and NATO operations of migration government in the Mediterranean", *Critical Military Studies*, **4** (2), 181–200.

Gregory, D. (2010), Seeing Red: Baghdad and the event-ful city. *Political Geography*, **29**(5), 266–79.

Hannah, M.G. (2000), *Governmentality and the Mastery of Territory in Nineteenth-century America*, Vol. 32. Cambridge: Cambridge University Press.

Harley, J.B. (1989), "Deconstructing the map", *Cartographica: The International Journal for Geographic Information and Geovisualization*, **26** (2), 1–20.

Harley, J.B. (2009), "Maps, knowledge, and power", in *Geographic Thought: A Praxis Perspective*. Cambridge: Cambridge University Press, pp. 129–48.

Heller, C. and L. Pezzani (2014), "A sea that kills, a sea that witnesses: making the sea account for the deaths of migrants at the maritime frontier of the EU", in *Forensic Architecture. Forensis: The Architecture of Public Truth*. Berlin: Sternberg Press, pp. 210–40.

Kitchin, R., J. Gleeson, and M. Dodge (2013), "Unfolding mapping practices: a new epistemology for cartography", *Transactions of the Institute of British Geographers*, **38** (3), 480–96.

Latour, B., V. November, and E. Camacho-Hübner (2010), "Entering a risky territory: space in the age of digital navigation", *Environment and Planning D: Society and Space*, **28** (4), 581–99.

Legg, S. (2007), "Beyond the European province: Foucault and postcolonialism", in *Space, Knowledge and Power: Foucault and Geography*. London: Routledge, pp. 265–89.

Malkki, L.H. (1995), "Refugees and exile: from 'refugee studies' to the national order of things", *Annual Review of Anthropology*, **24** (1), 495–523.

Mezzadra, S. and B. Neilson (2013), *Border as Method, or, the Multiplication of Labor*. Durham, NC: Duke University Press.

Mezzadra, S. and B. Neilson (2017), "On the multiple frontiers of extraction: excavating contemporary capitalism", *Cultural Studies*, **31** (2–3), 185–204.

Parker, N. and N. Vaughan-Williams (2012), "Critical border studies: broadening and deepening the 'lines in the sand' agenda", *Geopolitics*, **17** (4), 727–33.

Pickles, J. (2004), *A History of Spaces: Cartographic Reason, Mapping, and the Geo-coded World*. New York: Psychology Press.

Pinelli, B. (2017), "Borders, politics and subjects. Introductory notes on refugee research in Europe", *Etnografia Ricerca Qualitativa*, **1**, 5–24.

Said, E. (1995), *The Politics of Dispossession: The Struggle for Palestinian Self-determination, 1969–1994*. New York: Vintage Books.

Scheel, S. (2013), "Studying embodied encounters: autonomy of migration beyond its romanticization", *Postcolonial Studies*, **16** (3), 279–88.

Scott, J.C. (1998), *Seeing Like a State: How Certain Schemes to Improve the Human Condition have Failed*. New Haven, CT: Yale University Press.

Scott, Joan W. (1991), "The evidence of experience", *Critical Inquiry*, **17** (4), 773–97.

Sparke, M. (1995), "Between demythologizing and deconstructing the map: Shawnadithit's New-Found-Land and the alienation of Canada", *Cartographica: The International Journal for Geographic Information and Geovisualization*, **32** (1), 1–21.

Stoler, A.L. (2010), *Carnal Knowledge and Imperial Power: Race and the Intimate in Colonial Rule*. Oakland, CA: University of California Press.

Tsianos, V. and S. Karakayali (2010), "Transnational migration and the emergence of the European border regime: an ethnographic analysis", *European Journal of Social Theory*, **13** (3), 373–87.

Walters, W. (2017), "Deportation infrastructure", Paper presented at the Migrant Digitalities workshop, Swansea University, June.

Weizman, E. (2014), *Forensis: The Architecture of Public Truth*. Berlin: Sternberg.

32. The sanctuary network: transnational church activism and refugee protection in Europe
Katharyne Mitchell and Key MacFarlane

INTRODUCTION

In 2015, as unparalleled numbers of migrants arrived in Europe, Pope Francis called upon Catholic parishes, convents, and monasteries to provide sanctuary (Withnall, 2015). It wasn't enough to say, 'Have courage, hang in there,' he added. What was needed were tangible bundles of services, practice, and support: what the Pope called 'concrete hope.' This chapter is concerned with how concrete hope is organized across space. In Europe today many activist church actors work across national borders to consider how they can best protect refugees through various forms of sanctuary practices.[1] They learn from each other and share ideas across institutions and spatial boundaries; they also learn from church actions and sanctuary conferences of previous eras. Many of these learning practices include the sharing of data, stories, and contacts, strategizing about the most effective practices of persuasion and partnership with policy makers and the public, and discussion of efficacious forms of civil disobedience when deemed necessary.

These learning practices and transnational collaborations for and with refugees form what we call a sanctuary network. By this we mean a loose affiliation of activist churches and related institutions working with refugees, who share concrete information and strategies that are believed to be useful in protecting at-risk migrants. These practices often begin with local events, such as a conference or the provision of sanctuary in a specific church, but are then scaled up through forms of representation and activism on a considerably larger terrain. This form of upscaling is made possible through long-standing transnational church connections – often made on the basis of specific denominational or personal ties, the institutionalized relationships of church actors with other transnational activist networks, the connections between church-based migrant rights organizations and policy makers in government and the media.

In this chapter we investigate the formation and management of the sanctuary network in Europe by focusing on several key institutions and players and some critical events. The constitution of these types of relationships and practices over decades as well as across national borders is important to study because it can show us how counter-hegemonic ideas move over time and space, as well as how they become institutionalized, embedded in the landscape, and activated at different moments in time. Much of the literature on how contemporary ideas and rationalities move across space examines the development and movement of elite or punitive ideas such as broken windows policing (Mitchell, 2010) or laissez-faire economics (Peck, 2010) rather than those that are disruptive to dominant

---

[1] Our definition of refugees includes those who consider themselves refugees, and not just those who are categorized this way by state actors.

factions and/or developed from below. And while there is now a growing geographical literature on transnational activist social movements, these tend to focus on the formation of specific social relationships (Pratt, 2002; Perreault, 2003; Nagar, 2006, 2014) or on a transnational struggle in a particular time period, such as the struggle against climate change (Chatterton et al., 2013), war (Gillian and Pickerill, 2008), or nuclear armament (Routledge, 2003; Castree et al., 2008). Examining the development, management, and upscaling of activist, church-based sanctuary networks over time as well as across space gives us a different view of how these types of counter-hegemonic relationships and practices can be institutionalized and (re)activated on a larger scale and over a longer timeline. It also gives us a sense of the difference it makes for refugee protection to have a long-standing set of institutionalized spaces, facilities, and actors involved that are connected to yet also autonomous from dominant, 'orthodox' systems of refugee management.

In the next section of the chapter we introduce some of the literature on how neoliberal rationalities travel and become implemented. We then turn briefly to geographical work on transnational activist movements, showing how resistant practices and relationships can also be formed across national borders. We conclude this section by noting how these two literatures are important for theorizing transnational relationships and flows, but are inadequate on their own for conceptualizing the operations of the sanctuary network. Following this we provide a short historical and contemporary study of sanctuary practices, showing how earlier institutions and actors from the sanctuary movement of the 1980s in the US became important influences on the contemporary movement in Europe, particularly Germany. We then discuss some of the key institutionalized transnational relationships between church networks involved in migrant and refugee protection and between church organizations and policy makers in the European Union (EU).[2] We conclude by emphasizing the ongoing importance of collective memory and alternative understandings of justice and resistance (heterodoxy) that are bound up in church spaces and meanings and which faith actors and secular allies draw on in their struggles (heteropraxis) on behalf of refugees. More than an archipelago of safety, sanctuary networks trace a radically different geography of circulation and citizenship – one grounded in concrete hopes, everyday needs, and solidarities across both space and time.

FAST POLICY TRANSFER AND TRANSNATIONAL SOCIAL MOVEMENTS

Policy Mobilities

How do ideas travel and become articulated in larger networks and systems? And what are some of the material implications for society when hegemonic concepts flow and become institutionalized and activated across regional or national borders? Many geographers became interested in these questions in the context of the rapid dissemination of neoliberal rationalities and practices of governance from the late 1970s through the 1990s (e.g., McCann, 2008; Peck, 2010; Peck and Theodore, 2015). Jamie Peck (2006) traced

---

[2]   This section of the chapter draws on four months of fieldwork conducted from September 2016 to December 2016 in the following cities: Berlin, Brussels, Geneva, Lesbos, Mytilene, and Vienna.

the movement of neoliberal urbanism from its emergence in New York City following the fiscal crisis of 1975 to post-Katrina New Orleans. He and others have also charted these flows on a larger scale, showing how neoliberal rationalities of governance migrated from the Chicago School to other parts of the globe, such as Pinochet's Chile (Perreault and Martin, 2005; Harvey, 2007; Peck, 2010). What's highlighted here is the role played by free-market think tanks, starting with the foundation of the Mont Pelerin Society in 1947 (Hayter and Barnes, 2012) as well as the fiscal discipline and regulation imposed by multilateral agencies such as the International Monetary Fund, World Trade Organization, and World Bank (Ferguson and Gupta, 2002; Sparke, 2013).

Over the past decade, much of the geographic research on the cross-border circulation of ideas has focused on what Eugene McCann (2008) calls 'policy mobilities.' Part of the emerging interdisciplinary field of 'critical policy studies,' the mobilities approach challenges traditional understandings of policy found in political science. In thinking about how ideas move across distances political scientists tend to focus more on the idea of transfer (transfer of policy from point A to point B via a narrow set of rational actors, mainly operating at the scale of the nation-state). Geographers are interested in how policies move, how they are mobile – and what happens when they are mobile: how they are transformed and mutated in the process of motion. The importance of theorizing space and scale is apparent here. How do policies actually circulate across space and how do they both transcend scale and produce scale in the process? For example, Peck and Theodore wrote in 2010 (p. 170): 'mobile policies rarely travel as complete "packages", they move in bits and pieces – as selective discourses, inchoate ideas, and synthesized models – and they therefore "arrive" not as replicas but as policies already-in-transformation.' These transformations do not occur in a vacuum but are shaped by their local milieus. Such a theory has been helpful in accounting for how neoliberal policymaking takes place unevenly across multiple sites, 'absorbing domestic as well as transnational influences along the way' (Peck, 2011, p. 785).

In their recent work, Peck and Theodore (2015, p. 212) discuss mobility in terms of what they call 'fast policy.' While fast policies radiate across borders they 'are not free floating or self-propelling technologies that move through frictionless space before touching down. They are the objects of active advocacy and persuasion.' Peck and Theodore follow two such policies in particular: conditional cash transfers (CCTs) and participatory budgeting (PB). Originally developed in Latin America, CCTs and PB have since been touted by international agencies like the World Bank and United Nations, and propagated across a wide array of geographic contexts, yielding many different, sometimes unpredictable, results. What Peck and Theodore's case studies emphasize are the 'sticky' everyday realities of putting global policies to work. Never smooth, the movement of ideas across transnational space is shaped by its specific social and spatial contours.

This brings in the importance of actors: Who advocates and persuades? Who attempts to mold policies to their liking? Who is involved in this global policy chain and what are they doing to direct and push and alter and select and synthesize aspects of policies – so that they actually become something different in the process of movement? In Peck and Theodore's study, CCTs and PB were propagated and 'mutated' by a wide range of actors, from local and national government agencies to social movements and entrepreneurs. This process is not simply top-down. Larner and Laurie (2010) have written about the necessity to study the so-called 'middling technocrats' – those who are not necessarily 'elites' yet remain key in the calculations and technologies and the overall functioning of policy movements. Ananya Roy's interest has also been on the actors involved – but she's especially interested in the actors' situated practices through which policy is made globally mobile. For Roy (2012) this type of study requires a kind of global ethnography – a study of ethnographic circulations.

For most of these scholars, what is interesting and important to study are those who are making policy – and what happens in the various encounters between policy actors and policy-related movements and what policy does in the world. In some cases, normative policy models can, when taken up in different contexts, become repurposed to more radical ends. Peck and Theodore (2015, pp. xx–xxi) show how this occurred with CCTs. Once hailed by Washington Consensus agencies, CCT programs make welfare for the poor conditional on the monitored behavior of its recipients, addressing poverty through neoliberal means by encouraging individuals to build 'human capital.' In their dispersion, however, CCTs have become folded into 'neo-welfarist' policies and experiments with basic income, and in some instances have 'even threatened to evolve into the kind of no-strings-attached, unconditional cash transfers to the poor that are anathema to neoliberal policymakers' (Peck and Theodore, 2015, p. xxi).

It's important to study the mutations of normative policies as they are taken up by new actors. But equally important, we believe, are those who are producing counter-policies or what we might call alternative mobilities. These are actors who may use similar circuits and strategies to promote their own policies or to resist or alter hegemonic ideas (such as the ideas of the nation-state around appropriate migration and/or refugee management). In many cases these alternative policy circuits resist normative solutions or forms of consensus that do not address problems at their core.

Transnational Social Movements

Alternative mobilities are examined in the large body of scholarship on transnational social movements, which looks at how strategies, policies, and conceptions of resistance travel and transform across different sites. This literature is too vast to cover here so we will focus only on a few specific geographic contributions. What geographers bring to the discussion is an attention to what David Featherstone (2003) calls the 'spatialities of transnational resistance,' or the way in which the trajectories of oppositional movements are bound up with spatially constituted power relations.

We see two general tendencies in how geographers have addressed this issue. First, there are studies that map routes of resistance onto specific social linkages, which are often defined in terms of alliance (Pratt and Yeoh, 2003; Merrill, 2006) or relationality (see Nicholls, 2009). For example, in her work with the Philippine Women Centre in Vancouver, Geraldine Pratt (2002) outlines alliances or 'new bases for collaboration' between Filipina domestic laborers and white, 'middle-class' Canadian women. Engaging a similar feminist praxis in her books, Richa Nagar (2006, 2014) examines transnational alliances between non-governmental organization (NGO) activists in India and academics living elsewhere. Another example is Thomas Perreault's 2003 analysis of the multi-scalar networks that connect indigenous activists in the Ecuadorian Amazon with NGOs, ethnic rights organizations, development agencies, foreign researchers, and other actors. These studies remain primarily focused on the configuration of existing social groups, and emphasize alliances largely in terms of identity politics that are operative in a specific context.

The second tendency among geographers looking at transnational social movements has been to focus on a particular time period. Rather than highlighting a social relationship, this research emphasizes historical conjuncture. Chatterton et al. (2013), for instance, explore how the mobilizations that opposed the 2009 Copenhagen Climate Talks were the 'culmination of diverse forms of translocal organizing.' The emergence of climate change politics, they argue, 'generates solidarities between differently located struggles' (see also Anderson, 2004; Routledge, 2011). Gillian and Pickerill (2008) show how another event – the occupations in Afghanistan and Iraq – spurred international networks of anti-war activists across Australia, the US, and the UK. Others have looked at anti-nuclear mobilization during the Cold War, such as the European Nuclear Disarmament (END) movement which linked up activists in the Eastern bloc with those in Western and Northern Europe (Routledge, 2003; Castree et al., 2008).

The literatures on transnational social movements and on policy mobilities are useful in mapping out sanctuary practices today. Each provides different ways of thinking about the movement of ideas and the formation of transnational networks, whether those are neoliberal webs of governance or alternative forms of resistance. But they are ultimately insufficient for a holistic understanding of sanctuary networks because they do not fully account for what Allan Pred (1984, p. 284) referred to as the 'sedimentation' of cultural and social practices in the landscape, layered over time. Rather than imagining 'new' cross-border networks, we might look to the ones already at our feet, so to speak – buried under the dizzying flows of neoliberal globalization.

Church-based sanctuary networks contain an inherently embedded quality in terms of the ways that church buildings themselves are fixed in the context of an historical landscape of memory and ongoing social relationships. Even when policy mobilities are viewed as 'embedded' in the landscape, as they are for Peck (2011, p. 785), the analyses tend to gloss the historical nature of this embeddedness – the ways that policies are bound up with much older and often 'invisible' geographies of emotion and struggle. Similarly, the scholarship on social movements tends to downplay the historicity of resistance when it focuses on *present* alliances between social groups, often framing these groups ahistorically vis-à-vis identities that are fixed and/or taken for granted. On the other hand, when attention is directed to historical events like climate change or war, the temporal scope of activism can be limited. Sanctuary networks place resistance in a longer *durée*. They call upon a 'presence' that is not circumscribed by current mobilities, social relationships, or discrete events, but rather is layered in the landscape itself – in the very structure of the churches that provide refuge. Churches have both a solid physical base as well as a symbolic and spiritual set of meanings that grounds and gives concrete hope to the faith-based actors and their allies and networks that emerge from them (Snyder, 2012; Rabben, 2016).

THE SANCTUARY NETWORK

Churches in Europe were usually constructed on sites where it was believed that a miracle or other spiritually important event had occurred. As a result, the actual physical location where the church was built was considered to be on sanctified ground and thus holy. Additionally, because of the centrality of the altar in Christian religious traditions the area around the altar, called the *sanctuary*, is also considered especially sacred. These cultural and religious traditions that combine spatial location with a sense of the sacred qualities of Christianity permeate churches and create a bundle of collective memories that faith-based actors draw on and which often sustains them in their activist work on behalf of refugees (Raiser, 2010; Just, 2013; Mitchell, 2017).

In Europe, assumptions about the spiritual and sacred nature of church space opened up the possibility of protection and refuge from outside or 'profane' forces, including the law. Beginning around 600 AD, the practice arose whereby people accused of certain kinds of crimes could be offered sanctuary in a church and thus protected from arrest (Shoemaker, 2011). This concept of church asylum gained in momentum throughout the medieval period and was recognized in English law up until the seventeenth century. Even after Enlightenment rationalities of the importance of the rule of law and systems of good governance began to override these types of practices, there remained factions that held onto sanctuary ideals. Indeed, some nineteenth-century reformers hailed this way of thinking as one in which escape from 'justice' through the provision of church sanctuary could be conceptualized as an alternate or heterodox form of justice, noting that innocent people were often caught up in blood feuds or falsely accused during the Middle Ages (Shoemaker, 2011).

Today, even though church sanctuary was illegalized over three centuries ago and remains illegal in every country in Europe, there is still a strong contingent of both faith actors *and* secular reformers for whom the practices of church sanctuary make sense in certain situations, and for whom the collective memory and traditions of alternative justice hold sway (Marfleet, 2011). In concert with the Christian tradition of welcoming the stranger (e.g., Matthew 25: 31–40), these practices are often conceptualized as particularly relevant and justifiable when used for refugee protection. Against state-based acts of citizenship and legal safeguarding, they form a kind of heteropraxis.

The Central American Sanctuary Movement in the US

The European sanctuary movement of the contemporary moment has roots in the medieval period but also harkens back to the 1980s sanctuary movement in the US. This period of church asylum began in the context of protection offered to asylum seekers from Central America who were denied refugee status owing to the Cold War politics of the era. Churches in many cities around the US began to network together to shield and protect people fleeing from the growing violence in Guatemala, El Salvador, and other Central American countries. These kinds of activities took place between faith actors and other activists and non-profit organizations from cities in the southwest such as Tucson, spreading as far as the San Francisco Bay Area, Chicago, and Los Angeles (Crittenden, 1988; Coutin, 1993; Cunningham, 1995; Chinchilla et al., 2009; Carney et al., 2017).

These alliances were formed and sustained during the period that Central American refugees were seen to be in grave danger and, because of its geopolitical role in instigating the conflicts, the US was perceived as responsible for their plight. In this sense, the sanctuary practices of the time were strongly affiliated with a sense of alternative justice (alternative to hegemonic understandings of the rule of law and national sovereignty) drawing from the customs and cultural traditions of old English law. They were, or became, political acts as faith actors became more knowledgeable of the political circumstances surrounding the refugees' situations and as the church networks grew to encompass a broader set of allies (Coutin, 1993; Chinchilla et al., 2009). Smith (1996, p. 69) writes of this period: 'Sanctuary began as a movement of hospitality that aimed to provide for the humanitarian needs of vulnerable refugees. But Sanctuary quickly became more than that. It grew into a political movement that sought to end the human oppression generated by the U.S.-sponsored war in Central America.'

Key early organizers of this hybrid religious *cum* political movement were John Fife, a Presbyterian minister, and Jim Corbett, a Quaker. The movement became nationally and then globally known when Fife and Corbett declared the Southside Presbyterian Church, in Tucson, a sanctuary for refugees in March 1982. Through a deliberate strategy of activating their church affiliations and networks across the country, and as a result of increasingly strong and highly publicized retaliatory measures by the Immigration and Naturalization Service (INS), Corbett and Fife were able to expand the sanctuary movement rapidly, so that within a year, there were 45 sanctuary churches and synagogues involved, with an additional 600 groups providing added support. By mid-1984, the number of churches offering sanctuary had grown to 150 and there were endorsements from 18 national religious denominations and commissions. By 1987 this number had grown to 'over 420 Sanctuary groups, including 305 churches, 41 synagogues, 25 ecumenical religious groups, 24 cities, 15 universities, and 13 other secular groups' (Chinchilla et al., 2009, p. 107; see also Smith, 1996, p. 185). In addition to direct concrete aid to the refugees themselves, most movement coordinators were also deeply invested in raising awareness of the larger geopolitical context in which these events were occurring. Both the media-savvy relations and the sense of consciousness-raising responsibility of the US sanctuary movement became prominent features of European sanctuary networks in their work on behalf of refugees in the following years.

BAG *Asyl in der Kirche* and the New Sanctuary Movement in Berlin

Pastor Jurgen Quantz initiated the sanctuary movement in Berlin in the Heilig-Kreuz-Kirche (Holy Cross Church) in 1983. The church is located in Kreuzberg, a neighborhood that is home to many immigrants and which was one of the poorest boroughs of West Berlin in the late 1970s and 1980s. (It is now undergoing a rapid process of gentrification, but immigrants still make up a large percentage of the neighborhood's residents.) This was the beginning of the church network that later became known as the German Ecumenical Committee on Church Asylum (GECCA) (*BAG Asyl in der Kirche*).[3] Sanctuary practices in the church began as a result of Quantz's frequent contact with politically active young people in the district. He had heard about plans to deport Palestinians to Lebanon and then soon after that a group of young people came directly to him for help. The following description is from an author's interview with Quantz at the Heilig-Kreuz church on November 6, 2016:[4]

---

[3]   GECCA maintains a detailed and up-to-date website, available at: http://www.kirchenasyl.de/herzlich-willkommen/welcome/ (last accessed October 5, 2018).

[4]   The interview followed a religious ceremony in the church, which itself occurred at the tail end of a 2016 church conference on migration and sanctuary practices. These quotes are paraphrased from detailed notes that were taken at the time of the interview.

They asked us what can we do? I was a priest here since 1980. They asked, Can't you help us? I said, Yes, what should we do? They said, You have an old right – asylum in the church. It is from the medieval period. In the Bible you can find stories – come into the sanctuary. This is your tradition, you should do it. I initially said No. I said, Here we have modern laws and rights. But they said, We think you should. I said Okay, I'll discuss it with my members of council. I lived with my family here – one night they knocked. I opened the door and the young people came and said it had to happen now. So I let them in. They brought two families – then a third family into the Parish house. We were not prepared. There were 10 adults and 18 children! Then I asked the council and they said, Yes, and it led to a big public discussion. There was a huge media around it – a big event. We took them because we asked for a decision of the political senate – which lasted three to four months. Then they decided that this group could have permission (to stay). That was the beginning – then ten years later we started in 1994 with more again. Then we worked with young politicians from Kreuz and other congregations followed our lead – working groups came together and we discussed and formed a network of church leaders and politicians.

Some of the key church leaders of the 1980s sanctuary movement, such as the Presbyterian pastor John Fife, were important early role models, and also became directly involved in the European sanctuary movement. When one of the authors asked Pastor Quantz about this influence he spoke about the importance of the relationship and also its ongoing nature:

We knew about the sanctuary movement in the US. We knew John Fife. We are still Skyping with him. We have made a paper there – and they gave it to their senate and we gave it to our senate. We are discussing with him how to bring this public . . . We have connections now – We still work together. We had him come stay in our house to work together.

This involvement was informal, through ongoing relationships between ministers and pastors, but it also became more formalized in the early 2000s, as Fife was invited to be the inaugural speaker at the New Sanctuary Movement conference in Berlin in 2010. At that conference he was asked to talk about his experiences and his church's practices in the US sanctuary movement. In his Berlin speech Fife drew on a sense of alternative justice or allegiance to a 'higher' law (that of God), but also attributed his willingness to operate outside the parameters of the US legal system to the precedent set by the nineteenth-century abolition movement. When he gave his speech he invoked the model of the underground railroad (the Quakers were key actors in the underground railroad network) as a particular source of inspiration and justification for his church's sanctuary practices on behalf of refugees (cf. Chinchilla et al., 2009; Rabben, 2016). Moreover, after the Border Patrol ordered his church to stop giving sanctuary to Central American refugees in 1981 (with the additional threat that everyone involved in these practices would be indicted), he told the people in Berlin that his group made the decision to defy the police and continue to protect the refugees. He indicated that they made this political decision to contravene a national law based on their (alternative) faith-based understandings of what constitutes a moral act. He put it thus:

We can take our stand with the oppressed or we can take our stand with organized oppression. We can serve the Kingdom, or we can serve the kingdoms of this world – but we cannot do both. Maybe, as the gospel suggests, this choice is perennial and basic, but the presence of undocumented refugees here among us makes the definitive nature of our choice particularly clear and concrete. When the government itself sponsors the crucifixion of entire peoples and then makes it a felony to shelter those seeking refuge, a law-abiding protest merely trains us to live with atrocity. (Fife, 2011, pp. 7–8)

This direct invocation to draw inspiration from a 'higher' law in order to challenge national laws was reflected in the Charta of the New Sanctuary Movement, a document that was created following the 2010 Berlin conference. The two key church networks that helped to organize and coordinate the conference – GECCA and the Churches' Commission for Migrants in Europe (CCME) – created and affirmed the activist language of the Charta in the Annex to the conference documentation. They wrote:

> Because we want to welcome strangers we have agreed this Charta of the NSM in Europe . . . As Christians, we are unwilling to put up with this way of dealing with people in need. We stand together with them. They are made in God's image, as we are . . . Therefore we pledge: to use every opportunity to help refugees in need, where deportation looms and human dignity and lives are threatened, to grant refugees sanctuary in our churches until an acceptable solution is found for them. Not to shrink back, should open confrontation with civil authorities become necessary . . . All of Europe must become a safe haven, a 'sanctuary' for migrant men and women. To this we commit ourselves – in the conviction that God loves the strangers and that in them we encounter God herself/himself. (Annex, 2011, pp. 53–4)

Other key figures in the German network included Wolf Dieter Just and Claus Dieter Schulze. In separate interviews, both talked about the importance of church networking practices over time and space in keeping the sanctuary movement going. Schulze said in relation to a recent sanctuary case (a church asylum request in 2014 from a Somalian man), 'It was personal connections and experience from the 70s and 80s – the friendship network – that made it work' (Author's interview, November 5, 2016). Just also spoke of organized networking that he engaged in on a transnational basis. He mentioned starting a church asylum network of congregations in Berlin when they were supported with a left-leaning bishop and church leadership, and then living all over the world in ensuing years (Nairobi, Pittsburgh, the Netherlands). The combination of organizational experience and transnational living enabled him to write a book on church asylum in 1993 and organize a 1994 meeting on church asylum in Germany, with initiatives in Switzerland and the Netherlands. After writing letters to the Landeskirchen (Protestant national churches) and the Catholic Diocese, the ecumenical association for church asylum (GECCA) was officially formed, and began to have real 'political significance.' As with the US sanctuary movement, the group worked closely with the media to publish cases and make the plight of refugees and the practices of church asylum known to a broader public (Author's interview, November 6, 2016).

Just also had a powerful and ongoing relationship with John Fife. He said in an interview, 'We were impressed with the sanctuary movement in America.' He and several students from GECCA went to Tucson in 2008, and then again in 2010, where they lived in tents in the desert. Similarly, John Fife came to Berlin in 2010 to the New Sanctuary Movement conference, and visited Hamburg and the Ruhr area. 'We agreed to study our own pages – what is going on and happening. No more deaths.' When he was asked what he had learned from Fife and the US Sanctuary Movement, Just said:

> How practical they were! They had such a practical approach. Dropping water in the desert. Giving medical help. Even helping people to get into the country. This we don't do! It is a kind of 'ecumenical trafficking.' (He laughs). The geography is different – but churches here are an important lobby for the refugees.

When I asked him about the importance of his faith in guiding his sanctuary practices, he responded by referring to the Bible, specifically Matthew 25, to 'make clear that this is what churches have to do – actions founded in our faith' (Author's interview, November 6, 2016).

In this section we have noted some of the ways that faith plays a role in the sustainability of sanctuary practices and how the strong and abiding connections between faith actors and faith-based networks gives them the willingness and the courage to openly contest laws and policies that they believe are not moral. Their rationale for doing so often rests on basic assumptions about human dignity as well as a belief in a 'higher' law (God's law) that underpins their resistance and also gives it some degree of political power and legitimacy vis-à-vis the normative laws and policies of the state. It also rests on their trust and faith in each other and in the place-based solidarities (*Bünde*) that have been formed through struggle and sacrifice over time. This has not been a linear trajectory. In citing the past, from medieval asylum law to twentieth-century refugee movements, sanctuary networks reactivate traditions of insurgent citizenship buried in the strata 'beneath' today's neoliberal grids and orthodox assumptions of state sovereignty (cf. Tomba, 2017). This is not a matter of returning to the past but of bringing it into the present in ways that create heterodox spaces of resistance – spaces that expand.

Contemporary Sanctuary Practices in Europe

The 2010 New Sanctuary Movement in Berlin was a tangible transnational convocation of church networks and secular allies, which has expanded even further over the past eight years. There are now active sanctuary alliances in several cities and countries in Europe, including Germany, Belgium, Norway, Switzerland, France, the UK, and the Netherlands (Lippert and Rehaag, 2013). During the years 2015–16, when there was a rapid increase in migration to Europe as a result of wars in Syria and Iraq and other factors, these networks amplified their work together on behalf of refugees. Contemporary sanctuary practices in Europe range from hospitality, advocacy, and material assistance for asylum seekers to the provision of physical refuge for those at risk of detention or deportation. This risk is often incurred in the EU on the basis of those whose claims for asylum status have been denied owing to recent Dublin Regulations, which require asylum claimants to register and be processed for asylum in the first EU country in which they set foot (most often Greece, Italy, and Hungary). Asylum claimants in Germany and other Northern European countries now are often threatened with deportation to Hungary or Greece as the first country of arrival, despite the desperately bad conditions of many refugee camps in those countries.

In terms of advocacy and assistance, data compiled by scholars working for CCME indicates that the provision of assistance for migrants remains a core component of the work of European churches. Nearly half of church respondents to a recent survey wrote that they have someone working in the church administration who is responsible for migrant advocacy, and 65.7 percent of churches 'engage in advocacy work in partnership with other churches or their related agencies.' Moreover, the provision of 'practical and material assistance to migrants, refugees and asylum seekers is engaged in by approximately two out of every five churches at [the] national level' (Jackson and Passarelli, 2016, p. 102).

In terms of sanctuary practices where physical refuge is provided, GECCA documented 323 ongoing cases of church asylum for 547 persons in January 2017 (of whom 145 were children).[5] According to Dietlind Jochims, the head of GECCA and also the Church Minister for Refugees in Germany at the time, who spoke at a recent Berlin conference in the Heilig-Kreuz church in November 2016, the number of church asylum requests has grown rapidly in the last couple of years, and in late 2016 was ten times higher than in 2014.[6] While these numbers are relatively small, the provision of physical sanctuary in a church remains symbolically important in Europe. In one example of the type of refugee story that became big news in recent years, a violent removal from church asylum in Münster, Germany, in August 2016, made international headlines. This involved a Ghanaian asylum claimant who was forcibly taken from a monastery to be deported to Hungary under the Dublin regulations (DW, 2016). These types of stories are picked up and amplified by church networks such as GECCA, which work directly with journalists to make sure these events are covered. Church leaders and administrative assistants also make sure that there is constant media attention and communication with churches in the country and across Europe so that all are aware of sanctuary-related occurrences in any given week (Author's interview with administrative leader of GECCA, November 2016; see also Neufert, 2014).

These types of events spur discussions about EU policy within and between churches and church networks, including the EU designation of certain countries or regions as 'safe' spaces to which asylum claimants can be legally returned under international law. In the Berlin conference of 2016, the congregants spoke passionately about what constitutes real safety for migrants after learning that parts of Afghanistan were designated as safe spaces by EU officials in that year. The networked spaces of church asylum thus both have the capacity to physically protect individuals and families and also to serve as catalysts for wider discussions around what constitutes migrant safety in the context of geopolitically expedient policy decisions (cf. Mitchell and Sparke, 2018).

Up until 2016 the churches in Germany had a special relationship with the Federal Ministry of Migration and Refugees (BAMF), such that they generally agreed on what cases or individuals could and should be taken into church asylum. The churches provided refuge and basic support for asylum claimants for up to six months, a time in which immediate deportation under Dublin could not take place, and the asylum claimants were guaranteed another hearing in Germany. Through early summer 2016, they had a high success rate at these hearings of over 70 percent. However, according to Jochims, because of changes in leadership, the increased numbers of church asylum requests and cases, and the increased international attention, the ministry started cracking down on sanctuary practices involving this church-state relationship and the success rate at these hearings for asylum claimants declined dramatically.[7] Currently, Jochims indicated, more and more people are requesting church asylum, the number of cases accepted has decreased, and the procedure is now much stricter.

The organizing theme of the 2016 Berlin conference was Beyond Europe: Schützen wir

---

[5] See GECCA, available at: http://www.kirchenasyl.de/herzlich-willkommen/welcome/ (last accessed October 5, 2018).

[6] This information is drawn from participant observation at the Berlin conference in November 2016.

[7] Ibid.

Grenzen oder Menschenrechte? (Do we protect borders or human rights?). The title of the conference – '*Beyond* Europe' – itself represented a direct challenge to the EU and member-state norms of territory and sovereign rights to determine migration management. The title also utilized the languages of both German and English, indicating a direct effort to reach beyond the local context to attract international allies. The speakers at the workshop were likewise composed of a transnational, politically and linguistically mixed group, including politicians from the German government ministry involved with migration and refugee management (BAMF), secular activist groups such as Pro Asyl and Amnesty International, and liberal NGOs such as Sea-Watch, alongside church networks and other faith-based organizations.

Many of these faith-related networks working with and on behalf of refugees attempt to influence migration policy by writing policy briefs, press releases, reports, and papers and meeting with EU officials as often as possible. Doris Peschke, the head of CCME, said in an interview that her organization meets frequently with politicians and bureaucrats in the EU, and that lobbying for the rights of migrants was an important component of their organization's work. She also noted that the church network's influence had declined since the summer of 2015 as migration into Europe increased and politicians were becoming concerned about the rise of far-right political groups (Author's interview, November 23, 2016).

In addition to constant lobbying of EU bureaucrats, ministers, politicians, and policy makers at the local scale, both CCME and GECCA work closely with academics as well. The academic report, *Mapping Migration, Mapping Churches' Responses in Europe*, for example, provides contemporary demographic data on migration, along with specific information about church responses to migration. This report is just one of hundreds of academic papers, reports, policy briefs, and books that are churned out in both paper form and as resources available on the internet. Often these are produced by university-affiliated faculty and lecturers who are members of churches or other faith-based alliances themselves, and either do this work gratis or for a nominal amount. These types of documents and alliances manifest the importance of this polyglot network of actors, who are often held together by their faith, a strong belief in what they're doing, and in the possibilities of making a difference through their actions. Such networks recall the medieval German concept of *Bünde*, which was used half a millennium ago by the radical preacher Thomas Müntzer to describe a solidarity among the oppressed, replete with theological notions of sacredness and redemption (Koselleck, 2004).

CONCLUSION

> Sanctuary is a fundamentally collaborative practice, one that has the capacity to produce connections between individuals and institutions committed to the same values . . . The key point here is that, when combined with the fierce and durable commitment to the support of refugees and the undocumented, these ad-hoc, cross-border, multiply-scaled sanctuary networks produce a flexible and highly successful strategy of resistance that expands and contracts as needed. (Carney et al., 2017)

In this chapter we examined how ideas and policies travel across space and time. We addressed some of the previous literature in this area, looking at the movement of recent neoliberal technologies of governance, as well as some of the contemporary studies of transnational social movements. Our particular interest was in the question of how resistance to normative systems and programs of governance in migration can be transnationally engaged and sustained in the memories of past events and in the layering of those events in particular spaces. To answer some of these questions we took an empirical look at church-based forms of resistance to normative systems of refugee management in Europe – with a specific focus on sanctuary practices that protect and give refuge to those at risk of deportation and detention. We investigated the role of sanctuary networks, including faith-based practices situated in specific churches and church-based alliances or *Bünde*.

In the empirical study we found that many of the relationships and connections that were formed through sanctuary conferences in specific churches and neighborhoods influenced the creation of broader forms of solidarity. They also affected policy decisions with government actors and the EU, and connections that live on in mission statements, websites, reports, chartas, and people. For example, the transnational connections between the US and Europe and between countries in Europe were galvanized by the specific relationships between faith-based actors such as John Fife, Wolf Dieter Just, Jurgen Quantz, Doris Peschke, and Dietrich Jochims, who have traveled widely and who work to actively promote sanctuary practices within church-based networks and beyond. Such solidarities take place not only across space – but also across time. Critical for these sanctuary networks are the temporal connections between the past and present – from the medieval understandings of alternative justice to the underground railroad to the sanctuary movements of the 1980s, early 2000s, and the contemporary period. Such histories of struggle are bundled together and made concrete within the spaces of the church itself, where they become the sparks that are brought to bear on the present moment, permeating networks with heteropraxis, the electricity of hope.

The sanctuary movement continues to grow and change; it is reactivated and takes new forms in different contexts, yet many of the earlier ideas and practices remain critical for its ongoing growth and sustainability. We have demonstrated how this elastic capacity for renewal draws on the memory of successful social movements on behalf of refugees in the past and in other places, reflecting something unique owing to collective memories of alternative justice and shared practices vis-à-vis efficacious methods of consultation, confrontation, and resistance. A key geographical point here is how this memory becomes layered in the landscape – in the churches themselves and in the ways that faith-based actors and the relationships and networks they create have an ongoing physical and spiritual presence that gives them the faith, hope, and support they need to continue their work.

REFERENCES

Anderson, J. (2004), 'The Ties that Bind? Self- and Place-identity in Environmental Direct Action', *Ethics, Place and Environment*, **7** (1–2), 45–57.

Annex (2011), 'Charta of the New Sanctuary Movement in Europe', *New Sanctuary Movement in Europe: Healing and Sanctifying Movement in the Churches.* October, 7–10. CCME and Asyl in der Kirche, Berlin. Ed. German Ecumenical Committee on Church Asylum, February, Berlin.

Carney, M., R. Gomez, K. Mitchell, and S. Vannini (2017), 'Sanctuary Planet: A Global Sanctuary Movement for the Time of Trump', *Society & Space Online*. Available at: http://societyandspace.org/2017/05/16/sanctuary-planet-a-global-sanctuary-movement-for-the-time-of-trump/.

Castree, N., D. Featherstone, and A. Herod (2008), 'Contrapuntal Geographies: The Politics of Organizing Across Sociospatial Difference'. In K. Cox, M. Low, and J. Robinson (eds), *The SAGE Handbook of Political Geography* (pp. 305–22), Los Angeles, CA: SAGE.

Chatterton, P., D. Featherstone, and P. Routledge (2013), 'Articulating Climate Justice in Copenhagen: Antagonism, the Commons, and Solidarity', *Antipode*, **45** (3), 602–20.

Chinchilla, N., N. Hamilton, and J. Loucky (2009), 'The Sanctuary Movement and Central American Activism in Los Angeles', *Latin American Perspectives*, **169** (6), 101–26.

Coutin, S. (1993), *The Culture of Protest: Religious Activism and the US Sanctuary Movement*, Boulder, CO: Westview Press.

Crittenden, A. (1988), *Sanctuary: A Story of American Conscience and the Law in Collision*, New York: Grove Press.

Cunningham, H. (1995), *God and Caesar at the Rio Grande: Sanctuary and the Politics of Religion*, Minneapolis, MN: University of Minnesota Press.

DW (Deutsche Welle) (2016), 'Police Force Migrant Out of German Church', August 24. Available at: http://www.dw.com/en/police-force-migrant-out-of-german-church/a-19496599 (last accessed October 6, 2018).

Featherstone, D. (2003), 'Spatialities of Transnational Resistance to Globalization: The Maps of Grievance of the Inter-Continental Caravan', *Transactions of the Institute of British Geographers*, **28** (4), 404–21.

Ferguson, J. and A. Gupta (2002), 'Spatializing States: Towards an Ethnography of Neoliberal Governmentality', *American Ethnologist*, **29** (4), 981–1002.

Fife, J. (2011), 'Experiences of the Sanctuary Movement in the USA', *New Sanctuary Movement in Europe: Healing and Sanctifying Movement in the Churches*. October, 7–10. CCME and Asyl in der Kirche, Berlin. Ed. German Ecumenical Committee on Church Asylum, February, Berlin.

Gillian, K. and J. Pickerill (2008), 'Transnational Anti-war Activism: Solidarity, Diversity and the Internet in Australia, Britain and the United States after 9/11', *Australian Journal of Political Science*, **43** (1), 59–78.

Harvey, D. (2007), 'Neoliberalism as Creative Destruction', *American Academy of Political and Social Science*, **610**, 22–44.

Hayter, R. and T. Barnes (2012), 'Neoliberalization and its Geographic Limits: Comparative Reflections from Forest Peripheries in the Global North', *Economic Geography*, **88** (2), 197–221.

Jackson, D. and A. Passarelli (2016), *Mapping Migration, Mapping Churches' Responses in Europe: Belonging, Community and Integration: The Witness and Service of Churches in Europe*, CCME (Churches' Commission for Migrants in Europe) and Oikoumene: World Council of Churches Publications.

Just, W.D. (2013), 'The Rise and Features of Church Asylum in Germany: "I Will Take Refuge in the Shadow of Thy Wings Until the Storms are Past"'. In R. Lippert and S. Rehaag (eds), *Sanctuary Practices in International Perspectives: Migration, Citizenship and Social Movements* (pp. 135–47), New York: Routledge.

Koselleck, R. (2004), '*Begriffsgeschichte* and Social History'. In *Futures Past: On the Semantics of Historical Time* (pp. 75–92), New York: Columbia University Press.

Larner, W. and N. Laurie (2010), 'Travelling Technocrats, Embodied Knowledges: Globalising Privatisation in Telecoms and Water', *Geoforum*, **41** (2), 218–26.

Lippert, R. and S. Rehaag (eds) (2013), *Sanctuary Practices in International Perspectives: Migration, Citizenship and Social Movements*, New York: Routledge.

Marfleet, P. (2011), 'Understanding "Sanctuary": Faith and Traditions of Asylum', *Journal of Refugee Studies*, **24** (3), 440–55.

McCann, E. (2008), 'Expertise, Truth, and Urban Policy Mobilities: Global Circuits of Knowledge in the Development of Vancouver, Canada's "Four Pillar" Drug Strategy', *Environment and Planning A*, **40**, 885–904.

Merrill, H. (2006), *An Alliance of Women: Immigration and the Politics of Race*, Minneapolis, MN: University of Minnesota Press.

Mitchell, K. (2010), 'Ungoverned Space: Global Security and the Geopolitics of Broken Windows', *Political Geography*, **29**, 289–97.

Mitchell, K. (2017), 'Faith, Freedom, and Humanitarian Governance: The Spatial Politics of Church Asylum in Europe', *Space and Polity*, **21** (3), 269–88.

Mitchell, K. and M. Sparke (2018), 'Hotspot Geopolitics versus Geosocial Solidarity: Contending Constructions of Safe Space for Migrants in Europe', *Environment and Planning D: Society and Space*. Available at: https://doi.org/10.1177/0263775818793647.

Nagar, R. (2006), *Playing with Fire: Feminist Thought and Activism Through Seven Lives in India*, Minneapolis, MN: University of Minnesota Press.

Nagar, R. (2014), *Muddying the Waters: Coauthoring Feminisms Across Scholarship and Activism*, Urbana, IL: University of Illinois Press.

Neufert, B. (2014), 'Church Asylum', *Forced Migration Review*, **48**, 36–8.

Nicholls, W. (2009), 'Place, Networks, Space: Theorising the Geographies of Social Movements', *Transactions of the Institute of British Geographers*, **34** (1), 78–93.

Peck, J. (2006), 'Liberating the City: Between New York and New Orleans', *Urban Geography*, **27** (8), 681–713.

Peck, J. (2010), *Constructions of Neoliberal Reason*, Oxford: Oxford University Press.

Peck, J. (2011), 'Geographies of Policy: From Transfer-diffusion to Mobility-mutation', *Progress in Human Geography*, **35** (6), 773–97.

Peck, J. and N. Theodore (2010), 'Mobilizing Policy: Models, Methods, and Mutations', *Geoforum*, **41** (2), 169–74.

Peck, J. and N. Theodore (2015), *Fast Policy: Experimental Statecraft at the Thresholds of Neoliberalism*, Minneapolis, MN: University of Minnesota Press.

Perreault, T. (2003), 'Changing Places: Transnational Networks, Ethnic Politics, and Community Development in the Ecuadorian Amazon', *Political Geography*, **22**, 61–88.

Perreault, T. and P. Martin (2005), 'Geographies of Neoliberalism in Latin America', *Environment and Planning A*, **37**, 191–201.

Pratt, G. (2002), 'Collaborating Across Our Differences', *Gender, Place and Culture: A Journal of Feminist Geography*, **9** (2), 195–200.

Pratt, G. and B. Yeoh (2003), 'Transnational (Counter) Topographies', *Gender, Place and Culture: A Journal of Feminist Geography*, **10** (2), 159–66.

Pred, A. (1984), 'Place as Historically Contingent Process: Structuration and the Time-geography of Becoming Places', *Annals of the Association of American Geographers*, **74** (2), 279–97.

Rabben, L. (2016), *Sanctuary and Asylum: A Social and Political History*, Seattle, WA: University of Washington Press.

Raiser, K. (2010), 'Why Do We Do What We Do? The Theological Dimension of Sanctuary Work', *New Sanctuary Movement in Europe: Healing and Sanctifying Movement in the Churches*. October 7–10. CCME and Asyl in der Kirche, Berlin. Ed. German Ecumenical Committee on Church Asylum, February, Berlin.

Routledge, P. (2003), 'Anti-geopolitics'. In J. Agnew, K. Mitchell, and G. Toal (eds), *A Companion to Political Geography* (pp. 236–48), Malden, MA: Blackwell.

Routledge, P. (2011), 'Translocal climate justice solidarities'. In J. Dryzek, R. Norgaard, and D. Schlosberg (eds), *The Oxford Handbook of Climate Change and Society* (pp. 384–98), Oxford: Oxford University Press.

Roy, A. (2012), 'Ethnographic Circulations: Space–Time Relations in the Worlds of Poverty Management', *Environment and Planning A*, **44** (1), 31–41.

Shoemaker. K. (2011), *Sanctuary and Crime in the Middle Ages, 400–1500*, New York: Fordham University Press.

Smith, C. (1996), *Resisting Reagan: The US Central America Peace Movement*, Chicago, IL: University of Chicago Press.

Snyder, S. (2012), *Asylum-seeking, Migration and Church*, Farnham: Ashgate.

Sparke, M. (2013), *Introducing Globalization: Ties, Tensions, and Uneven Integration*, Oxford: Wiley-Blackwell.

Tomba, M. (2017), 'Politics Beyond the State: The 1918 Soviet Constitution', *Constellations*, **24**, 503–15.

Withnall, A. (2015), 'Pope Francis Promises to Take in Two Refugee Families and Urges Others to Follow His Example', *Independent*, September 6. Available at: https://www.independent.co.uk/news/people/pope-francis-promises-to-take-in-two-refugee-families-and-urges-others-to-follow-his-example-10488748.html (last accessed October 6, 2018).

Index